Essentials of Interactive
Computer Graphics

Chang Yaw.

Thank you for the
Years @ AW !!
Those experience form the
foundation for this book.

THANK you.

Kelvin
8/2009

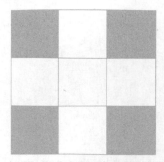

Essentials of Interactive
Computer Graphics
Concepts and Implementation

Kelvin Sung

Peter Shirley

Steven Baer

A K Peters, Ltd.
Wellesley, Massachusetts

Editorial, Sales, and Customer Service Office

A K Peters, Ltd.
888 Worcester Street, Suite 230
Wellesley, MA 02482
www.akpeters.com

Library of Congress Cataloging-in-Publication Data

Essentials of interactive computer graphics : concepts and implementation / Kelvin Sung, Peter Shirley, Steven Baer.   p. cm.
  Includes bibliographical references and index.
  ISBN 978-1-56881-257-1
    1. Computer graphics. 2. Interactive computer systems. I. Sung, Kelvin, 1964-
II. Shirley, P. (Peter), 1963- III. Baer, Steven.
  T385.E38565 2008
  006.6--dc22

                                                                          2008009675

Printed in India
12 11 10 09 08   10 9 8 7 6 5 4 3 2 1

To my father, Y. H. Sung, and in memory of my mother, T. C. Chang; his words
and her care shaped my life
— K. S.

To my wife Danna
— S. B.

Contents

Preface   xiii

List of Tutorials   xix

Introduction   1

I Elements of Interactive Programs   7

Introduction to Part I   9

1 Event-Driven Programming   13
   1.1 Control-Driven Programming 14
   1.2 Event-Driven Programming 19
   1.3 Triggering and Translation of Events 24
   1.4 Categories of Events 27
   1.5 Servicing of Events 30
   1.6 The Event-Driven Ball-Shooting Program 32
   1.7 Summary 35

2   Working with GUI APIs   37
     2.1   Our Application and Existing Libraries   38
     2.2   GUI Elements   39
     2.3   Building a GUI Application   41
     2.4   Examples: FLTK and MFC   43
     2.5   Implementation Notes   45
     2.6   Tutorials and Code Base   48

3   A Simple Graphics Program   75
     3.1   Coordinate Positions and Vertices   77
     3.2   A Computer Graphics Solution   79
     3.3   Lessons Learned   84
     3.4   Further Examples   85

4   Working with Graphics APIs   93
     4.1   Relationship between Graphics and GUI APIs   95
     4.2   Programming Graphics APIs   96
     4.3   Understanding Tutorials 3.1 and 3.2   100
     4.4   Abstraction of Graphics API   103

5   The Model-View-Controller Architecture   109
     5.1   The Model-View-Controller Framework   110
     5.2   Applying MVC to the Ball-Shooting Program   112
     5.3   Expanding the Ball-Shooting Program   118
     5.4   Interaction among the MVC Components   120
     5.5   Applying the MVC Concept   121
     5.6   Tutorials and Implementations   122

6   Applying to Real-World Applications   147
     6.1   PowerPoint   147
     6.2   Maya   149

II   Essential Concepts: Presented in 2D   153

Introduction to Part II   155

7   Attributes and Behaviors of Primitives   157
     7.1   Types of Primitives   158
     7.2   Working with Color   162
     7.3   Programming Geometric Primitives   163

7.4   Abstraction of Behavior: A Primitive Hierarchy   172
7.5   Collisions of Primitives   182
7.6   Collection of Primitives   188

8   Transformation Operators   193
8.1   The Translation Operator   194
8.2   The Scaling Operator   198
8.3   The Rotation Operator   204
8.4   Affine Transformations   209
8.5   Some Mathematics of the Transform Operators   210
8.6   Tutorials on Transformation Operators   215

9   Combining Transformation Operators   225
9.1   Concatenation of Operators   226
9.2   Inverse Transformation   229
9.3   Pivoted Transformations   231
9.4   Programming Transformations with Graphics APIs   236

10   Coordinate Systems   257
10.1   Understanding Tutorial 3.1   258
10.2   Device and Normalized Coordinate Systems   265
10.3   The World Coordinate System   266
10.4   The World Coordinate Window   273
10.5   Inverse Transformation   287

11   Hierarchical Modeling   293
11.1   Motivation   294
11.2   The SceneNode Class   299
11.3   Scene Trees and Scene Graphs   311
11.4   The Object Coordinate System   317
11.5   Simple Animation with the SceneNode Class   333

12   Making the Applications Interesting   337
12.1   Orientation of Objects   338
12.2   Alpha Blending and Transparency   345
12.3   File Texture Mapping   351

III   The Third Dimension   365

Introduction to Part III   367

13   A Simple 3D Application   369
  13.1 3D Coordinate Systems   371
  13.2 The Model and the Scene   372
  13.3 A Computer Graphics Simulation   374

14   The Camera   379
  14.1 A Computer Graphics Camera   380
  14.2 The Visible Volume   386
  14.3 The Coordinate Transformation Pipeline   396
  14.4 The World Transform: OC to WC   397
  14.5 The Eye Transform: WC to EC   398
  14.6 The Projection Transform: EC to NDC   402
  14.7 3D NDC–to-2D Device Transform   404
  14.8 Re-Examining Tutorial 13.1   405

15   Working with the Camera   409
  15.1 UWBGL Camera Implementation   413
  15.2 Working with Multiple Cameras   422
  15.3 Manipulating the Camera   422
  15.4 DC-to-WC Transformation   436
  15.5 2D Versus 3D Coordinate Transformation Pipeline   444

16   Graphics Programming in 3D   447
  16.1 Graphical Primitives for the Third Dimension   448
  16.2 Rotation in 3D   457
  16.3 Orientation in 3D   464
  16.4 Simple Scene Graph in 3D   479
  16.5 Scene Graph and Orientation   480
  16.6 Collision in 3D   485
  16.7 Selection in 3D   487

A   Material and Illumination   489

B   Vectors   493
    B.1   Vector Basics   493
    B.2   Vector Products   498
    B.3   Vector Examples   500
    B.4   Orthonormal Matrices   505

C   Summary of Library Version Changes   507

Index   537

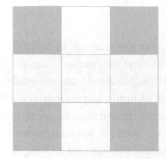

Preface

This book is designed for junior- or senior-level computer science, science, or engineering students with a basic background in linear algebra and experience with an object-oriented programming language. Working professionals with comparable background should be able to follow this book and learn the essential computer graphics concepts by themselves.

The technical content and organization of this book represent our answer to the question:

> If students can only schedule one elective computer graphics course in their undergraduate education, what should we teach in such a course?

When answering this question, we strive to achieve two major objectives:

- **To provide practical information.** The knowledge should be practical with potential applicability in the students' chosen field of profession.

- **To provide essential information.** The knowledge should be essential concepts that support students' future self-learning in the field of computer graphics.

Tutorials

We approach these objectives by focusing on topics that are relevant to popular computer graphics applications. To address the "one elective course" time restriction, only concepts that are relevant to interactive applications are covered. To maximize potential applicability, source code for example implementations (the tutorials) of the concepts is provided. These concept-demonstration tutorials are implemented using popular APIs. To ensure students learn the associated concepts together with the APIs, each tutorial has an OpenGL version and a DirectX version. We are in the process of porting the tutorials to the XNA Framework, a third graphics API.

The UWBGL Libraries

This book uses "the development of comprehensive software libraries suitable for building popular interactive computer graphics applications" as the central theme to connect and relate all the tutorials. All tutorials are implemented based on the UWBGL library system. Initially this library is trivial. As new concepts are introduced, corresponding sample implementation will be discussed and integrated into the UWBGL. In this way, the complexity of the library builds gradually as more concepts are presented in the book. There are a total of 18 different versions of the UWBGL library. This library system increases in complexity throughout the book and eventually enables fast prototyping of moderately complex interactive computer graphics applications.

Organization

We present the concepts associated with interactive graphics applications in three distinct parts.

1. Part I discusses the issues surrounding designing and implementing interactive applications based on a simple graphical user interface (GUI). To ensure the focus is on user interaction and software design topics, coverage of computer graphics is minimal in Part I.

2. Part II discusses the fundamental concepts for building graphics applications: graphical primitives, transformation, and (simple) applied linear algebra. To ensure the context is simple for understanding these concepts, the presentation is carried out in two dimensions.

3. Part III extends the discussion to the third dimension by introducing the computer graphics camera model and discussing techniques in software implementation.

Throughout the presentation, the independence of concepts from implementation is emphasized. The tutorials serve to reinforce this theme, where the same concepts are demonstrated in multiple versions based on competing APIs. Following this theme, we have chosen to omit the discussion of hardware shading and illumination. This is because the field is currently undergoing rapid changes and most of the materials involved are highly hardware- and API-dependent. Instead, implementation with the simple traditional Phong model is demonstrated in Appendix A. We believe that this field will continue to undergo rapid changes, and before it settles, the best source of up-to-date information will be online documentation and manuals.

Using This Book in a Course

The book organizes the topics above to support the gradual building of the UWBGL library system. It is important that the first four chapters of the book are covered in their given order. These chapters present the foundation and describe the requirements of the application/library that students will be building. Beyond the first four chapters, the topics can be covered in almost any order. In all cases, as soon as sufficient computer graphics topics are covered (by around Chapter 10 or 11), students should commence working on a final project based on the library system. In these final projects, students should demonstrate their knowledge and understanding by designing and developing an original and significantly complex application.

At the University of Washington, Bothell, two 10-week quarter courses are taught based on the contents of this book. The first course is a 2D graphics course concentrating on software infrastructure, user interaction, coordinate transformation, and 2D hierarchical modeling. This 2D course covers Parts I and II of the book. The first half of the second course covers the rest of the book. The second half of the second course covers topics in hardware shading and illumination based on up-to-date online documentation.

For more advanced students with a background in event-driven GUI programming, it is possible to review the topics in Part I with an initial programming assignment. In this case, Chapters 3 and 4 still need to be covered for an introduction to programming with graphics APIs.

This book can be used to teach building graphics applications to computer science (CS) major students, as well as non-major students with the appropriate programming background (experience with object-oriented programming). For CS majors, the course should concentrate on building and improving the UWBGL library system. For non-CS majors, the course should focus on using the UWBGL library system in developing applications (instead of developing the libraries).

Advantages of This Book

The major strength of this book is in the presentation of conceptual and practical insights required for the building of many popular interactive graphics applications. Essential concepts in interactive graphics application development are covered, including topics in software engineering, software design patterns, graphical user interfaces, real-time simulation, application programming interface (API) models, graphical primitives, coordinate transformations, scene nodes and hierarchies, blending, file texturing, and camera models and interaction. These issues are extremely important issues, especially for students who wish to pursue careers in computer graphics–related fields. This book offers readers a substantive learning experience designed to further enhance their computer graphics knowledge.

Software Update

We plan to continue improving and updating the tutorials and to include the support of additional APIs (e.g., XNA Framework and potentially Java and OpenGL) in the future. Please refer to http://depts.washington.edu/cmmr/biga/ for up-to-date source code of the tutorials.

Acknowledgments

First and foremost, thanks to all CSS 450 and CSS 451 students from the University of Washington, Bothell. Over the years, many brilliant students helped shape the design of the materials presented in this book. In 1999, after the raster-algorithm–based CSS 450 class, Jeff Wartes was the first to point out: "This course has been a disappointment. Drawing lines are only so interesting. I still have no idea how computer graphics relates to the games I play."

The development of the materials that eventually became this book was started in part as a reaction to these sincere comments. During the experimentation in the earlier years, the 2001 batch of CSS 450 students, especially Steve Baer, Jennifer Beers, Kazuko Hass, Gabriel Holmes, and Derek Gerstmann, critically evaluated the design of the library. Having done such a wonderful job, Steve has become an author of this book. Other significant contributions from students include Chris Dannunzio on working with DirectInput, Adam Smith and Sean Brogan on working with swap chains, Jack Nichols and Alexei Yatskov on programming in C#, and Peter Yiap and Robert Stone on programming with XNA. Jordan Phillips worked on the initial pass of the library organization; Jason Pursell, William Frankhouser, and Ethan Verrall developed detailed guides for the tutorials in Chapter 2; and Adrian Bonar built the documentation support system. A thank you also goes to colleagues in the community: Steve Cunningham for his guidance and support for this project, Edward Angel for the enlightening discussions on different approaches to teaching computer graphics, Charles Jackels for his encouragements, and Frank Cioch for the challenging pedagogical discussions. The supporting letters from Gladimir Baranoski, Peng-Ann Heng, Cary Laxer, Bob Lewis, Tiow-Seng Tan, Hung-Chuan Teh, and Herbert Yang on the initial ideas for this textbook helped secure a grant from the National Science Foundation that partially funded this project. Rebecca Reed-Rosenberg worked closely with Kelvin Sung on the evaluation of the materials. Ivan Lumala and John Nordlinger provided critical support toward the end of the writing of this book. We would like to thank our editors, Alice Peters and Kevin Jackson-Mead; thank you for the hard work, diligence, and timely feedback.

Kelvin Sung would like to thank the University of Washington, Bothell, for the sabbatical support for working on this book. The materials presented are based upon results from projects supported by the University of Washington, Bothell, Scholar Award 2004 and the National Science Foundation Grant No. DUE-0442420.[1] Toward the end, many of the tutorials were refined with support from Microsoft Research under the Computer Gaming Curriculum in Computer Science RFP, Award Number 15871.

Part I of this book is based liberally on Chapter 18 of the second edition of *Fundamentals of Computer Graphics*. Although the contents are reorganized with additional detail and extensive code examples that integrate smoothly with the rest of this book, the basic concepts on building interactive applications are the same.

---

[1] Any opinions, findings, and conclusions or recommendations expressed in this material are those of the author(s) and do not necessarily reflect the views of the National Science Foundation.

This book was written using the *LaTeX* document preparation software in the *WinEdt*[2]*/MiKTeX*[3] editing environment. The figures were made by the authors using *Autodesk Maya*, *Adobe Illustrator*, and *Jasc Paint Shop Pro*. The program source code documentation is built based on Doxygen.[4] The authors would like to thank the creators of these wonderful programs.

Kelvin Sung
Peter Shirley
Steven Baer

---

[2]http://www.winedt.com/
[3]http://www.miktex.org/
[4]http//www.doxygen.org/

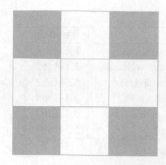

List of Tutorials

Tutorial	Project Name	Description	Based on
2.1(p. 49)	`SimpleDialog`	Demystify source files	-
2.2(p. 55)	`EchoButtonEvent`	GUI elements and controls	2.1
2.3(p. 58)	`SliderControls`	GUI control variables	2.2
2.4(p. 61)	`MouseAndTimer`	Application-defined events	2.3
2.5(p. 63)	`UpdateGUI`	Input/output GUI elements	2.4
2.6(p. 66)	`SliderCtrlWithEcho`	Extend GUI API with classes	2.5
2.7(p. 67)	`Library1`	Custom GUI library	2.6
2,8(p. 69)	`GroupControls`	Grouping GUI elements	2.7

Chapter 2. Tutorials on GUI API.

Tutorial	Project Name	Description	Based on
3.1(p. 79)	`Rectangles2D`	Drawing with D3D	2.8
3.2(p. 85)	`Rectangles2D`	Drawing with OGL	2.8
3.3(p. 87)	`RectangleClass`	Abstraction of drawing (D3D)	3.1
3.4(p. 87)	`RectangleClass`	Abstraction of drawing (OGL)	3.2
3.5(p. 90)	`CircleClass`	Apply drawing with abstraction	3.3

Chapter 3. Tutorials on drawing with graphics APIs.

Tutorial	Project Name	Description	Based on
4.1(p. 105)	`GraphicsSystem`	Abstraction Graphics API (D3D)	3.5
4.2(p. 107)	`SeparateLibrary`	Graphics API Interface Lib (D3D)	4.1
4.3(p. 107)	`GraphicsSystem`	Abstraction Graphics API (OGL)	3.4
4.4(p. 107)	`RectangleClass`	Graphics API Interface Lib (OGL)	4.3

Chapter 4. Tutorials on programming with graphics APIs.

Tutorial	Project Name	Description	Based on
5.1(p. 123)	ModelView	WindowHandler abstraction	Lib1
5.2(p. 131)	MouseInput	Mouse input via WindowHandler	5.1+Lib2
5.3(p. 135)	SimulateGravity	Real-time simulation/update	5.2+Lib2
5.4(p. 138)	TwoViews	Multiple independent views	5.3+Lib3
5.5(p. 141)	MultipleBalls	More complex application state	5.4+Lib3
5.6(p. 144)	BallShooting	Ball-Shooting program	5.5+Lib3

Chapter 5. Tutorials on model-view-controller architecture.

Tutorial	Project Name	Description	Based on
7.1(p. 163)	ObjectsAndAttributes	Graphical primitives	Lib4
7.2(p. 172)	ObjectClasses	Primitives class hierarchy	7.1+Lib5
7.3(p. 184)	Collisions	Collision of primitives	7.2+Lib6
7.4(p. 188)	ObjectCollections	Lists of primitives	7.3+Lib7
7.5(p. 191)	BallShoot2	Ball-Shooting with primitive	5.6+Lib7

Chapter 7. Tutorials on attributes and behaviors of graphical primitives.

Tutorial	Project Name	Description	Based on
8.1(p. 216)	TranslateSingleObject	Translation with one object	Lib8
8.2(p. 220)	TranslateObjects	Translation with two objects	Lib8
8.3(p. 222)	ScaleObjects	Scaling with two objects	Lib8
8.4(p. 222)	RotateObjects	Rotation with two objects	Lib8

Chapter 8. Tutorials on transformation operators.

Tutorial	Project Name	Description	Based on
9.1(p. 236)	TranslateScaleObj	Concatenate translate and scale	Lib8
9.2(p. 238)	MatrixMultiplyOrder	Order of concatenation	9.1+Lib8
9.3(p. 240)	MatrixStack	Matrix stack	9.2+Lib8
9.4(p. 242)	PivotedRotation	Pivoted scaling/rotation	9.3+Lib8
9.5(p. 245)	PerPrimitiveTrans	Pivoted transformation	9.4+Lib8
9.6(p. 250)	XformInfo	XformInfo class	9.5+Lib9
9.7(p. 251)	XformInfoControls	XformInfo GUI dialog	9.6+Lib9
9.8(p. 253)	BallShoot3	Ball-Shooting with XformInfo	7.5+Lib9
9.9(p. 255)	XformList	Reference for next chapter	9.6+Lib9

Chapter 9. Tutorials on concatenation of transformation operators.

Tutorial	Project Name	Description	Based on
10.1(p. 258)	ViewTransform0	World to NDC	3.1
10.2(p. 261)	ViewTransform1	Squares in NDC	10.1
10.3(p. 263)	ViewTransform2	Circle in NDC	10.2
10.4(p. 263)	ViewTransform3	Aspect ratio	10.3
10.5(p. 263)	ViewTransform4	Aspect ratio	10.3
10.6(p. 268)	XformListCoordSpace	World and device space	9.9+Lib9
10.7(p. 270)	ChangedCoordinates	World and device space	10.6+Lib9
10.8(p. 271)	TranslateWC	WC window center	10.7+Lib9
10.9(p. 278)	WCSupport	WC window with Lib10	10.8+Lib10
10.10(p. 280)	Panning	Moving WC window	10.9+Lib10
10.11(p. 283)	Zooming	Resizing WC window	10.10+Lib10
10.12(p. 285)	AspectRatio	Resizing UI drawing area	10.11+Lib10
10.13(p. 289)	BadMousePan	Mouse click input	10.12+Lib10
10.14(p. 289)	MousePan	Input with inverse transform	10.12+Lib10

Chapter 10. Tutorials on coordinate transformations.

Tutorial	Project Name	Description	Based on
11.1(p. 295)	SimpleArm	Arm object	Lib10
11.2(p. 297)	ParentChild	Parent/child group	11.1+Lib10
11.3(p. 303)	SceneNode	SceneNode class	11.2+Lib11
11.4(p. 305)	SceneNodeArm	Arm as a SceneNode	11.3+Lib11
11.5(p. 308)	SceneNodeMultiPrim	Multiple primitives in a node	11.4+Lib11
11.6(p. 312)	SceneNodeSiblings	Siblings nodes	11.5+Lib11
11.7(p. 327)	SceneNodePicking	Mouse click selection	11.6+Lib12
11.8(p. 329)	SceneNodeCollision	Object space collision	11.7+Lib12
11.9(p. 334)	SceneNodeAnimation	Animation with SceneNode	11.8+Lib12

Chapter 11. Tutorials on hierarchical modeling.

Tutorial	Project Name	Description	Based on
12.1(p. 338)	OrientationIn2D	Orientation of objects	11.8+Lib12
12.2(p. 343)	SceneNodeOrient	Orientation of scene nodes	12.1+Lib12
12.3(p. 350)	AlphaBlending	Simple alpha blending	Lib13
12.4(p. 355)	SimpleTexture	Simple texture mapping	-
12.5(p. 364)	TextureMapping	Integrate with library	12.3+12.4+Lib13

Chapter 12. Tutorials on more complex and interesting applications.

Tutorial	Project Name	Description	Based on
13.1(p. 374)	Rectangles3D	Simple 3D scene	3.1

Chapter 13. Tutorial on a simple 3D application.

Tutorial	Project Name	Description	Based on
14.1(p. 383)	AdjustCamera	Camera parameters	13.1
14.2(p. 389)	AdjustOrtho	Visible volume parameters	14.1
14.3(p. 393)	AdjustPersp	View frustum parameters	14.1
14.4(p. 395)	AdjustDepth	Near/far plane settings	14.3

Chapter 14. Tutorials on the computer graphics camera.

Tutorial	Project Name	Description	Based on
15.1(p. 416)	CameraLib	Integrate into library	14.3+Lib14
15.2(p. 422)	TwoCamera	Two cameras	15.1+Lib14
15.3(p. 425)	CameraMouseUI	Interactive camera manipulation	15.2+Lib14
15.4(p. 441)	CameraInvXform	DC to WC in 3D	15.3+Lib14

Chapter 15. Tutorials on working with the camera.

Tutorial	Project Name	Description	Based on
16.1(p. 455)	MeshSupport	D3D mesh resource	15.4+Lib15
16.2(p. 456)	CompoundMesh	Compound mesh Primitives	16.1+Lib15
16.3(p. 461)	RotateMatrix	Rotation with matrix	16.2+Lib16
16.4(p. 464)	RotateQuat	Rotation with quaternion	16.3+Lib17
16.5(p. 465)	Orientation	Working with quaternion	16.4+Lib17
16.6(p. 479)	SimpleHierarchy	Scene graph in 3D	16.5+Lib17
16.7(p. 480)	SceneGraphIn3D	Orientation in 3D	16.6+Lib17
16.8(p. 485)	CollisionIn3D	Collision in 3D	16.7+Lib17
16.9(p. 487)	SelectionIn3D	Mouse selection in 3D	16.8+Lib17

Chapter 16. Tutorials on working with the third dimension.

Tutorial	Project Name	Description	Based on
A.1(p. 490)	SimpleLighting	Simple lighting	14.1
A.2(p. 490)	Lighting	Integrate into library	16.9+Lib18
A.3(p. 491)	CustomMesh	Working with D3DMesh	A.2+Lib18

Appendix A. Tutorials on hardware illumination.

Introduction

Almost every laptop and desktop computer sold now has both a high-resolution screen and a mouse. Inside these systems there is usually a central processing unit (CPU) as well as a graphics processing unit (GPU). The GPU is of similar overall complexity to the CPU, but it has a very different overall architecture and purpose. Most of a programmer's education typically deals with the CPU and text and file input/output. This book, on the other hand, deals with the screen, the mouse, and the GPU. These are the essential entities that computer graphics programs control. Much of "standard" programming applies in graphics, but there are many additional things to be mastered by a graphics programmer. This book deals with those additional things.

The rest of this book develops graphics programs one step at a time and in full detail. This is not a book to sit and read and ponder, as the many mundane details presented are quite boring. However, they are vital details for actually doing graphics programming. So, as you read the book, test what you learn by doing. By the end of the book, you should have in your skill set the ability to write a simple—even complex—application. We begin with handling user input to the program, displaying 2D graphics, and then harnessing the full 3D power of the GPU.

Rather than discussing graphics at a high level, we will dive right in and begin programming starting with Chapter 2. Thus the rest of this introduction discusses some details to be aware of when using the book. These are important nuts and bolts and should not be skipped!

Although foundation concepts are covered, this book is the *how to* of computer graphics, rather than the more traditional *what is* text that usually covers computer graphics. More specifically, we concentrate on *how to* build interactive computer graphics applications. The book ensures sufficient foundation concepts are covered so that readers can begin coding interactive graphics applications as they read the text, thus providing readers with proper preparation in order to continue learning about foundations of computer graphics after finishing this book. As far as this book is concerned, an *application* is a *computer program*. We interchange the use of *application* and *program*.

The Tutorials

The presentation of the material in this book is tightly integrated with example programs. We refer to these examples as *tutorials*, because they are designed to teach and demonstrate the implementation of concepts. For each topic area, we typically study the concepts followed by discussion of implementations with source code snippets. Since the topic areas build on top of each other, so does the source code for the tutorials. Initially, the tutorials are bare-bones with a handful of files; as we learn more concepts, the complexity of the tutorials will also increase. Toward the end, the tutorials will be moderately elaborate software systems with thousands of lines of source code. It is important that you follow and understand the source code as you read the text. We have found that one of the best ways to follow this book is by practicing graphics program development based on the provided source code. In general, it may be difficult to understand this book without a good understanding of the tutorials.

Organization of the Tutorials

The tutorials and source code can be found on the accompanying CD.[5] The tutorials for each chapter are grouped under separate folders with the chapter being the name of the folder. Inside each chapter folder, the source code for each tutorial is separated into subfolders, with the tutorial's number and page number being the sub-folder's name. The final folder is named after the API and the programming language that the tutorial is implemented in. For example, Chapter 10 Tutorial 10.1 is first introduced on page 258, and there are two implementations

---

[5] Also available online at: http://depts.washington.edu/cmmr/biga/.

of this tutorial: OpenGL and D3D, both based on C++ and MFC. The source code for this tutorial is located at

```
chapter_tutorials/Chapter_10/Tutorial_10.1_OnPage258/C++_D3D_MFC/
chapter_tutorials/Chapter_10/Tutorial_10.1_OnPage258/C++_OGL_MFC/
```

We are currently working on

```
chapter_tutorials/Chapter_10/Tutorial_10.1_OnPage258/C#_XNA_UWBGUI/
```

IDE and APIs

We have chosen the Microsoft Visual Studio 2005 integrated development environment (IDE) as our target development environment. All tutorials are provided as separate Visual Studio projects. For this first edition of the book, we do not have support for any other IDEs.

The source code for the tutorials is in C++. We have developed two versions of most tutorials: one based on the OpenGL and the other based on the Microsoft DirectX Direct3D (D3D) graphics application programming interface (API). For now, the graphical user interface (GUI) library of most tutorials is based on the Microsoft Foundation Classes (MFC).

The choices for IDE, programming language, and libraries are based on the belief that these are probably the most widely available and most familiar environments to most of our readers. Our choices do not reflect endorsements for any of the systems we used. In fact, we believe that the concepts covered in this book, including implementation and specific skills, are independent of any particular software system. One should be able to port the learning from this book into any program or programming language and develop moderately complex interactive graphics programs, based on any modern IDE, object-oriented programming language, graphics library, and/or GUI library.

Our Libraries and Naming Conventions

In Chapter 2 we introduce a library to help abstract and customize the MFC library. In Chapter 4 we introduce another library to customize and interface to the OpenGL and D3D graphics libraries. From Chapter 5 onwards, we begin to work with the UWBGL libraries. We will work with one GUI library and two graphics libraries. The libraries have names of the form

UWBGL_**API_Type**_Lib**Version_Number**

UWB and UWBGL. UWB is the abbreviation for University of Washington, Bothell, the home institution of the first author where most of the design and initial development efforts took place. "UWBGL" stands for "UWB Graphics Library."

where **API_Type** can be

> MFC—Microsoft Foundation Classes (GUI library)
>
> D3D—Microsoft DirectX Direct3D (graphics library)
>
> OGL—OpenGL (graphics library)

and **Version_Number** is an integer. For example, UWBGL_D3D_Lib1 is the first D3D library, and UWBGL_OGL_Lib1 is the first OpenGL library we will develop. As we learn more concepts, we will continue to introduce new classes into each library, and the **Version_Number** of the corresponding library will increase.

We have established the following naming conventions to avoid collisions of identifiers.

- **Files.** Files have names that begin with uwbgl_**API_Type**. For example, uwbgl_D3DCircleGeom.h or uwbgl_OGLCircleGeom.h. For files that contain API-independent code, there will be no corresponding **API_Type**. For example, uwbgl_Utilitiy.h declares the utility functions (e.g., the random number functions) for the library.

- **File versions.** As we refine concepts, the contents of many files (e.g., classes) will continue to evolve. A *file version number* is attached to files to avoid confusion (e.g., wubgl_D3DCircleGoem**1**.h and uwbgl_D3DCircle Geom**2**.h). Notice that the file's version number is independent of the library's version number. For example, when evolving from UWBGL_D3D _Lib1 to UWBGL_D3D_Lib2, the file uwbgl_D3DGraphicsSystem1.h did not change. The same file version 1 file exists in both versions of the libraries.

- **Classes.** Classes have names that begin with the following.

  - UWB. General classes that are common to all Graphics APIs (OGL and D3D). These classes typically define pure virtual interfaces that specify functionality. For example, we will discuss the UWB_WindowHandler interface to the windowing system.

  - UWBD3D. Classes that customize and build on top of D3D functionality. For example, the UWBD3D_CircleGeometry class is built on top of D3D drawing routines and encapsulates the functionality of a circle.

  - UWBOGL. Classes that customize and build on top of OpenGL functionality. For example, the UWBOGL_CircleGeometry class is built on top of OpenGL drawing routines and encapsulates the functionality of a circle.

  – UWBMFC. Classes that customize and build on top of MFC functionality. For example, the UWBMFC_UIWindow class extends the MFC window class with customized support for our graphics applications.

  • **Utility functions.** General utility function names begin with UWB. For example, UWB_RandomNumber() returns a random number.

When necessary, we refer to each class/file by its entire identifier string (e.g., UWB_RandomNumber()). However, for readability, we refer to the names without the "UWB_" prefix, (e.g., RandomNumber() instead of UWB_RandomNumber()).

Appendix C summarizes the changes of the library, when necessary, with associated static class UML diagrams. As new libraries are introduced in the text, refer to this appendix.

Library Design Trade-Off

The UWBGL library is designed to present graphics concepts. Although we are concerned with efficiency issues, execution speed is always of lower priority when compared with logical organization for presenting graphics concepts. For example, our simple organization of resetting/setting all attributes before drawing each primitive necessarily means that the graphics rendering context must be updated many times during each redraw. The alternative of collecting similar primitives and setting the attributes once for all these primitives during redraw would be much more efficient. However, such organization would introduce complexity independent of graphics concepts. In all cases, we opted for simplicity at the expense of efficiency in order to provide clear and simple presentation of graphics concepts.

Learning with the Provided Source Code

While reading this book, it is absolutely important to constantly remember that the elaborated source code is provided as a tool for learning and demonstrating the underlying concepts. We believe it is easier to grasp the foundations if readers can experience and experiment with the concepts in moderately complex environments. As stated, the other goal of this book is for readers to begin to develop moderately complex interactive computer graphics applications. The source is provided as a demo.

There are different levels of using the source code and the elaborate libraries provided. Readers are encouraged to be:

- **Users of the source code.** Readers should be encouraged to start from Chapter 2, where we demonstrate how to be a programmer of and use the source code provided to experience concepts and develop applications. You don't need to understand every single line of the provided code to be a proficient user of the library and to program something complex as well as experience and learn the underlying computer graphics concepts.

- **Evaluators of the source code.** For those who can understand the source system, we encourage you to critically evaluate our solutions to implementing the graphics concepts. We believe we have a pretty good solution, but as in all design problems, there are no perfect answers. For example, we believe the IWindowHandler hierarchy (introduced in Chapter 5) is a pretty solution for abstracting graphics and GUI APIs while supporting view/controller functionality. However, we certainly understand that this is not a perfect solution, and readers are encouraged to evaluate the merits of our solution and to seek out alternative ideas.

- **Developers of their own systems.** From our experience using this source system in the classroom, the best students often challenge the provided source code and develop their own libraries while using the provided source as an example. Many students choose to implement their systems based on different programming languages with different APIs, for example, Java, Java Swing, and OpenGL, C++, MFC, and OpenGL, C#, WinForm, and XNA Framework, and so on.

In all cases, the most important point we hope to make is that readers should avoid getting bogged down with our implementation and being unable to continue learning as a result of our source code system. That would be the worst-case scenario. Always remember: find ways to use the source code and examples to experience and experiment with the concepts. You don't have to like the implementation. In fact, you are welcome to hate it and critically evaluate it; just don't allow your attitude toward the source code to hinder your learning of the subject matter.

Elements of Interactive Programs

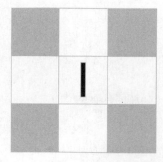

Introduction to Part I

This book is about building interactive computer graphics applications. In Part I, we concentrate on studying interactivity and the building of applications.

Interactivity. Chapter 1 shows us that interactivity demands the event-driven programming model and discusses the elements of the event-driven model. Chapter 2 shows us how to work with specialized graphical user interface (GUI) application programming interface (API) libraries in implementing event-driven interactive programs.

Graphics. Chapter 3 shows us how to draw simple geometric shapes with computer graphics. Chapter 4 shows us the principles of working with specialized graphics API libraries.

Building of applications. Chapter 5 shows us the model-view-controller (MVC) software architecture and demonstrates how to apply this architecture in organizing the GUI API, the graphics API, and our programming code to facilitate readability, maintainability, and expandability of our application. Chapter 6 uses the MVC architecture to explain the software structure of some real-world interactive graphics applications.

We will use the development of a simple example to organize our discussion: a program that allows the user to simulate the shooting of a ball under the influence of gravity. The user can specify initial velocity, create balls of different

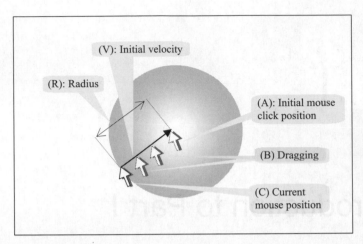

Figure I.1. Dragging out a ball.

sizes, shoot the ball, and examine the parabolic free fall of the ball. For clarity, we avoid graphics-specific complexities in 3D space and confine our discussion to 2D space. Obviously, our simple program is neither sophisticated nor representative of real applications. However, with slightly refined specifications, this example contains all the essential components and behavioral characteristics of more complex real-world interactive systems. We will use the design and development of the ball-shooting program throughout all chapters in Part I to help us consolidate the concepts.

Details of the Ball-Shooting Program

Our simple program has the following elements and behaviors.

- **The balls (objects).** The user can left-mouse-button-click and drag out a new ball (circle) anywhere on the screen (see Figure I.1). Dragging out a ball includes:

  - (A): initial mouse-button-click position defines the center of the circle;

  - (B): mouse-button-down and moving the mouse is the dragging action;

  - (C): current mouse position while dragging allows us to define the radius and the initial velocity. The radius R (in pixel units) is the dis-

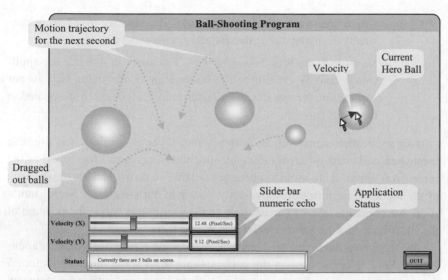

Figure I.2. The ball-shooting program.

tance to the center defined in (A). The vector from the current position to the center is the initial velocity V (in units of pixels per second).

Once created, the ball will begin traveling with the defined initial velocity.

- HeroBall **(hero/active object).** The user can also right-mouse-button-click to select a ball to be the current HeroBall. The HeroBall's velocity can be controlled by the slider bars (discussed below) where its velocity is displayed. A newly created ball is by default the current HeroBall. A right-mouse-button-click on unoccupied space indicates that no current HeroBall exists.

- **Velocity slider bars (GUI elements).** The user can monitor and control two slider bars (*x*- and *y*-directions with magnitudes) to change the velocity of the HeroBall. When there is no HeroBall, the slider-bar values are undefined.

- **The simulation.**

  - *Ball traveling/collisions (object intrinsic behaviors).* A ball knows how to travel based on its current velocity, and one ball can potentially collide with another. For simplicity, we will assume that all balls have identical mass and that all collisions are perfectly elastic.

- *Gravity (external effects on objects).* The velocity of a ball is constantly changing due to the defined gravitational force.

- *Status bar (application-state echo).* The user can monitor the application state by examining the information in the status bar. In our application, the number of balls currently on the screen is updated in the status bar.

Our application starts with an empty screen. The user clicks and drags to create new balls with different radii and velocities. Once a ball travels off of the screen, it is removed. To avoid unnecessary details, we do not include the drawing of the motion trajectories or the velocity vector in our solutions. Notice that a slider bar communicates its current state to the user in two ways: the position of the slider knob and the numeric echo (see Figure I.2).

We have now described the behavior of a simple interactive graphics application. We can begin learning the concepts that support the implementation of this type of application. We concentrate on issues concerned with interaction and software engineering practices.

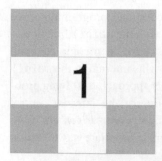

Event-Driven Programming

This chapter introduces the event driven programming model. This chapter

- explains the deficiencies of designing user-interface applications based on the traditional control-driven programming model;

- introduces the event-driven programming model and examines how this new model addresses the above deficiencies;

- demonstrates the development of user-interface solutions based on the event-driven programming model.

After this chapter, you should

- understand the parameters and principles of event-driven programming;

- understand the process for designing an event-driven solution;

- understand, at a conceptual level, the interactions between GUI APIs and our solution;

- be able to design an event-driven programming solution based on given specifications.

However, because this chapter does not cover the details of any API, we will *not* be able to implement the solutions we have designed. For that, we will wait for the next chapter.

For many of us, when we were first introduced to computer programming, we learned that the program should always start and end with the `main()` function—when the `main()` function returns, all the work must have been completed and the program terminates. Since the overall control remains internal to the `main()` function during the entire lifetime of the program, this approach to solving problems is referred to as the *control-driven programming* or the *internal control model* approach. As we will see, an alternative paradigm, *event-driven programming* or an *external control model* approach, is the more appropriate way to design solutions to interactive programs.

In this chapter, we will first formulate a solution to the (2D) ball-shooting program based on the perhaps more familiar control-driven programming model. We will then analyze the solution, identify shortcomings, and describe the motivation for the external control model or event-driven programming approach.

An event-driven program that interacts with users requires the support of a graphical user interface (GUI) system. A GUI system implements standard functionality of event-driven user-interactive programs and presents this functionality as a software library through an application programming interface (API). Examples of GUI APIs include Java Swing Library, OpenGL Utility ToolKit (GLUT), The Fast Light ToolKit (FLTK), and Microsoft Foundation Classes (MFC). Through the discussion in this chapter, we will gain insights into GUI systems. We will understand the standard functionality of event-driven user-interactive programs and the functionality that the GUI API must include. In the next chapter, we will look at examples of popular modern GUI APIs, analyze how these GUI systems support concepts learned in this chapter, and experiment with implementing programs with these GUI APIs.

The pseudocode that follows is C++/Java-like. We assume typical functionality from the operating system (`OperatingSystem::`) and from a GUI system (`GUISystem::`). The purpose of the pseudocode is to assist us in analyzing the foundation control structure (i.e., if/while/case) of the solution. For this reason, the details of application- and graphics-specific operations are intentionally glossed over. For example, the details of how to implement `UpdateSimulation()` are purposely omitted.

1.1 Control-Driven Programming

The main advantage of control-driven programming is that it is fairly straightforward to translate a verbal description of a solution to a program control structure. In this case, we verbalize our solution as follows:

(A): As long as user is not ready to quit

```
while UserCommand != Quit
```

(B): Parse the user command

```
    ParseAndExecute(UserCommand)
```

(C): Periodically update positions and velocities of the balls

```
    if (OperatingSystem::SufficientClockTimeHasElapesd)
      // update the positions and velocities of all the balls
      // in AllWorldBalls
      UpdateSimulation()
```

(D): Draw all balls to the computer screen

```
    // all the balls in AllWorldBalls set
    DrawBalls(AllWorldBalls)
```

(E): Set status bar with number of balls

```
    // Sets status bar: number of balls on screen
    EchoToStatusBar()
```

Listing 1.1. Programming structure from a verbalized solution.

- while the user does not want to quit (A);

- parse and execute the user's command (B);

- update the velocities and positions of the balls (C);

- then draw all the balls (D);

- and finally before we poll the user for another command, tell the user what is going on by echoing current application state to the status bar (E).

If we translate this verbal solution into a simple programming structure, we get something like Listing 1.1. In Listing 1.1 we introduce the set of AllWorldBalls to represent all the balls that are currently active in the application's window. The only other difference between the pseudocode in Listing 1.1 and our verbalized solution is in the added elapsed time check in Step (C): SufficientClockTime HasElapsed. (Recall that the velocities are defined in pixels per second.) To support proper pixel displacements, we must know real elapsed time between updates.

```
main() {
(A):  while ( GUISystem::UserAction != Quit )   {

    (B):  switch (GUISystem::UserAction)   {

            // Begins creating a new Hero Ball
      (B1):  case GUISystem::LeftMouseButtonDown:
                // hero not in AllWorldBalls set
                HeroBall = CreateHeroBall()
                DefiningNewHeroBall = true

            // Drags out the new Hero Ball
     (B1-1): case GUISystem::LeftMouseButtonDrag:
                RefineRadiusAndVelocityOfHeroBall()
                SetSliderBarsWithHeroBallVelocity()

            // Finishes creating the new Hero Ball
     (B1-2): case GUISystem::LeftMouseButtonUp:
                InsertHeroBallToAllWorldBalls()
                DefiningNewHeroBall = false

            // Selects a current hero ball
      (B2):  case GUISystem::RightMouseButtonDown:
                HeroBall = SelectHeroBallBasedOnCurrentMouseXY()
                if (HeroBall != null)
                    SetSliderBarsWithHeroBallVelocity()

            // Sets hero velocity with slider bars
      (B3):  case GUISystem::SliderBarChange:
                if (HeroBall != null)
                    SetHeroBallVelocityWithSliderBarValues()

            // Ignores all other user actions
      (B4):  default:
          } // end of switch(userAction)
          if (OperatingSystem::SufficientClockTimeHasElapsed)
                // Move balls by velocities and remove off-screen ones
```

Listing 1.2. Programming solution based on the control-driven model.

```
       (C):  UpdateSimulation()
             // Draw the new Hero Ball that is currently being defined
    (D):  DrawBalls(AllWorldBalls)


          if (DefiningNewHeroBall)
         (D1):  DrawBalls(HeroBall)


          // Sets Status Bar with number of balls currently on screen
    (E):  EchoToStatusBar


      } // end of while(UserAction != Quit)


    } // end of main() function. Program terminates.
```

Listing 1.2. (cont.)

As we add additional details to parse and execute the user's commands (B), the solution must be expanded. The revised solution in Listing 1.2 shows the details of a central parsing switch statement (B) and the support for all three commands a user can issue: defining a new HeroBall (B1), selecting a HeroBall (B2), and adjusting the current HeroBall velocity with the slider bars (B3). Undefined user actions (e.g., mouse movement with no button pressed) are simply ignored (B4).

Notice that HeroBall creation (B1) involves three user actions: mouse down (B1), followed by mouse drag (B1-1), and finally mouse up (B1-2). The parsing of this operation is performed in multiple consecutive passes through the outer while-loop (A): the first time through, we create the new HeroBall (B1); in the subsequent passes, we process the actual dragging operation (B1-1). We assume that mouse drag (B1-1) will never be invoked without the mouse-button-down (B1) action, and thus the HeroBall is always defined during the dragging operation. The LeftMouseButtonUp action (B1-2) is an implicit action not defined in the original specification.

In our implementation, we choose this implicit action to activate the insertion of the new HeroBall into the AllWorldBalls set. In this way, the HeroBall is not a member of the AllWorldBalls set until the user has completed the dragging operation. This delay ensures that the HeroBall's velocity and position will not be affected when the UpdateSimulation() procedure updates each ball in the AllWorldBalls set (C). This means that a user can take the time to drag out a new HeroBall without worrying that the ball will free fall before the release of the mouse button. The simple change in the drawing operation (D1) ensures proper drawing of the new HeroBall before it is inserted into the AllWorldBalls set.

When we examine this solution in the context of supporting user interaction, we have to concern ourselves with efficiency issues as well as the potential for increased complexity.

Efficiency concerns.   Typically a user interacts with an application in bursts of activity. These are continuous actions followed by periods of idling. This can be explained by the fact that as users, we typically perform some tasks in the application and then spend time examining the results. For example, when working with a word processor, our typical work pattern consists of bursts of typing/editing followed by periods of reading (with no input action). In our example application, we can expect the user to drag out some circles and then observe the free falling of the circles. The continuous while-loop polling of user commands in the main() function means that when the user is not performing any action, our program will still be actively running and wasting machine resources. During activity bursts, at the maximum, users are capable of generating hundreds of input actions per second (e.g., mouse-pixel movements). If we compare this rate to the typical CPU instruction capacities that are measured at 10^9 per second, the huge discrepancy indicates that, even during activity bursts, the user command-parsing switch statement (B) is spending most of the time in the default case not doing anything.

Complexity concerns.   Notice that our *entire solution* is in the main() function. This means that all relevant user actions must be parsed and handled by the user command-parsing switch statement (B). In a modern multiprogram shared-window environment, many actions performed by users are not application-specific. For example, if a user performs a left mouse-button click and drag in the drawing area of the program window, our application should react by dragging out a new HeroBall. However, if the user performs the same actions in the title area of the program window, our application must somehow implement moving the entire program window. As experienced users in window environments, we understand that there are numerous such operations, and we expect all applications to honor these actions (e.g., iconize, resize, raise or lower a window). Following the solution given in Listing 1.2, for every user action that we want to honor, we must include a matching supporting case in the parsing switch statement (B). This requirement quickly increases the complexity of our solution and becomes a burden to implementing any interactive applications.

To support the development of efficient interactive applications, we need system support where we could remain idle by default (not taking up machine resources) and only become active in the presence of interesting activities (e.g., user-input actions). Furthermore, to integrate interactive applications in sophisticated multiprogramming window environments, it is important that our system support automatically takes care of mundane and standard user actions. This is the basic functionality of a modern GUI system.

1.2 Event-Driven Programming

Event-driven programs are typically implemented based on an existing GUI system. GUI systems remedy the efficiency and complexity concerns by defining a default `MainEventLoop()` function. For event-driven programs, the `MainEvent Loop()` replaces the `main()` function, because all programs start and end in this function. Just as in the case of the `main()` function for control-driven programming, when the `MainEventLoop()` function returns, all work should have been completed, and the program terminates. The `MainEventLoop()` function defines the central control structure for all event-driven programming solutions and typically cannot be changed by a user application. In this way, the overall control of an application is actually external to the user's program code. For this reason, event-driven programming is also referred to as the external control model. Listing 1.3 shows a typical `MainEventLoop()` implementation. In this case, our program is the user application that is based on the `MainEventLoop()` function. Structurally, the `MainEventLoop()` is very similar to the `main()` function of Listing 1.2, with a continuous loop (B) containing a central parsing switch statement (D). The important differences between the two functions are the following.

- **(A) SystemInitialization().** Recall that event-driven programs start and end in the `MainEventLoop()` function. `SystemInitialization()` is a mechanism defined to invoke the user program from within the `MainEvent Loop()`. It is expected that user programs implement the function `System Initialization()` to initialize the application state and to register *event service routines* (refer to the discussion in (D)).

- **(B) Continuous outer loop.** Because this is a general control structure to be shared by all event-driven programs, there is no way to determine the termination condition. User programs are expected to override appropriate event service routines and terminate the program from within the service routine.

- **(C) Stop and wait.** Instead of actively polling the user for actions (wasting machine resources), the `MainEventLoop()` typically stops the entire

```
GUISystem::MainEventLoop() {
    // For initialization of application state and
    // registration of event service routines
(A): SystemInitialization()


    // continuous outer loop
(B): loop forever {


        // Program will stop and wait for next event
    (C): WaitFor(GUISystem::NextEvent)


        // Central parsing switch statement
    (D): switch (GUISystem::NextEvent) {
            case GUISystem::LeftMouseButtonDown:
                if (user application registered for this event)
                    Execute user defined service routine.
                else
                    Execute default UISystem routine.


            case GUISystem::Iconize:
                if (user application registered for this event)
                    Execute user defined service routine.
                else
                    GUISystem::DefaultIconizeBehavior()


            case ...
            Every possible event and the default services are included.
        } // end of switch(GUISystem::NextEvent)
    } // end of loop forever
} // end of GUISystem::MainEventLoop() function. Program terminate
```

Listing 1.3. The default MainEventLoop() function.

application process and waits for asynchronous operating-system calls to
re-activate the application process in the presence of relevant user actions.

- **(D) Events and central parsing switch statement.** Included in this statement are all possible actions/events (cases) that a user can perform. Associated with each event (case) is a default behavior and a toggle that allows

---

(A) System Initialization:

(A1): **Define Application State:**

      AllWorldBalls: A set of defined Balls, initialze to empty
      HeroBall: current active ball, initialize to null

(A2): **Register Event Service Routines:**

      Register **for:** **Left Mouse Button Down** Event
      Register **for:** **Left Mouse Button Drag** Event
      Register **for:** **Left Mouse Button Up** Event

(D) Events Services:

      // We care about these events, inform us if these events happen

      // service routine left mouse button click-down

(D1): **Left Mouse Button Down**

      HeroBall = Create a **new** ball at current mouse position
      // Draw all balls (including HeroBall)
      DrawAllBalls(AllWorldBalls, HeroBall)

      // service routine for left mouse button drag

(D2): **Left Mouse Button Drag**

      RefineRadiusAndVelocityOfHeroBall()
      // Draw all balls (including HeroBall)
      DrawAllBalls(AllWorldBalls, HeroBall)

      // service routine for left mouse button release

(D3): **Left Mouse Button Up**

      InsertHeroBallToAllWorldBalls()
      // Draw all balls
      DrawAllBalls(AllWorldBalls, null)

Listing 1.4. A simple event-driven program specification.

user applications to override the default behavior. During `SystemInitiali`
`zation()`, the user application can register an alternate service routine for
an event by toggling the override.

To develop an event-driven solution, our program must first register event service routines with the GUI system. After that, our entire program solution is
based on waiting for and servicing user events. While control-driven program-

ming solutions are based on an algorithmic organization of control structures in the main() function, an event-driven programming solution is based on the specification of events that cause changes to a defined application state. These are different paradigms for designing programming solutions. The key here is that, as programmers of an event-driven program, we have no explicit control over the algorithmic organization of the events: over which, when, or how often an event should occur.

Application state. This is the collection of information that describes the computational purpose of the application. For example, in the ball-shooting program, the application is defined to create a HeroBall and simulate the collection of balls in the application window. Thus, these objects are defined at Label (A1) in Listing 1.4.

Listing 1.4 shows an event-driven program that implements the left mouse button operations for our ball-shooting program. We see that during system initialization (A), the program defines an appropriate application state (A1) and registers left mouse button (LMB) down/drag/up events (A2). The corresponding event service routines (D1, D2, and D3) are also defined. At the end of each event service routine, we redraw all the balls to ensure that the user can see an up-to-date display at all times. Notice the absence of any control structure organizing the initialization and service routines. Recall that this is an event-driven program: the overall control structure is defined in the MainEventLoop(), which is external to our solution.

Listings 1.5–1.6 show how our program from Listing 1.4 is linked with the pre-defined MainEventLoop() from the GUI system. The MainEventLoop() calls the SystemInitialization() function defined in our solution (A). As described, after the initialization, our entire program is essentially the three event service routines (D1, D2, and D3). However, we have no control over the invocation of these routines. Instead, a user performs actions that trigger events that drive these routines. These routines in turn change the application state. In this way, an event-driven programming solution is based on specification of events (LMB events) that cause changes to a defined application state (AllWorldBalls and HeroBall). Since the user command-parsing switch statement (D in Listing 1.5) in the MainEventLoop() contains a case and the corresponding default behavior for every possible user actions, without any added complexity, our solution honors the non–application-specific actions in the environment (e.g., iconize, moving of application window).

In the context of event-driven programming, an event can be perceived as an asynchronous notification that something interesting has happened. The messenger for the notification is the underlying GUI system. The mechanism for receiving an event is via overriding the corresponding event service routine.

From the above discussion, we see that the registration for services of appropriate events is the core of designing and developing solutions for event-driven programs. Before we begin developing a complete solution for our ball-shooting program, let us spend some time understanding events.

MainEventLoop: *We, as GUI programmers, are users of this function. We* ***cannot*** *change this function.*

```
GUISystem::MainEventLoop() {
        // This will call the user defined function
```
(A): `SystemInitialization()`

(B): `loop forever {`

```
            // stop and wait for the next event
```
(C): `WaitFor ( GUISystem::NextEvent) {`

(D): `switch (GUISystem::NextEvent) {`

(D1): `case GUISystem::LeftMouseButtonDown:`
```
                if (user application registered for this event)
                    Invoke LeftMouseButtonDownServiceRoutine( currentMousePosition )
                else
                    Execute default GUISystem routine.
```

(D2): `case GUISystem::LeftMouseButtonDrag:`
```
                if (user application registered for this event)
                    Invoke LeftMouseButtonDragServiceRoutine( currentMousePosition )
                else
                    Execute default GUISystem routine.
```

(D3): `case GUISystem::LeftMouseButtonUp:`
```
                if (user application registered for this event)
                    Invoke LeftMouseButtonUpServiceRoutine( currentMousePosition )
                else
                    Execute default GUISystem routine.
```

```
            // There are many other events that do not concern us
            ⋮
```

```
        } // end of switch(GUISystem::NextEvent)
    } // end of loop forever
} // end of GUISystem::MainEventLoop() function. Program terminates.
```

Listing 1.5. MainEventLoop() to which our solution links.

User solution program: We, as GUI programmer, will program the following.

```
                    // will be invoked from the MainEventLoop during initialization.
(A):   SystemInitialization() {
       (A1):   // Defines Application State
               AllWorldBalls=NULL; // A set of defined Balls, initialze to empty
               HeroBall = null
       (A2):   // Registers event service routines
               GUISystem::RegisterServiceRoutine(GUISystem::LMBDown, LMBDownRoutine)
               GUISystem::RegisterServiceRoutine(GUISystem::LMBDrag, LMBDragRoutine)
               GUISystem::RegisterServiceRoutine(GUISystem::LMBUp, LMBUpRoutine)
               // "LMB": Left Mouse Button
       }


               // invoked from MainEventLoop when corresponding events are triggered.
(D):   Event Service Routines:
       D1:   LMBDownRoutine( mousePosition ) {
                   HeroBall = new ball at mousePosition
                   // Draw all balls (including HeroBall)
                   DrawAllBalls(AllWorldBalls, HeroBall)
             }
       D2:   LMBDragRoutine( mousePosition ) {
                   RefineRadiusAndVelocityOfHeroBall( mousePosition )
                   // Draw all balls (including HeroBall)
                   DrawAllBalls(AllWorldBalls, HeroBall)
             }
       D3:   LMBUpRoutine( mousePosition ) {
                   InsertHeroBallToAllWorldBalls()
                   // Draw all balls
                   DrawAllBalls(AllWorldBalls, null)
             }
```

Listing 1.6. Our solution that will link to MainEventLoop().

1.3   Triggering and Translation of Events

A typical modern computer comes with two attached input devices: the mouse and the keyboard. However, our solution for the ball-shooting program requires input events generated by devices ranging from slider bars (for velocity control) to buttons (the quit button). On the one hand, we understand that mouse clicks over "on-screen slider bar area" or "on-screen button area" would result in "slider bar" and "button pressed" events being triggered. On the other hand, we also understand that clicking on a mouse and pressing a button are two distinct events. This section briefly discusses the propagation and translation process from the hardware mouse clicks to the slider bar knob position events or button click events that our application receives.

Event. *Event* is a highly overloaded term in our discipline. In this chapter, we use event to mean GUI system events: an asynchronous notification that something interesting in the GUI system has happened.

1.3.1 The Operating System and Window Manager

On a typical computer system, the operating system (OS) is responsible for monitoring the physical states of input devices (e.g., keyboard or mouse). When interesting state changes occur on these devices (e.g., key presses or mouse movements), the OS packages and sends this information to the window manager. The window manager is the system application that is in charge of the entire computer display screen. Just as the OS keeps track of all the processes running on a machine, the window manager keeps track of all the application windows on the computer display screen. The window manger is responsible for forwarding relevant information from the OS to the currently active application. The GUI API that our application is built upon is responsible for receiving information from the window manager and translating and repackaging any hardware state change information (e.g., mouse click or key press) into semantically meaningful events (e.g., button click) for our application.

In focus. Because all user-triggered hardware state changes are directed toward the currently active window, an active window is often referred to as being *in focus*.

In the Linux OS *X Window* environment, a user has the option of working with different window manager programs (e.g., twm, mwm). This is in contrast with the Microsoft Windows environment, where the OS is tightly coupled with a single window manager program. However, in both cases the window manager keeps track of all application windows on the display screen and forwards all relevant hardware input device state change information to the currently active window/application.

1.3.2 The GUI API

The GUI API defines icons or graphical objects to represent virtual input and output devices. For example, a GUI API may define a 3D-looking rectangle to represent a "button," or a horizontal line to represent the "range" with a small 3D-looking rectangle on top of the line to represent the "slider knob." These virtual devices are examples of GUI elements. Notice that the application's main window

In-focus GUI element. The in-focus terminology also applies to individual GUI elements. For example, one can refer to an active slider bar as being the in-focus GUI element.

is also an example of a GUI element, where a few rectangles are used to represent the title bar and work area with a few surrounding lines representing the window borders. Typical applications first create the main window GUI element and then place other GUI elements at strategic locations inside the application's window to associate semantic meanings with those locations. For example, the ball-shooting program in Figure I.2 has six GUI elements:

1. Container main window;

2. Drawing area for the balls;

3. Two slider bars;

4. Quit button;

5. Status bar.

As we will see in Tutorial 2.8, in general, it is possible to place a window GUI element within another window GUI element. As the complexity of our application increases, this is a convenient and powerful way to organize the large number of GUI elements involved.

After receiving hardware device state change information from the window manager, the GUI API translates this information into events and forwards the events to the currently active GUI element. For example, a mouse click on an in-focus "button GUI element" is translated into a "button-pressed event," whereas a mouse click over a "slider bar GUI element" is translated into a "slider bar position event" with an appropriate scroll values.

Sometimes it is not appropriate/meaningul for the GUI API to translate and forward hardware state change information. For example, a user performs a mouse click over the status bar area of Figure I.2. Because the status bar is an output-only GUI element, it is not capable of receiving any input events. In cases like this, the GUI API typically allows the application to choose between discarding the event or translating and forwarding the event to the GUI element that contains the in-focus element. In this case, the main application container window would receive the mouse click event.

In practice, events have many triggering origins. For example, the user can trigger input events; the window manager can decide to enter screensaver mode and trigger events to inform all applications; or the OS can detect hardware abnormality and trigger events via the window manager. Ultimately, relevant events will be sent to our applications. From within our applications, it can be impossible to determine the true origin of an event. For example, a system hardware failure may result in the window manager sending a "save and quit" event to our application. In this case, it would be impossible for our application to determine if the event was triggered by a user's action or from the OS. Fortunately, in general there is no need for our application to be aware of the true triggering origin of an event.

1.4 Categories of Events

We classify events into three categories: user events, application events, and GUI/window manager events. In this section, we describe each of these event category and discuss the application's role in servicing these events.

1.4.1 The User

These are events triggered by the actions a user performs on the input devices. Notice that input devices include actual hardware devices (e.g., mouse, keyboard) and/or software-simulated GUI elements (e.g., slider bars, combo boxes). Typically, a user performs actions for two very different reasons.

- **Application-specific.** These are input actions that are part of the application. Clicking and dragging in the application screen area to create a HeroBall is an example of an action performed on a hardware input device. Changing the slider bars to control the HeroBall's velocity is an example of an action performed on a software-simulated GUI element. Both of these actions and the resulting events are application-specific: the application (our program) is solely responsible for servicing these events.

- **General.** These are input actions defined by the windowing environment. For example, a user clicks and drags in the window title-bar area expecting to move the entire application window. The servicing of these types of events requires collaboration between our application and the GUI system. We will discuss the servicing of these types of events in more detail when explaining events that originate from the GUI system in Section 1.4.3.

Notice that the meaning of a user's action is context-sensitive. It depends on where the action is performed: click and drag in the application screen area vs. slider bar vs. application window title-bar area. In any case, the underlying GUI system is responsible for parsing the context and determining which GUI element should receive a particular event.

1.4.2   The Application

These are events defined by the application, typically depending on some run-time conditions. During run time, if and when the condition becomes favorable, the supporting GUI system triggers the event and conveys the favorable conditions to the application. A straightforward example is a periodic alarm. Modern GUI systems typically allow an application to define (sometimes multiple) timer events. Once defined, the GUI system will trigger an event to wake up the application when the timer expires. As we will see, this timer event is essential for supporting real-time simulations. Since the application (our program) requested the generation of these types of events, our program is solely responsible for serving them. The important distinction between application-defined and user-generated events is that application-defined events can be predictable and dependable: when properly defined, these are events that our application can depend on. Even when the user is not doing anything, our application can depend on application-defined events to trigger.

1.4.3   The Window Manager and the GUI System

These are events that originated from either the window manager or within the GUI system. These events typically convey state information to the application. There are typically three reasons for these events.

- **Internal GUI states change.** These are events signaling an internal state change of the GUI system. For example, the GUI system typically generates an event before the creation of the application's main window. This provides an opportunity for the application to perform the corresponding initialization. In some GUI systems (e.g., MFC) the `SystemInitializa tion()` functionality is accomplished with these types of events: user applications are expected to override the appropriate window's creation event and initialize the application state. Modern, general-purpose commercial GUI systems typically define a large number of events signaling detailed state changes in anticipation of supporting different types of applications and requirements. For example, for the creation of the application's main window, the GUI system may define events for the following states:

    - before resource allocation;
    - after resource allocation but before initialization;
    - after initialization but before initial drawing.

A GUI system usually defines meaningful default behaviors for such events. To program an effective application based on a GUI system, one must understand the different groups of events and only service the appropriate selections.

- **External environment requests attention.** These are events indicating that there are changes in the windowing environment that potentially require application attention. For example, a user has moved another application window to cover a portion of our application window, or a user has minimized our application window. The GUI system and the windowing environment typically have appropriate service routines for these types of events. An application would only choose to service these events when special actions must be performed. For example, for a real-time simulation program, the application may choose to suspend the simulation if the application window is minimized. In this situation, an application must service the minimize and maximize events.

- **External environment requests application collaboration.** These are typically events requesting the application's collaboration to complete the service of some *general user actions* (see Section 1.4.1). For example, if a user click-drags the application window's title bar, the window manager reacts by letting the user "drag" the entire application window. This "drag" operation is implemented by continuously erasing and redrawing the entire application window at the current mouse pointer position on the computer display. The GUI system has full knowledge of the appearance of the application window (e.g., the window frames, the menus), but it has no knowledge of the application window content (e.g., how many free-falling balls traveling at what velocity). In this case, the GUI system redraws the application window frame and generates a Redraw/Paint event for the application, requesting assistance in completing the service of the user's "drag" operation. As an application in a shared window environment, our application is expected to honor and service these types of events. The most common events in this category are Redraw/Paint and Resize. Redraw/Paint is the single most important event that an application must service because it supports the most common operations a user may perform in a shared window environment. Resize is also an important event to which the application must respond because the application is in charge of GUI element placement policy (e.g., if window size is increased, how the GUI elements should be placed in the larger window).

1.5   Servicing of Events

As we have seen, event service routines handle events forwarded to our application. These routines are the core of our programming solution. In the presence of relevant events, the `MainEventLoop()` calls these functions and passes the control *back* to our program code. For this reason, these service routines are also referred to as *callback* functions.

1.5.1   Registration of Event Service Routines

An application program registers callback functions with the GUI system by passing the address of the function to the GUI system. This is the registration mechanism implied in Listing 1.5. Simple GUI systems (e.g., GLUT or FLTK) usually support this form of registration mechanism. The advantage of this mechanism is that it is easy to understand, straightforward to program, and often contributes to a small memory footprint in the resulting program. The main disadvantage of this mechanism is the lack of organizational structure for the callback functions.

In commercial GUI systems, user applications typically must work with a large number of events. A structured organization of the service routines can greatly increase the programmability of the GUI system. Modern commercial GUI systems often present their APIs through an object-oriented language interface (e.g., C++ for MFC, Java for Java Swing). For these systems, many event service routines are integrated as methods in the class hierarchies of the GUI system. In these cases, registration of event service routines may be implemented as subclassing and overriding corresponding virtual functions in the GUI system. In this way, the event service routines are organized according to the functionality of GUI elements.

The details of the different registration mechanisms will be demonstrated in Chapter 2 when we examine the implementation details.

1.5.2   Characteristics of Event Service Routines

Event service routines are simply functions in our program. However, these functions also serve an important role as the server of events. The following are guidelines one should take into account when implementing event service routines.

- An event service routine should only service the triggering event and return the control back to the `MainEventLoop()` immediately. This may seem to be a no-brainer. However, because of our familiarity with control-driven programming, it is often tempting to anticipate/poll subsequent events with a control structure in the service routine. For example, when servicing the left mouse button down event, we know that the mouse drag event will happen next. After allocating and defining the circle center, we have properly initialized data to work with the HeroBall object. It may seem easier to simply include a while-loop to poll and service mouse drag events. However, because there are other external events that may happen at any time (e.g., Timer event, external Redraw events), this monopolizing of control becomes a bad design decision and may cause the program to malfunction.

- An event service routine should be stateless, and individual invocations should be independent. In terms of implementation, this essentially means that event service routines should not define local static variables to record application state information for subsequent invocations. Since the application has no control over when or how often events are triggered, it follows that it is not possible to predict the next invocation of a service routine. This means when a service routine is invoked, it can be difficult to evaluate the validity of state information stored in the local static variables. The use of static variables in event service routines can easily lead to disastrously and unnecessarily complex solutions. One can always define extra state variables in the application state to record temporary state information that must persist over multiple event services. As we will see in our final event-driven ball-shooting solution, the DefiningNewHeroBall flag in Listing 1.7 is one such example.

- An event service routine should check for invocation conditions regardless of common sense logical sequence. For example, logically, a mouse drag event should never happen unless a mouse down event has already occurred. In reality, a user may depress a mouse button from outside of our application window and then drag the mouse into our application window. In this case, we will receive a mouse drag event without the corresponding mouse down event. For this reason, the mouse drag service routine should check the invocation condition that the proper initialization has indeed happened. Notice that in Listing 1.7, we do not include proper invocation condition checking. For example, in the LMBDragRoutine(), we do not verify that LMBDownRotine() has been invoked (by checking the DefiningNewHeroBall flag). In a real system, this may cause the program to malfunction and/or crash.

1.6   The Event-Driven Ball-Shooting Program

In Section 1.1, we began developing a control-driven programming solution to the ball-shooting program based on verbalizing the conditions (controls) under which the appropriate actions should be taken:

> while favorable condition, parse the input ...

As we have seen, with appropriate modifications, we were able to detail the control structures for our solution.

From the discussion in Section 1.2, we see that to design an event-driven programming solution, we must

- define the application state;

- describe how user actions change the application state;

- map the user actions to events that the GUI system supports;

- register corresponding event service routines to service the user actions.

The specification from p. 10 detailed the behaviors of our ball-shooting program. The description is based on actions performed on familiar input devices (e.g., slider bars and mouse). These actions change the application state and thus the appearance of the application window. This specification describes the second and third items from the above list without explicitly defining the application state. Our job in designing a solution is to derive the implicitly defined application state and design the appropriate service routines.

Listing 1.7 presents our event-driven programming solution. As expected, the application state (A1) is defined in `SystemInitialization()`. The `AllWorld` `Balls` set and `HeroBall` can be derived from the specification on p. 10. The `DefiningNewHeroBall` flag is a transient (temporary) application state designed to support user actions across multiple events (click-and-drag). Using transient application states is a common approach to support consecutive interrelated events.

Listing 1.7 shows the registration of three types of service routines (A2):

1. user-generated application-specific events (A2S1);

2. an application-defined event (A2S2);

3. a GUI system–generated event requesting collaboration (A2S3).

---

*(A): The **SystemInitialization** function.*

```
SystemInitialization() {
```

(A1): Define Application State

```
    AllWorldBalls: A set of defined Balls, initialze to empty
    HeroBall = null
    DefiningNewHeroBall = false
```

(A2): Register Event Service Routines

A2S1: Application Specific User Events

```
    GUISystem::RegisterServiceRoutine(GUISystem:: LMBDown, LMBDownRoutine)
    GUISystem::RegisterServiceRoutine(GUISystem:: LMBDrag, LMBDragRoutine)
    GUISystem::RegisterServiceRoutine(GUISystem:: LMBUp, LMBUpRoutine)
    GUISystem::RegisterServiceRoutine(GUISystem:: RMBDown, RMBDownRoutine)
    GUISystem::RegisterServiceRoutine(GUISystem:: SliderBar, SliderBarRoutine)
```

A2S2: Application Define Event

```
    GUISystem::DefineTimerPeriod(SimulationUpdateInterval)

    // Triggers TimerEvent every: SimulationUpdateInterval period
    GUISystem::RegisterServiceRoutine(GUISystem:: TimerEvent, ServiceTimer)
```

A2S3: Honor collaboration request from the GUI system

```
    GUISystem::RegisterServiceRoutine(GUISystem:: RedrawEvent, RedrawRoutine)
}
```

D: Event Service Routines.

```
    // Left mouse button down service routine
```

D1:   `LMBDownRoutine(mousePosition)`

```
        HeroBall = CreateHeroBall(mousePosition)
        DefiningNewHeroBall = true
```
    D1L3   `GUISystem::GenerateRedrawEvent`

```
    // Left mouse button drag service routine
```

D2:   `LMBDragRoutine(mousePosition)`

```
        RefineRadiusAndVelocityOfHeroBall(mousePosition)
        SetSliderBarsWithHeroBallVelocity()
        GUISystem::GenerateRedrawEvent  // Generates a redraw event
```

Listing 1.7. Event-driven ball-shooting program.

```
           // Left mouse button up service routine
  D3:  LMBUpRoutine(mousePosition)
           InsertHeroBallToAllWorldBalls()
           DefiningNewHeroBall = false


           // Right mouse button down service routine
  D4:  RMBDownRoutine(mousePosition)
           HeroBall = SelectHeroBallBasedOn (mousePosition )
           if (HeroBall != null)  SetSliderBarsWithHeroBallVelocity()


           // Slider Bar change service routine
  D5:  SliderBarRoutine(sliderBarValues)
           if (HeroBall != null)
               SetSliderBarsWithHeroBallVelocity(sliderBarValues)


           // Timer expired service routine
  D6:  ServiceTimer()
           // Move balls by velocities  and remove off-screen ones
           UpdateSimulation()

           // Sets status bar with number of balls on screen
           EchoToStatusBar()

           // Generates a redraw event
           GUISystem:: GenerateRedrawEvent

           // Reflect propoer HeroBall velocity
           if (HeroBall != null)
               SetSliderBarsWithHeroBallVelocity(sliderBarValues)


           // Redraw event service routine
  D7:  RedrawRoutine()
           DrawBalls(AllWorldBalls)
           if (DefiningNewHeroBall)
               // Draw the new Hero Ball that is being defined
               DrawBalls(HeroBall)
```

Listing 1.7. (cont.)

The timer event definition (A2S2) sets up a periodic alarm for the application to update the simulation of the free-falling balls. The service routines of the user-generated application-specific events (D1–D5) are remarkably similar to the

corresponding case statements in the control-driven solution presented in Listing 1.2 (B1–B3). It should not be surprising that this is so, because we are implementing the exact same user actions based on the same specification. Line 3
of the LMBDownRoutine() (D1L3) demonstrates that when necessary, our application can request the GUI system to initiate events. In this case, we signal
the GUI system that an application redraw is necessary. Notice that event service routines are simply functions in our program. This means that at D1L3, we
could also call RedrawRoutine() (D7) directly. The difference is that a call to
RedrawRoutine() will force a redraw immediately, while requesting the generation of a Redraw event allows the GUI system to optimize the number of redraws. For example, if the user performs a LMB click and starts dragging immediately, with our D1 and D2 implementation, the GUI system can gather the many
GenerateRedrawEvent requests in a short period of time and only generate one
Redraw event. In this way, we can avoid performing more redraws than necessary.

To achieve a smooth animation, we should perform about 20 to 40 updates per
second. It follows that the SimulationUpdateInterval should be no more than
50 milliseconds so that the ServiceTimer() routine can be invoked more than
20 times per second. (Notice that a Redraw event is requested at the end of the
ServiceTimer() routine.) This means, at the very least, that our application is
guaranteed to receive more than 20 Redraw events in one second. For this reason,
the GenerateRedrawEvent requests in D1 and D2 are really not necessary. The
servicing of our timer events will guarantee us an up-to-date display screen at all
times.

One important lesson to learn here is that we have completed the design of a
solution without mentioning implementation. In later chapters, we will see how
we can map this solution to implementations based on different technologies. The
lesson to learn is to design a solution before coding.

1.7 Summary

In this chapter, we have discussed programming models that are simply strategies
for organizing statements of our program. We have seen that for interactive applications, in which an application continuously waits and reacts to a user's input
actions, organizing the program statements based on designing control structures
results in complex and inefficient programs. Existing GUI systems analyze all
possible user actions, design control structures to interact with the user, implement default behaviors for all user actions, and provide this functionality in GUI
APIs. To develop interactive applications, we take advantage of the existing con-

trol structure in the GUI API (i.e., the `MainEventLoop()`) and modify the default behaviors (via event service routines) of user actions. In order to properly collaborate with existing GUI APIs, the strategy for organizing the program statements should be based on specifying user actions that cause changes to the application state.

Now that we understand how to organize the statements of our program, let's examine how we can implement this.

Working with GUI APIs

This chapter introduces us to the principles of working with GUI APIs. This chapter:

- identifies the GUI element as the fundamental entity in GUI API programming;

- describes the process of building GUI applications: the front-end layout design and the back-end programming support;

- differentiates front-end GUI elements from the back-end control variables;

- demonstrates the above principles based on a GUI API;

- demonstrates how to extend, organize, and customize a GUI API for the needs of our application.

After this chapter we should:

- understand the approach to learning a modern GUI API;

- be able to design/discuss implementation of GUI applications independent from API technologies;

In addition, with respect to hands-on programming, we should:

- understand source code of simple GUI applications independent of the implementation API technologies;

- be able to implement simple GUI applications based on MFC.

In this chapter, we describe the *principles* of working with modern GUI APIs. We emphasize principles because we are going to rely heavily on the MFC API to illustrate the ideas presented. However, it is important to remember that our focus is not learning the skills of using any particular API. Instead, we are interested in understanding the basic capabilities of modern GUI APIs so that we can examine and implement the requirements of event-driven interactive programs. For example, we should be able to apply the lessons learned from this chapter to other GUI APIs (e.g., the Java Swing Library or the Microsoft Forms Library). After this chapter (and with some practice), we want to be able to pick up the reference manual of any modern GUI API and commence developing a simple interactive application.

The ultimate goal of this chapter is the understanding of GUI APIs' support for user interactivity and not the implementation of the ball-shooting program. A proper implementation of the ball-shooting program can only commence after we learn the software architecture for organizing our solution structure, which will be covered in Chapter 5.

2.1   Our Application and Existing Libraries

Graphical UI. Notice that the "graphical" in GUI refers to a user interface that is "graphically" oriented. For example, a user interface with visually pleasing "graphical" buttons or slider bars. This should not be confused with the "computer graphics" we are learning in this book.

When developing interactive computer graphics programs, we work with existing tools, or software libraries, to develop our applications. In this book, we are learning how to develop user interactive graphics applications, and thus we work with graphical user interface (GUI) libraries and graphics libraries. These libraries provide well-defined application programming interfaces (APIs) with well-documented functions and utility classes. The applications we develop use/-subclass from the utility classes and call appropriate functions through the APIs. In this way, our application interacts with the users through a GUI API and draws graphics through a graphics API.

Examples of popular GUI APIs include Graphics Utility Toolkit (GLUT), Fast and Light Toolkit (FLTK), and Microsoft Foundation Classes (MFC). Examples of popular graphics APIs include OpenGL API, Microsoft Direct X Direct3D (D3D), and Java 3D. In this book, we will work with MFC to interact with the user, and OpenGL and D3D to draw graphics. We show examples in more than one GUI API to demonstrate that although the utility classes and function names may be significantly different, the principles of working with GUI APIs are very similar. We show examples in more than one graphics API to demonstrate that although configuration procedures are different, and the functions have very different names, these APIs are designed based on the same fundamental graphics concepts. When reading this book, remember that the programming and APIs are there to help us learn the concepts and knowledge. In general, the skills in working with an API should be readily transferable to new APIs.

2.2 GUI Elements

As we saw in Chapter 1, after the initialization, event-driven programs are simply a collection of routines that are driven by asynchronous external events. For this reason, facilitating the generation of appropriate events is key to implementing event-driven programs. In our case, since our programs are built to interact with users, our users are the main source of asynchronous events. Modern GUI APIs are designed to facilitate users in triggering appropriate events for our applications.

Modern GUI APIs define an elaborate set of GUI elements and associate extensive event structures with these GUI elements to support interactivity with the users and programmability of event service routines. For example, a GUI API would define a button GUI element and associate events such as mouse over (no click), clicked, double clicked, and so on with the button GUI element. The GUI API would then allow application programmers to register and service these events.

Recall that GUI elements are virtual input/output devices, typically represented as graphical icons. Other examples of common GUI elements include slider bars, checkboxes, radio buttons, combo boxes, text boxes, and so on. A window, or an area with fancy borders, is also an example of a GUI element. A window GUI element is special because it serves as a container for other GUI elements. In general, a GUI-based application has at least one GUI element—the main application window. From the user's perspective, GUI elements should be the following.

- **Visually pleasing.** For example, representing a button with a 3D-looking icon.

- **Semantically meaningful.** For example, the button should be properly labeled, so that users understand to move the mouse pointer over the icon and click the left mouse button to activate (depress) the button.

On the opposite end, from the programmer's perspective, a GUI element should have the following.

- **A unique identifier.** The application must be able to uniquely identify each GUI element to differentiate the actual triggering source of individual events.

- **Default behaviors.** GUI elements should define default behaviors for mundane situations. For example, a depressed GUI button should look different from an unactivated button. As application programmers, we expect GUI elements to behave appropriately for these types of typical situations.

- **Customizable behaviors.** As application developers, we want to have the option of customizing the behaviors of GUI elements. For example, our application may demand a depressed button to have a special color.

- **State information.** Certain types of interactions with the users require the corresponding GUI element types to retain state information. For example, a slider bar should record the knob position, a checkbox should record if it is currently checked (true) or unchecked (false). When servicing events generated by these types of GUI elements, our application must poll the corresponding state information.

Control variables. Variables in our program code that are associated with and represent GUI elements.

- **Abstract representation.** Customizable behaviors and polling of state information imply that our program must have variables referencing the corresponding GUI elements. These types of variables are referred to as control variables, where through a control variable, our program code can control a GUI element. To properly reflect the different functionality, control variables for different GUI element types should be of different data types. For example, there should be a CButton class for buttons and CSliderBar class for representing slider bar GUI elements.

- **Event service registration mechanisms.** As we have seen many times, this is probably the single most important functionality we expect from GUI elements.

It is interesting to note that sometimes it is desirable to have GUI elements controlled by the application. For example, in the ball-shooting program, as the Hero Ball free falls under gravitational force, the slider bar GUI elements are controlled by the application to correctly reflect the HeroBall velocity.

2.3 Building a GUI Application

We can perceive a GUI application as being a collection of GUI elements, where through these GUI elements a user can trigger events to cause changes to an application state in accomplishing desired tasks. The event-driven programming model taught us the *back end* of a GUI application: how to react to events and cause changes to an application state. The GUI API provides the mechanism for building the *front end* of a GUI application: how to put together the collection of GUI elements to support the generation of appropriate events.

2.3.1 Front End: Layout of GUI Elements

The first step in building a GUI application is to design the layout of the user interface system. This is referred to as the front end because the results are the front of our application that the user can see and interact with. In this step, the application developer must determine the location and appearance of every GUI element. Modern GUI APIs typically support this process with a GUI builder program. A GUI builder is an interactive graphical editor that allows its user to interactively place and manipulate the appearances of all GUI elements. This layout process typically involves a developer placing icons representing GUI elements into a rectangular area representing the application window. The developer then adjusts each GUI element's appearance (e.g., color, size). The result of GUI element layout is usually stored in some data files. The developer includes these data files with the rest of the development source code. When compiled and linked appropriately, the resulting program displays the designed GUI layout.

The goal of this first step is to arrange and manipulate the GUI elements to present an aesthetically pleasing, logically meaningful, and intuitively easy-to-use user interface. These are the topics of user interface design, an entire field in computer science. In this book, we will only describe the basic process involved in building a GUI. Our GUI front ends are sufficient, but they may not be the best, or even very good.

2.3.2 Back End: Establish Semantic Correspondence

As we have already seen, the semantic meanings of GUI elements are defined by the corresponding event service routines. For example, a mouse click over a button has no real meaning. It is the event service routine that quits the application that defines the semantic meaning of the button. We refer to this as the back end because the results of this step are pieces of code that operate behind the visible user interface. Typically, GUI builder programs provide mechanisms for supporting the registration of event service routines. For example, a GUI builder displays a list of defined events for a particular GUI element. The developer has the option of registering for an event by entering a service function name.

Similar types of support are also available for defining control variables. The developer indicates to the GUI builder (e.g., by clicking on an appropriate property sheet) that a control variable should be defined for a particular GUI element. Based on the GUI element type (e.g., a button), the GUI builder typically predetermines the data type (e.g., CButton) for the control variable and prompt the developer for the variable name.

Notice that in both cases, the developer entered program code fragments (names of service functions and control variables) into the GUI builder program. As mentioned, at the conclusion of the GUI builder program, information is saved into some data files. It is important for the GUI builder to integrate these code fragments with the rest of the event-driven program source code. There are two different mechanisms for supporting this integration.

1. **External linkage.** Some GUI builders require the developer to enter the entire event service routine program code directly into the GUI builder program. The GUI builder then generates extra program modules in the form of source code files that contain the event service routines. The developer includes these source code files as part of the development project.

2. **Internal direct code modification.** Some GUI builders modify and insert function prototypes and/or control variable declaration/initialization directly into the source files in the development project. The developer then edits the same source file to enter event service routine program code.

The advantage of the external linkage mechanism is that the GUI builder has minimal knowledge of the application source code. This provides a simple and flexible development environment where the developer is free to organize the source code structure, variable names, and so on, in any appropriate way. However, the externally generated programming module implies a loosely integrated environment. For example, to modify the behavior of a GUI element, the application developer must invoke the GUI builder, modify code fragments, and regenerate the external program module.

The internal direct code modification mechanism, in contrast, provides a better integrated environment where the GUI builder modifies the application program source code directly. However, to support proper "direct code modification," the GUI builder must have intimate knowledge of, and often places severe constraints on, the application source code system (e.g., source code organization, file names, variable names).

Control Variables

There are two situations where the back-end event-driven program must define a control variable to represent a front-end GUI element.

- **Polling/setting of GUI element state information.** A control variable should be defined for GUI elements with state information that must be polled/set during run time. For example, a checkbox's state information is altered every time a user clicks it. When servicing a checkbox's click event, the service routine must poll the GUI element (through the control variable) for its state. Notice that in this case, the data type of the checkbox control variable should be of `bool`. To support polling and setting operations, the data type of the corresponding control variable should reflect the state information and not the GUI element type. For example, a slider bar's state information is the position of the knob, or a `float`. Thus, control variables for polling and setting a slider-bar GUI element should be a variable with `float` data type and not `CSliderBar`.

- **Customization of GUI element behavior.** A control variable should be defined for GUI elements when an application demands customized behaviors. For example, an application may demand that the state of a checkbox be associated with the color of the checkbox: green for checked and red for unchecked. In this case, during event servicing, we must first poll the GUI element state and then modify the color attributes of the checkbox. This means that the application needs to have access to the `CCheckBox` data type.

2.4 Examples: FLTK and MFC

2.4.1 FLTK—Fluid and External Service Linkage

Figure 2.1 shows a screenshot of working with Fluid, FLTK's GUI builder. In the lower-right corner of Figure 2.1, we see that (A) Fluid allows an application developer to interactively place graphical representations of GUI elements (3D-looking icons). (B) is an area representing the application window. In addition (C), the application developer can interactively select each GUI element to define its physical appearances (color, shape, size, etc.). In the lower-left corner of

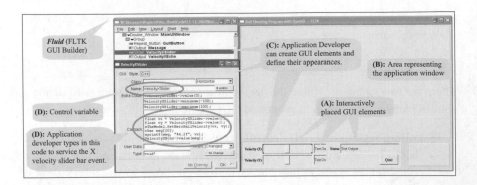

Figure 2.1. Fluid: FLTK's GUI builder.

Figure 2.1, we see that (D) the application developer has the option to type in program fragments to define a control variable for and to service events generated by the corresponding GUI element. In this case, we can see that the developer must type in the program fragment for handling the *x*-velocity slider bar events. This program fragment will be separated from the rest of the program source code system and will be associated with Fluid (the GUI builder). At the conclusion of the GUI layout design, the user can instruct Fluid to generate source code files to be included with the rest of the application development environment. In this way, some source code files are controlled and generated by the GUI builder, and the application developer must invoke the GUI builder in order to update/maintain the control variables and the event service routines. FLTK implements external service linkage.

2.4.2 MFC—Resource Editor and Direct Code Modification

Figure 2.2 shows a screenshot of the MFC resource editor, MFC's GUI builder. Similar to Fluid (Figure 2.1), in the middle of Figure 2.2, (A) we see that the resource editor also supports interactive designing of the GUI element layout in (B), an area representing the application window. Although the GUI builder interfaces operate differently, we observe that in (C), the MFC resource editor also supports the definition/modification of the physical appearance of GUI elements. However, unlike Fluid, the MFC resource editor is tightly integrated with the rest of the development environment. In this case, a developer can register event services by inheriting or overriding appropriate service routines. The MFC resource editor automatically inserts code fragments into the application source code system. To support this functionality, the application source code organization is

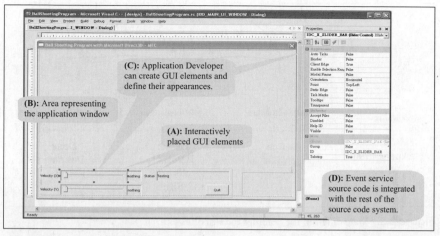

Figure 2.2. The MFC resource editor.

governed/shared with the GUI builder; the application developer is not entirely free to rename files/classes and/or to reorganize implementation source code file system structure. MFC implements internal direct code modification for event service linkage.

2.5 Implementation Notes

Before we begin examining examples of implementations in detail, it is important that we take note of a few important characteristics/pitfalls of programming with GUI APIs.

Application state.   The application state of an event-driven program must persist over the entire lifetime of the program. In terms of implementation, this means that the application state should be defined based on variables that are dynamically allocated during run time and that reside on the heap memory. These are in contrast to local variables that reside on the stack memory and that do not persist over different function invocations.

Implicit events.   The mapping of user actions to events in the GUI system often results in implicit and/or undefined events. In our ball-shooting solution, the actions to define a HeroBall involve left mouse button down and drag. When mapping these actions to events in our implementation (in Listing 1.2 and List-

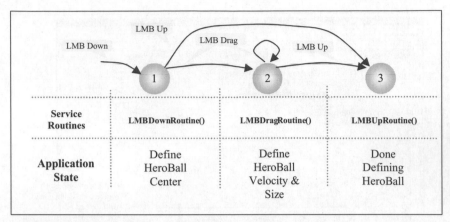

Figure 2.3. State diagram for defining the HeroBall.

ing 1.7), we realize that we should also pay attention to the implicit mouse button up event. Another example is the HeroBall selection action: right mouse button down. In this case, right mouse button drag and up events are not serviced by our application, and thus, they are undefined (to our application).

Consecutive user actions.   When one user action (e.g., "drag out the HeroBall" is mapped to a group of consecutive events (e.g., mouse button down, then drag, then up), a finite state diagram can usually be derived to help design the solution. Figure 2.3 depicts the finite state diagram for defining the HeroBall. The left mouse button down event puts the program into state 1 where, in our solution from Listing 1.7, LMBDownRoutine() implements this state and defines the center of the HeroBall, and so on. In this case, the transition between states is triggered by the mouse events, and we see that it is physically impossible to move from state 2 back to state 1. However, we do need to handle the case where the user action causes a transition from State 1 to State 3 directly (mouse button down and release without any dragging actions). This state diagram helps us analyze possible combinations of state transitions and perform appropriate initializations.

Input/output functionality of GUI elements.   An input GUI element (e.g., the quit button) is an artifact (e.g., an icon) for the users to generate events to cause changes in the application state, whereas an output GUI element (e.g., the status bar) is an avenue for the application to present application state information to the user as feedback. For both types of elements, information only flows in one direction—either from the user to the application (input) or from the application to the user (output). When working with GUI elements that serve both input and output purposes, special care is required. For example, after the user selects or defines a HeroBall, the slider bars reflects the velocity of the free-falling HeroBall (output), although at any time, the user can manipulate the slider bar to alter the HeroBall velocity (input). In this case, the GUI element's displayed state and the application's internal state are connected. The application must ensure that these two states are consistent. Notice that in the solution shown in Listing 1.2, this state consistency is not maintained. When a user clicks the right mouse button (B2 in Listing 1.2) to select a HeroBall, the slider bar values are updated properly; however, as the HeroBall free falls under gravity, the slider bar values are not updated. The solution presented in Listing 1.7 fixes this problem by calling the SetSliderBarWithHeroBallVelocity() function in the ServiceTimer() function.

Redraw/Paint events. In Section 1.4.3, it is stated that

> Redraw/Paint is the single most important event that an application must service . . .

Recall that the Redraw/Paint event is a reminder from the window manager that the content of our application window may be out-of-date. It is in our application's interests to update the window content as soon as possible, preferably before the user notices any inconsistency. On the other hand, as we have seen in the ball-shooting program solution presented in Section 1.6, to maintain smooth animation of simulated results, applications with real-time simulation must redraw the application state at a rate of more than 20 times in a second. With such high redraw rate, the application's window content can never be out-of-date for more than a few milliseconds. For this reason, applications with default high redraw rates do not need to service the Redraw/Paint event. Because most of the applications presented in this book involve real-time simulations with more than 20 redraws in a second, Redraw/Paint events are typically *not* serviced.

OnIdle events. Many GUI APIs define an OnIdle event to be triggered when nothing is happening or when the application is idling. An application with real-time simulation can choose to service this event to compute simulation updates. In this way, the application can take advantage of idle CPU cycles for simulation computations. The main disadvantage of this approach is that as the developer, we cannot predict the events.

1. If the application is completely idle, this event will be triggered continuously. As a result, the simulation process will be updated more frequently than necessary.

2. If the application gets busy (e.g., bursts of user activity) and is short on idle time, there is a chance that the simulation may lag behind real-time, resulting in an inconsistent display.

In practice, modern machines are fast enough that idle cycles are almost always available. Many commercial applications are developed with updates during the `OnIdle` events. For dependable and predictable update rates, we have chosen to compute simulations during the application-programmed `OnTimer` events.

2.6   Tutorials and Code Base

Modern GUI APIs are highly sophisticated, often with steep initial learning curves. When learning to work with a GUI API, we should constantly remind ourselves that ultimately, we are interested in building interactive graphics programs. Our goal is not to become an expert in GUI programming. Rather, we are interested in understanding the principles of working with the GUI API such that we can start building graphics applications. In this section, we use MFC to experience the different aspects of event programming studied. It is important to understand the underlying concepts behind the APIs and then be comfortable with using one of the APIs. The important lesson we should learn from the short history of our discipline is that APIs change and evolve rapidly; we must always be ready to learn new ones.

The tutorials from this section serve two purposes, to demonstrate how to work with a GUI API and how to work with MFC. In the beginning of each tutorial, explicit goal and approach statements identify the key ideas that will be demonstrated in the tutorial. These are API-independent statements, where to work with any GUI API, one must understand how to accomplish these tasks. Typically the procedures involved in programming with different GUI APIs may be different, but the end results contain similar elements (e.g., control variables with appropriate data types, event service routines via object-oriented override and/or via callback function registration, etc.).

In the following tutorials, we describe the results of working with MFC and relate these results to what we learned from earlier sections. For a detailed step-by-step how-to for working with the MFC resource editor and the details of building every tutorial in this chapter, see the MFC guide on the accompanying CD by William Frankhouser. To demonstrate the concepts presented are indeed language- and GUI API-independent, the following tutorials are also implemented in C# and the WinForm API. The corresponding detailed step-by-step

Tutorial	Demonstrates	Reusable Codebase
2.1	Demystify source code files	-
2.2	GUI elements and control variables	-
2.3	More with control variables	-
2.4	Application defined events	-
2.5	Input/output GUI elements	-
2.6	Extending GUI API with classes	`SliderCtrlWithEcho`
2.7	Custom GUI library	`MFC_Library`
2.8	Grouping of GUI elements	`ReplaceDialogControl()`

Table 2.1. Chapter 2 tutorials.

guide can also be found on the accompanying CD, written by Ethan Verrall. On-line resources are excellent avenues for learning basic skills in working with these software systems. Jason Pursell has developed an excellent step-by-step guide on working with the MFC editor that is tailored for the MFC-based tutorials in this book.[1]

Table 2.1 gives a brief summary of the tutorials in this section.

Tutorial 2.1. Demystifying the Files

- **Goal.** To demonstrate that while on first look, programming with a GUI API can appear to be overwhelming, with a systemic approach of analyzing the purpose of the files in the environment, we can gain significant understanding of the system.

- **Approach.** Familiarize and demystify the typically intimidating GUI development source code structure; create the simplest possible application with a GUI API and analyze every file; identify the purpose of files and draw attention to how these files are related/unrelated to GUI development.

Figure 2.4 is a screenshot of running Tutorial 2.1. This entire tutorial is automatically generated by the MFC wizard of the Microsoft Visual C++ (VC++) integrated development environment (IDE). When user clicks on the "OK" or the "Cancel" button, the application simply quits. This application does not do anything else.

Tutorial 2.1.
Project Name
  `MFC_SimpleDialog`

Figure 2.4. Tutorial 2.1.

---

[1]See Jason's home page at http://home.myuw.net/jpursell/ or http://faculty.washington.edu/ksung /biga/chapter_tutorials/VC_Guide/CreatingDialogAppWithMFC7.pdf

Purpose	Files	Folder
Source code	TutorialApp(.cpp,.h) TutorialDlg(.cpp,.h) stdafx(.cpp,.h), Resource.h	MFC_SimpleDialog (main project folder)
Documentation	Readme.txt	
GUI builder	*.rc	
IDE project	*.vcproj, *.sln	
IDE scratch	*.aps, *.ncb	
Icon	*.ico, *.rc2	\res
Debugging	*.exe, *.obj (compiled results)	\Debug
Release	*.exe, *.obj (compiled results)	\Release

Table 2.2. Source code structure for Tutorial 2.1.

Table 2.2 shows the source code structure for Tutorial 2.1. We will examine the files according to the purpose of the files.

- **Source code.** These are the files that contain the source code for the application. Notice that there are seven source files for this simple project! We will examine the details of these source files after examining the rest of the supporting files in this development project.

- **Documentation.** The ReadMe.txt file is a text file meant for the programmer to fill in comments.

- **GUI builder.** The .rc file is the data file of the MFC GUI builder (i.e., the resource editor). Listing 2.1 shows that this is a simple text file, where it is possible to open/edit this file with any simple text editor (e.g., Notepad). We see that among other data, this file includes information that describes the location and appearance of all the GUI elements on the application window.

- **IDE project.** The .vcproj/.sln files are used by the VC++ IDE for defining the source code project (e.g., what the source files are, how to compile the project). These are also text files; interested readers can open/edit these files with any text editor to examine the details.

- **IDE scratch.** The .aps/.ncb are temporary files kept/generated by the IDE while supporting our development process. These files can be deleted in between editing/development sessions.

- **Icon.** These are image files for describing the icon on the top left of the application window and when the application window is iconized.

Source listing. For the convenience of description, in general the presented source code has been significantly edited from the original source file. Readers should understand the source code in the book and expect to see the code fragments in different orders when examining the source code files.

```
// Microsoft Visual C++ generated resource script.
⋮
#include "Resource.h"
⋮
```

Source file.
MFC_SimpleDialog.rc file
in the *Resource Files* folder
of the MFC_SimpleDialog
project.

> **IDD_MFC_SIMPLEDIALOG_DIALOG** *is the identifier for the main application window. The following describes the dimension and appearance of this GUI element.*

```
IDD_MFC_SIMPLEDIALOG_DIALOG DIALOGEX  0, 0, 320, 200
STYLE DS_SHELLFONT | WS_POPUP | WS_VISIBLE | WS_CAPTION | DS_MODALFRAME
EXSTYLE WS_EX_APPWINDOW
CAPTION "MFC_SimpleDialog"
⋮
```

> *The following lines descrbe the locations and dimenstions of **OK** and **Cancel** buttons.*

```
BEGIN
    DEFPUSHBUTTON      "OK",IDOK,263,7,50,16
    PUSHBUTTON         "Cancel",IDCANCEL,263,25,50,16
⋮
```

Listing 2.1. Snippet from MFC_SimpleDialog.rc (Tutorial 2.1).

- **Debug.** The IDE uses this folder to record all the compile results, including all the .obj files and the eventual .exe file (executable program). The contents of this folder support interactive debugging in the IDE. All the .obj and the .exe files contain intermediate symbols for interactive debugging. As a result, files from this folder are much larger than they need be.

- **Release.** The IDE uses this folder to record all the compiled results. In contrast to the *Debug* folder, the files in this folder are for supporting final release of the program (after development is done). The executable file from this folder is optimized for size and speed.

Here are the details of the seven source files:

- Resource.h. This file defines the symbolic names (or GUI ID) of GUI elements used in the resource editor. For example, as shown in Listing 2.2, IDD_MFC_SIMPLEDIALOG_DIALOG is the symbolic name of the GUI element that represents the main application window. In this case, we see that this symbol is being defined to be a unique integer. Notice that in List-

GUI ID. The *GUI ID* is
a unique identifier associated
with each GUI element. The
GUI ID is used mainly by the
MFC resource editor.

Source file. Resource.h file
in the *Header* file folder of the
MFC_SimpleDialog project.

```
// Microsoft Visual C++ generated include file.
// Used by MFC_SimpleDialog.RC
//
    ⋮
#define IDD_MFC_SIMPLEDIALOG_DIALOG        102
    ⋮
```

Listing 2.2. Snippet from Resource.h file (Tutorial 2.1).

Source file.
TutorialApp.h/cpp
file in the *Source* and
Header file folders of the
MFC_SimpleDialog project.

```
class CTutorialApp : public CWinApp {
    ⋮
   virtual BOOL InitInstance();
};
    ⋮
```

> **theApp:** *this is the abstraction of our application.*

```
    CTutorialApp theApp; // The one and only CTutorialApp object
    ⋮
BOOL CTutorialApp::InitInstance() {
    ⋮ // Code for intialization
   // Create and show our dialog
   CTutorialDlg dlg;    // This is the our main application window
   m_pMainWnd = &dlg;
    ⋮
   // display the main application window, when the application
   // window quits, the application should terminate.
    ⋮
}
```

Listing 2.3. The CTutorialApp class (Tutorial 2.1).

ing 2.1, the MFC_SimpleDialog.rc file includes the Resource.h file to define the IDD_MFC_SIMPLEDIALOG_DIALOG symbol.

- StdAfx.h/.cpp. These two files contain precompile header information. They help speed up the compilation process. These two files are important

```
class CTutorialDlg : public CDialog {
    ⋮
    CTutorialDlg(CWnd* pParent = NULL); // standard constructor
    virtual BOOL OnInitDialog();        // The SystemInitialization() function
    afx_msg void OnPaint();             // To Support Redraw/Paint event
    DECLARE_MESSAGE_MAP()               // Identify the events to override from super class
    virtual void DoDataExchange(CDataExchange* pDX); // GUI element input/output support
    ⋮
};
```

> **TutorialDlg.cpp**: *implementation file*

```
CTutorialDlg::CTutorialDlg( ⋯ ){⋯ }  // Constructor
A:  BOOL CTutorialDlg::OnInitDialog() { ⋯ }
    ⋮
B:  BEGIN_MESSAGE_MAP(CTutorialDlg, CDialog)
        ON_WM_PAINT()
    ⋮
C:  void CTutorialDlg::OnPaint()  { ⋯ }
    ⋮
D:  void CTutorialDlg::DoDataExchange(CDataExchange* pDX)  { ⋯ }
    ⋮
```

Source file.
TutorialDlg.h/cppfile
in the *Source* and
Header filefolders of the
MFC_SimpleDialog project.

Listing 2.4. The CTutorialDlg class (Tutorial 2.1).

and exist in all of our projects. Fortunately, the handling of the precompile
header is fairly transparent, and we will not change these files.

Working with the precompile header. After changing
and/or creating a header file
in a project, it is a good idea
first to recompile stdafx.cpp
to ensure up-to-date precompile header information.

- TutorialApp.h/.cpp. These two files define and implement the CTutori
  alApp class: Listing 2.3 shows that CTutorialApp subclasses from the
  API system CWinApp. This class represents our application. The global
  variable theApp represents the instance of our running program. Notice
  that our main application window is a CTutorialDlg object and is instantiated and invoked in the InitInstance() function. When our application
  window exits, the control will return to InitInstance() and the application terminates.

- TutorialDlg.h/.cpp. These two files define and implement the CTutori
  alDlg class. As shown in Listing 2.4, CTutorialDlg subclasses from the

MFC CDialog class. Recall that our main application window is a GUI
element, and that we can define control variables for GUI elements. Now,
refer to Listing 2.3: the dlg object instantiated in the InitInstance()
function is the control variable for our main application window, and the
data type for our main application window is CTutorialDlg. Listing 2.3
shows dlg is referenced by m_pMainWnd, an instance variable of theApp.

When we examine the structure of the TutorialDlg.cpp file (refer to Listing 2.4),
we observe the following.

- **Object-oriented mechanism.** CTutorialDlg subclasses from the MFC
  CDialog class; this means that our main application window inherits *vast*
  predefined functionality from CDialog (e.g., mouse events, timer events).
  Notice the virtual functions that are overridden (e.g., OnInitDialog());
  these are examples of modifying predefined GUI element behaviors.

- SystemInitialization **(A).** The OnInitDialog() is our opportunity to
  perform initialization for the application window, much like the functionality of the SystemInitialization() function discussed in Section 1.2.
  Because we are overriding a virtual function, it is important to follow the
  protocol. In this case, we must invoke the superclass method CDialog::On
  InitDialog(), and we must return TRUE upon successful operations.

- Redraw/Paint **event (B and C).** The BEGIN_MESSAGE_MAP macro **(B)** helps
  register events for services. Here we see the registration of ON_WM_PAINT,
  the Redraw/Paint event. In this case, CTutorialDlg must override the
  OnPaint() function to service the event. Because the application window
  is empty, this function does not do anything.

- **GUI element and control variable data exchange (D).** As we will see in
  later tutorials, this function helps maintain the consistency of state information between the front-end GUI elements and their corresponding control
  variables in the back end.

Source file naming convention.   Note that of the above file names, Resource
.h, StdAfx.h, and StdAfx.cpp are governed by MFC. We will name *all* of the tutorials TutorialApp.h/.cpp for the application and TutorialDlg.h/.cpp for
the main application window. For the rest of the tutorials in this chapter, we will
only need to work with the CTutorialDlg class (our main application window).

Source file. Pseudocode; no corresponding source file.

```
System Initialization:
 // Define Application State: count the number of button clicks
 int m_OkCount = 0;  // initialize to 0
 // Register Event Service Routines
 Register for:  ButtonClick Event
 Events Services:
 ButtonClick              // service routine for button click
   m_OKCount++;           // if button is clicked, increment the count
   EchoToScreen(m_OKCount) // echo this new count to the application window
```

Listing 2.5. Abstract event-driven programming solution (Tutorial 2.2).

Tutorial 2.2. GUI Elements and Control Variables

- **Goal.** Experience event-driven programming design and implementation and understand front-end GUI elements versus back-end control variables.

- **Approach.** Work with an output-only GUI element, where at run time, our application must change the state of the GUI element.

Figure 2.5 is a screenshot of running Tutorial 2.2. This is a slightly more interesting application where we count the number of times the "Click to Add" button has been clicked. If we have to design a solution for this tutorial, our experience from Section 1.2 and Listing 1.4 leads us to an application state with a simple integer counter and a button event service routine that increments the counter. To implement the solution of Listing 2.5, we must first design the layout of the GUI application and then register the event services with the appropriate GUI element.

Tutorial 2.2.
Project Name
   MFC_EchoButtonEvent

Figure 2.5. Tutorial 2.2.

Front-End GUI Layout Design

Figure 2.6 shows that in our Tutorial 2.2 implementation, the front-end user interface has the following five GUI elements.

- **The application window.** We assign IDD_ECHOBUTTONEVENT_DIALOG to be the GUI ID for the application window GUI element. As in Tutorial 2.1, the CTutorialDlg class represents this GUI element, and theApp.m_pMain Wnd is the control variable that references our main application window.

- **The "Click to Add" button.** We assigned ID_BTN_ADD to be the GUI ID of this button. This is an *input-only* GUI element because our application

theApp. Recall from Tutorial 2.1 that theApp is an instance of CTutorialApp; it represents our application. In TutorialApp.cpp, we set the m_pMainWnd instance variable to reference the control variable representing our application main window.

GUI ID. GUI IDs are defined in the Resource.h file.

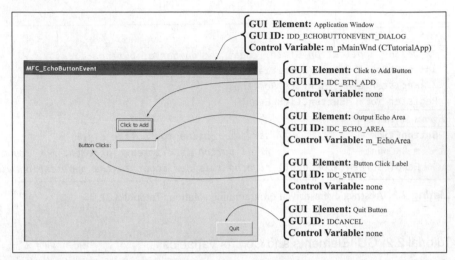

Figure 2.6. GUI elements of Tutorial 2.2.

never changes its state. Our application is only interested in receiving click events generated by this button. Because our application does not have any need to refer to this element, we do not need to define a control variable for this element.

- **The output echo area.** We assigned IDC_ECHO_AREA to be the GUI ID this element. This is the echo area where the application state information (number of clicks) will be displayed. At run time, our application needs to change the content of this GUI element. In our implementation, we define m_EchoText to be the control variable of this GUI element.

- **The "Button Clicks" label.** This is a static GUI element because it provides neither input nor output functionality. It is a simple label.

- **The "Quit" button.** This is the same button from Tutorial 2.1. Our application has no reference to this GUI element. This GUI element supports the default MFC service, where it reacts to a click event by quitting the application.

Back-End Implementation

The development environment structure for Tutorial 2.2 is identical to that of Tutorial 2.1 with the same folder structure and same seven source code files.

```
class CTutorialDlg : public CDialog {
    ⋮   // removed content similar to that from Listing 2.4 (Tutorial 2.1).
A1: int m_OkCount; // count of "Click to Add" button is clicked
B1: afx_msg void OnBnClickedBtnAdd(); // "Click to Add" service routine
C1: CString m_EchoText; // For controling the output GUI element
};
```

```
    ⋮   // removed content similar to that from Listing 2.4 (Tutorial 2.1).
    BOOL CTutorialDlg::OnInitDialog() {
A2: m_OkClick = 0; // initialize application state.
    ⋮

    BEGIN_MESSAGE_MAP(CTutorialDlg, CDialog)
B2: ON_BN_CLICKED(IDC_BTN_ADD, OnBnClickedBtnAdd)
    ⋮

    void CTutorialDlg::DoDataExchange(CDataExchange* pDX) {
C2: DDX_Text(pDX, IDC_ECHO_AREA, m_EchoText);
    ⋮
```

B3: *This is the "Click to Add" button service routine that we have registered with the MFC.*

```
void CTutorialDlg::OnBnClickedBtnAdd() {
A3: m_OkCount++; // update application state
C3: m_EchoText.Format("%d", m_OkCount); // convert to text for output
C4: UpdateData(FALSE); // flush count to window
    ⋮
```

Source file.
TutorialDlg.h/cpp file in the *Source* and *Header* files folders of the MFC_EchoButtonEvent project.

Listing 2.6. CTutorialDlg class (Tutorial 2.2).

In addition, following the naming convention of the source code files, we notice TutorialApp.h/.cpp defining the application and TutorialDlg.h/.cpp defining the main application window. When we compare the TutorialDlg.h/.cpp with those from Tutorial 2.1, we notice slight differences. These differences are the implementation of the functionality in Tutorial 2.2. Listing 2.6 highlights these differences. From Listing 2.6, we notice the following.

- **Application state (A).** As defined by the solution from Listing 2.5, at label A1 the application state is defined as an integer. At label A2, the application

OnInitDialog(). Recall that the OnInitDialog() function should implement the SystemInitialization() functionality.

state is initialized in the OnInitDialog() function. The application state is updated during the button event service routine (A3).

- **Support for the button GUI element (B).** The event service routine is declared at label B1 in the TutorialDlg.h file. At label B2, we register the ON_BN_CLICKED (on button click) event and associate the GUI element ID_BTN_ADD with the OnBnClickedBtnAdd() routine. This process registers the routine as a callback function for the click event on the button. The event service routine is implemented at label B3, where we update the application state and display the updated information to the output echo area.

ID_BTN_ADD. See Figure 2.6. This is the GUI ID for the "Click to Add" button.

- **Output GUI element (C).** At label C1, we define the variable m_EchoText, and at label C2, this variable is bound to the GUI element IDC_ECHO_AREA. Notice that before the binding statement at label C2, m_EchoText is simply just another instance variable. However, after the statement at C2, m_EchoText becomes the control variable of the IDC_ECHO_AREA. After the application state is updated in the button event service routine, at label C3, the m_EchoText is set with the updated application state. At this point, the value of the m_EchoText control variable is different from the state information presented in the IDC_ECHO_AREA. The statement at C4 flushes the content of m_EchoText to the GUI element to ensure consistency.

IDC_ECHO_AREA. See Figure 2.6. This is the GUI ID for the output echo area.

Tutorial 2.3. More with Control Variables

Tutorial 2.3.
Project Name
    MFC_SliderControls

- **Goal.** Understand that control variables can be complex data types and demonstrate working with control variables of input GUI elements.

- **Approach.** Work with slider bars, a fairly complex GUI element.

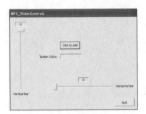

Figure 2.7. Tutorial 2.3.

Figure 2.7 is a screenshot of running Tutorial 2.3. This application is basically Tutorial 2.2 with two extra slider bar sets. From the GUI layout, we see that each slider bar set actually consists of three GUI elements: the label, the slider bar, and the echo area, as shown in Table 2.3. We worked with labels and the output echo area in Tutorial 2.2. In this tutorial, we will concentrate on working with the slider bar and servicing of slider bar events. When we examine the development environment, we see the familiar source code structure. Once again, we will concentrate on TutorialDlg.h/.cpp. Listing 2.7 highlights the new programming code fragments that are associated with the slider bars.

GUI Element	GUI ID	Control Variable
Slider Bars	IDC_V_SLIDER_BAR	m_VSliderBar
	IDC_H_SLIDER_BAR	m_HSliderBar
Slider Bar Labels	*Vertical Bar*	—
	Horizontal Bar	—
Slider Bar Echo Areas	IDC_V_SLIDER_ECHO	m_VSliderEcho
	IDC_H_SLIDER_ECHO	m_HSliderEcho

Table 2.3. The elements of Tutorial 2.3.

- **Slider bar echo control variables (A).** We see declaration of the variables at label A1. Note that m_HSliderEcho is simply another variable until the DDX_Text macro call at label A2. After this macro call, m_HSliderEcho becomes the control variable for IDC_H_SLIDER_ECHO GUI element. These control variables are initialized at label A3.

- **Slider bar control variables (B).** We see the declaration of the variables at label B1. These will be the control variables for the slider bars. Notice the CSliderCtrl data type. MFC predefines data types to support every type of GUI element (e.g., CButton for button GUI elements, CComboBox for combo-box GUI elements). At label B2, these variables are bound to the corresponding slider bar GUI elements. At label B3, during the initialization OnInitDialog() function call, we initialize the max, min, and initial position of the slider bar knobs. After the initialization function calls, the values of the control variables (e.g., m_VSliderBar) become out-of-sync with the state of the corresponding GUI element (e.g., IDC_V_SLIDER_BAR). The false parameter to the UpdateData() function call at label B4 flushes the control variables' values onto their corresponding GUI elements.

```
class CTutorialDlg : public CDialog {
      :  // removed content similar to that from
      // Listing 2.6 (Tutorial 2.2).
A1:   CString m_HSliderEcho, m_VSliderEcho;
B1:   CSliderCtrl m_VSliderBar, m_HSliderBar;
C1:   afx_msg void OnHScroll(UINT nSBCode, UINT nPos, CScrollBar* pScrollBar);
      afx_msg void OnVScroll(UINT nSBCode, UINT nPos, CScrollBar* pScrollBar);
};
```

Source file. TutorialDlg.h/cpp file in the *Source* and *Header* files folders of the MFC_SliderControls project.

Listing 2.7. CTutorialDlg class (Tutorial 2.3).

```
    : // removed content similar to that from Listing 2.6 (Tutorial 2.2).
    void CTutorialDlg::DoDataExchange(CDataExchange* pDX) {
A2: DDX_Text(pDX, IDC_H_SLIDER_ECHO, m_HSliderEcho);
    DDX_Text(pDX, IDC_V_SLIDER_ECHO, m_VSliderEcho);
B2: DDX_Control(pDX, IDC_V_SLIDER_BAR, m_VSliderBar);
    DDX_Control(pDX, IDC_H_SLIDER_BAR, m_HSliderBar);
    :

    BEGIN_MESSAGE_MAP(CTutorialDlg, CDialog)
C2: ON_WM_HSCROLL()
    ON_WM_VSCROLL()
    :

    BOOL CTutorialDlg::OnInitDialog() {
A3: m_VSliderEcho.Format("%d", 0); m_HSliderEcho.Format("%d", 0);
B3: m_VSliderBar.SetRange(0, 100, TRUE); m_VSliderBar.SetPos(0);
    :

B4: UpdateData(false);
    :
```

C3: *This is the* Horizontal *scroll bar serviceroutine we override from MFC.*

```
    void CTutorialDlg::OnHScroll(UINT nSBCode, UINT nPos, CScrollBar* pScrollBar) {
        // check to make sure we know which slider bar is generating the events
        if (pScrollBar == (CScrollBar *) &m_HSliderBar) {
    C4: int value = m_HSliderBar.GetPos();
    C5: m_HSliderEcho.Format("%d", value);
    C6: UpdateData(false);
        :
```

C7: *This is the* Vertical *scroll bar serviceroutine we override from MFC.*

```
    void CTutorialDlg::OnVScroll(UINT nSBCode, UINT nPos, CScrollBar* pScrollBar) {
        // content complements that of OnHScroll
```

Listing 2.7. (cont.)

H and V. To avoid repeating every sentence with an "*H*" for horizontal and an "*V*" for vertical, we omit the "*H/V*" characters and use one identifier to refer to both. For example, OnScroll() is referring to OnHScroll() and OnVScroll.

- **Slider bar service routines (C).** At label C1, we declare OnScroll() for servicing all horizontal and vertical scroll bars. Notice that before the service registration at label C2, these two are just simple functions. At label C2, we register for the ON_WM_SCROLL (on window scroll) event. Notice that no callback functions are passed in. The horizontal and vertical scroll event services are predefined by the MFC CDialog, and we override the OnScroll() functions to customize the services. The definition of event service routines can be found at labels C3 and C7. Notice that if our application has more than one horizontal scroll bar, *all* horizontal scroll events will be serviced by the the same OnHScroll() function. This means, as illustrated by the if statement in C3, that when servicing horizontal scroll events, we must identify which of the scroll bars triggered the event. At label C4, we call the GetPos() function on the control variable to obtain the up-to-date knob value, which is updated in the echo control variable at C5 and flushed to the corresponding GUI element at label C6.

Tutorial 2.4. Application-Defined Events

- **Goal.** Experience events triggered by the application; experience working with servicing events from the mouse.

- **Approach.** Work with GUI timer event; service all events from the mouse and echo all relevant information to the application window.

Figure 2.8 is a screenshot of running Tutorial 2.4. The source code of this application is based on that from Tutorial 2.3. When compared to the main application window from Tutorial 2.3, we can see two extra sets of outputs.

- **Mouse echo.** When the mouse pointer is inside the application window, this echo prints out the position of the mouse and the status (e.g., clicked) of the mouse buttons.

- **Timer echo.** We will enable the timer alarm to trigger an event for our application every second. This echo will print out the number of seconds elapsed since we started running this application.

Tutorial 2.4.
Project Name
MFC_MouseAndTimer

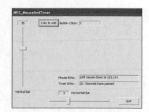

Figure 2.8. Tutorial 2.4.

```
class CTutorialDlg : public CDialog {
      ⋮  // removed content similar to that from Listing 2.7 (Tutorial 2.3).
A1:   int m_Seconds;
B1:   CString m_MouseEcho, m_TimerEcho;
C1:   afx_msg void OnTimer(UINT nIDEvent);
D1:   afx_msg void OnLButtonDown(UINT nFlags, CPoint point);
      afx_msg void OnMouseMove(UINT nFlags, CPoint point);
      afx_msg void OnRButtonDown(UINT nFlags, CPoint point);
};
```

Source file.
TutorialDlg.h/cpp
file in the *Source* and *Header* file folders of the MFC_MouseAndTimer project.

Listing 2.8. CTutorialDlg class (Tutorial 2.4).

```
// removed content similar to that from Listing 2.7 (Tutorial 2.3).
  BOOL CTutorialDlg::OnInitDialog() {
```
| A2: | `m_Seconds = 0;` |
| C2: | `SetTimer(0, 1000, NULL);` |
```
       ⋮

  void CTutorialDlg::DoDataExchange(CDataExchange* pDX) {
```
| B2: | `DDX_Text(pDX, IDC_MOUSEECHO, m_MouseEcho);` |
```
      DDX_Text(pDX, IDC_TIMERECHO, m_TimerEcho);

       ⋮

  BEGIN_MESSAGE_MAP(CTutorialDlg, CDialog)
```
| C3: | `ON_WM_TIMER()` |
| D2: | `ON_WM_LBUTTONDOWN()` |
```
    ON_WM_MOUSEMOVE()
    ON_WM_RBUTTONDOWN()

       ⋮
```

C4: *This is the timer service routine.*
```
  void CTutorialDlg::OnTimer(UINT nIDEvent) {
      // update time passed and echo to user
      m_Seconds++;
      m_TimerEcho.Format("%d: Seconds have passed", m_Seconds);
      UpdateData(false);

       ⋮
```

D3: *These are the left/right mouse button down service roune*
```
  void CTutorialDlg::OnLButtonDown(UINT nFlags, CPoint point)
  void CTutorialDlg::OnRButtonDown(UINT nFlags, CPoint point)
      // check if the control/alt/shift key is pressed
      if(nFlags & MK_CONTROL)

       ⋮

      m_MouseEcho.Format("%sLeft mouse down at %d,%d", prefix, point.x,
      point.y);
      UpdateData(false);

       ⋮
```

D4: *This is the mouse move service routine*
```
  void CTutorialDlg::OnMouseMove(UINT nFlags, CPoint point)
```

Listing 2.8. (cont.)

As in all previous tutorials, all changes in programming code are localized to the `TutorialDlg.h/.cpp` files. Listing 2.8 highlights the changes from the previous tutorial:

- **Application state (A).** Because the application counts the number of seconds elapsed, we must define (A1) and initialize (A2) a counter that we can count in seconds. This counter will be updated in the timer service routine in C4.

- **Mouse and timer echo (B).** These are simple output echo set-ups. As we saw in previous tutorials, we must declare the variables (B1) and associate the variables with the GUI IDs (B2). The content of these echo regions are updated during corresponding mouse and timer service routines.

- **Application timer events (C).** Label C1 shows the declaration of the `OnTimer()` service function. During the initialization in `OnInitDialog()`, at label C2, the alarm is set to go off every 1000 milliseconds (or 1 second). At label C3, we call the `ON_WM_TIMER` (on window timer) macro to register for the timer event. We do not see any callback function during the registration. Once again, the `OnTimer()` function is defined by the MFC `CDialog` class, and we will override it to customize to our application. The timer service routine is defined at label C4. This function is invoked once every second. We service the timer event by incrementing `m_Seconds` and echoing the new value to the defined echo area.

- **Mouse events (D).** Just like the timer in this tutorial and slider bars from previous tutorials, the `CDialog` class has default support for mouse events. We know we must override the functions (D1), register for the events (D2), and implement the functions (D3, D4). Notice that the mouse positions are passed in the `CPoint` structure. If you run the tutorial and move the mouse around in the application window, notice that the mouse positions are defined relative to the top-left corner (the origin is located at the top-left corner).

Hardware coordinate. The coordinate system where the top left is the origin with the *y*-axis increasing downward and the *x*-axis increasing to the right.

Tutorial 2.5. Input/output GUI elements.

- **Goal.** Experience working with GUI elements that serve both input (from user to application) and output (from application to user) functions for the application.

- **Approach.** Continue with the previous tutorial, where this tutorial will allow both the application and the user to control the slider bars.

Tutorial 2.5.
Project Name
   `MFC_UpdateGUI`

```
class CTutorialDlg : public CDialog {
      ⋮  // removed content similar to that from Listing 2.8 (Tutorial 2.4).
```
A1:
```
      BOOL m_TimerCtrlSliders;
      afx_msg void OnBnClickedTimerControlSliders();
};
```

```
⋮  // removed content similar to that from Listing 2.8 (Tutorial 2.4).
  void CTutorialDlg::DoDataExchange(CDataExchange* pDX) {
```
A2:
```
      DDX_Check(pDX, IDC_TIMER_CONTROL_SLIDERS, m_TimerCtrlSliders);
      ⋮
```

```
  BEGIN_MESSAGE_MAP(CTutorialDlg, CDialog)
```
A3:
```
      ON_BN_CLICKED(IDC_TIMER_CONTROL_SLIDERS, OnBnClickedTimerControlSliders)
      ⋮
```

```
  BOOL CTutorialDlg::OnInitDialog()
```
A4:
```
      m_TimerCtrlSliders = TRUE;
      UpdateData(false);
      ⋮
```

Timer service rouine: update slider bar and checkbox when appropriate.

```
  void CTutorialDlg::OnTimer(UINT nIDEvent) {
```
B1: *If the checkbox is checked:*
```
      if (m_TimerCtrlSliders)
```

Source file.
TutorialDlg.h/cpp file in the *Source* and *Header* file folders of the MFC_UpdateGUI project.

B2:
```
        int hvalue = m_HSliderBar.GetPos();
        if (hvalue > 0)
            m_HSliderBar.SetPos(hvalue-1);
            m_HSliderEcho.Format("$%$d", hvalue-1);
        // Do the same for the vertical slider bar \vdots
        int value = m_VSliderBar.GetPos();
        ⋮
```

B3:
```
      if ( (hvalue==0) && (vvalue==0) )
            m_TimerCtrlSliders = false;
            UpdateData(FALSE);
      ⋮
```

Listing 2.9. CTutorialDlg class (Tutorial 2.5).

Checkbox service routine: copy state from GUI element to control variable

```
void CTutorialDlg::OnBnClickedTimerControlSliders() {
A5:  UpdateData(true);
}
```

Listing 2.9. (cont.)

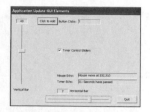

Figure 2.9. Tutorial 2.5.

Figure 2.9 is a screenshot of running Tutorial 2.5. Once again, this tutorial is very similar to Tutorial 2.4. From the front-end user interface, the only difference is the timer control (TC) checkbox located in the center of the application window. In this case, if the TC is checked, the application will decrement both of the slider bar's values one unit per second. When both slider bars have value zero, the application will uncheck TC. At any point, the user can check/uncheck the TC and change the slider bar values by adjusting the knobs on the slider bars. In this way, both of the slider bars and the TC can be controlled by both the application and the user.

Listing 2.9 highlights the changes in the `TutorialDlg.h`/`.cpp` files (from that of Tutorial 2.4).

- **The "Timer Control" (TC) checkbox (A).** The variable and the event service function are declared at label A1, the variable `m_TimerCtrlSliders` becomes the control variable of `IDC_TIMER_CONTROL_SLIDERS` (the checkbox GUI element) at label A2, the checkbox event is registered at label A3, the TC value is initialized to `TRUE` at label A4, and the service function is defined at label A5. At label A3, we see another example of event registration with a callback function.

  It is interesting that the checkbox service routine at A5 only has a single statement: `UpdateData(TRUE)`. When the user clicks on the TC checkbox, the front-end GUI will automatically flip the state of the checkbox GUI element. However, this information is not reflected in the control variable `m_TimerCtrlSldiers`. `UpdateData()` with the `TRUE` parameter sets the control variable according to the state of the GUI element.

  `UpdateData(FALSE)`. Recall from previous tutorials that `UpdateData()` with a `FALSE` parameter flushes control variable values to the GUI element.

- **The application controls GUI in the timer service routine (B).** On the per-second timer event, the timer service routine first checks to ensure that the sliders are under the control of the application with the if statement at label B1. If the condition is true, at label B2, the slider bar positions are polled and decremented accordingly. When both of the slider bars have value zero, at label B3, the control variable for the TC checkbox is updated and flushed to the front-end GUI element (with `UpdateData(FALSE)`).

As we continue to program with GUI APIs, we will begin to encounter repeated patterns of working with multiple GUI element types. For example, we will find ourselves constantly working with slider bars that require the numeric echoing functionality. The next few tutorials demonstrate how we can customize and/or organize our interface with the GUI API to better support programming in a moderately complex development environment.

Tutorial 2.6. The SliderCtrlWithEcho Class

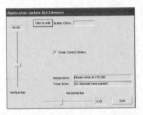

Figure 2.10. Tutorial 2.6.

- **Goal.** Demonstrate that when appropriate, we should apply knowledge from previous programming classes and define/customize new GUI element classes. In most cases, this will ease the programming effort and increase readability/maintainability of our system.

- **Approach.** Customize GUI behavior by creating new GUI element types. We will customize slider bar functionality to define a new slider bar type that supports a numeric echo area.

Figure 2.10 is a screenshot of running Tutorial 2.6. Notice that the application behaves identically to that of Tutorial 2.5. In this case, the only difference between these two applications is the support for the two slider bars. When we compare the source code of the two tutorials, we see one extra class in Tutorial 2.6: the SliderCtrlWithEcho.cpp/.h files. This new class extends the MFC CSliderCtrl class in two ways.

1. **Slider bar range.** CSliderCtrl only supports integer values. CSliderCtrlWithEcho presents a floating-point range with 10^5 unique positions.

2. **Numeric echo area.** It is convenient, and often important, for the user to know the exact numeric value of the slider bar knob position. SliderCtrlWithEcho supports the echoing of the bar knob numeric values.

Listing 2.10 shows the definition of the CSliderCtrlWithEcho class. We can see a simple public interface where the user can initialize, set, and get slider bar values. We also see familiar declarations of service routines and control variables. Initialize() is the only MFC-specific function where we must create and insert an echo GUI element for the numeric display. The rest of the classes are fairly straightforward, and you should explore the implementations.

```
class CSliderCtrlWithEcho : public CSliderCtrl {
  ┌─────────────────────────────┐
  │ A: public interface functions │
  └─────────────────────────────┘
    void Initialize(float min, float max, float init); // initialization
    bool SetSliderValue(float userValue); // set the slider bar for output
    float GetSliderValue();                // get user input value from the slider bar
  ┌───────────────────────────────────────────┐
  │ B: Internal representation and impelementation │
  └───────────────────────────────────────────┘
    int UserToMFCPos(float userValue); // translation from user (float) to MFC values (integer)
    float MFCToUserPos(int mfcValue);  // translation from MFC (integer) to user (float) values
    void UpdateSliderEcho();           // update current slider value to numeric echo area
    CStatic m_MessageWnd;              // control varaible for the echo area
  ┌──────────────────────────────────┐
  │ C: Override MFC event service routines │
  └──────────────────────────────────┘
    afx_msg void HScroll(UINT nSBCode, UINT nPos); // horizonatl scroll service routine
    afx_msg void VScroll(UINT nSBCode, UINT nPos); // vertical scroll service routine
};
```

Listing 2.10. The `CSliderCtrlWithEcho` class (Tutorial 2.6).

Source file.
`SliderCtrlWithEcho.h` file in the Controls folder of the `MFC_SliderCtrlWithEcho` project.

Tutorial 2.7. The MFC Library

- **Goal.** Demonstrate the advantage of collecting functionally related files into a separate software library.

- **Approach.** Gather all GUI API–specific functions and create a customized GUI library for our application.

The source code of Tutorial 2.7 is identical to that of Tutorial 2.6. The only difference here is in the organization of the source code listings. When we examine the source code for Tutorial 2.7, we see that we have collected all MFC-specific utilities and created the `MFC_Library1` software library. As the number of files grows in our development environment, creation of libraries to group functionally related files will become very important in maintaining a manageable source code structure. In all of our implementations, we call functions from `MFC_Library1` whenever possible. In this way, we have *customized* the GUI API, where instead of calling the underlying MFC functions, we call our library functions where the support is customized specifically for our applications.

As the developer of a software library, we must provide the following.

- **Manual and sample code.** This is to support ease of use by developers using our library. The manual should describe the functionality and document all classes/functions in the library. The sample code should illustrate

Tutorial 2.7.
Project Name:
  MFC_UseLibrary1
Library Support:
  MFC_Library1

examples of *how to use* the provided facilities in the library. In our case, the tutorials in this textbook serves as the sample code, whereas the explanation accompanying each tutorial serves as the manual for our libraries.

- **Header files.** This is to support compilation of the programming code based on our libraries. For example, if a programmer wants to declare a `CSliderCtrlWithEcho` object, she must include the `SliderCtrlWithEcho.h` file; otherwise, at compile time, the compiler will not understand what a `CSliderCtrlWithEcho` is. In all of our libraries, we have a library header file that includes all of the classes/functions defined in the library. For example, for `UWB_MFC_Lib1`, the file `uwbgl_MFC_Lib1.h` includes all the definitions for all the classes and functions defined in this library. A developer only needs to include this file to take advantage of facilities provided by this library.

  The advantage of one dedicated library header file is in its simplicity: developers only need to know about this single file. The main disadvantage comes in the form of compilation time; including all definitions in a library means the compiler must process much more information. We chose this approach mainly for the simplicity. In all of our tutorial projects, the library header files are included in the `StdAfx.h` file. Because all source files must include this precompiled header file, all source files have access to all functionality provided by our libraries.

Library file. Library files typically end with .lib or .dll in the Microsoft Windows environment. Other examples of library extensions include .a and .dso in the Unix environment.

- **The library.** This is to support *linking* of the programming code based on our library. In modern development environments, software libraries typically come in the form of a file. This file contains all the machine code for all the functions/classes defined in the library. At link time, a developer's compiled code will be linked with the contents of this library file. For example, if a programmer has properly included the `SliderCtrlWithEcho.h` file and declared an object for this class, at link time, the linker will locate and extract the machine code that implements the `SliderCtrlWithEcho` functionality.

  In modern development environments, there are two types of software libraries: statically linked and dynamically linked. Statically linked libraries are processed at link time, where the machine code is included in the executable program. Dynamically linked libraries support the loading of the library at run time. We have chosen to work with statically linked libraries for simplicity.

  The result of compiling our library project is a `.lib` file. For example, for the `MFC_Library1` project, the result of compilation is the `MFC_Library1`

.lib library file. A developer who uses our MFC_Library1 library must include this library file in the final linking of her program.

The library we have created, MFC_Library1, contains the SliderCtrlWith Echo class and a utility function (ReplaceDialogControl()). Let's examine this function in more detail.

Tutorial 2.8. Grouping of GUI Elements

- **Goal.** Demonstrate that sometimes it is advantageous to work with a container GUI element and the corresponding programming code to organize a user interface.

- **Approach.** Define a container object to contain related GUI elements and define a corresponding data type and control variable to manage the new container object.

Figure 2.11 is a screenshot of running Tutorial 2.8. The checkbox and the slider bar at the lower-left corner are meant for controlling the radius of a circle. Since we have not learned how to draw a circle, this application does not do anything. In this case, we are interested in the organization of the circle radius control GUI elements and the corresponding programming code.

Compile results. The Microsoft Visual Studio IDE stores the compile results from C++ projects in the *Debug* or the *Release* folder.

Tutorial 2.8.
Project Name:
    MFC_GroupControls
Library Support:
    MFC_Library1

Figure 2.11. Tutorial 2.8.

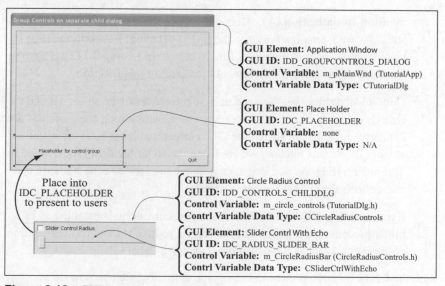

GUI Element: Application Window
GUI ID: IDD_GROUPCONTROLS_DIALOG
Control Variable: m_pMainWnd (TutorialApp)
Contrl Variable Data Type: CTutorialDlg

GUI Element: Place Holder
GUI ID: IDC_PLACEHOLDER
Control Variable: none
Contrl Variable Data Type: N/A

Place into
IDC_PLACEHOLDER
to present to users

GUI Element: Circle Radius Control
GUI ID: IDD_CONTROLS_CHILDDLG
Control Variable: m_circle_controls (TutorialDlg.h)
Contrl Variable Data Type: CCircleRadiusControls

GUI Element: Slider Contrl With Echo
GUI ID: IDC_RADIUS_SLIDER_BAR
Control Variable: m_CircleRadiusBar (CircleRadiusControls.h)
Contrl Variable Data Type: CSliderCtrlWithEcho

Figure 2.12. GUI elements in Tutorial 2.8.

Front-End GUI Layout Design

In all of the tutorials so far, the GUI elements are defined to be contained inside the default application window. Figure 2.12 shows the structure of the GUI elements in Tutorial 2.8. Notice that the GUI elements for controlling the circle radius are defined inside a separate container window (GUI ID: IDD_CONTROLS _CHILDDLG). As illustrated in Figure 2.12, a placeholder (GUI ID: IDC_PLACE HOLDER) is defined on the main application window for placing the container window.

Back-End Implementation

On the back end, we must define a new data type to support the new container window. Notice that our main application window is also an example of a container window, where the main application window is a GUI element that is defined to contain other GUI elements. We have been defining the CTutorialDlg class as the data type to support our main application window. When we examine the implementations (e.g., Listing 2.9 of Tutorial 2.5), we observe that CTutorialDlg is a subclass of the MFC CDialog class to take advantage of the vast predefined behaviors. Based on this experience, we can define a new data type for the new container window. Listing 2.11 shows that similar to the CTutorialDlg class, the new CCircleRadiusControls class is also a subclass of the MFC CDialog class. This means that all of our previous experiences can be applied. We observe the following.

- **Window initialization (A).** All container objects must initialize their contents. As we learned previously, the OnInitDialog() function will be invoked during the initialization of the window. In Listing 2.11, we observe the declaration (A1) and implementation (A2) of this function.

- **Control variables (B).** We need to have references to the slider bar and the checkbox during run time. As we have seen many times, the variables are defined at label B1, bound to the GUI elements at label B2, and initialized at label B3. In this tutorial, we are using the slider bar data type defined in Tutorial 2.6 (B1). Notice that even without any services, the numeric echo area reflects the knob positions correctly.

- **Event services (C).** The service of the checkbox event is established in familiar procedure: declaration of the service routine at label C1, registration of the event at label C2, and implementation at label C3.

With the CCircleRadiusControls data type definition, we can now define control variables for the container window in our main window. We have seen the

```
       class CCircleRadiusControls : public CDialog {
 A1:   virtual BOOL OnInitDialog();
 B1:   CSliderCtrlWithEcho m_CircleRadiusBar; // control variable for the slider bar
       BOOL m_bSliderControl;                 // control variable for the check box
 C1:   afx_msg void OnBnClickedControlRadiusCheck(); // service routine for the check box
       ⋮
};
```

```
   ⋮  // for the ease of reading, some code is removed (e.g. constructor, etc.)
 void CCircleRadiusControls::DoDataExchange(CDataExchange* pDX) {
 B2:   DDX_Control(pDX, IDC_RADIUS_SLIDER_BAR, m_CircleRadiusBar);
       DDX_Check(pDX, IDC_CONTROL_RADIUS_CHECK, m_bSliderControl);
       ⋮

 BEGIN_MESSAGE_MAP(CCircleRadiusControls, CDialog)
 C2:   ON_BN_CLICKED(IDC_CONTROL_RADIUS_CHECK, OnBnClickedControlRadiusCheck)
       ⋮

 A2:   BOOL CCircleRadiusControls::OnInitDialog() {
 B3:     m_CircleRadiusBar.Initialize(0.0f, 100.0f, 10.0f);
       ⋮

 C3:   void CCircleRadiusControls::OnBnClickedControlRadiusCheck()
       ⋮
```

Source file.
CircleRadiusControls.h/
.cpp file in the *Controls* folder
of the MFC_GroupControls
project.

Listing 2.11. The CCircleRadiusControls class (Tutorial 2.8).

```
class CTutorialDlg : public CDialog {
  ⋮
  CCircleRadiusControls m_circle_controls;
  ⋮
};
```

Source file.
TutorialDlg.h file in the
Header file folder of the
MFC_GroupControls project.

Listing 2.12. CTutorialDlg class (Tutorial 2.8).

definition of the two data types for the two container windows: CCircleRadius
Controls and CTutorialDlg. In addition, Listing 2.12 shows us that CTutorial
Dlg has the m_circle_controls control variable referencing a CCircleRadius
Controls window. However, we have also seen that during the front-end GUI
layout design, we did *not* place any CCircleRadiusControls GUI elements
into the main application window area. This means that at this point, after our
main application window starts, the back-end implementation will have a control
variable to a CCircleRadiusControls window; however, on the front-end GUI,
there will be no GUI element showing the window.

At run time, we must place the m_circle_controls at the region defined by
the placeholder GUI element (see Figure 2.12, GUI ID: IDC_PLACEHOLDER). The
ReplaceDialogControl() function defined in our MFC_Library1 is designed to
accomplish this task (see Listing 2.13). At run time, when CTutorialDlg initializes itself in the OnInitDialog() function, it calls ReplaceDialogControl()
(see Listing 2.14). In this way, the circle control window is replaced into the
region that was occupied by the placeholder GUI element. As we can see, defining separate GUI container windows involves significant effort; however, some
advantages include the following.

1. **Semantic mapping.** By grouping functionally related GUI elements into
   the a container window and defining a new class representing the container window, we have created a new user interaction object that supports
   a higher level of abstraction and interaction. For example, in this tutorial,
   we have created an *object* that is suitable for adjusting the radius of a circle.
   From this point on, we can work with the circle radius control object and
   not be concerned with slider bars and checkboxes.

2. **Code organization.** Instead of having a laundry list of every GUI element
   defined in the main application window, the main application window now
   contains a list of high-level interaction objects. This directly helps the organization of our source code system.

Source file.
UtilityFunctions.cpp file
in the *Source* file folder of the
MFC_Library1 project.

```
bool ReplaceDialogControl(CDialog& dlg, UINT placeholder_id,
                          CDialog& new_control_group, UINT control_group_id)
  // dlg  is the main application window
  // placeholder_id is ID of the place holder
  // new_control_group is control variable of the new container GUI element
  // control_group_id is ID of the new container GUI element
    Places the control_group_id GUI element in the area defined by placeholder_id.
```

Listing 2.13. The ReplaceDialogControl() function(Tutorial 2.8).

```
BOOL CTutorialDlg::OnInitDialog() {
    ⋮

    ReplaceDialogControl(*this, IDC_PLACEHOLDER, m_circle_controls, IDD_CONTROLS_CHILDDLG);
        // this -- is the main application window
        // IDC_PLACEHOLDER -- defines the region for the circle control
        // m_circle_controls -- control variable for the circle control
        // textbfIDD_CONTROLS_CHILDDLG -- GUI ID of the circle radius control window
    ⋮
```

Listing 2.14. CTutorialDlg::OnInitDialog() (Tutorial 2.8).

Source file.
TutorialDlg.cpp file in the *Source* file folder of the MFC_GroupControls project.

3. **Reuse.** We can instantiate multiple copies of the newly defined interaction object. For example, suppose I have an application with two circles and would like to have a separate radius control for each circle. In this case, we can instantiate two CircleRadiusControls objects to accomplish the task. In addition, it is straightforward to reuse the CircleRadiusControls in another application.

3

A Simple Graphics Program

This chapter introduces us to basic drawing with computer graphics. This chapter will:

- review coordinate systems;

- demonstrate simple applications built with different APIs;

- examine graphics API drawing procedures;

- begin the abstraction of working with graphics APIs.

After this chapter we should:

- understand how to apply our existing knowledge in understanding simple computer graphics programs in an API-independent manner;

- understand the fundamental steps of drawing in computer graphics programs;

- further appreciate the importance of technology-independent knowledge;

- gather sufficient knowledge to begin learning the principles of working with modern computer graphics libraries.

In addition, given the source of simple computer graphics programs, we should be able to:

Figure 3.1. Drawing two squares on a paper.

- locate and understand the structure of the drawing code independent from the implementation technology (e.g., programming language, specific graphics library);

- perform localized modifications to the program to introduce additional geometric objects.

If you want to draw two squares on a piece of paper, such as the ones shown in Figure 3.1, you must work with issues concerning the following.

- **Paper.** Prepare the piece of paper to draw on.

- **Size.** Determine the size of the squares.

- **Position.** Determine the location of the squares on the paper.

You would perform measurements similar to that of Figure 3.2, identify important positions (or vertices) similar to that of Figure 3.4, and then finally paint in the squares. We will see that the process of drawing shapes into a window on a computer monitor involves similar concepts. Let's begin by reviewing some familiar concepts involved.

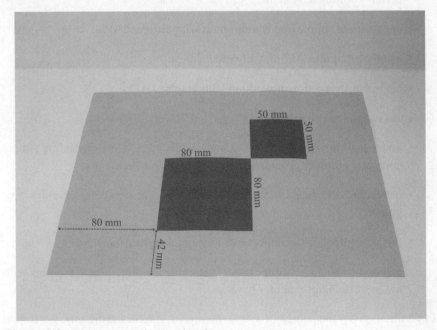

Figure 3.2. Measurement for drawing the two squares.

3.1   Coordinate Positions and Vertices

From our experience developing computer programs, we understand that we must somehow translate the measurements of Figure 3.2 into uniquely identifiable positions. Recall that the Cartesian coordinate system, with the origin and perpendicular axes measuring distances, is a convenient tool to uniquely identify positions in space. As illustrated in Figure 3.3, by the convention in 2D space, the upward direction is associated with the y-axis, the rightward direction is associated with the x-axis. We understand that the origin is located at the lower-left corner where the lines $x = 0$ and $y = 0$ intersect.

Figure 3.4 shows that we can overlay the 2D cartesian coordinate system over our paper, where we make choices about the following.

- **The origin.** This is the $(0,0)$ reference position. In this case, a convenient location for the origin is the lower-left corner of the paper.

- **The axes.** The choice of the origin and the Cartesian coordinate convention dictate that the x- and y-axes should follow the paper's edges, where the x-axis extends to the right and y-axis extends away.

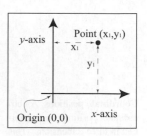

Figure 3.3.   The convention for a 2D coordinate system.

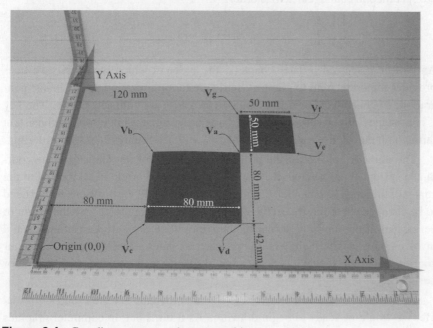

Figure 3.4.   Coordinate system and vertex positions.

- **Units on axes.** This is the measurement of distances on each of the axis. Because all measurements in Figure 3.2 are in millimeters (mm), it is obvious that the convenient choice should be mm.

With these choices, all the interesting positions of the squares can be conveniently identified:

Coordinate positions. All coordinate positions are specified in three dimensions. This ensures continuity as we develop our knowledge into the third dimension.

$$\text{Large square:} \begin{cases} V_a = & (160 \text{ mm}, & 122 \text{ mm}, & 0 \text{ mm}) \\ V_b = & (80 \text{ mm}, & 122 \text{ mm}, & 0 \text{ mm}) \\ V_c = & (80 \text{ mm}, & 42 \text{ mm}, & 0 \text{ mm}) \\ V_d = & (160 \text{ mm}, & 42 \text{ mm}, & 0 \text{ mm}) \end{cases},$$

$$\text{Small square:} \begin{cases} V_a = & (160 \text{ mm}, & 122 \text{ mm}, & 0 \text{ mm}) \\ V_e = & (210 \text{ mm}, & 122 \text{ mm}, & 0 \text{ mm}) \\ V_f = & (210 \text{ mm}, & 172 \text{ mm}, & 0 \text{ mm}) \\ V_g = & (160 \text{ mm}, & 172 \text{ mm}, & 0 \text{ mm}) \end{cases}.$$

Positions and vertices. In this book, both positions and vertices are used to refer to coordinate positions.

We refer to the storage associated with coordinate positions as *vertices*; for example, V_a is a vertex that stores the values of $(160, 122, 0)$. Notice that the vertices are specified in counterclockwise order:

$$V_a \to V_b \to V_c \to V_d.$$

As will be discussed in later chapters, the order in which we specify vertices provides important hints to graphics hardware for optimization during image generation. In general, clockwise or counterclockwise are both acceptable. The key is consistency: if you choose a specification ordering, it is important be consistent throughout the application. In this book, we will use counterclockwise ordering.

Choice of coordinate system. In general, as programmers we can perform transformations, and thus we have the freedom choosing any coordinate system to define our space. As we learn about transformations in the later chapters of this book, we will re-examine the choosing of coordinate systems in more detail.

The numeric values for the positions are results of our choice for the coordinate system. For example, if we were to choose the origin to be located at the center of the small square, then the numeric values for all the positions would need to be changed accordingly. On the other hand, if we were to choose the origin to be located at the top-right corner of the paper, then our vertex positions would involve many negative numbers. In this case, we can see that we have chosen our coordinate system so that it is convenient to specify locations and orientations for our scene.

At this point, we know exactly the size and location for the squares. In real life, we would be ready to begin drawing. As it turns out, in computer graphics programming, it is almost just as straightforward.

3.2 A Computer Graphics Solution

Tutorial 3.1. Drawing Squares with MFC and D3D

- **Goal.** Examine and learn the drawing procedures of a graphics API.

- **Approach.** Examine the drawing procedures of a simple program that draws the two squares form Figure 3.4.

Figure 3.5 is a screenshot of running Tutorial 3.1. This program draws the two squares with measurements from Figure 3.4 and waits for the user to click on the quit button. It is developed based on the D3D graphics API and the MFC GUI API.

Front-End GUI Layout

Figure 3.6 shows that there are four GUI elements in Tutorial 3.1: the application window, the quit button, the placeholder, and the D3D drawing area. This diagram illustrates a scheme similar to that of Tutorial 2.8, where we will replace the placeholder (IDC_GRFX_PLACEHOLDER) in the main window with the D3D drawing area.

Notice that the D3D drawing area does not have a GUI ID. Because this GUI element is dedicated for D3D drawing and this element's position is defined by the placeholder, we did not create any representation for this element during the

Tutorial 3.1.
Project Name
D3D_Rectangles2D

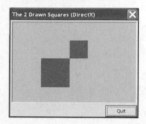

Figure 3.5. Tutorial 3.1.

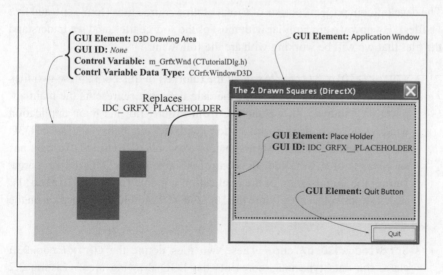

Figure 3.6. Front-end layout of Tutorial 3.1.

Source file.
TutorialDlg.h/cpp   file
in the *Source* and em-
phHeader folders of the
D3D_Rectangles2D project.

```
class CTutorialDlg : public CDialog {
    :
    :   // removed familiar content e.g., constructors etc.

    CGrfxWindowD3D m_GrfxWnd;
};
```

```
:   // removed familiar content e.g., constructors etc.
BOOL CTutorialDlg::OnInitDialog() {
    :
    :
    // Replaces IDC_GRFX_PLACEHOLDER on the application window
    m_GrfxWnd.ReplaceDialogControl(m_hWnd, IDC_GRFX_PLACEHOLDER);
    :
    :
```

Listing 3.1. CTutorialDlg class (Tutorial 3.1).

GUI layout design process. Our program code creates this GUI element during initialization of the main application window.

Back-End Programming Code

The development project consists of a total of nine source files (four .cpp and five .h files). By now we are familiar with most of the source files, and we understand the files that we will be working with are the following.

Quit Button. Because the quit button has the default behavior, no special supported is required.

- CTutorialDlg.h/.cpp. As in all the tutorials in this book, these two files define the CTutorialDlg class, the data type that represents the main application window. As we can see from Figure 3.6, the main application window only contains a quit button (with default behavior) and a D3D drawing area. Listing 3.1 shows that, as expected, CTutorialDlg only has an instance of m_GrfxWnd, the control variable to the D3D drawing area. During the initialization of the application window (in OnInitDialog()), m_GrfxWnd replaces itself into the IDC_GRFX_PLACEHOLDER position on the application window.

- GrfxWindowD3D.h/.cpp. These two files define the CGrfxWindowD3D class, the data type that represents the D3D drawing area. Listing 3.2 shows part of the definition of the CGrfxWndD3D class. We see that the

```
class CGrfxWindowD3D : public CWnd {
    ⋮
    bool ReplaceDialogControl(HWND hDialogHandle, int id);
    ⋮
    // this is the Paint/Redraw service function
    afx_msg void OnPaint();
    ⋮
    // this is the abstract D3D device
    LPDIRECT3DDEVICE9 m_pD3DDevice;
};
```

Source file. GrfxWindowD3D.h file in the *GrfxWindow* folder of the D3D_Rectangles2D project.

Listing 3.2. CGrfxWindowD3D class (Tutorial 3.1).

CGrfxWndD3Dclass is a subclass of the MFC CWnd class and thus is a simple generic window GUI element. We have already seen an implementation of the ReplaceDialogControl() function from Tutorial 2.8 where this function replaces itself into the area defined by the id GUI ID. In the rest of this section, we will concentrate on the redraw event service function OnPaint(). We will examine the rest of CGrfxWndD3D in the next chapter.

For now, we are going to concentrate on the programming code that actually draws the two squares. For the time being, we are going to assume that a graphics device is somehow created and initialized and properly referenced by m_pD3DDevice (the details will be covered in the next chapter). From our discussion in the previous chapters, we know drawing should occur when the window manager informs us that there is a Paint/Redraw event. As pointed out, the OnPaint() function is the event service routine for MFC's Paint/Redraw events. The two squares are drawn in this function. Listing 3.3 shows the programming code where the actual drawing occurs. We see that:

- **Step 1: select graphics hardware render buffer.** We have set up the graphics device to draw geometric shapes into an intermediate buffer. The content of this buffer will be presented to the application only after the drawing process is completed. In this way, our user will not see partially drawn images. In this step, we select the appropriate render buffer for subsequent drawings.

CWnd. The CWnd class is MFC's definition of a generic window GUI element. This class supports most default behaviors (e.g., mouse events, redraw/paint events) of a window.

Rendering. The process of converting geometries and related descriptions (e.g., light and material properties) into an image. We will discuss the details of the rendering process in later chapters.

Render buffer. Hardware buffers designed to support the rendering process. We will discuss these buffers in detail in later chapters.

```
void CGrfxWindowD3D::OnPaint() {
    ⋮ // check to ensure drawing area is defined
```

Step 1: *select graphics hardware render buffer.*

```
m_pD3DDevice->BeginScene();
    //perform all of our drawing
```

Step 2: *initialize selected hardware and set the coordinate system parameters.*

```
m_pD3DDevice->SetFVF(D3DFVF_XYZ | D3DFVF_DIFFUSE);
m_pD3DDevice->SetRenderState(D3DRS_CULLMODE, D3DCULL_NONE);
    ⋮
D3DXMATRIX world2ndc;
D3DXVECTOR3 scale(2.0f/width, 2.0f/height, 1.0f);
D3DXVECTOR3 translate(-1.0f, -1.0f, 0.0);
D3DXMatrixTransformation(&world2ndc, ..., scale, ..., translate);
m_pD3DDevice->SetTransform(D3DTS_VIEW, &world2ndc);
```

Step 3: *clear drawing buffer and draw two squares.*

```
m_pD3DDevice->Clear( ... );
DeviceVertexFormat v[4];  // Hardware device vertex format
    // First TRIANGLEFAN: The large square
v[0].m_point = D3DXVECTOR3(160,122,0);
v[1].m_point = D3DXVECTOR3( 80,122,0);
    ⋮
m_pD3DDevice->DrawPrimitiveUP(D3DPT_TRIANGLEFAN, 2, (CONST void *)v, ...);

    // Second TRIANGLEFAN: The small square
v[0].m_point = D3DXVECTOR3(160,122,0);
    ⋮
m_pD3DDevice->DrawPrimitiveUP(D3DPT_TRIANGLEFAN, 2, (CONST void *)v, ...);
```

Source file.
GrfxWindowD3D.cpp file in the *GrfxWindow* folders of the D3D_Rectangles2D project.

Step 4: *present the drawing buffer in the application window.*

```
m_pD3DDevice->EndScene();
m_pD3DDevice->Present(NULL, NULL, NULL, NULL);
}
```

Listing 3.3. CGrfxWndD3D::OnPaint() (Tutorial 3.1).

- **Step 2: initialize selected hardware and set the coordinate system parameters.** The `SetFVF()` and `SetRenderState()` functions initialize the hardware buffer. The next few lines of code are somewhat mysterious and may appear to be intimidating. However, with a closer look, we see scale and translate operations based on the width and height of the application window. As we will learn in Chapter 10, these few lines of code are defining an appropriate 2D cartesian coordinate system on the application window. The defined coordinate system has the origin located at the lower-left corner with x- and y-axes extending in the rightward and upward directions, respectively, and the implied units of measurement are in pixels.

The scene. Collection of all parameters that affect the rendering results. In this case, the scene is defined by the two squares.

- **Step 3: clear drawing buffer and draw two squares.** Notice that the first step in drawing is to ensure a clean buffer, like a clean piece of paper, with the `Clear()` command. For the actual drawing commands, we observe numeric values that corresponds to the measurements from Figure 3.4. In addition, we observe the following.

  - **Define hardware format** (`DeviceVertexFormat`). This is the graphics hardware vertex format. This structure is defined in the `CGrfxWnd D3D.cpp` file, where it has an (`x,y,z`) `m_point` location and an (`r,g, b`) `m_color` color. In this tutorial, all colors are set to (`0.4,0.4, 0.4`), or 40% gray.

  - **Specify geometric information.** The `v[]` array has four `DeviceVer texFormat` vertices. The `m_point` locations of these four vertices are filled with the measurements from Figure 3.4.

  - **Draw geometric information.** The `D3DPT_TRIANGLEFAN` parameter of the the `DrawPrimitive()` function tells the graphics device (`m_pD3DDevice`) that the geometric information should be interpreted and drawn as connecting triangles. The geometric information is passed to the graphics device in the (`CONST void*`)`v` parameter. In this way, the `m_pD3DDevice` will draw two connecting triangles into the hardware buffer representing the large square.

DrawPrimitive. Readers are encouraged to learn more about the `TRIANGLEFAN` parameter from D3D SDK manuals.

  - **Repeat for the small square.** The filling of geometric information and drawing operation are repeated for the small square.

- **Step 4: present the drawing buffer in the application window.** As mentioned, to prevent users from seeing partially drawn geometric shapes, all drawings are directed into internal hardware buffers. The contents of these buffers are not visible to the user until the `EndScene()` and `Present()` functions are called. In this way, users of the application will only observe completed images.

Double buffering. Dedicate two hardware render buffers to isolate the drawing process from the user. In this way, the users will never see partial drawing results on the application window.

In computer graphics, the drawing procedure from Steps 1 to 4 is referred to as the rendering process. The use of an internal drawing buffer to hide the drawing process from the user is referred to as double buffering. We refer to the collection of parameters that affects the appearance of rendered results as the scene. In this case, our scene is defined in Step 3, consisting of the geometries of the two squares. Although with many unknowns, we see that the rendering procedure of the D3D API is quite comprehensible! To ensure more thorough understanding, we will continue to examine `GrfxWndD3D.cpp` and `CGrfxWndD3D::OnPaint()` in the next few chapters.

3.3   Lessons Learned

After the detailed analysis of Tutorial 3.1, we can only claim partial understanding! This may seem overwhelming; however, at this point we have verified the following.

- **Computer graphics draws geometry.** Just like drafting technical drawings in real life, proper design and planning is essential when programming computer graphics. We have careful measurements and a design *prior* to actual programming.

- **Choice of coordinate system is important.** In the world of computer graphics, as the programmer, we choose the coordinate system that defines the space in the world. We have observed the importance of a convenient coordinate system. For Tutorial 3.1, if we had chosen the origin to be located at the center of the small square and inches to be the unit of measurement in Figure 3.2, then our solution in Listing 3.3 will become (1 inch = 2.54 cm)

$$V_a = (-\tfrac{25}{2.54}, -\tfrac{25}{2.54}, 0),$$
$$V_b = (-\tfrac{105}{2.54}, -\tfrac{105}{2.54}, 0).$$

Notice that different choices for coordinate systems will result in identical images being rendered. The choice we implemented did not result in a *more correct* solution, but it allowed for a *simpler* and *more elegant* solution.

More significantly, our current knowledge allows us to do the following.

- **Appreciate the distinctions between concepts and technologies.** For example, Tutorial 3.1 is an implementation based on a specific API technology. In the next section (Tutorial 3.2), we will examine another implementation of the scene from Figure 3.1 based on the OpenGL API. As we will see, all of our knowledge will apply in a straightforward manner.

- **Associate semantic meanings to the program source code.** This mapping of source code blocks allows us to design abstractions for the simple scene. In this way, we can achieve easier-to-comprehend source code with modular design and support for maintenance, modification, expansion, and reuse. We will explore this in Tutorial 3.3.

- **Understand the core of a simple graphics program.** We have sufficient knowledge to modify the scene and predict results. For example, we can imagine adding more squares, or even other geometric shapes. Notice that, without much knowledge of any API technologies, we can achieve a degree of understanding that allows us to modify the scene. We will explore this in Tutorial 3.5.

3.4   Further Examples

Tutorial 3.2. Drawing Squares with MFC and OpenGL

Tutorial 3.2.
Project Name
OGL_Rectangles2D

- **Goal.** Verify that the concepts of rendering procedure learned from Tutorial 3.1 are API-independent.

- **Approach.** Examine an OpenGL implementation of Figure 3.1 and apply our knowledge from Tutorial 3.1 in understanding the source code.

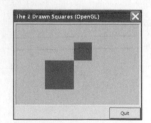

Figure 3.7. Tutorial 3.2.

Figure 3.7 is a screenshot of running Tutorial 3.2. As we can see, this program has the same front-end GUI layout as Tutorial 3.1 with exactly the same behavior where the program draws the scene from Figure 3.4 and quits when the user clicks on the button. However, unlike Tutorial 3.1, the computer graphics functionality of Tutorial 3.2 is based on the OpenGL API.

The back-end development source code structure of Tutorial 3.2 is similar to that of Tutorial 3.1. The only difference is that, instead of a D3D drawing area (CGrfxWndD3D), Tutorial 3.2 has an OpenGL drawing area defined by the CGrfxWndOGL class in the GrfxWindowOGL.h/.cpp files. Corresponding to the same GUI layout on the main application windows, the CTutorialDlg classes of Tutorials 3.1 and 3.2 are also very similar. Once again, the only difference is a CGrfxWndOGL control variable for drawing with OpenGL instead of the CGrfxWndD3D object. At this point, we can predict that the drawing routine for OpenGL should be located in CGrfxWndOGL::OnPaint() function.

Source file.
GrfxWindowOGL.cpp file in
the *GrfxWindow* folders of the
OGL_Rectangles2D project.

```
void CGrfxWindowOGL::OnPaint() {

    // check to ensure drawing area is defined
```
Step 1: select graphics hardware render buffer.
```
wglMakeCurrent(pDC->m_hDC, m_hRenderingContext);
```

Step 2: initialize selected hardware and set the coordinate system parameters.
```
glDisable( GL_CULL_FACE );

glMatrixMode(GL_PROJECTION);
glTranslated(-1.0, -1.0, 0.0);
glScaled(2.0/double(rect.Width()), 2.0/double(rect.Height()), 1.0);
```

Step 3: clear drawing buffer and draw two squares.
```
//clear the draw buffer to light gray
glClear( GL_COLOR_BUFFER_BIT );
glBegin(GL_QUADS);
    glColor4f(0.4f, 0.4f, 0.4f, 1.0f);
    // The large Square
    glVertex3d(160,122,0); // The vertices of the large square
    glVertex3d( 80,122,0);

    // The small square
    glVertex3d(...);          // The vertices of the small square
glEnd();
```

Step 4: present the drawing buffer in the application window.
```
SwapBuffers(pDC->m_hDC);
```

Listing 3.4. CGrfxWndOGL::OnPaint() (Tutorial 3.2).

Listing 3.4 shows that the OnPaint() function is significantly different. However, even with completely different function names, we can still apply the semantic structure derived from Tutorial 3.1.

- **Step 1: select graphics hardware render buffer.** The m_hRenderingCon text is a graphics device that was created and properly initialized. The wgl MakeCurrent() function associates the graphics device with the OpenGL drawing area (m_hDC). This function activates an implicit drawing device (or render context) for all drawing functions/commands.

- **Step 2: initialize selected hardware and set the coordinate system parameters.** Here we see that a parameter of the render context is being initialized to disable state. Once again, we see operations similar to those from Listing 3.3, where similar scale and translate operations are defining the same coordinate system as Tutorial 3.1.

- **Step 3: clear drawing buffer and draw two squares.** The vertices associated with the two squares are specified between the glBegin() and glEnd() scope. The GL_QUADS parameter informs the render context to process the positions specified by the glVertex3d() function as vertices of quadrilaterals. In this way, appropriate geometry can be drawn into the hardware buffers.

- **Step 4: present the drawing buffer in the application window.** Similar to Tutorial 3.1, our OpenGL implementation also supports double buffering. The contents of the internal drawing buffers are only presented to the application window after all drawing is done.

GL_QUAD. Readers are encouraged to read the OpenGL manual on the glBegin()/glEnd() functions and the corresponding format expected by the GL_QUAD parameter.

Notice that in OpenGL programming, all commands/functions are directed to an implicitly active graphics device, or the render context. For example, we call the glClear() function to clear the currently active drawing area. This is in contrast to the D3D approach (Listing 3.3) where functions are associated with an explicitly referenced graphics device. For example, to clear a D3D drawing area, we have to call the Clear() function referenced by the m_pD3DDevice (m_pD3DDevice→Clear()). Even with this difference, we see that we can apply the knowledge gained from Tutorial 3.1 to an implementation based on a completely different API technology. In the next chapter we will discuss the principles of working with graphics API technologies.

Tutorials 3.3 and 3.4. Reorganization with Classes

Tutorial 3.3.
Project Name
  D3D_RectangleClass

- **Goal.** Remind ourselves of the importance of building software systems with well-designed abstraction and a modularized interface.

Tutorial 3.4.
Project Name
  OGL_RectangleClass

- **Approach.** Reorganize the source code of Tutorial 3.1 to demonstrate better readability and to demonstrate that with a well-organized implementation, we can identify obvious potentials for expansion.

```
void CTutorialDlg::OnPaint() {
```
> *graphicsDevice: is the reference to the underlying graphics device.*
```
if ( graphicsDevice.GraphicsDeviceReady() ) {
    // Select a and clear graphics device
    graphicsDevice.BeginDeviceDraw();
    graphicsDevice.DefineCoordinateSystem(applicationWindowDimension);

        largeSquare.Draw(graphicsDevice);
        smallSquare.Draw(graphicsDevice);

    // Present the drawn result in the application window
    graphicsDevice.EndDeviceDraw();
}
}
```

Source file. Pseudocode; no corresponding source file.

Listing 3.5. API-independent rendering procedure.

Based on experience from Tutorial 3.1 and Tutorial 3.2, we can derive an API-independent rendering process and reimplement the OnPaint() function. It is obvious that to properly support Listing 3.5, we must define/implement the following classes.

- GraphicsDevice. This is the abstraction of the m_pD3DDevice of Listing 3.3 and m_hRenderContext of Listing 3.4. Unfortunately, at this point we do not understand how these devices were created/initialized. For this reason, we will defer the implementation of the GraphicsDevice class to the next chapter, after we understand the general principles of working with graphics APIs. We will derive a proper abstraction for GraphicsDevice in Tutorial 4.1.

- Rectangle. This is the class that must support the square geometries of our scene. Listing 3.6 shows a simple implementation of a D3D rectangle class. In this case, we choose simple SetCenter() and SetSize() public methods for setting the geometric information. Internally, we represent the rectangle by its center position (m_center_x, m_center_y) and its dimensions (m_width, m_height). This representation allows for straightforward scene specification. However, the drawing routines of D3D require vertex positions of the rectangle. As we can see, the CRectangle2D::Draw() function must compute the vertex positions before issuing the drawing requests to D3D.

In general, classes should be designed to support the semantics of the application and hide the requirements of the underlying API. For example, the public

```
class CRectangle2D {
public:
        ⋮ // constructor and destructor (not shown)
        void SetCenter(float x, float y);
        void SetSize(float width, float height);
        void Draw( LPDIRECT3DDEVICE9 pDevice ) const;

private:
        float m_center_x, m_center_y; // Center of the rectangle
        float m_width, m_height;      // Width and Height of the rectangle
};
```

*This is the implementation of **CRectangle2D** class.*

```
⋮ // constructor and destructor (not shown)
void CRectangle2D::SetCenter(float x, float y){ ... }
void CRectangle2D::SetSize(float width, float height) { ... }
```

Draw: This is the function that draws a rectangle to the graphics device.

```
void CRectangle2D::Draw(LPDIRECT3DDEVICE9 pDevice) const
{
    if(pDevice) { // if device is defined
        ⋮
```

Compute vertex positions from the center/width/height representation.

```
        v[0].m_point = D3DXVECTOR3(m_center_x - m_width/2.0f, m_center_y + m_height/2.0f, 0);
        v[1].m_point = D3DXVECTOR3(m_center_x - m_width/2.0f, m_center_y - m_height/2.0f, 0);
        v[2].m_point = D3DXVECTOR3(m_center_x + m_width/2.0f, m_center_y - m_height/2.0f, 0);
        v[3].m_point = D3DXVECTOR3(m_center_x + m_width/2.0f, m_center_y + m_height/2.0f, 0);
        pDevice->DrawPrimitiveUP(D3DPT_TRIANGLEFAN, 2, (CONST void *)v, ...);
    }
}
```

Listing 3.6. D3D Rectangle class (Tutorial 3.3).

Source file.
Rectangle2D.h/cpp file
in the *Primitives* folders of
the D3D_RectangleClass
project.

interface methods of the CRectangle2D class are designed for straightforward scene specification. The fact that data translation must occur before drawing is completely hidden from the rest of the application.

Tutorial 3.3 implements the CRectangle2D class as shown in Listing 3.6, and Tutorial 3.4 implements the same class based on the OpenGL API. For the interests of saving space and avoiding repetition, the details of the OpenGL implementation are not listed. Readers are encouraged to read the source code and explore similarities. The run-time screenshots from these tutorials are identical to the previous two.

Tutorials 3.5 and 3.6. The Circle Class

Tutorial 3.5.
Project Name
D3D_CircleClass

Tutorial 3.6.
Project Name
OGL_CircleClass

- **Goal.** Remind ourselves of an important strength of object-based design, where new types of objects with similar behaviors (public methods) can be easily integrated into the application.

- **Approach.** The structure of Listing 3.5 suggests that additional and different geometric types can be inserted in between BeginDeviceDraw() and EndDeviceDraw(). A circle geometric shape can support public methods similar to that of a CRectangle2D and thus can be integrated into Tutorial 3.3 in a straightforward manner.

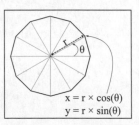

Figure 3.8 shows how to approximate a circle with 12 triangles. From trigonometry, we know that with a radius r, the vertex (x, y) positions of the triangles can be defined by θ, the angular offset from the x-axis, where:

$$x = r \times \cos(\theta),$$
$$y = r \times \sin(\theta).$$

Figure 3.8. Approximating a circle with 12 triangles.

This means that if we know how to draw a triangle, then we can approximate a circle. Recall that the CRectangle2D class approximates a rectangle with two triangles. Therefore, we know how to draw circles with both D3D and OpenGL.

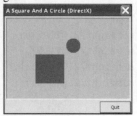

Figure 3.9 is a screenshot of running Tutorial 3.5. Notice the circle on the output window. This circle is an instance of the CCircle2D class. We have defined the public methods of the CCircle2D class to be similar to that of the CRectangle2D class. The significant difference is the Draw() function. In this case, we represented the circle with 100 triangles.

Figure 3.9. Tutorial 3.5.

Source file.
Circle2D.h/.cpp file in the *Primitives* folders of the D3D_CircleClass project.

```
class CCircle2D {
public:

    : // constructor and destructor (not shown)
    void SetCenter(float x, float y);
    void SetRadius(float radius);
    void Draw( LPDIRECT3DDEVICE9 pDevice ) const;
```

Listing 3.7. D3D Circle class (Tutorial 3.5).

```
private:
    float m_center_x,  m_center_y; // Center of the circle
    float m_radius;                 // Radius of the circle
};
```

> *This is the implementation of the **CCircle2D** class.*

```
⋮ // constructor and destructor (not shown)
void CCircle2D::SetCenter(float x, float y) { ... }
void CCircle2D::SetRadius(float radius) { ... }
```

> ***Draw:*** *This is the function that approximates a circle by drawing triangles.*

```
void CCircle2D::Draw(LPDIRECT3DDEVICE9 pDevice) const
{
    // the graphics device and the circle are both defined
    if (m_radius <= 0.0f || NULL == pDevice)
        return;
```

> *Approximate the circle with 100 triangles (TriangleFan)*

```
    DeviceVertexFormat v[100+2];
    float theta = (float)((2.0f * PI) / 100); // theta: angle increment for each triangle
    v[0].m_point = (m_center_x, m_center_y);  // Center of the TriangleFan
    for (int i=0; i<(kNumPts); i++) {
        v[i+1].m_point.x = m_center_x + (m_radius * sinf(i*theta));
        v[i+1].m_point.y = m_center_y + (m_radius * cosf(i*theta));
    }
    v[kNumPts+1] = v[1];
    pDevice->DrawPrimitiveUP(D3DPT_TRIANGLEFAN, kNumPts, (CONST void *)v,
                        sizeof(DeviceVertexFormat));
}
```

Listing 3.7. (cont.)

4

Working with Graphics APIs

This chapter introduces a framework for developing programs with modern graphics APIs. This chapter:

- discusses the relationships between graphics APIs and GUI APIs in interactive graphics applications;

- introduces a framework to encapsulate the principles of programming with modern graphics APIs;

- uses the framework to further explain the graphics API function calls from Tutorial 3.1;

- demonstrates tutorials that implement the framework abstraction.

After this chapter we should be able to:

- understand the principles of working with graphics APIs;

- understand approaches to abstract and customize graphics APIs for our applications to increase readability and to hide complexities.

In addition, given the source code of simple computer graphics programs, we should be able to

- identify and understand graphics API initialization and configuration calls, independent of the implementation technology (e.g. programming languages, APIs);

- categorize graphics API calls into semantic functionality (e.g., initialize, set up for drawing);

- use the abstraction we have developed in developing simple graphics applications.

If we re-examine the tutorials from Chapter 3, we observe the following.

- **APIs are complex.** The two APIs we worked with dictated a nine file source code project for drawing two simple squares!

- **Disciplinary concepts trump API.** In the Chapter 3 tutorials, we applied concepts from computer graphics to:

    - categorize API functions calls according to semantic functionality;

    - identify scene drawing functions;

    - implement a new class to modify the scene.

  We have parsed, partially understood, and designed new classes to modify the source code without knowing the details of the APIs.

Additionally, modern APIs are constantly evolving with frequent new releases and updates. These observations suggest that an efficient approach to work with modern APIs would be the following.

- Learn the disciplinary concepts.

- Derive the functionality required for our implementation.

- Examine appropriate APIs and design classes around API functions to fulfill the requirements of our implementations.

In this way, we approach working with an API based on the requirements for supporting our knowledge and our applications: we will only examine relevant API functions and classes. Because of the large numbers and the constant changes, studying and understanding each API function in detail may not be an efficient approach to learning how to work with an API.

In this chapter, we first examine the relationship between graphics APIs and GUI APIs, the two types of APIs we must work with in all of our applications. Then we introduce and implement a framework for programming with graphics APIs. Our goal is not to learn any particular graphics API; rather, we are interested in deriving an abstract framework that would allow us to use a graphics API without the details or the complexities.

4.1 Relationship between Graphics and GUI APIs

We say, "Tutorial 3.1 is based on two distinct types of APIs: the GUI API and the graphics API." By "based on" we refer to the fact that Tutorial 3.1 calls the functions and uses the utility classes provided by these two types of APIs. In practice, this means that we must include the appropriate header files to compile our source code, and we must include the appropriate library files to link our program.

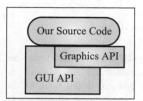

Figure 4.1. Relationship between our source code and the Graphics and GUI APIs.

Figure 4.1 shows the relationships between our source code and the two types of APIs. The fact that our source code sits on top of the graphics API and GUI API boxes indicates that our source code depends on the functionality of these two types of APIs. In our applications, we configured the graphics API to draw through the GUI API window. In this way, as illustrated in Figure 4.1, the Graphics API module rests on top of the GUI API module.

Figure 4.2 uses the simple scene from Tutorial 3.1 as an example to illustrate the functionality and responsibilities of the two APIs. A screenshot from Tutorial 3.1 is shown on the right of Figure 4.2 with the three GUI elements: the drawing area, the application window, and the button. From Chapter 2, we understand how to work with GUI API functions to create, initialize, and control the GUI elements to interact with the user. In this chapter, we will examine how the graphics API configures and initializes the graphics hardware and obtains a reference to the drawing area for presenting rendered images. We will carry out our examination with the familiar two-square scene from Tutorial 3.1. Before we begin analyzing the programming code, let's first develop a framework for understanding graphics APIs.

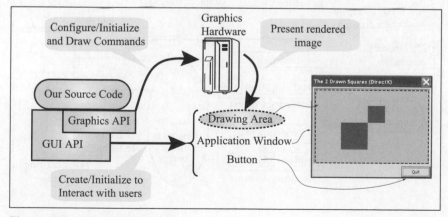

Figure 4.2. Relationship of APIs.

4.2   Programming Graphics APIs

GHC and RC. These are names and abbreviations introduced in this book for the convenience of discussion. In general, there is no industry standard or recommendation for organizing interfaces to graphics APIs.

Figure 4.3 illustrates that one way to understand a modern graphics API is by considering the API as a functional interface to the underlying graphics hardware. It is convenient to consider this functional interface as consisting of two stages: the graphics hardware context (GHC) and the rendering context (RC).

Graphics hardware context (GHC).   This stage is depicted as the vertical ellipse in Figure 4.3. We think of the GHC as a configuration that wraps over the hardware video display card. An application creates a GHC for each unique configuration (e.g., number of representable colors) of the hardware video card(s). When we issue drawing commands, geometries are rendered into hardware render buffers inside the GHC. The right side of Figure 4.3 shows that when a graphics API presents a rendered image, the image is flushed onto the GUI-created drawing area. For example, referring to Listing 3.3, where in Step 3 we clear the intermediate (hardware render) buffers and then in Step 4 the contents of the buffers are presented to the GUI-created drawing area. It is possible for an application to draw to multiple drawing areas. Figure 4.3 illustrates that one way would be associating multiple drawing areas (and buffers) with a single rendering context. Another way would be creating multiple rendering contexts to support drawings with different rendering parameters.

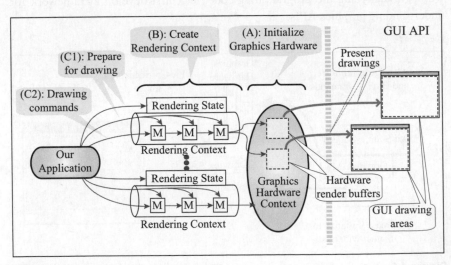

Figure 4.3. Working with a graphics API.

Rendering context (RC). This stage is depicted as the cylindrical pipes in Figure 4.3. The multiple pipes in the figure illustrates that an application can create multiple RCs to connect to the same GHC. As we saw above, through each RC an application can create and draw to multiple buffers/drawing areas. To properly support this functionality, each RC represents a complete rendering state. A rendering state encompasses all of the information that affects the final appearance of an image. This includes primitive attributes, illumination parameters, coordinate transformations, and so on. Color, size, pattern, and so on are examples of primitive attributes. Examples of illumination parameters include light source position/color, surface material properties, and so on. Graphics APIs typically support coordinate transformation with a series of two or three matrix processors. In Figure 4.3, the "M" boxes inside the RC pipes are the matrix processors. Each matrix processor is capable of transforming vertices. Because these processors operate in series, together they are capable of implementing multistage coordinate space transformations (e.g., object to world, world to eye, and eye to projected space). The application program must load these matrix processors with appropriate matrices to implement the desired transformations. For example, referring to Listing 3.3, in Step 2 we loaded the `world2ndc` matrix into the `D3DTS_VIEW` matrix processors of the D3D rendering pipe. Lastly, as shown in Figure 4.3, we can create multiple hardware buffers for each RC for drawing to different UI areas. However, in general, it is *not* possible to share hardware buffers across different RCs. This is because an RC usually represents a unique hardware configuration, and buffers created for different RCs will typically have different hardware resource demands (e.g., number of representable colors).

With this understanding, Figure 4.3 illustrates that to work with a graphics API, an application will do the following.

- **(A) Initialize one or more GHCs.** Each GHC represents a unique configuration of the graphics video card(s). In typical cases, one GHC is initialized and configured to be shared by the entire application.

- **(B) Create one or more RCs.** Typically, each RC represents a unique rendering configuration. For example, rendering with or without illumination, 2D versus 3D rendering, and so on. The application program must then create a hardware render buffer for the RC and associate the buffer with a GUI drawing area. If an application requires similar rendering to multiple drawing areas (e.g., a 3D world view and a 3D zoom view), multiple render buffers can be created for an RC.

- **(C) Draw into a render buffer.** An application draws to a desired GUI area via the corresponding RC and render buffer. Referring to Figure 4.3, an

Illumination. This is the process of creating nice-looking colors representing 3D objects. The topics related to illumination will be covered in Appendix A.

Matrix. This is a mathematical tool for transforming primitives. This will be discussed in detail in Chapter 8.

Coordinate transformation. This is a mathematical tool that allows convenient scene definition. This will be discussed in detail in Chapter 10.

`world2ndc` **and** `w2n`. We will abbreviate `world2ndc` as `w2n`. For example, the `world2ndc` matrix $\mathbf{M}_{world2ndc}$ will be written as $\mathbf{M}_{w2n}$.

```
void CGrfxWndD3D::OnPaint() {
    ⋮
```

C1: *with the selected render buffer set the render state and matrix processors.*

Step 2: *initialize selected hardware and set the coordinate system parameters.*

```
    ⋮
    m_pD3DDevice->SetRenderState(D3DRS_CULLMODE, D3DCULL_NONE);
    m_pD3DDevice->SetRenderState(D3DRS_LIGHTING, FALSE);
    ⋮
    m_pD3DDevice->SetTransform( D3DTS_WORLD, &identity);
    m_pD3DDevice->SetTransform( D3DTS_VIEW, &identity);
    m_pD3DDevice->SetTransform( D3DTS_PROJECTION, &identity);
    ⋮
    // Operations to compute the coordinate system
    m_pD3DDevice->SetTransform( D3DTS_VIEW, &world2ndc );
```

C2: *Send drawing commands to the RC (m_pD3DDevice).*

```
    ⋮
```

Step 3: *clear drawing buffer and draw two squares.*

```
    m_pD3DDevice->Clear( ... );
    ⋮
    // Set vertex information
    v[1].m_point = D3DXVECTOR3(160,122,0);
    ⋮
    // Send the vertex information and drawing command
    m_pD3DDevice->DrawPrimitiveUP(D3DPT_TRIANGLEFAN ... (CONST void *)v);
    ⋮
```

Source dile.
GrfxWindowD3D.cpp file in the *GrfxWindow* folders of the *D3D_Rectangles2D* project.

Listing 4.1. Re-examine drawing with D3D (Tutorial 3.1).

application sets the rendering state (C1) and then issues drawing commands to the RC (C2). Setting the rendering state involves activating the proper render buffer, setting all relevant primitive and illumination attributes, and computing/loading appropriate transformation matrices into the matrix processors. A drawing command is typically a series of vertex positions accompanied by instructions on how to interpret the vertices (e.g., two vertex positions with an instruction that these are endpoints of a line).

```
void CGrfxWindowOGL::OnPaint() {
   ⋮
```

C1: *with the selected render buffer set the render state and matrix processors.*

Step 2: *initialize selected hardware and set the coordinate system parameters.*

```
   glDisable( GL_CULL_FACE );
   ⋮

   glMatrixMode(GL_MODELVIEW);
   glLoadIdentity();
   glMatrixMode(GL_PROJECTION);
   glTranslated(-1.0, -1.0, 0.0);
   ⋮
```

C2: *Send drawing commands to the RC (render context: **m_hRenderContext**).*

   ⋮

Step 3: *clear drawing buffer and draw two squares.*

   ⋮

```
   glBegin(GL_QUADS);
      ⋮

      glVertex3d(160,122,0); // The vertices of the large square
      ⋮

   glEnd();
```

Source file.
GrfxWindowOGL.cpp file in the *GrfxWindow* folders of the OGL_Rectangles2D project.

Listing 4.2. Re-examine drawing with OpenGL (Tutorial 3.2).

The four-step drawing procedure we derived from Tutorials 3.1 and 3.2 (Listings 3.3 and 3.4) implements (C). For example, if we include comments from the GHC/RC framework in the D3D drawing routine (CGrfxWndD3D::OnPaint()), we get Listing 4.1. We observe the following.

- C1 maps nicely to Step 2 of the drawing procedure. At this point, although we still do not know what a D3DRS_LIGHTING is, we do know that it is per graphics device. In addition, we see that the D3D graphics device has three matrix processors: WORLD, VIEW, and PROJECTION. We observe that in our drawing, we only programmed the VIEW processor with the w2n matrix and left the other two processors initialized to identity.

- C2 is simply Step 3 of the four-step drawing procedure. In the case of the D3D API, DrawPrimitiveUP() is the drawing command. We see explicit filling of the v-array and the TRIANGLEFAN parameter of the drawing command instructing the RC to draw the vertices as connecting triangles.

When we apply the same analysis procedure to the OpenGL drawing routine (CGrfxWndOGL::OnPaint()), we get Listing 4.2. We observe the following.

(C1) GL_CULLFACE is a per-render-context state. In addition, we see that the OpenGL graphics device has two matrix processors: MODELVIEW and PROJECTION. In this case, we program the PROJECTION processor to implement our coordinate system and leave the MODELVIEW processor initialized to identity.

(C2) OpenGL implements drawing commands significantly differently from D3D. Instead of D3D's packaging all vertices and sending the RC one drawing command, OpenGL sets up the RC (with glBegin()) *before* sending the vertex information (with glVertex3d()).

4.3 Understanding Tutorials 3.1 and 3.2

We have derived a semantic framework for working with graphics APIs. However, disciplinary knowledge in computer graphics is necessary to fully understand the details of graphics API function calls. In the rest of this book, we will learn concepts in computer graphics, and we will begin to understand more graphics API function calls. Fortunately, as is the case in Chapter 3, we will see that the knowledge we have gathered thus far will allow us to do the following.

1. Apply the framework and understand the semantics of application source code independent of the graphics API.

2. Design classes to abstract the framework to increase readability, maintainability, and potential for expansion.

Continue with Tutorial 3.1

Tutorial 3.1. We will further examine the source code from Tutorial 3.1.

- **Goal.** Demonstrate how to apply the GHC/RC framework with the D3D graphics API.

- **Approach.** Apply the GHC/RC framework to a very simple D3D drawing example, for example, Tutorial 3.1.

```
int CGrfxWindowD3D::OnCreate(LPCREATESTRUCT lpCreateStruct) {
    (A). Initialize graphics hardware context (GHC).
    // Verify D3D SDK is installed.Conceptually, m_pD3D is the reference to the GHC.
    if(NULL == m_pD3D) m_pD3D = Direct3DCreate9( D3D_SDK_VERSION);
    if(NULL == m_pD3D) return FALSE;

    // Inquire the capabilities of graphics adapter. Results are stored in display_mode
    D3DDISPLAYMODE display_mode;
    m_pD3D->GetAdapterDisplayMode( D3DADAPTER_DEFAULT, &display_mode );

    (B). Create rendering context (RC).
    // present_params specifies hardware buffer mode for the RC we are about to create.
    D3DPRESENT_PARAMETERS present_params;
    ⋮
    present_params.BackBufferFormat = display_mode.Format;
    ⋮
    // Creating the RC. m_pD3DDevice is the reference to the RC.
    if( FAILED(m_pD3D->CreateDevice( ..., m_hWnd, ... &m_pD3DDevice) ) )
    ⋮
```

Source file.
GrfxWindowD3D.cpp file in
the *GrfxWindow* folders of the
D3D_Rectangles2D project.

Listing 4.3. CGrfxWindowD3D::OnCreate() (Tutorial 3.1).

We are finally ready to examine all of the graphics API calls encountered in Tutorial 3.1. Recall that in Tutorial 3.1, we introduced the CGrfxWndD3D class to represent the GUI drawing area. We examined drawing with a graphics API in the OnPaint() function. Here we want to examine the initialization of a graphics API. OnCreate() is called during MFC's window creation time. It is in this function that we create and initialize the D3D graphics device. Listing 4.3 shows the structure of the CGrfxWndD3D::OnCreate() function.

CGrfxWndD3D. Recall that this class is a subclass of the CWnd class, the generic MFC window class.

- **(A). Initialize graphics hardware context (GHC).** This operation ensures that there is a valid Direct3D development environment (or the *SDK*). Conceptually, the results stored in m_pD3D are a reference to the hardware graphics adapter (or the GHC). The GetAdapterDisplayMode() function returns the capabilities of the graphics hardware in display_mode.

- **(B). Create rendering context (RC).** We set the present_params variable with appropriate hardware render buffer specifications and call Create Device() to create the RC and the corresponding render buffer. The results are stored in m_pD3DDevice. The m_hWnd is the reference to the GUI drawing area. Notice that m_hWnd is a parameter of the CreateDevice() function call. In this way the hardware render buffer and the RC (m_pD3DDevice) are bound to the GUI API drawing area. This is the reason that the Present() function call in Step 4 of Listing 3.3 presents the intermediate hardware buffers in our application window.

Continue with Tutorial 3.2

Tutorial 3.2. We will further examine the source code from Tutorial 3.2.

- **Goal.** Demonstrate how to apply the GHC/RC framework with OpenGL Graphics API.

- **Approach.** Apply the GHC/RC framework to a very simple OpenGL drawing example, for example, Tutorial 3.2.

Recall that Tutorial 3.2 implements the same two-square scene as Tutorial 3.1 based on the OpenGL graphics API. Recall that the OpenGL drawing area was defined to be CGrfxWindowOGL with drawing defined in the OnPaint() function, and as in the case with D3D, the creation and initialization of the graphics API happened during the creation of the drawing area in the OnCreate() function. Listing 4.4 shows that although OpenGL has different function calls, the same graphics API programming framework applies.

CGrfxWindowOGL. Recall that this is the OpenGL drawing area and that this is a subclass of the MFC CWnd class.

- **(A). Initialize graphics hardware context (GHC).** The GetDC() function is defined by the CWnd class. In this case, we see that we use the results from the GetDC() call (pDC) to get the hardware adapter capabilities. This ensures the proper binding of GUI drawing area to the graphics rendering hardware buffers. Our program sets the desired render buffer format in the pfd structure and calls ChoosePixelFormat() to inquire if the GHC (m_hDC) is capable of supporting the specified format. The results of the inquiry are stored in nPixelFormat.

- **(B). Create rendering context (RC).** We call the SetPixelFomat() function to initialize the GHC (m_hDC) to the desired format, and call the wgl CreateContext() to create m_hRenderingContext, the RC. Notice that the created RC is based on the GHC (m_hDC), which is bound to the GUI drawing area via pDC (the results of GetDC() function call). As we have seen, all OpenGL commands are sent to the *currently active* RC.

```
int CGrfxWindowOGL::OnCreate() {
```
⋮

> *(A). Initialize graphics hardware context (GHC).*
>> *Get OpenGL hardware abstraction*

```
CDC* pDC = GetDC();
if(NULL == pDC) return FALSE;
```

>> *Inquire capabilities of adapter*

```
PIXELFORMATDESCRIPTOR pfd = { ... };
int nPixelFormat = ChoosePixelFormat(pDC->m_hDC, &pfd );
```

> *(B). Create rendering context (RC).*

```
if (nPixelFormat)
```

>> *Create and set the desired rendering buffer format*

```
    int pixel_format_index = SetPixelFormat(pDC->m_hDC, nPixelFormat, &pfd);
    if(pixel_format_index)
```

>>> *Creating the RC. **m_hRenderingContext** is the reference to the RC*

```
        m_hRenderingContext = ::wglCreateContext(pDC->m_hDC);
```
⋮

Source file.
`GrfxWindowOGL.cpp` file in the *GrfxWindow* folders of the `OGL_Rectangles2D` project.

Listing 4.4. `CGrfxWindowOGL::OnCreate()` (Tutorial 3.2).

4.4 Abstraction of Graphics API

In Tutorial 3.3 and 3.4, we applied our knowledge of object-based programming and encapsulated the functionality of a `Rectangle`. Based on the interface of the abstraction, we generalized the behavior of an abstract drawable object. Based on this abstraction, we designed the `Circle` class with similar interface methods. In this chapter, we have learned about graphics API programming. In the previous section, we applied the knowledge to associate semantic meanings with graphics API–specific programming code. In this section, we want to follow the learning process from Tutorial 3.5: we want to combine the new knowledge with object-based programming to design an abstraction for the graphics API functionality. Based on the GHC/RC framework, we can define a simple abstract interface to the graphics API (see Listing 4.5). With this `GraphicsSystem` class, the corresponding `OnCreate()` and `OnPaint()` functions would look like Listing 4.6.

```
class GraphicsSystem {
```

> *Functionality demanded by **OnCreate**() of Listings 4.3 and 4.4.*

```
    CreateGraphicsContext(); // Create and Initialize GHC and RC
```

> *Functionality demanded by the **OnPaint**() of Listings 4.1 and 4.2.*

```
    // Select and initialize the RC for drawing
    BeginDraw();
    // Present the drawn results on the GUI drawing area
    EndDrawAndShow();
};

GraphicsSystem TheAPI
```

Listing 4.5. The GraphicsSystem class.

```
bool OnCreate()  {
    :   // Initialize GUI system
    // Create and Initialize GHC and RC
    if (!TheAPI.CreateGraphicsContext() )
        return false;

    :

    return true;
}


void OnPaint() {
    TheAPI.BeginDraw();        // Initialize RC for drawing
        m_LargeSquare.Draw();      // Draw the large square
        :

    TheAPI.EndDrawAndShow();
        // Present the drawn results on the application window
};
```

Listing 4.6. Pseudocode for OnCreate() and OnPaint().

The functionality presented in Listing 4.5 is driven entirely by our experience from working with graphics APIs. The CreateGraphicsContext() function should create/initialize the GHC and create one instance of RC. The BeginDraw() and EndDrawAndShow() functions are designed to encapsulate graphics API initialization and configuration calls. As we can see from the OnPaint() function in Listing 4.6, in this way, application programmers can focus on specifying the scene geometries (e.g., the rectangles). TheAPI is the object representing our interface to the graphics API. Because there should be only one interface to the graphics API, we define a static singleton variable that is globally accessible. Now we can examine the actual implementation of the GraphicsSystem class.

Tutorial 4.1. The D3D GraphicsSystem Class

- **Goal.** Increase the readability of our source code by hiding low-level graphics API function calls.

- **Approach.** Design an abstraction for a graphics API based on the requirements of our applications. For example, in this tutorial we will implement the GraphicsSystem class of Listing 4.5 based on the D3D graphics API. We will integrate the new class into the source code of Tutorial 3.5.

Figure 4.4 is a screenshot of running Tutorial 4.1. Not surprisingly, this output is identical to that of Tutorial 3.5. However, if we compare the source code of

Tutorial 4.1.
Project Name
D3D_GraphicsSystem

Tutorial 3.5. Recall that in Tutorial 3.5 we worked with the CRectangle2D and CCircle2D classes to draw a scene with a rectangle and a circle.

Source file.
D3DGraphicsSystem.h file in the *GraphicsSystem* folders of the D3D_GraphicsSystem project.

```
class GraphicsSystemD3D {
A:  // class variable for representation of singleton interface to the D3D API.
    public:   static GraphicsSystemD3D& GetSystem();
    private:  static GraphicsSystemD3D m_TheAPI;

B:  // public interface for initialization/termination/accessing
    public:   bool CreateGraphicsContext(HWND hWindow);
              void ShutDown();
              LPDIRECT3DDEVICE9 GetActiveDevice();

C:  // public interface initializing the device for drawing
              bool BeginDraw(float width, float height);
              bool EndDrawAndShow();

D:  // private representation of the D3D interface.
    private:
        // This is the D3D Interface (GHC)
        LPDIRECT3D9       m_pD3D;
        // This is one drawing pipeline (RC)
        LPDIRECT3DDEVICE9 m_pD3DDevice;
};
```

Listing 4.7. The D3D GraphicsSystem class.

Source file.
GrfxWindowD3D.cpp file in
the *GrfxWindow* folders of
the D3D_GraphicsSystem
project.

```
BOOL CGrfxWindowD3D::OnInitDialog() {
    ⋮
    Initialize the D3D graphics system
    if ( !GraphicsSystemD3D::GetSystem().CreateGraphicsContext(m_hWnd) )
        return FALSE;
    ⋮

void CGrfxWindowD3D::OnPaint() {
    ⋮
    GraphicsSystemD3D& theAPI = GraphicsSystemD3D::GetSystem();
    if( theAPI.BeginDraw(width, height) ) {
        m_LargeSquare.Draw();
        m_SmallCircle.Draw();
        theAPI.EndDrawAndShow();
    }
    ⋮
```

Listing 4.8. D3D OnCreate() and OnPaint() (Tutorial 4.1).

these two tutorials, we notice a new class defined. Listing 4.7 is the D3D implementation of the GraphicsSystem class (from Listing 4.5). At Label A, m_TheAPI is declared as static, or a class variable. We take advantage of the class variable construct in object-oriented programming to enforce the singleton nature of the interface to the graphics API. At Label B, we see two new functions.

- ShutDown(). To release relevant memory at deletion time.

- GetActiveDevice(). To return the currently active graphics device. This function conveys the point that each graphics API can support multiple RCs (or drawing areas).

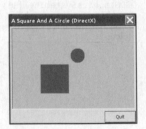

Figure 4.4. Tutorial 4.1.

In the interests of saving space and avoiding repetition, the implementation of the GraphicsSystemD3D methods are not shown here. These functions are basically copies of corresponding portions of code we saw in Listings 3.3 and 4.3. Listing 4.8 shows that the implementation of the OnCreate() and OnPaint() functions are almost identical to our prediction from Listing 4.6. With the new GraphicsSystemD3D class, the drawing routine of the CRectangle 2D class must be updated (from Tutorial 3.3, Listing 3.6). Listing 4.9 shows that with the GraphicsSystemD3D class, the CRectangle2D (and CCircle2D) classes can access the currently active graphics device directly for drawing.

```
void CRectangle2D::Draw() const {
    LPDIRECT3DDEVICE9 pDevice = GraphicsSystemD3D::GetSystem().GetActiveDevice();
    if(pDevice) {
        DeviceVertexFormat v[4];
        :
        :
        // set the vertices of the rectangle ...
        :
        :
        pDevice->DrawPrimitiveUP(D3DPT_TRIANGLEFAN, 2, (CONST void *)v, ...);
    }
}
```

Source file.
Rectangle2D.cpp file in
the *Primitives* folders of
the D3D_GraphicsSystem
project.

Listing 4.9. The D3D Rectangle2D class Draw() function.

Tutorial 4.2. The D3D Graphics Library

In Tutorial 2.7, we grouped GUI API–specific functions/classes into a separate software library to organize our source code structure. Here we define another separate software library to organize graphics API–specific functionality. We collect the files defining the GraphicsSystemD3D, Circle2D, and Rectangle2D classes and define the D3D_GraphicsLibrary. Our main source code project only contains files that are related to our scene definition.

As we learn more graphics concepts and implement more graphics-specific classes, our graphics library will continue to grow. In this way, not only do we learn graphics and use graphics APIs, we also implement our own API. This separation of source according to functionality simplifies solution development. In our case, this separation can also help focus our learning when we develop an isolated part of the code system. For example, as a program developed based on the D3D_GraphicsLibrary, when working with Tutorial 4.2 we can concentrate on designing the scene with circles and rectangles and not be concerned with graphics API–specific details.

In every sense, our graphics software library presents an API for our application. Interestingly, in this case we are both the API developer and the application developer. In this manner, we will learn how to use sophisticated APIs, and we will also gain experience designing our own API.

Tutorial 4.2.
Project Name:
   D3D_SeparateLibrary
Library Support:
   D3D_GraphicsLib

Tutorial 4.3.
Project Name
   OGL_GraphicsSystem

Tutorial 4.4.
Project Name:
   OGL_SeparateLibrary
Library Support:
   OGL_GraphicsLib

The OpenGL Tutorials

Tutorial 4.3 is an OpenGL version of Tutorial 4.1, and Tutorial 4.4 is an OpenGL version of Tutorial 4.2. Because of the similarities, the details of the OpenGL tutorials are not included here. Readers are encouraged to verify the learning from the D3D examples to examine and understand the source code of the OpenGL tutorials.

5

The Model-View-Controller Architecture

This chapter discusses the implementation of interactive graphics applications based on the model-view-controller (MVC) software architecture. This chapter:

- introduces the MVC software architecture for organizing interactive graphics application solution design;

- describes an MVC-based solution for the ball-shooting program;

- demonstrates the expandability of the MVC-based solution;

- develops software abstractions and library support for the implementation of our MVC-based ball-shooting solution.

After this chapter we should:

- understand the technology-independent MVC architecture;

- understand the process for designing interactive applications based on the MVC architecture;

- understand the concepts and implementation of having multiple view-controller pairs.

In terms of implementation, we should be able to:

- understand the software abstraction and libraries developed;

- understand how to utilize these resources in implementing MVC-based solutions;

- critically evaluate these resources and identify alternate solutions.

At this point we know the following.

- **The programming model.** We understand that the event-driven programming model better supports developing solutions for user interactive applications in shared windowing environments.

- **The GUI API.** We understand the principles of working with modern GUI APIs, and we understand the mechanisms for registration of events and the coordination between the front-end GUI elements and back-end programming code.

- **The graphics API.** We have gained some understanding and developed sufficient abstraction to begin simple drawing with graphics APIs.

These represent the foundation concepts and technology know-how for implementing the ball-shooting program. However, due to the practical complexities involved with programming and coordinating the functionality presented by the two APIs, it can be overwhelming to determine where or how to begin an implementation.

In this chapter, we learn the model-view-controller (MVC) software architecture where a framework is introduced to structure the collaborations of functionality between components. With this framework guiding our design and implementation, we will be better equipped to develop programs that are easier to understand, maintain, modify, and expand.

5.1   The Model-View-Controller Framework

Based on our experience developing solutions in Chapter 1, we understand that interactive graphics applications can be described as applications that allow users to interactively update their internal states. These applications provide real-time visualization of their internal states (e.g., the free-falling balls) with computer graphics (e.g., drawing circles). The model-view-controller (MVC) framework provides a convenient structure for discussing this type of application. In the

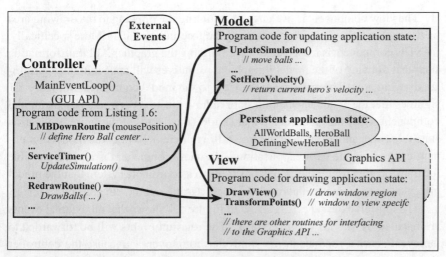

Figure 5.1. Components of an interactive graphics application.

MVC framework, the model component is the application state, the view component is responsible for providing the support for the model to present itself to the user, and the controller component is responsible for providing the support for the user to interact with the model. Within this framework, our solution from Section 1.6 (Listing 1.7) is simply the implementation of a controller. In this chapter, we will develop the understanding of the other two components in the MVC framework and how these components collaborate to support interactive graphics applications.

Figure 5.1 shows the details of an MVC framework to describe the behavior of a typical interactive graphics application. We continue to use the ball-shooting program as our example to illustrate the details of the components. The top-right rectangular box is the model, the bottom-right rectangular box is the view, and the rectangular box on the left is the controller component. These three boxes represent program code we, as application developers, must develop. The two dotted rounded boxes represent external graphics and GUI APIs.

The model component defines the persistent application state (e.g., `AllWorld Balls`, `HeroBall`) and implements interface functions for this application state (e.g., `UpdateSimulation()`). Because we are working with a "graphics" application, we expect graphical primitives to be part of the representation for the application state (e.g., `CirclePrimitives`). This fact is represented in Figure 5.1 by the application state (the ellipse) partially covering the graphics API box. In the rest of this section, we will use the terms *model* and *persistent application state* interchangeably.

The view component is in charge of initiating the drawing to the drawing area on the application window (e.g., drawing the free-falling balls). More specifically, the view component is responsible for initializing the graphics API transformation such that drawing of the model's graphical primitives will appear in the appropriate drawing area. The arrow from the view to the model component in Figure 5.1 signifies that the actual application state redraw must be performed by the model component. Only the model component knows the details of the entire application state (e.g., size and location of the free-falling circles), so only the model component can redraw the entire application. The view component is also responsible for transforming user mouse-click positions to a coordinate system that the model understands (e.g., mouse button clicks for dragging out the HeroBall).

The top-left external events arrow in Figure 5.1 shows that all external events are handled by the MainEventLoop(). The relevant events will be forwarded to the event service routines in the controller component. Because the controller component is responsible for interacting with the user, the design is typically based on the event-driven programming model. The solution presented in Section 1.6 and the event service routines from Listing 1.7 is an example of a controller component implementation. The arrow from the controller to the model indicates that most external events eventually change the model component (e.g., creating a new HeroBall or changing the current HeroBall velocity). The arrow from the controller to the view component indicates that the user input point transformation is handled by the view component. Controllers typically return mouse-click positions in the hardware coordinate system. In the application model, it is more convenient for us to work with a coordinate system with a lower-left origin. The view component with its transformation functionality has the knowledge to perform the necessary transformation.

Hardware coordinate. Recall that hardware coordinate is defined to be one where the origin is located at the top-left corner.

Because the model must understand the transformation set up by the view, it is important that the model and the view components are implemented based on the same graphics API. However, this sharing of an underlying supporting API does not mean that the model and view are an integrated component. On the contrary, as will be discussed in the following sections, it is advantageous to clearly distinguish between these two components and to establish well-defined interfaces between them.

5.2   Applying MVC to the Ball-Shooting Program

With the described MVC framework and the understanding of how responsibilities are shared among the components, we can now refine the solution presented in Listing 1.7 and complete the design of the ball-shooting program.

5.2.1   The Model

The model is the application state and thus this is the core of our program. When describing approaches to designing an event-driven program in Section 1.6, the first two points mentioned were:

1. define the application state;

2. describe how a user changes this application state.

These two points are the guidelines for designing the model component. In an object-oriented environment, the model component can be implemented as classes, and the state of the application can be implemented as instance variables, with "how a user changes this application state" implemented as methods of the classes.

Listing 5.1 shows that the instance variables representing the state are typically private to the model component. The CBall class is basically a circle that can travel based on a defined velocity. Listing 5.1 also shows the four categories of methods that a typical model component must support.

1. **Application state inquiries.** These are functions that return the application state. These functions are important for maintaining up-to-date GUI elements (e.g., echo number of balls on screen).

2. **Application state changes from user events.** These are functions that change the application state according to a user's input actions. Notice that the function names should reflect the functionality (e.g., CreateHero Ball()) and not the user event actions (e.g., ServiceLMBDown()). It is common for a group of functions to support a defined finite state transition. For example, CreateHeroBall(), ResizeHeroBall(), and AddHeroBall ToWorld() implement the finite state diagram of Figure 2.3.

3. **Application state changes from application (timer) events.** This is a function that updates the application state resulting from purposeful and usually synchronous application timer events. For the ball-shooting program, we update all of the velocities, displace the balls' positions by the updated velocities, and compute ball-to-ball collisions, as well as remove off-screen balls.

4. **Application state visualization.** This is a function that knows how to draw the application state (e.g., drawing the necessary number of circles at the corresponding positions). It is expected that a view component will initialize appropriate regions on the application window, set up transformations, and invoke this function to draw into the initialized region.

Source file. Pseudocode; no corresponding source file.

```
class CApplicationModel  {
    private:  Application's private state.
        Array<CBall*> AllBalls
            // World balls, initially empty
        CBAll         HeroBall
            // The Hero Ball
        bool          DefiningNewHero
            // If LMB drag is true


    public:  1. Application state inquires.
        bool   IsDefinningHeroBall()
            // If in the middle of defining a new hero ball
        CBall* SelectedBall()
            // Current hero ball is not null
        int    NumBallsOnScreen()
            // Number of balls currently on screen


          2. Application state change from user events.
        void   CreateHeroBall(mousePosition)
            // center=mousePosition; radius=0; velocity=0
        void   ResizeHeroBall(mousePosition)
            // compute new radius and velocity
        void   MoveSelectedBallTo(mousePosition)
            // move hero to mousePosition, if no current hero NO-Op
        void   AddHeroBallToWorld()
            // done with current hero, insert into world balls
        void   SelectBallAt(mousePosition)
            // hero=ball at mousePosition, if none hero=NULL


          3. Applicaiton state changes from application events.
        void   UpdateSimulation()
            // Move balls by their velocities,
            // update velocity by gravity and remove off-screen ones


          4. Application state visualization.
        void   DrawModel( )
            // Draw all the freefalling balls (including the HeroBall)
}
```

Listing 5.1. The model of the ball-shooting program.

It is important to recognize that the user's asynchronous events are arriving in between synchronous application timer events. In practice, a user observes an instantaneous application state (the graphics in the application window) and generates asynchronous events to alter the application state for the next round of simulation. For example, a user sees that the HeroBall is about to collide with another ball and decides to change the HeroBall's velocity to avoid the collision. This means that before that synchronous timer update, we must ensure that all existing asynchronous user events are processed. In addition, the application should provide continuous feedback to ensure that users are observing an up-to-date application state. This subtle handling of event arrival and processing order is not an issue for simple, single-user applications like our ball-shooting program. On large-scale multi-user networked interactive systems, where input event and output display latencies may be significant, the UpdateSimulation() function is often divided into pre-update, update, and post-update.

5.2.2   The View

```
class  CUIDrawArea {
     private:  An area on application window for drawing. Actual implemenation is API dependent.

     public:
         void  ActivateForDrawing()
             // All subsequent Graphics API draw commands will show up in this area
}
```

Source file. Pseudocode; no corresponding source file.

```
class  CApplicationView {
     private:
         CUIDrawArea TargetDrawArea
             // An area of the application main window for drawing

     public:
         void HardwareToModelXform(mousePtInHardware, outputPtForModel)
             // transform the input mouse points for the model

         void DrawGraphics(ApplicationModel TheModel)
             // Set up TargetDrawArea and call TheModel.DrawModel() to draw all balls
}
```

Listing 5.2. The view component of the ball-shooting program.

Listing 5.2 shows the CApplicationView class supporting the two main func-
tionalities of a view component: coordinate space transformation and initialization for redraw. As discussed earlier, the controller is responsible for calling the HardwareToModelXform() function to communicate user input points to
the model component. The CUIDrawArea class is introduced to encapsulate the
highly API-dependent device initialization and drawing procedures.

5.2.3   The Controllers

We can improve the solution of Listing 1.7 to better support the specified functionality of the ball-shooting program. Recall that the application window depicted in
Figure I.2 has two distinct regions for interpreting events: the upper application
drawing area where mouse button events are associated with defining/selecting the
HeroBall and the lower GUI element area where mouse button events on the GUI
elements have different meanings (e.g., mouse button events on the slider bars
generate SliderBarChange events). We also notice that the upper application
drawing area is the exact same area where the CApplicationView must direct
the drawings of the CApplicationModel state. Listing 5.3 introduces two types
of controller classes: a CViewController and the CMainAppController. Each
controller class is dedicated to receiving input events from the corresponding region on the application window. The CViewController creates a CApplication
View during initialization such that the view can be tightly paired for drawing of
the CApplicationModel state in the same area. In addition, the CViewControl
ler class also defines the appropriate mouse event service routines to support the
interaction with the HeroBall. The CMainAppController is meant to contain
GUI elements for interacting with the application state.

The bottom of Listing 5.3 illustrates that the GUI API MainEventLoop()
will still call the SystemInitialization() function to initialize the application.
In this case, we create one instance each of CViewController and CMainApp
Controller. The CViewController is initialized to monitor mouse button events
in the drawing area of the application window (e.g., left mouse button click to define HeroBall), whereas the CMainAppController is initialized to monitor the
GUI element state changes (e.g., left mouse button dragging of a slider bar). Notice that the service of the timer event is global to the entire application and should
be defined in only one of the controllers (either one will do).

In practice, the GUI API MainEventLoop() *dispatches* events to the controllers based on the *context* of the event. The context of an event is typically
defined by the location of the mouse pointer or the current *focus* of the GUI

```
class CViewController  {
    private: CApplicationModel TheModel = null // Reference to the application state
             CApplicationView  TheView  = null // for drawing to the desirable region

    public:
        void Initialize(CApplicationMode aModel, CUIDrawArea anArea) {
            // anArea on the application window for drawing
            TheView  = new CApplicationView( anArea )
            TheModel = aModel
            // Register Event Service Routines
            GUISystem::RegisterServiceRoutine(GUISystem::LMBDown, LMBDownRoutine)
            GUISystem::RegisterServiceRoutine(GUISystem::LMBDrag, LMBDragRoutine)
            GUISystem::RegisterServiceRoutine(GUISystem::LMBUp, LMBUpRoutine)
            GUISystem::RegisterServiceRoutine(GUISystem::RMBDown, RMBDownRoutine)
            GUISystem::RegisterServiceRoutine(GUISystem::RedrawEvent, RedrawRoutine)
        }
}
```

Source file. Pseudocode; no corresponding source file.

```
class CMainAppController {
    private: CViewController aViewController; // For drawing and mouse interaction

    public:
        void Initialize(CApplicationModel aModel)  {
            TheModel = aModel
            // initialize the drawing area
            aViewController.Initialize(aModel, areaForDrawing)
            // Register Event Service Routines
            GUISystem::DefineTimerPeriod(SimulationUpdateInterval)
            GUISystem::RegisterServiceRoutine(GUISystem:: SliderBar, SliderBarRoutine)
            GUISystem::RegisterServiceRoutine(GUISystem:: TimerEvent, ServiceTimer)
        }
}


SystemInitialization() {
    CApplicationModel aModel = new CApplicationModel();
    CMainAppController mainApp = new CAppController()

    mainApp.Initialize(aModel)
}
```

Listing 5.3. The controller of the ball-shooting program.

element (i.e., which element is active). The application is responsible for creating a controller for any region on the window for which it wants to receive events directly from the GUI API.

5.3   Expanding the Ball-Shooting Program

One interesting characteristic of the MVC solution presented in Section 5.2 is that the model component does not have any knowledge of the view or the controller components. This clean interface allows us to expand our solution by inserting additional view/controller pairs. For example, Figure 5.2 shows an extension to the ball-shooting program given in Figure I.2. It has an additional small view next to the quit button. The small view is exactly the same as the original large view, except that it covers a smaller area on the application window. Listing 5.4 shows that, with our MVC solution design, we can implement the small view by creating a new instance of CViewController in the CMainAppController class. The only other requirement is to define a new CUIDrawArea (smallDrawingArea). Because this is a highly GUI API–dependent operation, as in Listing 5.3, we defer the details of this operation to the actual implementation.

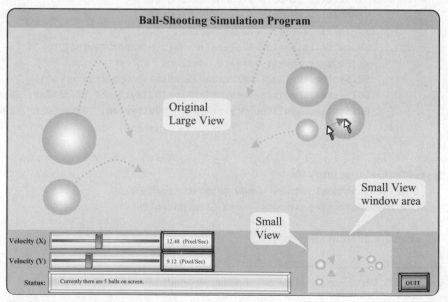

Figure 5.2. The ball-shooting program with large and small views.

```
class CMainAppController {
    private: CViewController aViewController; // For drawing and mouse interaction
    CViewController aSmallView;       // For the small view

    public:
        void Initialize(CApplicationModel aModel)  {
            TheModel = aModel
            // initialize the drawing area
            aViewController.Initialize(aModel, areaForDrawing)
            // ... identical to the event service registration as Listing 5.3
            aSmallView.Initialize(aModel, smallDrawingArea)
        }
    }
```

| Define aSmallView: | (margin annotation for `CViewController aSmallView;`) |
| Init aSmallView: | (margin annotation for `aSmallView.Initialize(aModel, smallDrawingArea)`) |

Source file. Pseudocode; no corresponding source file.

Listing 5.4. Implementing the small view for the ball-shooting program.

For simplicity, Figure 5.2 shows two identical view/controller pairs. In general, a new view/controller pair can be created to present a different visualization of the application state. For example, with slight modifications to the view component's transformation functionality, the large view of Figure 5.2 can be configured into a zoom view, and the small view can be configured into a work view, where the zoom view can zoom into different regions (e.g., around the HeroBall) and the work view can present the entire application space (e.g., all the free-falling balls).

Figure 5.3 shows the components of the solution in Listing 5.4 and how these components interact. We see that the model component supports the operations of all the view and controller components, and yet it does not have any knowledge of these components. This distinct and simple interface has the following advantages.

- **Simplicity.** The model component is the core of the application and usually is the most complicated component. By keeping the design of this component independent from any particular controller (user input/events) or view (specific drawing area), we can avoid unnecessary complexity.

- **Portability.** The controller component typically performs the translation of user actions to model-specific function calls. The implementation of this translation is usually simple and specific to the underlying GUI API. Keeping the model clean from the highly API-dependent controller facilitates portability of a solution to other GUI platforms.

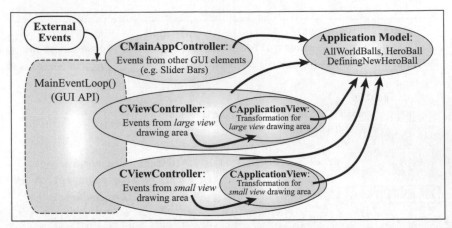

Figure 5.3. Components of the ball-shooting program with small view.

- **Expandability.** The model component supports changing of its internal
  state and understands how to draw its contents. As we saw in Listing 5.4,
  this means that it is straightforward to add new view/controller pairs to
  increase the interactivity of the application.

5.4   Interaction among the MVC Components

The MVC framework is a tool for describing general interactive systems. One
of the beauties of the framework is that it is straightforward to support multiple
view/controller pairs. Each view/controller pair shares responsibilities in exactly
the same way: the view presents the model, and the controller allows the events
(user-generated or otherwise) to change the model component.

For an application with multiple view/controller pairs, like the one depicted
in Figure 5.3, we see that a user can change the model component via any of the
three controllers. In addition, the application itself is also capable of changing the
model state. All components must, however, ensure that a coherent and up-to-date
presentation is maintained for the user. For example, when a user drags out a new
`HeroBall`, both the large- and small-view components must display the dragging
of the ball, whereas the `CMainAppController` component must ensure that the
slider bars properly echo the implicitly defined `HeroBall` velocity. In the classical
MVC model, the coherency among different components is maintained with an
elaborate protocol (e.g., via the observer design pattern). Although the classical
MVC model works very well, the elaborate protocol requires that all components
communicate or otherwise keep track of changes in the model component.

In our case, and in the case of most modern interactive graphics systems, the application defines the timer event for simulation computation. To support smooth simulation results, we have seen that the timer event typically triggers within real-time response thresholds (e.g., 20–50 milliseconds). When servicing the timer events, our application can take the opportunity to maintain coherent states among all components. For example, in the `ServiceTimer()` function in Listing 1.7, we update the velocity slider bars based on current `HeroBall` velocity. In effect, during each timer event service, the application pushes the up-to-date model information to all components and forces the components to refresh their presentation for the user. In this way, the communication protocol among the components becomes trivial. All components keep a reference to the model, and each view/controller pair in the application does not need to be aware of the existence of other view/controller pairs. In between periodic timer events, the user's asynchronous events change the model. These changes are only made in the model component, and no other components in the application need to be aware of the changes. During the periodic timer service, besides computing the model's simulation update, the model flushes up-to-date state information to all components. For example, when the user clicks and drags with the left mouse button pressed, a new `HeroBall` will be defined in the model component. During this time, the large- and small-view components will not display the new `HeroBall`, and the velocity slider bars will not show the new `HeroBall`'s velocity. These components will get and display up-to-date `HeroBall` information only during the application timer event servicing. Since the timer event is triggered more than 30 times per second, the user will observe a smooth and up-to-date application state in all components at all times.

5.5 Applying the MVC Concept

The MVC framework is applicable to general interactive systems. As we have seen in this chapter, interactive systems with the MVC framework result in clearly defined component behaviors. In addition, with clearly defined interfaces among the components, it becomes straightforward to expand the system with additional view/controller pairs.

An interactive system does not need to be an elaborate software application. For example, the slider bar is a fully functional interactive system. The model component contains a current value (typically a floating-point number), the view component presents this value to the user, and the controller allows the user to interactively change this value. A typical view component draws rectangular icons (bar and knobs) representing the current value in the model component, whereas the controller component typically supports mouse down and drag events to interactively change the value in the model component. With this understanding, we can describe the `CSliderBarWithEcho` class based on the MVC framework: the numeric echo area is an extra view component. Notice that because we cannot change the slider bar value by typing in the echo area, this view component does not have a complementary controller component.

5.6 Tutorials and Implementations

There are many approaches to implementing the MVC architecture. In our case, based on our previous experience working with GUI and graphics APIs, we notice that drawing (view functionality) and mouse events (controller functionality) are typically targeted toward the same GUI window element. This suggests that when implementing a view/controller pair on top of a modern GUI API, both the view and the controller components must reference the same GUI window object.

Figure 5.4 shows the major components and classes of our MVC implementation. The wire-frame box on the right represents the GUI API. As illustrated, in the front end of the GUI API we can see the drawing area and the application window. From the previous tutorials, we understand that at run time, the drawing area will replace itself into the application window. As in all our implementations, in the back end the application window is represented by the `CTutorialDlg` class. Here, we see the introduction of the `UIWindow` class as the

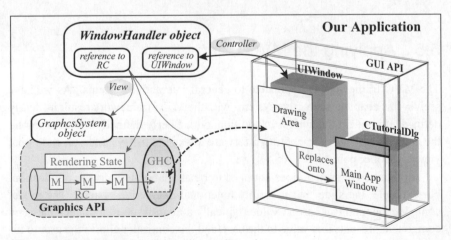

Figure 5.4. Implementing the view/controller pair.

back-end programming representation of the drawing area. As will be discussed, the `UIWindow` subclasses from the MFC `CWnd` class and implements the run-time `ReplaceDialogControl()` functionality.

The left side of Figure 5.4 illustrates that the `GraphicsSystem` object, introduced in Section 4.4 (Tutorial 4.2), will be our abstraction for interfacing with the graphics API. From our experience working with previous tutorials, we understand that during graphics API initialization, we establish a correspondence between the hardware buffer and the UI drawing area. This correspondence is illustrated by the dotted line connecting the buffer in the GHC and the front-end UI drawing area. It is this drawing area that a user can direct GUI API mouse events to and observe graphics API drawings. The center of Figure 5.4 is the `WindowHandler` class, where it has a reference to the `UIWindow` drawing area and behaves as a view/controller pair for our application. The `WindowHandler` has a reference to the RC and works with the `GraphicsSystem` to present the view component drawing functionality. For the controller component functionality, the `WindowHandler` class supports the mouse events generated from the `UIWindow`.

The tutorials in this chapter derive and develop the `WindowHandler` and the `GraphicsSystem` classes. Our final ball-shooting program will be based on the results of these classes. Our main gaols are to understand how the MVC architecture can be supported and how we can achieve code re-use from our design. All the tutorials in the rest of this book will be based on these classes.

Tutorial 5.1. Interface to APIs

- **Goals.** Become familiar with the `UWBGL` libraries; more specifically, develop understanding for the structure of the MFC and D3D libraries, and for the following classes:

  - `MFC_UIWindow`

  - `UWBD3D_WindowHandler`

  - `UWBD3D_GraphicsSystem`

- **Approach.** Implement a simple interactive graphics application with `UWBGL` libraries and examine how the familiar functionality is implemented in the different classes in the `UWBGL`.

Figure 5.5 is a screenshot of running Tutorial 5.1. Notice the familiar control located at the lower-left corner. This is identical to the control form Tutorial 2.8 (`CCircleRadiusControls` class). In this tutorial, this control manipulates the

GHC and RC. Recall from Section 4.2: GHC, the *graphics hardware context*, represents the hardware rendering buffer; and RC, the *rendering context*, roughly defines the appearance.

Tutorial 5.1.
Project Name:
  D3D_ModelView
Library Support:
  UWBGL_MFC_Lib1
  UWBGL_D3D_Lib1

Figure 5.5. Tutorial 5.1.

radius of the circle when the checkbox is enabled. When we examine the source code, we observe two support libraries: `UWB_MFC_Lib1` and `UWB_D3D_Lib1`.

UWB_MFC_Lib1

Reference. See p. 508 for a summary of the `UWBGL_MFC_Lib1` library.

There are nine source files in this library.

- `uwbgl_MFCDefines.h`. This include file defines compilation parameters. We will not change this file.

- `uwbgl_MFC_Lib1.h`. This is the header file that declares all the symbols and functions defined in this library. Developers (us) should include this header file when working with this library.

- `uwbgl_MFCUtility.h/.cpp`. These two files declare and implement the `ReplaceDialogControl()` function. As we saw in Tutorial 2.8, this function is capable of replacing a GUI window element onto the application window. We have experience with this functionality for the purpose of organizing and grouping of GUI elements in Tutorial 2.8.

- `uwbgl_MFCSliderCtrlWithEcho1.h/.cpp`. These two files implement the `SliderCtrlWithEcho` class as detailed in Tutorial 2.6.

`UWBMFC_UIWindow`. Because it will not cause any ambiguity, we will refer to this class simply as `UIWindow`. In general, for readability, we will try to avoid the identifier string "UWBxxx".

- `uwbgl_MFCUIWindow1.h/.cpp`. These two files implement the `UIWindow` class. `UIWindow` is a subclass of `CWnd` and implements the `ReplaceDialogControl()` functionality. As illustrated in Figure 5.4, this class is designed to represent a GUI drawing area for our application.

UWBGL_D3D_Lib1

Reference. See p. 509 for a summary of the `UWBGL_D3D_Lib1` library.

math3d++. This is a separate self-contained inline library that supports mathematics operations for 3D computer graphics. All of the basic data types (e.g., vector, matrix) and their corresponding operations (e.g., addition, substraction, transformation) are supported.

There are 14 files organized into three folders: *Common Files*, *D3D Files*, and *Header Files*.

Folder	Subfolder	Purpose
Header Files	-	D3D-specific .h files
D3D-specific classes		
D3D Files	D3D_Geoms	classes to draw D3D geometries
	D3D_GraphicsSystem	`D3DGraphicsSystem` files
	D3D_WindowHandler	`D3DWindowHandler` files
Graphics API–independent source code files		
Common Files	WindowHandler	`WindowHandler` files

```
struct UWB_IWindowHandler {
    A: Working with Graphics and GUI API
    virtual bool IsGraphicsDeviceValid() = 0;
    virtual bool InitializeHandler(HWND hAttachedWindow)=0;
    virtual void ShutDownHandler()=0;
    ...
    B: View component functionality
    // Support drawing
    virtual void BeginDraw()=0;
    virtual void EndDrawAndShow()=0;
    virtual void DrawGraphics()=0;
    ...
    C: Controller component functionality
    virtual void OnMouseButton(bool down, unsigned int nFlags, int hwX, int hwY)=0;
    virtual void OnMouseMove(unsigned int nFlags, int hwX, int hwY)=0;
};
```

Listing 5.5. The `UWB_IWindowHandler` class (Tutorial 5.1).

Source file. uwbgl_IWindowHandler.h file in the *Common Files/WindowHandler* subfolder of the UWBGL_D3D_Lib1 project.

The files in the *Header Files* and the *D3D Files* folders are specific to the D3D library. The files in the *Common Files* folder are shared between OGL and D3D graphics libraries. There are four files in the *Common Files* folder.

- `uwbgl_Common.h`. This header file defines general constants (e.g., pi), macros (e.g. degree-to-radian conversion), and compilation parameters. We will not change this file.

- `uwbgl_IWindowHandler.h` (**in *Common Files/WindowHandler* subfolder**). This file defines the `UWB_IWindowHandler` class, a pure abstract description encapsulating the view/controller pair functionality of the MVC framework. This is the class illustrated in Figure 5.4. Listing 5.5 shows the pure virtual functions defined in the `IWindowHandler` class. We can identify three major categories of functionality:

  - **(A) Graphics and GUI API.** As illustrated in Figure 5.4, this class is responsible for establishing the *connection* between graphics and GUI APIs. These functions are for proper initialization and shut down of these two APIs.

  - **(B) View component.** These are graphics API functionality, for drawing and for transformation.

UWB_IWindowHandler. The *I* in front of the `IWindowHandler` signifies this is an *interface*, or a pure virtual class. Once again, for readability we will refer to this class as `IWindowHandler`.

– **(C) Controller component.** These are GUI window element mouse events; these routines report the status of the mouse when it is inside the GUI drawing area.

UWB_WindowHandler.
Notice that in this case,
UWB_WindowHandler does
not have the *I*.

- uwbgl_WindowHandler1.h/.cpp (**in** *Common Files/WindowHandler* **subfolder**). This is a subclass of and defines an API-independent implementation of the pure virtual IWindowHandler. As illustrated in Figure 5.6, the WindowHandler is meant to be subclassed by each application to customize view/controller functionality. We will discuss the functions declared here in detail as we encounter their implementation in the tutorials.

There are two files in the *Header Files* folder.

- uwbgl_D3DDefines.h. This include file defines compilation parameters. We will not change this file.

- uwbgl_D3D_Lib1.h. This is the complement of the uwbgl_MFC_Lib1.h header file. When developing programs based on this library, we must include this header file in our source file.

There are eight files in the *D3D Files* folder.

- uwbgl_D3DCircleGeom1.h/.cpp **and** uwbgl_D3DRectangleGeom1.h/.cpp (**in** *D3D_Geoms* **subfolder**). These four files define the basic functionality for drawing of circles and rectangles. We saw the details of these classes in Tutorial 3.3 and Tutorial 3.5.

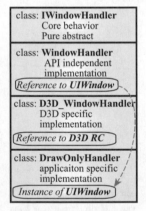

Figure 5.6. The Win dowHandler hierarchy.

uwbgl_D3D_Lib.h
uwbgl_MFC_Lib.h. In all tutorials, these two files are included by the StdAfx.h file.
Since all of our source files
must include StfAfx.h for
a precompiled header, these
two library header files are included by all of our source
files.

- uwbgl_D3DGraphicsSystem1.h/.cpp (**in** *D3D_GraphicsSystem* **sub-folder**). These two files implement the interface to the graphics API (see Figure 5.4). We developed the earlier version of this class in Tutorial 4.3. The major difference here is that we have delegated the drawing functionality BeginDraw() and EndDrawAndShow() to the WindowHandler class.

- uwbgl_D3DWindowHandler1.h/.cpp (**in** *D3D_WindowHandler* **subfolder**). These two files implement the UWBD3D_WindowHandler class. As illustrated in Figure 5.6, this is the D3D API–specific implementation of the WindowHandler. This class establishes the reference to the D3D device and supports D3D-specific BeginDraw() and EndDrawAndShow() functions.

The ModelView Project

With the support from the above two libraries, the actual project source code is relatively straightforward. There are two classes we should pay attention to.

```
class CModel {
    public:
        // Draws the square and the circle
        void Draw();
        // For interaction with the radius control slider bar
        float GetCircleRadius() const;
        void SetCircleRadius(float radius);
    private:
        // content of the world: a square and a circle
        UWBD3D_RectangleGeometry m_LargeSquare;
        UWBD3D_CircleGeometry    m_SmallCircle;
};
```

Source files. Model.h/.cpp files in the *Model* folder of the D3D_ModelView project.

Listing 5.6. The CModel class (Tutorial 5.1).

```
class CDrawOnlyHandler : public UWBD3D_WindowHandler {
    public:
        :
        bool Initialize(... control_id ...);
            // Place m_window into the application main window
        void DrawGraphics();
            // Invoke CModel to redraw into the m_window
    private:
        UWBMFC_UIWindow m_window;
            // This is the GUI drawing area
};
```

Source file. DrawOnlyHandler.h file in the *WindowHandler* folder of the D3D_ModelView project.

Listing 5.7. CDrawOnlyHandler (Tutorial 5.1).

- CModel. In this case, the model is a very simple scene of a square and a circle. From Listing 5.6, we notice that the public interface of the CModel class is driven completely by the functionality of the application, where the only requirements are the ability of getting and setting the radius of the circle.

  The CModel object is defined as an instance variable in the CTutorialApp class. Because the CTutorialApp class represents the running process, there can only be one instance, and thus there can only be a single instance of the model.

- CDrawOnlyHandler. This a subclass of the UWBD3D_WindowHandler. As the name of the class suggests, this class can only support drawing (the

Source file.
DrawOnlyHandler.cpp
file in the *WindowHandler*
folder of the D3D_ModelView
project.

```
void CDrawOnlyHandler::DrawGraphics() {
    A: Configuring to draw to m_window
    BeginDraw();

         ⋮

    // Set up proper transformation (to be covered later)
    D3DXMatrixTransformation(&world2ndc, ... );
    m_pD3DDevice->SetTransform(D3DTS_VIEW, &world2ndc);

    // clear the draw buffer to light gray
    // Clear the drawing area to background color
    m_pD3DDevice->Clear( ... );

    B: Invoke the Model to draw itself
    theApp.GetModel().Draw();

    C: Present the draw result in the m_window area
    EndDrawAndShow();

}
```

Listing 5.8. CDrawOnlyHandler::DrawGraphics() (Tutorial 5.1).

' view functionality). We will examine the input mouse functionality in Tutorial 5.2. The private data m_window from Listing 5.7 is the GUI drawing area. During GUI element layout design time, on the application window we define a placeholder GUI element with GUI ID of control_id. At run time, the placeholder will be replaced by the m_window in the Initialize() function call. Listing 5.8 shows the details of the CDrawOnlyHandler:: DrawGraphics() function, where the following happens.

BeginDraw() **and**
EndDrawAndShow(). These
functions belongs to the
UWBD3D_WindowHandler
(D3DWindowHandler1.cpp
in *D3D Files/D3D_Window
Handler* subfolder of the
UWBGL_D3D_Lib1 project).

 – (A) Call BeginDraw() to configure the graphics API for drawing to the area referenced by m_window.

 – (B) Inform the model to redraw itself.

 – (C) Present the drawing results and reconfigure the graphics API to get ready for the next drawing operation (potentially to a different GUI drawing area).

Listing 5.9 shows that the implementation of the main application window (CTutorialDlg) includes an instance of CCircleRadiusControls and an instance of CDrawOnlyHandler representing the view/controller pair. The important opera-

```
class CTutorialDlg : public CDialog {
    :
    private:  // Data to be displayed in the application window
        CCircleRadiusControls  m_controls; // The is the control class from Tutorial 2.8
        CDrawOnlyHandler       m_view;     // This is the View/Controller pair
};
```

Source Files.
TutorialDlg.h file in the *Header Files* folder of the *D3D_ModelView* project.

Listing 5.9. CTutorialDlg.h (Tutorial 5.1).

```
BOOL CTutorialDlg::OnInitDialog() {
    :
```
| *A: Create the graphics context for Graphics API* |
```
    if(!UWBD3D_GraphicsSystem::GetSystem().CreateGraphicsContext(m_hWnd) ) return FALSE;
```

| *B: Place the circle radius controls at **IDC_PLACEHOLDER** position.* |
```
    if(!UWBMFC_ReplaceDialogControl(*this, IDC_PLACEHOLDER, m_controls, ... ) ) return FALSE;
```

| *C: Initialize the WindowHandler and place the drawing area at **IDC_PLACEHODER2** position.* |
```
    if(!m_view.Initialize(*this, IDC_PLACEHOLDER2) ) return FALSE;
    :
```

| *D: Initialize the timer with 40 updates per second (25 milliseconds).* |
```
    SetTimer( ... );     // Program the timer to go-off every 25 millisecond
    :
}
```

Source files.
TutorialDlg.cpp file in the *Source Files* folder of the D3D_ModelView project.

Listing 5.10. CTutorialDlg::OnInitDialog() (Tutorial 5.1).

tions of the CTutorialDlg class are the initialization (OnInitDia log()) and servicing of the timer events (OnTimer()).

- CTutorialDlg::OnInitDialog(). Listing 5.10 shows that during initialization, the main application window must do the following.

    - (A) Create the graphics context of the graphics API.

    - (B and C) Replace the placeholder GUI elements and place the circle radius control (m_control) and the drawing area (wrapped in the m_View object) into the main application window.

    - (D) Initialize the timer events.

```
void CTutorialDlg::OnTimer(UINT nIDEvent) {
```
> A: *when enabled, update the circle's radius*
```
    if (m_controls.m_bSliderControl)
        theApp.GetModel().SetCircleRadius( m_controls.m_CircleRadiusBar.GetSliderValue() );
```

> B: *Redraw the entire model*
```
    m_view.DrawGraphics();

}
```

Listing 5.11. CTutorialDlg::OnTimer() (Tutorial 5.1).

Source files.
TutorialDlg.cpp file in the
Source Files folder of the
D3D_ModelView project.

- CTutorialDlg::OnTimer(). Listing 5.11 shows that when the timer goes off, our application must do the following.

    - (A) Update the CModel according to the user's action during the previous timer period (25 millisecond).

    - (B) Invoke the CDrawOnlyHandler to display the updated CModel.

This tutorial is a very simple MVC implementation. Notice the following.

- **Model.** Defined in the CModel class, a simple model with simple interface methods.

- **Controllers.** There are two controllers objects and a view/controller pair. The two controllers are the main application window (CTutorialDlg) and the circle radius controls (CCircleRadiusControls). Both of these controllers are capable of generating events for the model.

- **View/controller pair.** We get experience with subclassing from the Window Handler abstraction. We see that in the simplest form, we must define a GUI area for drawing (UIWindow), and we must define the drawing routine (DrawGraphics()).

- **Collaborations of the components.** The main application window contains components. However, the components do not have knowledge of each other. The only collaboration comes during the timer event, where the main application window (CTutorialDlg) polls the controllers, updates the application model, and triggers redraws. We continue to keep the components clean from each other. In this way, it becomes straightforward to insert/remove components from the main application window.

- **Inconsistent state.** When a user adjusts the radius control slider bar, for a short amount of time, the state of the model (radius of the small circle) and that of the GUI elements (slider bar value) will be inconsistent. This is because we do not update the model's state during event services in the `CCircleRadiusControls` class. Instead, this update is deferred until the timer service routine. Because the timer goes off every 25 msec, the user cannot notice this inconsistency. The advantage of this approach is that the model and the controller are loosely coupled and it is easy for maintenance and upgrade.

- `Paint/Redraw` **event.** Since we are triggering redraw at 25 msec intervals, the user always sees an up-to-date display. There is no need to service the `Paint/Redraw` events.

Tutorial 5.2. Processing Mouse Events

- **Goals.** Become familiar with the controller functionality of the `Window Handler` class: processing the mouse events.

- **Approach.** Design and develop a simple application with simple mouse events. This tutorial is a simple circle editor, where:

  - left mouse button click position defines the center of the circle;
  - left mouse button drag defines the radius of the circle to be from the center to the current mouse position;
  - right mouse button click/drag moves the center of circle to the current mouse position;
  - the application must display the up-to-date circle for the user at all times.

The Model

Figure 5.7 is a screenshot of editing a circle with Tutorial 5.2. From the above event specifications, we know that the model component of Tutorial 5.2 should look like Listing 5.12, which shows that the `CModel` class has a single circle and has an interface that supports the creation, resizing, and moving of the circle.

The Controller

Design. With the `CModel` designed as shown in Listing 5.12, the mouse event services can now be defined as in Listing 5.13.

Tutorial 5.2.
Project Name:
   D3D_MouseInput
Library Support:
   UWBGL_MFC_Lib1
   UWBGL_D3D_Lib2

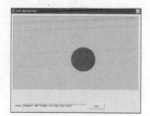

Figure 5.7. Tutorial 5.2.

Hardware coordinate. Recall that the mouse positions returned to us are defined with origin located at the top-left corner, whereas our output device coordinate system has the origin at the lower-left corner. In the Win32 environment, the *WindowsClient* coordinate also defined the origin to be the top-left corner.

```
class CModel {
    void CreateCircleAt( int centerX, int centerY);
        // Create circle at (centerX, centerY)
    void ResizeCircle( int perimeterX, int perimeterY);
        // Resize such input point is on the circumference
    void MoveCirceTo( int centerX, int centerY);
        // Move center of circle to (centerX, centerY)
    void DrawModel();
        // Draw the circle


    private:
        UWBD3D_CircleGeometry m_Circle; // Simple world with one circle
};
```

Source files. Model.h/cpp in the *Model* folder of the D3D_MouseInput project.

Listing 5.12. The model for Tutorial 5.2.

```
A: Left Mouse Click (atX, atY)
    Convert HadwareCoordinate to DeviceCoordinate(atX, atY -> dcX, dcY)
    getTheModel().CreateCircleAt(dcX, dcY)
B: Left Mouse Drag (atX, atY)
    Convert HadwareCoordinate to DeviceCoordinate(atX, atY -> dcX, dcY)
    getTheModel().ResizeCircle(dcX, dcY)
C: Right Mouse Click (atX, atY)
    Convert HadwareCoordinate to DeviceCoordinate(atX, atY -> dcX, dcY)
    getTheModel().MoveCircleTo(dcX, dcY)
D: Right Mouse Drag (atX, atY)
    Convert HadwareCoordinate to DeviceCoordinate(atX, atY -> dcX, dcY)
    getTheModel().MoveCircle(dcX, dcY)
```

Listing 5.13. Mouse event services (Tutorial 5.2).

Implementation. We once again subclass from WindowHandler to implement the desired view/controller pair functionality. With the single circle application state, the output view component functionality is identical to that from Tutorial 5.1. However, in this tutorial we must support mouse events. Listing 5.14 shows the definition of the CDrawAndMouseHandler class. Similar to the CDraw OnlyHandler calss, the CDrawAndMouseHandler view/controller pair also subclasses from the UWBD3D_WindowHandler. In this case, the view component functionality is identical to that of CDrawOnlyHandler from Tutorial 5.1. Listing 5.15 shows the two new mouse event service routines implementing the event services defined in Listing 5.13. With the new CDrawAndMouseHandler, the CTutorialDlg main application window class is similar to that from Tutorial 5.1.

HardwareToDevice(). The implementation of this function can be found in *uwbgl_WindowHandler2.cpp* in the *Common* folder of the *UW-BGL_D3D_Lib2* project.

```
class CDrawAndMouseHandler : public UWBD3D_WindowHandler {
```
Identical to CDrawOnlyHandler from Tutorial 5.1
```
    bool Initialize(CDialog& parent_dlg, int control_id);
    void DrawGraphics();
    UWBMFC_UIWindow m_window;
```
Override from UWB_WindowHandler to implement Listing 5.13
```
    void OnMouseButton(bool down, unsigned int nFlags, int hwX, int hwY);
    void OnMouseMove(unsigned int nFlags, int hwX, int hwY);
    // down - TRUE (mouse button when down) or FALSE (mouse button went up)
    // nFlags - Which buttons (e.g. left, right, center, etc.)
    // hwX/hwY - Mouse Position (in hardware coordinate where upper-left is origin)
};
```

Source file.
DrawAndMouseHandler.h in the *WindowHandler* folder of the D3D_MouseInput project.

Listing 5.14. CDrawAndMouseHandler class (Tutorial 5.2).

```
void CDrawAndMouseHandler::OnMouseButton(bool down, unsigned int nFlags, int hwX, int hwY)
```
Transforms origin from the upper left to the lower left corner
```
    HardwareToDevice(hwX, hwY, deviceX, deviceY);    // hardware to device coordinate
```
*Left Mouse Button Down: this is condition **A:** of Listing 5.13.*
```
    if (nFlags & MK_LBUTTON)
        if (down) theApp.GetModel().CreateCircleAt(deviceX, deviceY);
        ⋮
```
*Right Mouse Button Down: this is condition **C:** of Listing 5.13.*
```
    if (nFlags & MK_RBUTTON)
        if (down) theApp.GetModel().MoveCirceTo(deviceX, deviceY);
        ⋮
```

Source file.
DrawAndMouseHandler.cpp in the *WindowHandler* folder of the D3D_MouseInput project.

```
void CDrawAndMouseHandler::OnMouseMove(unsigned int nFlags, int hwX, int hwY)
    HardwareToDevice(hwX, hwY, deviceX, deviceY); // hardware to device coordinate
    ⋮
```
*Left Mouse Button Down: this is condition **B:** of Listing 5.13.*
```
    if(nFlags & MK_LBUTTON)
        theApp.GetModel().ResizeCircle(deviceX, deviceY);
        ⋮
```
*Left Mouse Button Down: this is condition **D:** of Listing 5.13.*
```
    if(nFlags & MK_RBUTTON)
        theApp.GetModel().MoveCirceTo(deviceX, deviceY);
```

Listing 5.15. CDrawAndMouseHandler mouse event services (Tutorial 5.2).

Inconsistent state.   Notice that the mouse events are serviced as soon as they are triggered. This is in contrast with Tutorial 5.1, where the effects of user actions to the circle radius controls were delayed until the periodic timer events. However, in both cases, redraw of application window only occurs at the timer event. In this case, after the user causes changes to the circle and before the timer event triggers, the application window will be showing an out-of-date circle. The graphics display and the application state may be inconsistent. However, once again, we emphasize that the timer events will trigger every 25 msec. This means that the maximum period of inconsistency will be less than 25 msec. This is undetectable by the user.

UWBGL_D3D_Lib2

Change summary. See p. 511 for a summary of changes to the library.

Tutorial 5.2 is linked with version 2 of the UWB D3D library (UWB_D3D_Lib2). There are two changes between versions 1 and 2.

1. WindowHandler::HardwareToDevice().   As we saw in Listing 5.15, this function transforms points with origin at upper-left corner (hardware coordinate) to origin located at lower-left corner (device coordinate).

UWB_EchoToStatusArea(). The implementation of this function can be found in the UWB_D3D_Lib2 project in files uwbgl_Utility1.h/.cpp in the *Common* folder.

2. UWB_EchoToStatusArea(const char*) **function.**   This is a general-purpose function that is capable of echoing string messages to a designated status area. We, as the programmer, must create the GUI element to represent the designated status area and connect the appropriate control variable for this function to operate properly.

   (a) During the layout of GUI elements, create a GUI element with GUI ID of IDC_STATUS in the main application window (CTutorialDlg).

   (b) During initialization of CTutorialDlg, in the OnInitDialog() function, connect the GUI element to UWB_hEchoWindow control variable with the following code.

Source file. TutorialDlg.cpp in the *Source Files* folder of the D3D_MouseInput project.

```
// obtain the reference to the GUI element
CWnd* pWnd = GetDlgItem(IDC_STATUS);
// connect the GUI element to control variable
if (pWnd) UWB_hEchoWindow = pWnd->m_hWnd;
// at this point the function
UWB_EchoToStatusArea( "OnInitDialog_Complete" );
    // will echo the message to the GUI element
```

(c) We can now invoke `UWB_EchoToStatusArea()` to echo the status of our application from anywhere in our application to the `IDC_STATUS` area.

Tutorial 5.3. Effects of Real-Time Simulation

- **Goals.** Demonstrate working with real-time changes to the model in our development framework.

- **Approach.** Continue working with Tutorial 5.2; we will simulate how the created circle may drop under gravitational force. Because this is a simple example with a simple model, it is straightforward to focus on the increased complexity of the model component and the process of simulating real-time events in our development environment.

- **Application specification.** The application reacts to mouse events in a similar manner to that of Tutorial 5.2. In addition, when all mouse buttons are released, the defined circle will free fall toward the bottom of the application window. Our application must detect the situation when the circle drops outside of the window and stop any further computations.

Figure 5.8 is a screenshot of the free-falling circle from Tutorial 5.3.

Tutorial 5.3.
Project Name:
  D3D_SimulateGravity
Library Support:
  UWBGL_MFC_Lib1
  UWBGL_D3D_Lib2

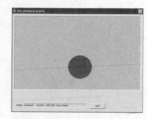

Figure 5.8. Tutorial 5.3.

Model

Our application is now about creating a circle that *moves*. We define a `CBall` to be a circle with a velocity. Notice that a `CBall` object understands if it is within a rectangular width × height bound. Our application model contains a `CBall` object (instead of the `CircleGeometry` in Tutorial 5.2). In addition, anticipating support for the ball-shooting program, we name our interface functions accordingly.

```
class CBall : public UWBD3D_CircleGeometry {
    public:
        ⋮
        vec3 GetVelocity() const;
        void SetVelocity(const vec3& velocity);
        bool IsOutsideBounds(width, height) const;
            // in/out side a bound defined by: width by height
    private:
        vec3 m_velocity;
}
```

Source file. `Ball.h` file in the *Model* folder of the `D3D_SimulateGravity` project.

Listing 5.16. The `CBall` class (Tutorial 5.3).

Source File. Model.h file in the *Model* folder of the D3D_SimulateGravity project.

```
class CModel {
```
┌───┐
│ *A: Similar to* **CModel** *from Tutorial 5.2* │
└───┘
```
    void CreateHeroBall(x, y);
        // Create the Ball/Circle at (x,y)
    void ResizeHeroBall(x, y);
        // Resize the Ball such that (x,y) passes through circumference
    void MoveHeroBallTo(x, y);
        // Move the center of the Ball to (x,y)
    void DrawModel();
        // Draw the Ball (circle)
```

┌──┐
│ *B: Methods to support behaviors of the free-falling ball.* │
└──┘
```
    void SetWorldSize(float width, float height);
    void SetHeroBallAnimation(bool on);
```

┌──────────────────────────────┐
│ *C: Simulate the free falling ball.* │
└──────────────────────────────┘
```
    void UpdateSimulation();
```

┌──────────────────────────┐
│ *D: Internal representations.* │
└──────────────────────────┘
```
    CBall   m_Ball;
        // the ball
    bool m_bAnimatingBall;
        // should the ball free fall?
    float m_WorldWidth, m_WorldHeight;
        // bounds of the window
    clock_t m_previous_update_time;
        // how much time has passed between UpdateSimulation calls
};
```

Listing 5.17. The CModel class (Tutorial 5.3).

In this case, the CModel has the following.

- (A) Familiar functionality to support the creation and editing of the circle (or HeroBall).

- (B) Proper support for simulation: the model must know when to begin simulation (after the mouse button releases) and the bounds for the simulation (size of the application window).

```
void CModel::UpdateSimulation() {
    float elapsed_seconds = // compute wall-clock elapse time
    if(m_bAnimatingBall)  {
```

> **C1:** *Update hero ball velocity.*

```
        vec3 velocity = m_Ball.GetVelocity(); // get the ball velocity
        velocity.y += ...                     // increment the y-component
        m_Ball.SetVelocity(velocity);         // set the new velocity to ball
```

> **C2:** *Compute new hero ball position.*

```
        update_vector = m_Ball.GetVelocity() * elapsed_seconds; // compute displacement
        center = m_Ball.GetCenter() + update_vector;            // compute new center
        m_Ball.SetCenter(center);                               // set new center to ball
```

> **C3:** *Stop the ball if outside of bound.*

```
        if(m_Ball.IsOutsideBounds(m_WorldWidth, m_WorldHeight)) { // if outside the bound
            m_Ball.SetVelocity(zero_velocity);       // set velocity to zero to stop the ball
            m_bAnimatingBall = false;                // set flag to avoid any future computation
        ⋮
```

Source file. `Model.cpp` file in the *Model* folder of the `D3D_SimulateGravity` project.

Listing 5.18. `CModel::UpdateSimulation()` (Tutorial 5.3).

- (C) A function that simulates real-time behavior of the model. As illustrated in Listing 5.18 to simulate the free-falling ball, we must do the following.

    - (C1) Accelerate the downward velocity.

    - (C2) Update the `HeroBall` position according to its velocity.

    - (C3) Detect if the `HeroBall` is out of bounds and, if so, stop any future animation/computation/free falling.

    The `m_bAnimatingBall` flag is switched on at the end of creation of the ball, when the left mouse button is released.

- (D) Internal representation of the application model. In this case, the model must be aware of the size of the world and the *wall-clock* time in between updates.

Because the specification of Tutorial 5.3 does not include extra user actions, we do not need any other controllers or view/controller pairs. The only work left is to ensure proper triggering of the model simulation. The main window timer event service function (`CTutorialDlg::OnTimer()`) is shown in Listing 5.19.

Source file.
TutorialDlg.cpp file in
the *Source Files* folder of
the D3D_SimulateGravity
project.

```
void CTutorialDlg::OnTimer(UINT nIDEvent) {
    theApp.GetModel().UpdateSimulation(); // update the model state

    m_view.DrawGraphics();    // Draw the view that shows our model
}
```

Listing 5.19. CTutorialDlg::OnTimer() (Tutorial 5.3).

Timer event versus wall clock. We have programmed the timer event to trigger every 25 msec. Unfortunately, due to the shared windowing environment, the actual triggering period is only *roughly* 25 msec. For supporting real-time display, updating user events, and so on, *roughly* 25 msec is sufficient (e.g., a ± 5 msec difference will not result in observable inconsistencies). However, for real-time simulation, ± 5 msec is 20% of 25 msec and may potentially result in 20% error! To ensure more reliable simulation results, we poll the system clock to compute an accurate elapsed *wall-clock* time in between update simulations.

Tutorial 5.4. Multiple View/Controller Pairs

Tutorial 5.4.
Project Name:
  D3D_TwoViews
Library Support:
  UWBGL_MFC_Lib1
  UWBGL_D3D_Lib3

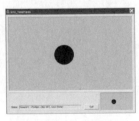

Figure 5.9. Tutorial 5.4.

- **Goals.** Demonstrate incorporating multiple view/controller pairs in our development environment.

- **Approach.** Continue working with Tutorial 5.3. With the same model component, we will add an extra view/controller pair. Once again, with the relatively simple application, we can focus on examining the extra support that is required for the multiple view/controller pairs.

- **Application specification.** With a user interaction identical to that of Tutorial 5.3, we will add an additional small window to display the free-falling circle.

Figure 5.9 is a screenshot of the free-falling circle from Tutorial 5.4. This tutorial focuses on developing the support for *multiple* output draw areas in the main application window. We know that each view/controller pair requires the support of a UIWindow for drawing, and that each UIWindow is associated with a hardware drawing buffer from the graphics API. This means that in order to support multiple view/controller pairs, we must be able to create multiple hardware drawing buffers from the graphics API.

Graphics API: The GraphicsSystem Class

Recall the graphics hardware context (GHC) and rendering context (RC) framework we developed from Section 4.2. Figure 4.3 illustrates that it is possible to

```
class UWBD3D_GraphicsSystem {
    ⋮
    bool CreateGraphicsContext(HWND hMainWindow);
    // similar to verion 1 from UWB_D3D_Lib1
    ⋮
```

Create an additional **Swap Chain** for the RC (m_pD3DDevice).

```
        LPDIRECT3DSWAPCHAIN9 CreateSwapChain(HWND hWindow);
    private:
        ⋮

        LPDIRECT3DDEVICE9    m_pD3DDevice;
};
```

Source file.
uwbgl_D3DGraphicsSystem2
.h file in the *D3D Files/
GraphicsSystem* subfolder of
the UWBGL_D3D_Lib3 project.

Listing 5.20. GraphicsSystem class (Tutorial 5.4).

create multiple hardware drawing buffers in the GHC to be associated with the rendering states of each RC. So far, our GraphicsSystem class creates only one hardware drawing buffer during the creation of GHC/RC in CreateGraphics Context(). We need to extend the GraphicsSystem class to support the creation of multiple hardware drawing buffers.

OpenGL.   OpenGL dictates that each RC must be associated with one unique hardware drawing buffer. In this case, a new RC (HGLRC) must be created for each GUI drawing area. The data type representing OpenGL rendering contexts is HGLRC. To support multiple GUI drawing areas, we create a new HGLRC for each GUI drawing area by calling the wglCreateContext() function.

D3D.   D3D supports the creation of *swap chains* to associate multiple drawing buffers with each RC. For D3D release 9, the data type representing a swap chain is DIRECT3DSWAPCHAIN9, and the data type representing the RC is Direct3D Device9. To support multiple GUI drawing areas, we create one RC (DIRECT3D Device9), and then for each GUI drawing area, we create a new DIRECT3DSWAP CHAIN9 object based on the same RC. Listing 5.20 shows that version 2 of the UWBD3D_GraphicsSystem class supports the creation of additional swap chains for each RC. The detailed procedure of creating the swap chain is D3D-specific and is not shown here.

Interface to GUI: The WindowHandler Class

In Figure 5.4, we saw that the WindowHandler class is designed to bridge the graphics API and GUI API to implement the view/controller functionality.

Source file.
uwbgl_D3DWindowHandler3
.h file in the *D3D Files/
WindowHander* subfolder of
UWBGL_D3D_Lib3 project.

```
class UWBD3D_WindowHandler : public UWBGFX_WindowHandler {
    // ... similar to earlier verion from UWB_D3D_LIB2
    ⋮
    // must create and initialize m_pSwapChain
    virtual bool InitializeHandler(HWND hAttachedWindow);
    ⋮
    virtual void BeginDraw();
        // must activate the proper swap chain
    virtual void EndDrawAndShow();
        // present the proper hardware drawing buffer
  protected:
    LPDIRECT3DDEVICE9    m_pD3DDevice;
        // This is the reference to the D3D RC Device
    LPDIRECT3DSWAPCHAIN9 m_pSwapChain;
        // This is the reference to the swap chain.
    ⋮
};
```

Listing 5.21. UWBD3D_WindowHandler class (Tutorial 5.4).

Figure 5.6 illustrates that to fulfill this bridging function, the UWBD3D_WindowHand
ler keeps references to the UIWindow and to the RC (DIRECT3DDEVICE9). Now,
to support drawing to multiple hardware buffers, the UWBD3D_WindowHandler
must also keep a reference to the DIRECT3DSWAPCHAIN9. Listing 5.21 shows
that the new WindowHandler class must invoke the GraphicsSystem to create a
new swap chain during InitializeHandler(). Notice that BeginDraw() and
EndDrawAndShow() must now coordinate and activate proper swap chains to direct the rendering of the RC to the proper hardware drawing buffer.

Implementation

With the new GraphicsSystem and WindowHandler support in the D3D library,
the changes to our application code are actually relatively straightforward.

Source file.
DrawAndMouseHandler.h
file in the *WindowHandler*
folder of the D3D_TwoViews
project.

- CDrawOnlyHandler **and** CDrawAndMouseHandler. We want the small
  window to be a *draw-only* window. These two classes are identical to the
  ones from Tutorial 5.1 and Tutorial 5.2. The CTutorialDlg class has one
  instance of each type of the handlers.

- **GUI placeholders.** During layout design, we created two GUI placeholder elements, one for the area of the large drawing area and the other for the area of the small drawing area. During `CTutorialDlg` initialization (in `OnInitDialog()`), the `WindowHandlers` replace themselves onto the corresponding areas.

- **OnTimer.** During `OnTimer` event services, besides calling the model component's `UpdateSimulation()` function, `CTutorialDlg` must also ensure that both of the handlers redraw their display.

UWBGL_D3D_Lib3

The third version of the library also includes the following utilities in the *Common Files* folder:

Change Summary. See p. 514 for a summary of changes to the library.

Utility	Function	Files
UWB_Array	STL Dynamic array	`uwbgl_Containers.h`
UWB_RandomNumbers	Randon number	`uwbgl_Utility2.h/.cpp`
UWB_Clock	Stop watch in msec	`uwbgl_Clock.h/.cpp`
UWB_Color	Color	`uwbgl_Color1.h/.cpp`

Tutorial 5.5. Application State Complexity

- **Goals.** Demonstrate working with a more complex model component; understand that the `UpdateSimulation()` function can be complex.

- **Approach.** Continue working with Tutorial 5.4. In this tutorial, we allow the user to work with multiple free-falling balls.

- **Application specification.** With an application similar to that of Tutorial 5.4, our application should support:

  - Left mouse button:
    * down event—define the center of a new ball;
    * drag event—define the radius of the new ball (similar to that of Tutorial 5.3);
    * up event—new ball starts to free fall.
  - Right mouse button:
    * down event—select the ball under the mouse pointer;

Tutorial 5.5.
Project Name:
   D3D_MultipleBalls
Library Support:
   UWBGL_MFC_Lib1
   UWBGL_D3D_Lib3

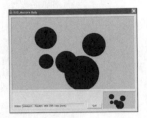

Figure 5.10.   Tutorial 5.5.

* drag event—move the center of the selected ball to the current mouse pointer position;
* up event—ignored.

We allow the selected ball to continue free falling during the dragging of the right mouse button.

Figure 5.10 is a screenshot of the free-falling balls from Tutorial 5.5. Upon close examination of the application specification, we realize that our software libraries are fully capable of supporting all the operations defined. All the programming of this tutorial is limited to source code files located in the `D3D_MultipleBalls` project.

- **Model.** When comparing to Tutorial 5.4, we have a significantly more complex model. We must extend the `CModel` class functionality.

- **Controller.** With more than one ball to work with, the service routines for the left and right mouse button events must be updated accordingly.

Implementation

Examine the implementation of the model component in Listing 5.22. From the `private` representation section of the `CModel` class, we see the `m_pHeroBall`

Source file.   `Model.h` file in the *Model* folder of the `D3D_MultipleBalls` project.

```
// not shown are functions similar to Listing 5.17 from Tutorial 5.3
class CModel {
    ⋮
    ⋮
    void MoveSelectedBallTo(float x, float y);
        // move the selected ball to (x,y)
    void AddHeroBallToWorld();
        // insert the hero ball into the worldSet
    int SelectBallAt(float x, float y);
        // select the ball under position (x,y)

    ⋮
    ⋮
private:
    CBall* m_pHeroBall;           // newly created hero ball
    UWB_Array<CBall> m_AllBalls;  // the collection of all balls
    int m_selected_index;         // index of the selected ball

    ⋮
    ⋮
};
```

Listing 5.22. `CModel` class (Tutorial 5.5).

```
int CModel::SelectBallAt(float x, float y) {
    m_selected_index = -1;                    // assume none selected
    for(int i=0; i<m_AllBalls.Count(); i++)   // loop through all balls
        CBall& ball = m_AllBalls[i];
        distance = ball.GetCenter() to (x, y) // distance from center of ball to (x,y)
        if(distance < ball.GetRadius())       // if distance is less than radius
            m_selected_index = i;             // ball is selected
        ⋮

    return m_selected_index;
}
```

Source file. `Model.cpp` file in the *Model* folder of the the `D3D_MultipleBalls` project.

Listing 5.23. `CModel::SelectBallAt()` Function (Tutorial 5.5).

being defined to support the left mouse button definition of a new ball. The `m_AllBalls` and the `m_selected_index` define a collection of balls and the support for a currently selected ball among the collection. We also see public interface functions to support manipulating these new application states. The interesting changes involved in the implementation of the new `CModel` class are shown in Listing 5.23. Listing 5.23 shows that to select a ball at position (x, y), we must loop through all balls in the world collection and compute the distance for each of the balls. This is an $O(n)$ operation, where n is the number of balls in the world collection. In real-time applications, whenever we encounter requirements of looping through all world elements, we must be acutely aware of the complexities. In general, any computations involving more than linear-time $(O(n))$ complexity run the danger of sub-real-time responses. Listing 5.24 shows the implementation of the `UpdateSimulation()` function. It is important to realize that before we return from this function, *no* events of any kind can arrive at our application. This means that as far as computing the application state is concerned, it is guaranteed that nothing will change before we return from this function. For example, before we return from this function, because the control of the process is within this function, a user will *not* be able to trigger any events. Notice that in our implementation, we compute the new velocities, positions, and membership validity in three separate loops. Because no events can interrupt this function, the order of these loops is not important. If we had chosen to compute the membership validity before updating the velocities/positions, the visible balls on the screen would be different by one update, or a difference of 25 msec.

With the definition of the `CModel` class, mouse button event services becomes a simple calling of corresponding functions. For example, the right mouse button down event can be serviced by calling `CModel::SelectBallAt()`, and so on.

Source file. Model.cpp file in the *Model* folder of the the D3D_MultipleBalls project.

```
void CModel::UpdateSimulation() {
    // Compute elapsed second since previous update
    float elapsed_seconds = ...
    // update ball velocities based on gravity
    float accel_y = -15.0f * elapsed_seconds;
    ┌──────────────────────────────────────────┐
    │ Velocity: Update all balls' velocity      │
    └──────────────────────────────────────────┘
    foreach ball in m_AllBalls
        // accelerated velocity
        velocity = ball.GEtVelocity() + accel_y
        // set the new velocity to the ball
        ball.SetVelocity(velocity);
    ┌──────────────────────────────────────────┐
    │ Position: Update all balls' position      │
    └──────────────────────────────────────────┘
    foreach ball in m_AllBalls
        // compute new position based on current + velocity
        center = ball.GetCenter() + ball.GetVelocity()
        // Set the new position to the ball
        ball.SetCenter(center);
    ┌──────────────────────────────────────────────────────┐
    │ Membership: Destroy balls that travel outside of the world │
    └──────────────────────────────────────────────────────┘
    foreach ball in m_AllBalls
        if(ball.IsOutsideBounds(m_WorldWidth, m_WorldHeight))
            m_AllBalls.DeleteItem(ball);
```

Listing 5.24. CModel::UpdateSimulation() Function (Tutorial 5.5).

When compared with previous tutorials, Tutorial 5.5 supports more user actions, and the output is more graphically oriented (more displayed balls). However, to support these extra user actions and graphical outputs, we see that the corresponding programming code has not much to do with the specific GUI API or graphics API. This observation is true in general. As the complexity of our application increases, we would be spending more programming efforts in developing and maintaining the model component, and in most cases, the programming involved will be API-independent.

Source file. Mouse button service routines are defined by the view/controller pair CDrawAndMouseHandler class. The implementation can be found in DrawAndMouseHandler.h/cpp in the *WindowHandler* folder of the D3D_MultipleBalls project.

Tutorial 5.6. The Ball-Shooting Program

Tutorial 5.6.
Project Name:
  D3D_BallShooting
Library Support:
  UWBGL_MFC_Lib1
  UWBGL_D3D_Lib3

- **Goals.** Demonstrate the implementation of the ball-shooting program as specified on p. 10.

- **Approach.** Continue working with Tutorial 5.5 to complete the implementation of the ball-shooting program.

```
void CModel::UpdateSimulation() {
    // compute elapsed second since previous update
    float elapsed_seconds = ...

    //check for collisions between all of the existing balls
    foreach test_ball in m_AllBalls
        foreach other_ball in m_AllBalls
            if(test_ball.Intersects(other_ball)) // if the two balls intersect
                // computer new velocities for both
                // detail description can be found in Section B.1

    // not shown code identical to Listing 5.24 (Tutorial 5.5)
}
```

Source file. Model.cpp file in the *Model* folder of the D3D_BallShoot project.

Listing 5.25. CModel::UpdateSimulation() function (Tutorial 5.6).

Figure 5.11 is a screenshot from interacting with the ball-shooting program implemented in Tutorial 5.6. When comparing to Tutorial 5.5 we notice two major differences: interball collision and slider-bar control of ball velocity.

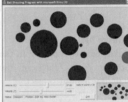

Figure 5.11. Tutorial 5.6.

Interball Collision

In order to compute interball collision, we must collide each ball with every other ball in the world. Listing 5.25 shows the nested for loops required to compute intersections between every ball in the world. Notice that this is an $O(n^2)$ operation, where n is the number of balls in the m_AllBalls array. As the number of balls increases in the world, this collision routine would quickly cause sub-real-time responses. In this case, because the user must click and drag to create a ball and because balls free fall out of the application window rapidly, the total number of balls in the m_AllBalls array does not grow very large (e.g., less than 100). For these reasons, we can still experience real-time response.

Slider-Bar Controls

As discussed in Tutorial 2.3, if registered, MFC will call the OnHScroll() function for servicing of the horizontal scroll bar events. Listing 5.26 shows that the servicing of the scroll-bar events involves setting the velocity of the currently selected ball. In this case, the user changes the selected ball velocity in between timer events, and during the servicing of timer event the UpdateSimulation() function will move the selected ball by its new velocity. Notice that the Update Simulation() and OnHScroll() functions will *never* execute concurrently.

```
void CTutorialDlg::OnHScroll(UINT nSBCode, UINT nPos, CScrollBar* pScrollBar) {
    // Determine which of the scroll bars triggered the event
    if (pScrollBar == (CScrollBar *) &m_VelocityXSlider)  {
        pBall = theApp.GetModel().SelectedBall();
        if(pBall) {
            pBall->SetVelocity( // with value updated from the slider bar );
        }
    } else if (pScrollBar == (CScrollBar *) &m_VelocityYSlider) {
        // code similar to above, operating on the y-component of velocity
        :
    }
}
```

Listing 5.26. CTutorial::OnHScroll() function (Tutorial 5.6).

Source file.
TutorialDlg.cpp file in the *Source Files* folder of the D3D_BallShoot project.

6

Applying to Real-World Applications

We have seen that the event-driven programming model is well-suited for designing and implementing programs that interact with users. In addition, we have seen that the model-view-controller (MVC) framework is a convenient and powerful structure for organizing functional modules in an interactive graphics application. In developing a solution to the ball-shooting program, we have demonstrated that knowledge from event-driven programming helps us design the controller component (e.g., handling of mouse events), computer graphics knowledge helps us design the view component (e.g., transformation and drawing of circles), whereas the model component is highly dependent upon the specific application (e.g., free-falling and colliding circles). Our discussion so far has been based on a very simple example. We will now explore the applicability of the MVC framework and its implementation in real-world applications.

6.1 PowerPoint

Figure 6.1 shows how we can apply our knowledge in analyzing and gaining insights into Microsoft PowerPoint,[1] a popular interactive graphics application. A

---
[1] Powerpoint is a registered trademark of Microsoft.

147

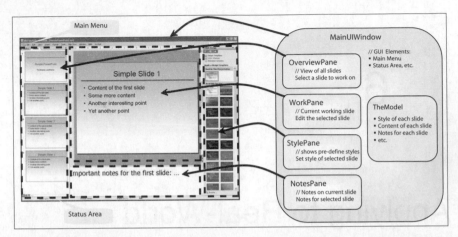

Figure 6.1. Understanding PowerPoint using the MVC implementation framework.

screenshot of a slide creation session using the PowerPoint application is shown at the left of Figure 6.1. The right side of Figure 6.1 shows how we can apply the implementation framework to gain insights into the PowerPoint application. The `MainUIWindow` at the right of Figure 6.1 is the GUI window of the entire application, and it contains the GUI elements that affect/echo the entire application state (e.g., main menu, status area). We can consider the `MainUIWindow` as the module that contains the `TheModel` component and includes the four view/controller pairs.

Recall that `TheModel` is the state of the application and that this component contains all the data that the user interactively creates. In the case of PowerPoint, the user creates a collection of presentation slides, and thus `TheModel` contains all the information about these slides (e.g., layout design style, content of the slides, notes associated with each slide). With this understanding of the `TheModel` component, the rest of the application can be considered as a convenient tool for presenting `TheModel` (the view) to the user and changing `TheModel` (the controller) by the user. In this way, these convenient tools are precisely the view/controller pairs (e.g., `ViewController` components from Figure 5.3).

In Figure 6.1, each of the four view/controller pairs (i.e., `OverviewPane`, `WorkPane`, `StylePane`, and `NotesPane`) supports the changing of different aspects of the `TheModel` component.

- `OverviewPane`. The view component displays multiple consecutive slides from all the slides that the user has created; the controller component supports the user scrolling through all these slides and selecting one for editing.

- **WorkPane.** The view component displays the details of the slide that is currently being edited; the controller supports selecting and editing the content of this slide.

- **StylePane.** The view component displays the layout design of the slide that is currently being edited; the controller supports selecting and defining a new layout design for this slide.

- **NotesPane.** The view component displays the notes that the user has created for the slide that is currently being edited; the controller supports editing of this notes.

As is the case with most modern interactive applications, PowerPoint defines an application timer event to support user-defined animations (e.g., animated sequences between slide transitions). The coherency of the four view/controller pairs can be maintained during the servicing of this application timer event. For example, the user works with the StylePane to change the layout of the current slide in the TheModel component. In the meantime, before servicing the next timer event, OverviewPane and WorkPane are not aware of the changes and display an out-of-date design for the current slide. During the servicing of the timer event, the MainUIWindow forces all view/controller pairs to poll TheModel and refresh their contents. As discussed in Section 5.4, because the timer events are typically triggered more than 30 times in a second, the user is not able to detect the brief out-of-date display and observes a consistent display at all times. In this way, the four view/controller pairs only need to keep a reference to the TheModel component and do not need to have any knowledge of each other. Thus, it is straightforward to insert and delete view/controller pairs into/from the application.

6.2   Maya

We now apply our knowledge in analyzing and understanding Maya,[2] an interactive 3D modeling/animation/rendering system. The left side of Figure 6.2 shows a screenshot of Maya in a simple 3D content creation session. As in the case of Figure 6.1, the right side of Figure 6.2 shows how we can apply the implementation framework to gain insights into the Maya application. Once again, we see that the MainUIWindow is the GUI window of the entire application containing GUI elements that affect/echo the entire application state, the TheModel component, and all the view/controller pairs.

---

[2] Maya is a registered trademark of Autodesk.

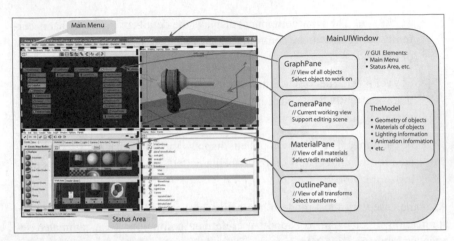

Figure 6.2. Understanding Maya with the MVC implementation framework.

Because Maya is a 3D media creation system, the `TheModel` component contains 3D content information (e.g., scene graph, 3D geometry, material properties, lighting, camera, animation). Once again, the rest of the components in the `MainUIWindow` are designed to facilitate the user's view and to change `TheModel`. Here is the functionality of the four view/controller pairs.

- `GraphPane.` The view component displays the scene graph of the 3D content; the controller component supports navigating the graph and selecting scene nodes in the graph.

- `CameraPane.` The view component renders the scene graph from a camera viewing position; the controller component supports manipulating the camera view and selecting objects in the scene.

- `MaterialPane.` The view component displays all the defined materials; the controller component supports selecting and editing materials.

- `OutlinePane.` The view component displays all the transform nodes in the scene; the controller component supports manipulating the transforms (e.g., create/change parent-child relationships).

Once again, the coherency among the different view/controller pairs can be maintained while servicing the application timer events.

We do not speculate that PowerPoint or Maya is implemented according to our framework. These are highly sophisticated commercial applications, and the underlying implementation is certainly much more complex. However, based on the knowledge we have gained from Part I of this book, we can begin to understand how to approach discussing, designing, and building such interactive graphics applications. Remember that the important lesson we want to learn is how to organize the functionality of an interactive graphics application into components and understand how the components interact so that we can better understand, maintain, modify, and expand an interactive graphics application.

Essential Concepts:
Presented in 2D

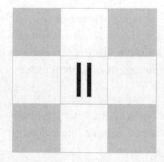

Introduction to Part II

In Part I, we studied "building interactive applications," where we concentrated on interaction with the user and software architectures. We are now ready to include computer graphics in our programs. It is important to clarify once again that we are learning computer graphics concepts in the context of building interactive applications. In this way, we will only concentrate on a relevant subset of topics. For simplicity and ease of presentation, all topics will be presented in 2D. As we will see in Chapter 16 (in Part III), except for rotation, all concepts learned (including all tutorials) generalize to 3D in straightforward ways.

Essential computer graphics concepts for building interactive graphics applications include understanding of graphics primitives and approaches to organize these primitives with transformation operators for interaction purposes.

- **Graphics primitives.** Chapter 7 discusses the different types of graphics primitives and their attributes. The associated tutorials develop an object-oriented class hierarchy to encapsulate the functionality and behaviors for graphics primitives.

- **Transformation operators.** Chapter 8 introduces (and reviews) the basic affine transformation operators. Chapter 9 discusses approaches and motivations for combining (concatenating) these transformation operators.

- **Coordinate systems.** Chapter 10 discusses approaches to take advantage of the graphics hardware to create virtual coordinate spaces that are convenient for designing graphical scenes and for interacting with graphical objects.

- **Hierarchical modeling.** Chapter 11 introduces the idea of organizing graphical primitives and transformation operators as nodes in a tree-like hierarchy. The chapter then demonstrates how to build complex objects where users can control and interact with different components of such objects.

- **Appearance and intelligence.** Chapter 12 introduces texture and blending, simple hardware strategies to increase the visual complexity of applications. This chapter also demonstrates how to apply simple linear algebra to increase the apparent intelligence of our application.

Attributes and Behaviors of Primitives

This chapter discusses the fundamentals of working with graphics primitives—how to modify their appearances and how to abstract their behaviors. This chapter:

- introduces the different types of primitives that are supported by graphics APIs;

- describes how we can efficiently program with these primitives;

- explains some of the attributes that can affect the appearances of the primitives;

- develops abstractions for simple physical behaviors of primitives.

After this chapter we should:

- understand the approaches to drawing different types of primitives with graphics APIs;

- understand the advantages of designing a hierarchy for graphics primitives;

- understand how to work with simple physical behaviors of graphics primitives (motion and collision).

In addition, with respect to hands-on programming, we should:

- understand the `Primitive` hierarchy;

- be able to implement interactive graphics applications based on the `Primi tive` hierarchy.

Listing 4.1 in Chapter 4 shows that after proper initializations, drawing with graphics APIs involves the following.

- **C1.** Setting of the render state.

- **C2.** Issuing of the drawing commands.

We have already worked with drawings where we issued drawing commands to draw triangle primitives. In addition, we have seen that an example attribute of the triangle primitive is its color. In this chapter, we explore the different primitives that can be drawn with graphics APIs and their corresponding attributes.

To support programming, in the tutorials we will design abstractions for the graphics API primitives and introduce simple but commonly encountered behaviors for these primitives: motion, collision, and collection.

7.1   Types of Primitives

Most modern computer graphics hardware can only process/draw points, lines, and triangles. These are the fundamental shapes that are capable of approximating the vast majority of graphical objects that the end users are familiar with. Graphics hardware is optimized to process these basic shapes efficiently. Modern graphics APIs typically define simple collection structures to support an efficient description of the basic shapes. For example, graphics APIs typically support the drawing of a point list, where an application would specify n coordinate positions and in one drawing command request the graphics API to draw n individual points. When compared to issuing individual drawing commands for drawing individual points separately, the point list command optimizes the number of graphics API calls. This becomes an important optimization when the application program is trying to draw a very large (e.g., 10^6) number of points. In this section, we briefly describe some of the common structures used for each of the basic shapes.

It is important to note that our goal here is to present the most commonly supported primitives and their attributes. The following discussion provides a conceptual framework for understanding graphics APIs and is not an exhaustive list. For example, we do not describe the OpenGL convex polygon (approximated with triangles) primitive type. With the discussion of triangle stripe and fan, we expect the readers to understand the idea of approximating a convex polygon with triangles. In addition, graphics APIs typically only support some of the following. For example, D3D does not support line style or line width.

7.1.1   Points

Points are simple and yet can be powerful for approximating physical effects. For example, a particle system is an approach that uses a large number of points to approximate physical effects like fire, water, and so on. Figure 7.1 shows a simple example of approximating fireworks with fast-moving, colorful points. Graphics APIs typically support specifying individual points or a collection of points, that is, point lists.

Attributes of a point include the following.

- **Color.** This is the color that the point should be drawn.

- **Size.** This is how large the point should be drawn.

- **Texture coordinate.** This attribute allows each point to be displayed in more than one color. For example, a large point may cover a few pixels, and it is possible to display different colors for those pixels. We will learn about texture mapping in Chapter 12.

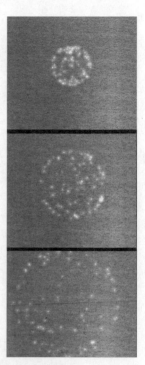

Figure 7.1.   Simple approximation of firework with points (Image from Jordan Philips CSS450 Final Project (Fall 2004)).

7.1.2   Lines

Lines are important for approximating curves, which in turn can be used to model objects like hair, fur, and so on. To optimize the specification of lines, graphics APIs typically support the drawing of the following.

- **One line segment.** An application program will specify two points and request the graphics API to draw one line.

- **Line segments or line lists.** An application program will specify $2n$ points and request the graphics API to draw n line segments where each pair of points define a separate line segment.

- **Line strips or polylines.**   An application program will specify n points (where $n > 2$) and request the graphics API to draw $n - 1$ connected line segments. The *polyline* drawing command optimizes the number of vertices an application program must specify. This drawing command is important

Figure 7.2. Gouraud shaded line with a black endpoint and a white endpoint.

Gouraud shading. Linear color interpolation between endpoints with different color values.

Illumination computation. Compute the color of an object based on its *material properties* and geometric relationship with light sources.

Flat shading. Filling the interior of a geometric shape (e.g., line or triangle) with the same color.

for approximating the outline of connected shapes (e.g., approximating the outline of a circle).

A line segment has two types of attributes: per-vertex and per–drawing command attributes.

Per-vertex attributes. These are attributes that can be different for each vertex. Examples of per-vertex attributes include the following.

- **Color.** This defines the color for the vertex. When the endpoints of a line have different colors, the graphics hardware can perform *Gouraud shading* and linearly interpolate the color while drawing the line segment. For example, a line segment can be set to have a white endpoint and a black endpoint. When Gouraud shading is enabled, the graphics hardware will draw a line where the color of the line changes gradually from white to black along the line. Figure 7.2 shows such a line.

- **Texture coordinate.** Similar to a point's texture coordinate attribute, when texture mapping is enabled, this attribute allows us to control the color along the line. Once again, we will study texture mapping in Chapter 12.

- **Normal vector.** This attribute supports illumination computation for the line, that is, how a light source illuminates the line. We will describe illumination models and computation in Appendix A.

Per–drawing command attributes. These are attributes that are associated with each drawing command. For example, the following attributes will be applied to all the line segments in a polyline drawing command.

- **Line color.** When Gouraud shading, illumination computation, and texture mapping are all disabled, this color defines the color of the entire line (or line segments for a polyline).

- **Material property.** When illumination computation is enabled, this attribute defines how the line segments will be illuminated by light sources. Once again, we will learn about illumination models and illumination computation in Appendix A.

- **Line style/width.** These define the style (e.g., dotted versus solid line) and width of a line.

7.1.3 Triangles

The triangle is one of the most important primitives in computer graphics. Triangles can be used to approximate many geometric objects in 2D and 3D. For example, we have already experienced approximating 2D circles with triangles. Figure 7.3 shows approximating a tiger's geometric shape with triangles, and Figure 7.4 shows approximating a teapot's geometric shape with strips of triangles that are arranged in an orderly manner. There are many drawing commands defined to optimize the drawing of triangles, some examples of which include the following.

Figure 7.3. Approximating a tiger with triangles.

Figure 7.4. Approximating a teapot with triangle strips.

- **Triangle list.** An application program will specify $3n$ vertices and request the graphics API to draw n individual triangles.

- **Triangle fan.** An application program will specify $n + 2$ vertices and request the graphics API to draw n triangles where all triangles are connected to the first specified vertex. Figure 7.5 shows an example of specifying a triangle fan.

- **Triangle strips.** An application program will specify $n + 2$ vertices and request the graphics API to draw n connected triangles. Figure 7.6 shows an example of specifying a triangle strip.

Figures 7.5 and 7.6 are examples of how the triangles can be specified. In general, the exact order is highly graphics API–dependent. In addition, each graphics API may have additional requirements/restrictions to ensure clockwise and/or counterclockwise ordering of individual triangles in the collection.

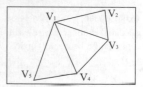

Figure 7.5. Specifying a triangle fan.

Attributes of triangles. A triangle can have up to three types of attributes: per-vertex, per-edge, and per–drawing command attributes. The per-vertex attributes of a triangle are identical to the per-vertex attributes of a line. The per-edge attributes of a triangle define the appearance of the edges of a triangle. Examples include width, style, color, and so on. Because triangles are meant to approximate more complex objects, edge attributes are typically not supported by graphics APIs. The per–drawing command attributes for a triangle are similar to those of a line segment.

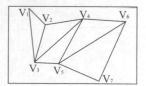

Figure 7.6. Specifying a triangle strip.

- **Triangle color.** When Gouraud shading, illumination computation, and texture mapping are all disabled, this color defines the color for *flat shading* the entire triangle (or triangles in the triangle fan/strip).

- **Material property.** This is identical to that of the line.

- **Fill style.** This attribute defines if the interior of the triangle should be filled. When switched to wire-frame mode, only the outline edges of the triangles will be drawn.

Wire frame. Draw the outlines of the primitives, leaving the interior unfilled.

7.2 Working with Color

Normalized number. This is a floating-point number defined between 0.0 and 1.0. For example, the number 1.2 is not a valid normalized number.

Typically, color is expressed as a (red,green,blue) triplet (or (r, g, b)). We refer to each of the red, green, and blue as a color channel, or a color component. Each of the color components is defined either as a normalized floating-point number:

$$0.0 \leq r, g, b \leq 1.0$$

or as an integer:

$$0 \leq r, g, b \leq 255.$$

In either case, the minimum number represents no intensity for the corresponding component, and the maximum number represents full intensity. For example:

0x00FF0000. This is a hexadecimal number where each digit can be between 0 and F (15).

Color	Floating point	Integer	Packed unsigned integer
white	$(1.0, 1.0, 1.0)$	$(255, 255, 255)$	0x00FFFFFF
red	$(1.0, 0.0, 0.0)$	$(255, 0, 0)$	0x00FF0000
green	$(0.0, 1.0, 0.0)$	$(0, 255, 0)$	0x0000FF00
blue	$(0.0, 0.0, 1.0)$	$(0, 0, 255)$	0x000000FF
black	$(0.0, 0.0, 0.0)$	$(0, 0, 0)$	0x00000000

The maximum intensity of the integer representation is limited to 255 and can be represented by an unsigned 8-bit integer. A packed unsigned integer packs the three 8-bit integers into bit positions of a 32-bit unsigned integer. This is a compact way to represent color. The limited and discrete range of 256 (or 2^8) intensity levels of the integer representation reflects the capability of a typical graphics device. The underlying hardware elements of a typical graphics device are capable of displaying 256 distinct shades for each of the three colors. For this reason, these types of graphics displays can display a total of

$$2^8 \times 2^8 \times 2^8 = 2^{24} \approx 16 \text{ million unique colors.}$$

7.3 Programming Geometric Primitives

Tutorial 7.1. Primitives and Attributes

Tutorial 7.1.
Project Name:

D3D_ObjectsAndAttributes
Library Support:
    UWBGL_MFC_Lib1
    UWBGL_D3D_Lib4

- **Goals.** Get experience with some attributes for drawing geometric primitives; understand that the actual programming of geometric primitives is independent of the graphics API.

- **Approach.** Study the implementation of a simple graphics primitive editor; analyze an approach to decouple the general programming abstraction of primitives from the API-dependent drawings.

Figure 7.7 is a screenshot of running Tutorial 7.1. This tutorial allows the user to create/edit a point, a line, or a circle. In addition, the user can adjust the color, (Gouraud) shading color, and point size attributes for these primitives. We will analyze the library support for this tutorial and then study the CModel source code.

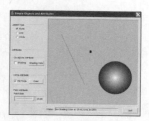

Figure 7.7. Tutorial 7.1.

UWBGL_D3D_Lib4

As in all UWBGL libraries, the source files to this library are organized into three groups.

Change summary. See p. 514 for a summary of changes to the library.

- *Common Files* **folder.** Contains files that implement API-independent functionality. For example, we have worked with WindowHandler.h/.cpp, which implement abstract view/controller pair functionality; or Clock.h/.cpp, which implement wall-clock stopwatch functionality. In this case, because of the large number of files, we further subdivide this folder into four subfolders.

  - *DrawHelper* **subfolder.** Contains DrawHelper1.h/.cpp, which define the DrawHelper abstraction that allow us to decouple API-specific primitive drawing from API-independent primitive behaviors. We will examine this class in detail.

  - *Geoms* **subfolder.** Contains the source and header files for the Point Geom, LineGeom, and CircleGeom classes. These classes implement the API-independent behavior of primitives. We will examine these classes in detail.

  - *Utilities* **subfolder.** Contains Containers.h, Utility2.h/.cpp, Color1.h/.cpp, and Clock.h/.cpp. These files are identical to the files from the previous library (UWBGL_D3D_Lib3).

- *WindowHandler* **subfolder.** Contains `IWindowHandler`, and `Window Handler.h/.cpp`, the abstract and API-independent definition of the `WindowHandler` class. These file are identical to the files from the previous library (`UWBGL_D3D_Lib3`).

- *Header Files* **folder.** Contains the header files that support D3D API-specific functionality.

- *D3D Files* **folder.** Contains files that define D3D-specific classes. For example, we have already seen `D3DWindowHandler.h/.cpp` implementing D3D-specific `WindowHandler` functionality.

  - *D3D_DrawHelper* **subfolder.** Contains `D3DDrawHelper1.h/.cpp`. These two files implement D3D-specific drawing functionality for the `DrawHelper` abstraction. This new subfolder replaces the previous *D3D_Geoms* subfolder.

  - *D3D_GraphicsSystem* **subfolder.** Contains `D3DGraphicsSystem.h/ .cpp`. These files implement the abstract graphics API. These files are identical to the ones from the previous library.

  - *D3D_WindowHandler* **subfolder.** Contains `D3DWindowHandler.h/ .cpp`. These files implement the view/controller pair for the D3D API. These files are identical to the ones from the previous library.

`DrawHelper` **class.** The `DrawHelper` class defines drawing attributes and pure virtual drawing functions. As we can see from Listing 7.1, under label A are the drawing functions that do not do anything. Under label B are the functions and the instance variables that are capable of recording the desired attributes for drawing. Label C shows examples of the attribute-setting functions. To support graphics API–specific drawing commands, each graphics API should subclass from `DrawHelper` and override the drawing functions. Label D shows that the `DrawHelper` class has support for modeling transformations. We will discuss working with the transformation functions in Chapter 9.

OGLDrawHelper. Similar to the D3DDrawHelper class, the OGLDrawHelper class implements OpenGL-specific primitive drawings.

RC. Rendering context. Recall that this context contains the entire rendering state.

`D3DDrawHelper` **class.** The `D3DDrawHelper` class subclasses from the `Draw Helper` class to implement D3D-specific attribute setting and primitive drawing. Listing 7.2 shows the `D3DDrawHelper` class override the drawing and attribute-setting functions. The implementation of the attribute-setting functions (e.g., `SetFillMode()`) shows that we do indeed invoke the D3D `GraphicsSystem` to set the render state of the D3D RC. Listing 7.3 shows the draw functions for line

Source file.
uwbgl_DrawHelper1.h/cpp files in the *Common Files/ DrawHelper* subfolder of the UWBGL_D3D_Lib4 project.

```
class UWB_DrawHelper  {
    A: Functions to draw geometric primitives
    virtual bool DrawPoint(vec3 position) {return false;}
    virtual bool DrawLine(vec3 start, vec3 end) {return false;}
    virtual bool DrawCircle(vec3 center, float radius) {return false;}
    :

    B: Functions to set the attributes of the primitives
    virtual void ResetAttributes();
    virtual void SetShadeMode(eShadeMode mode); // Gouraud or Flat shading
    virtual void SetFillMode(eFillMode mode);   // Wire frame or fill solid
    UWB_Color SetColor1(UWB_Color color);       // color to draw
    D: Functions for supporting model transformations
    virtual bool InitializeModelTransform();
    :

  private:  ...
    eShadeMode m_ShadeMode;      // enum data type for shading
    eFillMode  m_FillMode;       // enum data type of fill mode
    UWB_Color  m_Color1, m_Color2; // storing the color setting
    :

};
```

```
C: Implementation of attribute setting functions
void UWB_DrawHelper::SetShadeMode(eShadeMode mode) {  m_ShadeMode = mode; }
void UWB_DrawHelper::SetFillMode(eFillMode mode) {  m_FillMode = mode; }
:
```

Listing 7.1. The UWB_DrawHelper class (Tutorial 7.1).

and circle. As we can see, in both cases, at label A, we obtain the reference to the D3D RC. At labels B and C, we compute the vertex positions and per-vertex attributes (e.g., color). At label E, we issue the drawing command. At label D, we define the results of Gouraud shading, where for a line we define linear interpolation between m_Color1 from the starting vertex to m_Color2 at the ending vertex. Although for a circle, we define all the circumference vertices to be m_Color1 with the center of the circle being m_Color2; this causes color changing gradually from the center toward the circumference showing continuous concentric circles with gradual color changes. The DrawPoint() function has a similar structure and is not shown here.

```cpp
class UWBD3D_DrawHelper : public UWB_DrawHelper {
    // virtual function overrides

    // draws D3D points
    bool DrawPoint(vec3 position);

    // draws a D3D line
    bool DrawLine(vec3 start, vec3 end);

    // approximates circle with Friangle Fan
    bool DrawCircle(vec3 center, float radius);
    ⋮


    // Sets D3D Render State
    void SetShadeMode(eShadeMode mode);
    void SetFillMode(eFillMode mode );
};
```

```cpp
⋮
void UWBD3D_DrawHelper::SetShadeMode(eShadeMode mode) {
    LPDIRECT3DDEVICE9 pDevice = UWBD3D_GraphicsSystem::GetSystem().GetD3DDevice();
    ⋮


    if( smGouraud == m_ShadeMode )
        pDevice->SetRenderState(D3DRS_SHADEMODE, D3DSHADE_GOURAUD);
    ⋮

void UWBD3D_DrawHelper::SetFillMode(eFillMode mode) {
    LPDIRECT3DDEVICE9 pDevice = UWBD3D_GraphicsSystem::GetSystem().GetD3DDevice();
    ⋮


    if( fmSolid == m_FillMode )
        pDevice->SetRenderState(D3DRS_FILLMODE, D3DFILL_SOLID);
    ⋮
```

Source file.
uwbgl_D3DDrawHelper1.h/
.cpp files in the *D3D Files/-
DrawHelper* subfolder of the
UWBGL_D3D_Lib4 project.

Listing 7.2. The UWBD3D_DrawHelper class (Tutorial 7.1).

```
bool UWBD3D_DrawHelper::DrawLine(vec3 start, vec3 end) {
A:  LPDIRECT3DDEVICE9 pDevice = UWBD3D_GraphicsSystem::GetSystem().GetD3DDevice();
    ⋮

    // Set the start point positions
B:  draw_points[0].m_point.x = start.x;
    ⋮

    // Per vertex color
C:  draw_points[0].m_color = m_Color1.ARGB();
    ⋮

    // Gouraud shading interpolates
D:  if (m_ShadeMode == smFlat)
        draw_points[1].m_color = m_Color1.ARGB(); // from m_Color1 to m_Color2
    else                                          // along the line
        draw_points[1].m_color = m_Color2.ARGB();
    ⋮

E:  pDevice->DrawPrimitiveUP(D3DPT_LINELIST, 1, (CONST void *)(&draw_points), sizeof(⋮));
    ⋮


bool UWBD3D_DrawHelper::DrawCircle(vec3 center, float radius) {
A:  LPDIRECT3DDEVICE9 pDevice = UWBD3D_GraphicsSystem::GetSystem().GetD3DDevice();
    ⋮

B/C: // Compute vertex positions for the TriangleFan,
     // fill the circumference vertices with m_Color1

    ⋮

    // for Gouraud shading, set the center color to m_Color2
D:  if( smGouraud == m_ShadeMode )
        v[0].m_color = m_Color2.ARGB(); // causing interploation from
                                        // circumference toward the center
    ⋮

E:  pDevice->DrawPrimitiveUP(D3DPT_TRIANGLEFAN, kNumPts-2, (CONST void *)v, sizeof(⋮));
    ⋮
```

Source file.
uwbgl_D3DDrawHelper1.cpp file in the *D3D Files/DrawHelper* subfolder of the UWBGL_D3D_Lib4 project.

Listing 7.3. The UWBD3D_DrawHelper draw functions (Tutorial 7.1).

```
class UWB_PointGeometry {
    ⋮
    // sets m_point instance variable
A:  void SetLocation(float x, float y, float z=0.0f);
    ⋮
    // sets m_color instance variable
B:  void SetColor(const UWB_Color& color);
    ⋮

C:  void Draw(UWB_DrawHelper* pDrawHelper) const;
    ⋮

  protected:
    ⋮

    vec3 m_point;          // to store the location of the point
    UWB_Color m_color;     // color attribute of the point
    ⋮
```

Source file.
uwbgl_PointGeom1.h/cpp
files in the *Common Files/-Geoms* subfolder of the
UWBGL_D3D_Lib4 project.

```
void UWB_PointGeometry::Draw(UWB_DrawHelper* pDrawHelper) const {
    ⋮
    pDrawHelper->ResetAttributes();
    pDrawHelper->SetColor1(m_color);
    pDrawHelper->SetPointSize(m_point_size);
    pDrawHelper->DrawPoint(m_point);
}
```

Listing 7.4. The UWB_PointGeometry class (Tutorial 7.1).

Point/line/circle geometries. When a geometric primitive has access to the DrawHelper class, it can draw itself to the API-specific device by calling the appropriate attribute-setting and primitive-drawing functions. For example, Listing 7.4 shows an API-independent PointGeometry class, where this class does not contain any graphics API–specific function calls. We see that in this case, the point class has a simple public behavior where we can set its geometry (A) and attribute (B). The Draw() function simply delegates the responsibilities to the DrawHelper class. If the pDrawHelper pointer references a D3DDrawHelper class (as shown in Listing 7.2), then the corresponding D3D drawing would occur.

```
class CModel {
  public:
    ⋮
A:  void SetObjectColor(const UWB_Color& color);
    void SetCircleFillMode(bool filled);
B:  void StartDefineGraphicsObject(float world_x, float world_y);
    void EndDefineGraphicsObject(float world_x, float world_y);
    void MoveGraphicsObject(float world_x, float world_y);
C:  void DrawModel();
    ⋮

  private:
    ⋮
D:  UWB_CircleGeometry m_Circle;
    UWB_PointGeometry  m_Point;
    UWB_LineGeometry   m_Line;
E:  UWBD3D_DrawHelper m_DrawHelper;
    ⋮
};
```

Source file. Model.h file in the *Model* folder of the D3D_ObjectsAndAttributes project.

Listing 7.5. The CModel class (Tutorial 7.1).

Alternatively, if an OGLDrawHelper is passed to the Draw() function, then the corresponding OpenGL drawing would occur. LineGeometry and CircleGeometry have similar class structures, and the details are not shown here.

The CModel class. With the functionality defined in UWB_D3D_Lib4, the core application state (or the CModel class) of Tutorial 7.1 can be defined. From Listing 7.5, we can see that public interface of the model class includes (A) methods for setting primitive attributes, (B) methods for interactively drawing the primitives, and (C) drawing of the model. Privately, we see instances of geometric primitives at label D, and the D3DDrawHelp object (m_DrawHelper) that will support the drawing in D3D. The implementation of these methods is shown in Listing 7.6. At label A, we see that the attribute-setting methods (e.g., SetObjectColor()) are implemented by straightforward calling of public methods supported by the corresponding primitive type (e.g., m_Circle's SetColor() method). At label B, we see that to properly support primitive editing, we must determine the currently active primitive type and then set the vertex/geometric properties accordingly. Lastly at label C, we see that the D3D graphics API–

A:
```cpp
void CModel::SetObjectColor(const UWB_Color& color) {
    if(gotCircle == m_CurrentObjectType)  m_Circle.SetColor(color);
    else if(gotPoint == m_CurrentObjectType)  m_Point.SetColor(color);
    ⋮
```

B:
```cpp
void CModel::StartDefineGraphicsObject(float world_x, float world_y) {
    if(gotCircle == m_CurrentObjectType) {
        m_Circle.SetCenter(world_x, world_y);
        m_Circle.SetRadius(0);
    } else if(gotPoint == m_CurrentObjectType)
    ⋮
```

Source file. Model.cpp file in the *Model* folder of the D3D_ObjectsAndAttributes project.

```cpp
void CModel::EndDefineGraphicsObject(float world_x, float world_y) {
    if(gotCircle == m_CurrentObjectType) {
        ⋮
    } else if(gotPoint == m_CurrentObjectType) {
        ⋮
```

C:
```cpp
void CModel::DrawModel() {
    m_Circle.Draw(&m_DrawHelper);
    m_Line.Draw(&m_DrawHelper);
    ⋮
```

Listing 7.6. Example implementation of CModel (Tutorial 7.1).

```cpp
class CTutorialDlg : public CDialog {
```
A:
```cpp
    afx_msg void OnTimer(UINT nIDEvent);
    afx_msg void OnHScroll(UINT nSBCode, UINT nPos, CScrollBar* pScrollBar);
    afx_msg void OnBnClickedColorButton();
private:
    ⋮
```

Source file. CTutorialDlg.cpp file in the *Source Files* folders of the D3D_ObjectsAndAttributes project.

```cpp
    // Control variables for GUI elements
```
B:
```cpp
    UWBMFC_SliderCtrlWithEcho m_PointSizeSlider;
    BOOL m_bFillCircle, m_Shading;
```
C:
```cpp
    CDrawAndMouseHandler m_view;
};
```

Listing 7.7. The CTutorialDlg class (Tutorial 7.1).

specific drawing is implemented by calling the primitive draw routine through the D3DDrawHelper object (m_DrawHelper).

The Tutorial 7.1 application. As in all the tutorials, an instance of CModel is defined in the CTutorialApp class. Recall that the CTutorialApp class is the abstract representation of the running program and that there is only one instance of this object. By defining the CModel instance in the CTutorialApp class, we are guaranteed that there will only be one instance of the CModel object. Once again, the CTutorialDlg class represents the application dialog window. Listing 7.7 shows the declarations of GUI event service routines (at label A) and GUI control variables (at label B). At label C, the CDrawAndMouseHandler class is similar to that from Tutorial 5.2 (Listing 5.14), where this is the view/controller pair abstraction and implements the drawing area in the application main window. Listing 7.8 shows the CDrawAndMouseHandler methods for drawing (A1) and handling of mouse events (B1). At label A2, we see the the implementation of DrawGraphics() invokes the CModel::DrawModel() function for drawing. At label B2, we see that mouse events are translated into appropriate methods on the CModel class for the definition of the primitive geometries.

Source file.
DrawAndMouseHandler.h/ .cpp files in the *WindowHandler* folder of the D3D_ObjectsAndAttributes project.

```
class CDrawAndMouseHandler : public UWBD3D_WindowHandler {
        :
A1:     bool Initialize(CDialog& parent_dlg, int control_id);
        void DrawGraphics();
        :

B1:     void OnMouseButton(bool down, unsigned int nFlags, int windowX, int windowY);
        void OnMouseMove(unsigned int nFlags, int windowX, int windowY);
        :


A2:     void CDrawAndMouseHandler::DrawGraphics() {
            // initialize Graphics API RC and sets up transformation processors
            m_pD3DDevice->SetTransform(D3DTS_VIEW, &world2ndc);
            :

            theApp.GetModel().DrawModel();          // Get the instance of CModel and redraw
            :
```

Listing 7.8. The CDrawAndMouseHandler class (Tutorial 7.1).

```
B2:   void CDrawAndMouseHandler::OnMouseButton(bool down, unsigned int nFlags,
                                               int hwX, int hwY) {
          // hardware to device coordinate transform
          HardwareToDevice(hwX, hwY, deviceX, deviceY);

          if(nFlags & MK_LBUTTON) {
              // Left mouse button click
              theApp.GetModel().StartDefineGraphicsObject(deviceX, deviceY);
          } else if(nFlags & MK_RBUTTON) {
              // Right mouse button click
              theApp.GetModel().MoveGraphicsObject(deviceX, deviceY);
          ⋮
      void CDrawAndMouseHandler::OnMouseMove(unsigned int nFlags, int hwX, int hwY) {
          ⋮
```

Listing 7.8. (cont.)

7.4   Abstraction of Behavior: A Primitive Hierarchy

From Tutorial 7.1, we understand that the general behaviors of primitives (e.g., geometric definition, moving of a primitive) are independent of the graphics API–specific drawing operations. We saw that the DrawHelper class supports graphics API–specific implementation of primitive-drawing functions and that the general primitive classes can work with the DrawHelper class and be defined in a graphics API–independent manner.

Tutorial 7.2. The Primitive Hierarchy

Tutorial 7.2.
Project Name:
  D3D_ObjectClasses
Library Support:
  UWBGL_MFC_Lib1
  UWBGL_D3D_Lib5

- **Goals.** To practice object-oriented design and implementation with the geometric primitives; experience graphics programming based on abstract behavior.

- **Approach.** To study the implementation of a simple primitive hierarchy; analyze a simple primitive editor design/implementation based on interaction with abstract Primitive class.

Figure 7.8 is a screenshot of running Tutorial 7.2. This tutorial is similar to the previous one except that the primitives move around in the application window and that the primitive attributes are accessible via GUI elements. For example, we can separately enable and disable the shading of the line and the circle. This tutorial is implemented based on UWBGL_D3D_Lib5 and a corresponding new CModel class.

UWBGL_D3D_Lib5

As in all previous UWBGL_D3D libraries, source code of this library is stored in three folders:

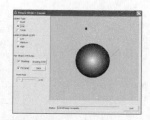

Figure 7.8. Tutorial 7.2.

Change summary. See p. 515 for a summary of changes to the library.

Folder	Subfolder	Purpose
Header Files	-	D3D specific .h files
D3D Files	-	D3D specific classes
Graphics API–independent source code files:		
Common Files	Utilities	general utilities (e.g., Clock, Color)
	DrawHelper	DrawHeler implementation files
	WindowHandler	WindowHandler implementation files
	Primitives	Primitive hierarchy implementation files

When compared to UWBGL_D3D_Lib4, the only difference is that the *Primitives* subfolder has replaced the *Geoms* subfolder in the *Common Files* folder. There are four classes in the *Primitive* subfolder:

Class	Source Files
UWB_Primitive	uwbgl_Primitive1.h/.cpp
UWB_PrimitivePoint	uwbgl_PrimitivePoint1.h/,cpp
UWB_PrimitiveLine	uwbgl_PrimitiveLine1.h/.cpp
UWB_PrimitiveCircle	uwbgl_PrimitiveCircle1.h/.cpp

The Primitive class defines the pure virtual behavior for all primitives, and the other three classes implement the actual functionality.

The Primitive class. Listing 7.9 shows the Primitive class implementation and definitions. We see the following.

- **A: The Draw() function.** Notice that this is *not* a virtual function. As shown in the implementation A1, the procedure for drawing for *any* primitive is the same: set the attributes (SetDrawAttributes()) and draw the primitive (DrawPrimitive()). Notice that DrawPrimitive() is a *pure* virtual function. In this way, the Primitive base class defines the drawing procedure but does not implement the actual functions. Subclasses must implement the DrawPrimitive() function to complete the implementation of the Draw() function.

```
class UWB_Primitive {
  public:
A:  void Draw( eLevelOfDetail lod, UWB_DrawHelper& draw_helper ) const;

B:  virtual void Update(float elapsed_seconds);

C:  virtual void MouseDownVertex(int vertexID, float x, float y);
    virtual void MoveTo(float x, float y);
D:  void SetVelocity(vec3 velocity); // Set/Get velocity attribute
    vec3 GetVelocity() const;
    bool IsStationary() const;
    ⋮

  protected:
E:  vec3 m_velocity; // instance variables for storing the attributes
    UWB_Color m_FlatColor; // color for flat shading
    float  m_PointSize;    // If primitive is a point this is the size,
                           // otherwise, not used
F:  virtual void SetupDrawAttributes(UWB_DrawHelper& draw_helper) const;
    virtual void DrawPrimitive( ... UWB_DrawHelper& draw_helper ) const = 0;
    ⋮
};
```

Source file.

uwbgl_Primitive1.h/cpp files in the *Common Files/ Primitives* subfolder of the UWBGL_D3D_Lib5 project.

Listing 7.9. The UWB_Primitive class (Tutorial 7.2).

- **B: The** Update() **function.** The elapsed_seconds parameter is the wall-clock time since the previous invocation of this function. A subclass with a time-varying internal state should override this function and update its internal states accordingly.

- **C: The mouse edit support functions.** These functions are defined to support abstract mouse interactions. For example, vertexID can be used to represent the number of editing mouse clicks performed on behalf of a primitive. We will examine how to use these functions to support general editing of point, line, and circle primitives.

- **D and E: The attributes and the corresponding set/get functions.** All primitive attributes are represented by instance variables in the Primitive base class. As shown at label D1, attribute setting and getting functions simply set/get the corresponding internal instance variables.

$\vdots$

```
A1:   void UWB_Primitive::Draw(eLevelOfDetail lod, UWB_DrawHelper& draw_helper) const {

         :

         SetupDrawAttributes(draw_helper);
         DrawPrimitive(lod, draw_helper);

         :

D1:   void UWB_Primitive::SetVelocity(vec3 velocity){ m_velocity = velocity; }
         bool UWB_Primitive::IsStationary() const {
         return ( UWB_ZERO_TOLERANCE >= fabs(m_velocity.x) && ...

         :

F1:   void UWB_Primitive::SetupDrawAttributes(UWB_DrawHelper& draw_helper) const {
         draw_helper.ResetAttributes();
         draw_helper.SetColor1(m_FlatColor);

         :
```

Listing 7.9. (cont.)

We made a design decision where for the ease of programming, we have defined the superset of all primitive attributes in the base class. For example, the m_PointSize attribute is defined. However, this attribute is only meaningful for a point primitive, and all non-point subclasses will ignore this attribute. In this way, our implementation is not optimized for memory efficiency. However, because all attributes and their corresponding set/get functions are defined in the Primitive base class, all subclass objects can have uniform public interface functions. As we will see in the CModel implementation, this uniform interface simplifies programming with the Primitive hierarchy.

The m_Velocity is an unusual attribute to be defined in a primitive hierarchy. This is because all other primitive attributes affect the appearance of the attribute, whereas the velocity affects the physical behavior of the primitive object. Once again, we define this physical attribute in the base class for the uniformity of public methods and the ease of programming with the hierarchy.

- **F: The subclass-responsible functions for supporting drawing.** As discussed, the Draw() function specifies the drawing procedure in the form of pure virtual functions, and the subclass must override these functions to implement the actual drawing operations. As illustrated at label F1, by default, the `Primitive` base class resets all drawing attributes and sets the flat shading color. Subclasses must override this function to set individual primitive-specific attributes.

Because some of the functions in the `Primitive` class are undefined (e.g., `Draw Primitive()`), this is a pure virtual class and we cannot instantiate objects of this class.

The concrete `Primitive` classes. The `PrimitivePoint` class subclasses from the `Primitive` class and implements the behavior of a point primitive. Listing 7.10 shows that the `PrimitivePoint` class overrides the update (A) and the mouse editing functions (B). As illustrated at label A1, the update function assumes that the velocity is defined as units per second and simply moves the position of the point. The mouse editing support functions at B1 always set the point location. The set/get location functions (at label C1) are defined to support the definition of vertex position for the point. Notice the implementation of the `DrawPrimitive()` function (D1) and the collaboration with the superclass of the set attribute function (D2). These two functions are called when the `Draw()` method tries to draw a point.

Listing 7.11 shows that the `PrimitiveLine` class is similar to the `Primitive Point` class. The line class overrides the update (A) and mouse editing functions (B) and implements the set-up draw attribute and draw primitive functions (D). In this case, the line class has different vertex geometry accessing functions at label C for setting and getting the endpoints (defined at label E). The implementation of the `Update()` function at label A1 shows behavior similar to the point primitive, where in this case, both of the endpoints are moved (the entire line will move). The implementation of mouse editing functions at B1 shows that the `vertexID` can be used to encode the nth mouse click. In this case, during the first (`vertexID= 0`) mouse click, both of the points on the line are set. In subsequent mouse clicks, only the endpoint of the line is affected. As will be shown in the `CModel` implementation, this functionality allows us to always draw a line from the first mouse click position to the current mouse position for line editing. Lastly, the implementation of the attribute setting function at label D2 shows the line collaborating with the superclass and setting Gouraud shading attributes.

Listing 7.12 shows that the `PrimitiveCircle` class is similar to the point and line classes. In fact, all concrete subclasses of the `Primitive` class will have this similar structure. In this case, at label A1 we see that the `Update()` function moves the center of the circle. At label B1, once again we see that the `vertexID` is being treated as the nth mouse click, where we define the circle center and zero radius for the initial mouse click. For subsequent mouse clicks, we compute radius based on the distance between the mouse position and the center of the circle.

```cpp
class UWB_PrimitivePoint : public UWB_Primitive {
  public:
A:  virtual void Update(float elapsed_seconds);
B:  virtual void MouseDownVertex(int vertexID, float x, float y);
    virtual void MoveTo(float x, float y);
C:  void SetLocation(float x, float y, float z=0.0f);
    vec3 GetLocation() const;

  protected:
D:  void DrawPrimitive( eLevelOfDetail lod, UWB_DrawHelper& draw_helper ) const;
    void SetupDrawAttributes(UWB_DrawHelper& draw_helper) const;
E:  vec3 m_point; // for storing the vertex of the point
};
```

Source files.
uwbgl_PrimitivePoint1.h
/.cpp files in the *Common Files/ Primitives* subfolder of the UWBGL_D3D_Lib5 project.

```cpp
A1: void UWB_PrimitivePoint::Update(float elapsed_seconds)
        vec3 adjust_vec = m_velocity * elapsed_seconds;
        m_point += adjust_vec;
B1: void UWB_PrimitivePoint::MouseDownVertex(int vertexID, float x, float y) {
        SetLocation(x,y);
    }
    void UWB_PrimitivePoint::MoveTo(float x, float y) { SetLocation(x,y); }
C1: void UWB_PrimitivePoint::SetLocation(float x, float y, float z) {
        m_point = vec3(x,y,z);
    }
    vec3 UWB_PrimitivePoint::GetLocation() const { return m_point; }
    ⋮
D1: void UWB_PrimitivePoint::DrawPrimitive(eLevelOfDetail lod,
                                    UWB_DrawHelper& draw_helper) const
        draw_helper.DrawPoint(m_point);
D2: void UWB_PrimitivePoint::SetupDrawAttributes(UWB_DrawHelper& draw_helper) const
        // super class to set common attributes (color)
        __super::SetupDrawAttributes(draw_helper);
        // the only other attribute a point support
        draw_helper.SetPointSize(m_PointSize);
```

Listing 7.10. The UWB_PrimitivePoint class (Tutorial 7.2).

```
class UWB_PrimitiveLine : public UWB_Primitive {
  public:
A:  virtual void Update(float elapsed_seconds);
B:  virtual void MouseDownVertex(int vertexID, float x, float y);
    virtual void MoveTo(float x, float y);
C:  void SetStartPoint(float x, float y, float z=0.0f);
    vec3 GetStartPoint() const;
      ⋮
  protected:
D:  void DrawPrimitive( eLevelOfDetail lod, UWB_DrawHelper& draw_helper ) const;
    void SetupDrawAttributes(UWB_DrawHelper& draw_helper) const;
E:  vec3 m_start, m_end;   // the end points on the line
};
```

```
A1:  void UWB_PrimitiveLine::Update(float elapsed_seconds)
        vec3 adjust_vec = m_velocity * elapsed_seconds;
        m_start += adjust_vec;   m_end += adjust_vec;
B1:  void UWB_PrimitiveLine::MouseDownVertex(int vertexID, float x, float y)
        if(0 == vertexID) SetStartPoint(x,y);
        SetEndPoint(x,y);
     void UWB_PrimitiveLine::MoveTo(float x, float y) { SetEndPoint(x,y); }
      ⋮
D2:  void UWB_PrimitiveLine::SetupDrawAttributes(UWB_DrawHelper& draw_helper) const
        // super class to set color
        __super::SetupDrawAttributes(draw_helper);
        // set current shading mode, and
        draw_helper.SetShadeMode(m_ShadeMode);
        // set the shading color
        draw_helper.SetColor2(m_ShadingColor);
```

Source files.
uwbgl_PrimitiveLine1.h/cpp
files in the *Common Files/
Primitives* subfolder of the
UWBGL_D3D_Lib5 project.

Listing 7.11. The UWB_PrimitiveLine class (Tutorial 7.2).

```
class UWB_PrimitiveCircle : public UWB_Primitive {
  public:
A:  virtual void Update(float elapsed_seconds);
B:  virtual void MouseDownVertex(int vertexID, float x, float y);
    virtual void MoveTo(float x, float y);
```

Listing 7.12. The UWB_PrimitiveCircle class (Tutorial 7.2).

```
C:    void SetCenter(float x, float y, float z=0.0f);
      vec3 GetCenter() const;
      ⋮
    protected:
D:    void DrawPrimitive( eLevelOfDetail lod, UWB_DrawHelper& draw_helper ) const;
      void SetupDrawAttributes(UWB_DrawHelper& draw_helper) const;
E:    vec3 m_center; float m_radius;   // the end points on the line
    };
```

Source files.
uwbgl_PrimitiveCircle1.h
/.cpp files in the *Common
Files/Primitives* subfolder of
the UWBGL_D3D_Lib5 project.

```
A1:   void UWB_PrimitiveCircle::Update(float elapsed_seconds)
          vec3 adjust_vec = m_velocity * elapsed_seconds;
          m_center += adjust_vec;
B1:   void UWB_PrimitiveCircle::MouseDownVertex(int vertexID, float x, float y)
          if(0 == vertexID) // SetCenter(x,y); SetRadius(0);
          else  // compute radius from (x,y) to center and call SetRadius()
      void UWB_PrimitiveCircle::MoveTo(float x, float y) { SetCenter(x,y); }
      ⋮
```

Listing 7.12. (cont.)

The CModel **class.**   To support the primitive-editing functionality, we understand
that the application state must support instances of the point, line, and circle primitives. However, unlike in Tutorial 7.1 where we worked with three distinct objects
and therefore had to be constantly aware of which primitive was currently active,
in this case, with the support of the Primitive hierarchy, all primitives have identical public methods, and the application only need to work with the interface of
the Primitive class. Listing 7.13 shows the details of the CModel class. Let's
first examine the *private* representation at label F. Besides the peripheral support
information of world size, stopwatch, and draw helper, we see three instances of
concrete Primitives (point, line, and circle) and the m_pCurrentObject pointer
to the virtual Primitive class. The CModel class interacts with the controller via
this pointer exclusively, enforcing a uniform implementation for the editing of
all primitives. At labels A and A1, we see that CModel allows the setting of the
currently active primitive (by pointing the m_pCurrentObject pointer to the corresponding object). After setting the currently active primitive, labels B and B1
show that the implementation of the set/get attribute functions are simply mapped
to calling the corresponding primitive functions. Label C shows the declaration of
functions for editing the geometric information of the primitives. At label C1, we

see a direct mapping to public methods defined by the Primitive hierarchy. We observe the capability of a carefully designed object-oriented hierarchy where, based on the mouse-click-drag metaphor, we have designed two interface functions. Here we see that with the same two-function interface, we can create/edit three different types of primitives. At labels D and E are update and draw functions. It is expected that these two functions should be called more than real-time thresholds in each second (e.g., more than 20 times). In this case, at labels D1 and E1, we call the corresponding functions for the three primitives to accomplish the display of smooth motion.

Source files. Model.h/cpp files in the *Model* folder of the D3D_ObjectClasses project.

```
class CModel {
A: void SetCurrentTypeToPoint();
   void SetCurrentTypeToLine();

      ⋮

B: void SetShadeMode( eShadeMode mode );
   eShadeMode GetShadeMode();

      ⋮

C: void StartDefineGraphicsObject(float world_x, float world_y);
   void EndDefineGraphicsObject(float world_x, float world_y);
   void MoveGraphicsObject(float world_x, float world_y);
D: void UpdateSimulation();
E: void DrawModel();

   private:
F: float m_WorldWidth, m_WorldHeight; // size of the world
   UWB_Clock m_stop_watch;           // wall-clock elapses in between updates
   UWBD3D_DrawHelper m_DrawHelper;   // helper for D3D drawing

   UWB_Primitive* m_pCurrentObject; // pointer to primitive currently being edited
   UWB_PrimitiveCircle m_Circle;    // instance of circle
   UWB_PrimitivePoint m_Point;      //        line and
   UWB_PrimitiveLine m_Line;        //        point
};
```

Listing 7.13. The CModel class of Tutorial 7.2.

```
A1:   void CModel::SetCurrentTypeToPoint() { m_pCurrentObject = &m_Point; }
      void CModel::SetCurrentTypeToLine() {  m_pCurrentObject = &m_Line; }
      ⋮

B1:   void CModel::SetShadeMode( eShadeMode mode ) { m_pCurrentObject->SetShadeMode(mode); }
      eShadeMode CModel::GetShadeMode() { return m_pCurrentObject->GetShadeMode(); }
      ⋮

C1:   void CModel::StartDefineGraphicsObject(float world_x, float world_y)
          m_pCurrentObject->MouseDownVertex(0, world_x, world_y);
          m_pCurrentObject->SetVelocity(vec3(0,0,0));
      void CModel::EndDefineGraphicsObject(float world_x, float world_y)
          m_pCurrentObject->MouseDownVertex(1, world_x, world_y);
      void CModel::MoveGraphicsObject(float world_x, float world_y)
          m_pCurrentObject->MoveTo(world_x, world_y);

D1:   void CModel::UpdateSimulation()

          ⋮ // Check for boundary conditions to bounce the primitives by negating velocities
          float elapsed_seconds = m_stop_watch.GetSecondsElapsed();
          m_Point.Update(elapsed_seconds);

          ⋮ // calls m_Circle and m_Line Update(elapsed_seconds);
E1:   void CModel::DrawModel()
          // calls m_Circle, m_Point and m_Line.Draw() function
```

Listing 7.13. (cont.)

The `CDrawAndMouseHandler` **class.**   Listing 7.14 shows the mouse event service routines for the view/controller pair (`CDrawAndMouseHandler`) where the left and right mouse button events are mapped directly to the `CModel` editing functionality.

```
void CDrawAndMouseHandler::OnMouseButton(bool down, unsigned int nFlags, int hwX, int hwY)
    // Hardware to device transform
    HardwareToDevice(hwX, hwY, deviceX, deviceY);
    if(nFlags & MK_LBUTTON)
        if(down) // LMB down event
            theApp.GetModel().StartDefineGraphicsObject(...);
        else    // LBM Up event
            theApp.GetModel().PlaceGraphicsObjectInMotion();
```

Source file.
`DrawAndMouseHandler.cpp` file in the *WindowHandler* folder of the `D3D_ObjectClasses` project.

Listing 7.14. Mouse event services (`CDrawAndMoseHandler` Tutorial 7.2).

```
else if(nFlags & MK_RBUTTON)
    if(down) // RMB down event
        theApp.GetModel().MoveGraphicsObject(...);

void CDrawAndMouseHandler::OnMouseMove(unsigned int nFlags, int hwX, int hwY)
    // Hardware to device transform
    HardwareToDevice(hwX, hwY, deviceX, deviceY);
    if(nFlags & MK_LBUTTON)
        // LMB drag event
        theApp.GetModel().EndDefineGraphicsObject(...);
    else if(nFlags & MK_RBUTTON)
        // RMB drag event
        theApp.GetModel().MoveGraphicsObject(...);
```

Listing 7.14. (cont.)

7.5 Collisions of Primitives

We have presented a primitive hierarchy with an interface that supports uniform interactions with different primitive types. From Tutorial 7.2, we have experienced that it is straightforward to work with the hierarchy to create/edit different primitives with the same set of mouse-click events. We have also seen that the Primitive base class supports all attributes (e.g., color, fill mode) that affect the appearance of the primitives. The velocity attribute is different from the rest because this attribute affects the physical behavior instead of the appearance of the primitive. In this section, we examine one other physical behavior of primitives: collision. In a complex library system, physical behavior should be defined as a separate hierarchy that collaborates with the primitive hierarchy. In the interests of learning graphics without extensively studying the physical behavior of objects, we will only work with two physical behaviors in our primitive class: velocity and collision. We have already seen the straightforward effects of velocity, and in this section, we will examine collision between primitives.

To detect collision between two primitives, we need to compute if the primitives overlap in space. Note that detecting overlapping in space is different from intersecting primitives. For example, we have experience with detecting circle collision mathematically in the ball-shooting program, where we compared the distance between the centers of two circles with the sum of their radii. This is very different from mathematically intersecting the two circles by computing the roots to the quadratic functions. In general, when working with many primitive types, there are two major challenges to detecting collisions based on mathematics.

- **Tedious mathematics**. The mathematics of determining if two different geometric shapes occupy the same space can be tedious, and the implementation can be complex (e.g., between a triangle and a rectangle). Often, the mathematics can deteriorate into intersecting edges of the primitives. In addition, to successfully participate in collision computation, every geometric shape must know how to collide with every other supported geometric shape (e.g., circle against line, point, triangle, rectangle; line against point, triangle, rectangle). In general, to support n different types of primitives, we would need to implement $O(n^2)$ collision routines! For example, to properly support collision between our point, line, and circle primitives, we must define 3 collision routines. If we wish to introduce a new primitive type (e.g., triangle) we must implement additional three new collision routines, i.e., triangle against circle, line, and point!

- **Complex invocation**. At run time, based on the participating primitives in a collision, we must determine which of the n^2 routines to invoke!

For these reasons, interactive graphics applications typically do not support true collision between objects. Instead, simpler geometric shapes, referred to as bounding volumes, are defined to bound the primitives. During a collision process, instead of intersecting the actual primitives, application programs compute the intersection of the corresponding bounding volumes. A collision is deemed successful when the bounding volumes of two primitives overlap in space. For example, if we choose to use circles as the bounding volume primitive, then we would bound a circle around a primitive by computing a center and a radius such that the primitive is entirely within the circle. In this case, if we wish to compute the collision between two triangles, we would compute the collision between the bounding circles of the two triangles.

In general, bounding volumes can be any geometric shape or shapes. For example, circles (2D), spheres (3D), boxes, and so on. When choosing the shape for bounding volumes, we should pay attention to the following.

- **Simplicity**. The bounding volume must be simple to compute. The bounding volumes are typically computed during run time to approximate the primitives. We cannot afford excessive computation when determining the values for the bounding volume. In addition, it should be straightforward to determine if two bounding volumes occupy the same space. After all, mathematic simplicity is one of the main reasons for working with bounding volumes.

Void space. Spaces that are inside the bounding volume but outside of the actual primitive.

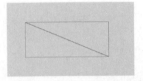

Figure 7.9. Bounding a line with a bounding box.

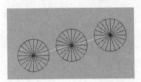

Figure 7.10. Bounding a line with three bounding circles.

• **Tightness of bound**. A bounding volume should closely represent the space that is occupied by the actual primitive.

Directly related to these are the characteristics of collision with bounding volumes.

• **Approximation**. Bounding volumes can only approximate the bounds of a primitive. For example, Figure 7.9 shows an example of bounding a line primitive with a box, and Figure 7.10 shows bounding a line with three circles. Notice that in both cases, there are relatively large *void spaces*. In general, bounding volume collision tests can only approximate collision results. In Figure 7.9, a collision would be considered successful when the bounding volume of another primitive is within the bound of the box. Whereas in the Figure 7.10, a successful collision happens when overlap occurs with any of the three bounding circles. Notice that in Figure 7.10, because there are gaps between the bounding circles, it is actually possible to intersect with the line primitive without causing a successful collision!

• **Collision point.** The collision result is a boolean true or false. Since the collision result is approximated, the bounding volume cannot pinpoint the position where a collision would occur.

Tutorial 7.3. Collision Support

Tutorial 7.3.
Project Name:
  D3D_Collisions
Library Support:
  UWBGL_MFC_Lib1
  UWBGL_D3D_Lib6

• **Goals.** Get experience with programming bounding volumes for graphics primitives; understand approaches to approximating primitive collisions;

• **Approach.** Using a bounding box as an example, study an implementation and an approach to integrate bounding volumes into our primitive hierarchy.

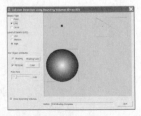

Figure 7.11. Tutorial 7.3.

Figure 7.11 is a screenshot of running Tutorial 7.3. This tutorial extends Tutorial 7.2, where in addition to creating/editing primitives with motion, the primitives are capable of colliding with each other and reacting with some defined behaviors. In this case, primitives react to collision by moving away from each other. Once again, we will study this tutorial by first examining the library support, and then we will look at how the library functionality is applied in the project.

UWBGL_D3D_Lib6

Change summary. See p. 516 for a summary of changes to the library.

In this library, we introduce the UWB_BoundingVolume class to support bounding volume collision computation. When compared to UWBGL_D3D_Lib5, there are two changes.

1. *Bounding Volumes* **folder.** A new subfolder is created in the *Common Files* folder. There are two new source files in this folder, uwbgl_Intersect1.h /cpp, which define and implement the UWB_BoundingVolume functionality.

2. Primitive **hierarchy.** All files in the Primitive hierarchy are updated to support the new collision functionality.

The BoundingVolume **class.** As in the case of Primitive hierarchy, the bounding volume abstraction also has a pure virtual base class. Label A in Listing 7.15 shows that a UWB_BoundingVolume object must know what type of bounding volume it is (e.g., a bounding sphere or a bounding box). At label B are the general behaviors. Notice that the Intersects() function can only return a true/false status. This function answers the bounding volume overlap-in-space question without any intersection details. The Add() function allows the bounding volume to grow by inserting additional volumes. The Draw() function at label C allows the drawing of the bounding volumes. As we will see, this is a useful option for debugging.

Source files.
uwbgl_Intersect1.h/cpp files in the *Common Files/ Bounding Volumes* subfolder of the UWBGL_D3D_Lib6 project.

```
class UWB_BoundingVolume {
    // types of bounding volume
A:  enum volume_type { box, sphere};
    // subclass returns the appropriate from above
    virtual volume_type GetType() const = 0;
    virtual vec3 GetCenter() const = 0;
B:  virtual bool Intersects(const UWB_BoundingVolume& other) const = 0;
    // subclass returns the appropriate from above
    virtual ContainsPoint(vec3) const = 0;
    virtual void Add(const UWB_BoundingVolume* pBV) const = 0;
C:  virtual void Draw(UWB_DrawHelper* pDrawHelper) const{}
};
```

Listing 7.15. The UWB_BoundingVolume class (Tutorial 7.3).

Source files.
uwbgl_Intersect1.h/cpp
files in the *Common Files
/BoundingVolumes* subfolder
of the UWBGL_D3D_Lib6
project. Notice that in this
case the UWB_BoundingBox
class is also defined/im-
plemented in the uwbgl_
Intersect1.h/cpp files.

```
class UWB_BoundingBox : public UWB_BoundingVolume {
A:  volume_type GetType() const {return box;}
    vec3 GetMin() const {return m_min;}
    :
B:  void SetCorners(vec3 corner1, vec3 corner2);
    :
C:  bool Intersects(const UWB_BoundingVolume& other) const;
    bool ContainsPoint(vec3 location) const;
    :
D:  void Draw(UWB_DrawHelper* pDrawHelper) const;

  private:
E:  vec3 m_min, m_max;
};
```

Listing 7.16. The UWB_BoundingBox class (Tutorial 7.3).

Listing 7.16 shows that UWB_BoundingBox subclasses from the UWB_Bounding Volume class. We see that besides implementing all the pure virtual functions defined in the base class, additional information-accessing functions are defined at label A, and information-setting functions are defined at label B. At label E, we see that a bounding box is represented internally by the max and min positions.

Primitive collision response support. With the UWB_BoundingBox class support, all primitives that know how to set the min/max bounds can participate in colliding with other primitives. Listing 7.17 shows the modification of the Primitive base class to support collisions. Listing 7.18 shows that to collide two primitives, we first determine if their bounding volumes overlap, and if so, we call the CollisionResponse() functions to allow the primitives to update their behavior as a result of successful collision. Subclasses from the Primitive class are responsible for defining the actual bounding volume. However, the Primitive base class does define simple behavior for CollisionResponse(). Listing 7.19 shows that by default, primitives respond to a collision by traveling at the same speed but away from the colliding primitive. In this version of the D3D library, all concrete primitive classes (point, line, circle) implement the UWB_BoundingBox as their bounding volume.

```
class UWB_Primitive {
    // exactly the same as Listing 7.9...
    // except the following three additional functions
    ⋮
    // Collision Detection / Response
    virtual const UWB_BoundingVolume* GetBoundingVolume( eLevelOfDetail lod ) const;
    virtual void CollisionResponse(const UWB_Primitive* pOther, vec3 other_location);
    void DrawBoundingVolume( eLevelOfDetail lod, UWB_DrawHelper* pRenderer,
                             UWB_Color color ) const;
};
```

Source file.
uwbgl_Primitive2.h file in the *Common Files/Primitives* subfolder of the UWBGL_D3D_Lib6 project.

Listing 7.17. The UWB_Primitive class (Tutorial 7.3).

```
// assume ... pPrimA and pPrimB are pointers to Primitives
// Get the bounding volume from pPrimA
UWB_BoundingVolume *pBVA = pPrimA->GetBoundingVolume();
// Get the bounding volume from pPrimB
UWB_BoundingVolume *pBVB = pPrimB->GetBoundingVolume();

// Test if the two bounding volumes overlaps
if ( pBVA->Intersects(pBVB) ) {
    // pPrimA responses to the collision
    pPrimA->CollisionResponse( pPrimB, pPrimB->GetLocation() );
    // pPrimB responses to the collision
    pPrimB->CollisionResponse( pPrimA, pPrimA->GetLocation() );
}
⋮
```

Source file.
Sample code for working with bounding volumes and primitive collision response. No source file.

Listing 7.18. Working with the Primitive collision interface (Tutorial 7.3).

```
void UWB_Primitive::CollisionResponse(const UWB_Primitive* pOther, vec3 other_location) {
    // vector points from the other_location towards the primitive
    dir = GetLocation() - other_location;
    // direction pointing away from other_location
    dir = normalize(dir);
    // speed of the current velocity
    mySpeed = length(GetVelocity());
    // new velocity is the same speed, but away from other_location
    SetVelocity(mySpeed * dir);
}
```

Source file.
uwbgl_Primitive2.cpp file in the *Common Files/Primitives* subfolder of the UWBGL_D3D_Lib6 project.

Listing 7.19. The default primitive CollisionResponse() function (Tutorial 7.3).

```
void CModel::UpdateSimulation() {
    ⋮
    // check if primitive is going out of world bound

    // Get the bounding volumes ready for collision detection
    const UWB_BoundingVolume* pCircleBV = m_Circle.GetBoundingVolume(lod);
    const UWB_BoundingVolume* pPointBV  = m_Point.GetBoundingVolume(lod);
    const UWB_BoundingVolume* pLineBV   = m_Line.GetBoundingVolume(lod);
    ⋮

    // Colliding circle and point
    if(pCircleBV && pPointBV && pCircleBV->Intersects(*pPointBV))
        m_Circle.CollisionResponse(&m_Point, ptLoc);  // circle to response
        m_Point.CollisionResponse(&m_Circle, cirLoc); // point to response
    // Colliding circle and line
    if(pCircleBV && pLineBV && pCircleBV->Intersects(*pLineBV)) ...
    // Colliding line and point
    if(pPointBV && pLineBV && pPointBV->Intersects(*pLineBV)) ...
    ⋮
    // update the position of each object
```

Source file.
Model.cpp   file   in   the
Model   folder   of   the
D3D_Collisions project.

Listing 7.20. The CModel::UpdateSimulation() function (Tutorial 7.3).

Working with the collision functionality.   With the collision functionality supported by the library, the source code of Tutorial 7.3 differs from that of Tutorial 7.2 only in the CModel::UpdateSimulation() function. Listing 7.20 shows that during periodic timer updates, we must intersect all primitive objects against each other to ensure that we have tested all the potential collisions.

7.6   Collection of Primitives

Tutorial 7.4.
Project Name:
   D3D_ObjectCollections
Library Support:
   UWBGL_MFC_Lib1
   UWBGL_D3D_Lib7

From Listing 7.20, it is obvious that we need some form of collection structure such that we can use a loop programming construct to iterate through each primitive to test for the collision between all the primitives.

Tutorial 7.4. Primitive List

- **Goals.**   To introduce the idea of having a collection structure itself be a Primitive; experience working with such structures.

- **Approach.** To introduce the `PrimitiveList` class, a `Primitive` subclass that has a collection of `Primitive` references; examine how to work with this class.

Figure 7.12 is a screenshot of running Tutorial 7.4. This tutorial extends Tutorial 7.3 by supporting the creation of any number of point, line, and circle primitives with motion and by supporting the collision between these primitives.

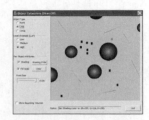

Figure 7.12. Tutorial 7.4.

UWBGL_D3D_Lib7

When we examine the supporting library for this tutorial, we see that only two files are added to the *Common Files/Primitives* subfolder: uwbgl_Primitive List.h/cpp. These two files implement the `UWB_PrimitiveList` class. Listing 7.21 shows that `UWB_PrimitiveList` is a subclass of the `Primitive` class. At label D, we notice that this class has an array of references to `Primitive`. With the corresponding interface methods at label B, this class can behave just like a linked list of `Primitive` pointers. The functions defined at label A ensure the update of all primitives in the list when appropriate and proper support of collision functionality. The overrides at label C ensure that all primitives in this list can be drawn when the `Primitive::Draw()` function is called.

Change summary. See p. 517 for a summary of changes to the library.

```
class UWB_PrimitiveList : public UWB_Primitive {
A:   virtual void Update(float elapsed_seconds);
     virtual const UWB_BoundingVolume* GetBoundingVolume( eLevelOfDetail lod ) const;
     void DrawChildBoundingVolumes(... UWB_DrawHelper*, UWB_Color color) const;
B:   int Count() const;
     UWB_Primitive* PrimitiveAt(int index);
     void Append(UWB_Primitive* pPrimitive);
     void DeletePrimitiveAt(int index);
   protected:
        ⋮
C:   virtual void DrawPrimitive( eLevelOfDetail lod, UWB_DrawHelper& draw_helper ) const;
     virtual void SetupDrawAttributes(UWB_DrawHelper& draw_helper) const;
D:   UWB_PointerArray<UWB_Primitive*> m_list;
     UWB_BoundingBox m_bounds;       // union of all primitive bounds
};
```

Source file. uwbgl_PrimitiveList1.h file in the *Common Files/ Primitives* subfolder of the UWBGL_D3D_Lib7 project.

Listing 7.21. The `UWB_PrimitiveList` class (Tutorial 7.4).

Working with the primitive list.   To support an unlimited number of primitives in the world, the CModel class is modified from previous tutorials. Listing 7.22 shows that the CModel has an instance of the PrimitiveList class. From previous tutorials, we have already seen working through the m_pCurrentObject pointer for editing/creating different types of primitive objects. In this case, a new primitive is created each time StartDefineGraphicsObject() is called, whereas at the end of primitive creation, when the left mouse button releases, the EndDefineGraphicsObject() will insert the newly created primitive into the m_AllPrimitives list. Listing 7.23 shows that updating the model involves three steps. At label A, we loop through each primitive in the m_AllPrimitives list and delete those that are outside of the world bound. At label B is a nested loop where we collide each primitive with all other primitives. Finally at label C, we update all the primitives. Listing 7.23 also shows that to draw all the primitives, we can simply call the list's Draw() function.

Examining this tutorial closer, we realize that its behavior is similar to that of the ball-shooting program, where instead of colliding balls only, this program supports colliding any primitive type.

Source file.   Model.h file in the *Model* folder of the D3D_ObjectCollections project.

```
class CModel {
    ⋮
    // similar to previous tutorials (e.g. Listing 7.13).
    void StartDefineGraphicsObject(float world_x, float world_y);
    void EndDefineGraphicsObject(float world_x, float world_y);
    ⋮

private:
    ⋮
    UWB_Primitive* m_pCurrentObject;   // currently editing primitive
    UWB_PrimitiveList m_AllPrimitives; // list of all the created primitives
};
```

Listing 7.22. The CModel class (Tutorial 7.4).

```
void CModel::UpdateSimulation()
A:  for(int i=count-1; i>=0; i--)
        const UWB_Primitive* pPrimitive = m_AllPrimitives.PrimitiveAt(i);
        const UWB_BoundingVolume* pBV = pPrimitive->GetBoundingVolume(lod);
        if(!pBV->Intersects(m_WorldBounds)) m_AllPrimitives.DeletePrimitiveAt(i);
```

Listing 7.23. The CModel implementation (Tutorial 7.4).

```
B:  for(int i=0; i<count; i++)
        UWB_Primitive* pTestPrimitive = m_AllPrimitives.PrimitiveAt(i);
        const UWB_BoundingVolume* pTestBV = pTestPrimitive->GetBoundingVolume(lod);
        for(int j=i+1; j<count; j++)
            UWB_Primitive* pOtherPrimitive = m_AllPrimitives.PrimitiveAt(j);
            const UWB_BoundingVolume* pOtherBV = pOtherPrimitive->GetBoundingVolume(lod);
            if(pOtherBV && pTestBV->Intersects(*pOtherBV))
                pTestPrimitive->CollisionResponse(pOtherPrimitive, pOtherBV->GetCenter());
                pOtherPrimitive->CollisionResponse(pTestPrimitive, pTestBV->GetCenter());
C:  m_AllPrimitives.Update(elapsed_seconds);
    ⋮

void CModel::DrawModel()
    m_AllPrimitives.Draw( lod, m_DrawHelper );
    if(m_bShowBoundingVolumes)
        m_AllPrimitives.DrawChildBoundingVolumes(lod, &m_DrawHelper, color);
```

Source file. Model.cpp file in the *Model* folder of the D3D_ObjectCollections project.

Listing 7.24. (cont.)

Tutorial 7.5. Re-implementing the Ball-Shooting Program

Figure 7.13 is a screenshot of running Tutorial 7.5. This tutorial re-implements the ball-shooting program based on the new library (UWB_D3D_Lib7). We modify Tutorial 7.4 such that the GUI front end resembles that of the ball-shooting program, and in this case we only support the creation of the CBall (a subclass of PrimitiveCircle) primitive type. The CModel of the source code is very similar to Tutorial 7.4. When comparing the core implementation of our application state (CModel) to that from Tutorial 5.6, we see a more general solution (we can support shooting/colliding of any primitives) with fewer details (all collisions and mathematics are hidden in class implementations).

Tutorial 7.5.
Project Name:
    D3D_BallShoot2
Library Support:
    UWBGL_MFC_Lib1
    UWBGL_D3D_Lib7

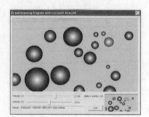

Figure 7.13.   Tutorial 7.5.

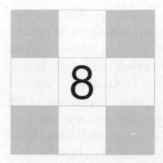

8

Transformation Operators

This chapter presents the fundamentals of the transformation operators used in computer graphics. This chapter:

- presents the row vector to represent vertex positions, the matrix to represent transformation operators;

- explains in details the translation, scaling, and rotation transformation operators;

- reviews the simple mathematics regarding vectors and matrices;

- demonstrates how to program transformation operators with modern graphics API.

After this chapter we should:

- understand the effects of the basic transformation operators;

- be ready to examine how to combine transformation operators to accomplish more complex effects.

In addition, with respect to hands-on programming, we should:

- have insights into the matrix processors of the graphics APIs;

- be able to use the matrix processors to accomplish simple transformation operations.

One simple way to describe an interactive computer graphics application is that it is a program that allows the user to interactively manipulate geometric objects. Indeed, as we have experience from the ball-shooting program, where we create balls of different sizes (scales) and watch them fall (move) under the influence of gravity. Here we see that by "manipulate," we mean move, scale, rotate, and so on. In computer graphics, we refer to these manipulation operations as the transformation operations. It is interesting that in this entire book, we only work with three different transformation operators: *translate*, *scale*, and *rotate*. These three basic operators are sufficient for most real-world complex graphical environments. Even more remarkable is the fact that these three operators are very simple and that they operate on points. In this chapter, we introduce the mathematical tools borrowed from linear algebra to help us describe these operators.

In this book, we are not interested in the general theories behind the transformation operators. We will not present the general theories nor any proof associated with the tools we learn. We are only interested in learning the facts and experiencing how to apply these facts in computer graphics applications. Readers interested in the theories behind the materials presented in this chapter should consult an introductory linear algebra textbook.

In our discussion, we express all coordinate values in two dimensions. For example, a vertex position

$$V = (x, y),$$

is expressed as a vector:

$$\mathbf{V} = \begin{bmatrix} x\, y \end{bmatrix}.$$

For simplicity, the third dimension of $z = 0$ is left out. Although all our examples are given in two dimensions, the results we derive are generally applicable in three dimensions. At the end of the discussion for each transformation operator, we present a brief discussion on how to generalize our results to the third dimension.

Vector representation.

$$\mathbf{V} = \begin{bmatrix} x\, y \end{bmatrix}$$

represents the vertex position $V = (x, y)$ by the *vector* $\mathbf{V}$. As will be discussed in Section 8.5, this representation supports convenient mathematics operations for transformation of vertex positions.

8.1   The Translation Operator

Translation means moving. The translation operator:

$$\mathbf{T}(t_x, t_y)$$

moves a point V_a from

$$\mathbf{V}_a = \begin{bmatrix} x_a\, y_a \end{bmatrix}$$

to a new position V_{at}:

$$\begin{aligned} \mathbf{V}_{at} &= \begin{bmatrix} x_{at}\, y_{at} \end{bmatrix} \\ &= \begin{bmatrix} x_a + t_x\ y_a + t_y \end{bmatrix}, \end{aligned}$$

where t_x and t_y are the displacements in the x-axis and y-axis directions, respectively. We represent this operation as

$$\mathbf{V}_{at} = \mathbf{V}_a \, \mathbf{T}(t_x, t_y).$$

In this case, the translate operator process V_a to generate V_{at}. We refer to V_a as the *input* (point) to the operator and V_{at} as the *output* of the operator. Figure 8.1 shows an example of the translation operator with $t_x = 5$ and $t_y = -3$, or

$$\mathbf{T}(t_x, t_y) = \mathbf{T}(5, -3)$$

operating on the point V_a

$$\mathbf{V}_a = \begin{bmatrix} x_a \, y_a \end{bmatrix} = \begin{bmatrix} 3 \, 7 \end{bmatrix}$$

and *moving* the point to the new position V_{at} at:

$$\begin{aligned}
\mathbf{V}_{at} &= \begin{bmatrix} x_{at} \, y_{at} \end{bmatrix} \\
&= \mathbf{V}_a \, \mathbf{T}(t_x, t_y) \\
&= \begin{bmatrix} x_a + t_x \, y_a + t_y \end{bmatrix} \\
&= \begin{bmatrix} 3 + 5 \, 7 - 3 \end{bmatrix} \\
&= \begin{bmatrix} 8 \, 4 \end{bmatrix}.
\end{aligned}$$

As we can see from this example, a positive displacement moves a point in the positive direction along the corresponding axis. For example, from Figure 8.1 we see that a positive t_x moves the point in the positive x-axis (right) direction from $x = 3$ to $x = 8$. The negative t_y value moves the point's y in the negative y-axis (down) from $y = 7$ to $y = 4$.

Notice that the translation operator moves a point relative to its initial position and that this operation is independent from any other points. This means that we can apply the same translation operator to any number of points and the results of the operation on each point will be independent from the other points. Figure 8.2 shows that we can apply the same $\mathbf{T}(5, -3)$ operator to the point

$$\mathbf{V}_c = \begin{bmatrix} x_c \, y_c \end{bmatrix} = \begin{bmatrix} 1 \, 4 \end{bmatrix},$$

and the results of the translation would, as expected, be

$$\begin{aligned}
\mathbf{V}_{ct} &= \begin{bmatrix} x_{ct} \, y_{ct} \end{bmatrix} \\
&= \mathbf{V}_c \, \mathbf{T}(5, -3) \\
&= \begin{bmatrix} x_c + t_x \, y_c + t_y \end{bmatrix} \\
&= \begin{bmatrix} 1 + 5 \, 4 - 3 \end{bmatrix} \\
&= \begin{bmatrix} 6 \, 1 \end{bmatrix}.
\end{aligned}$$

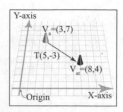

Figure 8.1. The translation operator.

Implied parameters. The parameters for the displacement, (t_x, t_y), are an integral part of the translation operator. For simplicity and readability, these parameters are often left out and are implied in expressions. For example,

$$\mathbf{V}_{at} = \mathbf{V}_a \, \mathbf{T}(t_x, t_y)$$

may be written as

$$\mathbf{V}_{at} = \mathbf{V}_a \, \mathbf{T}.$$

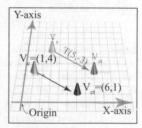

Figure 8.2. Translating two points with the $T(5, -3)$ operator.

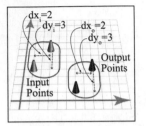

Figure 8.3. Relative distances between input and output points.

Figure 8.3 shows that if we examine the relative distances between the two input points (i.e., V_a and V_c), we see that the distance in the x-direction is dx_i:

$$dx_i = |x_c - x_a| = |1 - 3| = |-2| = 2,$$

whereas the distance in the y-direction is dy_i:

$$dy_i = |y_c - y_a| = |4 - 7| = |-3| = 3.$$

When we compare these distances to that from the output points (i.e., V_{at} and V_{ct}) dx_o and dy_o:

$$dx_o = |x_{ct} - x_{at}| = |6 - 8| = |-2| = 2,$$
$$dy_o = |y_{ct} - y_{at}| = |1 - 4| = |-3| = 3.$$

We observe that

$$dx_o = dx_i,$$
$$dy_o = dy_i.$$

Translation operator. Maintains the shape, size, and orientation of an object.

This observation should not be surprising because the translate operator offsets *all* input points by the same displacements and thus should not alter the relative distances between the input and output positions. In general, if input vertices to a translation operator are from a geometric shape (e.g., a triangle), then the results of the translate operation would be a displaced triangle with the exact same dimensions (edge lengths) and orientation. Figure 8.4 shows the effect of applying the $\mathbf{T}(5,-3)$ translation operator on four vertices that form a rectangle:

Edges. Describe the *adjacency* between vertices. For example, in Figure 8.4, vertex V_a is adjacent to V_b and V_c. In this case, we say $\overline{V_a V_b}$ is an edge and $\overline{V_a V_c}$ is another edge.

Direction of edges. If we treat an edge as a vector connecting two vertices, then each edge has a unique direction.

Angles between edges. These are angles between connecting edges. For example, in Figure 8.4, $\angle V_a V_b V_c$ is a 90-degree angle.

$$\text{Input points}: \begin{cases} V_a = & (3,7), \\ V_b = & (1,7), \\ V_c = & (1,4), \\ V_d = & (3,4). \end{cases}$$

We see that applying the $\mathbf{T}(5,-3)$ operator on the input points

$$\begin{aligned} \mathbf{V}_{at} &= \mathbf{V}_a\,\mathbf{T}(5,-3), \\ \mathbf{V}_{bt} &= \mathbf{V}_b\,\mathbf{T}(5,-3), \\ \mathbf{V}_{ct} &= \mathbf{V}_c\,\mathbf{T}(5,-3), \\ \mathbf{V}_{dt} &= \mathbf{V}_d\,\mathbf{T}(5,-3) \end{aligned}$$

results in

$$\text{Output points}: \begin{cases} V_{at} = & (8,4), \\ V_{bt} = & (6,1), \\ V_{ct} = & (6,4), \\ V_{dt} = & (8,1). \end{cases}$$

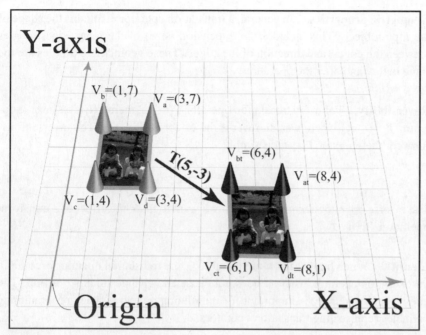

Figure 8.4. The translation operator.

As expected, the output points form the exact same geometric shape with the exact same dimensions. Now, if the four input positions (V_a, V_b, V_c, V_d) are the vertices of an object (e.g., a rectangular photograph), then the operations of Figure 8.4 would *translate* (or move) the photograph to the location defined by the output positions $(V_{at}, V_{bt}, V_{ct}, V_{dt})$.

Summary of the Translation Operator

Order of operations. In general, for *all transformation operators*, the order of operations is important. For example,

$$V_a \, T(t_x, t_y)$$

is different from

$$T(t_x, t_y) \, V_a.$$

In fact, as will be discussed in Section 8.5,

$$T(t_x, t_y) \, V_a$$

is an undefined operation.

Geometric properties. In general, a translation operator maintains the shape of the input object. This includes the dimension (size) of the input edges, angles between the edges, and direction of the edges. These geometric attributes are the same before and after the operation.

Reversibility. For every translation operator $\mathbf{T}(t_x, t_y)$, there exists an inverse operator $\mathbf{T}^{-1}(t_x, t_y)$ where we can reverse the effect of $\mathbf{T}(t_x, t_y)$. The inverse transform for the operator $\mathbf{T}(t_x, t_y)$ is simply

$$\mathbf{T}^{-1}(t_x, t_y) = \mathbf{T}(-t_x, -t_y).$$

The inverse operator is important when we want to *undo* the effect of a transform operation.

Identity. When both t_x and t_y are equal to 0, the translation operator becomes a no-operation operator, where it does not cause any changes to any position. The knowledge of identity is important for initializing operators when programming variables representing translation operators.

Extension to 3D. All of our discussions are valid in the third dimension, and we can extend our results in a straightforward manner by simply including a third parameter t_z:

$$\mathbf{T}(t_x, t_y, t_z),$$

where the t_z parameter describes the displacement in the z-axis direction.

8.2   The Scaling Operator

Scaling means change of size. The scaling operator

$$\mathbf{S}(s_x, s_y)$$

scales a point V_a from

$$V_a = \begin{bmatrix} x_a & y_a \end{bmatrix}$$

to a new position V_{as}:

$$
\begin{aligned}
V_{as} &= \begin{bmatrix} x_{as} & y_{as} \end{bmatrix} \\
&= \begin{bmatrix} x_a \times s_x & y_a \times s_y \end{bmatrix},
\end{aligned}
$$

Implied parameters. As in translation operators, and in general for all transform operators for simplicity and readability, the scaling factor parameters, (s_x, s_y), are often left out and are implied in expressions. For example,

$$V_{as} = V_a \, \mathbf{S}(s_x, s_y)$$

may be written as:

$$V_{as} = V_a \, \mathbf{S}.$$

where s_x and s_y are the factors of scaling in the x-axis and y-axis directions, respectively. We represent this scaling operation as

$$\mathbf{V}_{as} = \mathbf{V}_a\,\mathbf{S}(s_x, s_y) = \mathbf{V}_a\,\mathbf{S}.$$

Figure 8.5 shows an example where the scaling operator has scale factors of $s_x = 3$ and $s_y = 0.5$, or

$$\mathbf{S}(s_x, s_y) = \mathbf{S}(3, 0.5),$$

operating on the point V_a:

$$\mathbf{V}_a = \begin{bmatrix} x_a\ y_a \end{bmatrix} = \begin{bmatrix} 3\ 8 \end{bmatrix}$$

and *resizing* the point to the new position V_{as}:

$$\begin{aligned}
\mathbf{V}_{as} &= \begin{bmatrix} x_{as}\ y_{as} \end{bmatrix} \\
&= \mathbf{V}_a\,\mathbf{S}(s_x, s_y) \\
&= \begin{bmatrix} x_a \times s_x\ y_a \times s_y \end{bmatrix} \\
&= \begin{bmatrix} 3 \times 3\ 8 \times 0.5 \end{bmatrix} \\
&= \begin{bmatrix} 9\ 4 \end{bmatrix}.
\end{aligned}$$

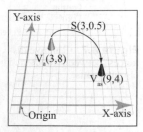

Figure 8.5. The scale operator.

Notice that we can work with the x and the y scaling factors independently: the amount of size change in the x-axis direction is defined solely by the s_x parameter and is unrelated to s_y in any way. Typically, scaling factors are positive floating-point numbers. A scaling factor greater than 1.0 has the effect of *stretching* a point in the positive direction of the corresponding axis, whereas a factor less than 1.0 has the effect of compressing a point toward the origin. From Figure 8.5, we see that $s_x = 3$ stretches x_a (the x-component of V_a) from $x = 3$ to $x = 9$, whereas $s_y = 0.5$ compresses y_a from $y = 8$ to $y = 4$. Scaling factors of $\mathbf{S}(0, 0)$ will push *all* input points to the origin. As in the case of the translation operator, the scaling operator repositions a point relative to the point's initial position, and this operation is independent of any other points.

As we saw in the case of translation, this property allows us to apply the same operator on any number of points. Figure 8.6 shows that we can apply the same $\mathbf{S}(3, 0.5)$ operator on the point V_c:

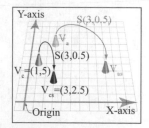

Figure 8.6. Scaling two points with $\mathbf{S}(3, 0.5)$.

$$\mathbf{V}_c = \begin{bmatrix} x_c\ y_c \end{bmatrix} = \begin{bmatrix} 1\ 5 \end{bmatrix},$$

and the results of the resizing would, as expected, be V_{cs}:

$$\begin{aligned}
\mathbf{V}_{cs} &= \begin{bmatrix} x_{cs} \; y_{cs} \end{bmatrix} \\
&= \mathbf{V}_c \, \mathbf{S}(3,0.5) \\
&= \begin{bmatrix} x_c \times s_x \; y_c \times s_y \end{bmatrix} \\
&= \begin{bmatrix} 1 \times 3 \; 5 \times 0.5 \end{bmatrix} \\
&= \begin{bmatrix} 3 \; 2.5 \end{bmatrix}.
\end{aligned}$$

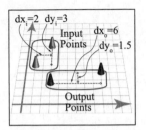

Figure 8.7. Relative distances between input and output points.

Figure 8.7 shows that if we examine the relative distances between the two input points (i.e., $\mathbf{V}_a$ and $\mathbf{V}_c$), we see that the distance in the x-direction is dx_i:

$$dx_i = |x_c - x_a| = |1 - 3| = |-2| = 2,$$

whereas the distance in the y-direction is dy_i:

$$dy_i = |y_c - y_a| = |5 - 8| = |-3| = 3.$$

When we compare these distances to those of the output points (i.e., $\mathbf{V}_{at}$ and $\mathbf{V}_{ct}$), we observe the x and y direction distances to be dx_o and dy_o:

$$\begin{aligned}
dx_o &= |x_{cs} - x_{as}| = |3 - 9| = |-6| = 6, \\
dy_o &= |y_{cs} - y_{as}| = |2.5 - 4| = |-1.5| = 1.5.
\end{aligned}$$

We observe that

$$\begin{aligned}
dx_o &= s_x \times dx_i = 3 \times 2 = 6, \\
dy_o &= s_y \times dy_i = 0.5 \times 3 = 1.5.
\end{aligned}$$

Scaling operator. Changes the x and y size of objects according to the scale factors.

We see that when we apply the same scale operator to V_a and V_c, in effect we are also applying the scale operator on the distances between these points. In this way, by repositioning each individual point, we have resized the relative distances between these points. Figure 8.8 shows applying the $\mathbf{S}(3,0.5)$ operator on four vertices that form a rectangle:

$$\text{Input points}: \begin{cases} V_a = & (3,8), \\ V_b = & (1,8), \\ V_c = & (1,5), \\ V_d = & (3,5). \end{cases}$$

We see that the scale operator will reposition the input points to

$$\begin{aligned}
\mathbf{V}_{as} &= \; \mathbf{V}_a \, \mathbf{S}(3,0.5), \\
\mathbf{V}_{bs} &= \; \mathbf{V}_b \, \mathbf{S}(3,0.5), \\
\mathbf{V}_{cs} &= \; \mathbf{V}_c \, \mathbf{S}(3,0.5), \\
\mathbf{V}_{ds} &= \; \mathbf{V}_d \, \mathbf{S}(3,0.5),
\end{aligned}$$

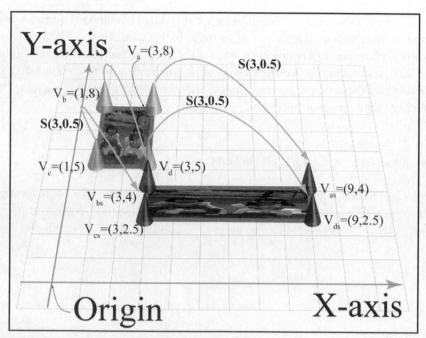

Figure 8.8. Applying the $S(3, 0.5)$ operator on four points.

which results in

$$\text{Output points}: \begin{cases} V_{as} = & (9, 4), \\ V_{bs} = & (3, 4), \\ V_{cs} = & (3, 2.5), \\ V_{ds} = & (9, 2.5). \end{cases}$$

When we examine the size of the input and output rectangles, indeed we observe the scaling of width (size in the x-direction) by a factor of 3, from 2 to 6, and the scaling of height by a factor of 0.5, from 3 to 1.5. This scaling of dimension is true in general, where we can apply the scaling operator to *resize* geometric shapes to the desired dimension. In the case of Figure 8.8, one worrying observation is that although the $S(3, 0.5)$ operator has accomplished the desired/expected result of resizing the 2×3 rectangle into a 6×1.5 rectangle, the operator has also moved the resulting rectangle in a counterintuitive manner. We note that the moving of the scaled rectangle is the result of the repositioning of the points with respect to the x- and y-axes, or scaling of x- and y-values based on their respective distances measured from the x- and y-axis.

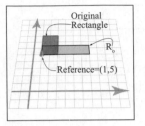

Figure 8.9. Example of an "intuitive" scaling operation.

Figure 8.9 shows an example of what we may expect, intuitively, from a scaling operation with scaling factors of $(3, 0.5)$. In this case, the 2×3 rectangle is scaled with respect to a *reference* position at the lower-left corner of the rectangle at $(1, 5)$, resulting in the rectangle (R_o). We will describe how to accomplish this kind of transformation in the next chapter after we have a good understanding of the basic transformation operators.

Negative Scaling Factors: Reflections

Applying a scaling operator with negative scaling factor has the effect of reflecting the input points across axes. For example, if we apply a scale operator with $s_x = -1$ and $s_y = 1$ (or $\mathbf{S}(-1, 1)$) on the point $V_a = (3, 4)$, we get

$$
\begin{aligned}
\mathbf{V}_{as} &= \begin{bmatrix} x_{as} \ y_{as} \end{bmatrix} \\
&= \mathbf{V}_a \, \mathbf{S}(s_x, s_y) \\
&= \begin{bmatrix} x_a \times s_x \ y_a \times s_y \end{bmatrix} \\
&= \begin{bmatrix} 3 \times -1 \ 4 \times 1 \end{bmatrix} \\
&= \begin{bmatrix} -3 \ 4 \end{bmatrix}.
\end{aligned}
$$

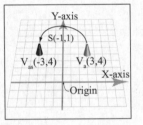

Figure 8.10. Effect of negative scaling factor.

This result is illustrated in Figure 8.10. We see that with an s_x of -1, the input point V_a is reflected across the y-axis and not the x-axis. Reflection is a special case of the scaling operator, and we have learned that the scaling operator can be applied to multiple points. Figure 8.11 shows the results of reflecting four vertices of a rectangle:

$$
\text{Input points:} \begin{cases} V_a = & (3, 4), \\ V_b = & (1, 4), \\ V_c = & (1, 1), \\ V_d = & (3, 1). \end{cases}
$$

We have already seen that scaling by $\mathbf{S}(-1, 1)$ simply flipped the x-coordinate value of V_a to $V_{as} = (-3, 4)$. In this example, we see that the flipping applies to the rest of the vertex positions:

$$
\text{Output points:} \begin{cases} V_{as} = & (-3, 4), \\ V_{bs} = & (-1, 4), \\ V_{cs} = & (-1, 1), \\ V_{ds} = & (-3, 1). \end{cases}
$$

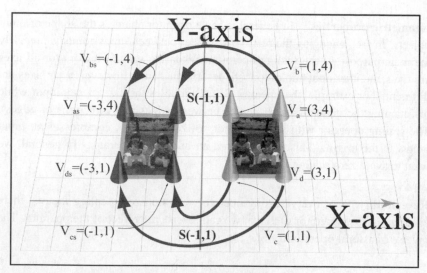

Figure 8.11. Reflecting a photograph across the y-axis.

Notice that the resulting rectangle formed by the scaled vertices is a mirror image of the original rectangle. This fact can be observed by the mirrored photograph in Figure 8.11. This mirror reflection can be generalized, where

$$\mathbf{S}(1, -1)$$

mirror reflects vertices/objects across the x-axis, and

$$\mathbf{S}(-1, 1)$$

mirror reflects vertices/objects across the y-axis.

Summary of the Scaling Operator

Order of operations. Once again, in general for all transformation operators, the order of operations is important. In this case,

$$\mathbf{V}_a \, \mathbf{S}$$

is different from

$$\mathbf{S} \, \mathbf{V}_a.$$

Geometric properties. In general, a scale operator changes the shape of input objects. In fact, changing the relative distances between input points is precisely the main purpose of the scaling operator. When the scaling factors for all axes are the same, the input and output shapes are the same; however, their sizes are different. For example, the operator $\mathbf{S}(2,2)$ doubles the size of any input while maintaining the general shape (angles between edges and directions of edges). The scaling operator with scaling factors of zero, $\mathbf{S}(0,0)$, compresses all input points to the origin. This is considered an undefined operator. In general, we want to avoid zero scaling factors.

Reversibility. For every scaling operator with non-zero scaling factors, there exists an *inverse* operator such that we can reverse the effect of the operator. The inverse transform operator for $\mathbf{S}(s_x, s_y)$ is

$$\mathbf{S}^{-1} = \mathbf{S}\left(\frac{1}{s_x}, \frac{1}{s_y}\right).$$

Identity. Unlike the translation operator where 0 displacement is the identity operator, the scaling operator is a no-operation operator when both the s_x and s_y scaling factors are 1.0.

Extension to 3D. For positive scaling factors, the extension to the third dimension is straightforward. In 3D, the scaling operator simply has the third parameter $S(s_x, s_y, s_z)$, where s_z is the scaling factor in the z-axis. Negative scaling factor in 3D space is an interesting way of creating mirrored objects.

8.3 The Rotation Operator

Rotation means turning. The rotation operator

$$\mathbf{R}(\theta)$$

rotates a point V_a from

$$\mathbf{V}_a = \begin{bmatrix} x_a & y_a \end{bmatrix}$$

to a new position V_{ar}:

$$\begin{aligned} \mathbf{V}_{ar} &= \begin{bmatrix} x_{ar} & y_{ar} \end{bmatrix} \\ &= \begin{bmatrix} x_a \cos\theta - y_a \sin\theta & y_a \cos\theta + x_a \sin\theta \end{bmatrix}, \end{aligned}$$

where θ is the angle that is rotated in the counterclockwise direction measured with respect to the origin. As in the case for translation and scaling, we represent the rotation operation as

$$\mathbf{V}_{ar} = \mathbf{V}_a \, \mathbf{R}(\theta) = \mathbf{V}_a \, \mathbf{R}.$$

Figure 8.12 shows an example where the rotation angle $\theta = 45°$, or

$$\mathbf{R}(\theta) = \mathbf{R}(45°),$$

operating on V_a:

$$\mathbf{V}_a = \begin{bmatrix} x_a & y_a \end{bmatrix} = \begin{bmatrix} 8 & 4 \end{bmatrix}$$

and turning the point to the new position $\mathbf{V}_{ar}$ at

$$\begin{aligned}
\mathbf{V}_{ar} &= \begin{bmatrix} x_{ar} & y_{ar} \end{bmatrix} \\
&= \mathbf{V}_a \mathbf{R}(\theta) \\
&= \begin{bmatrix} x_a \cos\theta - y_a \sin\theta & y_a \cos\theta + x_a \sin\theta \end{bmatrix} \\
&= \begin{bmatrix} 8\cos(45) - 4\sin(45) & 4\cos(45) + 8\sin(45) \end{bmatrix} \\
&\approx \begin{bmatrix} 2.83 & 8.49 \end{bmatrix}.
\end{aligned}$$

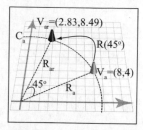

Figure 8.12. The rotate operator.

Notice that unlike translation and scaling operators, in the case of rotation operator, both the input x- and y-coordinate values affect the x- and y-coordinates of the output point. From Figure 8.12, we can see that the rotation operator turns V_a counterclockwise 45 degrees. This turning is performed with respect to the origin $(0,0)$ such that R_a, the distance between V_a and the origin:

$$R_a = \sqrt{x_a^2 + y_a^2} = \sqrt{8^2 + 4^2} \approx 9.0,$$

is the same as R_{ar}, the distance between V_{ar} and the origin:

$$R_{ar} = \sqrt{x_{ar}^2 + y_{ar}^2} = \sqrt{2.83^2 + 8.49^2} \approx 9.0.$$

This equidistance to the origin of input and output points of the rotation operator is always true. When we vary the values of θ, the results rotating V_a will always be located on the circumference of the circle C_a in Figure 8.12. The center of this circle is always the origin, and the radius is always equal to the distance between V_a and the origin (or R_a). In this way, the rotation operator slides input point V_a on the circumference of the circle C_a. With a positive θ, the rotation operator slides the input point on the circumference counterclockwise by θ degrees, whereas a negative θ will cause V_a to be slid clockwise along the circumference. As in the case of the translation and scaling operators, we observe that the output position from the rotation operator only depends on the corresponding input point. As in previous cases, this observation tells us that we can apply the rotation operator to any number of points. Figure 8.13 shows that we can apply the same $\mathbf{R}(45°)$ to the point

$$\mathbf{V}_c = \begin{bmatrix} x_c & y_c \end{bmatrix} = \begin{bmatrix} 5 & 2 \end{bmatrix},$$

and the results of the rotation would, as expected, be

$$\begin{aligned}
\mathbf{V}_{cr} &= \begin{bmatrix} x_{cr} & y_{cr} \end{bmatrix} \\
&= \mathbf{V}_c\,\mathbf{R}(45°) \\
&= \begin{bmatrix} x_c\cos(45) - y_c\sin(45) & y_c\cos(45) + x_c\sin(45) \end{bmatrix} \\
&= \begin{bmatrix} 5\cos(45) - 2\sin(45) & 2\cos(45) + 5\sin(45) \end{bmatrix} \\
&\approx \begin{bmatrix} 2.12 & 4.95 \end{bmatrix}.
\end{aligned}$$

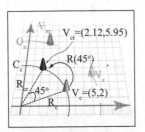

Figure 8.13. Rotate two individual points with the rotate operator.

Once again, we notice that the distance between the input point V_c and the origin (R_c) is

$$\begin{aligned}
R_c &= \sqrt{x_c^2 + y_c^2} \\
&= \sqrt{5^2 + 2^2} \\
&\approx 5.4,
\end{aligned}$$

which is the same as R_{cr}, the distance between V_{cr} and the origin:

$$\begin{aligned}
R_{cr} &= \sqrt{x_{cr}^2 + y_{cr}^2} \\
&= \sqrt{2.12^2 + 4.95^2} \\
&\approx 5.4.
\end{aligned}$$

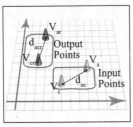

Figure 8.14. Distance between input points and output points.

In this way, we see that V_c is slid along the circumference of circle C_c counterclockwise by 45 degrees to V_{cr}. Figure 8.14 shows that if we examine the distance d_{ac} between the two input points V_a and V_c, we have

$$\begin{aligned}
d_{ac} &= \sqrt{(x_a - x_c)^2 + (y_a - y_c)^2} \\
&= \sqrt{(8 - 5)^2 + (4 - 2)^2} \\
&\approx 3.6.
\end{aligned}$$

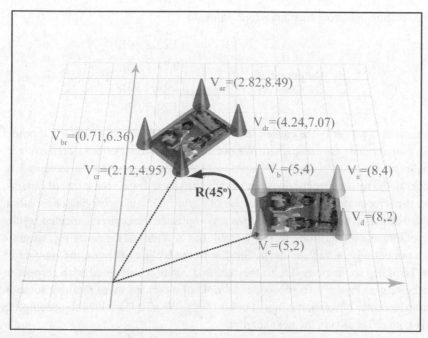

Figure 8.15. Applying the $\mathbf{R}(45°)$ operator on four points.

Now, if we examine the distance d_{acr} between the two output points V_{ar} and V_{cr}, we have

$$d_{acr} = \sqrt{(x_{ar} - x_{cr})^2 + (y_{ar} - y_{cr})^2}$$

$$\approx \sqrt{(2.8 - 2.1)^2 + (8.5 - 4.9)^2}$$

$$\approx 3.6.$$

From this example, we see that although V_a and V_c are rotated along the circumferences of circles with different radii (C_a and C_c), and the orientation of output points (V_{ar} and V_{cr}) appear to be very different from that of the input points, the distance between points remains constant. In general, this property of constant distance (size) is true for any rotation. Figure 8.15 shows the effect of applying the $\mathbf{R}(45°)$ operator on four vertices that form a rectangle:

Rotation operator. Maintains the size and shape of an object, but not the orientation.

$$\text{Input points}: \begin{cases} V_a = & (8,4), \\ V_b = & (5,4), \\ V_c = & (5,2), \\ V_d = & (8,2). \end{cases}$$

The rotation operator turns these four points to

$$\text{Output points}: \begin{cases} V_{ar} = & (2.82, 8.49), \\ V_{br} = & (0.71, 6.36), \\ V_{cr} = & (2.12, 4.95), \\ V_{dr} = & (4.24, 7.07). \end{cases}$$

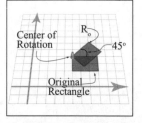

Figure 8.16. Example of an "intuitive" rotation operation.

In this case, we verify the earlier observation that distances between input points and output points are maintained. We notice that the output vertices define a rectangle that is the same size as the input rectangle, only at a rotated orientation. In general, the rotate operator does not change the shape or the area (size) of objects, just the orientation is altered. In the case of Figure 8.15, one worrying observation is that although the $R(45)$ operator has accomplished the desired/expected results of rotating the input rectangle, the operator has also moved the resulting rectangle in a not entirely intuitive manner. Similar to the scaling operator, the moving of the resulting rectangle is due to the fact that rotation is defined with respect to to the origin. Figure 8.16 shows an example of a perhaps more intuitive rotation with the center of rotation being at point $(5,4)$. We will learn how to accomplish this kind of rotation in the next chapter.

Summary of the Rotation Operator

Order of operations.   As in previous operators, with our vector representation,

$$\mathbf{R}\,\mathbf{V}_a$$

is an undefined operation.

Geometric properties.   In general, all corresponding input and output edges will be of the same length. In addition, the angles formed by the input edges will be exactly the same as the corresponding output angles.

Reversibility. $\mathbf{R}^{-1}(\theta) = \mathbf{R}(-\theta)$.

Identity. $\mathbf{R}(0)$.

Extension to 3D.   Rotation in three dimensions is a much more complex operation. For example, instead of a center of rotation position (e.g., origin), in 3D, rotation is defined with respect to an axis. We will examine rotations in 3D space in Chapter 16.

8.4   Affine Transformations

The three transformation operators we have discussed are examples of *affine transformations*. In general, an affine transformation transforms parallel lines to parallel lines, and finite points to finite points. These types of transformations do not unproportionately warp geometric objects, and they do not introduce or reduce geometric elements (i.e., vertices and edges). These characteristics are intuitive to humans and are easier for humans to relate to.

Affine transformations are *linear*, or in simpler terms, they leave geometric relationships unchanged. For example, a midpoint before a transformation operation will be a midpoint after a transformation. An intuitive way to understand this is: if an operator works on a point, then the operator also works on an object that is defined by a group of points. For example, if an operator operates properly on a vertex position, then this operator would operate properly on a triangle (defined by a group of three vertices), and this same operator would also operate properly on a teapot that is defined by a group of triangles. This linearity is an important property. In our discussions, we have taken advantage of this linearity property by first studying the effect of each operator on one vertex position, and then two, before generalizing to geometric shapes. In subsequent chapters, we will continue to examine transformation operations based on simple vertex positions and then generalize our learning.

As we can see, the three operators we have studied are indeed very simple. It is interesting that highly complex graphical environments can be defined and supported based on these operators. In the next few chapters, we will learn to combine these operators in non-trivial manners to accomplish more complex transformations. It is important that we review some of the fundamental mathematics before we generalize the utilization of these simple operators. In the next section, we will review some formal notations that will help us further discuss the transformation operators. We want to examine how to generalize the utilization of these operators and, more specifically, how to do the following.

- Apply these operators on more interesting geometric objects we have worked with (e.g., circles and rectangles).

- Combine these operators to accomplish interesting effects.

- Work with graphics APIs in using these operators in our source code library.

Once again, for brevity and readability, in the rest of the book we may not explicitly list the parameters of the transformation operators. For example, we will use $\mathbf{T}$ to mean $\mathbf{T}(t_x, t_y)$, $\mathbf{S}$ to represent $\mathbf{S}(s_x, s_y)$, and $\mathbf{R}$ to mean $\mathbf{R}(\theta)$. Before

we continue, here is a summary of the properties of the transformation operators
we have studied:

Operator	Inverse	Identity	Maintains Shape
$\mathbf{T}(t_x, t_y)$	$\mathbf{T}(-t_x, -t_y)$	$\mathbf{T}(0,0)$	Yes
$\mathbf{S}(s_x, s_y)$	$\mathbf{S}(\frac{1}{s_x}, \frac{1}{s_y})$	$\mathbf{S}(1,1)$	No
$\mathbf{R}(\theta)$	$\mathbf{R}(-\theta)$	$\mathbf{R}(0)$	Yes

8.5 Some Mathematics of the Transform Operators

This section is not meant to present a complete mathematical background for the
transformation operators. Instead, we list some relevant facts and properties for
these operators. Our discussion is limited to vectors in two or three dimensions
and 4×4 matrices representing the well-defined affine transformations. For a
discussion of more involved operations with vectors, see Appendix B. To learn
more about the mathematics of vectors and matrices, see a classic textbook on
linear algebra.

Triangles. A triangle is the simplest geometric shape with area that can be defined by vertices, and thus it is the most straightforward to process. Triangles have many elegant properties; for example, the three vertices of a triangle are guaranteed to form a flat plane.

We have seen that it is straightforward to represent vertex positions as vectors.
We have also seen that the transformation operators are well-defined mathematical
operations that manipulate vectors. The mathematical foundation allows custom-
designed hardware processors to efficiently implement these operations. Today,
virtually all commercial graphics hardware is based on transforming and processing vertices. As a direct result, all popular graphics APIs are also defined based
on processing vertices. To simplify hardware implementation, only triangles are
explicitly processed by the hardware. In all cases, the vast majority of graphical objects we encountered are defined based on collections of triangles. For this
reason, we will concentrate on working with a collection of vertices (or vectors).
Typically, the vertices represent a collection of triangles, which in turn represent
some meaningful geometrical shape (e.g., a sphere, a car).

8.5.1 A Word about Vectors

In the beginning of this chapter, when we first introduced transformation operators, we said that we can represent a vertex position V_a:

$$V_a = (x_a, y_a, z_a)$$

with the vector representation $\mathbf{V}_a$:

$$\mathbf{V}_a = \begin{bmatrix} x_a & y_a & z_a \end{bmatrix}.$$

Because the x_a, y_a, and z_a coordinate values are lined up in a row, we refer to this vector representation as a row vector. $\mathbf{V}_a^T$ is the *transpose* of vector $\mathbf{V}_a$:

$$\mathbf{V}_a^T = \begin{bmatrix} x_a \\ y_a \\ z_a \end{bmatrix},$$

and $\mathbf{V}_a^T$ is also a vector. Because the coordinate values are written one on top another, or in a column, we refer to this representation as a column vector. In general, the transpose of a row vector is a column vector, and the transpose of the column vector is the original row vector:

$$(\mathbf{V}_a^T)^T = \mathbf{V}_a.$$

Geometrically, there is no difference between representing a vertex as a column vector or a row vector. However, as will be discussed in Section 8.5.3, in the case of transformation, column and row vectors must be treated with care.

8.5.2   A Word about Matrices

The transformation operators we have studied are represented by 4×4 matrices $\mathbf{M}$, where:

$$\mathbf{M} = \begin{bmatrix} a_{00} & a_{01} & a_{02} & a_{03} \\ a_{10} & a_{11} & a_{12} & a_{13} \\ a_{20} & a_{21} & a_{22} & a_{23} \\ a_{30} & a_{31} & a_{32} & a_{33} \end{bmatrix}.$$

We say that this is a matrix with four rows by four columns (or 4×4) of elements. Each of the 16 elements

$$a_{ij} = \text{element at} \begin{cases} i\text{th row,} & \text{where } 0 \le i \le 3, \\ j\text{th column,} & \text{where } 0 \le j \le 3, \end{cases}$$

is a floating-point number. Each of the transformation operators we have studied is simply a 4×4 matrix with different values in these 16 elements. In this book, we are not interested in the details of this 4×4 matrix. However, it is interesting to relate the transformation operators we have learned to the internals of a 4×4 matrix. Figure 8.17 shows that the 4×4 matrix can be partitioned into two regions:

- **Top-left 3 × 3 region.** This region encodes the scaling and rotation operations. In addition, we can consider the 0th row/column to be affecting the

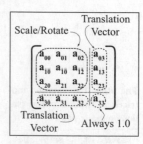

Figure 8.17. Decomposing the transformation operator: the 4×4 matrix. The fourth dimension of the matrix is introduced to support translation and homogeneous coordinate system for perspective projection.

x-coordinate values, the first row/column to be affecting the *y*-coordinate values, and the second row/column mainly affecting the *z*-coordinate values.

- **Translation vector.** Depending on the order of operations (as will be discussed later), the translation operation is either encoded in fourth row or the fourth column.

In our case, the matrix for the translation operator is

$$\mathbf{T}(t_x, t_y, t_z) = \begin{bmatrix} 1 & 0 & 0 & 0 \\ 0 & 1 & 0 & 0 \\ 0 & 0 & 1 & 0 \\ t_x & t_y & t_z & 1 \end{bmatrix},$$

the matrix for the scaling operator is

$$\mathbf{S}(s_x, s_y, s_z) = \begin{bmatrix} s_x & 0 & 0 & 0 \\ 0 & s_y & 0 & 0 \\ 0 & 0 & s_z & 0 \\ 0 & 0 & 0 & 1 \end{bmatrix},$$

and the matrix for the rotation operator on the *xy*-plane is

$$\mathbf{R}(\theta) = \begin{bmatrix} \cos\theta & \sin\theta & 0 & 0 \\ -\sin\theta & \cos\theta & 0 & 0 \\ 0 & 0 & 1 & 0 \\ 0 & 0 & 0 & 1 \end{bmatrix}.$$

The other two rotation matrices. The matrix for rotation on the *xz*-plane is

$$\begin{bmatrix} \cos\theta & 0 & -\sin\theta & 0 \\ 0 & 1 & 0 & 0 \\ \sin\theta & 0 & \cos\theta & 0 \\ 0 & 0 & 0 & 1 \end{bmatrix},$$

and the matrix for rotation on the *yz*-plane is

$$\begin{bmatrix} 1 & 0 & 0 & 0 \\ 0 & \cos\theta & \sin\theta & 0 \\ 0 & -\sin\theta & \cos\theta & 0 \\ 0 & 0 & 0 & 1 \end{bmatrix}.$$

Another very important operator is the no-operation, or the identity operator **I**:

$$\mathbf{I}_4 = \begin{bmatrix} 1 & 0 & 0 & 0 \\ 0 & 1 & 0 & 0 \\ 0 & 0 & 1 & 0 \\ 0 & 0 & 0 & 1 \end{bmatrix}.$$

The identity operator is especially important when it comes to initialization of variables for accumulation.

Mathematically, we can multiply (or concatenate) multiple 4×4 matrices into a single 4×4 matrix. For example, if $\mathbf{M}_1$ and $\mathbf{M}_2$ are two 4×4 matrices, then $\mathbf{M}_a$,

$$\mathbf{M}_a = \mathbf{M}_1 \mathbf{M}_2,$$

is also a 4×4 matrix. Notice that if we switch the multiplication order, then $\mathbf{M}_b$,

$$\mathbf{M}_b = \mathbf{M}_2 \mathbf{M}_1,$$

is also a 4×4 matrix; however, in general,

$$\mathbf{M}_a \neq \mathbf{M}_b,$$

or in general,

$$\mathbf{M}_1\mathbf{M}_2 \neq \mathbf{M}_2\mathbf{M}_1.$$

Interestingly, the order of matrix multiplication is not important, or in general,

$$\mathbf{M}_1\mathbf{M}_2\mathbf{M}_3 = \mathbf{M}_1(\mathbf{M}_2\mathbf{M}_3) = (\mathbf{M}_1\mathbf{M}_2)\mathbf{M}_3.$$

8.5.3 Matrices and Vectors

All transformation operators we have studied are 4×4 matrices; for example, we have seen that the translation operator $\mathbf{T}$ is a 4×4 matrix. When we apply this transformation operator on a vertex position $\mathbf{V}$:

$$\mathbf{V} = \begin{bmatrix} x & y & z \end{bmatrix},$$

mathematically, we are computing vector-matrix multiplication. We have already seen that the result of this multiplication is another vector. With the row vector representation, the mechanics of vector-matrix multiplication governs that the vector must appear on the left side of the matrix, as:

$$\mathbf{V}_c = \mathbf{V}\,\mathbf{T} = \begin{bmatrix} x_c & y_c & z_c \end{bmatrix}.$$

Because this vector appears on the left side before the matrix, the row-vector/matrix multiplication is also referred to as "pre-multiplying a vector." In the case of row-vector representation, $\mathbf{T}\,\mathbf{V}$ is an undefined operation. If the vertex position is represented as a column vector $\mathbf{V}^T$,

$$\mathbf{V}^T = \begin{bmatrix} x \\ y \\ z \end{bmatrix},$$

then the vector must appear on the right side of the matrix:

$$\mathbf{V}_r = \mathbf{T}\,\mathbf{V}^T = \begin{bmatrix} x_r \\ y_r \\ z_r \end{bmatrix}.$$

Since this vector appears on the right side after the matrix, the column-vector/matrix multiplication is also referred to as "post-multiplying a vector." Notice that in the case of column-vector representation,

$$\mathbf{V}^T\,\mathbf{T}$$

is undefined. In general, with the same transformation operator $\mathbf{M}$ and the same vertex position $V = (x, y, z)$, the results from pre- and post-multiplication will be different, or:

$$\mathbf{V}_r = \begin{bmatrix} x\ y\ z \end{bmatrix} \mathbf{M} = \begin{bmatrix} x_r\ y_r\ z_r \end{bmatrix},$$

and

$$\mathbf{V}_c = \mathbf{M} \begin{bmatrix} x \\ y \\ z \end{bmatrix} = \begin{bmatrix} x_c \\ y_c \\ z_c \end{bmatrix}.$$

Then, in general,

$$\mathbf{V}_r \neq \mathbf{V}_c^T \text{ or } \begin{bmatrix} x_r\ y_r\ z_r \end{bmatrix} \neq \begin{bmatrix} x_c\ y_c\ z_c \end{bmatrix}.$$

When programming with graphics APIs, we as the programmer can choose to work with either row- or column-vector representation. Because the results of the two approaches are not interchangeable, it is important that we choose one and be consistent throughout our programming. One important and dangerous caveat is that most modern graphics APIs represent row and column vectors with the same data structure (e.g., a three-element array, or a three-element vector class) and typically support both pre- and post-vector/matrix multiplication with that same data structure. As programmers, we must be extremely careful with coding vector-matrix multiplication.

It is interesting that D3D chose pre-multiplication, wheras OpenGL supports post-multiplication. Because most of the tutorials in this book are based on D3D, we will follow the pre-multiplication convention.

8.5.4   Homogeneous Coordinate Representation

It is interesting that the mathematics required to support 3D graphics operations are in four dimensions. We have already seen that the fourth dimension of the 4×4 matrix encodes translation information. In addition, the fourth dimension of the matrix is needed for encoding perspective projection. Perspective projection is the mathematical foundation for displaying 3D objects on 2D displays.

Because the underlying matrices are defined in four dimensions, mathematically, the vectors representing coordinate positions must also be defined in four dimensions. The homogeneous coordinate system represents a point,

$$V_a = (x_a,\ y_a,\ z_a),$$

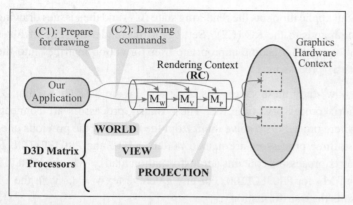

Figure 8.18. The D3D matrix processors.

in 3D space with a four-dimensional vector:

$$\mathbf{V}_h = \begin{bmatrix} x_h\ y_h\ z_h\ w_h \end{bmatrix} = \begin{bmatrix} \frac{x_h}{w_h} & \frac{y_h}{w_h} & \frac{z_h}{w_h} & 1.0 \end{bmatrix} = \begin{bmatrix} x_a\ y_a\ z_a\ 1.0 \end{bmatrix},$$

where w_h is a nonzero floating-point number. Strictly speaking, all of the vectors we have encountered should be expressed in the homogeneous coordinate system with the fourth component $w_a = 1.0$. In practice, this fact that the fourth component of the homogeneous coordinate has $w_a = 1.0$ is true for the vast majority of the cases one encounters in computer graphics. For example, all of the examples we will encounter in this book will have $w_a = 1.0$. For this reason, when discussing/implementing computer graphics programs, the fourth component of the homogeneous coordinate is assumed and typically left out. In this book, we will always work with three component vectors. In typical vector-matrix multiplications, the fourth-dimension $w_a = 1.0$ will be assumed. This is also the case for modern graphics API libraries; typically all vectors are defined as a three-component data structure with the fourth component assumed to be 1.0.

8.6   Tutorials on Transformation Operators

Recall that when learning about graphics APIs in Chapter 4, Figure 4.3 illustrated that the rendering context (RC) contains matrix processors to process/transform vertex positions. In Section 4.2, when describing how to draw with graphics APIs, we said that:

RC. Rendering context. See Section 4.2 for more details.

... an application sets the rendering state (C1) and then issues drawing commands to the RC (C2). Setting of the rendering state involves ... computing/loading appropriate transformation matrices into the matrix processors ...

We can now study these statements in detail. Figure 8.18 shows that D3D has three matrix processors in the RC. These matrix processors are connected in a series, where processors receive input from the output of the previous one.

These three processors are named WORLD, VIEW, and PROJECTION. Each of these matrix processors contains a transformation matrix: $\mathbf{M}_W$ for WORLD, $\mathbf{M}_V$ for VIEW, and $\mathbf{M}_P$ for PROJECTION. For any given vertex $V = (x, y, z)$, the D3D RC implements the transformation

$$V \, \mathbf{M}_W \, \mathbf{M}_V \, \mathbf{M}_P,$$

where the vertex V will be transformed first by $\mathbf{M}_W$ of the WORLD processor, followed by $\mathbf{M}_V$ of the VIEW processor, and lastly by $\mathbf{M}_P$ of the PROJECTION processor. One of our jobs as the graphics API programmer is to compute and load these matrix processors.

UWBGL_D3D_Lib8

Change summary. See p. 518 for a summary of changes to the library.

All tutorials in this chapter are developed based on version 8 of the UW_D3D_Lib library. The only change in this library is the inclusion of the PrimitiveRect angleXY class with the uwbgl_PrimitiveRectXY1.h/cpp source files in the *Primitives* subfolder of the *Common Files* folder. PrimitiveRectangleXY defines/draws rectangles on the 2D *xy*-plane.

Tutorial 8.1. Translating an Object

Tutorial 8.1.
Project Name:
D3D_TranslateSingleObj
Library Support:
  UWBGL_MFC_Lib1
  UWBGL_D3D_Lib8

- **Goals.** Experience with programming matrix processors of the graphics APIs.

- **Approach.** Examine the simplest case of using the matrix processor: programming one simple translation.

Figure 8.19 is a screenshot of running Tutorial 8.1. This tutorial translates the rectangle by the scroll-bar values in the *x*- and *y*-directions. Instead of changing the geometric values in the PrimitiveRectangleXY object, the translation is accomplished by programming the D3D WORLD matrix processor. The solution

```
class CModel {
    ⋮
    // called by the slider bars service functions
A:  void SetTranslation(float x, float y);
    ⋮
    // to redraw the rectangle (and the grid)
    void DrawModel();

  private:  ⋮
    // the rectangle
B:  UWB_PrimitiveRectangle m_Rectangle;
    // the x/y displacement from the GUI slider bars
C:  float m_TranslateX, m_TranslateY;
};

CModel::CModel() : m_TranslateX(0), m_TranslateY(0) {
D:  m_Rectangle.SetCorners(vec3(0,0,0), vec3(2,3,0));
    ⋮
```

Source file. Model.h file in the *Model* folder of the D3D_TranslateSingleObject project.

Listing 8.1. The CModel class of Tutorial 8.1.

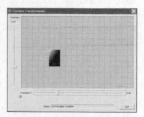

Figure 8.19. Tutorial 8.1.

structure of this tutorial is similar to the ones we have worked with previously. The CTutorialDlg class represents the application main window with the Draw OnlyHandler implementing the draw-only functionality of the view/controller pair UI drawing area. The model of this tutorial is straightforward. At label B in Listing 8.1, we see that the model has a simple rectangle. The SetTranslation() function at label A is called by the event service routines for the GUI translation slider bars to set the model's representation for the translation at label C. Label D shows that the rectangle is initialized with corners of $(0,0)$ and $(2,3)$. From interacting with the Tutorial 8.1 program, we verify that the rectangle is indeed 2×3 in size, and with both slider bars set to 0, the rectangle does indeed appear at the lower-left corner of the drawing area. Before we examine the CModel::DrawModel() function, let us refresh our memory by examining the matrix processors that we have programmed in all of our tutorials.

Initialization of the matrix processors. Recall that during the CTutorialDlg initialization, in the CTutorialDlg::OnInitDialog() function, we call the

```
bool UWBD3D_GraphicsSystem::CreateGraphicsContext(HWND hMainWindow) {

    : // create m_pD3D the graphics hardware context (GHC)
    m_pD3D = Direct3DCreate9( D3D_SDK_VERSION);

    : // create m_pD3DDevice the rendering context (RC)
    if( FAILED(m_pD3D->CreateDevice( D3DADAPTER_DEFAULT, ... &m_pD3DDevice ) ) )

    :
```

> *Programming the matrix processors: initialize all with the identity.*

```
    D3DXMATRIX identity; D3DXMatrixIdentity(&identity);
    m_pD3DDevice->SetTransform(D3DTS_WORLD, &identity);
    m_pD3DDevice->SetTransform(D3DTS_VIEW, &identity);
    m_pD3DDevice->SetTransform(D3DTS_PROJECTION, &identity);

}
```

Listing 8.2. Initialization of the matrix processors (Tutorial 8.1).

Source file.
uwbgl_D3DGraphicsSystem2.cpp file in the *D3D Files/GraphicsSystem* subfolder of the UWBGL_D3D_Lib8 project.

GraphicsSystem::CreateGraphicsContext() function to create the graphics contexts and initialize the GraphicsSystem to abstract our interaction with the graphics API. Listing 8.2 shows that at the end of CreateGraphicsContext(), we initialize all three matrix processors to the identity matrix (I_4) with the SetTransform() function calls. At this point, all three matrix processors implement the no-operation transformation.

Programming of the M_V (VIEW) matrix. Recall that to redraw the UI drawing area, we invoke the WindowHandler::DrawGraphics() function. In this case, the DrawOnlyHandler class implements the DrawGraphics() function. Listing 8.3 shows that the DrawGraphics() function computes the world2ndc matrix based on the current world width and height and loads the world2ndc matrix into the VIEW processor. These few lines of code compute the appropriate coordinate transformation to support the CModel drawing. We will study the mathematics and logic behind this computation in Chapter 10.

Programming of the M_W (WORLD) matrix. Following the programming of the matrix processors, by the time the CModel::DrawModel() function is invoked, the D3D RC matrix processors have:

$$\begin{aligned} M_W &= I_4 && (4 \times 4 \text{ identity matrix}), \\ M_V &= M_{world2ndc} && (\text{or } M_{w2n}), \\ M_P &= I_4. \end{aligned}$$

```
void CDrawOnlyHandler::DrawGraphics() {
    :
    : // obtain the width and height for the world
    ┌─────────────────────────────────────────┐
    │ Programming the VIEW matrix processor:  │
    └─────────────────────────────────────────┘

    D3DXMATRIX world2ndc;
    D3DXVECTOR3 scale(2.0f/width, 2.0f/height, 1.0f);
    D3DXVECTOR3 translate(-1.0f, -1.0f, 0.0);
    D3DXMatrixTransformation(&world2ndc, ... &scale, ... &translate);
    m_pD3DDevice->SetTransform(D3DTS_VIEW, &world2ndc);

    : // calls the model to perform the actual drawing
    theApp.GetModel().DrawModel();
    :
```

Source file. DrawOnlyHandler.cpp file in the *WindowHandler* folder of the D3D_TranslateSingleObject project.

Listing 8.3. Programming the $\mathbf{M}_V$ matrix (Tutorial 8.1).

```
void CModel::DrawModel() {
    :
    : draws the grid ... // DrawGrid( m_DrawHelper, m_WorldBounds );
    LPDIRECT3DDEVICE9 pDevice = UWBD3D_GraphicsSystem::GetSystem().GetD3DDevice();
    D3DXMATRIX translate_matrix;
    A: D3DXMatrixTranslation( &translate_matrix, m_TranslateX, m_TranslateY, 0);
    B: pDevice->SetTransform( D3DTS_WORLD, &translate_matrix );
    C: m_Rectangle.Draw( lod, m_DrawHelper );
    :
```

Source file. Model.cpp file in the *Model* folder of the D3D_TranslateSingleObject project.

Listing 8.4. Programming the $\mathbf{M}_W$ matrix (Tutorial 8.1).

When we examine the implementation of the CModel::DrawModel() function in Listing 8.4, we see that at label A, we call the D3DXMatrixTranslation() function to compute the translate_matrix matrix based on the m_TranslateX/Y values set by the GUI slider bars. The translate_matrix encodes our translation operator $\mathbf{T}$. At label B, we call the SetTransform() function to load the computed translate_matrix into the WORLD matrix processor. By the time the rectangle Draw() function is invoked, the D3D RC matrix processors have

$$\mathbf{M}_W = \mathbf{T},$$
$$\mathbf{M}_V = \mathbf{M}_{w2n},$$
$$\mathbf{M}_P = \mathbf{I}_4.$$

The vertices of the rectangle $\mathbf{V}_i$ are transformed by

$$
\begin{aligned}
\mathbf{V}_i \, \mathbf{M}_W \, \mathbf{M}_V \, \mathbf{M}_P & \\
= \quad \mathbf{V}_i \, \mathbf{T} \, \mathbf{M}_{w2n} \, \mathbf{I}_4 & \\
= \quad \mathbf{V}_i \, \mathbf{T} \, \mathbf{M}_{w2n}. &
\end{aligned}
$$

Because the $\mathbf{M}_{w2n}$ matrix is not changing, the translation effect we observed when changing the slider bar is accomplished by the computed $\mathbf{T}$ translation operator (or `translate_matrix`). This tutorial verifies that by properly computing and loading the matrix processors before sending the vertices and the drawing commands to the graphics API, we can indeed control the location of the rectangle.

Tutorial 8.2. Per-Primitive Translation

Tutorial 8.2.
Project Name:
  D3D_TranslateObjects
Library Support:
  UWBGL_MFC_Lib1
  UWBGL_D3D_Lib8

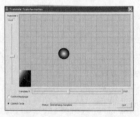

Figure 8.20.   Tutorial 8.2.

- **Goals.** Further experiment with programming the matrix processors; more specifically, we want to understand that the matrix processor can be changed in between drawing commands.

- **Approach.** Examine the drawing of two primitives, with and without user-controlled transformations.

Figure 8.20 is a screenshot of running Tutorial 8.2. This tutorial is similar to the previous one except that the user has the option of choosing to translate either the circle or the rectangle by selecting the two radio control buttons located at the lower left of the application window. We can verify that with the "Control Rectangle" button selected, the circle remains at the origin, whereas the slider bars control the location of the rectangle in exactly the same manner as in the previous tutorial. If we activate the "Control Circle" button, we notice a swap between the rectangle and the circle, where the rectangle jumps to and remains at the lower-left origin and the slider bars control the location of the circle. Except for the `CModel` class, the solution of this tutorial is identical to that of the previous one.

From the described behaviors of this tutorial and from the tracing of the matrix processors from the previous tutorial, we can derive that, in this case, when a primitive (circle or rectangle) is under the slider translation control, its vertices V_i should be transformed by

$$\mathbf{V}_i \, \mathbf{T}(t_x, t_y) \, \mathbf{M}_{w2n},$$

where t_x and t_y are the corresponding slider-bar values. The vertices of the primitive that is *not* controlled by the slider bars should be transformed by

$$\mathbf{V}_i \, \mathbf{M}_{w2n}.$$

```
A:  void SetUpTranslationMatrix(float x, float y) {
        LPDIRECT3DDEVICE9 pDevice = UWBD3D_GraphicsSystem::GetSystem().GetD3DDevice();
        D3DXMATRIX translate_matrix;
        D3DXMatrixTranslation(&translate_matrix, x, y, 0);
        pDevice->SetTransform(D3DTS_WORLD, &translate_matrix );
        ⋮
B:  void CModel::DrawModel() {
        ⋮
        ⋮ draws the grid ... // DrawGrid(m_DrawHelper, m_WorldBounds);
C:      if(m_bTransformCircle)
            SetUpTranslationMatrix(m_TranslateX, m_TranslateY);
        m_Circle.Draw(lod, m_DrawHelper);
D:      SetUpTranslationMatrix(0,0);
        if(!m_bTransformCircle)
            SetUpTranslationMatrix(m_TranslateX, m_TranslateY);
        m_Rectangle.Draw(lod, m_DrawHelper );
        SetUpTranslationMatrix(0,0);
        ⋮
```

Source file. Model.cpp file in the *Model* folder of the D3D_TranslateObjects project.

Listing 8.5. The CModel::DrawModel() function of Tutorial 8.2.

This suggests that we can control the drawing of the circle and the rectangle by loading the WORLD matrix either with the proper translation operator or with the identity matrix. In Listing 8.5 at label A, the SetUpTranslationMatrix() function computes the translation operator **T**, and the results are stored in trans late_marix. We see that this operator is loaded into the WORLD matrix processor by the SetTransform() function. When the input parameters to this function are $(0,0)$, the computed results are the identity matrix. In the DrawModel() function (B), when the "Control Circle" radio button is selected (m_bTransformCircle is true), at label C we compute the translation operator **T** based on the slider-bar values. In this way, the circle is drawn according to the transform

$$\mathbf{T}(t_x, t_y)\, \mathbf{M}_{w2n}.$$

At label D, we compute and load the WORLD matrix processor with the identity matrix, and the rectangle is drawn with translation being identity. That is why the rectangle always remains at the origin when the "Control Circle" button is activated. When the "Control Circle" button is not selected, m_bTransformCircle is false, and the transformations experienced by the circle and the rectangle would swap. From this tutorial, we see that it is possible to program the matrix processors and control the transformations for individual primitives we draw.

Tutorials 8.3 and 8.4. The Scaling and Rotation Operators

Tutorial 8.3.
Project Name:
  D3D_ScaleObjects
Library Support:
  UWBGL_MFC_Lib1
  UWBGL_D3D_Lib8

Tutorial 8.4.
Project Name:
  D3D_RotateObjects
Library Support:
  UWBGL_MFC_Lib1
  UWBGL_D3D_Lib8

- **Goals.** Experience with scaling and rotation operators.

- **Approach.** Examine the drawing of primitives with the scaling/rotation operators.

Figures 8.21 and 8.22 are screen-shots of running Tutorials 8.3 and 8.4. These two tutorials are structurally identical to Tutorial 8.2. The only difference is in the transformation operator control, whereas in Tutorial 8.2 we allow user controls translation, Tutorial 8.3 lets user controls the scaling, and Tutorial 8.4 lets user controls the rotation operators. The behavior of the tutorials are also similar, that depending on the radio control button settings, the slider bars control one of the primitives. In the case of these two tutorials, we are interested in examine the D3D function calls to compute the scaling/rotation operator. Listing 8.6 shows the transformation-setting functions from Tutorials 8.3 and 8.4. At label A, we see the D3D function D3DXMatrixScaling(), which computes the scaling operator $S(s_x, s_y)$ and stores the results in scale_matrix. As in the case of the translation operator in Listing 8.5, this operator is stored into the WORLD matrix processor by the SetTransform() function call. If the parameters of SetUpScaleMatrix() are $(1,1)$, the result is the identity matrix. At label B, we see the D3DXMatrixRotationZ() function, which computes the rotation operator $R(\theta)$. Notice that the unit on the angle is in *radians* (and *not* degrees). As with translation and scaling, the rotation operator is represented by rotate_matrix, and this operator can be stored into the WORLD matrix processor. These tutorials show us that we can load the WORLD matrix processor with any appropriate operators (represented by a matrix) to accomplish desired transformations on the primitive we wish to draw. We are now ready to learn the theory that allows us to construct powerful transformation operators with matrices.

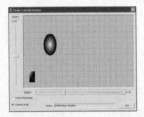

Figure 8.21.   Tutorial 8.3.

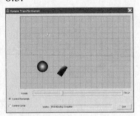

Figure 8.22.   Tutorial 8.4.

Source file. Model.cpp file in the *Model* folder of the D3D_ScaleObjects and D3D_RotateObjects projects.

Tutorial 8.3: Model.cpp: working with the Scaling opeartor.

```
void SetUpScaleMatrix(float x, float y) {
    LPDIRECT3DDEVICE9 pDevice =
        UWBD3D_GraphicsSystem::GetSystem().GetD3DDevice();
    D3DXMATRIX scale_matrix;
A:  D3DXMatrixScaling(&scale_matrix, x, y, 0);
    pDevice->SetTransform( D3DTS_WORLD, &scale_matrix );
}
```

Listing 8.6. The CModel::DrawModel() function of Tutorial 8.3 and 8.4.

---

*Tutorial **8.4**: Model.cpp: working with the **Rotation** opeartor*

```
void SetUpRotateMatrix(float angle_radians) {
    LPDIRECT3DDEVICE9 pDevice = UWBD3D_GraphicsSystem::GetSystem().GetD3DDevice();
    D3DXMATRIX rotate_matrix;
B:  D3DXMatrixRotationZ(&rotate_matrix, angle_radians);
    pDevice->SetTransform( D3DTS_WORLD, &rotate_matrix );
}
```

Listing 8.6. (cont.)

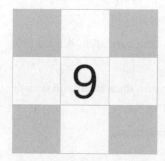

9

Combining Transformation Operators

This chapter discusses the effects of and strategies for combining basic transformation operators. This chapter:

- analyzes the advantages and costs of combining transformation operators;

- describes the process of inverting a combined transformed operator;

- explains approaches to combine and design new transformation operators to accomplish specific scaling and rotation tasks;

- derives graphics API support for programming transformations and develops an abstraction to assist in the programming of transformations with graphics APIs.

After this chapter we should:

- understand the effects and results of combined transformation operators;

- understand how to design new transformation operators to manipulate basic geometric shapes based on simple specifications.

In addition, with respect to hands-on programming, we should:

- be able to comprehend existing graphics API transformation-related programming code;

- be able to program and take advantage of the matrix stack facility in reusing and combining transformation operators.

Transformation operator vs. transformation matrix. In the rest of this book, we will use *transformation operator* and *transformation matrix* interchangeably.

As discussed in Section 8.6, the D3D RC pipeline implements

$$\mathbf{V} \, \mathbf{M}_W \, \mathbf{M}_V \, \mathbf{M}_P,$$

where the input vertex $\mathbf{V}$ is operated on by three separate transformation operators. In this chapter, we will study what it means to combine transformation operators and how to strategically combine these operators to accomplish more complex transformation operations.

9.1 Concatenation of Operators

We observe that both the input and output of the three transformation operators are vectors (representing vertex positions). For example, the translation operator $\mathbf{T}(t_x, t_y)$:

$$\mathbf{V}_{at} = \mathbf{V}_a \, \mathbf{T}(t_x, t_y),$$

or

$$\mathbf{V}_{at} = \mathbf{V}_a \, \mathbf{T},$$

where both $\mathbf{V}_a$ and $\mathbf{V}_{at}$ are vectors, representing coordinate positions. Because all operators accept vectors and compute vectors, in general, we can feed the output of one operator into the input of another operator. For example, we can direct the output of the above translation as the input of a scaling operator $\mathbf{S}$:

$$\mathbf{V}_{ats} = \mathbf{V}_{at} \, \mathbf{S}.$$

In this case, if

$$\mathbf{V}_a = \begin{bmatrix} x_a \ y_a \end{bmatrix},$$

then we know that

$$\mathbf{V}_{at} = \begin{bmatrix} t_x + x_a \ t_y + y_a \end{bmatrix}$$

and that

$$\begin{aligned}
\mathbf{V}_{ats} &= \mathbf{V}_{at} \, \mathbf{S}(s_x, s_y) \\
&= \begin{bmatrix} x_a + t_x \ y_a + t_y \end{bmatrix} \mathbf{S}(s_x, s_y) \\
&= \begin{bmatrix} (x_a + t_x) \times x_s \ (y_a + t_y) \times y_s \end{bmatrix}.
\end{aligned} \tag{9.1}$$

Note that Equation (9.1) is the same as

$$\mathbf{V}_a \; \mathbf{T}(t_x, t_y) \; \mathbf{S}(s_x, s_y)$$

or

$$\mathbf{V}_{at} \; \mathbf{S}(s_x, s_y) = \mathbf{V}_a \; \mathbf{T}(t_x, t_y) \; \mathbf{S}(s_x, s_y).$$

Figure 9.1 shows an example where

$$\mathbf{V}_a = \begin{bmatrix} 3 & 8 \end{bmatrix},$$

$$\mathbf{T} \quad \text{with} \begin{cases} t_x = -1 \\ t_y = -5 \end{cases},$$

$$\mathbf{S} \quad \text{with} \begin{cases} s_x = 3 \\ s_y = 0.5 \end{cases}.$$

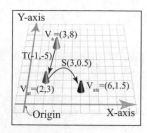

Figure 9.1. The results of applying translate and scale operators in succession.

If we apply the two operators separately, with translate first:

$$\begin{aligned}
\mathbf{V}_{at} &= \begin{bmatrix} x_{at} & y_{at} \end{bmatrix} \\
&= \begin{bmatrix} x_a + t_x & y_a + t_y \end{bmatrix} \\
&= \begin{bmatrix} 3 - 1 & 8 - 5 \end{bmatrix} \\
&= \begin{bmatrix} 2 & 3 \end{bmatrix},
\end{aligned}$$

followed by the scale operator:

$$\begin{aligned}
\mathbf{V}_{ats} &= \mathbf{V}_{at} \; \mathbf{S}(s_x, s_y) \\
&= \begin{bmatrix} x_{at} \times s_x & y_{at} \times s_y \end{bmatrix} \\
&= \begin{bmatrix} 2 \times 3 & 3 \times 0.5 \end{bmatrix},
\end{aligned}$$

we get

$$\mathbf{V}_{ats} = \begin{bmatrix} 6 & 1.5 \end{bmatrix}.$$

We can verify this result with Equation (9.1):

$$\begin{aligned}
\mathbf{V}_{ats} &= \begin{bmatrix} (x_a + t_x) \times x_s & (y_a + t_y) \times y_s \end{bmatrix} \\
&= \begin{bmatrix} (3 - 1) \times 3 & (8 - 5) \times 0.5 \end{bmatrix} \\
&= \begin{bmatrix} 6 & 1.5 \end{bmatrix}.
\end{aligned}$$

This result is applicable to all the transformation operators we have studied, where given two or more transformation operators, it is possible to combine (or concatenate) these operators into a single operator. This concatenated operator has the same net effect on vertices as applying the individual operators in the concatenation order. For the above given example, we can define a new operator $\mathbf{M}_a$ to encode the translation followed by scaling operation:

$$\mathbf{M}_a = \mathbf{T} \, \mathbf{S}. \tag{9.2}$$

The discussion in Section 8.5 tells us that both $\mathbf{T}$ and $\mathbf{S}$ are 4×4 matrices, and $\mathbf{M}_a$ is also a 4×4 matrix. Now when applying $\mathbf{M}_a$ to any vertex position $V_1 = (x_1, y_1)$, the net effect is the same as applying the $\mathbf{S}$ and $\mathbf{T}$ operators in succession:

Cost of concatenation. It costs exactly 16 floating-point multiplications and nine floating-point additions to compute the concatenation of two 4×4 matrices.

$$
\begin{aligned}
\mathbf{V}_2 &= \mathbf{V}_1 \, \mathbf{M}_a \\
&= \left[(x_1 + t_x) \times x_s \quad (y_1 + t_y) \times y_s \right].
\end{aligned}
$$

The advantages of concatenating multiple operators (matrices) into a single operator (matrix) include the following.

- **Compact representation.** Instead of writing $\mathbf{TS}$, we can simply express the combined operation as $\mathbf{M}_a$. This more compact representation allows simpler and more precise expression for the desired operations.

Vector-to-matrix multiplications. Depending on the actual implementation, in 3D space, this operation typically involves nine floating-point multiplications and nine floating-point additions, or 18 floating-point operations.

- **Computation efficiency.** From the given example, we see that there are two ways to compute $\mathbf{V}_{ats}$, either by applying $\mathbf{T}$ and $\mathbf{S}$ separately or by applying the concatenated matrix $\mathbf{M}_a$. Mathematically, the results from the two approaches are identical. Computationally, the first approach involves two vector-matrix multiplications, while the second approach involves one matrix-matrix multiplication and one vector-matrix multiplication. If we need to compute this same operation for a large number of vertices (e.g., n vertices), the first approach would take $2n$ vector-matrix multiplications, whereas the second approach can reuse the same concatenated matrix and would only need to perform n extra vector-matrix multiplications. In general, the characteristics of computer graphics applications are such that we often perform the same sequence of transformations on a large number of vertices. Usually, it is more cost efficient to concatenate matrices.

Order of concatenation. As discussed in Section 8.5, the order is important in matrix multiplication. In general,

$$\mathbf{M}_1 \, \mathbf{M}_2 \neq \mathbf{M}_2 \, \mathbf{M}_1.$$

Notice that in Equation (9.2), the translation is on the left side of the scaling operator. This means that the translation matrix will operate on the input vertex position before the scaling operator. If we switch the order of the two transform operators, we get

$$\mathbf{M}_b = \mathbf{ST}.$$

Notice that the operator $\mathbf{M}_b$ applies scaling before translation. In general,

$$\mathbf{M}_a \neq \mathbf{M}_b,$$

or

$$\mathbf{TS} \neq \mathbf{ST}.$$

In transformation operations, the order of applying the operators, or the order of concatenation, is very important! For example, we can easily verify the effects of

M_a and M_b with our example of $V_a = (3,8)$ and $T(-1,-5)$, $S(3,0.5)$. We have already seen that

$$\begin{aligned} V_a\, M_a &= [3\ 8]\, T(-1,-5) S(3,0.5) \\ &= [6\ 1.5]. \end{aligned}$$

As for M_b, where the order of the two transform operators are switched,

$$\begin{aligned} V_a\, M_b &= [3\ 8]\, S(3,0.5) T(-1,-5) \\ &= [(3 \times 3) - 1\ \ (8 \times 0.5) - 5] \\ &= [8\ -1]. \end{aligned}$$

The results are very different!

9.2 Inverse Transformation

Figure 9.2 shows that in order to undo the transformation M_a, we would:

1. Undo the scaling by performing the inverse transform of of $S(3,0.5)$:

$$S^{-1}(3,0.5) = S(\tfrac{1}{3},2).$$

2. Undo the translation by performing the inverse transform of $T(-1,-5)$:

$$T^{-1}(-1,-5) = T(1,5).$$

From this example, we see that the operator to undo M_a, or the *inverse transform* of M_a, is

$$M_a^{-1} = S^{-1}\, T^{-1}. \tag{9.3}$$

Recall from Equation (9.2) that M_a is defined as

$$M_a = T\, S.$$

We see that M_a^{-1} is applying the inverse transform of each of the operators in M_a in the reverse order. Instead of translate followed by scale, we apply the inverse scale first, followed by the inverse translate.

In general, for any concatenated affine transform operator, the inverse of the transform is always the inverse of each operator applied in reverse order. For

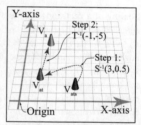

Figure 9.2. M_a^{-1}: undoing M_a.

Order of operation. Remember that the operator on the leftmost of a concatenation expression will operate on input vertices *first*. For example, when applying

$$M = TS$$

to a point V,

$$VM = VTS,$$

the translation operator will operate on the point V first.

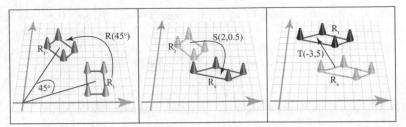

Figure 9.3. Applying $\mathbf{M}_{n1}$ on the vertices of a rectangle.

example, if we define a new transform operator $\mathbf{M}_n$, where we want to rotate a point, then scale, and finally translate:

$$\mathbf{M}_n = \mathbf{RST},$$

then the inverse $\mathbf{M}_n^{-1}$ would be

$$\mathbf{M}_n^{-1} = \mathbf{T}^{-1}\mathbf{S}^{-1}\mathbf{R}^{-1}$$

Figure 9.3 shows an example of applying $\mathbf{M}_{n1}$, with

$$\mathbf{M}_{n1} = \mathbf{R}(45°)\mathbf{S}(2,0.5)\mathbf{T}(-3,5),$$

to the vertices of a rectangle. Notice the following in Figure 9.3.

- **Left diagram.** The rotation of $\mathbf{R}(45°)$ is applied to the input vertices of rectangle R_i. The results of this operation are the vertices of rectangle R_r.

- **Center diagram.** The scale of $\mathbf{S}(2,0.5)$ resizes the vertices of R_r to those of R_s.

- **Right diagram.** The translate of $\mathbf{T}(-3,5)$ moves the vertices of rectangle R_s to that of R_t.

Now, to undo the transform effect of $\mathbf{M}_{n1}$, we must transform the vertices of rectangle R_t back to that of R_i. From the three diagrams of Figure 9.3, we can see that one straightforward way to *undo* the effect would be to apply the inverse operators of Figure 9.3, from the right diagram to the left diagram:

$$\mathbf{M}_{n1}^{-1} = \mathbf{T}^{-1}(-3,5)\mathbf{S}^{-1}(2,0.5)\mathbf{R}^{-1}(45°),$$

or

$$\mathbf{M}_{n1}^{-1} = \mathbf{T}(3,-5)\mathbf{S}(0.5,2)\mathbf{R}(-45°).$$

Figure 9.4 shows the details of the inverse operation. In this case, the input vertices are those correspond to R_t on the left diagram. The left, center, and right diagram of Figure 9.4 illustrate the effects of the $\mathbf{T}(3,-5)$, $\mathbf{S}(2,0.5)$, and $\mathbf{R}(-45°)$ of the $\mathbf{M}_{n1}^{-1}$ operator.

Scaling of a rectangle. In the center diagram of Figure 9.3, R_r is a rectangle where the edges are not parallel to the x- or y-axis. In this case, we see that when applying different scaling factors in the x- and y- directions, the right-angle property of R_r is not preserved.

Uniqueness of transform. Transformation operators are *not* unique. In general, there are an infinite number of ways to define operators for any transformation operation. For example, the operator $\mathbf{R}(45°)$, or any $\mathbf{R}(\theta)$ where

$$\theta = (360 \times n) + 45°$$

for any integer n, will transform vertices from R_i to R_r.

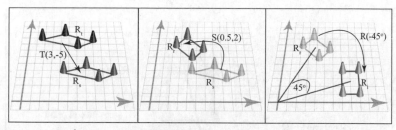

Figure 9.4. $\mathbf{M}_{n1}^{-1}$: the inverse transform of $\mathbf{M}_{n1}$.

9.3 Pivoted Transformations

We are now ready to address the concerns brought up by the illustrations of Figure 8.9 and Figure 8.16. Recall that in these cases, we observed unexpected moving side effects from the scaling and rotation operators. This moving side effect hinders the effectiveness of these operators where the results of the operation depend upon the initial positions of the vertices. We are now ready to address this side effect by working with concatenation of operators.

Figure 9.5 uses the same four vertices as in Figure 8.9 to illustrate how to accomplish the more intuitive scaling operation by strategically combining translation and scaling operators. In Figure 9.5, we first apply the $T(-1,-5)$ operator followed by the $S(3,0.5)$ operator on the four corners of the input rectangle R_i, where:

$$\text{Input points:} \begin{cases} V_a = & (3,8), \\ V_b = & (1,8), \\ V_c = & (1,5), \\ V_d = & (3,5). \end{cases}$$

The result of the translate operation is rectangle R_t:

$$\text{Output from translation:} \begin{cases} V_{at} = & (2,3), \\ V_{bt} = & (0,3), \\ V_{ct} = & (0,0), \\ V_{dt} = & (2,0). \end{cases}$$

Here we notice that the translated rectangle has the left (e_{bct}) and the bottom edges (e_{cdt}) reside along the y- and x-axes. The following serve as input to the scaling operation:

- **Edge e_{bct}.** This is the edge formed by vertices V_{bt} and V_{ct}. By definition, all vertices on the y-axis have value 0 for the x-coordinate. Recall that the scaling operator resizes by multiplying the scaling factor s_x by the x-coordinate

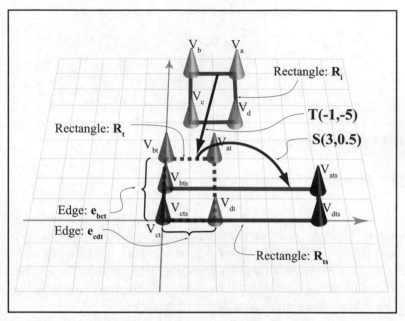

Figure 9.5. Combining translate and scale operators on a rectangle.

values. Now, if a vertex has 0 for its x-coordinate value (e.g., V_{bt} and V_{ct}), then the scaling in the x-direction will not affect these vertices. Notice that this has the effect of keeping the left side of the rectangle stationary while stretching the right side of the rectangle by s_x. As a result, the scaling operation will change the size of the rectangle by a factor of s_x. Because the left side of the rectangle does not move under the scaling operation, we have eliminated the horizontal component of the moving side effect.

- **Edge e_{cdt}.** This edge resides on the x-axis. Similar to the reason given above for e_{bct}, since the vertices (i.e., V_{bt} and V_{ct}) that define this edge have 0 for y-coordinate values, these vertices are not affected by s_y. As a result, when applying the scaling factor s_y, we press down the edge e_{cdt} and compress the other vertices along the y-axis direction. This has the effect of keeping the bottom edge of the rectangle stationary when stretching/compressing the top edge of the rectangle by a factor of s_y. Once again, because the bottom edge of the rectangle does not move, we have eliminated the vertical component of the moving side effect.

- **Vertex V_{ct}.** This vertex is at the origin and is not affected by any scaling operation.

From the above discussion, we understand that both the left and bottom edges of rectangle R_t will be kept stationary under scaling. As a result, when we apply $S(3,0.5)$ on the vertices of rectangle, we get rectangle R_{ts}:

$$\text{Output from scaling}: \begin{cases} V_{ats} = & (6,1.5), \\ V_{bts} = & (0,1.5), \\ V_{cts} = & (0,0), \\ V_{dts} = & (6,0). \end{cases}$$

When comparing to R_t, R_{ts} is the result of stretching the right edge by three times and the compressing the top edge by half the original height. Notice that there is no counterintuitive movement when scaling R_t into R_{ts}. Figure 9.6 shows that by applying the inverse of the original translation operator

$$\mathbf{T}^{-1}(-1,-5) = \mathbf{T}(-(-1),-(-5)) = \mathbf{T}(1,5)$$

to the vertices of rectangle R_{ts}, we get:

$$\text{Vertices of } R_o: \begin{cases} V_{ao} = & (7,6.5), \\ V_{bo} = & (5,6.5), \\ V_{co} = & (5,5), \\ V_{do} = & (7,5). \end{cases}$$

Transforming from rectangle R_i to R_o, we have accomplished the effects of Figure 8.9.

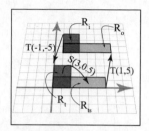

Figure 9.6. Achieving the effect of Figure 8.9.

9.3.1 Scaling with Arbitrary Pivot

In the above example, we applied a series of three operators,

$$\mathbf{T}(-1,-5)\mathbf{S}(3,0.5)\mathbf{T}^{-1}(-1,-5),$$

to the input vertices of the original rectangle R_i. Notice that the last operator $(\mathbf{T}^{-1})$ is the inverse transform of the first translation operator $(\mathbf{T})$. In practice, the above three operators are used in the following way.

1. **Translation.** Translates all vertices such that the center of scaling becomes the origin. In the above example, the scaling operation was defined with respect to the lower-left corner of rectangle R_i, and thus the translation is

$$\text{displacement} = \begin{cases} t_x = -5, \\ t_y = -1. \end{cases}$$

This operation translates the lower-left corner to the origin.

Order of operation. Remember that the *leftmost* operator is the one that operates on input vertices *first*. In the case of

$$\mathbf{TST}^{-1},$$

$\mathbf{T}$ will be the first to be applied on the input.

2. **Scaling.** Scales the results of the above translation, where the center of scaling is now located at the origin.

3. **Translation.** Translates the results of the scaling operation back to the original location. In our example with the translation,

$$\text{displacement} = \begin{cases} t_{xi} = -t_x = 5, \\ t_{yi} = -t_y = 1, \end{cases}$$

the origin is translated back to the lower-left corner of the original input rectangle R_i.

In this way, the above three operations strategically *selected* the reference position $((5,1))$ on the input rectangle for scaling. In general, the reference position for the scaling operation is defined by the displacements (t_x, t_y) of the first and last translation operations. We refer to this *reference position* for scaling operation as the *pivot* position for scaling. We define the operator $\mathbf{S}_{pt}(s_x, s_y)$:

$$\mathbf{S}_{pt}(s_x, s_y) = \mathbf{T}(-pt.x, -pt.y)\mathbf{S}(s_x, s_y)\mathbf{T}(pt.x, pt.y), \tag{9.4}$$

where

$$\mathbf{pt} = \begin{bmatrix} pt.x & pt.y \end{bmatrix}$$

is the pivot position. Notice that the simple scale operator $\mathbf{S}(s_x, s_y)$ introduced in Section 8.2 is simply

$$\mathbf{S}(s_x, s_y) = \mathbf{S}_{pt0}(s_x, s_y),$$

where

$$pt0 = \text{origin} = \begin{cases} pt0.x = 0, \\ pt0.y = 0. \end{cases}$$

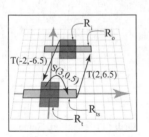

Figure 9.7. Scaling with pivot at the center of R_i.

In general, for any enclosed area, if the pivot position is outside of the area, the scaling operation will have the side effect of moving the entire area. For example, in Figure 8.8, the pivot position was the origin (and outside of the rectangle area), and we have seen that the scaling operation caused counterintuitive moving of the entire output rectangle.

Figure 9.7 shows applying the pivoted scaling operator $\mathbf{S}_{pt}(3, 0.5)$ to the vertices of R_i in Figure 9.5. In this case, we chose the pivot position to be

$$\mathbf{pt} = \begin{bmatrix} 2 & 6.5 \end{bmatrix},$$

or the center of R_i. This is another example of a more intuitive scaling of a rectangular area. It is left as an exercise for the reader to verify the vertex positions of R_t, R_s, and eventually R_o of Figure 9.7.

9.3.2   Rotation with Arbitrary Pivot

We can apply the lessons we have learned in scaling directly to rotation. Recall
that when operating on an input vertex $\mathbf{V}_a$, the rotate operator $\mathbf{R}(\theta)$ would:

$$\mathbf{V}_a \mathbf{R}(\theta) = \begin{bmatrix} x_a \cos\theta - y_a \sin\theta & y_a \cos\theta + x_a \sin\theta \end{bmatrix}.$$

Now, if $\mathbf{V}_a$ is the origin, where

$$\mathbf{V}_a = \begin{bmatrix} x_a & y_a \end{bmatrix} = \begin{bmatrix} 0 & 0 \end{bmatrix},$$

then

$$\begin{aligned} \mathbf{V}_a \mathbf{R}(\theta) &= \begin{bmatrix} 0 \times \cos\theta - 0 \times \sin\theta & 0 \times \cos\theta + 0 \times \sin\theta \end{bmatrix} \\ &= \begin{bmatrix} 0 & 0 \end{bmatrix} \\ &= \mathbf{V}_a. \end{aligned}$$

This observation says that the origin position will not be changed by a rotation
operator. In another words, by default, the origin is the center of rotation, or the
pivot position. Based on what we have learned from scaling, we know that we
can apply translation before and after the rotate operator to strategically select the
pivot position. Now we can define the pivoted rotation operator $\mathbf{R}_{pt}(\theta)$, where

$$\mathbf{R}_{pt}(\theta) = \mathbf{T}(-pt.x, -pt.y)\mathbf{R}(\theta)\mathbf{T}(pt.x, pt.y). \qquad (9.5)$$

Once again,

$$\mathbf{pt} = \begin{bmatrix} pt.x & pt.y \end{bmatrix}$$

is the pivot position. With the pivoted rotation operator, we can now rotate any
collection of vertices centered at any chosen pivot position. For example, Figure 9.8 shows the results of applying

$$\mathbf{R}_{pr}(45°),$$

where

$$\mathbf{pr} = \begin{bmatrix} 3 & 8 \end{bmatrix},$$

or rotating R_i with the top-right corner being the pivot position. As we saw in
pivoted scaling, by translating the pivot vertex to the origin before we apply the
rotation, we can accomplish the desired and more intuitive rotation. Figure 9.9
shows another example of $\mathbf{R}_{pc}(45°)$, with

$$\mathbf{pc} = \begin{bmatrix} 2 & 6.5 \end{bmatrix},$$

the center of the rectangle R_i.

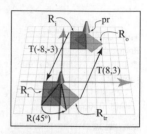

Figure 9.8.   Rotation
with pivot at the top right
of R_i. R_t is the translated
R_i, R_{tr} is the rotated rectangle from R_t, and R_o is the
rotation result.

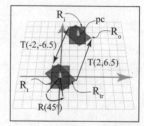

Figure 9.9.   Rotation
with pivot at the center of
R_i. As in Figure 9.8, R_t is
the translated rectangle R_i,
R_{tr} is the rotated rectangle,
and R_o is the result.

9.4   Programming Transformations with Graphics APIs

Tutorial 9.1. Concatenation of Matrices

Tutorial 9.1.
Project Name:
  D3D_TranslateScaleObj
Library Support:
  UWB_MFC_Lib1
  UWB_D3D_Lib8

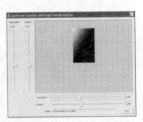

Figure 9.10.   Tutorial 9.1.

- **Goals.** Understand graphics APIs' support for concatenation of transformation operators (matrices).

- **Approach.** Use simple translation and scaling as examples to examine how concatenation can be implemented.

Figure 9.10 is a screenshot of running Tutorial 9.1. This tutorial implements and visualizes the concatenated results of scaling and translation matrices:

$$\mathbf{V}_i \, \mathbf{S}(s_x, s_y) \, \mathbf{T}(t_x, t_y),$$

where $\mathbf{V}_i$ are the vertices of a rectangle. In this case,

$$\text{rectangle vertices:} \begin{cases} V_a = & (0,0), \\ V_b = & (2,0), \\ V_c = & (2,3), \\ V_d = & (0,3). \end{cases}$$

Because V_a is the origin, from our discussion, we know that the scaling operation will be carried out with respect to V_a. In this case, we would expect the rectangle to be scaled by (s_x, s_y) with the left and bottom edges being stationary and the scaled rectangle to be translated by (t_x, t_y). By manipulating the slider bars, we can verify this behavior and that each of the four slider bars controls the corresponding displacements or scaling factors.

    Listing 9.1 shows the CModel class of this tutorial. At label A are the functions that the slider-bar event service functions will call to set the corresponding values for the displacements (i.e., t_x, t_y) and/or scaling factors (i.e., s_x, s_y) at label B. The rectangle we see in the application window is defined at label C. Listing 9.2 is the function that computes and draws the rectangle. At label A, we see the declaration of three transformation operators (matrices). It is important to note that all three operators are of the same D3DXMATRIX data type (all transformation operators are matrices). At label B, as we saw in tutorials from the previous chapter, these two functions compute the translation and scaling matrices. At label C, we call the function D3DXMatrixMultiply() to concatenate the translation and scaling operators into the combined_matrix operator. At this point, combined_matrix ($\mathbf{M}_a$) implements

$$\mathbf{M}_a = \mathbf{S}(s_x, s_y) \, \mathbf{T}(t_x, t_y). \tag{9.6}$$

```
class CModel {
    ⋮
    // called by the slider bar event service routines
A:  void SetTranslation( float x, float y );
    // to update the m_Transate/m_Scale variables
    void SetScale( float x, float y );
  private:
    ⋮
    // These are the tx and ty displacements
B:  float m_TranslateX, m_TranslateY;
    // These are the sx and sy scaling factors
    float m_ScaleX, m_ScaleY;
C:  UWB_PrimitiveRectangle m_Rectangle;    // The rectangle
};
```

Source file. Model.h file in the *Model* folder of the D3D_TranslateScaleObject project.

Listing 9.1. The CModel class of Tutorial 9.1.

```
void CModel::DrawModel() {
    ⋮
    // the operators
A:  D3DXMATRIX translate_matrix, scale_matrix, combined_matrix;
    // compute T(tx,ty)
B:  D3DXMatrixTranslation(&translate_matrix, m_TranslateX, m_TranslateY, 0);
    // compute S(sx,sy)
    D3DXMatrixScaling( &scale_matrix, m_ScaleX, m_ScaleY, 1);
    // Ma = ST
C:  D3DXMatrixMultiply(&combined_matrix, &scale_matrix, &translate_matrix);
D:  LPDIRECT3DDEVICE9 pDevice=UWBD3D_GraphicsSystem::...GetD3DDevice();
    // MW ← ST
    pDevice->SetTransform(D3DTS_WORLD, &combined_matrix);
E:  m_Rectangle.Draw(lod, m_DrawHelper);
    ⋮
}
```

Source file. Model.cpp file in the *Model* folder of the D3D_TranslateScaleObject project.

Listing 9.2. The CModel::DrawModel() function of Tutorial 9.1.

At label D, the combined_matrix is loaded into the WORLD (M_W) matrix processor. Recall that when drawing with D3D, all vertices (V) go through the transformation

$$V\, M_W\, M_V\, M_P.$$

In this case, because M_P and M_V remain unchanged in between updates, and because we are loading M_a into M_W before each redraw, the transformation that affects the rectangle is

$$V_i\, M_a = V_i S(s_x, s_y) T(t_x, t_y).$$

Tutorial 9.2. Order of Matrix Concatenation

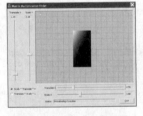

Figure 9.11.   Tutorial 9.2.

- **Goals.** Verify that the order of matrix concatenation is important and that different concatenation ordering would result in different transformation operators.

- **Approach.** Continue with previous tutorial, and allow the user to control the order to concatenate the translation and scaling operators.

Figure 9.11 is a screenshot of running Tutorial 9.2. This tutorial extends Tutorial 9.1 by allowing the user to the control of the order of concatenation for the translation and scaling operators. By clicking on the corresponding radio button in the lower-left corner, the user can select to apply either the M_a operator (Equation (9.6)) from Tutorial 9.1:

$$M_a = S(s_x, s_y) T(t_x, t_y)$$

or

$$M_b = T(t_x, t_y) S(s_x, s_y) \tag{9.7}$$

to the vertices (V_i) of the rectangle. We have already experienced M_a in the previous tutorial. For M_b, notice that the input vertices will be translated before being scaled. For any non-zero (t_x, t_y), the output of the translation operation is a rectangle with non-zero vertex coordinates. From previous discussions, we would expect the scaling operation to change the size of and move the translated rectangle. We can verify these behaviors by manipulating the four slider bars. The implementation of this tutorial is identical to that of Tutorial 9.1 except for the CModel::DrawModel() function, shown in Listing 9.3. When comparing to the DrawModel() function from Listing 9.2, we observe the same computation for the translation and scaling operators (A), the same loading of the WORLD matrix with

```
void CModel::DrawModel() {
      ⋮
A:    D3DXMatrixTranslation(&translate_matrix, m_TranslateX, m_TranslateY, 0);
      D3DXMatrixScaling( &scale_matrix, m_ScaleX, m_ScaleY, 1);
B:    if(!m_bTranslateFirst)
          // computes Mₐ = ST
          D3DXMatrixMultiply(&combined_matrix, &scale_matrix, &translate_matrix);
      else
          // computes M_b = TS
          D3DXMatrixMultiply(&combined_matrix, &translate_matrix, &scale_matrix);
      ⋮
C:    pDevice->SetTransform(D3DTS_WORLD, &combined_matrix);
D:    m_Rectangle.Draw(lod, m_DrawHelper);
}
```

At labels B:
// computes $\mathbf{M}_a = \mathbf{ST}$
// computes $\mathbf{M}_b = \mathbf{TS}$

Source file. Model.cpp file in the *Model* folder of the D3D_MatrixMultipleOrder project.

Listing 9.3. The CModel::DrawModel() function of Tutorial 9.2.

the concatenated results from combined_matrix(C), and the drawing of the rectangle (D). In this case, depending on the radio button selected, at label B we either compute the $\mathbf{M}_a$ or the $\mathbf{M}_b$ operator and store the result in combined_matrix for loading into the WORLD matrix.

Graphics API Matrix Stacks

The concatenation of matrices we experienced in the previous tutorials is a frequently performed operation in interactive computer graphics applications. In addition, as we will see in Chapter 11, we often need to save and restore transformation matrices. Modern graphics APIs typically define a matrix stack to support these operations. A matrix stack is a push-down stack where the basic element of the stack is a transformation matrix. In other words, the matrix stack supports the pushing and popping of an entire transformation matrix onto/off a stack. Furthermore, the matrix stack typically supports operations for concatenating transformation matrices with the top of the stack element. For example, the Direct3D API defines the ID3DXMatrixStack to support the following functions.

- Push(). Duplicates the top of the stack matrix and then performs a typical stack push operation. In this way, the top of the stack matrix is duplicated, and as programmers, we have a copy of the top stack matrix to work with. This operation is important for saving transformation matrices.

- **Pop().** Pops off the current top of the stack. This is a typical stack pop operation, where the current top of the stack is eliminated from the stack. This operation is important for restoring previous transformation matrices.

- **Concatenation.** The ID3DXMatrixStack defines many transformation operators (e.g., TranslateLocal(), ScaleLocal()) where the results of the transformation operation is concatenated with the top of the stack matrix.

Tutorial 9.3. Working with the D3D Matrix Stack.

Tutorial 9.3.
Project Name:
  D3D_MatrixStack
Library Support:
  UWB_MFC_Lib1
  UWB_D3D_Lib8

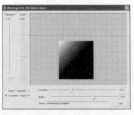

Figure 9.12. Tutorial 9.3.

- **Goals.** Understand the matrix stack utility for concatenating, saving, and restoring of transformation matrices.

- **Approach.** Experience using the D3D matrix stack in a simple application; in this case, we will re-implement Tutorial 9.2 based on the D3D matrix stack utility.

Figure 9.12 is a screenshot of running Tutorial 9.3. The behavior of this tutorial is identical to that of Tutorial 9.2. The only difference between these two tutorials is in the implementation of the CModel::DrawModel() function. In this case, instead of computing and loading transformation matrices explicitly, we take advantage of the D3D matrix stack utility. Listing 9.4 shows that, at label A, we request D3D to create a ID3DXMatrixStack object, pMatrixStack. At label B1, we load an identity matrix to the top of the stack and perform a Push() operation to duplicate this identity matrix for later use. At this point, the pMatrixStack has two elements, and both are identity matrices. Depending on the GUI radio button selection, either the operations at label C or D will be performed. In either case, the TranslateLocal() and ScaleLocal() functions compute the appropriate operator *and* concatenate the operator to the top of the pMatrixStack. At label E, we call the GetTop() function to access and load the concatenated matrix to the WORLD matrix processor. With the WORLD matrix processor properly loaded, at label F we send the rectangle vertices to the D3D RC for drawing. Recall that at label B1, we have pushed and saved a copy of the identity matrix on the stack. Now at label B2, we pop off the concatenated matrix that we no longer need and re-initialize the WORLD matrix with the saved identity matrix at label G.

It is important to understand the order of concatenation for the matrix stack transformation function calls, that

```
pMatrixStack->TranslateLocal( ... )
```

```
    void CModel::DrawModel() {
    ⋮
        // reference to a matrix stack
A:  ID3DXMatrixStack *pMatrixStack;
        // Creates a matrix stack object
        D3DXCreateMatrixStack(0, &pMatrixStack);
        // Loads identity to the top of stack
B1: pMatrixStack->LoadIdentity();
        // duplicate the top of the stack and push
        pMatrixStack->Push();
            if (!m_bTranslateFirst)
                // concatenate translation
        C:  pMatrixStack->TranslateLocal(m_TranslateX,m_TranslateY);
                // and scaling with top of stack
                pMatrixStack->ScaleLocal(m_ScaleX, m_ScaleY);
            else
        D:  pMatrixStack->ScaleLocal(m_ScaleX, m_ScaleY);
                pMatrixStack->TranslateLocal(m_TranslateX, m_TranslateY);
        // Load WORLD with top of stack
    E:  pDevice->SetTransform(D3DTS_WORLD, pMatrixStack->GetTop());
            // Draw the rectangle
    F:  m_Rectangle.Draw(lod, m_DrawHelper);
            // pop-off computed transform and restore the saved identity matrix
B2: pMatrixStack->Pop();
        // Load identity in to WORLD
  G:  pDevice->SetTransform( D3DTS_WORLD, pMatrixStack->GetTop() );
    ⋮
```

Source file. `Model.cpp` file in the *Model* folder of the D3D_MatrixStack project.

Listing 9.4. The `CModel::DrawModel()` function of Tutorial 9.3.

computes

$$\text{top of stack matrix} = \mathbf{T}\,\mathbf{M}_t,$$

where $\mathbf{M}_t$ is the current matrix at the top of the stack. The important detail is that the operator $\mathbf{T}$ is concatenated on the left of $\mathbf{M}_t$. This concatenation on the left side of the top of stack matrix is true for all `Local` transformations functions in D3D. For example, at label C, after the `TranslateLocal()` function call, the computed top of stack matrix $\mathbf{M}_{t1}$ is

$$\mathbf{M}_{t1} = \mathbf{T}\,\mathbf{M}_t,$$

and after the `ScaleLocal()` function call, the concatenated matrix at the top of the stack, $\mathbf{M}_{t2}$, is

$$\mathbf{M}_{t2} = \mathbf{S}\,\mathbf{M}_{t1} = \mathbf{S}\,\mathbf{T}\,\mathbf{M}_{t}.$$

Because in this case the top of matrix stack was initialized to the identity matrix, or $\mathbf{M}_{t} = \mathbf{I}_4$,

$$\mathbf{M}_{t2} = \mathbf{I}_4\,\mathbf{S}\,\mathbf{T} = \mathbf{S}\,\mathbf{T}.$$

We see that at label C, we are computing the $\mathbf{M}_a$ operator of Equation (9.6). In exactly the same manner, at label D we are computing the $\mathbf{M}_b$ operator of Equation (9.7).

In this tutorial, we observe the push and pop functionality for saving and restoring matrices. In addition, we see that the matrix stack can be used as an implicit target for concatenating transformation operators. In this case, we compute transformation operators without explicitly managing matrices. From now on, we will work almost exclusively with the matrix stack when computing transformation operators.

Tutorial 9.4. Pivoted Scaling/Rotation

Tutorial 9.4.
Project Name:
  D3D_PivotedRotation
Library Support:
  UWB_MFC_Lib1
  UWB_D3D_Lib8

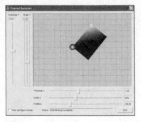

Figure 9.13.   Tutorial 9.4.

- **Goals.** Verify and implement the pivoted scaling and rotation transformation.

- **Approach.** Allow the user to select pivot positions; construct the corresponding transformation operator; examine the transformation results.

Figure 9.13 is a screenshot of running Tutorial 9.4. This tutorial implements the transformation

$$\mathbf{M}_c = \mathbf{S}(s_x, s_y)\,\mathbf{R}(\theta)\,\mathbf{T}(t_x, t_y) \tag{9.8}$$

and draws

$$\mathbf{V}_i\,\mathbf{M}_c,$$

where, similar to Tutorial 9.1, $\mathbf{V}_i$ are

$$\text{rectangle vertices:} \begin{cases} V_a = & (0,0), \\ V_b = & (2,0), \\ V_c = & (2,3), \\ V_d = & (0,3). \end{cases}$$

Once again, the slider bars on the application window control the corresponding transformation parameters (e.g., `TranslateX` controls t_x). By manipulating the

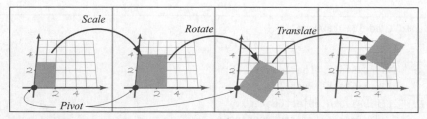

Figure 9.14. Transforming rectangle pivot at lower-left corner ($\mathbf{M}_c$).

slider bars, a user can specify the parameters for the transformation and observe the transformed rectangle. Recall the discussion in Tutorial 9.1 that by default with the specified vertices, the given rectangle's pivot position is its lower-left corner, V_a. Figure 9.14 details the effect of each of the operators in the $\mathbf{M}_c$ transformation on the rectangle. A detail that may be slightly counterintuitive is the fact that the scaling operator $\mathbf{S}$ is the leftmost operator in Equation (9.8), and yet this operator is applied first. In our case, the leftmost operator in a concatenated operator always operates on input vertices first.

In addition to implementing $\mathbf{M}_c$, this tutorial also allows the user to choose the pivot position for the scaling and rotation transformations to be the center of the rectangle. Figure 9.15 illustrates that, as discussed, we must first translate the *pivot* position to the origin before applying scaling and rotation operators. Because both scaling and rotation have the same pivot position,

$$\mathbf{M}_d = \mathbf{T}(-pt_x, -pt_y)\,\mathbf{S}(s_x, s_y)\,\mathbf{R}(\theta)\,\mathbf{T}(pt_x, pt_y)\,\mathbf{T}(t_x, t_y), \qquad (9.9)$$

where (pt_x, pt_y) is the pivot position. In this case, the pivot position is the center of the rectangle, or $pt = (1.0, 1.5)$. Listing 9.5 shows the implementation of the `CModel::DrawModel()` function where we implement the $\mathbf{M}_d$ transform. At label A, the top of the matrix stack is initialized to be the identity matrix. At label B, we determine what the user's choice of pivot position is. The $\mathbf{M}_d$ operator is computed at label C. Notice that if the user chooses the lower-left corner

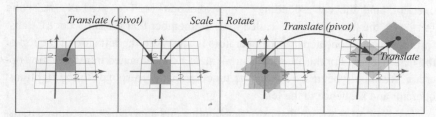

Figure 9.15. Transforming rectangle pivot at center.

Source file. `Model.cpp` file in the *Model* folder of the `D3D_PivotedRotation` project.

```
void CModel::DrawModel() {
    ⋮
```

A:
```
    pMatrixStack->LoadIdentity();
    pMatrixStack->Push()
```

B:
```
    if(m_bPivotAtObjectCenter)
        // center of the rectangle
        pivot = vec3(1.0, 1.5, 0.0);
    else
        // default pivot position is the lower left corner
        pivot = vec3(0.0, 0.0, 0.0);
    // Mt1 ← T(tx,ty,0)Mt
```

C:
```
    pMatrixStack->TranslateLocal(m_TranslateX, m_TranslateY, 0.0f);
    // Mt2 ← T(px,py,0)Mt1
    pMatrixStack->TranslateLocal(pivot.x, pivot.y, 0.0f);
    // Mt3 ← R(θ)Mt2
    pMatrixStack->RotateAxisLocal( &z_axis, m_RotateAngleRadians );
    // Mt4 ← S(sx,sy,1)Mt3
    pMatrixStack->ScaleLocal(m_ScaleX, m_ScaleY, 1.0f);
    // Mt5 ← T(-px,-py,0)Mt4
    pMatrixStack->TranslateLocal(-pivot.x, -pivot.y, 0.0f);
    // MW ← Mt5
```

D:
```
    pDevice->SetTransform(D3DTS_WORLD, pMatrixStack->GetTop());
    m_Rectangle.Draw(lod, m_DrawHelper);
    ⋮
```

Listing 9.5. The `CModel::DrawModel()` function of Tutorial 9.4.

to be the pivot position, we would perform two translation operations with zero displacements and effectively compute $\mathbf{M}_c$ of Equation (9.8). Lastly at label D, the computed matrix is loaded into the WORLD matrix processor, and the rectangle is drawn. Notice the correspondence between the ordering of operators in Equation (9.9) and the sequence of function calls at label C: $\mathbf{T}(t_x,t_y)$ is the *rightmost* operator, and the corresponding `TranslateLocal(m_TranslateX, m_TranslateY)` is the function that is called *first*. Remember that for D3D Local transform functions, concatenation of operators is always to the left side of the top of the matrix stack. For this reason, to implement a concatenated transformation operator, we should begin by calling the function that corresponds to the rightmost operator and sequence to the left.

In this tutorial, we see that by understanding and analyzing the required transform operator carefully, the actual implementation can be rather straightforward.

Tutorial 9.5. Transforming Individual Primitives

- **Goals.** Experience applying different transformations to different primitives; understand that we can load and change the matrix processors during each redraw of the application window.

- **Approach.** Work with two primitives and allow the user to specify different transforms for each primitive; examine how we support programming the setting of different transformations.

Figure 9.16 is a screenshot of running Tutorial 9.5. From manipulating the slider bars, we can verify that the translation slider bars control the positions of both of the rectangles, whereas the scale/rotate slider bars control only one of the rectangles. In this case, the vertices of the two rectangles, R_1 and R_2, are

$$R_1 \text{ vertices:} \begin{cases} V_a = & (0,0), \\ V_b = & (2,0), \\ V_c = & (2,3), \\ V_d = & (0,3), \end{cases} \quad R_2 \text{ vertices:} \begin{cases} V_e = & (5,5), \\ V_f = & (8,5), \\ V_g = & (8,6), \\ V_h = & (5,6). \end{cases}$$

Tutorial 9.5.
Project Name:
  D3D_PerPrimitiveTrans
Library Support:
  UWB_MFC_Lib1
  UWB_D3D_Lib8

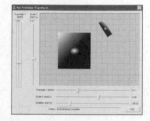

Figure 9.16. Tutorial 9.5.

Notice that in both cases, the scaling and rotation is performed with respect to the center of the rectangles. At this point, we can derive the two transformations for the two rectangles to be

$$\mathbf{M}_1 = \mathbf{T}(-p1.x, -p1.y)\,\mathbf{S}(s_x, s_y)\,\mathbf{T}(p1.x, p1.y)\,\mathbf{T}(t_x, t_y),$$
$$\mathbf{M}_2 = \mathbf{T}(-p2.x, -p2.y)\,\mathbf{R}(\theta)\,\mathbf{T}(p2.x, p2.y)\mathbf{T}(t_x, t_y),$$

where $p1 = (1, 1.5)$ and $p2 = (6.5, 5.5)$ are the center (pivot) positions of the rectangles. We see that in this case, we must apply different transformation operators to each of the rectangles. The solution structure of this tutorial is identical to the others from this chapter except for the CModel class. Listing 9.6 shows the relevant definition of the CModel class. As in all previous tutorials from this chapter, the slider bars' event service routines call the functions defined at label A to set the parameters for transformation (defined at label C). The two rectangles are defined at label B. Listing 9.7 shows the details of transformation setup and drawing. At label A, we initialize the top of the matrix stack and save a copy of the identity matrix. At label B, we concatenate the translation operator, $\mathbf{T}(t_x, t_y)$, to the top of the matrix stack. Since both $\mathbf{M}_1$ and $\mathbf{M}_2$ need this operation, at label C1 we duplicate and push a copy of this matrix onto the stack. At this point, there are three elements on the matrix stack: an initial identity matrix saved by the Push() operation at label A and two copies of the TranslateLocal() matrix resulting from the Push() operation at label C1. At label D, we proceed to

Source file. Model.h file
in the *Model* folder of the
D3D_PerPrimitiveTransform
project.

```
class CModel {
    ⋮
    // Called by the slider bar event service routines
A:  void SetTranslation( float x, float y );
    // these functions set the corresponding
    void SetScale( float x, float y );
    // transformation parameters defined below
    void SetRotation( float angle_radians );
  private:
    ⋮
    // The rectangles on screen
B:  UWB_PrimitiveRectangle m_Rectangle1, m_Rectangle2;
    // parameters for transformation: (t_x,t_y)
C:  float m_TranslateX, m_TranslateY;
    float m_ScaleX, m_ScaleY, m_RotateAngleRadians; // (s_x,s_y), and θ
};
```

Listing 9.6. The CModel class of Tutorial 9.5.

Source file. Model.cpp
file in the *Model* folder of the
D3D_PerPrimitiveTransform
project.

```
void CModel::DrawModel() {
    ⋮
A:  pMatrixStack->LoadIdentity();
    pMatrixStack->Push();
B:  pMatrixStack->TranslateLocal(m_TranslateX, m_TranslateY, 0.0f);
C1: pMatrixStack->Push();
        vec3 pivot = m_Rectangle1.GetLocation();
    D:  pMatrixStack->TranslateLocal(pivot.x, pivot.y, 0.0f);
        pMatrixStack->ScaleLocal(m_ScaleX, m_ScaleY, 1.0f);
        pMatrixStack->TranslateLocal(-pivot.x, -pivot.y, 0.0f);
    E:  pDevice->SetTransform( D3DTS_WORLD, pMatrixStack->GetTop() );
        m_Rectangle1.Draw( lod, m_DrawHelper );
C2: pMatrixStack->Pop();
F1: pMatrixStack->Push();
    G:  // calls matrix stack translate/rotate functions
        // loads the D3D WORLD matrix processor and draws m_Rectangle2
F2: pMatrixStack->Pop();
    ⋮
```

Listing 9.7. The CModel::DrawModel() function of Tutorial 9.5.

compute the $\mathbf{M}_1$ operator, and at label E, the concatenated matrix at the top of the stack is loaded into the WORLD processor for drawing of rectangle R_1. The Pop() operation at label C2 eliminates the $\mathbf{M}_1$ operator at the top of the matrix stack and restores the $\mathbf{T}(t_x, t_y)$ operator that was saved by the Push() operation at label C1. The code at labels F and G computes $\mathbf{M}_2$ and draws R_2 in a similar manner as that for $\mathbf{M}_1$ and R_1.

This tutorial demonstrates using the matrix stack for saving/restoring shared transform operators, and that we can load/override the matrix processor (e.g., the WORLD matrix processor) to change the transformations of different primitives.

UWBGL_D3D_Lib9

This library extends from Lib8 by extending the D3D_DrawHelper class to support the matrix stack and by designing the new XformInfo class to abstract the programming of transformations.

Change summary. See p. 521 for a summary of changes to the library.

The D3D_DrawHelpler **class.** As shown in Listing 9.8, the updated implementation of UWBD3D_DrawHelper class has an instance of the D3D matrix stack (B) and implements the transformation functions of the DrawHelper class (A). Listing 9.9 shows the implementation of the transformation functions. First, notice that for all cases, before the functions return, we load the top of the matrix stack to

```
class UWBD3D_DrawHelper : public UWB_DrawHelper {
    ⋮

    A: transformation functions defined by UWB_DrawHelper (the parent class)
    bool InitializeModelTransform();
    bool AccumulateModelTransform(vec3 translation, vec3 scale,
                                  float rotation_radians, vec3 pivot);
    bool PushModelTransform();
    bool PopModelTransform();
  private:
    ⋮

    B:   ID3DXMatrixStack* m_pMatrixStack;
};
```

Listing 9.8. The UWBD3D_DrawHelper class (Lib9).

Source file. uwbgl_D3DDrawHelper3.h file in the *D3D Files/ DrawHelper* subfolder of the UWBGL_D3D_Lib9 project.

Source file.
uwbgl_D3DDrawHelper3.cpp
file in the *D3D Files/
DrawHelper* subfolder of
the UWBGL_D3D_Lib9 project.

```
A:   bool UWBD3D_DrawHelper::PushModelTransform()
        m_pMatrixStack->Push();
        pDevice->SetTransform(D3DTS_WORLD, m_pMatrixStack->GetTop());
B:   bool UWBD3D_DrawHelper::PopModelTransform()
        m_pMatrixStack->Pop();
        pDevice->SetTransform(D3DTS_WORLD, m_pMatrixStack->GetTop());
C:   bool UWBD3D_DrawHelper::InitializeModelTransform()
        m_pMatrixStack->LoadIdentity();
        pDevice->SetTransform(D3DTS_WORLD, m_pMatrixStack->GetTop());
D:   bool UWBD3D_DrawHelper::AccumulateModelTransform(trans, scale,
                                                     rotate, pivot)
        // Mt1 ← T(tx,ty,tz)Mt
        m_pMatrixStack->TranslateLocal( trans.x, trans.y, trans.z);
        // Mt2 ← T(px,py,pz)Mt1
        m_pMatrixStack->TranslateLocal(pivot.x, pivot.y, pivot.z);
        // Mt3 ← R(θ)Mt2
        m_pMatrixStack->RotateAxisLocal(&z_axis, rotation_radians);
        // Mt4 ← S(sx,sy,sz)Mt3
        m_pMatrixStack->ScaleLocal(scale.x, scale.y, scale.z);
        // Mt5 ← T(-px,-py,-pz)Mt4
        m_pMatrixStack->TranslateLocal(-pivot.x,-pivot.y,-pivot.z);
        // MW ← Mt5
        pDevice->SetTransform(D3DTS_WORLD,m_pMatrixStack->GetTop());
```

Listing 9.9. Transformation functions UWBD3D_DrawHelper (Lib9).

the D3D WORLD matrix processor. This ensures the synchronization of the top of the matrix stack with the WORLD processor. We see that at labels A and B, the Push() and Pop() functions save and restore the top of the matrix stack. At label C, the InitializeModelTransform() function loads the matrix stack with the identity matrix. At label D, the AccumulateModelTransform() function computes a new operator at the top of the matrix stack. The transformation operator being computed is

$$
\begin{aligned}
\mathbf{M}_{t5} &= \mathbf{T}(-p_x,-p_y)\,\mathbf{M}_{t4} \\
&= \mathbf{T}(-p_x,-p_y)\,\mathbf{S}(s_x,s_y)\,\mathbf{M}_{t3} \\
&= \mathbf{T}(-p_x,-p_y)\,\mathbf{S}(s_x,s_y)\,\mathbf{R}(\theta)\mathbf{M}_{t2} \\
&= \mathbf{T}(-p_x,-p_y)\,\mathbf{S}(s_x,s_y)\,\mathbf{R}(\theta)\mathbf{T}(p_x,p_y)\mathbf{M}_{t1},
\end{aligned}
$$

or

$$\mathbf{M}_{t5} = \mathbf{T}(-p_x, -p_y)\mathbf{S}(s_x, s_y)\mathbf{R}(\theta)\mathbf{T}(p_x, p_y)\mathbf{T}(t_x, t_y)\mathbf{M}_t, \qquad (9.10)$$

where $\mathbf{M}_{t5}$ is the final top of the matrix stack, $\mathbf{M}_t$ is the initial top of the matrix stack, and (p_x, p_y) is the pivot position. In this way, this function concatenates (or accumulates) the scaling, rotation, and translation operators with the top of the matrix stack. Notice the following

- **Pivot position.** Scaling and rotation have the same pivot position. This is more restrictive then the general pivoted scaling and rotation of Equations (9.4) and (9.5). However, we do have a simpler interface to the function, and in most cases we require the same pivot position for scaling and rotation operations.

- **Order of operation.** The scaling operation is applied before the rotation operation, with the translation operation being applied last. This ordering computes more intuitive results.

Once again, the `AccumuateModelTransform()` function changes the D3D WORLD matrix by loading it with the accumulated results from the top of the matrix stack.

The `UWB_XformInfo` class. The `UWB_XformInfo` class is shown in Listing 9.10. At label D, we see that the `XformInfo` class defines instance variables to represent the transformation parameters. This class then provides the set/get functions (A and A1) to support accessing the translation, rotation, scaling, and pivot settings.

```
class UWB_XformInfo {
A:   vec3 GetTranslation() const;
     void SetTranslation(vec3 translation);
     ⋮
     // Get/Set functions for scaling, rotation, and pivot
     ⋮
B:   void SetUpModelStack(UWB_DrawHelper& draw_helper) const;
C:   void DrawPivot(UWB_DrawHelper&, float size=1.0f);

   protected:
D:   vec3 m_translation, m_scale; // (tx,ty) and (sx,sy)
     float m_rotation_radians;    // θ in radians
     vec3 m_pivot;                // pivot position for scaling and rotation
};
```

Source file.
uwbgl_XformInfo1.h/cpp files in the *Common Files/ XFormInfo* subfolder of the UWBGL_D3D_Lib9 project.

Listing 9.10. The `UWB_DrawHelper` class (Lib9).

A1: `vec3 UWB_XformInfo::GetTranslation() const{ return m_translation; }`
`void UWB_XformInfo::SetTranslation(vec3 translation){ m_translation = translation; }`

B1: `void UWB_XformInfo::SetUpModelStack(UWB_DrawHelper& draw_helper) const`
`    draw_helper.AccumulateModelTransform(m_translation,m_scale,m_rotation_radians,m_pivot);`

C1: `void UWB_XformInfo::DrawPivot(UWB_DrawHelper &draw_helper, float size)`

⋮

`    draw_helper.DrawCircle( m_pivot, size);`

Listing 9.10. (cont.)

At labels B and B1, we see that these transformation parameters are sent to the `DrawHelper` class for setting the corresponding graphics API–dependent matrix processors (e.g. the `WORLD` matrix of D3D). At labels C and C1, for debugging purposes, we support the drawing of a circle at the pivot position.

In the next tutorial, we examine how to use these new facilities to coordinate the transformation of primitives.

Tutorial 9.6. Using the `XformInfo` Abstraction

Tutorial 9.6.
Project Name:
 D3D_XformInfo
Library Support:
 UWB_MFC_Lib1
 UWB_D3D_Lib9

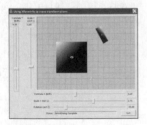

Figure 9.17. Tutorial 9.6.

- **Goals.** Understand how to use the `UWB_XformInfo` abstraction for supporting transformations.

- **Approach.** Examine the implementation of Tutorial 9.5 based on the `Xform Info` class.

Figure 9.17 is a screenshot of running Tutorial 9.6. By manipulating the slider bars, we can verify that this tutorial has exactly the same behavior as that of Tutorial 9.5. The only difference is that our implementation is based on the `XformInfo` class. Listing 9.11 details the `CModel` class of Tutorial 9.6. At label A, `RectWithXform` is introduced to clearly illustrate the association between `XformInfo` and `Primitive`. At label B, we see the declaration of the two rectangles. In this case, the set transformation functions selectively update the rectangles' `XformInfo`. We see that at label C the translation information is updated into both; at label D, the scaling information is updated into only R_1; whereas at label E, the rotation information is only updated in R_2's `XformInfo`. At label F, we call the transformation functions of the `DrawHelper` class to initialize and set up the D3D `WORLD` matrix processor before issuing the draw command.

This tutorial demonstrates how to use the new `XformInfo` class to record transformation information and work with the transformation functions in the `DrawHelper` class to accomplish the desired transformed effects.

Source file. Model.h file in the *Model* folder of the D3D_XformInfo project.

```
class CModel {
    ⋮
  private:
    ⋮
    // a struct: For simplicity and clarity of illustration
```
`A:`
```
    struct RectWithXform {
        UWB_PrimitiveRectangle m_rect; // A rectangle
        UWB_XformInfo m_xform; };        // The associated transformation information
    // R₁ and R₂ rectangles with transformation information
```
`B:`
```
    RectWithXform m_Rect1, m_Rect2;
};
```

`C:`
```
    void CModel::SetTranslation(float x, float y) {
        m_Rect1.m_xform.SetTranslation(vec3(x,y,0));    // set the same translation to both
        m_Rect2.m_xform.SetTranslation(vec3(x,y,0)); } // R₁ and R₂
    // R₁ only
```
`D:`
```
    void CModel::SetScale(float x, float y) { m_Rect1.m_xform.SetScale(vec3(x,y,0)); }
    // R₂ only
```
`E:`
```
    void CModel::SetRotation(float theta) { m_Rect2.m_xform.SetRotationRadians(theta); }
```
`F:`
```
    void CModel::DrawModel()
        ⋮
        m_DrawHelper.InitializeModelTransform();
        m_DrawHelper.PushModelTransform();
        m_Rect1.m_xform.SetUpModelStack( m_DrawHelper );
        m_Rect1.m_rect.Draw( lod, m_DrawHelper );
        m_DrawHelper.PopModelTransform();
        // ... similar operations for m_Rect2
```

Listing 9.11. The CModel class of Tutorial 9.6.

Tutorial 9.7. Supporting User Interaction with XformInfo

Tutorial 9.7.
Project Name:
D3D_XformInfoControls
Library Support:
  UWB_MFC_Lib1
  UWB_D3D_Lib9

- **Goals.** Examine the effects of changing the parameters in the XformInfo class.

- **Approach.** Implement a GUI class that allows the user to interactively change every parameter in the XformInfo class.

Source file. `Model.h` file in the *Model* folder of the `D3D_XformInfoControls` project.

```
class CModel {
    ⋮
    // sets the m_pSelectedRect reference
    // to either R₁ or R₂
A:  void SelectRect1();
    void SelectRect2();
    // returns xform of m_pSelectedRect
B:  UWB_XformInfo GetSelectedXform() const;
    // sets xform to m_pSelectedRect
    void SetSelectedXform( const UWB_XformInfo& xform );

    private:
    ⋮
C:  RectWithXform m_Rect1, m_Rect2; // Rectangles: R₁ and R₂
D:  RectWithXform* m_pSelectedRect; // points to either R₁ or R₂
}
```

Listing 9.12. The `CModel` class of Tutorial 9.7.

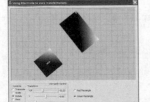

Figure 9.18. Tutorial 9.7.

Source file.
`XformInfoControl.h/cpp` in the *Controls* folder of the `D3D_XformInfoControls` project.

Figure 9.18 is a screenshot of running Tutorial 9.7. The implementation is very similar to that of Tutorial 9.6 with an *identical* `CModel::DrawModel()` routine. The main differences are illustrated in Listing 9.12. At label A, the `CModel` class lets its user *select* a rectangle. The selected rectangle is pointed to by the `m_pSelectedRect` reference defined at label D. The user of the `CModel` class can call the get/set functions at label B to access the `XformInfo` of the selected rectangle. The service functions of the "Red/Green Rectangle" radio button call the corresponding select functions at label A.

The `XformInfo` of the selected rectangle is controlled by the GUI elements of the `XformInfo` control located at the lower-left corner of the application window. The `XformInfo` control is a GUI element *container window* based on the idea introduced in Tutorial 2.8 (on p. 69): related GUI elements are grouped inside a container window for better interaction and for reuse. In this case, on the GUI front end, the `IDD_XFORMCONTROL_DIALOG` is created to contain all the GUI elements necessary to control each element in an `XformInfo` object. A placeholder (`IDD_XFORM_CONTROL_PLACEHOLDER`) is created on the application window to support run-time placing of the container window with the `ReplaceDialog Control()` function. In the back-end implementation, the `CXformInfoControl` class is created to implement the necessary GUI functionality. The `CXformInfo`

Control class is capable of controlling any XformInfo object inside a CModel class that implements SetSelected Xform() and GetSelectedXform():

Source file. Model.h file in the *Model* folder of the D3D_XformInfoControls project.

```
// Access the currently selected XformInfo object
UWB_XformInfo GetSelectedXform() const;
// Sets the currently selected XformInfo object
void SetSelectedXform(const UWB_XformInfo& xform);
```

The tutorials in the rest of this book will reuse the XformInfo control GUI container window and the corresponding XformInfoControl class for controlling transformations.

Tutorial 9.8. The Ball-Shooting Program with XformInfo

- **Goals.** Understand that we can accomplish all primitive movements and size changes by working with transformations.

- **Approach.** Re-implement the CBall class in the ball-shooting program to include an instance of XformInfo and support interaction via updating transformations.

Tutorial 9.8.
Project Name:
  D3D_BallShoot3
Library Support:
  UWB_MFC_Lib1
  UWB_D3D_Lib9

Figure 9.19 is a screenshot of running Tutorial 9.8. Notice that the behavior of this program is identical to the ball-shooting program we have worked with. In fact, the only difference in this implementation is in the CBall implementation. Listing 9.13 shows the details of the CBall class. In this implementation, whereas the CBall class still subclasses from the PrimitiveCircle, we will support all geometry changes via the m_Xform (an XformInfo) object defined at label C. Notice that at label D, the constructor, we initialize the superclass circle to be a unit circle located at the origin. This unit circle is the reference for all transformation and will remain constant throughout the lifetime of the CBall object. At label A, we override all of the geometry-related functions. At label A1, we implement the corresponding functions by manipulating the m_Xform object with respect to the underlying unit circle. For example, instead of changing the center position of the circle, we implement the MoveTo() function by translating the unit circle; changing the radius of a circle is implemented as scaling the unit circle; and so on. With the proper transformation settings, label B1 shows that we draw the CBall object by first setting up the model transformation and then sending the vertices of a unit circle down.

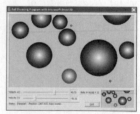

Figure 9.19. Tutorial 9.8.

In this tutorial, we observe that transformation can be a valuable tool for supporting user interaction. In general, if a user wants to manipulate the geometry of a complex object with a large number of vertices, it can become expensive to recompute the object's position and update all the vertices. For example, if the

```
    class CBall : public UWB_PrimitiveCircle
A:      virtual void MoveTo(float, float);
        virtual void MouseDownVertex(int, float, float);
        virtual vec3 GetLocation() const;
        virtual void Update(float elapsed_seconds);
    protected:
B:      virtual void DrawPrimitive(eLevelOfDetail lod,
                                   UWB_DrawHelper& draw_helper) const;

    private:
C:      UWB_XformInfo   m_Xform;
```

```
D:  CBall::CBall() { SetCenter(vec3(0, 0, 0));  SetRadius(1.0f); }
A1: vec3 CBall::GetLocation() const { return m_Xform.GetTranslation();}
    void CBall::MoveTo(float x, float y)
        { m_Xform.SetTranslation(vec3(x, y, 0.0f));}
    void CBall::MouseDownVertex(int id, float x, float y)
        ⋮
        vec3 center = m_Xform.GetTranslation();
        vec3 pt(x, y, 0.0f);
        m_Xform.SetScale(length(center-pt));
        ⋮
    void CBall::Update(float elapsed_seconds)
        ⋮
        vec3 displacement = elapsed_seconds * GetVelocity();
        m_Xform.SetTranslation(m_Xform.GetTranslation() + displacement);
        ⋮
        ⋮
B1: void CBall::DrawPrimitive(eLevelOfDetail lod,
                               UWB_DrawHelper& draw_helper) const
        draw_helper.PushModelTransform();
        draw_helper.InitializeModelTransform();
        m_Xform.SetUpModelStack(draw_helper);  // sets up matrix stack
        __super::DrawPrimitive(lod, draw_helper);  // circle's draw function
        draw_helper.PopModelTransform();
```

Source file. CBall.h file in the *Model* folder of the D3D_BallShoot3 project.

Listing 9.13. The CBall class of Tutorial 9.8.

user wants to scale a teapot object with thousands of vertices, it can be inefficient to go through all vertices to compute their new positions. In general, it is more efficient to manipulate the geometry of objects via the transformation operators.

Tutorial 9.9. A Face for Reference

- **Goal.** Define a reference object to assist in the studying of coordinate transformation, and have some fun when doing so.

- **Approach.** Draw a face based on simple geometric shapes, and then program the face with our library.

Figure 9.20 is a screenshot of running Tutorial 9.9. This tutorial implements the simple geometric face as defined by Figure 9.21. We will use this as reference geometry for studying coordinate transformation in Chapter 10.

Tutorial 9.9.
Project Name:
  D3D_XformList
Library Support:
  UWB_MFC_Lib1
  UWB_D3D_Lib9

Figure 9.20.   Tutorial 9.9.

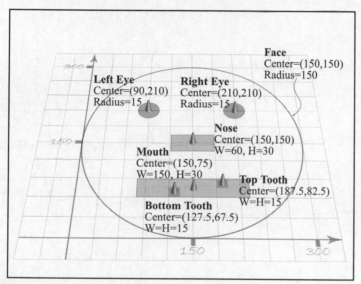

Figure 9.21. Measurements of the simple geometric face.

10

Coordinate Systems

This chapter discusses coordinate systems and the transformation between different coordinate systems. This chapter:

- analyzes the world2ndc matrix we have worked with in all of the tutorials;
- explains the need for world and normalized device coordinate systems;
- describes and experiments with the world coordinate window;
- derives all essential coordinate transformation operators and demonstrates how to implement these operators.

After this chapter we should:

- understand the difference between modeling design space and device drawing space;
- understand the need for transforming mouse click positions to the world coordinate space.

In addition, with respect to hands-on programming, we should:

- be able to program $\mathbf{M}_{w2n}$ operators to support any user-specified world coordinate window;
- be able to utilize graphics API matrix processors in supporting necessary coordinate transformation operations;
- be able to transform mouse clicks to the world coordinate space.

10.1   Understanding Tutorial 3.1

Recall that in the first tutorial of Chapter 3, we began by measuring and discussing how to draw two squares with the following measurements:

$$\text{LargeSquare}_{\text{wc}} = \begin{cases} V_a = & (160, \quad 122), \\ V_b = & (80, \quad 122), \\ V_c = & (80, \quad 42), \\ V_d = & (160, \quad 42), \end{cases} \tag{10.1}$$

wc. Abbreviation for world coordinate. We will study the details of this coordinate system in Section 10.3.

and

$$\text{SmallSquare}_{\text{wc}} = \begin{cases} V_a = & (160, \quad 122), \\ V_e = & (210, \quad 122), \\ V_f = & (210, \quad 172), \\ V_g = & (160, \quad 172). \end{cases} \tag{10.2}$$

Tutorial 3.1 displayed these squares where each millimeter was represented with a pixel on the application window.

Tutorial 10.1. The world2ndc (w2n) Transform

Tutorial 10.1.
Project Name
   D3D_ViewTransform0

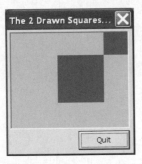

Figure 10.1.   Tutorial 10.1: Re-implement Tutorial 3.1 with 200×160 drawing area.

- **Goal.** Understand the w2n transformation operator we have encountered in all of the tutorials.

- **Approach.** Analyze the simplest tutorials we have worked with and study the effect of the operator.

Figure 10.1 is a screenshot of running Tutorial 10.1. This tutorial is identical to Tutorial 3.1 except that the UI drawing area is 200 pixels $\times$ 160 pixels. We can verify that vertices V_e, V_f, and V_g are outside of the UI drawing area and are not visible. Recall that before we developed the UWBGL_D3D_Lib support, drawing was performed during the GrfxWindowD3D::OnPaint() function call, as shown in Listing 10.1. We are now equipped with sufficient knowledge to completely understand this very first graphics API tutorial. In particular, we are interested in understanding the mysterious Step 2 of setting and computing the parameters for the coordinate systems. Based on the knowledge learned from the previous chapters, we understand that in Step 2, we first initialize all three of the D3D matrix processors (WORLD, VIEW, and PROJECTION) to the identity matrix. We then compute the w2n matrix by concatenating a translation and a scaling matrix. Finally, we load the w2n matrix into the VIEW matrix processor. In fact, a similar code

---

```
void CGrfxWindowD3D::OnPaint()
```
> **Step 1:** *select graphics hardware render buffer.*

⋮

> **Step 2:** *initialize selected hardware and set the coordinate system parameters.*

⋮

```
// Initialize D3D matrix processors setting all three
// matrix processors to identity matrix
m_pD3DDevice->SetTransform(D3DTS_WORLD, &identity);
m_pD3DDevice->SetTransform(D3DTS_VIEW, &identity);
m_pD3DDevice->SetTransform(D3DTS_PROJECTION, &identity);

D3DXMATRIX world2ndc;                      // Coordinate Transformation operator
D3DXVECTOR3 scale(2.0f/width, 2.0f/height, 1.0f); // Parameters for the operator
D3DXVECTOR3 translate(-1.0f, -1.0f, 0.0);          //
// compute the coordinate transformation operator
D3DXMatrixTransformation(&world2ndc, scale, translate);
// Load the operator into the D3D VIEW matrix
m_pD3DDevice->SetTransform(D3DTS_VIEW, &world2ndc);
```

> **Step 3:** *clear drawing buffer and draw two squares.*

⋮

```
v[0].m_point = D3DXVECTOR3(160,122,0);
v[1].m_point = D3DXVECTOR3( 80,122,0);
```

⋮

```
m_pD3DDevice->DrawPrimitiveUP(D3DPT_TRIANGLEFAN, 2, (CONST void *)v, ...);
```

⋮

Source file.
GrfxWindowD3D.cpp file in the *GrfxWindow* folder of the D3D_ViewTransform0 project.

Listing 10.1. `CGrfxWndD3D::OnPaint()` (Tutorial 10.1)

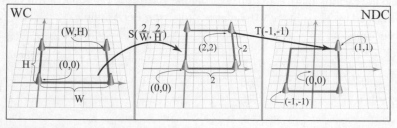

Figure 10.2. The operations of w2n.

fragment exists in every tutorial we have worked with. We perform these operations each time we initialize the graphics API for redraw: in the earlier tutorials when servicing the Redraw/Paint events (in the OnPaint() function); and in the later tutorials, when redrawing the WindowHandler UI drawing area (in the DrawGraphics() function). Figure 10.2 shows the details of the transformation operation that is implemented by the w2n matrix:

- **Scale factor.** Recall that the width and height parameters are the dimensions of the application window. In Listing 10.1, the scaling factors are defined to be $s_x = \frac{2.0}{\texttt{width}}$ and $s_y = \frac{2.0}{\texttt{height}}$. The diagram on the left of Figure 10.2 shows that this scaling factors will shrink a width × height rectangle into a 2×2 rectangle. For example, in this case we have defined the dimension of the application window to be 200 pixels × 160 pixels.

- **Displacement.** The displacements of the translation operator are constants for all cases: $t_x = -1$ and $t_y = -1$. The diagram on the right of Figure 10.2 shows how this translation operator moves the 2×2 rectangle resulting from the scaling operation.

- w2n **matrix.** We will refer to this matrix (or the transformation operator) as $\mathbf{M}_{w2n}$. We see that this is a concatenated operator with a scaling followed by a translation, or

$$\mathbf{M}_{w2n} = \mathbf{ST} = \mathbf{S}\left(\frac{2}{200}, \frac{2}{160}\right)\mathbf{T}(-1, -1). \tag{10.3}$$

Notice that $\mathbf{M}_{w2n}$ is loaded into the VIEW matrix processor (or $\mathbf{M}_V$) of the D3D rendering context (RC). In the case of D3D, we know that all vertices $\mathbf{V}_i$ will be transformed by

$$\mathbf{V}_{it} = \mathbf{V}_i\, \mathbf{M}_W\, \mathbf{M}_V\, \mathbf{M}_P.$$

In this case, both the WORLD ($\mathbf{M}_W$) and the PROJECTION ($\mathbf{M}_P$) matrices are initialized to the identity matrix. For this reason, the vertices of the squares will only be transformed by $\mathbf{M}_{w2n}$ in the VIEW matrix processor. For example, $V_a = (160, 122)$ will become V_{at}:

$$\begin{aligned}
\mathbf{V}_{at} &= \mathbf{V}_a\, \mathbf{M}_{w2n} \\
&= \begin{bmatrix} 160 & 122 \end{bmatrix} \mathbf{S}(\tfrac{2}{200}, \tfrac{2}{160})\mathbf{T}(-1, -1) \\
&= \begin{bmatrix} \frac{160\times 2}{200} - 1 & \frac{160\times 2}{150} - 1 \end{bmatrix} \\
&= \begin{bmatrix} 0.6 & 0.525 \end{bmatrix}.
\end{aligned}$$

When applying $\mathbf{M}_{w2n}$ to all of the vertices, we get

$$\text{LargeSquare}_{ndc} = \begin{cases} V_{at} = & (0.6, & 0.525), \\ V_{bt} = & (-0.2, & 0.525), \\ V_{ct} = & (-0.2, & -0.475), \\ V_{dt} = & (0.5, & -0.475), \end{cases} \qquad (10.4)$$

and

$$\text{SmallSquare}_{ndc} = \begin{cases} V_{at} = & (0.6, & 0.525), \\ V_{et} = & (1.1, & 0.525), \\ V_{ft} = & (1.1, & 1.15), \\ V_{gt} = & (0.6, & 1.15). \end{cases} \qquad (10.5)$$

ndc. Abbreviation for *normalized device coordinate*. We will study the details of this coordinate system in Section 10.2.

Here we see that Direct3D actually transforms the input vertices into much smaller numbers. It is interesting that we defined the vertices of the squares according to LargeSquare$_{wc}$ (Equation (10.1)) and SmallSquare$_{wc}$ (Equation (10.2)), only to define the transform operator $\mathbf{M}_{n2w}$ (Equation (10.3)) to ensure that the D3D API transforms these input vertices to LargeSquare$_{ndc}$ (Equation (10.4)) and SmallSquare$_{ndc}$ (Equation (10.5)). Based on these observations, it is logical to conclude the following.

- **The effects of $\mathbf{M}_{n2w}$.** If we define the input vertices by LargeSquare$_{ndc}$ and SmallSquare$_{ndc}$, then there would be no need for the $\mathbf{M}_{w2n}$ operator of Equation (10.3).

Tutorial 10.2. Drawing without the w2n Transform

- **Goal.** Verify the effects of the w2n matrix.

- **Approach.** Draw the two squares defined by the vertices of LargeSquare$_{ndc}$ and SmallSquare$_{ndc}$ with identity in the D3D VIEW matrix processor.

Figure 10.3 is a screenshot of running Tutorial 10.2. We observe the output to be identical to that of Tutorial 10.1. However, the drawing routines of these two tutorials are different in significant ways. From Listing 10.2, we observe the following differences.

- **Step 2.** We do not compute the w2n matrix. Instead, we initialize all three matrix processors to identity and proceed to drawing the squares.

Tutorial 10.2.
Project Name
D3D_ViewTransform1

Figure 10.3. Tutorial 10.2.

```
void CGrfxWindowD3D::OnPaint()
```
⋮

Source file.
GrfxWindowD3D.cpp file in
the *GrfxWindow* folder of
the   D3D_ViewTransform1
project.

Step 2: *initialize selected hardware and set the coordinate system parameters.*

⋮

```
// Initialize D3D matrix processors setting all three
// matrix processors to identity matrix
m_pD3DDevice->SetTransform(D3DTS_WORLD, &identity);
m_pD3DDevice->SetTransform(D3DTS_VIEW, &identity);
m_pD3DDevice->SetTransform(D3DTS_PROJECTION, &identity);
```

Step 3: *clear drawing buffer and draw two squares.*

⋮

```
// Vertices of the LargeSquare_ndc
v[0].m_point = D3DXVECTOR3(0.60f,0.525f,0);   // V_at
v[1].m_point = D3DXVECTOR3(-0.2f,0.525f,0);   // V_bt
v[2].m_point = D3DXVECTOR3(-0.2f,-0.475f,0);  // V_ct
v[3].m_point = D3DXVECTOR3(0.60f,-0.475f,0);  // V_dt
m_pD3DDevice->DrawPrimitiveUP(D3DPT_TRIANGLEFAN, 2, (CONST void *)v,...);

// Vertices of the SmallSquare_ndc
v[0].m_point = D3DXVECTOR3(0.6f,0.525f,0);    // V_at
v[1].m_point = D3DXVECTOR3(1.1f,0.525f,0);    // V_et
v[2].m_point = D3DXVECTOR3(1.1f,1.15f,0);     // V_ft
v[3].m_point = D3DXVECTOR3(0.6f,1.15f,0);     // V_gt
m_pD3DDevice->DrawPrimitiveUP(D3DPT_TRIANGLEFAN, 2, (CONST void *)v,...);
```

⋮

Listing 10.2. `CGrfxWndD3D::OnPaint()` (Tutorial 10.2)

- **Step 3.** The two squares are specified by vertices defined by LargeSquare$_{ndc}$ (Equations (10.4)) and SmallSquare$_{ndc}$ (Equations (10.5)).

In this tutorial, we verify our observations that we can reproduce the effects of the $\mathbf{M}_{w2n}$ operator of Equation (10.3). Based on the results of this tutorial, we further observe the following.

- When all three matrix processors in the D3D RC are initialized to be the identity matrix, only vertices between the range of ± 1.0 are displayed.

Tutorial 10.3. Verify the ±1.0 Drawing Area

- **Goal.** Verify that the application window displays all vertices inside the range of ±1.0.

- **Approach.** With all matrix processors set to the identity matrix, draw a circle with center located at the origin $((0,0))$ and radius of 1.0.

Figure 10.4 is a screenshot of running Tutorial 10.3. In this case, the output UI drawing area is defined to be 200 pixels × 200 pixels. Once again, we initialize all the matrix processors of the D3D API to identity and proceed to draw a unit circle located at the origin. Recall that we approximate a circle with a triangle fan where vertices of the triangles are located on the circumference of the circle. We observe that the circle perfectly fits within the application drawing area. This tutorial verifies that the reason we need the $\mathbf{M}_{w2n}$ transform is that the D3D graphics API automatically transforms all vertices from within the range of

$$\begin{cases} -1.0 \leq x \leq 1.0, \\ -1.0 \leq y \leq 1.0, \end{cases}$$

to the entire application drawing area. In computer graphics, we refer to this square area covered by ±1 as the normalized space, or normalized device coordinate (NDC).

Tutorials 10.4 and 10.5. Experimenting with the NDC

- **Goal.** Understand that the entire NDC is mapped onto the application drawing area, regardless of the dimensions of the application window.

- **Approach.** Draw the unit circle onto application draw areas with drastically different dimensions and observe the results.

To further understand the transformation performed internally (and automatically) by D3D, in Tutorials 10.4 and 10.5 we define the UI drawing areas to be 100 pixels × 200 pixels and 200 pixels × 100 pixels, respectively. In both tutorials, the drawing routines are identical to that of Tutorial 10.3, where the same unit circle with center located at the origin is drawn in each case. Figures 10.5 and 10.6 are screenshots of running Tutorials 10.4 and 10.5. It is interesting that in both cases, just as in the case of Tutorial 10.3, the unit circles fit perfectly within the bounds of the application windows. Of course, in this case, because the application windows are rectangular, the circles are squashed into corresponding ellipses.

Tutorial 10.3.
Project Name
D3D_ViewTransform2

Figure 10.4. Tutorial 10.3: Drawing a circle of radius 1.0 and center at $(0,0)$ with D3D

Tutorial 10.4.
Project Name
D3D_ViewTransform3

Tutorial 10.5.
Project Name
D3D_ViewTransform4

Figure 10.5. Tutorial 10.4: Drawing the same circle onto a 100 × 200 window.

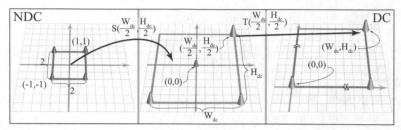

Figure 10.7. D3D's M_{n2d} operator.

The M_{n2d} transform. From our discussions, we observe that the D3D API must be performing

$$\mathbf{M}_{n2d} = \mathbf{S}\left(\frac{W_{dc}}{2}, \frac{H_{dc}}{2}\right) \mathbf{T}\left(\frac{W_{dc}}{2}, \frac{H_{dc}}{2}\right) \tag{10.6}$$

on all vertices, where

$$\begin{aligned}
W_{dc} &= \text{Width of drawing area (on device)}, \\
H_{dc} &= \text{Height of drawing area (on device)}.
\end{aligned}$$

Figure 10.7 illustrates the transformation described by Equation (10.6). On the left diagram we see that the $\mathbf{S}(\frac{W_{dc}}{2}, \frac{H_{dc}}{2})$ operator scales the 2×2 NDC space into an $H_{dc} \times W_{dc}$ region. The center and right diagrams of Figure 10.7 show that the translation operator moves the region to the proper device location. In general, any vertex V_i we specify to the D3D graphics API undergoes the transform

$$\mathbf{V}_{dc} = \mathbf{V}_i \, \mathbf{M}_W \, \mathbf{M}_V \, \mathbf{M}_P \, \mathbf{M}_{n2d},$$

where $\mathbf{M}_W$, $\mathbf{M}_V$, and $\mathbf{M}_P$ are the WORLD, VIEW, and PROJECTION matrix processors of the D3D RC and $\mathbf{V}_{dc}$ is the vertex on the UI drawing area. A very important lesson we have learned so far is that whereas the matrix processors ($\mathbf{M}_W$, $\mathbf{M}_V$, and $\mathbf{M}_P$) are under our program's control, $\mathbf{M}_{n2d}$ will be applied internally by the D3D graphics API automatically and is not under our program's control. Another important observation is that the graphics API (D3D) knows what the underlying display device resolution is (width/height) and computes $\mathbf{M}_{n2d}$ accordingly.

   We see the that the $\mathbf{M}_{w2n}$ operator we construct in Step 2 of Listing 10.1 for Tutorial 10.1 (and for every single tutorial we have worked with so far) is to complement the $\mathbf{M}_{n2d}$ transform (Equation (10.6)) that D3D performs automatically. An obvious question is, "Why would D3D automatically perform the $\mathbf{M}_{n2d}$ operation?" To answer this question, we must first understand coordinate systems.

Linearity of affine transformation. Before we leave this section, notice that we analyzed the $\mathbf{M}_{w2n}$ operator from Equation (10.3) based on transforming the

Figure 10.6. Tutorial 10.5: Drawing the circle onto a 200×100 window.

$(0,0)$ to $(200,160)$ rectangular area to the area within the ± 1 range (NDC) (Figure 10.2). This same operator also proportionally transforms the two squares inside the rectangular area where the transformed squares are proportionally located inside the NDC space. This is an example of the linear property of affine transformation: if the transform operator works for a rectangle, then all geometric contents inside the rectangle will also transform appropriately. For this reason, when deriving coordinate transformations, we only need to consider the operator that transforms the enclosing rectangular region of interest.

10.2   Device and Normalized Coordinate Systems

In Section 3.1 when we wanted to describe vertex positions of the squares, we borrowed concepts from the Cartesian coordinate system with the horizontal and vertical axes and units on the axis. From the discussion in the previous section, we see two examples of applying the concepts associated with the Cartesian coordinate system.

1. **Device coordinate (DC).** When we draw and refer to positions on the application window, implicitly, we assume a coordinate system. We assume that the origin is located at the lower-left corner of the window, with units being pixels. Note that the DC is a variable coordinate system, where it can be changed even during the lifetime of an application (e.g., by resizing the application window size). The DC has dimension width (W_{dc}) by height (H_{dc}). The application's drawing area is the DC space.

2. **Normalized (device) coordinate (NDC).** With center at the origin and x/y ranges between -1 and $+1$, the NDC defines a 2×2 square area. This is the internal coordinate system of the D3D graphics API. We have seen that, as programmers working with D3D, we are responsible for programming the matrix processors such that all vertices are transformed into the NDC (i.e., the $\mathbf{M}_{w2n}$ operator). In turn, D3D will automatically transform vertices from NDC to DC when processing the vertices (i.e., the $\mathbf{M}_{n2d}$). The NDC never changes.

Although the internal NDC representation causes extra complexity and processing, the NDC representation is also very important for the following reasons.

- **Consistency and flexibility.** A well-defined constant coordinate system is important for the internal implementation of the D3D API. As programmers of the API, such a well-known coordinate system provides a fixed reference

Coordinate system and space. Coordinate *systems* and coordinate *spaces* are used interchangeably in this book. For example, device coordinate *system* and device coordinate *space* are both referred to as the DC.

NDC and OpenGL. For similar reasons as discussed here, the OpenGL API also defines the NDC as its internal coordinate system. The OpenGL API also performs the exact same $\mathbf{M}_{n2d}$ operator (as defined by Equation (10.6)) on every input vertices.

as the rest of the application changes: as the DC window size changes, we can continue to communicate to the D3D API based on the NDC. In this way, our solution can be completely independent of the size of the UI drawing area. Because our solution is designed with reference to the NDC, our program can run in the same way with a 200×200 or a 500×500 UI window.

- **Convenience.** With the strategically chosen center (origin) and the coordinate ranges (of ± 1), it is straightforward to transform the NDC square to other rectangular regions. For example, we have already seen in Equation (10.6) that it takes simple scaling and translation operations to transform the NDC to DC. In general, it is convenient to transform NDC to any coordinate space, for example, to the coordinate space defined for paper on printouts.

However, for humans, the ± 1 range of NDC is not always intuitive and often inconvenient to work with. For example, it is not straightforward to design a geometric face (e.g., Figure 9.21) where all vertex information must be constraint to between -1 and 1. To compensate for this rigid constraint, we introduce the *world coordinate* space for our programs to work in.

10.3   The World Coordinate System

When designing the geometric face of Figure 9.21, the implicit unit of measurement was the pixel. The implementation of Tutorial 9.9 conformed to this assumption where, for example, the drawing area is exactly 300 pixels $\times$ 300 pixels. It would seem that if we want to display this face design on an application window with a different dimension, we would have to re-measure and re-define all vertex positions. However, if we examine the implementation of Tutorial 9.9 more closely, in the CDrawOnlyHandler::DrawGraphics() function, the w2n matrix is the $\mathbf{M}_{w2n}$ operator:

$$\mathbf{M}_{w2n} = \mathbf{S}\left(\frac{2}{\text{width}}, \frac{2}{\text{height}}\right)\mathbf{T}(-1, -1),$$

where

$$\begin{cases} \text{width} &= \quad 300 \text{ pixels}, \\ \text{height} &= \quad 300 \text{ pixels}. \end{cases}$$

```
void CDrawOnlyHandler::DrawGraphics()
    float width = 300.0f, height=300.0f;
    :
    // Construct the matrix that will transform from the world bounds
    // to NDC
    D3DXVECTOR3 scale(2.0f/width, 2.0f/height, 1.0f);
    D3DXVECTOR3 translate(-1.0f, -1.0f, 0.0);
    D3DXMatrixTransformation(&world2ndc, ... &scale, ... &translate);
    m_pD3DDevice->SetTransform(D3DTS_VIEW, &world2ndc);
    :
```

Source file.
DrawOnlyHandler.cpp
file in the *WindowHandler*
folder of the D3D_XformList
project.

Listing 10.3. The DrawGraphics() function of Tutorial 9.9.

Figure 10.8 illustrates the transformation that takes place. Note the following.

- **Step 1.** The M_{w2n} operator transforms all vertices from our *design space* into the NDC. In this case, the design and measurements are based on a drawing area of width = 300 and height = 300. In the implementation of Tutorial 9.9, the values for the width and height are fixed based on the width and height of the application window. However, notice that the input of the M_{w2n} transformation is our design space and that the output is the NDC space. In fact, neither the input nor the output is related to the DC dimension!

- **Step 2.** The M_{n2d} operator is internal to the D3D graphics API. This operator transforms all vertices from the NDC to the final application drawing area, or the device coordinate (DC). Notice that this transformation, M_{n2d},

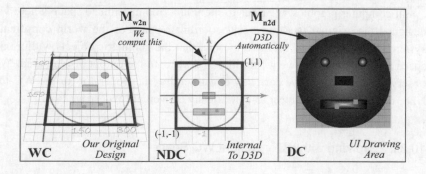

Figure 10.8. Transformation for drawing of the face in Figure 9.21.

is governed by the dimensions of the application window and is independent of the values we used for the $\mathbf{M}_{w2n}$ operator.

These observations indicate that, in fact, our 300×300 design space need not be related to the application window size. Indeed, the D3D internal NDC space helped separate $\mathbf{M}_{w2n}$ and $\mathbf{M}_{n2d}$ into independent operators, where

$$\text{Design space} \xrightarrow{\mathbf{M}_{w2n}} \text{NDC} \xrightarrow{\mathbf{M}_{n2d}} \text{DC}.$$

As application programmers, we only need to be concerned with the $\mathbf{M}_{w2n}$ operator, which is independent of the DC!

10.3.1   Design Space versus Drawing Area

Tutorial 10.6. DC-Independent Design Space

Tutorial 10.6.
Project Name:
D3D_XformListCoordSpace
Library Support:
  UWB_MFC_Lib1
  UWB_D3D_Lib9

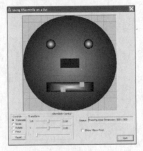

Figure 10.9.   Running Tutorial 10.6.

- **Goal.** Verify that the 300×300 design space of Figure 9.21 is indeed independent of the dimensions of the UI drawing area.

- **Approach.** Change the dimension of the UI drawing area to 500×500 and observe the output.

Figure 10.9 is a screenshot of running Tutorial 10.6. Although the UI front end of this tutorial appears to be significantly different from that of Tutorial 9.9, these two tutorials have identical back-end implementations! The only significant difference is that in this case, the UI drawing area is 500×500 pixels. From the output of this tutorial, we see a larger but the same geometric face as the one observed in Tutorial 9.9. In this tutorial, we display a 300×300 design space in a 500×500 drawing area; we have verified that our design space is indeed independent of the device dimensions.

In computer graphics, we refer to the 300×300 coordinate space where we designed the original face the world coordinate space or the world coordinate system (WC). The world refers to the fact that the geometric objects within this space are the world that we would like to draw onto the output display area. We observe that as long as we correctly construct the $\mathbf{M}_{w2n}$ operator (or the WC-to-NDC operator), we can select to work in any convenient WC space.

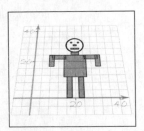

Figure 10.10.   A full-figure geometric person.

10.3.2   Working with a Convenient WC Space

It is important to select a design space or the WC such that it is convenient to specify our geometric objects. For example, in anticipation of specifying the full-

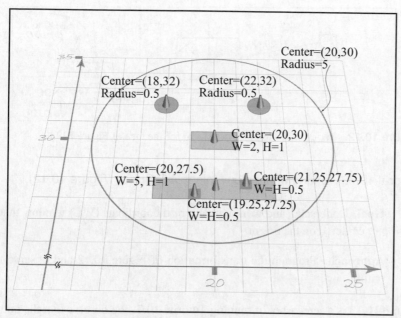

Figure 10.11. WC window of the face from Figure 10.10.

figure geometric person of Figure 10.10, we can choose a more convenient WC space to specify the face of Figure 9.21. Figure 10.11 shows a Window into the WC to illustrate the details of the new geometric face. In this case, the rectangular WC window is bounded by

$$\text{WC window} = \left\{ \begin{array}{l} 15 \leq x \leq 25 \\ 25 \leq y \leq 35 \end{array} \right. = \left\{ \begin{array}{l} \text{center} = (cx_{wc}, cy_{wc}) = (20, 30), \\ \text{width} = W_{wc} = 10, \\ \text{height} = H_{wc} = 10. \end{array} \right.$$

If we want to display the content of this WC window, we must construct an appropriate $\mathbf{M}_{w2n}$ operator. As we saw in Figure 10.8, as programmers of the D3D graphics API, our goal is to construct the $\mathbf{M}_{w2n}$ operator to transform the WC window into D3D's internal coordinate system, i.e., the NDC. In turn, D3D will automatically transform the content of the NDC to the drawing area on the application window.

Figure 10.12 illustrates one way to construct the $\mathbf{M}_{w2n}$ operator, where we first move the center of the region to the origin and then scale the region into a 2×2 area, or

$$\mathbf{M}_{w2n} = \mathbf{T}(-20, -30)\mathbf{S}\left(\frac{2}{10}, \frac{2}{10}\right). \tag{10.7}$$

Linearity of affine transformation. Recall that to transform geometric contents between rectangular regions, we can concentrate on constructing the operator that transforms between the rectangles that surround the regions. The contents inside the rectangles will transform proportionally.

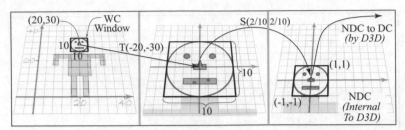

Figure 10.12. $\mathbf{M}_{w2n}$: world-to-NDC transform for the face of Figure 10.11.

Tutoral 10.7. Working with a Convenient WC Space (Figure 10.12)

Figure 10.13. Tutorial 10.7.

- **Goal.** Understand and work with a world coordinate (WC) window that is *not* centered on the origin.

- **Approach.** Program the transformation of Figure 10.12 and observe the output.

Figure 10.13 is a screenshot of running Tutorial 10.7. We observe that the output of this tutorial is identical to that of Tutorial 10.6. However, this tutorial implements the geometric face as defined by Figure 10.11 (in CModel.cpp). The DrawGraphics() function shown in Listing 10.4 defines the $\mathbf{M}_{w2n}$ transform operator of Equation 10.7. We see that although the world coordinate spaces and the actual geometric values specified in this tutorial are very different from that of Tutorial 10.6, the output from the two tutorials are identical to each other. This tutorial verifies that we can define the WC window to support a convenient WC space for designing our world and that the WC space is independent of the dimensions of the UI drawing device.

```
void CDrawOnlyHandler::DrawGraphics()
    ⋮
    // Translate the center of WC to the origin
    D3DXMatrixTranslation(&toPlace, -20.0f, -30.0f, 0.0);
    // Scale to 2x2
    D3DXMatrixScaling(&toSize, 2.0f/10.0f, 2.0f/10.0f, 1.0);
    // build M_{w2n} operator of Equation 10.7
    D3DXMatrixMultiply(&world2ndc, &toPlace, &toSize);
    // Load to the VIEW matrix (M_V)
    m_pD3DDevice->SetTransform(D3DTS_VIEW, &world2ndc);
```

Listing 10.4. The DrawGraphics() function of Tutorial 10.7.

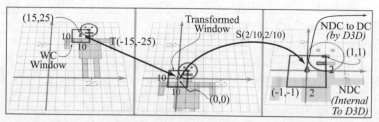

Figure 10.14. Location of WC window as defined by Equations (10.8) and (10.9).

Notice that there are no physical boundaries around the WC window. As programmers, we choose the WC window and program the $\mathbf{M}_{w2n}$ operator accordingly. For example, in Tutorial 10.7, we could easily choose to select a different WC window:

$$\text{WC window} \begin{cases} \text{center} = (15, 25), \\ \text{width} = \text{height} = 10, \end{cases} \tag{10.8}$$

and define the $\mathbf{M}_{w2n}$ to be

$$\mathbf{M}_{w2n} = \mathbf{T}(-15, -25)\mathbf{S}\left(\frac{2}{10}, \frac{2}{10}\right). \tag{10.9}$$

Tutorial 10.8. Translating the WC Window (Figure 10.14)

- **Goal.** Verify our understanding that we can move the WC window in the WC system to show a different part of the WC system.

- **Approach.** Program Equation (10.9) to verify our understanding.

Figure 10.15 is a screenshot of running Tutorial 10.8. The implementation of this tutorial is identical to that of Tutorial 10.7, except we program the $\mathbf{M}_{w2n}$ according Equation (10.9) as shown in Listing 10.5. The image output of the the program does reflect our predictions from Figure 10.14. In this case, we can see the greyish outline of the rest of the geometric person of Figure 10.10. If we examine the class definition in Listing 10.6, at label A we observe that the CModel class defines the geometries for the entire human of Figure 10.10 in the m_figure PrimitiveList object. At label B, we see that the CModel::Draw() function draws all the geometries that are defined in the m_figure object. However, from the output of this tutorial in Figure 10.15, we see that only the geometries inside the WC window are displayed in the UI drawing area. From this tutorial, we see that the graphics API clips away all the geometries outside of the NDC ±1 range.

Tutorial 10.8.
Project Name:
   D3D_TranslateWC
Library Support:
   UWB_MFC_Lib1
   UWB_D3D_Lib9

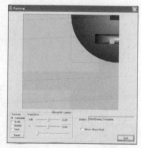

Figure 10.15. Running Tutorial 10.8.

Clipping. Graphics APIs only process and display geometries inside the ±1 range of the NDC space. Geometries outside of this range are clipped and/or otherwise guaranteed to not show up in the UI drawing area.

Source file.
DrawOnlyHandler.cpp file
in the *WindowHandler* folder
of the D3D_TranslateWC
project.

```
void CDrawOnlyHandler::DrawGraphics()
    ⋮
    // Translate the center of WC to the origin
    D3DXMatrixTranslation(&toPlace, -15.0f, -25.0f, 0.0);
    // Scale to 2x2
    D3DXMatrixScaling(&toSize, 2.0f/10.0f, 2.0f/10.0f, 1.0);
    // build M_w2n operator of Equation 10.9
    D3DXMatrixMultiply(&world2ndc, &toPlace, &toSize);
    // Load to the VIEW matrix (M_V)
    m_pD3DDevice->SetTransform(D3DTS_VIEW, &world2ndc);
```

Listing 10.5. The DrawGraphics() function of Tutorial 10.8.

Source file. Model.cpp file
in the *Model* folder of the
D3D_TranslateWC project.

A:
```
CModel::CModel()  { // CModel class constructor
    ⋮
    // geometry for the torso
    UWB_PrimitiveRectangle* pTorso = new UWB_PrimitiveRectangle();
    pTorso->SetCorners( vec3(15,11,0), vec3(25,24,0) );
    ⋮
    // geometry for the left leg
    UWB_PrimitiveRectangle* pLeftLeg = new UWB_PrimitiveRectangle();
    ⋮
    // defines the entire geometry for the simple person of Figure 10.10
    ⋮
    // m_figure is a PrimitiveList
    m_figure.Append(pTorso);  m_figure.Append(pLeftLeg);
    ⋮
    // append all defined goemetry into the m_figure PrimitiveList
}
```

B:
```
void CModel::DrawModel()  // CModel draw function
    ⋮
    // Set up the WORLD matrix
    m_xform.SetUpModelStack( m_DrawHelper );
    // draws the entire goemetric human of Figure 10.10
    m_figure.Draw( lod, m_DrawHelper );
    ⋮
```

Listing 10.6. The CModel class of Tutorial 10.8.

10.4 The World Coordinate Window

In order to properly support WC design space, in our programs we must identify a rectangular region of interest, or the *window* inside the WC:

$$\text{WC window} = \begin{cases} \text{center} & = (cx_{wc}, cy_{wc}), \\ \text{width} & = W_{wc}, \\ \text{height} & = H_{wc}. \end{cases}$$

We must then construct a corresponding $\mathbf{M}_{w2n}$ to transform this region to the NDC space. In general, we transform the center of the region to the origin ($T(-cx_{wc}, -cy_{wc})$) and then scale the width and height of the region to the NDC 2×2 square ($S(\frac{2}{W_{wc}}, \frac{2}{H_{wc}})$):

$$\mathbf{M}_{w2n} = \mathbf{T}(-cx_{wc}, -cy_{wc})\mathbf{S}(\frac{2}{W_{wc}}, \frac{2}{H_{wc}}). \qquad (10.10)$$

10.4.1 Vertices in Different Coordinate Spaces

As programmers working with graphics APIs, we specify vertices in the WC, or $\mathbf{V}_{wc}$. As illustrated in Figure 10.16, this vertex undergoes different transforms until it reaches the DC, or $\mathbf{V}_{dc}$, before being displayed on the output drawing area:

$$\mathbf{V}_{wc} \xrightarrow{\mathbf{M}_{w2n}} \mathbf{V}_{ndc} \xrightarrow{\mathbf{M}_{n2d}} \mathbf{V}_{dc},$$

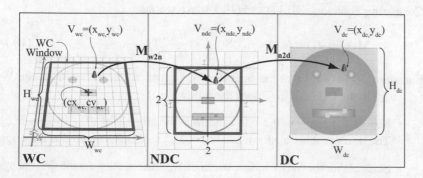

Figure 10.16. Transformation of a vertex between different coordinate systems.

where

$$\begin{aligned}
\mathbf{V}_{wc} &= \begin{bmatrix} x_{wc} & y_{wc} \end{bmatrix}, \\
\mathbf{V}_{ndc} &= \mathbf{V}_{wc}\,\mathbf{M}_{w2n}, \\
\mathbf{V}_{dc} &= \mathbf{V}_{ndc}\,\mathbf{M}_{n2d},
\end{aligned}$$

or

$$\begin{aligned}
\mathbf{V}_{dc} &= \mathbf{V}_{ndc}\,\mathbf{M}_{n2d} \\
&= \mathbf{V}_{wc}\,\mathbf{M}_{w2n}\,\mathbf{M}_{n2d}.
\end{aligned}$$

If we let

$$\mathbf{M}_{w2d} = \mathbf{M}_{w2n}\,\mathbf{M}_{n2d}, \tag{10.11}$$

then

$$\mathbf{V}_{dc} = \mathbf{V}_{wc}\,\mathbf{M}_{w2d}. \tag{10.12}$$

Recall that $\mathbf{M}_{n2d}$ is defined by Equation (10.6) and that $\mathbf{M}_{w2n}$ is defined by Equation (10.10) (re-listing the two equations):

$$\mathbf{M}_{n2d} = \mathbf{S}(\frac{W_{dc}}{2}, \frac{H_{dc}}{2})\mathbf{T}(\frac{W_{dc}}{2}, \frac{H_{dc}}{2}), \tag{10.6}$$

$$\mathbf{M}_{w2n} = \mathbf{T}(-cx_{wc}, -cy_{wc})\mathbf{S}(\frac{2}{W_{wc}}, \frac{2}{H_{wc}}). \tag{10.10}$$

Consecutive scaling operators. Two consecutive scaling operators:

$$S(s_{x1}, s_{y1})S(s_{x2}, s_{y2})$$

have the same effect as scaling once by the combined effect of the scaling factors:

$$S(s_{x1}s_{x2}, s_{y1}s_{y2}).$$

In this way,

$$\begin{aligned}
\mathbf{V}_{dc} &= \mathbf{V}_{wc}\,\mathbf{M}_{w2d} \\
&= \mathbf{V}_{wc}\,\mathbf{M}_{w2n}\,\mathbf{M}_{n2d} \\
&= \mathbf{V}_{wc}\,\mathbf{T}(-cx_{wc}, -cy_{wc})\,\mathbf{S}(\frac{2}{W_{wc}}, \frac{2}{H_{wc}})\,\mathbf{S}(\frac{W_{dc}}{2}, \frac{H_{dc}}{2})\,\mathbf{T}(\frac{W_{dc}}{2}, \frac{H_{dc}}{2}),
\end{aligned}$$

or

$$\mathbf{V}_{dc} = \mathbf{V}_{wc}\,\mathbf{T}(-cx_{wc}, -cy_{wc})\,\mathbf{S}(\frac{W_{dc}}{W_{wc}}, \frac{H_{dc}}{H_{wc}})\,\mathbf{T}(\frac{W_{dc}}{2}, \frac{H_{dc}}{2}). \tag{10.13}$$

Comparing Equations (10.12) and (10.13), we see that

$$\mathbf{M}_{w2d} = \mathbf{T}(-cx_{wc}, -cy_{wc})\mathbf{S}(\frac{W_{dc}}{W_{wc}}, \frac{H_{dc}}{H_{wc}})\mathbf{T}(\frac{W_{dc}}{2}, \frac{H_{dc}}{2}). \tag{10.14}$$

Equation (10.14) says that the operator $\mathbf{M}_{w2d}$, which transforms from the WC (x_{wc}, y_{wc}) to the DC (x_{dc}, y_{dc}), does the following.

- **Move.** The center of the WC window to the origin with ($\mathbf{T}(-cx_{wc}, -cy_{wc})$). The result of this transform is a $W_{wc} \times H_{wc}$ rectangle centered at the origin.

- **Scale.** With the WC window width of W_{wc}, the scaling factor $\frac{W_{dc}}{W_{wc}}$ changes the width to W_{dc}. In a similar fashion, the height becomes H_{dc}. After the scaling operator, we have a $W_{dc} \times H_{dc}$ rectangle centered at the origin.

- **Move.** The rectangle centered at the origin has half its width/height on either side of the y/x axis. The translation of $\mathbf{T}(\frac{W_{dc}}{2}, \frac{H_{dc}}{2})$ moves the lower-left corner of the rectangle to the origin, with the upper-right corner located at (W_{dc}, H_{dc}). This is the definition of the DC space.

If we expand the operators in Equation (10.13), then, to transform a point (x_{wc}, y_{wc}) from our design space (WC) to a point (x_{dc}, y_{dc}) on the device drawing area (DC),

$$
\begin{aligned}
x_{dc} &= ((x_{wc} - cx_{wc})\frac{W_{dc}}{W_{wc}}) + \frac{W_{dc}}{2}, \\
y_{dc} &= ((y_{wc} - cy_{wc})\frac{H_{dc}}{H_{wc}}) + \frac{H_{dc}}{2},
\end{aligned}
\tag{10.15}
$$

where

$$
\text{Device drawing area} \begin{cases} \text{width} & = W_{dc}, \\ \text{height} & = H_{dc}, \end{cases}
$$

and

$$
\text{WC window} = \begin{cases} \text{center} & = (cx_{wc}, cy_{wc}), \\ \text{width} & = W_{wc}, \\ \text{height} & = H_{wc}. \end{cases}
$$

From Equation (10.15), we see that when the size of the device drawing remains constant (i.e., W_{dc} and H_{dc} do not change), then the transformation from WC to DC is governed by the parameters of the WC window as follows.

1. **Center** (cx_{wc}, cy_{wc}). Defines the location of the WC window. Intuitively, by changing the center we are moving the WC window and thus should observe different rectangular regions in the WC system, or panning of the view. Tutorial 10.10 will examine panning in detail.

2. **Dimension** $(W_{wc} \; H_{wc})$. Defines the size of the WC window. Intuitively, by changing the dimension, we increase/decrease the rectangular region to be displayed. With a fixed-size UI drawing device, increasing the size of the WC window means showing a larger amount of the WC system in the fixed-size DC drawing area, or a zooming-out effect. With the same logic, decreasing the size of the WC window creates a zooming-in effect. Tutorial 10.11 will examine zooming in detail.

3. **Ratio of scaling factors** ($\frac{W_{dc}}{W_{wc}}$ versus $\frac{H_{dc}}{H_{wc}}$). We scale the width of the WC window by $\frac{W_{dc}}{W_{wc}}$ and the height by $\frac{H_{dc}}{H_{wc}}$. When these two scaling factors are different, the proportion of the results in DC space will also be different from that of the original WC space. For example, a square will be transformed into a rectangle. Section 10.4.4 will examine this effect in detail.

We remind ourselves that Equation (10.15), or the $\mathbf{M}_{w2d}$ operator, is the *net* transformation that would be applied to vertices specified in WC space. From Equation (10.11), we observe that, as programmers, we are only responsible for $\mathbf{M}_{w2n}$, or half of the $\mathbf{M}_{w2d}$ operator. The other half of the operator, $\mathbf{M}_{n2d}$, is computed automatically by the graphics API. In this case, we analyze Equation (10.15) and the $\mathbf{M}_{w2d}$ operator to understand the details of the images generated in the UI drawing device. We will examine the effects of changing the WC window based on tutorial implementations. Let us first extend our library to support working with the WC window.

UWBGL_D3D_Lib10

Change summary. See p. 522 for a summary of changes to the library.

This library extends from Lib9 by extending the UWB_WindowHandler class to support the definition of the WC window and programming of the $\mathbf{M}_{w2n}$ operator. Recall that the WindowHandler object is defined to abstract a view/controller pair. For the WindowHandler object to properly display different regions of the

Source file.
uwbgl_WindowHandler3.h file in the *Common Files/WindowHandler* subfolder of the UWBGL_D3D_Lib10 project.

```cpp
class UWB_WindowHandler : public UWB_IWindowHandler {
    :
    // Set/Get methods for accessing the m_WCWindow object
A:  virtual void SetWCWindow(const UWB_BoundingBox &window);
    virtual const UWB_BoundingBox* GetWCWindow();
    // Set/Get methods for the drawing device (via m_hAttachedWindow)
B:  virtual void SetDeviceSize(int width, int height);
    virtual void GetDeviceSize(int &width, int &height);
    // wcPt -> dcPt (Equation 10.13)
C:  virtual void WorldToDevice(float wcX wcY, int &dcX &dcY);
    // dcPt -> wcPt (Equation 10.19)
    virtual void DeviceToWorld(int dcX dcY, float &wcX &wcY);
    // Drawing the WCWindow
D:  virtual void DrawWCWindow(UWB_DrawHelper&);
    // Compute Mw2n and load to API matrix processor
E:  virtual void LoadW2NDCXform() = 0;
  protected:
    :
    HWND m_hAttachedWindow; // The UI drawing device (a MFC Window)
F:  UWB_BoundingBox m_WCWindow; // Window for the World Coordinate
};
```

Listing 10.7. The WindowHandler class of UWBGL_D3D_Lib10.

```
void UWB_WindowHandler::WorldToDevice(float wcx, float wcy, int &dcx, int &dcy) const {
    ⋮
    GetDeviceSize(dcW, dcH); // dcW/dcH are the width/height of the drawing device
    center = m_WCWindow.GetCenter(); // center of the WCWindow
    // Equation 10.13
    dcx = (m_WCWindow.Width() / 2.0f) + ((dcW/m_WCWindow.Width())  * (-center.x + wcx));
    dcy = (m_WCWindow.Height()/ 2.0f) + ((dcH/m_WCWindow.Height()) * (-center.y + wcy));


void UWB_WindowHandler::DeviceToWorld(int dcx, int dcy, float &wcx, float &wcy) const
    ⋮
    GetDeviceSize(dcW, dcH); // dcW/dcH are the width/height of the drawing device
    vec3 center = m_WCWindow.GetCenter(); // center of the WCWindow
    // Equation 10.19
    wcx = center.x + ((m_WCWindow.Width()/dcW)  * (dcx - (dcW/2.0f)));
    wcy = center.y + ((m_WCWindow.Height()/dcH) * (dcy - (dcH/2.0f)));
```

Source file.
uwbgl_WindowHandler3.cpp
file in the *Common Files/Win-
dowHandler* subfolder of the
UWBGL_D3D_Lib10 project.

Listing 10.8. The WindowHandler transform and draw functions.

```
class UWBD3D_WindowHandler : public UWB_WindowHandler {
    ⋮
    virtual void LoadW2NDCXform() const; // Computes and loads VIEW matrix with M_{w2n}
    ⋮
```

```
void UWBD3D_WindowHandler::LoadW2NDCXform() const
    // center of the m_WCWindow (cx_{wc},cy_{wc})
    vec3 center = m_WCWindow.GetCenter();
    // T(-cx_{wc},-cy_{wc})
    D3DXMatrixTranslation(&toPlace, -center.x, -center.y);
    // S(2/W_{wc}, 2/H_{wc})
    D3DXMatrixScaling(&toSize, 2.0f/m_WCWindow.Width(), 2.0f/m_WCWindow.Height());
    // M_{w2n} = T(-cx_{wc},-cy_{wc})S(2/W_{wc}, 2/H_{wc})
    D3DXMatrixMultiply(&world2ndc, &toPlace, &toSize);
    // M_V ← M_{w2n}
    m_pD3DDevice->SetTransform(D3DTS_VIEW, &world2ndc);
    ⋮
```

Source file.
uwbgl_D3DWindowHandler4.h
/.cpp files in the *D3D Files/
WindowHandler* folder of the
UWBGL_D3D_Lib10 project.

Listing 10.9. The LoadW2NDCXform() functions.

model, it must support the WC window and the associated transformations. From Listing 10.7, we see that, at label F, we define a `UWB_BoundingBox` object to represent the WC window. The get/set access functions for the `m_WCWindow` are defined at label A. Because the UI drawing area (drawing device) is supported by the MFC GUI API (`m_hAttachedWindow`), the device get/set functions at label B are implemented by interacting with the `m_hAttachedWindow` object. The two functions at label C implements the WC-to-DC transformations (more details to follow). The drawing function at label D allows us to visualize the WC window as a wire-framed rectangle. The function at label E should compute the $\mathbf{M}_{w2n}$ matrix and load the graphics API with this matrix. Note that this function is a pure virtual function; since `WindowHandler` is a graphics API–independent class, we do not know how to implement this function. This function will be implemented by the `D3DWindowHandler` class. Listing 10.8 shows the implementations of the transformation functions. We see that in both cases, the functions are faithful implementations of equations we have derived. We will derive Equation (10.19) in Section 10.5 and discuss how to work with these functions to handle mouse inputs. Listing 10.9 shows the implementation of the `LoadW2NDCXform()` function in the `D3D_WindowHandler` class. From the listing, we observe step-by-step implementation of Equation (10.10). The computed $\mathbf{M}_{w2n}$ operator is loaded into the `VIEW` ($\mathbf{M}_V$) matrix processor of the D3D API.

Tutorial 10.9. Working with `UWBGL_D3D_Lib10`

Tutorial 10.9.
Project Name:
  D3D_WCSupport
Library Support:
  UWB_MFC_Lib1
  UWB_D3D_Lib10

- **Goal.** Demonstrate how to work with the new `UWBGL_D3D_Lib10` library.

- **Approach.** Re-implement Tutorial 10.8 based on the new library to understand how to work with the new functions.

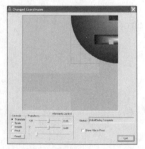

Figure 10.17. Running Tutorial 10.9.

Figure 10.17 is a screenshot of running Tutorial 10.9. This tutorial is identical to Tutorial 10.8 except that the new implementation takes advantage of the new WC window functionality provided by the `UWBGL_D3D_Lib10` library. Listing 10.10 shows that, in the `CTutorialDlg::OnInitDialog()` function, at label A we initialize the view/controller pair WC window (`m_view`) as part of the application state initialization process. When redrawing the view/controller pair in the `DrawGraphics()` function, at label B we call the `LoadW2NDCXform()` function to compute and load the $\mathbf{M}_{w2n}$ operator into the D3D `VIEW` matrix processor.

```
BOOL CTutorialDlg::OnInitDialog()
    ⋮
    // m_view is a DrawOnlyHandler (D3DWindowHandler)
    if(!m_view.Initialize(*this, IDC_PLACEHOLDER))
        return FALSE;
    UWB_BoundingBox wcWindow(vec3(10, 20),vec3(20, 30)); // initialize the wcWindow
    // set the m_WCWindow of WindowHandler object
A:  m_view.SetWCWindow( wcWindow );
    ⋮
```

```
void CDrawOnlyHandler::DrawGraphics()
    ⋮
    BeginDraw();
B:  LoadW2NDCXform();    // compute and load the Mw2n to the VIEW matrix processor

    m_pD3DDevice->Clear( ⋮ ); // Clears the device for drawing
    theApp.GetModel().DrawModel(); // Tells the Model to draw itself
    EndDrawAndShow();
    ⋮
```

Source file. TutorialDlg.cpp file in the *Source Files* folder of the D3D_WCSupport project.

Listing 10.10. Working with UWBGL_D3D_Lib10 (Tutorial 10.9).

10.4.2 WC Window Position: Panning

Recall that Equation (10.15) defines the transformation of a point from WC space (x_{wc}, y_{wc}) to DC space (x_{dc}, y_{dc}):

$$
\begin{aligned}
x_{dc} &= ((x_{wc} - cx_{wc})\tfrac{W_{dc}}{W_{wc}}) + \tfrac{W_{dc}}{2}, \\
y_{dc} &= ((y_{wc} - cy_{wc})\tfrac{H_{dc}}{H_{wc}}) + \tfrac{H_{dc}}{2},
\end{aligned} \quad (10.15)
$$

where $W_{dc} \times H_{dc}$ is the drawing device dimension and

$$
\text{WC window} = \begin{cases} \text{center} & = (cx_{wc}, cy_{wc}), \\ \text{width} & = W_{wc}, \\ \text{height} & = H_{wc}. \end{cases}
$$

In Tutorial 10.8, we observed that by changing the WC center position (cx_{wc}, cy_{wc}), we can show different regions of the model defined in the WC system. Based on our discussions, we can predict that a continuous changing of WC window position would create an effect of panning through the WC system.

Tutorial 10.10.
Project Name:
  D3D_Panning
Library Support:
  UWB_MFC_Lib1
  UWB_D3D_Lib10

Figure 10.18.   Running
Tutorial 10.10.

Tutorial 10.10. Moving the WC Window Center $((cx_{wc}, cy_{wc}))$

- **Goal.** Verify that the effect of changing the center position of a WC window does indeed correspond to continuous displaying of different regions in the WC system.

- **Approach.** Allow the user to interactively change the center position of a WC window and examine the results.

Figure 10.18 is a screenshot of running Tutorial 10.10. In this tutorial, the large (main) view displays a larger region of the WC system (the entire geometric person), while the small view only displays part of the WC system visible in the main view. The red wire-framed rectangle in the main view represents the WC window of the small view. The two slider bars on the lower-right of the application window control the center position $((cx_{wc}, cy_{wc}))$ of the WC window for the small view. By changing these two slider bars, we can observe the red rectangle in the main view and the image showing in the small view pan across the main view. This tutorial verifies that changing the WC window position creates the panning effect. Figure 10.19 illustrates that the implementation of Tutorial 10.10 involves two different types of `CWindowHandler` objects. The top-center rectangle represents the `CDrawOnlyHandler` of the small view, whereas the bottom-center rectangle is the `CMainHandler` of the main view. As we can see, the `CMainHandler` maintains a reference to the small view. This reference provides the small view WC window information for the main view to draw the wire-framed red rectangle. With the `UWBGL_D3D_Lib10` support, both of the `Handler` objects have an instance of `UWB_BoundingBox` representing their corresponding WC window. As in the case of Listing 10.10, during `DrawGraphics()`, each

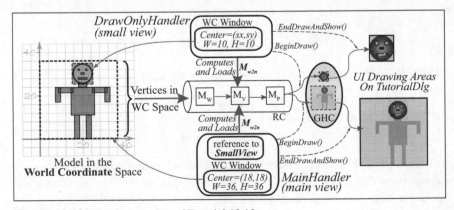

Figure 10.19.   Implementation of Tutorial 10.10.

```
class CDrawOnlyHandler : public UWBD3D_WindowHandler {
    ⋮
    UWBMFC_UIWindow m_window; // the UI drawing area (device)
};

class CMainHandler : public CDrawOnlyHandler {
    ⋮
    void SetLinkedHandler(CDrawOnlyHandler* pHandler) { m_pLinkedHandler = pHandler; }
    ⋮
  protected:
    CDrawOnlyHandler* m_pLinkedHandler; // reference to the small view
};
```

Source file.
DrawOnlyHandler.h file in the *WindowHandler* folder of the D3D_Panning project.

Listing 10.11. The WindowHandler classes of Tutorial 10.10.

```
class CTutorialDlg : public CDialog {
    ⋮
A:  CMainHandler      m_main_view; // the main view
    CDrawOnlyHandler  m_small_view;  // the small view
};
```

Source file.
TutorialDlg.h/cpp file in the *Source Files* folder of the D3D_Panning project.

```
BOOL CTutorialDlg::OnInitDialog() {
    ⋮
    if( !m_main_view.Initialize(*this, IDC_PLACEHOLDER) ) return FALSE;
    if( !m_small_view.Initialize(*this, IDC_PLACEHOLDER3) ) return FALSE;
    ⋮
B:  m_small_view.SetWCWindow(theApp.GetModel().GetWorldBounds());
    m_main_view.SetWCWindow( UWB_BoundingBox( vec3(0,0,0), vec3(36,36,0) ) );
C:  m_main_view.SetLinkedHandler( &m_small_view );
    ⋮
```

Listing 10.12. The CTutorialDlg classes of Tutorial 10.10.

Handler object calls the LoadW2NDCXform() function to compute and load the D3D RC $\mathbf{M_V}$ matrix with their corresponding $\mathbf{M}_{w2n}$ operator before drawing. The left side of Figure 10.19 shows that the model is defined in the WC space. When the model draws, it sends *all* the vertices of all the geometries to the D3D RC.

Source file.
DrawAndMouseHandler.cpp
file in the *WindowHandler*
folder of the D3D_Panning
project.

```
void CMainHandler::DrawGraphics()
    ⋮
    BeginDraw();
    ⋮
A: LoadW2NDCXform(); // compute Mw2n and load to MV
    ⋮
    m_pD3DDevice->Clear( ⋮ ); // clears the UI drawing area (device)
    theApp.GetModel().DrawModel();    // model sends all geometries
    ⋮
    // draws the red wire-frame rectangle
B: m_pLinkedHandler->DrawWCWindow(helper);
    EndDrawAndShow();
```

Listing 10.13. The CMainHandler::DrawGraphics() function of Tutorial 10.10.

As we have learned, the M_{w2n} operator ensures that only the region defined by the corresponding WC window is transformed into the ±1 NDC space where the rest of the geometries will be clipped away by the graphics API. The right side of Figure 10.19 reminds us that that each Handler object is responsible for initializing the swapchain links with BeginDraw() and flushing the hardware buffer to the UI draw area with the EndDrawAndShow() function calls. Listing 10.11 shows the definition of the CDrawOnlyHandler and CMainHandler classes of Tutorial 10.10. We see that indeed both of the classes subclass from the UWBD3D_WindowHandler class and that the CMainHandler has a reference to the small view (m_pLinkedHandler). Referring to Listing 10.12, at label A we see that the main application window (CTutorialDlg) has an instance of each of the Handler objects representing the main and the small views. At label B, the WC window for each of the views is initialized. At label C, the main view gets a reference to the small view. Listing 10.13 shows the DrawGraphics() function of MainHandler calling LoadW2NDCXForm() to compute and load the corresponding M_{w2n} operator at label A (before drawing the model). At label B, the WC window of the m_pLinkedHandler (small view) is drawn (as the red wire-frame rectangle) in the main view.

With this structure, the two slider bars are connected to the small view's WC window center position. When the user adjusts the slider bars, the changes are immediately updated to the m_small_view's m_WCWindow. In the subsequent redraw, the updated WC window computes an appropriate M_{w2n} operator that corresponds to the user input.

10.4.3   WC Window Dimension: Zooming

If we double the WC window size of the small view from Tutorial 10.10 such that

$$\text{WC window} \begin{cases} \text{center} = (15,25), \\ W_{wc} = H_{wc} = 20, \end{cases}$$

then the WC window covers a larger region in the WC system. From Equation (10.15):

$$\begin{aligned} x_{dc} &= ((x_{wc} - cx_{wc})\tfrac{W_{dc}}{W_{wc}}) + \tfrac{W_{dc}}{2}, \\ y_{dc} &= ((y_{wc} - cy_{wc})\tfrac{H_{dc}}{H_{wc}}) + \tfrac{H_{dc}}{2}, \end{aligned} \quad (10.15)$$

we see that as W_{wc} and H_{wc} are the denominators in the scale factors, doubling these effectively halves the scaling factors. This implies that we should expect the elements on the DC display to decrease in size. As illustrated in Figure 10.20, we see that if we increase the WC window size, more elements in the WC are displayed in the output display area. Correspondingly, each individual element does indeed appear to be smaller on the output display. We see that increasing the WC window size results in the zooming-out sensation. For the same reasons, we can expect a zooming-in effect when we decrease the WC window size.

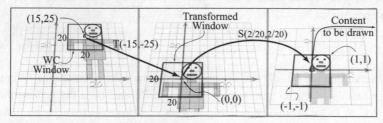

Figure 10.20.   Double the WC window size.

Tutorial 10.11. Scaling the WC Window (W_{wc}, H_{wc})

- **Goal.** Verify zooming effect in relation to the WC window dimensions.

- **Approach.** Extend Tutorial 10.10 and allow user to adjust the width and height of the small view WC window.

Figure 10.21 is a screenshot of running Tutorial 10.11. This tutorial extends Tutorial 10.10 with two more slider bars at the lower right of the application window. The two new sliders are connected directly to the width (W_{wc}) and height (H_{wc}) of

Tutorial 10.11.
Project Name:
  D3D_Zooming
Library Support:
  UWB_MFC_Lib1
  UWB_D3D_Lib10

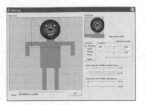

Figure 10.21. Running
Tutorial 10.11.

the m_small_view's m_WCWindow. Based on the previous discussions, we understand that as the user adjust the slider bars, the resulting changes will be reflected
in the subsequent $\mathbf{M}_{w2n}$ (Equation (10.10)) operator that is loaded into the $\mathbf{M}_V$ matrix. In this tutorial, we can interactively adjust and observe the expected zooming
effects. In addition, we observe the following.

- Changing W_{wc} without corresponding changes to H_{wc} (or changing H_{wc}
  without corresponding changes to W_{wc}) creates an annoying squeezing effect. We will examine this closely in the next section.

- The zooming effect appears to be defined with respect to the center of the
  WC window. That is, as we zooming in, it appears we are getting closer
  to the center of the WC window. This is a direct result of our scaling the
  width and height of the WC window with respect to the center of the WC
  window. It is left as an exercise for the reader to derive implementations to
  support zooming with respect to some other position in the WC window.

10.4.4 WC Window Width-to-Height Ratio: Aspect Ratio

Recall that the WC-to-DC transformation is governed by Equation (10.14), the
$\mathbf{M}_{w2d}$ operator, or

$$\mathbf{M}_{w2d} = \mathbf{T}(-cx_{wc}, -cy_{wc})\,\mathbf{S}(\frac{W_{dc}}{W_{wc}}, \frac{H_{dc}}{H_{wc}})\,\mathbf{T}(\frac{W_{dc}}{2}, \frac{H_{dc}}{2}). \quad (10.14)$$

We observe that the middle scaling operator controls the zoom factor. When the
scaling factors in the x- and y-directions are different, then the transformation
from WC to DC will involve resizing objects in x- and y-directions by different
amounts. In the cases of Tutorials 10.4 and 10.5, we worked in the NDC space
directly with a WC window size of

$$\begin{cases} W_{wc} = 2 \text{ with } & -1 \le x \le 1, \\ H_{wc} = 2 \text{ with } & -1 \le y \le 1. \end{cases}$$

For both tutorials,

$$W_{dc} \ne H_{dc}.$$

This means that the factors of the scaling operator in Equation (10.14) are different
in the x- and y-directions. For this reason, in both cases we observed the squashed
circles. In order to maintain proportional shapes from WC to DC, the x and y
scaling factors in the $\mathbf{M}_{w2d}$ operator must be the same, or

$$\frac{W_{dc}}{W_{wc}} = \frac{H_{dc}}{H_{wc}}.$$

Collecting WC and DC terms on either sides of the equation,

$$\frac{W_{dc}}{H_{dc}} = \frac{W_{wc}}{H_{wc}}. \tag{10.16}$$

We define aspect ratio to be:

$$\text{aspect ratio} = \frac{\text{width}}{\text{height}}.$$

Equation (10.16) says that to maintain proportional shapes when transforming from WC to DC, the aspect ratio of the WC window must be the same as that of the device drawing area.

Tutorial 10.12. Experimenting with Aspect Ratios

Tutorial 10.12.
Project Name:
  AspectRatio
Library Support:
  UWB_MFC_Lib1
  UWB_D3D_Lib10

- **Goal.** Understand WC window and DC aspect ratios and verify the artifacts when the ratios do not match.

- **Approach.** Extend Tutorial 10.11 and allow interactive changing of UI drawing dimension.

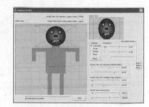

Figure 10.22 is a screenshot of running Tutorial 10.12. This tutorial extends Tutorial 10.11 by including two more slider bars at the lower right of the application window. These two new slider bars control the device dimension of the small-view UI drawing area, or W_{dc} and H_{dc}. Recall that the other four slider bars control the small-view WC window location (cx_{wc} and cy_{wc}) and dimension (W_{wc} and H_{wc} sliders). From Equation (10.16) we understand that the image displayed in the small view will be distorted if/when we adjust the sliders bars such that

Figure 10.22. Running Tutorial 10.12.

$$\frac{W_{dc}}{W_{wc}} \neq \frac{H_{dc}}{H_{wc}}.$$

We note that in general these four numbers can be controlled by the following.

- **Our application.** As the programmer of the application, we can design our application to allow user control of these values. For example, our application could allow the user to zoom in the world by allowing the WC window to change size, or our application could allow the user to increase/decrease the UI drawing area. In these cases, in order to maintain object proportions, it is important that our application presents a coherent and meaningful user interface. For example, we should implement zooming functionality by providing the user with one single zoom factor. The single zoom factor would ensure that the ratio $\frac{W_{dc}}{W_{wc}}$ remains constant and thus avoid the situation where WC and DC aspect ratios are different.

- **Window manager.** Because our application runs in a shared windowing environment, it is always possible that the environment may change the size of the UI drawing area and inform our application about the changes. In this case, if the DC aspect ratio is changed, then in order to maintain proper proportions, we must change the WC window dimension accordingly. For example, initially our application may have a WC window size of 10×10 and a DC displaying area of 200×200. If for some reason, the window manager decides to change the DC drawing area to 200×100, we must update the WC window to match the 0.5 DC aspect ratio. In this case, we can:

  - *increase the WC window size* to 10×20 and show more of the WC space; or
  - *decrease the WC window size* to 5×10 and show less of the WC space.

  The first option guarantees that we will show at least the original WC window, whereas the second option guarantees that we will show at most the original WC window. The choice between the above two options is a policy decision: neither choice is more correct. We should program our application to support the behavior specified by the user.

10.4.5 Summary

The world coordinate (WC) system is introduced to dissociate our model design space from the dimensions of the UI drawing area. As we have seen, this is advantageous for the following reasons.

- With the WC, we can define any coordinate system that is convenient for designing the geometric models and not be concerned with the dimensions of the eventual output drawing area.

- With the WC *window*, we can control the parameters (center, width, and height) to select the exact regions of the WC space to be displayed in the UI drawing area.

To properly support the WC system, the graphics API introduces the normalized device coordinate (NDC) system, a coordinate system bounded by ± 1. Our job as the graphics API programmer is to compute the $\mathbf{M}_{w2n}$ (Equation (10.10)) operator for each of the WC window regions we wish to display. The graphics API will automatically clip away all geometries outside of the ± 1 range and will automatically compute the $\mathbf{M}_{n2d}$ (Equation (10.6)) operator for drawing the geometries to the output device. In our library design, the $\mathbf{M}_{w2n}$ operator is computed by the WindowHandler class and loaded into the VIEW matrix processor (M_V) of the D3D RC. Finally, we have seen that when defining the WC window, we must ensure that the WC window aspect ratio is the same as that of the UI drawing device. Otherwise, disproportional scaling will occur, resulting in images that appear squeezed.

10.5   Inverse Transformation

So far, we have concentrated on learning the output of geometric elements. To build interactive applications, we must interact with the user. In particular, we must understand how the added window coordinate system affects a user's picking or selecting an on-screen object by clicking the mouse buttons (in DC space).

In the Tutorial 5.6 implementation of the ball-shooting program, we compared mouse click positions with circles in the AllWorldBalls collection to locate the selected one. Notice that this simple operation involves a comparison across two distinct coordinate systems.

- **Mouse-click position** (pt_{dc}). This is a point on the display device (that the user's mouse clicked on). In the case of MFC, this position is returned to us in the hardware coordinate space. As described in Chapter 2 (Tutorial 2.4), we *flipped* the y-axis by subtracting the y-value from the height of the device and thereby converting the point into the device coordinate space with the origin at the lower-left corner. In all of the following discussions, we assume that the hardware-to-device transform has already been performed and we will work with points in DC space, pt_{dc}.

- AllWorldBalls **collection.** This is the set of all geometries in the world. By definition, these geometries are defined in the world coordinate (WC) space.

In the case of Tutorial 5.6, although we did not distinguish between these two coordinate systems, the selection operation functioned correctly because we have carefully defined the WC window to coincide exactly with the DC space. In general, we must transform input mouse positions to the WC space before working with them. For example, in the Tutorial 10.7 implementation of displaying the

Hardware coordinate. Recall that the MFC API returns mouse click positions in the hardware coordinate system where the top-left is the origin with y-axis incrementing downward and x-axis increase rightward.

Hardware-to-device transform. This transformation is performed by the HardwareToDevice() function defined in the WindowHandler class.

geometric face of Figure 10.11, we know

$$\text{DC coordinate:} \begin{cases} 0 \le x_{dc} \le 300, \\ 0 \le y_{dc} \le 300, \end{cases}$$

whereas

$$\text{WC window:} \begin{cases} 15 \le x_{wc} \le 25, \\ 25 \le y_{wc} \le 35. \end{cases}$$

In this case, the user's mouse clicks (pt_{dc}) will return points in DC space with range $[0, 300]$. Clearly, this is very different from where the features of the face are defined in the WC space. In this case, we must perform the inverse of the $\mathbf{M}_{w2d}$ operator to transform pt_{dc} into a point in WC space. If we express

$$pt_{dc} = (x_{dc}, y_{dc})$$

as a vector

$$\mathbf{V}_{dc} = \begin{bmatrix} x_{dc} & y_{dc} \end{bmatrix},$$

then we must compute $\mathbf{V}_{wc}$, where

$$\mathbf{V}_{wc} = \mathbf{V}_{dc}\, \mathbf{M}_{w2d}^{-1}.$$

From Equation (10.14), recall that $\mathbf{M}_{w2d}$ is

$$\mathbf{M}_{w2d} = \mathbf{T}(-cx_{wc}, -cy_{wc})\mathbf{S}(\frac{W_{dc}}{W_{wc}}, \frac{H_{dc}}{H_{wc}})\mathbf{T}(\frac{W_{dc}}{2}, \frac{H_{dc}}{2}). \quad (10.14)$$

From the discussion in Section 9.2, we know that the inverse of a concatenated operator is simply the inverse of each element concatenated in the reverse order:

$$\mathbf{M}_{w2d}^{-1} = \mathbf{M}_{d2w} = \mathbf{T}^{-1}(\frac{W_{dc}}{2}, \frac{H_{dc}}{2})\mathbf{S}^{-1}(\frac{W_{dc}}{W_{wc}}, \frac{H_{dc}}{H_{wc}})\mathbf{T}^{-1}(-cx_{wc}, -cy_{wc}),$$

which is

$$\mathbf{M}_{d2w} = \mathbf{T}(-\frac{W_{dc}}{2}, -\frac{H_{dc}}{2})\mathbf{S}(\frac{W_{wc}}{W_{dc}}, \frac{H_{wc}}{H_{dc}})\mathbf{T}(cx_{wc}, cy_{wc}) \quad (10.17)$$

or

$$\mathbf{V}_{wc} = \mathbf{V}_{dc}\mathbf{T}(-\frac{W_{dc}}{2}, -\frac{H_{dc}}{2})\mathbf{S}(\frac{W_{wc}}{W_{dc}}, \frac{H_{wc}}{H_{dc}})\mathbf{T}(cx_{wc}, cy_{wc}). \quad (10.18)$$

Equation (10.18) says that to transform a point (x_{dc}, y_{dc}) from the device drawing area (DC) to a point (x_{wc}, y_{wc}) in our design space (WC):

$$\begin{aligned} x_{wc} &= ((x_{dc} - \tfrac{W_{dc}}{2})\tfrac{W_{wc}}{W_{dc}}) + cx_{wc}, \\ y_{wc} &= ((y_{dc} - \tfrac{H_{dc}}{2})\tfrac{H_{wc}}{H_{dc}}) + cy_{wc}, \end{aligned} \quad (10.19)$$

where

$$\text{Device drawing area} \begin{cases} \text{width} &= W_{dc}, \\ \text{height} &= H_{dc}, \end{cases}$$

```
void UWB_WindowHandler::DeviceToWorld(int dcx, int dcy, float &wcx, float &wcy) const
    ⋮
A:  GetDeviceSize(dcW, dcH);                    // Get the UI drawing device dimension
    vec3 center = m_WCWindow.GetCenter();       // Center position of the WC Window
    float wcW = m_WCWindow.Width();             // Width of the WC Window
    float wcH = m_WCWindow.Height();            // Height of the WC Window
B:  wcx = center.x + ((wcW/dcW) * (dcx - (dcW/2.0f))); // implement Equation 10.17
    wcy = center.y + ((wcH/dcH) * (dcy - (dcH/2.0f))); // by computing Equation 10.19
```

Listing 10.14. The `WindowHandler::DeviceToWorld()` implementation.

Source file.
uwbgl_WindowHandler3.cpp file in the *Common Files/ WindowHandler* subfolder of the UWBGL_D3D_Lib10 project.

and

$$\text{WC window} = \begin{cases} \text{center} & = (cx_{wc}, cy_{wc}), \\ \text{width} & = W_{wc}, \\ \text{height} & = H_{wc}. \end{cases}$$

Listing 10.14 shows the implementation of Equation (10.19) in the `DeviceToWorld()` transform function of the `UWB_WindowHandler` class in `D3D_UWB_Lib10`. At label A, we obtain the dimension of the drawing device and the parameters for the WC window. Label B is a direct implementation of Equation (10.19). In general, we must transform all user mouse-click positions by Equation (10.17) before comparing with points in the WC space.

Tutorials 10.13 and 10.14. Mouse Positions and Inverse Transforms

- **Goal.** Verify mouse positions and the need for device-to-world transformations.

- **Approach.** Extend Tutorial 10.12 to support moving of the small-view WC window by dragging with the left mouse button in the main view.

Figure 10.23 is a screenshot of running Tutorials 10.13 and 10.14. In these tutorials, left mouse button drag in the main view defines the center position for the WC window of the small view. For example, from Figure 10.11 we know that the nose position of the geometric person is $(20, 30)$ in WC space. Now, if the user left mouse button clicks at the nose position in the main view, our application will react by moving the center of the small-view WC window to $(20, 30)$. If the user left mouse button drags towards the right-eye position, $(22, 32)$, our application will track the position by moving the center of the small-view WC window. Notice

Tutorial 10.13.
Project Name:
    D3D_BadMousePan
Library Support:
    UWB_MFC_Lib1
    UWB_D3D_Lib10

Tutorial 10.14.
Project Name:
    D3D_MousePan
Library Support:
    UWB_MFC_Lib1
    UWB_D3D_Lib10

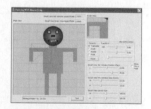

Figure 10.23. Running Tutorial 10.13 and 10.14.

```
// Mouse button services
void CMainHandler::OnMouseButton(bool down, unsigned int nFlags, int hwX, int hwY)
        :

A:   HardwareToDevice(hwX, hwY, deviceX, deviceY); // hwXY -> deviceXY
        :

B:   if(nFlags & MK_LBUTTON) // Left Mouse Button down
           // Compute new center for small view WC Window
           ComputeBoundPosition(deviceX, deviceY);


// Mouse move services
void CMainHandler::OnMouseMove(unsigned int nFlags, int hwX, int hwY)
        :

A:   HardwareToDevice(hwX, hwY, deviceX, deviceY);
        :

B:   if(nFlags & MK_LBUTTON) // Left Mouse Button drag
           // Compute new center for small view WC Window
           ComputeBoundPosition(deviceX, deviceY);
```

Source file.
DrawAndMouseHandler.cpp
file in the *WindowHan-*
dler folder of the
D3D_BadMousePan project.

Listing 10.15. The MainHandler mouse event service routines of Tutorial 10.13.

that in our discussion, these are in WC coordinate units, while we know that the mouse positions are in device coordinates. Tutorial 10.13 shows us the results of not transforming points to the WC space and using the mouse positions in the DC space directly. Listing 10.15 shows the mouse button click (OnMouseButton) and mouse move (OnMouseMove) service routines of Tutorial 10.13. In both service routines, at label A we transform the mouse click position from hardware to device coordinate, and then use the DC position to compute the center position for the small-view WC window. For this reason, in Tutorial 10.13, if we click around the top region of the main view, the corresponding DC points will have values around 300, and thus the small-view WC window will be moved to corresponding positions. Because nothing is defined in the 300 range in the WC space, nothing will show up in the small-view drawing area. Recall from Figure 10.10 that the geometric person is defined within the range of $[0, 40]$. This means if we left mouse button click/drag around the lower-left region of the main view, limiting our DC position to within the range of $[0, 40]$, we will see the small-view WC window panning around the geometric person. Clearly we must transform the DC positions to WC before computing the WC window position. Tutorial 10.14 extends from Tutorial 10.13 with the simple inclusion of the DeviceToWorld() function calls. Listing 10.16 shows the mouse event source routines of Tutorial 10.14. As we can see at label A, the `DeviceToWorld()` function is called (for both mouse button and mouse move event service routines). By running Tutorial 10.14, we can verify that this tutorial functions as expected.

```
// Mouse button services
void CMainHandler::OnMouseButton(bool down, unsigned int nFlags, int hwX, int hwY)
    ⋮
    HardwareToDevice(hwX, hwY, deviceX, deviceY); // hwXY -> deviceXY
A:  DeviceToWorld(deviceX, deviceY, wcX, wcY); // deviceXY -> wcXY
    ⋮

    if(nFlags & MK_LBUTTON) // Left Mouse Button down
        // Compute new center of small view WC Window based on wcXY
        ComputeBoundPosition(wcX, wcY);


// Mouse move services
void CMainHandler::OnMouseMove(unsigned int nFlags, int hwX, int hwY)
    ⋮
    HardwareToDevice(hwX, hwY, deviceX, deviceY); // hwXY -> deviceXY
A:  DeviceToWorld(deviceX, deviceY, wcX, wcY); // deviceXY -> wcXY
    ⋮

    if(nFlags & MK_LBUTTON) // Left Mouse Button down
        // Compute new center of small view WC Window based on wcXY
        ComputeBoundPosition(wcX, wcY);
```

Source file.
DrawAndMouseHandler.cpp file in the *WindowHandler* folder of the D3D_MousePan project.

Listing 10.16. The `MainHandler` mouse event service routines of Tutorial 10.14.

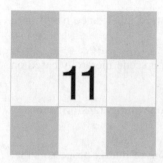

Hierarchical Modeling

This chapter discusses approaches to build hierarchical models, compound geometric objects where independent components can be controlled by transformations. This chapter:

- analyzes the technical requirements for building hierarchical models and derives the concept of a scene node;

- presents approaches to organize scene nodes into scene graphs and scene trees as hierarchical models;

- describes the scene node parent-child relationship where the child inherits the parent's transformation;

- describes object coordinate spaces in a scene graph/tree and experiments with transforming from object to device coordinate spaces.

After this chapter we should:

- understand how to design and define a compound object with independently controllable components;

- understand how to control and interact with the different components in a hierarchical model.

In addition, with respect to hands-on programming, we should:

- be able to implement parent-child transformation inheritance based on a matrix stack and the WORLD matrix processor;

- be able to implement a compound object with a scene hierarchy based on the SceneNode class;

- be able to define simple animations based on controlling transformations in scene nodes.

We have learned that graphics APIs provide a *pipeline* of matrix processors that assists us in controlling the drawing of our geometric model.

For example, we have seen that in the case of D3D, this pipeline consists of the WORLD ($\mathbf{M}_W$), VIEW ($\mathbf{M}_V$), and PROJECTION ($\mathbf{M}_P$) matrix processors. We have learned that, for D3D, the vertex $\mathbf{V}_i$ that we wish to draw will be transformed into $\mathbf{V}_o$, where

Grayed-out matrices. The $\mathbf{M}_P$ and $\mathbf{M}_V$ matrices are grayed out to indicate the assumption that they have been properly initialized and will not be changed.

$$\mathbf{V}_o = \mathbf{V}_i \, \mathbf{M}_W \, \mathbf{M}_V \, \mathbf{M}_P. \tag{11.1}$$

We have learned that graphics APIs typically compute and apply $\mathbf{M}_{n2d}$ to $\mathbf{V}_o$ such that if $\mathbf{V}_o$ is within the bounds of the NDC, it will show up in the drawing device. So far the PROJECTION matrix $\mathbf{M}_P$ has been left as the identity matrix $\mathbf{I}_4$.

$\mathbf{M}_{w2n}$. In the *UWB_GL* library, the $\mathbf{M}_{w2n}$ matrix is computed and loaded to the $\mathbf{M}_V$ matrix processor by the LoadW2NXform() function defined in the WindowHandler class.

In Chapter 10, we learned the details of how to compute the world-to-NDC matrix ($\mathbf{M}_{w2n}$) to load into the VIEW matrix processor ($\mathbf{M}_V$) to allow us to work in a convenient design space. Chapter 9 discussed how we can work with the WORLD matrix processor in controlling the transformation (e.g., size and location) of geometric primitives.

In this chapter, we focus our attention back on the WORLD ($\mathbf{M}_W$) matrix processor. We are interested in efficient and effective defining and controlling of our geometric model. This chapter will introduce SceneNode and SceneTree as a layer of abstraction between our programming code and the underlying WORLD matrix processor.

11.1 Motivation

The discussion from Chapter 9 showed us that if we want to draw a circle with a triangle fan of radius r_i centered at location (x_i, y_i), we can do one of two things.

1. Set the WORLD matrix to identity:

$$\mathbf{M}_W = \mathbf{I}_4$$

and define a triangle fan centered at (x_i, y_i) with radius of r_i.

2. Set the WORLD matrix processor to be

$$\mathbf{M}_W = \mathbf{S}(r_i, r_i)\, \mathbf{T}(x_i, y_i)$$

and define a triangle fan centered at the origin $((0,0))$ with radius of 1.0.

While both approaches draw the exact same circle, the second approach supports interactive changing of the circle more efficiently, where we can simply change the translation and scale factors to move or resize the circle. This is the approach we will learn about. Tutorial 9.6 introduced the XformInfo class to implement

$$\mathbf{M}_W = \mathbf{T}(-p_x, -p_y)\, \mathbf{S}(s_x, s_y)\, \mathbf{R}(\theta)\, \mathbf{T}(p_x, p_y)\, \mathbf{T}(t_x, t_y)$$

to support translation and pivoted scaling/rotation of primitives. In this chapter, we will continue with this discussion. In particular, we will examine controlling of the transformation of defined geometric primitives. In computer graphics applications, we typically define geometric primitives to represent a physical object and then work with transformation matrices to control the defined object. For example, Figure 11.1 shows a simple geometric model of an arm and a connected palm. In this simple example, the arm is represented by the 2×3 rectangle

$$R_{a0} = \left\{ \begin{array}{l} (0, -1), \\ (3, -1), \\ (3, 1), \\ (0, 1), \end{array} \right.$$

and the palm is represented by the circle

$$C_{p0} = \left\{ \begin{array}{l} \text{center} = (4, 0), \\ \text{radius} = 1.0. \end{array} \right.$$

As illustrated in Figure 11.1, we define the pivot position to be located at $P_a = (0, 0)$ such that the rotation of the arm can resemble that of a real physical arm.

Tutorial 11.1. Controlling the Simple Arm

- **Goal.** Work with a set of defined geometric primitives and with controlling the transformation of the defined primitives.

- **Approach.** Define the geometry of the simple arm in Figure 11.1 and manipulate transformations to control the arm.

Figure 11.2 is a screenshot of running Tutorial 11.1. We see that we can interactively control the transformation of the arm, where the rotation and scaling operations are performed with respect the P_a pivot position.

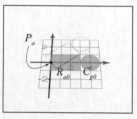

Figure 11.1. The simple arm geometry of Tutorial 11.1.

Tutorial 11.1.
Project Name:
  D3D_SimpleArm
Library Support:
  UWB_MFC_Lib1
  UWB_D3D_Lib10

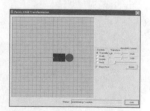

Figure 11.2. Tutorial 11.1.

Source file. Model.h/cpp
files in the *Model* folder of the
D3D_SimpleArm project.

```
class CModel {
    ⋮
```
A:
```
    UWB_PrimitiveRectangle m_Arm; // Rectangle Ra0
    UWB_PrimitiveCircle m_Palm;   // Circle Cp0
    // Transformation operator: Ma = T(-Pa)SaRaT(Pa)Ta
```
B:
```
    UWB_XformInfo m_ArmXform;

    void DrawModel(); // To draw the arm (Ra0 and Cp0)
    ⋮
    ⋮
};
```

```
void CModel::DrawModel() {
    ⋮
    // Initialize top of matrix stack (Mt = I4)
```
C:
```
    m_DrawHelper.InitializeModelTransform();
    // Push the matrix stack
    m_DrawHelper.PushModelTransform();
    // Mt1 = MaMt and then MW = Mt1
```
D:
```
    m_ArmXform.SetUpModelStack(m_DrawHelper);
    // Draw the two triangles in Ra0
    m_Arm.Draw(lod, m_DrawHelper);
    // Draw the triangle Fan of Cp0
    m_Palm.Draw(lod, m_DrawHelper);
    // Pop off the top of the matrix stack
    m_DrawHelper.PopModelTransform();
    ⋮
```

Listing 11.1. The CModel class of Tutorial 11.1.

Listing 11.1 shows that in our implementation, we follow Figure 11.1 and define the R_{a0} rectangle and C_{p0} circle (at label A). In addition, we define the m_ArmXform (at label B), an XformInfo object, to implement

$$\mathbf{M}_a = \mathbf{T}(-P_a)\, \mathbf{S}_a(s_x, s_y)\, \mathbf{R}_a(\theta)\, \mathbf{T}(P_a)\, \mathbf{T}_a(t_x, t_y).$$

Through interacting with the slider bars, the user sets the m_ArmXform object to control the translation (t_x, t_y) and pivoted (P_a) rotation (θ) and scaling (s_x, s_y) of the simple arm. During DrawModel(), at label C, we initialize the top of the matrix stack $(\mathbf{M}_t)$ to identity (with the InitializeModelTransform() function call), then at label D, the m_ArmXform object concatenates $\mathbf{M}_a$ with the top of the matrix stack and loads the concatenated result into the WORLD ($\mathbf{M}_W$) matrix. The concatenated top of stack $\mathbf{M}_{t1}$ is

$$\mathbf{M}_{t1} = \mathbf{M}_a \, \mathbf{M}_t = \mathbf{M}_a \, \mathbf{I}_4 = \mathbf{M}_a.$$

In this way, the top of the stack $\mathbf{M}_{t1}$ is simply $\mathbf{M}_a$ and is loaded into the $\mathbf{M}_W$ matrix processor. As pointed out by Equation (11.1), all vertices $\mathbf{V}_i$ of triangles that represent R_{a0} and C_{p0} will be transformed into $\mathbf{V}_{io}$ according to

$$\begin{aligned} \mathbf{V}_{io} \;&= \mathbf{V}_i \, \mathbf{M}_W \, \mathbf{M}_V \, \mathbf{M}_P \\ &= \mathbf{V}_i \, \mathbf{M}_a \, \mathbf{M}_V \, \mathbf{M}_P. \end{aligned} \qquad (11.2)$$

The important lesson this tutorial demonstrates is that to control geometric objects in computer graphics applications, we typically:

- **Do not** alter the basic geometry of the primitives (i.e., we do not change the vertex positions of R_{a0} or C_{p0}).

- **Do** define a transformation operator to transform the defined geometric primitives (i.e., we defined m_ArmXform ($\mathbf{M}_a$) to transform R_{a0} and C_{p0}).

We can increase the complexity of the simple arm of Tutorial 11.1 by supporting independent transformation control over the palm (C_{p0}). As illustrated in Figure 11.3, we want the palm to be transformed with respect to the end of the arm, or pivoted at the location P_p. Notice that, in addition to the independent transformation of the palm, when we transform the arm by changing $\mathbf{M}_a$, we would expect the palm to follow $\mathbf{M}_a$.

Tutorial 11.2. Independent Control of the Palm

- **Goal.** Work with two levels of transformations where the second level follows the transformation from the first level.

- **Approach.** Implement the arm/palm control as defined by Figure 11.3.

Figure 11.4 is a screenshot of running Tutorial 11.2. In this tutorial, by activating the appropriate radio button, we can choose to interactively control the *entire* object (i.e., R_{a0} and C_{p0}) or to independently transform only the palm object (i.e., C_{p0}). Listing 11.2 shows that the implementation of Tutorial 11.2 is similar to that of Tutorial 11.1 with two important differences.

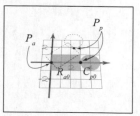

Figure 11.3. Independent transformation of the palm.

Tutorial 11.2.
Project Name:
  D3D_ParentChild
Library Support:
  UWB_MFC_Lib1
  UWB_D3D_Lib10

Figure 11.4. Tutorial 11.2.

Source file. Model.h/cpp files in the *Model* folder of the D3D_ParentChild project.

```
class CModel {
    // ... similar to Tutorial 11.1 ...
        ⋮
    // Rectangle R_{a0}
    UWB_PrimitiveRectangle m_Arm;
    // Circle C_{p0}
    UWB_PrimitiveCircle m_Palm;
    // Transformation operator: M_a = T(-P_a)S_aR_aT(P_a)T_a
    UWB_XformInfo m_ArmXform;
    // Transformation opeator: M_p = T(-P_p)S_pR_pT(P_p)T_p
A:  UWB_XformInfo m_PalmXform;
        ⋮
};
```

```
void CModel::DrawModel() {
    // ... similar to Tutorial 11.1 ...
    // Initialize top of matrix stack (M_t = I_4)
    m_DrawHelper.InitializeModelTransform();
    // Push the matrix stack
    m_DrawHelper.PushModelTransform();
    // M_{t1} = M_aM_t and then M_W = M_{t1}
B:  m_ArmXform.SetUpModelStack(m_DrawHelper);
    // Draw the two triangles in R_{a0}
    m_Arm.Draw(lod, m_DrawHelper);
    // M_{t2} = M_pM_{t1} and then M_W = M_{t2}
C:  m_PalmXform.SetUpModelStack(m_DrawHelper);
    // Draw the triangle Fan of C_{p0}
    m_Palm.Draw(lod, m_DrawHelper);
    // Pop off the top of the matrix stack
    m_DrawHelper.PopModelTransform();
}
```

Listing 11.2. The CModel class of Tutorial 11.2.

The first difference is at label A of the CModel class definition. We have defined m_PalmXform, a second XformInfo object, to support the independent transformation of the palm (C_{p0}). When the corresponding radio button is selected, the m_PalmXform object records the transformation values interactively set by the user. These transformation values together define

$$\mathbf{M}_p = \mathbf{T}(-P_p)\,\mathbf{S}_p\,\mathbf{R}_p\,\mathbf{T}(P_p)\mathbf{T}_p,$$

where $\mathbf{T}_p$, $\mathbf{R}_p$, and $\mathbf{S}_p$ are the translation, rotation, and scaling matrices, respectively, defined by the user's interactive settings, and $P_p = (3,0)$ is the pivot position defined in Figure 11.3.

The second important difference between the implementations of Tutorial 11.1 and Tutorial 11.2 is in the CModel::DrawModel() function. Similar to Tutorial 11.1, after the InitializeModelTransform() and the SetUpModelStack() function calls at label B, the top of the matrix stack $\mathbf{M}_{t1}$ becomes

$$\mathbf{M}_{t1} = \mathbf{M}_a,$$

and $\mathbf{M}_{t1}$ is loaded into the WORLD matrix processor ($\mathbf{M}_W$). In this way, the triangles of R_{a0} are transformed according to Equation (11.2). However, at label C, m_PalmXform is invoked to compute and concatenate $\mathbf{M}_p$ onto the top of the matrix stack $\mathbf{M}_{t2}$:

$$\begin{aligned} \mathbf{M}_{t2} &= \mathbf{M}_p \, \mathbf{M}_{t1} \\ &= \mathbf{M}_p \, \mathbf{M}_a, \end{aligned}$$

and $\mathbf{M}_{t2}$ is loaded into the WORLD matrix. In this way, the vertices of C_{p0} triangle fan, $\mathbf{V}_c$, are transformed to $\mathbf{V}_{co}$ according to

$$\begin{aligned} \mathbf{V}_{co} &= \mathbf{V}_c \, \mathbf{M}_W \, \mathbf{M}_V \, \mathbf{M}_P \\ &= \mathbf{V}_c \, \mathbf{M}_{t2} \, \mathbf{M}_V \, \mathbf{M}_P \qquad\qquad (11.3) \\ &= \mathbf{V}_c \, \mathbf{M}_p \, \mathbf{M}_a \, \mathbf{M}_V \, \mathbf{M}_P. \end{aligned}$$

Notice that $\mathbf{V}_c$ is first transformed by m_PalmXform ($\mathbf{M}_p$) and then by m_ArmXform ($\mathbf{M}_a$). In this way, the C_{p0} circle is transformed as an integral element of the arm object (by $\mathbf{M}_a$), whereas it is also independently transformed as a component on the arm's object (by $\mathbf{M}_p$).

In general, since the palm inherits the transform from the arm object, we refer to the palm as the child and the arm as the parent. We observe that one way to define independently transformable components in objects is to apply the involved primitive transform operators in a tree-like ordering. In the next section, we introduce the SceneNode class to support the building of a tree-like structure to support the appropriate hierarchical concatenation of transformation operators.

11.2   The SceneNode Class

Tutorials 11.1 and 11.2 demonstrated the following.

- Graphical objects (e.g., the arm) are defined by geometric primitives (e.g., the rectangle R_{a0} and circle C_{p0}). In addition, to control the graphical object, we typically *do not* change the basic geometry of the primitives (e.g., we do not change the vertices of R_{a0} to rotate it).

- Interactive control of a graphical object is accomplished via manipulating transformation operators (e.g., the m_ArmXform, $\mathbf{M}_a$).

- Components on a graphical object (e.g., the palm on the arm) can be independently transformed when separate transformation operators (e.g., the m_PalmXform, $\mathbf{M}_p$) are concatenated in a tree-like hierarchical ordering.

UWBGL_D3D_Lib11

This library introduces the SceneNode class to extend Lib10. As illustrated in Figure 11.5, the SceneNode class encapsulates the functionality of the above observations.

- **PrimitiveList.** This list references the primitives that define the graphical object (e.g., R_{a0} of the arm, or C_{p0} of the palm).

- **XformInfo.** This is the transformation operator with which we can control the graphical object (e.g., the m_ArmXform for the arm or the m_PalmXform for the palm).

- **Child** SceneNodes. These are references to child SceneNode objects allowing the building of a tree structure to support ordered concatenation of the transformation operator.

- **Velocity.** This is defined for the convenience of moving the SceneNode. For example, to implement constant movement of a SceneNode object, our program code can periodically update the translation operator in the XformInfo object with this velocity.

Listing 11.3 shows the implementation of the structure illustrated by Figure 11.5, where m_pPrimitive at label A can reference UWB_PrimitiveList for a list of geometric primitives. The m_xform object at label B is designed to support transforming all geometries referenced by m_pPrimitive. The m_child_nodes array at label C allows the definition of child nodes for building a tree-like hierarchy of SceneNodes. As explained, the velocity at label D is meant for updating the translation of the m_xform object. As will be shown later, to support a friendly user interface, the m_Name at label E allows definition of a meaningful name for each node.

Change summary. See p. 523 for a summary of changes to the library.

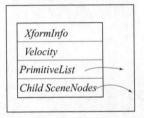

XformInfo
Velocity
PrimitiveList
Child SceneNodes

Figure 11.5. A Scene Node.

```
class UWB_SceneNode {
  public:
    // constructor/destructor and the set/access methods for:
    // Primitives/XformInfo/Children/Velocity/Name ... etc.


    // draws all primitives and children nodes
    void Draw(eLevelOfDetail, UWB_DrawHelper&) const;
      ⋮

  protected:
    // Geometric primitives of the graphics object
A:  UWB_Primitive* m_pPrimitive;
    // Children nodes (components)
B:  UWB_PointerArray<UWB_SceneNode*> m_child_nodes;
    // This operator computes: Mcn
C:  UWB_XformInfo m_xform;
    // Velocity of the node (updates m_xform->m_translation)
D:  vec3 m_velocity;
    // Optional name of this node: for GUI support
E:  std::string m_Name;
};
```

Source file.
uwbgl_SceneNode1.h   file
in the *Common Files/ Sce-neNode* subfolder of the
UWBGL_D3D_Lib11 project.

Listing 11.3. The UWB_SceneNode class definition.

Listing 11.4 shows the two important aspects of the implementation of the SceneNode class:

1. **Memory management.** The destructor at label A shows that the SceneNode class expects that the memory associated with the m_pPrimitive reference is allocated from the heap (via the new() operation). Notice that the SceneNode class does not make assumptions with respect to the references in the m_child_node array. It is the responsibility of the programmer to delete() child nodes that are allocated on the heap.

2. **Transformation operator concatenation.** The Draw() function shows how the transformation operator is concatenated with the top of the matrix stack ($\mathbf{M}_t$) to control the geometric primitives, where at label:

   - **B.** The top of the matrix stack, $\mathbf{M}_t$, is pushed and duplicated. At this point, we know that the top two entries on the matrix stack are $\mathbf{M}_{t1}$ and $\mathbf{M}_t$, and we know that these two matrices are the same.

```
UWB_SceneNode::~UWB_SceneNode           // Destructor
A:   if(m_pPrimitive)
         // Releasing memory => m_pPrimitive must be allocated on the Heap!
         delete m_pPrimitive;
         m_pPrimitive = NULL;


void UWB_SceneNode::Draw(eLevelOfDetail lod, UWB_DrawHelper& draw_helper) const
     // duplicate the top of the matrix stack (Mₜ₁ = Mₜ)
B:   draw_helper.PushModelTransform();
         // Mₜ₂ = MₛₙMₜ₁  and  M_W = Mₜ₂
     C:  m_xform.SetUpModelStack(draw_helper);
     D:  if(m_pPrimitive)
             // Draw the primitives of this node
             m_pPrimitive->Draw( lod, draw_helper );
         // Draw all the children nodes
     E:  for(int i=0; i<m_child_nodes.Count(); i++)
             m_child_nodes[i]->Draw(lod, draw_helper);
     // Pop off the current top of stack (pop off Mₜ₂)
F:   draw_helper.PopModelTransform();
```

Source file.
uwbgl_SceneNode1.cpp
file in the *Common Files/*
SceneNode subfolder of the
UWBGL_D3D_Lib11 project.

Listing 11.4. The UWB_SceneNode class implementation.

- **C.** The transformation operator m_xform ($\mathbf{M}_{cn}$) is concatenated with the current top of the matrix stack, such that the new top of the matrix stack becomes

$$\mathbf{M}_{t2} = \mathbf{M}_{sn}\mathbf{M}_{t1}.$$

  In addition, this new top of the matrix stack $\mathbf{M}_{t2}$ is loaded into the WORLD matrix processor ($\mathbf{M}_W$).

- **D.** The geometric primitives referenced by m_pPrimitive are drawn where all these primitives will be transformed by the $\mathbf{M}_{t2}$ matrix that was loaded in the WORLD matrix processor.

- **E.** The child nodes are invoked to draw themselves. Because the current top of the matrix stack $\mathbf{M}_{t2}$ is concatenated with the $\mathbf{M}_{cn}$ matrix of this node, all geometric primitives of child nodes will be affected by this transformation operator. In this way, this invoking node becomes the parent node. We will examine this hierarchical transformation concatenation in more detail in Tutorial 11.3.

- **F.** The concatenated top of matrix stack $\mathbf{M}_{t2}$ is popped off, thus restoring the original $\mathbf{M}_t$ as the top of the matrix stack. In this way, the matrix stack is unchanged before and after this drawing routine.

Notice that the nodes and the matrices are concatenated in order, where the current node is always processed before that of the child nodes. In addition, the above drawing routine traverses the hierarchy in a depth-first manner. The depth-first in-order traversal of the Draw() routine is hard-coded; the routine does not support run-time re-configuration of traversal order. This fixed traversal implies a fixed drawing sequence where children's primitives are always drawn after those from the parents. As a result, children's primitives always cover those of parents'. This is a limitation of the SceneNode class.

In computer graphics, a scene node typically refers to the combination of a transformation operator with its associated primitives, or simply the functionality of our SceneNode class. An interconnected hierarchy of scene nodes is typically referred to as a scene tree. When sharing of scene nodes is allowed, the scene tree can be generalized to a scene graph.

In the rest of this section, we study scene nodes by examining how to work with the SceneNode class. We will examine building hierarchical models with scene nodes and including multiple primitives in each scene node. Scene trees/-graphs will be examined in more detail in the next section.

Tutorial 11.3. Working with the SceneNode Class

- **Goal.** Gain insight and understanding of how to work with the SceneNode class.

- **Approach.** Implement the arm/palm hierarchy from Tutorial 11.2 based on the SceneNode class.

Tutorial 11.3 runs and behaves identically to Tutorial 11.2. The only differences between these two tutorials are in the implementation of the arm and the palm graphical objects. The top portion of Listing 11.5 shows that the definition of the CModel class is mostly similar to that of Tutorial 11.2. The exception here is that at label A, the m_scene SceneNode object replaces the rectangle, circle, and XformInfo objects. During the construction of the CModel object, at labels B, C, and D, a SceneNode hierarchy that corresponds to the illustration of Figure 11.6 is constructed. At label B, the memory of R_{a0} (pRectangle) is allocated and geometric information is initialized and set to be referenced by m_pPrimitive

Tutorial 11.3.
Project Name:
    D3D_SceneNode
Library Support:
    UWB_MFC_Lib1
    UWB_D3D_Lib11

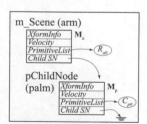

Figure 11.6. The SceneNode structure of Tutorial 11.3.

Source file. Model.h/cpp files in the *Model* folder of the D3D_SceneNode project.

```
class CModel {
    // ... similar to Tutorial 11.2 ...
    :
A:  UWB_SceneNode m_scene;  // This is the arm
    // Draw all of the geometry that is part of this model.
    void DrawModel();
};
```

```
CModel::CModel() ...       // Constructor
    // Allocate memory for R_{a0}
B:  UWB_PrimitiveRectangle* pRectangle = new UWB_PrimitiveRectangle();
    :

    // Set the geometric information of R_{a0} (pRectangle)
    // m_scene->m_pPrimitive = R_{a0}
    m_scene.SetPrimitive(pRectangle);
    // SceneNode for the palm
C:  UWB_SceneNode* pChildNode = new UWB_SceneNode();
    // Allocate memory for C_{p0}
    UWB_PrimitiveCircle* pCircle = new UWB_PrimitiveCircle();
    :

    // Set the geometric information of C_{p0} (pCircle)
    // pChildNode->m_pPrimitive = pCircle
    pChildNode->SetPrimitive( pCircle );
    // Set pChildeNode into m_scene->m_child_node array
D:  m_scene.InsertChildNode( pChildNode );
    :
```

```
void CModel::DrawModel()
    // Draws the SceneNode hierarchy
E:  m_scene.Draw(lod, m_DrawHelper);
    :
```

Listing 11.5. The CModel class of Tutorial 11.3.

of m_scene. At label C, the child scene node pChildNode and circle C_{p0} are allocated and appropriately initialized. At label D, pChildNode is set to become a child node of m_scene. In this way, as illustrated in Figure 11.6, m_scene references the arm geometry (R_{a0}) and has the transformation operator ($\mathbf{M}_a$) that controls the entire arm. The child of m_scene references the palm geometry (C_{p0}) and has the transformation operator that controls only the palm object.

Label E in Listing 11.5 shows that in this case, drawing of the entire arm can be accomplished by simply calling the m_scene.Draw() function. From Listing 11.4, we know that the SceneNode::Draw() routine does the following.

- **C.** Concatenates $\mathbf{M}_a$ with the top of matrix stack and loads the top of matrix stack to the WORLD matrix.

- **D.** Draws R_{a0}; with $\mathbf{M}_a$ loaded in the WORLD matrix, the triangles of R_{a0} are transformed according to Equation (11.2).

- **E.** Invokes the child node Draw() function with $\mathbf{M}_a$ on the top of the matrix stack. In this case, the child node concatenates $\mathbf{M}_p$ with $\mathbf{M}_a$, loads the result to the WORLD matrix processor, and draws C_{p0}. With the concatenated results of $\mathbf{M}_p$ and $\mathbf{M}_a$ on the top of the matrix stack, the triangles of C_{p0} are transformed according to Equation (11.3).

In this way, although with very different implementations, Tutorials 11.2 and 11.3 behave in identical manners. This tutorial demonstrates that the SceneNode class is convenient for building and controlling graphical objects with independently transformable components.

Notice that the identifiable and controllable "graphical objects" (e.g., the arm, or the palm) are usually associated with SceneNode objects. Recall that at label E of Listing 11.3, the SceneNode class has a m_Name instance variable reserved for naming of individual components in an object.

Tutorial 11.4. Subclassing from the SceneNode Class

- **Goal.** Demonstrate different ways of working with the SceneNode class, including design reuse.

- **Approach.** Show a different approach to implementing the arm/palm hierarchy from Tutorial 11.3 with the same SceneNode class.

Tutorial 11.4.
Project Name:
   D3D_SceneNodeArm
Library Support:
   UWB_MFC_Lib1
   UWB_D3D_Lib11

Tutorial 11.4 runs and behaves identically to Tutorial 11.3. In this case, we subclass from SceneNode to create individual classes for the arm and the palm objects. Listing 11.6 shows the CPalm class, a general palm object designed to be attached to the arm object of Figure 11.3. Taking advantage of the functionality defined by the SceneNode class, the CPalm class only needs to define the constructor (at label A). The first parameter of the constructor, the vec3 at position, defines the location of the palm object. This is to ensure that it is possible to define and attach a CPalm object to an arm object at any location. In the implementation

Source file. Palm.h/cpp files in the *Model* folder of the D3D_SceneNodeArm project.

```
class CPalm : public UWB_SceneNode {
A:   Palm(vec3 at, const char* name = "Palm");
        ⋮
}
```

```
CPalm::CPalm(vec3 at, const char *name) : UWB_SceneNode(name)
     // Pivot of Mp is 1 unit in X from the Palm location
B:   m_xform.SetPivot(vec3(at.x-1,at.y,0.0f));
     // memory for Cp0
C:   UWB_PrimitiveCircle* pCircle = new UWB_PrimitiveCircle();
     // set Cp0 geomtry based on at position
        ⋮

     // Memory for a PrimitiveList
D:   UWB_PrimitiveList* pPalmPrim = new UWB_PrimitiveList();
     // insert Cp0 into the list
     pPalmPrim->Append(pCircle);
     // m_pPrimitive is a PrimitiveList
E:   SetPrimitive(pPalmPrim);
        ⋮
```

Listing 11.6. The CPalm class of Tutorial 11.4.

of the constructor at label B, the at position is used to define the pivot position of the transform. Referring to Figure 11.3, the pivot position of the palm P_p is 1 unit to the left of the center of the circle C_{p0}. At label C, the circle C_{p0} is allocated and initialized based on the values of at.

Recall from Section 7.6 that we have defined the PrimitiveList to be a subclass of the Primitive class. For this reason, the m_pPrimitive pointer of SceneNode can also reference a PrimitiveList (list of primitives). In Listing 11.6 at label D, a PrimitiveList object is allocated to contain the C_{p0} circle, and at label E the list is set to be a primitive of the CPalm class. Listing 11.7 shows the definition and implementation of the CArm class. As in the case of the CPalm class, we only need to support the constructor of the CArm class (at label A). Once again, the first parameter of the constructor allows the arm to be at any location. The implementation of the constructor corresponds to that of the CPalm, where the transformation pivot (at label B) and the R_{a0} geometry (at label C) are both defined with respect to the at position. Once again, a list is created for R_{a0} to represent the primitive of CArm (at labels D and E). Finally, at label F, a CPalm object

Source file. Arm.h/cpp files in the *Model* folder of the D3D_SceneNodeArm project.

```
class CArm : public UWB_SceneNode {
A:   CArm(vec3 at, const char* name = "Arm");
     ⋮
}
```

```
CArm::CArm(vec3 at, const char *name) : UWB_SceneNode(name)
B:   m_xform.SetPivot(at); // Pivot of Ma is the Arm location
C:   UWB_PrimitiveRectangle* pRectangle = new UWB_PrimitiveRectangle(); // memory for Ra0
     // sets Ra0 geometry based on at position
     ⋮
D:   UWB_PrimitiveList* pArmPrim = new UWB_PrimitiveList(); // Memory for a PrimitiveList
     pArmPrim->Append(pRectangle); // insert Ra0 into list
E:   SetPrimitive(pArmPrim); // m_pPrimitive is a PrimitiveList
     ⋮
F:   UWB_SceneNode* pPalm=new CPalm(vec3(at.x+4,at.y,at.z); // Palm is at 4 unit in X from Arm
     InsertChildNode(pPalm); // insert the allocated CPalm as a child
```

Listing 11.7. The CArm class of Tutorial 11.4.

Source file. Model.h/cpp files in the *Model* folder of the D3D_SceneNodeArm project.

```
class CModel {
     // ... similar to Tutorial 11.3 ...
A:   CArm m_OneArm;          // This is the arm
     void DrawModel();       // Draw everything in the CModel
};
```

```
CModel::CModel() : ...        // Constructor:
B:   m_OneArm(vec3(0,0,0) )   // initialize the arm to locate at (0,0,0)
     { ... }
```

```
void CModel::DrawModel()
C:   m_OneArm.Draw(lod, m_DrawHelper);          // Draws the SceneNode hierarchy
     ⋮
```

Listing 11.8. The CModel class of Tutorial 11.4.

is created and inserted as a child of the CArm object. Listing 11.8 shows that with the CArm class, the CModel class only needs to define (label A) and instantiate the CArm object at a proper location (label B). As in the case of Tutorial 11.3, the drawing of the arm is accomplished by calling the Draw() function (label C).

This tutorial demonstrates how to subclass from the SceneNode class to create *general* graphical objects that can be reused. As will be demonstrated in later tutorials, we can instantiate multiple CArm objects in more complex graphical models.

Tutorial 11.5. The SceneTreeControl GUI Object

Tutorial 11.5.
Project Name:
D3D_SceneNodeMultiPrim
Library Support:
UWB_MFC_Lib1
UWB_D3D_Lib11

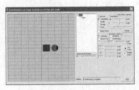

Figure 11.7. Tutorial 11.5.

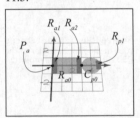

Figure 11.8. Design of the arm of Tutorial 11.5.

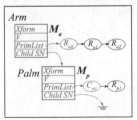

Figure 11.9. SceneNode structure for Tutorial 11.5.

- **Goal.** Demonstrate that it is possible to include multiple primitives in a SceneNode and examine the effects of changing transformation parameters in a scene node hierarchy.

- **Approach.** Increase the primitive complexity of the arm's model and introduce the CSceneTreeControl class to support general user interaction with scene nodes.

Figure 11.7 is a screenshot of running Tutorial 11.5. Compared to the previous tutorial, the two main differences are: (1) the more complex arm/palm design, and (2) the more elaborate user interface.

Figure 11.8 shows the detailed design of the arm/palm objects of this tutorial. In this case, the palm object consists of two primitives (C_{p0}, R_{p1}), and the arm object has three primitives (R_{a0}, R_{a1}, R_{a2}). Figure 11.9 shows the SceneNode implementation of the design.

With the scene node hierarchy from Figure 11.9, this tutorial implements the SceneTreeControl GUI container to support user interaction with the different scene nodes and primitives. As illustrated in Figure 11.10, the SceneTreeControl itself contains two GUI containers, the PrimitiveControl and XformInfo Control. Together, these GUI containers support the following

- **Selection of** SceneNode. Displays the tree structure of a SceneNode. A user can click on any of the nodes in the displayed tree structure to select a current SceneNode.

- **Selection of primitive.** Allows a user to select a current primitive from the primitive list of the currently selected SceneNode by scrolling the slider bar at the bottom of the SceneTreeControl.

- **Control of transformation.** Through the XformInfoControl GUI container, controls the XformInfo transformation operator of the selected Scene Node.

- **Control of primitive attributes.** Through the PrimitiveControl GUI container, controls the attributes of the selected primitive.

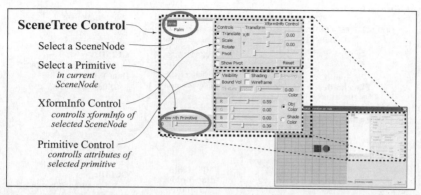

Figure 11.10. Tutorial 11.5 user interface details.

Recall that a *GUI container* is a subwindow that contains functionally related GUI elements for organization and reuse purposes. To create GUI containers with the MFC GUI API, on the front end we must do the following.

1. Create a separate GUI ID (GUI element) to contain all the GUI elements.

2. Create a placeholder on the application window for placing the subwindow.

In the back-end implementation, we must do the following.

1. Create a data type, that is a class, to define the functionality of the GUI elements.

2. Call the ReplaceDialogControl() function at run time to place the GUI container into the application window.

In this case, as illustrated in Figure 11.11, SceneTreeControl contains two separate GUI containers, XformInfoControl and PrimitiveControl:

GUI Container	GUI Front End (GUI ID)	Implementation Back End
SceneTreeControl	IDD_SCENETREE_CONTROL	data type: CSceneTreeControl
PrimitiveControl	IDD_PRIMITIVE_CONTROL	data type: CPrimitiveControl
XformInfoControl	IDD_XFORMINFO_CONTROL	data type: CXformInfoControl

Listing 11.9 reminds us that in our implementations, a GUI container data type (CSceneTreeControl) typically subclasses from the MFC CDialog class. At label A, we are reminded that the OnInitDialog() function will be called during the MFC CDialog creation. At label B, we see that the CSceneTreeControl class has an instance of CXformInfoControl and an instance of CPrimitive

GUI container. See Tutorial 2.8 on p. 69 for more details of working with GUI containers using MFC.

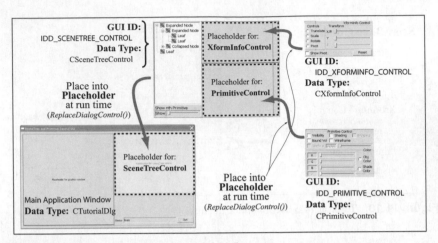

Figure 11.11. GUI containers of Tutorial 11.5.

```
class CSceneTreeControl : public CDialog {
    // ... details related to MFC not shown ...
```
A:
```
    virtual BOOL OnInitDialog(); // Called by MFC during initialization
    ⋮
```
B:
```
    CXforomInfoControl m_XformControl;
    CPrimitiveControl m_PrimitiveControl; // support PrimitiveControl
    // build the GUI scene tree structure
    void BuildSceneTree(UWB_SceneNode*, HTREEITEM);

    // ... other GUI event service routines not shown ...
};
```

```
BOOL CSceneTreeControl::OnInitDialog() {
    ⋮
    // Builds GUI SceneTree structure
```
C:
```
    BuildSceneTree(theApp.GetModel().GetRootNode());
```
D:
```
    UWBMFC_ReplaceDialogControl(...,m_XformControl, IDD_XFORMCONTROL_DIALOG);
    UWBMFC_ReplaceDialogControl(...,m_PrimitiveControl, IDD_PRIMITIVE_CONTROL);
    ⋮
```

Source file.
SceneTreeControl.h   file
in the *Controls* folder of the
D3D_SceneTreeControl
project.

Listing 11.9. The CSceneTreeControl class of Tutorial 11.5.

```
class CPrimitiveControl : public CDialog {
    // ... details related to MFC not shown ...
A:  void SetPrimitive(UWB_Primitive *p); // Sets the m_Primitive pointer at label B

    protected:
B:  UWB_Primitive *m_Primitive; // GUI event service functions would change
                                // the attributes referenced by this pointer
    // ... GUI event service functions not shown ...
};
```

Source file.
PrimitiveControl.h   file
in the *Controls* folder of the
D3D_SceneTreeControl
project.

Listing 11.10. The CPrimitiveControl class of Tutorial 11.5.

Control. During the CSceneTreeControl construction, in the OnInitDialog() function at label C, the BuildSceneTree() function is called with the root node of the model (the arm). This function builds the tree structure on the left of the SceneTreeControl (see Figure 11.10). At label D, the ReplaceDialog Control() functions are called to place the XformInfoControl and Primitive Control into their respective placeholders in the SceneTreeControl.

The implementation of CXformInfoControl was discussed in Tutorial 9.7 (p. 251). CPrimitiveControl is similar to CXFormInfoControl where an appropriate GUI element is defined for each controllable attribute in a UWB_ Primitive class. As illustrated in Listing 11.10, the user of the CPrimitive Control class calls the SetPrimitive() function (label A) to set the m_Primi tive pointer (label B). The GUI elements in the PrimitiveControl container set the attributes of the primitive referenced by the m_Primitive pointer.

The CSceneTreeControl class will be reused in tutorials throughout the rest of this book.

11.3   Scene Trees and Scene Graphs

In general, a hierarchical model is a geometric model built based on generations of transformation operators and primitives, where the user has independent control over components in the model. In our case, with the functionality defined in the SceneNode class, a hierarchical model is simply a scene node hierarchy.

In the previous section, we introduced and worked with the SceneNode class to abstract and become familiar with the functionality of a scene node. In this section, we concentrate on the hierarchy that interconnects scene nodes. We will see that the scene tree, a straightforward tree hierarchy of scene nodes, can easily be constructed and maintained to model objects with independently controllable

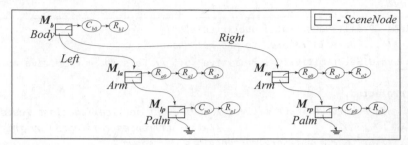

Figure 11.14. SceneNode structure for Tutorial 11.6.

components. The scene graph is a more general hierarchy where either scene nodes or groups of primitives are shared. The sharing of scene nodes or primitives is referred to as instancing. As we will see, instancing allows more efficient resource utilization; however, the resulting scene graph becomes tricky to control and maintain. Our source code library does not support instancing.

Tutorial 11.6. Working with a General Scene Tree

Tutorial 11.6.
Project Name:
  D3D_SceneNodeSiblings
Library Support:
  UWB_MFC_Lib1
  UWB_D3D_Lib11

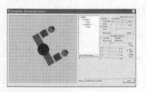

Figure 11.12. Tutorial 11.6.

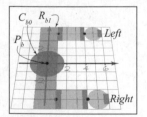

Figure 11.13. Model for Tutorial 11.6.

- **Goal.** Demonstrate that we can build an arbitrarily complex scene tree based on the SceneNode class.

- **Approach.** Design and work with a scene tree hierarchy with multiple child branches involving more than one generation of descendants.

Figure 11.12 is a screenshot of running Tutorial 11.6. In this tutorial, the simple arm scene hierarchy is replaced with a more complex two-arm human model. Figure 11.13 shows the details of the model. The base of the model is defined by the torso (rectangle R_{b1}) and the head (circle C_{b0}) with pivot position located at P_b (the origin). We see that the CArm hierarchy defines the left and right arms of the model. In this case, we would like to have control over the entire human model (e.g., rotating the entire model) while retaining the independent arm and palm control over the left and right arms.

Figure 11.14 shows an implementation of the human model of Figure 11.13 with five SceneNode objects. In this implementation, the two children of the Base scene node are both instances of the CArm object from Tutorial 11.5. Notice that each of the scene nodes has its own transformation operator. In this case, M_b is the transformation operator of the Body node, and M_{la} and M_{lp} are the operators for the left Arm and Palm nodes, whereas M_{ra} and M_{rp} are the operators for the right Arm and Palm nodes. Listing 11.11 shows the implementation of Figure 11.14 in the CModel class. At label A, we see the m_Body defining

```
class CModel {
    // ... similar to Tutorial 11.5 ...
A:  UWB_SceneNode m_Body;  // This is the body (base of root node of tree)
    ⋮
};
```

Source file. Model.h/cpp
files in the *Model* folder of the
D3D_SceneNodeSiblings
project.

```
CModel::CModel() : m_Body("Body") {           // The CModel class constructor
    ⋮
    // list for geometries of the body
B:  UWB_PrimitiveList* pList = new UWB_PrimitiveList();
    // Circle Cb0
    UWB_PrimitiveCircle* pC = new UWB_PrimitiveCircle();
    // Rectangle Rb1
    UWB_PrimitiveRectangle* pR = new UWB_PrimitiveRectangle();
    // initialize the attributes of Cb0 and Rb1
    ⋮
    // insert Cb0 into the primitive list
C:  pList->Append(pC);
    // insert Rb1 into the primitive list
    pList->Append(pR);
    // pList is the primitive of mBody
D:  m_Body.SetPrimitive(pLase);
    // Instantiate left CArm object
E:  CArm *left = new CArm(vec3(1.0f,4.0f,0.0f), "LeftArm");
    // Instantiate the right CArm object
    CArm *right = new CArm(vec3(1.0f,-4.0f,0.0f), "RightArm");
    // left and right arms are set to be
F:  m_Body.InsertChildNode(left);
    // children of the m_Body
    m_Body.InsertChildNode(right);
    ⋮
}
```

Listing 11.11. The CModel class of Tutorial 11.6.

the root scene node of the human model. The scene tree is initialized during the
construction of the CModel class. At label B, the primitive list, the head (circle
C_{b0}), and the torso (rectangle R_{b1}) are allocated and initialized. At label C, the

primitives are inserted into the primitive list, and the list is set to be the primitive of m_Body at label D. The left and right arms are allocated at label E and set to be the children of m_Body at label F. In this way, the scene node hierarchy (or simply the scene) is constructed. The entire scene hierarchy is drawn when we invoke the SceneNode::Draw() routine of the m_Body object. In this case, the primitives of the Body node (e.g., R_{b0}) will be transformed by $\mathbf{M}_{db}$:

$$\mathbf{M}_{db} = \mathbf{M}_b \, \mathrm{M}_V \, \mathrm{M}_P. \tag{11.4}$$

Right Arm/Palm. Correspondingly, primitives of the right Arm/Palm will be transformed by

$\quad \mathbf{M}_{ra} \, \mathbf{M}_b \, \mathrm{M}_V \, \mathrm{M}_P$

and

$\quad \mathbf{M}_{rp} \, \mathbf{M}_{ra} \, \mathbf{M}_b \mathrm{M}_V \, \mathrm{M}_P.$

The primitives of the left Arm (e.g., R_{a0}) will be transformed by $\mathbf{M}_{dla}$:

$$\mathbf{M}_{dla} = \mathbf{M}_{la} \, \mathbf{M}_b \mathrm{M}_V \, \mathrm{M}_P, \tag{11.5}$$

whereas the primitives of the left Palm (e.g., R_{p0}) will be transformed by $\mathbf{M}_{dlp}$:

$$\mathbf{M}_{dlp} = \mathbf{M}_{lp} \, \mathbf{M}_{la} \, \mathbf{M}_b \mathrm{M}_V \, \mathrm{M}_P. \tag{11.6}$$

The SceneTreeControl user interface construct allows the user select one of the $\mathbf{M}_b$, $\mathbf{M}_{rp}$, $\mathbf{M}_{ra}$, $\mathbf{M}_{lp}$, or $\mathbf{M}_{la}$ transformations for interactive manipulation. In this way, the user can have independent control of each of the components in the scene hierarchy.

This tutorial presents a straightforward extension to Tutorial 11.5 in building a scene tree with the SceneNode class. Through working with the SceneTree Control GUI container, the user can select any of the five scene nodes and control the selected transformation operator. In addition, the user can select any of the primitives in the selected scene node to interactively adjust the attributes of the selected primitive.

11.3.1   Instancing: Scene Graph

From Figures 11.13 and 11.14, we can observe that the scene hierarchies under the left and the right arms are identical. Indeed, in Listing 11.11, the two arms are implemented based on the same CArm class. For efficiency purposes, it is logical to examine the possibilities of sharing the CArm object, that is, implement the two arms based on sharing the memory of one instance of the CArm object.

Sharing of Scene Node Hierarchy

Figure 11.15 shows a straightforward approach to sharing an instance of the CArm hierarchy. Notice that in order to retain the independent control over the two separate arms, the CArm object must have two separate parents with two independent

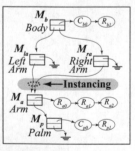

Figure 11.15. Instancing: sharing of scene nodes.

transformation operators. To satisfy this requirement, two new scene nodes are introduced in Figure 11.15 (LeftArm and RightArm) parenting the shared CArm instance. Recall from Listing 11.4 that the SceneNode::Draw() routine performs in-roder depth-first matrix concatenation. In this case, for the LeftArm,

$$\mathbf{M}_{l1} = \mathbf{M}_a\, \mathbf{M}_{la}\, \mathbf{M}_b,$$
$$\mathbf{M}_{l2} = \mathbf{M}_p\, \mathbf{M}_a \mathbf{M}_{la}\, \mathbf{M}_b,$$

$\mathbf{M}_b\, \mathbf{M}_{la}\, \mathbf{M}_{ra}\, \mathbf{M}_a\, \mathbf{M}_p$. Transformation operators of the Base, LeftArm, RightArm, Arm, and Palm nodes, respectively.

where $\mathbf{M}_{l1}$ is the transformation matrix for drawing of primitives in the Arm node (e.g., R_{a0}) and $\mathbf{M}_{l2}$ is for the primitives of the Palm node (e.g., C_{p0}). For the RightArm,

$$\mathbf{M}_{r1} = \mathbf{M}_a\, \mathbf{M}_{ra}\, \mathbf{M}_b,$$
$$\mathbf{M}_{r2} = \mathbf{M}_p\, \mathbf{M}_a\, \mathbf{M}_{ra}\, \mathbf{M}_b.$$

Notice that although there is only one instance of the CArm node, the primitives of this node will be drawn twice, once for each of the LeftArm and RightArm parent. Because each time the primitives will be drawn with different matrices, $\mathbf{M}_{l1}$ and $\mathbf{M}_{l2}$ versus $\mathbf{M}_{r1}$ and $\mathbf{M}_{r2}$, the primitives will appear in different locations with distinct orientations. In this way, by drawing the scene node twice, we can create the illusion of two distinct objects (the two arms) in the application window.

When a user manipulates the LeftArm transformation operator ($\mathbf{M}_{la}$), only $\mathbf{M}_{l1}$ and $\mathbf{M}_{l2}$ are affected, and thus only the primitives drawn associated with the left arm will be affected. In this way, by manipulating the LeftArm ($\mathbf{M}_{la}$) and RightArm ($\mathbf{M}_{ra}$) transformation operators, the user can control the left and right arms independently.

When implementing instancing by sharing of scene node hierarchy, there is *no* straightforward way of supporting independent control over components inside the hierarchy. For example, in our case, the CArm hierarchy is shared, and an example of an "independently controllable component" in the hierarchy is the Palm object. Notice that the transformation operator for controlling the Palm, $\mathbf{M}_p$, is shared between the left and the right arms. This is verified from the fact that the transformation operators for the left palm ($\mathbf{M}_{l2}$) and the right palm ($\mathbf{M}_{r2}$) do not include dedicated transformation operators for controlling the primitives associated with the left and right palms. Without separate transformation operators, the user will not be able to control the two palms independently. In this case, if the user manipulates the $\mathbf{M}_p$ operator, in the application window the palms on both arms will change in an identical manner!

Supporting instancing by sharing scene node hierarchy is only viable when the instances do not change, or when all instances behave in exactly the same manner. Examples of instances that do not change would include stationary objects, e.g., identical tables/chairs. These objects can be highly complex with definitions that involve many scene nodes, and yet we would not expect any of their components to change. Examples of instances that behave in exactly the same manner may include engines of a commercial airplane, tires on a car, and so on. These types of objects contain moving components, for example, the rotating tires, or jet-engine blades, and we expect movement to be synchronized and identical.

Sharing of Geometries

An approach to overcome the lack of control over components in the shared scene node hierarchy is to avoid any sharing of scene nodes (or transformation operators). Instead, instancing is supported via sharing of geometric primitives only. Figure 11.16 shows this alternative approach of implementing instancing for the human model from Figure 11.13. In this case, instead of sharing the entire CArm scene node hierarchy of Figure 11.9, only the involved geometric primitives are shared. Because all of the left/right arm/palm objects now have independent scene nodes (and thus separate transformation operators), the user is able to control each of the components in exactly the same manner as Tutorial 11.6. In fact, from the standpoint of user interaction, the scene node structure of Figure 11.16 and that of Figure 11.14 behave in an identical manner.

Implementing instancing by sharing of geometries retains the exact independent control of components while also conserving memory. This is especially important for complex geometric objects with high degrees of symmetry where there are identical components that must support independent controls. For example, the geometries of the left and right limbs of a detailed human model are highly symmetrical with many reusable components (e.g., the geometries of left and right index fingers, calves), where it is important to retain independent control over the components.

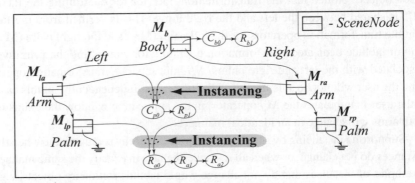

Figure 11.16. Instancing: sharing of geometries.

11.3.2   Discussion

When compared to instancing by sharing of scene node hierarchy, sharing of geometries is more complex to implement and to work with in general. For example, we may want to create a new instance of the human model of Figure 11.13. With the sharing by scene node approach of Figure 11.15, after the creation of the Base, LeftArm, and RightArm nodes, we can simply reference an existing CArm object without any knowledge of the interior structure of the CArm object. This is compared to the sharing by geometries approach of Figure 11.16, where in order to share the geometries of the CArm object, we must traverse the CArm hierarchy to duplicate all internal nodes and create necessary references to the geometries. However, sharing by geometries does have the important advantage of retaining independent control over all components. The sharing of scene nodes generalizes the scene tree structure into a general directed graph, or a scene graph. In general, as programmers, we must avoid creating cycles in scene graphs. An example of a scene graph supported in a commercial product is the directed acyclic graph (DAG) of the Maya Animation System. The UWB_GL software library does not support instancing. In other words, we only support the building of scene trees and not scene graphs. As programmers, when programming with the UWB_GL API, we must ensure the integrity of the scene tree structure.

An important aspect of instancing that is not discussed here is the sharing of primitive attributes. In real commercial systems, users should be given the option of manipulating the attributes of any primitives independently from the instancing structure. For example, the user may want the left and right arms to have slightly different colors. The grouping functionality in graphical editors can be implemented by creating a parent node common to all group members.

11.4   The Object Coordinate System

We have learned that a scene hierarchy (or a scene tree, or a scene graph) is defined by interconnected scene nodes and provides a framework for interpreting transformation operators and the drawing of corresponding geometric primitives. By strategically traversing this hierarchy of scene nodes, with appropriate concatenation of transformation operators before the drawing of corresponding geometric primitives, we can create geometric models of objects while supporting independent control over components of objects.

To abstract the functionality of a node in the scene hierarchy (or simply the scene), we have designed the SceneNode class to include a transformation op-

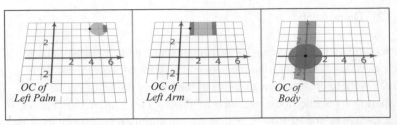

Figure 11.17. Different OC spaces of Figure 11.13.

erator, a primitives list, and an array of child node pointers. When designing a geometric model with a `SceneNode` object, we define the primitives in the most convenient coordinate space and then rely on the transformation operator to position and manipulate the geometric models. For example, when designing the arm of Figure 11.8, the geometric primitives (e.g., R_{a0}, C_{p0}) are defined with respect to the origin located at P_a. This arm object is included and positioned into the human model of Figure 11.14 where the transformation operator in the Arm node supports the interactive manipulation of the arm object. Recall that in Section 10.3, we introduced the idea of a world coordinate (WC) system to provide a convenient coordinate space for working with graphical objects. In a similar manner, we can consider the transformation operators in a scene hierarchy creating convenient coordinate spaces for defining components of objects. We refer to these coordinate spaces as the object coordinate (OC) spaces. Figure 11.17 illustrates that there are typically many OC spaces in a scene hierarchy. For example, the OC space for the primitives of the left palm, the OC space for the primitives of the left arm, and so on.

Modeling coordinate space. Because objects are defined, or modeled, in OC space, sometimes OC space is also called *modeling coordinate space.*

As with any coordinate space, the OC space provides a convenient space for designing graphical objects. However, the extra coordinate space also means that the primitives are defined in a coordinate space that is independent from where they will appear. This is similar to the case of WC space, where:

- **Drawing.** We must compute and perform extra transformation operations before drawing of primitives. We have already worked with this in the `Scenenode::Draw()` function (label C in Listing 11.4) where we must concatenate the transformation operator and load the results into the WORLD matrix processor before drawing the primitives.

- **Selection.** We must perform inverse transformations to compute the user's mouse-click position in the primitive coordinate spaces. For the WC space, in Section 10.5, we discussed how to transform points from device coordinate space to WC space. In this case, with the OC space, additional inverse

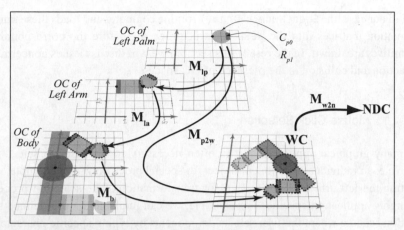

Figure 11.18. Transformation of the left palm OC space.

transformations that correspond to the transformation operators in the scene hierarchy must be considered. We will discuss this issue in Section 11.4.1.

- **Collision.** We must transform primitives into a common coordinate space before the primitives can interact. For example, if we want the left palm in the human model of Figure 11.13 to bounce off a ball, we would need to detect collisions between the primitives that define the palm and the ball. In order to perform the collision detection, we must transform all primitives into a common coordinate space (e.g., WC). We will discuss this issue in Section 11.4.2.

As mentioned, thus far we have worked with the drawing aspect of OC spaces. For example, when drawing the left palm of Figure 11.13, we computed $\mathbf{M}_{dlp}$ (Equation (11.6)):

$$\begin{aligned} \mathbf{M}_{dlp} &= \mathbf{M}_{lp}\,\mathbf{M}_{la}\,\mathbf{M}_b\,\mathbf{M}_V\,\mathbf{M}_P \\ &= \mathbf{M}_{p2w}\,\mathbf{M}_{w2n}. \end{aligned}$$

Figure 11.18 shows that one way to understand $\mathbf{M}_{dlp}$ is that

$$\mathbf{M}_{w2n} = \mathbf{M}_V\,\mathbf{M}_P$$

is the WC-to-NDC transformation (as discussed in Section 10.3), and we can consider

$$\mathbf{M}_{p2w} = \mathbf{M}_{lp}\,\mathbf{M}_{la}\,\mathbf{M}_b$$

to be the palm-OC-to-WC transformation that transforms the left palm primitives (C_{p0} and R_{p1}) into the WC space.

In our case, the `SceneNode::Draw()` routine computes and loads these transformation matrices into the `WORLD` matrix processor before the corresponding primitives are drawn. In the rest of this section, we will discuss issues concerning selection and collision in the presence of OC spaces.

11.4.1   Mouse-Click Selection

In many graphical applications, it is often necessary for the user to select, or activate, an individual component/object for special processing. For example, selecting the left arm of Tutorial 11.6 for transformation. The selection process is highly application-specific. For example, we can implement a pre-defined selection scheme where the user selects components by typing specific characters, or as in Tutorial 11.6 where the user selects components via a custom GUI interface (the `SceneTreeControl`). In addition, the results of selection are also application-dependent. For example, the user can select an entire graphical object (e.g., the human model), a component in the object (e.g., the left palm), or an individual primitive of a component (e.g., the C_{p0} circle).

An intuitive way for the user to select an object is by moving and clicking the mouse over an object. To support this functionality, we must process every object in the scene hierarchy to determine if the object is sufficiently close to the mouse-click position. For example, the mouse-click position pt_{dc} of Figure 11.19 should select the left palm or the C_{p0} circle. From this example, we see that to support

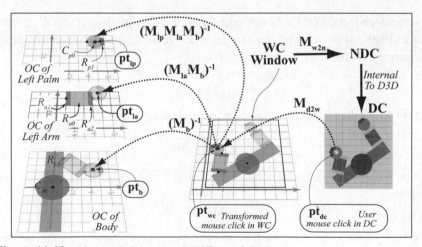

Figure 11.19. Mouse-click position in different OC spaces.

the mouse-click selection operation , our program must perform the following.

- **Coordinate space conversion.** As illustrated in Figure 11.19, mouse-click positions are typically defined in the device coordinate space while primitives of components are usually defined in individual OC spaces. Our program must convert these positions into a common coordinate space for the proximity test.

- **Proximity test.** Our program must determine if the mouse-click position is within the bounds of or sufficiently close to each graphical object.

Coordinate Space Conversion

The problem at hand is that we need to perform proximity tests between the DC space mouse-click position and the primitive vertices that are in different OC spaces. The solution, of course, is to transform the mouse-click position and/or the primitive vertices into a common coordinate space for the proximity tests. In general, there are three strategies to implement this solution. For the following discussion, the mouse-click position,

$$pt_{dc} = (x_{dc}, y_{dc}),$$

is expressed as a vector,

$$\mathbf{V}_{dc} = \begin{bmatrix} x_{dc} & y_{dc} \end{bmatrix}.$$

1. **Only transform mouse-click position.** Transform the mouse-click position to each of the OC spaces for proximity test. For example, in Figure 11.19 we compute the following.

   - **Body OC space.** Transform $\mathbf{V}_{dc}$ to the body's OC space by

   $$\begin{aligned} \mathbf{V}_b &= \mathbf{V}_{dc}\,\mathbf{M}_{d2w}\,(\mathbf{M}_b)^{-1} \\ &= \mathbf{V}_{dc}\,\mathbf{M}_{d2w}\,\mathbf{M}_b^{-1} \end{aligned}$$

   and use $\mathbf{V}_b$ (or pt_b) for performing proximity tests with the vertices of C_{b0} and R_{b1}.

   - **Left arm OC space.** Transform $\mathbf{V}_{dc}$ to the left arm's OC space by

   $$\begin{aligned} \mathbf{V}_{la} &= \mathbf{V}_{dc}\,\mathbf{M}_{d2w}\,(\mathbf{M}_{la}\mathbf{M}_b)^{-1} \\ &= \mathbf{V}_{dc}\,\mathbf{M}_{d2w}\,\mathbf{M}_b^{-1}\,\mathbf{M}_{la}^{-1} \end{aligned}$$

   and use $\mathbf{V}_{la}$ (or pt_{la}) for performing proximity tests with the vertices of R_{a0}, R_{a1}, and R_{a2}.

Mouse-click position. Mouse-click positions are often defined in the hardware coordinate space (see Section 10.5). Once again, in the following discussion, we assume that the `Hard wareToDevice()` function has already been called and that the mouse-click position is defined in the device coordinate (DC) space.

$\mathbf{M}_{d2w}$. This is the DC-to-WC transform as defined by Equation (10.17) on p. 288.

$\mathbf{M}_b, \mathbf{M}_{la}, \mathbf{M}_{lp}$. These are the transformation matrices of the `Body`, `LeftArm`, and `LeftPalm` as illustrated in Figure 11.14

$pt_b = (x_b, y_b).$
$$\mathbf{V}_b = \begin{bmatrix} x_b & y_b \end{bmatrix}.$$

$pt_{la} = (x_{la}, y_{la}).$
$$\mathbf{V}_{la} = \begin{bmatrix} x_{la} & y_{la} \end{bmatrix}.$$

- **Left palm OC space.** Transform $\mathbf{V}_{dc}$ to the left palm's OC space by

$$\begin{aligned}
\mathbf{V}_{lp} &= \mathbf{V}_{dc}\,\mathbf{M}_{d2w}(\mathbf{M}_{lp}\mathbf{M}_{la}\mathbf{M}_{b})^{-1} \\
&= \mathbf{V}_{dc}\,\mathbf{M}_{d2w}\,\mathbf{M}_{b}^{-1}\,\mathbf{M}_{la}^{-1}\,\mathbf{M}_{lp}^{-1}
\end{aligned}$$

and use $\mathbf{V}_{lp}$ (or pt_{lp}) for performing proximity tests with the vertices of C_{p0}, and R_{p1}.

$pt_{lp} = (x_{lp}, y_{lp})$.

$\mathbf{V}_{lp} = [x_{lp}\ \ y_{lp}]$.

Notice that in order to correctly determine which component is closest to the mouse-click position pt_{dc}, we must perform the above computations for every primitive in the scene hierarchy. In this case, we must also perform the corresponding computations for the primitives of the right arm and right palm.

The main advantage of this approach is that only the mouse-click position needs to be transformed. The disadvantage is that the inverse transform of every OC space must be computed.

2. **Only transform primitive vertices**. Leave the mouse-click position in DC space and transform the primitive vertices of every component in the scene hierarchy into the DC space for proximity tests. Notice that the transformation computation involved is similar to the drawing of primitives where vertices are transformed from individual OC spaces into the DC space. The OpenGL API takes advantage of this similarity and defines functionality to approximate results of proximity tests based on drawing of primitives.

3. **Transform both mouse-click position and primitive vertices.** Transform all positions to a convenient coordinate space for proximity tests. Recall that when drawing primitives, our program computes and transforms vertices to the NDC space. The graphics API is responsible for transforming primitives from NDC to DC space. In this way, our program supports the functionality of transforming vertices to NDC space but not to DC space. In the absence of hardware-assisted proximity testing functionality, it is more convenient to transform the mouse-click position into the NDC (or WC) space and perform the proximity tests in the NDC (or WC) space.

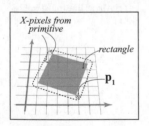

Figure 11.20. A rectangle with boundaries not aligned with the axis.

Proximity Tests

Once all primitive vertices and the mouse-click position are in the same coordinate space, we must determine if the mouse-click position is sufficiently close to any of the primitives for a successful selection. Notice that the mouse-click position can be represented as a point primitive, and in effect we are determining if the point primitive is sufficiently close to other primitives. In this way, the issues involved here are similar to those of collisions between primitives (as discussed in Section 7.5). The only difference here is that sufficiently close does not necessarily mean that two primitives have collided. For example, an application can define that to select an object, the mouse click must be within at least x pixels of the edges of the object. The more refined the criteria of "sufficiently close," the more difficult it is to implement the computations involved. For example, the dotted lines around the rectangle of Figure 11.20 show that the "within x pixels from the edges" criteria results in circular boundaries around the rectangle vertices. In this case, a mouse click at position p_1 should be considered hitting the rectangle; however, the computation involved is expensive.

In general, in the absence of a data structure dedicated to support searching, selection is an $O(n)$ operation where n is the number of primitives in the scene hierarchy. This is to say that we must process every primitive to determine the results of each selection operation. When there is more than one graphical object under the mouse-click position, there will be more than one successful result from the proximity tests. In this case, it is the responsibility of the application to determine the most logical object to be selected by the user. For example, when there are overlapping objects, our program can decide to select the top-most visible object.

UWBGL_D3D_Lib12

This library extends `Lib11` to support selection (and collision) functionality in the `SceneNode` class. We have chosen the world coordinate (WC) space to perform proximity tests. The implementation is based on the `BoundingBox` class. As discussed in Section 7.5, although it is simple and efficient to implement, bounding primitives with axis-aligned boxes may result in large void spaces. For this reason, `BoundingBox` based selection/collision computation limits our results to rough approximations. This is especially the case for non-axis aligned rectangles and lines. The choice of WC space for proximity tests means that we must transform mouse-click positions and primitive bounding boxes to the WC space. Listing 11.12 shows that the `SceneNode` class has been extended to include two new functions for computing WC space bounding boxes. The `GetBounds()` function at label A computes a WC space bounding box that bounds all the primitives, including those from the child nodes. The `GetNodeBounds()` function at label B returns the WC bounding box of `pSearchNode`, a descendent of the current node. Listing 11.13 shows the implementation of the `SceneNode::GetBounds()` function. Figure 11.21 uses the body and left arm node from the human model hierarchy of Figure 11.14 to help explain the `GetBounds()` function.

Change summary. See p. 524 for a summary of changes to the library.

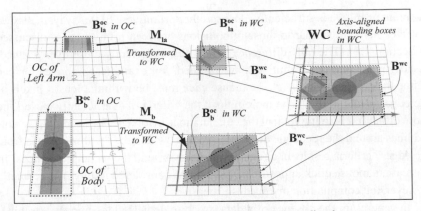

Figure 11.21. Coordinate transformations of scene node bounding boxes.

Source file.
uwbgl_SceneNode2.h file in the *Common Files/ SceneNode* subfolder of the UWBGL_D3D_Lib12 project.

```
class UWB_SceneNode {
    ⋮
A:  UWB_BoundingBox GetBounds(...) const;
    // Compute a Bounding Box in WC space that encloses all the
    // primitives of this node including that of all children nodes
B:  bool GetNodeBounds(const UWB_SceneNode* pSearchNode ...) const;
    // pSearchNode is a children of this node, this function
    // computes a Bounding Box in WC space that encloses all the
    // primitives of pSearchNode including that of all it children
    // nodes
}
```

Listing 11.12. The SceneNode bounding box support.

To compute the WC bounding box for this hierarchy, we invoke the GetBounds() function of the body node:

- **Compute bounding box in OC (A).** At label A, the OC bounding box $\mathbf{B}_b^{oc}$ is computed.

- **Compute OC-to-WC transformation (B).** At label B, the $\mathbf{M}_b$ matrix is concatenated to the top of the matrix stack. At this point, the top of the matrix stack contains the OC-to-WC transformation matrix.

```
UWB_BoundingBox UWB_SceneNode::GetBounds( ...    ) const
     UWB_BoundingBox bbox; // This is the bounding box (bbx)
     ⋮
A:   if(m_pPrimitive)
          bbox.Add(m_pPrimitive->GetBoundingVolume( ... )); // bbox from primitives in OC space
B:   helper.PushModelTransform();     // set up OC-to-WC transform on matrix stack
     m_xform.SetUpModelStack(helper);
     ⋮
C:   helper.TransformPoint(...)       // transform each bbox vertex from OC to WC
     // computes the bounding box in WC
     ⋮
     for(int i=0; i<NumChildren(); i++)        // compute bbox for all children
D:       bbox.Add(m_child_nodes[i]->GetBounds()); // extend bbox to bound all children's bbox
E:   helper.PopModelTransform();               // restore the top of the matrix stack
     return bbox;
```

Source file.
uwbgl_SceneNode2.cpp
file in the *Common Files/
SceneNode* subfolder of the
UWBGL_D3D_Lib12 project.

Listing 11.13. The `SceneNode::GetBounds()` function.

- **Transform the OC bounding box to WC (C).** At label C, each of the eight vertices of the bounding box is transformed from OC to WC. Notice that, as illustrated in Figure 11.21, the result of transforming $\mathbf{B}_b^{oc}$ to WC space is a rotated rectangle. However, by definition, a bounding box must be axis-aligned. For this reason, the bounding box in WC space is the axis-aligned box $\mathbf{B}_b^{wc}$ (lower middle of Figure 11.21).

- **Compute and combine with children's bounding boxes (D).** At label D, the child node of body, the left arm's `GetBounds()` function is invoked. The `GetBounds()` function will be executed on behalf of the left arm, and at label A, the left arm computes the OC bounding box $\mathbf{B}_{la}^{oc}$ (top left of Figure 11.21). At label B, the left arm node concatenates $\mathbf{M}_{la}$ with the top of the matrix stack. Recall that at this point, the top of the matrix stack contains the $\mathbf{M}_b$ matrix. In this way, the OC-to-WC transformation matrix at the top of the matrix stack becomes the concatenation of $\mathbf{M}_b\mathbf{M}_{la}$. As a result, the WC bounding box returned from the left arm is $\mathbf{B}_{la}^{wc}$ (upper middle of Figure 11.21). The `box.Add()` function at label D combines the body's bounding box $\mathbf{B}_b^{wc}$ with the left arm's bounding box $\mathbf{B}_{la}^{wc}$ to form the final bounding box $\mathbf{B}^{wc}$ (right side of Figure 11.21).

```
bool UWB_SceneNode::GetNodeBounds( const UWB_SceneNode* pSearchNode ... ) const
    // helper function implementing WC bbox computation
    return GetNodeBoundsHeler(pSearchNode ... )


bool UWB_SceneNode::GetNodeBoundsHelper( const UWB_SceneNode* pSearchNode ... ) const
    :
    :
    // when successfully find the target node
    if( this == pSearchNode )
        // compute the WC bounding box and return
A:  box = this->GetBounds( ... )

    // otherwise set up OC-to-WC xform and continue searching
    else
        // concatenate transforamtion onto matrix stack
B:      helper.PushModelTransform();
        // to allow computation of OC-to-WC xform
        this->GetXformInfo().SetUpModelStack(helper);

        // search all children for the target node
        for(int i=0; i<this->NumChildren(); i++)
B1:         if(this->GetChildNode(i)->GetNodeBoundsHelper( pSearchNode, ...))
            :
            :
                found = true;
    // restore trop of matrix stack
C:  helper.PopModelTransform();

    return found;
```

Listing 11.14. The SceneNode::GetNodeBounds() function.

Source file.
uwbgl_SceneNode2.cpp
file in the *Common Files/
SceneNode* subfolder of the
UWBGL_D3D_Lib12 project.

- **Restore the top of matrix stack (E).** At label E, we restore the top of the matrix stack before returning the results of the computed bounding box in WC space.

Observe from the above discussion that in order to compute the WC bounding box of a scene node, we need to know all of its ancestors' transformations. For example, the left arm's WC bounding box, $\mathbf{B}_{la}^{wc}$, is computed by transforming the bounding box in OC, $\mathbf{B}_{la}^{oc}$, based on its parent's transformation $\mathbf{M}_b$. If we want to determine if the mouse-click position is within the bounds of the left arm (independent of that of the body node), we still have to begin the OC-to-WC transformation computation starting from the body node. In our implementation, the ancestor's transformation matrices are concatenated on the top of the matrix stack. Listing 11.14 shows the implementation of the GetNodeBounds() function designed to compute the WC bounding box of a *branch* of the scene hierarchy rooted at pSearchNode. As in all cases, the OC-to-WC transformation is maintained at the top of the matrix stack (at label B) while the hierarchy is traversed in search of the target pSearchNode (at label B1). When the target node is found at label A, the WC bounding box rooted at this node is computed by the GetBounds() function. At this point, all the transformations of the ancestors of this target node are concatenated at the top of the matrix stack. For this reason, it is possible to correctly compute the WC bounding box. The PopModelTransform() function call at label C ensures that the proper matrix stack is maintained.

Tutorial 11.7. Mouse-Hit Detection

Tutorial 11.7.
Project Name:
   D3D_SceneNodePicking
Library Support:
   UWB_MFC_Lib1
   UWB_D3D_Lib12

- **Goal.** Demonstrate the coordinate transformations and proximity tests computations involved to support the implementation of mouse-click selection.

- **Approach.** Support mouse-click selection of scene nodes in the human model from Figure 11.13.

Figure 11.22 is a screenshot of running Tutorial 11.7. As in previous tutorials, this tutorial allows the user to select a current scene node via the SceneTreeControl GUI element. In addition, this tutorial computes and shows the WC bounding box of the branch of the hierarchy that is rooted at the currently selected scene node. For example, in Figure 11.22, the user has selected the left arm node in SceneTreeControl, and the WC bounding box drawn is the branch of the hierarchy rooted at the left arm, including that of the child, the left palm node. Finally, this tutorial is capable of determining if a mouse click is within the currently highlighted WC bound. Notice that the WC bounding box is an axis-aligned rectangle, which may include significant void spaces. Listing 11.15 shows the definition of the CModel class of Tutorial 11.7. The function SetActiveNode() at label A selects a currently active scene node. This function is called when the user clicks in the SceneTreeControl GUI element to activate a different scene node to work with. Recall that the currently active scene node is the one that we compute the WC bounding box for. The PickNodeAt() function at label B accepts the (wcX, wcY) point in WC space and determines if the point is within the bounds of the currently selected scene node. The m_Body at label C is the root node of the entire human model hierarchy, whereas the m_pActiveNode is the currently selected scene node. Listing 11.16 shows the implementation of the PickNodeAt() function. Local variables for this function are defined at label A. The matrix stack is

Figure 11.22. Tutorial 11.7.

Source file. Model.h file in the *Model* folder of the D3D_SceneNodePicking project.

```
class CModel {  // ... similar to Tutorial 11.6  ...
   public:
      // sets the currently selected scene node
A:    void SetActiveSceneNode(UWB_SceneNode *);
      // test if (wcX, wcY) is inside the WC Bbox of the currently
      // selected scene node
B:    void PickNodeAt(float wcX, float wcY);
   private:
      // root of the enture human model hierarchy
C:    UWB_SceneNode m_Body;
      // pointer to the scene node that is selected in the
      // SceneTreeControl GUI element
D:    UWB_SceneNode* m_pActiveNode;
         ⋮
};
```

Listing 11.15. The CModel class of Tutorial 11.7.

Source file. Model.cpp file in the *Model* folder of the D3D_SceneNodePicking project.

```
void CModel::PickNodeAt(float worldX, float worldY)
      // bbox of the currently selected scene node
A:    UWB_BoundingBox bbox;
      // mouse click position in WC
      vec3 pick_point(worldX, worldY, 0);
      // initialize matrix stack for OC-to-WC computation
B:    m_DrawHelper.InitializeModelTransform();
      // compute WC bbox for the selected scene node
C:    m_Body.GetNodeBounds(m_pActiveNode, bbox ...);
      // test if bbox contains the mouse click position
D:    if(bbox.ContainsPoint( pick_point ) )
         ⋮
         // all positions are in WC space
         sets bbox draw color and prints appropriate message
```

Listing 11.16. The implementation CModel class of Tutorial 11.7.

initialized at label B for the proper concatenation of the OC-to-WC transformation matrix. At label C, we call the GetNodeBounds() function on the m_Body node. As illustrated in Listing 11.14, the GetNodeBounds() function will maintain a correct OC-to-WC transformation matrix on the matrix stack while traversing the hierarchy in search of the target node. In this case, the m_pActiveNode is the tar-

```
void CDrawAndMouseHandler::OnMouseButton(bool down, unsigned int nFlags, int hwX, int hwY)
        // variable for point in DC space
A:    int dcX, dcY;
        // variable for point in WC space
    float wcX, wcY;
        // Transform from hardware space (hwX,hwY) to DC (dcX, dcY)
B:    HardwareToDevice(hwX, hwY, dcX, dcY);
        // Transform from DC (dcX,dcY) to WC (wcX,wcY)
    DeviceToWorld(dcX, dcY, wcX, wcY);
C:    if(MK_LBUTTON && down) // if left mouse button is clicked
            // Calls the PickNodeAt() function with mouse click in WC
            theApp.GetModel().PickNodeAt(wcX,wcY)
```

Source file.
DrawAndMouseHandler.cpp
file in the *WindowHandlers* folder of the
D3D_SceneNodePicking
project.

Listing 11.17. The mouse-click service routine of Tutorial 11.7.

get pSearchNode. In this way, the bbox returned will be the WC bounding box of the currently selected scene node. Because all positions are in the WC space, we can perform the simple containment test at label D to determine if pick_point is within the bounds of bbox. Listing 11.17 shows the mouse event service routine implemented in CDrawAndMouseHandler.cpp. In this case, we can see that the mouse-click position is forwarded to the service routine in hardware coordinate space, (hwX, hwY). At label B, the mouse-click position is transformed into DC space, (dcX, dcY), and then to WC space, (wcX, wcY). At label C, we see that when the left mouse button is clicked, the CModel::PickNodeAt() function is called with the mouse-click position in the WC space.

11.4.2 Collision

In Section 7.5, we discussed the issues involved with colliding primitives. Our conclusion is that it is more efficient to approximate collisions with intersections of simple volumes that bound the colliding primitives. The UWB_BoundingVolume class (Listing 7.15 on p. 185) was introduced to approximate primitive collision. In the previous section, we learned how to compute WC bounding boxes for scene node objects based on the UWB_BoundingBox class to support mouse-click selection. We can now approximate the collision between scene nodes based on the intersection of their corresponding bounding boxes.

Tutorial 11.8. Collision Detection

- **Goal.** Demonstrate colliding scene node objects based on the WC bounding boxes.

Tutorial 11.8.
Project Name:
D3D_SceneNodeCollision
Library Support:
 UWB_MFC_Lib1
 UWB_D3D_Lib12

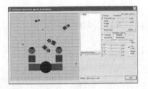

Figure 11.23. Tutorial 11.8.

- **Approach.** Collide the left and right palm scene nodes of Figure 11.13 with different types of primitives.

Figure 11.23 is a screenshot of running Tutorial 11.8. On the lower side of the drawing area is the human model hierarchy of Figure 11.14. As in previous tutorials, the user can select and manipulate the transformation operators of any node in this hierarchy. Recall that in this hierarchy, the palm nodes are located at the end of the corresponding arms. UWB_Primitive objects that we will refer to as bullets are generated at the top of the drawing area and dropped vertically towards the human model. This tutorial counts the number of times the bullets collide with the left and right palm scene nodes. When a collision is detected, the bullet object reacts by bouncing away from the colliding palm scene node.

This tutorial implements two types of bullets: balls and arms. A ball bullet is a simple circle primitive, whereas an arm-bullet is a CPrimitiveArm object. Listing 11.18 shows that CPrimitiveArm is a subclass of UWB_Primitive. This object wraps over an instance of the CArm scene node object (as defined in Listing 11.7 on p. 306). The Update() function at label A moves/rotates the CPrimitiveArm object by modifying the CArmXformInfo object; the GetBoundingVolume() function at label B calls SceneNode::GetNodeBounds() to compute the WC bounding box, whereas the DrawPrimitive() function at label C draws the CArm object. In this way, from the public interface, CPrimitiveArm behaves exactly like a UWB_Primitive object. Listing 11.19 highlights the main

Source file.
PrimitiveArm.h/cpp file in the *Model* folder of the D3D_SceneNodeCollision project.

```
class CPrimitiveArm : public UWB_Primitive {
  public:
         ⋮
      // periodic update of primitive
A:    virtual void Update(float elapsed_seconds);
      // Compute WC bbox
B:    virtual const UWB_BoundingVolume* GetBoundingVolume( ... )
  protected:
      // draw the CArm scene node
C:    virtual void DrawPrimitive( ... );
      // Scene node as defined in Listing 11.7 for storing the WC bbox
D:    CArm m_Arm;
      UWB_BoundingBox m_Bound;
};
```

Listing 11.18. The CPrimitiveArm class of Tutorial 11.8.

```
class CModel {
    // ... similar to that of Tutorial 11.7
    // pointers to the left/right palm scene nodes
A:  UWB_SceneNode *m_pLeftPalmNode, *m_pRightPalmNode;
    // all the bullets in the world
B:  UWB_PrimitiveList *m_bullets;
}
```

Source file. Model.h file in the *Model* folder of the D3D_SceneNodeCollision project.

Listing 11.19. The CModel class of Tutorial 11.8.

```
void CModel::UpdateSimulation() {
    UWB_BoundingBox left_palm_bounds, right_palm_bounds; // variables for WC bboxes
A:  m_DrawHelper.InitializeModelTransform(); // initialize for OC-WC transformation
    // WC bbox of left palm scene node
B:  m_Body.GetNodeBounds(m_pLeftPalmNode, left_palm_bounds ...)
    // WC bbox of right palm scene node
    m_Body.GetNodeBounds(m_pRightPalmNode, right_palm_bounds ...)
C:  for( every primitive in the m_bullet list )
        // pTestPrimitive is current bullet
   C1:  UWB_Primitive* pTestPrimitive = m_bullets.PrimitiveAt(i);
        const UWB_BoundingVolume* pVolume = pTestPrimitive->GetBoundingVolume();
        // left palm collides current bullet
   C2:  if(left_palm_bounds.Intersects(*pVolume))
            pTestPrimitive->CollisionResponse( ... ); // current bullet should bounce away
            m_hit_count++; // increment the on screen hitCount
   C3:  // Test right palm node for intersection and perform similar
        // operations to that of Left Palm
        ⋮
    // Create new bullets about every 0.5 seconds
D:  if(m_second_counter > 0.5f) CreateNewBullet();
E:  // destroy all bullets that are outside the world
}
```

Source file. Model_Simulation.cpp file in the *Model* folder of the D3D_SceneNodeCollision project.

Listing 11.20. The CModel::UpdateSimulation() function of Tutorial 11.8.

difference of the CModel class from that of Tutorial 11.7. In this tutorial, during the creation of the human model hierarchy, the references to the left and right palm scene nodes are kept in the m_pLeftPalmNode and m_pRightPalmNode variables (at label A of Listing 11.19). These two pointers are used to compute WC bounding boxes for collision detections. The m_bullets primitive list at label B is defined to maintain all the bullets in the world. Listing 11.20 shows the implementation of the `CModel::UpdateSimulation()` function of Tutorial 11.8. Recall that this function is called at about 25 msec intervals from the timer event service routine. In this function, we must collide all the bullets with the two palm nodes, generate new bullets, and remove all the bullets that are outside of the world boundaries. With the matrix stack properly initialized at label A, the `GetNodeBounds()` functions are called at label B to compute the WC bounding box of the left and right palm node. At label C, we loop through every bullet in the world to compute the bounding volume of the bullet (label C1) and intersect the bounding volume with the left and right arm bounding box (labels C2 and C3). New bullets are created at about 0.5 sec intervals (at label D), and finally at label E, bullets that are outside the world bounds are removed from the `m_bullets` list.

There are three details we should notice from this tutorial.

1. **Rough approximations.** Collision approximations of non-axis aligned rectangular objects have relatively low accuracy. Try rotating the arm and the palm such that these scene nodes are about 45 degrees from the *x/y* axes. Notice that successful collisions of the palm with the dropping arm bullet often have relatively large gaps in between the actual primitives. This low accuracy in intersection approximation is a direct result of the large void spaces in axis-aligned bounding boxes. In many cases, using strategic bounding circles/spheres would result in much better results.

2. **Multiple collisions.** The `hitCount` echoed in the status area may be incremented by several counts for one actual collision. This is a result of multiple successful intersections between a bullet and the palm over several timer update cycles. For example, within one update cycle, a fast-traveling bullet would move from outside to well inside the bounds of a palm object. In this case, the bullet's velocity will be updated after the successful collision. However, during the subsequent timer update cycle, before the bullet has the opportunity to move outside the palm's bound, another successful intersection may result. This problem becomes especially prominent when the human model hierarchy is also moving. For example, try rotating the left arm scene node while observing the `hitCount`; it will increase at a higher rate than the actual number of intersections. One easy way to fix this problem is to test the bullet's velocity direction and only perform intersection tests on bullets that are moving *towards* a palm object.

3. **Collision limitations.** The `SceneNode::GetNodeBounds()` function returns the WC bounding box of a *branch*, or subtree, rooted at the target scene node. This means that with the current functionality of the `SceneNode`

class, we cannot compute the WC bounding box for an internal node of the model hierarchy. For example, for the human model hierarchy of Figure 11.14, we cannot compute the WC bounding box of the body node without including the arm and the palm nodes. This means that we cannot compute the collision between internal nodes of a scene hierarchy. It is relatively straightforward to implement this functionality by modifying the GetNodeBounds() function. This is left as an exercise.

11.4.3 Discussion

In general, each of the XformInfo operators in a scene node introduces a new object coordinate space. This section pointed out that we must transform all geometries involved in selection and collision operations to a common coordinate space. We have also noticed that selection and collision functionality can be approximated by the intersections of corresponding bounding volumes. In our implementation, we have chosen the WC to be the common coordinate space for intersection computations, and we have chosen the bounding box to approximate the bounds of scene nodes. Readers are reminded that these choices are decisions for implementations. The general discussion applies regardless of the implementation decisions. For example, we can choose the NDC to be the common coordinate space for intersection computation, and bounding spheres to approximate the bounds of scene nodes. In fact, bounding spheres are capable of defining much tighter bounds for non-axis aligned primitives. It is left as an exercise for you to implement bounding spheres for the SceneNode class.

In practice, invisible collision primitives (and/or scene nodes) are often built into scene hierarchies. These primitives are typically easy to collide with mathematically and are placed at strategic positions in the hierarchy. For example, Figure 11.24 shows that we can define collision primitives to simplify collision computation for the arm of Figure 11.8. In this case, circles C_a and C_p are invisible and thus will never be drawn. During collision computations, instead of processing every primitives to compute the bounding box, we could simple return C_a and C_p as the bounding spheres of the arm and the palm nodes.

11.5 Simple Animation with the SceneNode Class

As we have seen in the CPrimitiveArm class (Listing 11.18 on p. 330), we can update the XformInfo operator in a SceneNode object to move or rotate the ob-

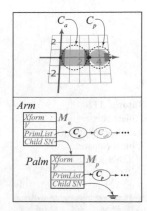

Figure 11.24. The arm with collision primitives.

ject. If we modify the `XformInfo` operator of selective nodes in a scene hierarchy during each timer update, then a continuous animation will be observed by the user.

Tutorial 11.9. Animating the `SceneNodes`

Tutorial 11.9.
Project Name:
D3D_SceneNodeAnimation
Library Support:
UWB_MFC_Lib1
UWB_D3D_Lib12

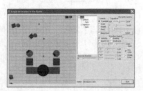

Figure 11.25.   Tutorial 11.9.

Source file.
Model_Siumulation.cpp
file in the *Model* folder of the
D3D_SceneNodeAnimation
project.

- **Goal.** Demonstrate that simple animation of scene nodes can be implemented by modifying the `XformInfo` operators of scene nodes during timer events.

- **Approach.** Continuously update the palm nodes' rotation operator in the human model from Figure 11.13.

Figure 11.25 is a screenshot of running Tutorial 11.9. This tutorial runs and behaves very similar to that of Tutorial 11.8. The only difference is that the two palms on the human model and the palm of the arm bullet spin continuously. Listing 11.21 shows that in order to create the spinning animation of the palms on the human model, the rotation value in the `XformInfo` operator of the left and right palm nodes must be incremented during each timer update. We see that at label A, a copy of the left palm `XformInfo` node is obtained; at label B, the rotation value is incremented; and at label C, the new rotation value is copied back to the left palm node. With the increased rotation value, the next redraw will rotate the left palm with an additional angle from its original position. In this way, during timer events, the rotation value is continuously incremented, and the incremented value shows up as additional rotation when the palm is drawn, resulting in an apparent spinning animation of the palm node.

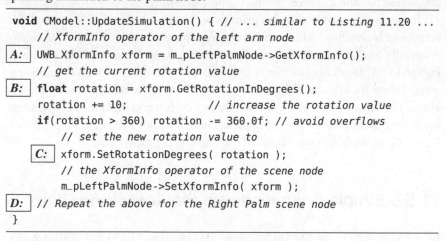

```
void CModel::UpdateSimulation() { // ... similar to Listing 11.20 ...
    // XformInfo operator of the left arm node
A:  UWB_XformInfo xform = m_pLeftPalmNode->GetXformInfo();
    // get the current rotation value
B:  float rotation = xform.GetRotationInDegrees();
    rotation += 10;              // increase the rotation value
    if(rotation > 360) rotation -= 360.0f; // avoid overflows
        // set the new rotation value to
    C:  xform.SetRotationDegrees( rotation );
        // the XformInfo operator of the scene node
        m_pLeftPalmNode->SetXformInfo( xform );
D:  // Repeat the above for the Right Palm scene node
}
```

Listing 11.21. The `CModel::UpdateSimulation()` function of Tutorial 11.9.

The `PrimitiveArm::Update()` function performs similar operations on the palm node of the arm bullet. You are encouraged to examine the implementation in the `PrimitiveArm.cpp` file, in the *Model* folder of the `D3D_SceneNodeAnima tion` project.

12

Making the Applications Interesting

This chapter discusses some mathematics background and advanced computer graphics concepts that allow the building of more intelligent and visually appealing applications. This chapter:

- presents the mathematics to orient and move objects toward any given directions/positions;

- explains the basic ideas of simulating transparency with alpha blending;

- describes the essential concepts and procedures of working with file texture mapping.

After this chapter we should:

- understand simple and practical applications of vector dot products and cross products;

- understand the basic concepts behind alpha blending and file texturing.

In addition, with respect to hands-on programming, we should:

- be able to program the motion of objects to follow and/or home in on any position;

337

  • be able to utilize alpha blending and file texture mapping to increase the apparent complexity of a graphics scene.

We have learned many technical details of building interactions and designing geometric manipulations of graphical objects. We need two important areas to make our applications interesting: intelligence and visual appearance. To be intelligent, our application must be aware of its state and react meaningfully. To be visually appealing, the graphical objects in our program should include appropriate real-life complexity. In general, these two topic areas are highly application-specific and can involve knowledge and skills from diverse backgrounds (e.g., artificial intelligence, machine learning, computer arts).

In many interactive applications, one of the most important application states is the notion of orientation of the graphical objects, the knowledge of which way is front, left, and right, such that the application can steer or move the objects accordingly. In this chapter, we present tutorials that apply simple linear algebra to orient graphical objects and individual nodes in a scene graph. To address visual appearance, we extend the library to support simple transparency effects (via blending) and texture mapping. In these ways, we can increase the sophistication of our applications in intelligence and in appearance.

12.1   Orientation of Objects

One important operation shared by many intelligent applications is to move graphical objects purposefully. For example, moving an object forward or turning an object towards its left or right. To implement this operation, we first recall that objects are defined in individual OC spaces. These objects are then placed into the world coordinate (WC) space with an OC-to-WC transformation matrix. Recall that with the UWBGL implementation, the OC-to-WC matrix is stored in the SceneNode class. In addition, we must remember that user mouse clicks are in device DC space. When computing orientations to navigate objects, it is important to make sure that all geometries and positions are transformed to a common coordinate space where computations are performed. In the following tutorials, we choose to work in the WC space.

Tutorial 12.1.
Project Name:
  D3D_OrientationIn2D
Library Support:
  UWB_MFC_Lib1
  UWB_D3D_Lib12

Tutorial 12.1. Automatic Arm Object Navigation

  • **Goal.** Understand how to compute orientation and navigate graphics objects.

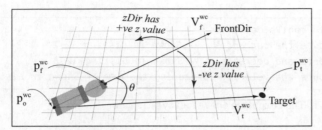

Figure 12.4. Compute turning direction.

- **Approach.** Implement the home-in seeking operation to demonstrate how to compute front and how to turn objects to the left and right.

Figure 12.1 is a screenshot of running Tutorial 12.1. We can enable navigation of the arm object by checking the "Allow Arm Movements" checkbox. When enabled, the arm object will move toward the gray target. We can relocate the target by left mouse button dragging in the drawing area. Observe that the arm object always turns toward the target while continuously moving toward the target. The arm object will stop moving when its origin overlaps the target position. The arm object always seeks out and homes in on the target position. Figure 12.2 shows the details of the arm object and the origin (p_o^{oc}) and front (p_f^{oc}) positions defined for this tutorial. The scene graph design for the arm object is shown in Figure 12.3. Recall that the $\mathbf{M}_a$ matrix is responsible for transforming points in arm OC space to the WC:

$$
\begin{aligned}
p_o^{wc} &= p_o^{oc}\,\mathbf{M}_a, \\
p_f^{wc} &= p_f^{oc}\,\mathbf{M}_a.
\end{aligned}
\tag{12.1}
$$

In this case, the front direction of the arm in WC is defined as

$$\mathbf{V}_f^{wc} = p_f^{wc} - p_o^{wc}.$$

In this way, "moving the arm forward" in the WC space can be implemented by adding $\mathbf{M}_a$ translation to the $\mathbf{V}_f^{wc}$ vector. As shown in Figure 12.4, if we let the target position in WC be p_t^{wc}, then the direction from the arm origin (p_o^{wc}) toward the target is

$$\mathbf{V}_t^{wc} = p_t^{wc} - p_o^{wc},$$

where "turning the arm toward the target" can be implemented by decreasing the θ-angle in Figure 12.4 (the angle between vectors $\mathbf{V}_f^{wc}$ and $\mathbf{V}_t^{wc}$). If we normalize the vectors, then

$$\theta = \cos^{-1}(\hat{\mathbf{V}}_f^{wc} \cdot \hat{\mathbf{V}}_t^{wc}).$$

Figure 12.1. Tutorial 12.1.

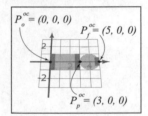

Figure 12.2. The front of the arm object (from Tutorial 11.5, Figure 11.8 on p. 308).

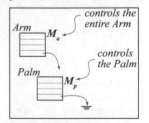

Figure 12.3. The arm with OC-to-WC transforms (from Tutorial 11.5, Figure 11.9 on p. 308).

Angle between vectors. See Section B.2.1 for details.

Source file.
Pseudocode; no
corresponding source file.

```
bool CModel::ComputeFrontVelocity()
// Step 1. Compute the current Vf -- Shown in Listing 12.2
// Step 2. Compute and decrease θ -- Shown in Listing 12.3
// Step 3. Compute the velocity for moving the Arm -- Shown in Listing 12.4
```

Listing 12.1. The `ComputeFrontVelocity()` function.

Source file.
`Model_MoveToTarget.cpp`
file in the *Model* folder of
the `D3D_OrientationIn2D`
project.

```
bool CModel::ComputeFrontVelocity(float sec) {
       ⋮
       // initPos=p_o^wc; front=p_f^wc; frontDir=V_f^wc
A:     vec3 front(1,0,0), initPos(0,0,0), frontDir;
       // Arm's OC to WC Xform (M_a from Figure 12.3)
       UWB_XformInfo axf = m_pArmDrive->GetXformInfo();
       // Initiate scene graph traversal
       dh.PushModelTransform();
       // to compute OC->WC xform
B:     dh.InitializeModelTransform();
       // TopofStack=M_a (Arm's OC->WC xform matrix)
       axf.SetUpModelStack(dh);
       // Compute p_f^wc = p_f^oc M_a
C:     dh.TransformPoint(front);
       // Compute p_o^wc = p_o^oc M_a
       dh.TransformPoint(initPos);
       dh.PopModelTransform();
       // Compute V_f^wc = p_f^wc - p_o^wc
D:     frontDir =  front - initPos;
       ⋮ //contiune with code from Listing 12.3: compute and decrease θ
```

Listing 12.2. Step 1: Compute the forward direction ($\mathbf{V}_f^{wc}$).

Target position (p_t). Notice that the target position p_t is specified by the user's left mouse button click (in DC). As discussed in Section 10.5 and demonstrated in Tutorial 10.14, the `WindowHandler` supports the DC-to-WC transform. We must transform mouse click p_t to the WC space.

We can decrease θ by changing the rotation angle of $\mathbf{M}_a$ accordingly. In our Tutorial 12.1 implementation, we call `CModel::ComputeFrontVelocity()` during every timer event service to turn and move the arm object gradually toward the target position. Listing 12.1 shows that our implementation can be described as three main steps, to be detailed in the following listings. Listing 12.2 shows the details of the first step. The OC positions are defined at label A. At label B, we imitate the scene graph traversal procedure by setting up the matrix stack and loading the $\mathbf{M}_a$ matrix to the top of the matrix stack. At label C, the WC positions are computed. Finally, at label D, the front direction of the arm in WC is

```
bool CModel::ComputeFrontVelocity(float sec) {
        ⋮ // code from Listing 12.2: that computed frontDir=Vᶠʷᶜ in WC
        // Target gray circle's transform
```
A: `txf = m_pMoveToTarget->GetXformInfo();`
```
        // movePt=pₜʷᶜ (target position)
        vec3 movePt = txf.GetTranslation();
        // dir=Vₜʷᶜ = pₜʷᶜ − pₒʷᶜ (direction towards target)
```
B: `vec3 dir = movePt - initPos;`
```
        // pₒ is very close to pₜ => done.
        if (length(dir) < 0.1f) return false;
        // vector normalization: compute V̂ᶠʷᶜ and V̂ₜʷᶜ
```
C: `normalize(frontDir); normalize(dir);`
```
        // cosθ = V̂ᶠʷᶜ · V̂ₜʷᶜ, or θ = acos(V̂ᶠʷᶜ · V̂ₜʷᶜ)
        theta = fabs(acosf(dot(frontDir, dir)));
        // θ is not very small (zero)
```
D: `if (theta > 0.001f) {`
```
        // zDir = V̂ᶠʷᶜ × V̂ₜʷᶜ
```
E: `vec3 zDir = cross(frontDir, dir);`
```
            // aTheta is the current Arm rotation
            float aTheta = axf.GetRotationInRadians();
            // check sign of z-component from cross product
            // to turn clockwise or counterclockwise
```
F: `if (zDir.z > 0) aTheta += theta*TURN_RATE;`
```
            else        aTheta -= theta*TURN_RATE;
        axf.SetRotationRadians(aTheta);
        // sets new rotation to Mₐ of Figure 12.3
        m_pArmDrive->SetXformInfo(axf);
    }
}
⋮ // continue with code from Listing 12.4: to update new velocity for Arm
```

Source file.
Model_MoveToTarget.cpp
file in the *Model* folder of
the D3D_OrientationIn2D
project.

Listing 12.3. Step 2: Compute and decrease θ.

computed. Listing 12.3 shows the details of the second step of ComputeFrontVel
ocity() (from Listing 12.1). At label A, the target position p_t^{wc} in WC is re-
trieved from the appropriate transform. At label B, $\mathbf{V}_t^{wc}$ is computed. The length
of this vector is the distance between the arm origin (p_o^{wc}) and the target. When
this distance is small, the arm has arrived at the target position and we are done.
At label C, the $\mathbf{V}_f^{wc}$ and $\mathbf{V}_t^{wc}$ vectors are normalized, and the angle θ between these
two vectors is computed. A small θ value represents that the arm is pointing ap-
proximately toward the target. The checking at label D ensures that we do not

Source file.
Model_MoveToTarget.cpp
file in the *Model* folder of
the D3D_OrientationIn2D
project.

```
bool CModel::ComputeFrontVelocity(float sec) {
    ⋮ // code from Listing 12.2: Computed front direction (V_f^wc)
    ⋮ // code from Listing 12.3: Computed and decreased θ
    // fronDir=V̂_f^wc (normalized)
    vec3 velocity = frontDir * ARM_SPEED * sec;
    m_pArmDrive->SetVelocity(velocity);
}
```

Listing 12.4. Step 3: Compute and set arm velocity.

Left versus right turns. See
Section B.2.2 for details of
applying the cross product in
differentiating left from right
sides of a given vector.

overshoot when rotating the arm toward the target. At label E, we compute the cross product of $\mathbf{V}_f^{wc}$ and $\mathbf{V}_t^{wc}$ in order to determine if the arm object should be turning left or right to face the target position p_t^{wc}. At label F, the arm's rotation is updated by a percentage of the computed θ value. In this way, we can accomplish the effect of turning the arm object gradually toward the target in subsequent updates. Listing 12.4 shows the final computation of the velocity for the arm object. Recall that frontDir has been normalized. Here, we are setting the appropriate scene node velocity such that the arm object will move at constant speed (ARM_SPEED) toward the current front direction ($\hat{\mathbf{V}}_f^{wc}$).

This tutorial demonstrates some valuable lessons.

- **Coordinate system.** We must be acutely aware of the different coordinate systems involved. We have chosen the world coordinate (WC) system to carry out all computations.

- **Directions.** In this case, the front direction of the arm object in OC space is defined trivially to be along the x-axis. However, as the arm navigates in the WC space, we must continuously recompute the current front direction in the WC space. As we have seen, we:

    - identify appropriate positions in the OC space, that is, identify p_f^{oc} and p_o^{oc};
    - transform these positions from OC to WC, that is, compute p_f^{wc} and p_o^{wc};
    - compute the WC direction vector by subtracting the WC positions, that is, compute $\mathbf{V}_f^{wc} = p_f^{wc} - p_o^{wc}$.

- **Turning.** Given a forward-facing direction ($\mathbf{V}_f^{wc}$) and a target position (p_t^{wc}), we use the vector dot product to determine the amount of turning that must be performed (θ), and we use the cross product to determine if we should turn left or right.

4. **Gradual effect.** Instead of setting the transformation operator with the computed final value, we update the operator with a fraction of the computed value. In this way, subsequent updates will gradually transform our object toward the ultimate goal.

Tutorial 12.2.
Project Name:
   D3D_SceneNodeOrient
Library Support:
   UWB_MFC_Lib1
   UWB_D3D_Lib12

Tutorial 12.2. Automatic Navigation with Independent Aiming

• **Goal.** Demonstrate and understand that the lessons learned from Tutorial 12.1 can be applied to individual scene nodes in a scene graph.

• **Approach.** Building on Tutorial 12.1, implement a second target position for aligning the palm component.

Figure 12.5 is a screenshot of running Tutorial 12.2. Once again checking the "Allow Arm Movement" checkbox will enable the navigation of the arm object. In addition to the left mouse button controlled gray target, in this tutorial right mouse button drag controls the position of the red target position. Similar to the previous tutorial, the arm object will automatically navigate toward the gray target. In this tutorial, as the arm object travels, its palm component will continuously point toward the red target.

Figure 12.5. Tutorial 12.2.

In Figure 12.2, the origin position of the palm component is located at p_p^{oc}, whereas the front is also defined by p_f^{oc}. For the palm component, the OC-to-WC transformation is defined by the concatenation of the palm transform ($\mathbf{M}_p$) and the arm transform ($\mathbf{M}_a$), so

$$\begin{aligned} p_f^{wc} &= p_f^{oc}\,\mathbf{M}_p\,\mathbf{M}_a, \\ p_p^{wc} &= p_p^{oc}\,\mathbf{M}_p\,\mathbf{M}_a. \end{aligned} \tag{12.2}$$

As depicted in Figure 12.6, in this case the front-facing vector of the palm object is

$$\mathbf{V}_p^{wc} = p_f^{wc} - p_p^{wc}.$$

If the red target's WC position is defined to be p_r, then the vector from the palm object toward the red target is

$$\mathbf{V}_r^{wc} = p_r^{wc} - p_p^{wc}.$$

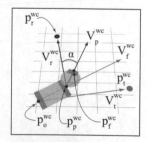

Figure 12.6. Implementing the aiming functionality.

Source file.
ArmPalmGaze.cpp file in
the *Model* folder of the
D3D_SceneNodeOrient
project.

```
void CArm::ComputePalmGaze(vec3 gazePt, float sec) {  // gazePt=p_r^{wc}
    // front=p_f^{oc}; palmPos=p_p^{oc}
A:  vec3 front(5,0,0), palmPos(4,0,0);
    // This is M_a of Figure 12.3
    UWB_XformInfo xf = GetXformInfo();
    // This is M_p of Figure 12.3
    UWB_XformInfo pxf = GetPalmNode()->GetXformInfo();
    // Imitate scene graph traversal
    dh.PushModelTransform();
    // to compute OC->WC xform
B:  dh.InitializeModelTransform();
    // M_a (parent) gets on stack first
    xf.SetUpModelStack(dh);
    // top of matrix stack now = M_a M_p
    pxf.SetUpModelStack(dh);
    // Compute p_f^{wc} = p_f^{oc} M_a M_p
C:  dh.TransformPoint(front);
    // Compute p_p^{wc} = p_p^{oc} M_p M_a
    dh.TransformPoint(palmPos);
    dh.PopModelTransform();
    // currentPalmGaze=V_p^{wc} = p_f^{wc} - p_p^{wc}
D:  vec3 currentPalmGaze = front - palmPos;
    // newPalmGaze=V_r^{wc}
    vec3 newPalmGaze = gazePt - palmPos;
    // palm overlaps the gaze position, we are done
    if (length(newPalmGaze) < 0.1f)  return;
        .
        .
        .
    // remaining code is similar to Listing 12.3
}
```

Listing 12.5. Computing the aim direction for the palm.

Our goal here is to rotate the $\mathbf{V}_p^{wc}$ direction to align with the $\mathbf{V}_r^{wc}$ vector. We can expect the solution to the fundamental problem of rotating one vector ($\mathbf{V}_f^{wc}$) to align with another ($\mathbf{V}_t^{wc}$) to be similar to that in Listing 12.3. In this case, we must pay attention to the slightly different OC-to-WC transformation. Listing 12.5 shows the details of computing the front direction for the palm component ($\mathbf{V}_p^{wc}$). At label A, the palm's front (p_f^{oc}) and origin (p_p^{oc}) positions are defined in the OC space. At label B, we imitate the scene graph traversal procedure and set up the OC-to-WC transformation matrix on the matrix stack. At label C, the front and origin positions are transformed into WC space (p_f^{wc} and p_p^{wc}). And finally at label

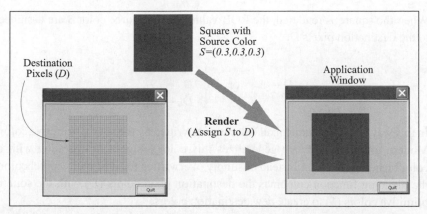

Figure 12.7. Rendering a dark gray square.

D, we compute the vectors in WC space. From this point on, the remaining code is very similar to that of Listing 12.3, where one vector is turned gradually into another.

Notice that the p_f^{wc} in Tutorial 12.1 is different from the one computed in this tutorial. Although in the previous case, p_f^{oc} was transformed by Equation (12.1) based on the arm's OC-to-WC transformation matrix ($\mathbf{M}_a$), in this tutorial, the same p_f^{oc} position is transformed in Equation (12.2) based on the palm's OC-to-WC transformation matrix ($\mathbf{M}_p\mathbf{M}_a$). In this way, although based on the same OC space front position (p_f^{oc}), we can obtain two different front positions for computing the front vectors for arm ($\mathbf{V}_f^{wc}$) and palm ($\mathbf{V}_p^{wc}$).

12.2 Alpha Blending and Transparency

At this point, from having worked with graphics APIs quite extensively, we understand that the rendering of a primitive involves assigning appropriate colors to the corresponding pixels. For example, Figure 12.7 shows a dark gray square being rendered into appropriate pixels. In this case, the source color of the squares is S,

$$S = (S_r, S_g, S_b) = (0.3, 0.3, 0.3).$$

Those pixels that will be covered by the square are the destination pixels, D,

$$D = (D_r, D_g, D_b).$$

0.0 to 1.0 color representation. The following discussion assumes that each channel of the color is specified as a normalized floating-point number where 0.0 means off and 1.0 is the maximum.

When the square is rendered, the RGB values of the source color S are assigned to the destination pixels D:

$$D \leftarrow S \quad \text{or} \quad \begin{cases} D_r \leftarrow S_r, \\ D_g \leftarrow S_g, \\ D_b \leftarrow S_b. \end{cases}$$

In this way, the destination pixel color is overwritten by the source primitive color. Modern graphics hardware generalizes this color assignment operation with a color blending function. Instead of simply overwriting the destination pixel color, the blending function combines the destination pixel colors (D) with the source primitive colors (S) to create new destination colors:

$$D \leftarrow f(D \times A_d, S \times A_s), \tag{12.3}$$

where

$$\begin{cases} D & - & \text{destination pixel color,} \\ A_d & - & \text{destination blending factor,} \\ S & - & \text{source primitive color,} \\ A_s & - & \text{source blending factor,} \\ f() & - & \text{blending function.} \end{cases}$$

For example, with blending factors

$$\begin{cases} A_d = (0.2, 0.2, 0.2), \\ A_s = (0.8, 0.8, 0.8), \end{cases}$$

and a blending function of addition

$$\begin{aligned} D & \leftarrow & f(D \times A_d, S \times A_s), \\ D & \leftarrow & (D \times 0.2) + (S \times 0.8), \end{aligned}$$

we get

$$\begin{cases} D_r \leftarrow D_r \times 0.2 + S_r \times 0.8, \\ D_g \leftarrow D_g \times 0.2 + S_g \times 0.8, \\ D_b \leftarrow D_b \times 0.2 + S_b \times 0.8. \end{cases}$$

In this case, the final destination pixel colors are a blend of 20% (0.2) original destination pixel colors with 80% (0.8) source primitive colors.

To properly support this blending functionality, modern graphics hardware introduced a forth channel to the color representation, the α channel:

$$\text{color} = (r, \quad g, \quad b, \quad \alpha),$$

so

$$S = (S_r, \quad S_g, \quad S_b, \quad S_\alpha),$$
$$D = (D_r, \quad D_g, \quad D_b, \quad D_\alpha).$$

Notice that although defined as the fourth channel of color, the α channel cannot affect the color of a pixel directly. Only the R, G, and B channels can change the color of a pixel. The α channel is designed to be used as the blending factor in achieving transparency effects. For example, Figure 12.8 shows a semitransparent circle drawn over a square. Notice that we can see through and observe colors/objects behind the circle. The final color of pixels covered by the circle is actually a blend of the circle color and that of the original destination pixel color: the colors of the square and the grid. In this case, the circle is the source primitive with color S; before rendering the circle, the destination pixels' colors are D. In this example, the source blending factor A_s is

$$A_s = S_\alpha,$$

and the destination blending factor A_d is

$$A_d = (1 - S_\alpha),$$

whereas the blending function is the addition function

$$D \leftarrow D \times A_d + S \times A_s,$$
$$D \leftarrow D \times (1 - S_\alpha) + S \times S_\alpha,$$

or

$$\begin{cases} D_r & \leftarrow D_r \times (1 - S_\alpha) + S_r \times S_\alpha, \\ D_g & \leftarrow D_g \times (1 - S_\alpha) + S_g \times S_\alpha, \\ D_b & \leftarrow D_b \times (1 - S_\alpha) + S_b \times S_\alpha, \\ D_\alpha & \leftarrow D_\alpha \times (1 - S_\alpha) + S_\alpha \times S_\alpha. \end{cases} \quad (12.4)$$

In this way, S_α approximates the opacity effect of the circle: when $\alpha = 1$, we will not see any color behind the circle; when $\alpha = 0.5$, we will see an equal blend; and when $\alpha = 0$, the circle will be completely transparent.

Typical modern graphics hardware supports the following blending factors (A_d and A_s) for source and destination:

Constant 0	$(0,0,0,0)$
Constant 1	$(1,1,1,1)$
Source color	$(S_r, S_g, S_b, S_\alpha)$
Inverse source color	$(1 - S_r, 1 - S_g, 1 - S_b, 1 - S_\alpha)$
Source alpha	$(S_\alpha, S_\alpha, S_\alpha, S_\alpha)$
Inverse source alpha	$(1 - S_\alpha, 1 - S_\alpha, 1 - S_\alpha, 1 - S_\alpha)$
Destination alpha	$(D_\alpha, D_\alpha, D_\alpha, D_\alpha)$
Inverse destination alpha	$(1 - D_\alpha, 1 - D_\alpha, 1 - D_\alpha, 1 - D_\alpha)$

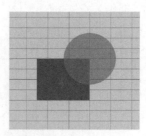

Figure 12.8. A semitransparent circle.

High-end hardware. Specialized graphics hardware may support additional options for blending factor and function types.

Typical supported blending functions include:

Addition	$D = DA_d + SA_s$
Subtract	$D = SA_s - DA_d$
Reverse subtract	$D = DA_d - SA_s$
Min	$D = \min(SA_s, DA_d)$
Max	$D = \max(SA_s, DA_d)$

Because the α channel often controls the blending factors, this blending of source primitive color with destination pixel color is often referred to as alpha blending. To work with alpha blending, our program must:

1. enable alpha blending functionality;

2. define A_s, the source blending factor;

3. define A_d, the destination blending factor;

4. define the blending function ($f(DA_d, SA_s)$ of Equation (12.3)).

For example, the blending operation from Equation (12.4) is defined as:

A_s:	Source alpha
A_d:	Inverse source alpha
Blend function:	Addition

UWBGL_D3D_Lib13

Change summary. See p. 525 for a summary of changes to the library.

This library supports per-primitive alpha blending and texture mapping. The major changes to this library are the inclusion of texture file resource management, primitive attribute support, and `DrawHelper` extension for blending and texturing. The details of texture support will be discussed in the next section. Listing 12.6 shows the modification to the `Primitive` class to support the blending and texture mapping attributes. At labels A and B are the public interface methods for setting and querying the protected instance variables representing the new attributes. Recall that in the `UWBGL` design, the `Primitive` class stores the attributes for the `DrawHelper` class during graphics API–dependent rendering of the primitives. Label C shows the modification to the `SetupDrawAttributes()` method that passes the new attributes to the `DrawHelper` class. Listing 12.7 shows the D3D support for enabling alpha blending. At label A, with the alpha blending enabled, we enable and program the D3D alpha blending functionality according to the list in the previous section. At label B, when alpha blending is disabled, we do not have to worry about blending factors or the blending function. Notice that the `DrawHelper::EnableBlending()` function is called during `SetupDrawAttributes()` for *each* primitive object. in this way, the alpha-blending functionality is enabled/disabled for each of the `UWBGL` primitives.

Once again, the support for texture mapping of `UWB_Lib13` will be discussed in the next section.

```
class UWB_Primitive {
    ⋮
```

A:
```
   public:
       void EnableBlending( bool on ); // Enable/disable primitive blending
       bool IsBlendingEnabled() const; // Query the prmitive's blending state

   protected:
       bool m_bBlendingEnabled; // storage of primitive's blending state
```

B:
```
   public:
       void SetTextureFileName(const wchar_t*); // Set texture file name
       const wchar_t* GetTextureFileName();      // Query texture file name
       void EnableTexturing(bool on);   // enable/disable primitive file texture mapping
       bool IsTexturingEnabled() const; // Query file texture mapping state

   protected:
       bool m_bTexturingEnabled;   // storage of primitive's textere mapping state
       std::wstring m_TexFileName; // if enabled, texture file name
    ⋮
};
```

Source file.
`uwbgl_Primitive3.h/cpp` files in the *Common Files/ Primitives* subfolder of the `UWBGL_D3D_Lib13` project.

```
void UWB_Primitive::SetupDrawAttributes(UWB_DrawHelper& draw_helper) {
    ⋮
```

C:
```
   draw_helper.EnableBlending( m_bBlendingEnabled );
   draw_helper.SetTextureInfo( m_TexFileName.c_str() );
   draw_helper.EnableTexture( m_bTexturingEnabled );
    ⋮
```

Listing 12.6. Modification to `Primitive` for supporting blending and texturing.

Source file.
uwbgl_D3DDrawHelper5.cpp
file in the *D3D Files/
D3D_DrawHelper* subfolder
of the UWBGL_D3D_Lib13
project.

```
bool UWBD3D_DrawHelper::EnableBlending( bool on ) {
        :
    // Alpha blending is enabled for this primitive
A:  if( on ) {
        // 1. Enable D3D alpha blending
        pDevice->SetRenderState(D3DRS_ALPHABLENDENABLE,TRUE);
        // 2. Define As = Sα
        pDevice->SetRenderState(D3DRS_SRCBLEND,D3DBLEND_SRCALPHA);
        // 3. Define Ad = 1 - Sα
        pDevice->SetRenderState(D3DRS_DESTBLEND,D3DBLEND_INVSRCALPHA);
        // 4. Blending function=Addition
        pDevice->SetRenderState(D3DRS_BLENDOP,D3DBLENDOP_ADD);
    // Alpha blending is disabled for this primitive
B:  } else
        // Disable D3D Alpha blending
        pDevice->SetRenderState(D3DRS_ALPHABLENDENABLE, FALSE);
        :
```

Listing 12.7. Enabling blending for the D3D API.

Tutorial 12.3.
Project Name:
    D3D_AlphaBlending
Library Support:
    UWB_MFC_Lib1
    UWB_D3D_Lib13

Figure 12.9.   Tutorial
12.3.

Tutorial 12.3. Alpha Blending

- **Goal.** Demonstrate alpha blending by allowing the user to change the blending factors interactively.

- **Approach.** Implement a simple scene with a circle and a square that allows the user to set the α channel for both of the primitives.

Figure 12.9 is a screenshot of running Tutorial 12.3. This tutorial has enabled the "Blending" checkbox in the PrimitiveControl. This checkbox directly controls the EnableBlending() attribute of the primitive highlighted in the SceneTree Control. Now, select the "Circle" object from the SceneTreeControl and enable the "Blending" checkbox. Notice that the circle becomes semi-transparent where we can see through it and observe the blue square behind it. Now, if we adjust the α channel via the "A" slider bar, we can adjust the degree of transparency of the circle. In this tutorial, we see that the transparency/opacity functionality can be accomplished with the blending functionality programmed in Listing 12.7.

12.3   File Texture Mapping

As illustrated in Figure 12.10, one way to understand file texture mapping is that we stretch/compress an image from a file and paste this image like a label onto a primitive. The main goal of texture mapping is to increase the apparent complexity of a scene. For example, Figure 12.11 is a simple scene with a circle and a rectangle. Figure 12.12 shows the same scene with the same simple circle and rectangle primitives except that in this case both primitives are *pasted* (or mapped) with file textures. When we compare these two images, the image from Figure 12.12 appears to be more complex. For many interactive applications, appropriately texture-mapped primitives can lead to significantly more appealing application and can contribute directly to positive user experience.

For the case of Figure 12.10, we refer to the images as texture maps and describe the primitives as texture-mapped primitives. Just like a pixel is the basic element in an image, we refer to each element of a texture map as a texel. In all of the examples we will work with, texel values are colors. However, in general, a texel can contain any arbitrary floating-point value. To understand the basic concepts behind file texture mapping, in the following discussion we will first clarify what a texture file is. We then explain the two coordinate systems that enable the mapping process. The actual texture lookup and pixel color computation are presented last.

12.3.1   File Texture: Image Files

As depicted in Figure 12.10, the rectangular photograph on the lower-left corner of Figure 12.12 is actually a simple rectangle primitive pasted with an image. In this case, the image happens to be a digital photograph stored in the jpeg format.

File texture mapping. In this book, we use the terms *file texture mapping* and *texture mapping* interchangeably. While this is acceptable in our context, be aware that there are many forms of mapping or calculating texture on primitives. For example, *procedural texture mapping* computes textures with no reference to files.

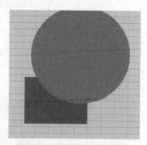

Figure 12.11. A simple scene of a circle and a square.

Figure 12.12. Simple scene with texture maps.

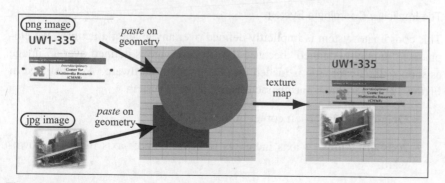

Figure 12.10. Pasting images on primitives.

In our context, an image (or an image file) is simply a formatted file containing a 2D array of colors. When we view this file with an image viewer application, an image will be displayed. The color of each pixel on the displayed image will correspond to an element in the 2D array of the formatted file. Some popular file formats for storing images include: jpg, tiff, gif, png, and so on. In this way, "an image" or a "file texture" is simply a file that contains a digital photograph, a creative art drawing, or the results of a scanner operation. As long as a file contains a 2D array of colors and is formatted according to some image file format, we can use it as a file texture.

File texture mapping treats an image file as a texture and maps this texture onto a primitive. In this chapter, we are interested in understanding the basic concepts of file texture mapping such that we can incorporate textures into our applications.

12.3.2 Texture Coordinates

Two coordinate systems are defined on the texture image and on the primitive to enable the mapping.

1. **The *st* coordinate system on file textures.** Graphics hardware implicitly defines a normalized coordinate system over a file texture.

2. **The *uv* coordinate system on primitives.** Our programs must explicitly define texture coordinate positions for each vertex of our primitive.

Based on these two coordinate systems, correspondence between pixel and texel positions is established, and the color identified by the texel is used in computing the final color of the pixel.

Figure 12.13. The *st* coordinate system.

The Implicit *st* Coordinate System.

This coordinate system is implicitly defined over any given file texture. We emphasize "implicitly defined" because the *st* coordinate is defined over an image as soon as the texture file is loaded into the graphics hardware. As illustrated in Figure 12.13, here are some characteristics of the *st* system.

- **Origin.** The upper-left corner of the image.

- **Axis directions.** *s*-axis increases rightward, and *t*-axis increases downward.

- **Normalized.** Values for *st* are always in the range 0 to 1.0.

- **Coverage.** The coordinate system is always defined over the entire image.

These properties of the *st* coordinate system are true independent of the resolution of the image. For example,

Position in an image	*st* coordinate value
top-left corner	(0.0, 0.0)
bottom-left corner	(0.0, 1.0)
middle	(0.5, 0.5)
top-right corner	(1.0, 0.0)
bottom-right corner	(1.0, 1.0)

In this way, depending on the resolution of the texture image, the same *st* coordinate position may identify very different texel positions. For example, independent of the resolution of a texture image, $st = (0.5, 0.5)$ indentifies the texel in the center: texel $(5,5)$ for an 11×11 pixel image; or texel $(50, 50)$ for a 101×101 pixel image; or texel $(50, 5)$ for a 101×11 pixel image.

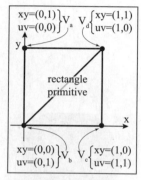

Figure 12.14. The *uv* coordinate system.

The Explicit *uv* Texture Coordinate System

We, as the programmers, are responsible for defining and assigning *uv* texture coordinate values to each vertex position on the primitives. Figure 12.14 shows an example of texture coordinate assignments at the vertices of a rectangle primitive. We observe that in addition to the *xy* geometric position, each vertex also has a *uv* texture position. These two coordinate positions identify points in two completely independent domains, and yet together they serve a complementary role in computing final colors for the pixels: the *xy* geometric positions assist in determining which of the pixels are covered, whereas the *uv* texture positions assist in determining the color for these pixels. The process of defining and assigning *uv* texture coordinate values to vertex positions is referred to as texture placement. In general, high-quality texture placement is a laborious process involving highly experienced artists spending long hours manipulating the *uv* values at individual vertex positions to accomplish specific artistic effects.

12.3.3   Texel Value Look-up

As illustrated in Figure 12.15, during rendering, for each pixel inside a primitive, the following happens.

- Compute *uv* coordinate values based on interpolation from the surrounding vertices.

- Reference *st* coordinate with the computed *uv* values to identify a texel.

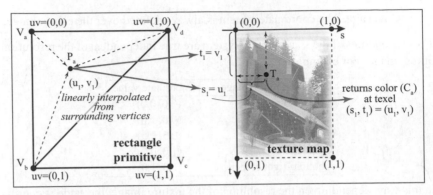
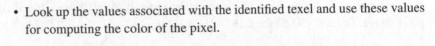

Figure 12.15. Texel value look-up.

- Look up the values associated with the identified texel and use these values for computing the color of the pixel.

For example, as illustrated in Figure 12.15, at pixel position P_a the texture coordinate (u_1, v_1) is computed based on interpolating the uv values from the surrounding three vertices: V_a, V_b, and V_d. The (u_1, v_1) values are then used as reference into the st coordinate space to identify a texel T_a. The value of the texel C_a is returned for computing the color of the pixel.

12.3.4 Using the Texel Values

The most straightforward usage of the looked-up texel value C_a is to treat it as a color and simply assign it into the destination pixel D:

$$D \leftarrow C_a$$

The square in Figure 12.12 is computed based on this straightforward assignment. From the discussion in Section 12.2 and from Equation (12.3), we understand that modern graphics hardware supports more interesting functions in computing the color of the destination pixel. For example, it is virtually impossible to identify the circle primitive in Figure 12.12. Figure 12.16 shows the same image with α blending disabled for the circle primitive. We see that in addition to basic (r, g, b), a file texture can also contain α information for each pixel. In this case, with the per-pixel α information, when blending is enabled the portions of the circle with file texture of $\alpha = 0$ become completely transparent.

Figure 12.16. Simple scene with blending disabled.

Alpha channel in image files. Not all image file formats support the storing of the α channel for each pixel. For example, the jpg file format does not support storing of α channel, whereas the png file format supports the storing of α channel.

12.3.5   Implementation

To work with file texture mapping, our program must:

1. define texture coordinate on all vertices;

2. select and load the file texture into graphics hardware;

3. define how texel values are used to compute pixel colors;

4. enable texture-mapping functionality.

Tutorial 12.4. Simple File Texture Mapping

- **Goal.** Demonstrate how to work with graphics API file texture mapping.

- **Approach.** Implement a simple program without the UWBGL library to clearly illustrate the steps required for working with graphics API texture mapping.

Figure 12.17 is a screenshot of running Tutorial 12.4. In this tutorial, we can select a current file texture by clicking the "Select File Texture" button to select an image file. The texture-mapping functionality can be enabled by the "Enable Texture" checkbox. Select any image file and enable the texture mapping. Now, try transforming the primitive. Observe that the texture map behaves as though it is a flexible sticker pasted on the geometry: the textured image stretches, rotates, and moves with the primitive. In addition, notice that negative scaling flips the texture image.

The implementation of this tutorial is purposefully independent of the UWBGL library. In this case, all texture-mapping functionality is implemented in the Model.cpp file. With this simple tutorial, we can examine and understand the programming of texture-mapping functionality in a continuous linear sequence. After this understanding, in the next tutorial the texture-mapping functionality will be abstracted into different modules of the UWBGL library.

To ensure clear and focused presentation, the Model.cpp file is divided according to functional/logical modules in the following different listings. Listing 12.8 shows the DeviceVertexFormat defined in Model.cpp for drawing the textured rectangle and circle. At label A, we see that besides position and color, we must associate a *uv* coordinate with each vertex position. Label B defines the corresponding code for programming the D3D API. Listing 12.9 shows the draw functions of the rectangle (DrawUnitSquare()) and the circle

Tutorial 12.4.
Project Name:
   D3D_SimpleTexture
Library Support:
   UWB_MFC_Lib1
   UWB_D3D_Lib13

Figure 12.17.   Tutorial 12.4.

DeviceVertexFormat. See Step 3 in Listing 3.3 (on p. 82); this is the mechanism for a program to communicate vertex size and content to the D3D API.

```
struct DeviceVertexFormat {
    D3DXVECTOR3 m_Point; // x,y,z position
    D3DCOLOR    m_Color; // color of vertex (actually a DWORD)
A:  FLOAT       m_U, m_V; // Texture coordinate
};
B:  static DWORD DeviceVertexFormatCode = D3DFVF_XYZ|D3DFVF_DIFFUSE|D3DFVF_TEX1;
```

Source file. `Model.cpp` file in the *Model* folder of the `D3D_SimpleTexture` project.

Listing 12.8. Vertex format for texture-mapping support.

```
static void DrawUnitSquare(LPDIRECT3DDEVICE9 pDevice) {

A:  DeviceVertexFormat v[4]; // now includes texture cooridnate position
B:  v[0].m_Point = D3DXVECTOR3(-1.0f, 1.0f, 0.0f); // V0.Point ← (-1,1,0)
    v[0].m_U = 0.0f; v[0].m_V = 0.0f;              // V0.UV ← (0,0)
```

Source file. `Model.cpp` file in the *Model* folder of the `D3D_SimpleTexture` project.

```
    // V1.Point ← (-1,-1,0), V1.UV ← (0,1)

    // V2.Point ← ( 1,-1,0), V2.UV ← (1,1)

    // V3.Point ← ( 1, 1,0), V3.UV ← (1,0)
    // Inform D3D of the vertex format
C:  pDevice->SetFVF(DeviceVertexFormatCode);

    // Draw 2 triangles in Triangle Fan
    pDevice->DrawPrimitiveUP(D3DPT_TRIANGLEFAN,...);

static void DrawUnitCircle( LPDIRECT3DDEVICE9 pDevice ) {

    for (int i=0; i<kNumPts; i++)
D:  v[i+1].m_Point.x = cosf(i*delta); // (x,y) position of a circle
    v[i+1].m_Point.y = sinf(i*delta); // is defined by (cosθ,sinθ)
F:  v[i+1].m_U = (v[i+1].m_Point.x)*0.5f+0.5f;      // u = x×0.5+0.5
    v[i+1].m_V = 1.0f-((v[i+1].m_Point.y*0.5)+0.5) // v = 1-(y×0.5+0.5)

    // Inform D3D of the vertex format and approximate the circle by 100
    // trianges in a fan
```

Listing 12.9. Primitive *uv* texture coordinate assignments.

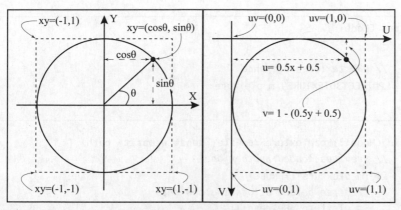

Figure 12.18. The circle xy position and uv texture placement.

(`DrawUnitCirce()`). At label A, we see the declaration of four vertices with the new vertex format (`DeviceVertexFormat`) from Listing 12.8. At label B, each vertex is assigned with the corresponding geometric xy values and the appropriate uv texture-placement values according to Figure 12.14. At label C, we first inform the API about the vertex format with the `SetFVF()` function, and then we draw the vertices as a triangle-fan. At label D, we compute the geometric xy vertex positions for the unit circle, whereas the uv texture placements are computed at label F. The left side of Figure 12.18 shows the xy position of a circle with unit radius centered around the origin. The right side of Figure 12.18 shows that our uv texture placement strategy is to maximize the image in the circle. In this case, the xy coordinate space covered by the circle is

$$xy \text{ geometric range } = \begin{cases} \text{center } = (c_x, c_y) = (0,0), \\ \text{width } = W_x = 2.0, \\ \text{height } = H_y = 2.0, \end{cases}$$

and our texture-placement strategy is to define the same circle to occupy the maximum uv texture coordinate space, or

$$uv \text{ texture coordinate range } = \begin{cases} \text{center } = (c_u, c_v) = (0.5, 0.5), \\ \text{width } = W_u = 1.0, \\ \text{height } = H_v = 1.0. \end{cases}$$

Coordinate transformation. See Figure 10.16 (on p. 273) and Equation (10.14), where we learned about transforming positions between bounded coordinate regions.

Notice that we have an almost identical situation to the coordinate transformation in Chapter 10. The only difference here is the fact that the y-axis and v-axis directions are opposite. Similar to the hardware-to-device coordinate transform, we will have to flip the y-axis values. If v' is defined with respect to the lower-left

```
class CModel {
    ⋮
    // D3D texture reference
A:  LPDIRECT3DTEXTURE9 m_pTexture;
    ⋮
```

```
void CModel::LoadTextureFromFile( const wchar_t* path) {
    // Previous loaded another one?
B:  if (m_pTexture != NULL)
        // free before allocating new ones
        m_pTexture->Release();
    // Load file to graphics hardware
C:  if(FAILED(D3DXCreateTextureFromFile(pDevice,path,&m_pTexture)))
        // loading failed
        m_pTexture = NULL;
}
```

Source file. `Model.cpp` file in the *Model* folder of the D3D_SimpleTexture project.

Listing 12.10. Loading texture into graphics hardware.

corner, or

$$v = 1 - v',$$

then

$$[uv'] = [xy]\, T(-c_x, -c_y) S(\frac{W_u}{W_x}, \frac{H_v}{H_y}) T(c_u, c_v),$$

in this case,

$$[uv'] = [xy]\, T(0,0) S(\frac{1}{2}, \frac{1}{2}) T(0.5, 0.5).$$

In this way,

$$\begin{cases} u & = x \times 0.5 + 0.5, \\ v & = 1 - v' = 1 - (y \times 0.5 + 0.5). \end{cases}$$

With *uv* texture placements defined on vertices, Listing 12.10 shows the D3D support for loading file textures. At label A, the `m_pTexture` is a reference to a D3D-specific texture structure. Our job as a D3D programmer is to load an appropriate texture into this structure and enable this structure for texture mapping while rendering primitives. At label B, we see that this D3D-specific structure is a limited resource, and we must properly manage (release) previously

```
void CModel::DrawModel() {
    // user has selected texture mapping
A:  if (m_EnableTexture && (m_pTexture != NULL))
        // Enable graphics API texture mapping
        pDevice->SetTextureStageState(... D3DTOP_SELECTARG1);
        // Select a current texture map
        pDevice->SetTexture(0, m_pTexture);
    // slider bars transformation setting
B:  m_xform.SetUpModelStack(draw_helper);
        // either draw the circle
C:  if(dt_circle==m_DrawType) DrawUnitCircle( pDevice );
    // or draw the square
    else DrawUnitSquare( pDevice );
        // Switch off texture when done
D:  if (m_EnableTexture && (m_pTexture != NULL))
        // Disable graphics API texture mapping
        pDevice->SetTextureStageState(... D3DTOP_DISABLE);
        // Set curren texture map to NULL
        pDevice->SetTexture(0, NULL);
}
```

Source file. Model.cpp file in the *Model* folder of the D3D_SimpleTexture project.

Listing 12.11. Drawing with file texture.

allocated versions. At label C, we see the utility function that, given a valid path to an image file, properly loads the m_pTexture structure into the D3D pDevice. Listing 12.11 shows that to draw with the loaded texture, we must enable the texture-mapping functionality and define how to use the texel values (at label A). At label B, we set up the WORLD matrix processor to support user-specified transformations. At label C, either the circle or square will be drawn. At label D, to ensure the proper rendering state, texture-mapping functionality is switched off after the primitive is drawn.

This tutorial shows us that we can switch texture mapping on/off at any point before/after drawing primitives. This means that in our primitive hierarchy, we can define texture mapping as a per-primitive attribute and control the texturing of each primitive independently.

UWBGL_D3D_Lib13 Support for File Texture

As pointed out in Section 12.3.5 and demonstrated in Tutorial 12.4, the important three steps in programming with file texture mapping are as follows.

Change summary. See p. 525 for a summary of changes to the library.

1. **Define *uv* texture placements.** Recall that in the UWBGL library, all API-specific drawing operations are implemented in the DrawHelper class. In this case, we have merged the new DeviceVertexFormat and primitive *uv* texture placement computation into the D3D_DrawHelper5.cpp file. The changes involved are very similar to those of Listing 12.8 and Listing 12.9, and we will not re-list them here.

2. **Load image file as texture.** As discussed in the following, Lib13 introduces functionality to support working with any simple file resource. This is in anticipation that we will work with other types of file resources (e.g., mesh files). The texture files are stored in a resource table defined in the GraphicsSystem class.

3. **Enable texture functionality.** As discussed in the following, Lib13 supports per-primitive texture attributes by defining appropriate attributes in the Primitive base class and extending the D3D_DrawHelper class.

File Resource Loading and Management

Listing 12.12 shows a simple base class for searching and loading files. Load Resource() (at label A) receives a fileName, calls FindFilePath() (at label B) to find the full path to this file, and calls the pure virtual function LoadResource FromFile() to load the file into D3D as a resource. Listing 12.13 shows the implementation of loading a texture file as resource. At label C, we see that the loaded file will be bound to this D3D texture structure. Label A defines the func-

```
class UWBD3D_Resource {
      ⋮
      // find/load the file
A:    virtual bool LoadResource(LPDIRECT3DDEVICE9, fileName);
   protected:
      // find fullPath from filename
B:    void FindFilePath(filename, fullPath);
      // subclass responsibility
C:    virtual bool LoadResourceFromFile(fullPathName) = 0;
      ⋮
```

Listing 12.12. Abstract support for file resource loading.

```
class UWBD3D_TextureResource : public UWBD3D_Resource {
    ⋮
    // Access the D3D Texture Structure
A:  LPDIRECT3DTEXTURE9 GetD3DTexture();
  protected:
    // To load image file
B:  virtual bool LoadResourceFromFile(fullPathName);
    // D3D Texture structure
C:  LPDIRECT3DTEXTURE9 m_pTexture;
    ⋮
```

Source file. uwbgl_D3D
TextureResource1.h
file in the *D3D Files/
D3D_Resources* subfolder
of the UWBGL_D3D_Lib13
project.

Listing 12.13. Texture resource support.

tion for accessing the D3D texture structure. At label B, `LoadResourceFrom File()` is overridden to load the specified image file into the D3D texture structure defined at label C (similar to the texture loading shown in Listing 12.10).

Texture Resource Storage and Activation

At label B of Listing 12.14, we see an array of file texture resources. The `FindTex tureResource()` function searches the file texture resource array for a texture file name. If the name is not found, the image file will be opened, and a new texture resource will be created and stored into the file texture resource table. Listing 12.15 shows the implementation of the activate/deactivate texture methods. At label A,

```
class UWBD3D_GraphicsSystem {
    ⋮
A:  bool ActivateTexture(texName ...); // enable texture mapping
    void DeactivateTexture();          // disable texture mapping
    ⋮
    // table (array) of file textures
B:  UWB_PointerArray<UWBD3D_TextureResource*> m_texture_resources;
    // find texture in table
    UWBD3D_TextureResource* FindTextureResource(texture_name ...);
    ⋮
```

Source file.
uwbgl_GraphicsSystem3.h
file in the *D3D Files/
D3D_GraphicsSystem*
subfolder of the
UWBGL_D3D_Lib13 project.

Listing 12.14. Array of texture resources in UWBGL.

```
bool UWBD3D_GraphicsSystem::ActivateTexture( ... texFile ) {

        // find in table, or load
   A:   UWBD3D_TextureResource* pTexture = FindTextureResource( texFile );

        // Use of Color in Texel
   B:   m_pD3DDevice->SetTextureStageState(... D3DTSS_COLOROP ...);

        // Use of α in Texel
        m_pD3DDevice->SetTextureStageState(... D3DTSS_ALPHAOP ...);

        // select texture resource
        m_pD3DDevice->SetTexture(stage, pTexture->GetD3DTexture() );
        ⋮

void UWBD3D_GraphicsSystem::DeactivateTexture( DWORD stage ) {

        // Disable texture
   C:   m_pD3DDevice->SetTexture(stage, NULL);
        m_pD3DDevice->SetTextureStageState(...D3DTOP_DISABLE...);
        ⋮
```

Source file.
GraphicsSystem_TextureControls1.h
file in the *D3D Files/
D3D_GraphicsSystem* sub-
folder of the
UWBGL_D3D_Lib13 project.

Listing 12.15. Enabling and disabling texture mapping in UWBGL.

we search the texture resource table (label B of Listing 12.14) for the texFile.
This file will be opened and loaded if it does not already exist in the table. At label
B, we see code similar to that from Listing 12.11 that enables texture mapping.
The difference is that in this case, the α channel is also enabled to support alpha
blending with texels.

Per-Primitive Texture Attribute Support

Label C of Listing 12.16 shows two new attributes defined for all primitives:
whether file texture is enabled, and if so, the image file name. Label B shows the
access functions for the new attributes. At label A, we are reminded that before
drawing of a primitive, the SetupDrawAttribute() function is always called to
pass the attribute information to the DrawHelper class. Listing 12.17 shows the
D3D_DrawHelper class activating and deactivating texture-mapping functionality based on the primitive attribute. In this way, by the time a primitive is being
drawn, the D3D rendering state will have been properly programmed according
to the corresponding texture attributes.

```
class UWB_Primitive {
    ⋮
    // Sets attribute with DrawHelper
A:  virtual void SetupDrawAttributes(UWB_DrawHelper&);
    ⋮
    // Set file texture name
B:  void SetTextureFileName(texFile);
    // Get file texture name
    const wchar_t* GetTextureFileName();
    // Enable/disable texture mapping
    void EnableTexturing(bool on);
    ⋮
    bool IsTexturingEnabled() const;
  protected:
    ⋮
    // Texture map on/off attribute
C:  bool m_bTexturingEnabled;
    // Name of file texture
    std::wstring m_TexFileName;
    ⋮
```

Source file.
uwbgl_Primitive3.h
file in the *Common Files/
Primitives* subfolder of the
UWBGL_D3D_Lib13 project.

Listing 12.16. Per-primitive texture attributes.

```
bool UWBD3D_DrawHelper::EnableTexture(bool on)
    ⋮
  if( on )
      // Enable file texture
A:    UWBD3D_GraphicsSystem::GetSystem().ActivateTexture(m_TexFileName);
  else
      // Disable texturing
B:    UWBD3D_GraphicsSystem::GetSystem().DeactivateTexture();
    ⋮
```

Source file.
uwbgl_D3DDrawHelper5.cpp
file in the *D3D Files/
D3D_DrawHelper* subfolder
of the UWBGL_D3D_Lib13
project.

Listing 12.17. File texture attribute control.

Tutorial 12.5.
Project Name:
  D3D_TextureMapping
Library Support:
  UWB_MFC_Lib1
  UWB_D3D_Lib13

Figure 12.19.   Tutorial
12.5.

Tutorial 12.5. Alpha Blending and File Texturing with UWBGL

- **Goal.** Demonstrate programming primitives with alpha blending and file texture mapping.

- **Approach.** Support alpha blending and file texture mapping in the Primi tiveControl such that the user can control these attributes interactively.

Figure 12.19 is a screenshot of running Tutorial 12.5. Notice that all of the attribute controls are now enabled in the PrimitiveControl. Because *uv* placement is defined for each of the primitive types—point, line, rectangle, and circle—the user can examine texturing effects on all primitives types.

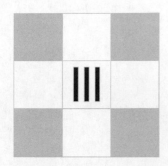

The Third Dimension

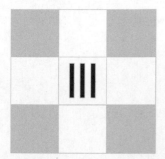

Introduction to Part III

By now, we know how to build moderately complex interactive graphics applications in 2D space. Part III of this text shows that the concept of a camera is the component required to extend our learning into the third dimension. All concepts learned in 2D space are generalized to 3D.

- **Simple application in 3D.** Chapter 13 uses a simple 3D scene to introduce the important elements in 3D interactive computer graphics application.

- **3D viewing.** Chapter 14 discusses different types of viewing volumes and projections. The coordinate system concepts learned in 2D are extended to accommodate the camera in 3D space.

- **Working with the computer graphics camera.** Chapter 15 extends our graphics library to support interaction with the camera in 3D space and working with multiple cameras.

- **Extending all concepts to 3D.** Chapter 16 extends the concepts learned into the third dimension. As we will see, with the exception of rotation, all concepts generalize into 3D in a straightforward manner.

13

A Simple 3D Application

Similar to Chapter 3, where we were introduced to 2D graphics programming with a minimal program, this chapter introduces us to 3D graphics programming with a minimal 3D program. This chapter:

- reviews that the model, camera, and scene are the basic elements in a 3D composition;

- presents the left- and right-handed coordinate systems;

- describes approaches to define a simple scene composition;

- demonstrates a simple computer graphics simulation of the defined scene.

After this chapter we should:

- understand the basic elements in a 3D scene composition;

- understand the basic approaches to define a simple scene composition.

In addition, with respect to hands-on programming, we should:

- be able to parse and understand a simple 3D program.

The photograph of Figure 13.1 shows two pieces of square paper on a desk. This photograph is the 3D version of the two drawn squares from Figure 3.1. Recall that in Chapter 3, we use Figure 3.1 as an example to illustrate the similarities between drawing two squares on a piece of paper and drawing two squares in an

Figure 13.1. The paper scene. A photograph of two pieces of papers on a desk (the larger one is 8 cm × 8 cm, and the smaller one is 5 cm × 5 cm).

application window. In this case, we will use the simple scene from Figure 13.1 to help us begin developing 3D computer graphics programs.

Figure 13.2 shows the set-up that took the photograph of Figure 13.1. Based on this simple set-up, we can identify some important elements in creating this photograph.

- **The model.** This is the subject of the photograph. In this case, we custom tailored two pieces of papers with specific sizes (8×8 and 5×5 cm).

- **The camera.** This is the imaging device. In this case, we have a simple pinhole-like camera with no focusing capability.

- **The scene.** This is the composition, or arrangement of the model, the camera, and the light sources. In this case, we have arranged the two pieces of paper to touch at their corners and placed the camera 25 cm away from the center of the large piece of paper. There is no light source in this scene.

As we will see, developing a 3D computer graphics program involves all of the above elements. The goal of this chapter is to analyze a computer graphics solution of Figure 13.1 such that we can relate programming code to these elements.

Light sources. We will examine examples of illumination models and light sources in Appendix A.

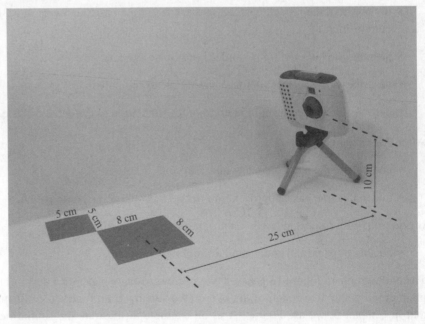

Figure 13.2. The set-up that took the picture of Figure 13.1.

We will learn the details of a typical computer graphics camera in the next chapter. At that point, we will integrate our solution with the UWBGL library.

13.1   3D Coordinate Systems

In order to configure the scene of Figure 13.2 in a computer program, we need to uniquely identify positions in 3D space. Recall from the discussion in Section 3.1 that the Cartesian coordinate system as illustrated in Figure 13.3 is a convenient tool to uniquely identify positions. To extend this coordinate system to the third dimension, we can introduce a new axis, the z-axis, that is perpendicular to both the x- and y-axes. As illustrated in Figure 13.4, we notice that there are two possible directions for the z-axis. On the left of Figure 13.4 the z-axis points inward, into the paper, and the z-axis on the right of the figure points outward, out of the paper. In this case, we see that with the same origin, for the position that is

- x_1 distance to the right of the origin;

- y_1 distance above the origin;

- z_1 distance *outward* from the origin;

the coordinate system on the left, with z-direction pointing inward, identifies the position as

$$(x_1, y_1, -\mathbf{z_1}),$$

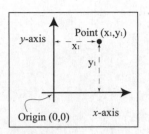

Figure 13.3. The convention for a 2D coordinate system.

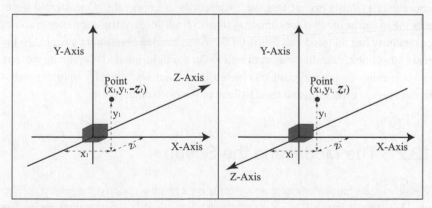

Figure 13.4. The two options for the z-axis direction to extend the 2D coordinate system to the third dimension.

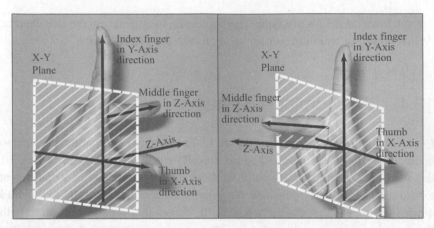

Figure 13.5. The left-handed and right-handed coordinate systems.

and because of the opposite z-axis direction, the system on the right identifies the position as

$$(x_1, y_1, \mathbf{z_1}).$$

In order to uniquely identify a position in 3D space, we must distinguish between these two options.

Figure 13.5 illustrates that if we let our thumb point in the x-direction, our index finger point in the y-direction, and our middle finger point in the z-direction, then the two options of Figure 13.4 can be represented by these three fingers of our left and right hands. For this reason, we term the two options of describing positions in three dimensional space the left-handed coordinate system and the right-handed coordinate system. There is no real difference between these two coordinate systems except that the z-directions are opposite. One should never mix the usage of the two coordinate systems. Traditionally, the computer graphics community has adopted and followed the right-handed coordinate system. In the rest of this book, coordinate system will mean the right-handed coordinate system.

One other computer graphics convention is that we typically map the y-axis to the vertical direction, and the xz-plane to the horizontal plane.

13.2   The Model and the Scene

With the right-handed coordinate system, we can now specify the set-up of Figure 13.2. Just as in the 2D case, our first task is to identify a convenient coordinate system. Once again, by convenience we are referring to a coordinate system that

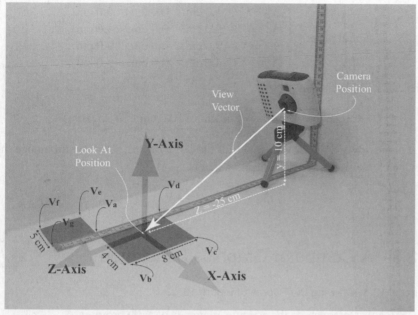

Figure 13.6.   The coordinate system and the positions of the model for the scene of Figure 13.1.

allows straightforward description of the location and orientation of the model and camera in the scene. Figure 13.6 shows a coordinate system where the following are true.

- The origin is located at the center of the 8 cm × 8 cm paper.

- The x- and z-axes are parallel to the edges of the papers. Notice that we have followed the computer graphics convention where the y-axis points upward from the xz horizontal plane.

- The unit of measurement is in centimeters.

With these choices, all the vertex positions of the papers can be conveniently identified:

$$
\text{Large paper:}
\begin{cases}
V_a = & (-4.0\,\text{cm}, \quad 0.0\,\text{cm}, \quad 4.0\,\text{cm}), \\
V_b = & (4.0\,\text{cm}, \quad 0.0\,\text{cm}, \quad 4.0\,\text{cm}), \\
V_c = & (4.0\,\text{cm}, \quad 0.0\,\text{cm}, \quad -4.0\,\text{cm}), \\
V_d = & (-4.0\,\text{cm}, \quad 0.0\,\text{cm}, \quad -4.0\,\text{cm}),
\end{cases}
$$

$$\text{Small paper:} \begin{cases} V_a = & (-4.0\,\text{cm}, & 0.0\,\text{cm}, & 4.0\,\text{cm}), \\ V_e = & (-9.0\,\text{cm}, & 0.0\,\text{cm}, & 4.0\,\text{cm}), \\ V_f = & (-9.0\,\text{cm}, & 0.0\,\text{cm}, & 9.0\,\text{cm}), \\ V_g = & (-4.0\,\text{cm}, & 0.0\,\text{cm}, & 9.0\,\text{cm}). \end{cases}$$

The camera is located at

$$\text{Camera position} = (0.0\,\text{cm}, \quad 10.0\,\text{cm}, \quad -25.0\,\text{cm})$$

and points toward the origin (center of the large paper). Once again, notice the counterclockwise vertex specification, that is,

$$V_a \rightarrow V_b \rightarrow V_c \rightarrow V_d.$$

13.3   A Computer Graphics Simulation

Tutorial 13.1.
Project Name:
  Rectangles3D
Library Support:
  UWB_MFC_Lib1

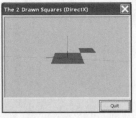

Figure 13.7. Rendered image of the two pieces of paper from Figure 13.1 with D3D.

Tutorial 13.1. Drawing the Papers of Figure 13.1

- **Goal.** Demonstrate the essential elements of a 3D program.

- **Approach.** Examine the drawing procedures of a simple program that simulates the photograph of Figure 13.1.

Figure 13.7 is a screenshot of running Tutorial 13.1. The source code of this tutorial is based on that from Tutorial 3.1 where there was *no* UWBGL library support. Recall that Tutorial 3.1 was our first 2D graphics program to draw the two squares of Figure 3.1. In this tutorial, we modify the source code to show a similar scene with two squares in a 3D graphics program. The simplicity of these two programs allows the clear illustration of the changes involved between similar 2D and 3D graphics programs. The source code shown in Listing 13.1 is identical to that of Listing 3.2 (on p. 81). To refresh our memories, this listing shows that the drawing area of Tutorial 13.1, GrfxWindowD3D, is a subclass of the MFC CWnd class. Recall from Figure 3.6 that in the absence of the elaborate UWBGL abstractions, we *replace* the drawing area into the application window (label A) and service the OnPaint() event (label B) to draw in this drawing area. The D3D-specific variables at label C are properly initialized during the construction of GrfxWindowD3D. Listing 13.2 is the OnPaint() service routine that renders the image of Figure 13.7. When compared with the same function from Tutorial 3.1 (Listing 3.3 on p. 82), we notice the identical four-step procedure. Once again, we verify that independent of the actual application, the principle of working

```
class CGrfxWindowD3D : public CWnd {
    :
A:  bool ReplaceDialogControl(:);    // Re-Places this window into the application
    :
B:  afx_msg void OnPaint();          // Event signifying redraw should occure
    :
C:  LPDIRECT3DDEVICE9 m_pD3DDevice; // D3D Device Context
};
```

Source file.
GrfxWindowD3D.h file in the *GrfxWindow* folder of the D3D_Rectangles3D project.

Listing 13.1. The GrfxWindowD3D class of Tutorial 13.1.

```
void CGrfxWindowD3D::OnPaint() {
    : // check to ensure drawing area is defined
```
Step 1: select graphics hardware render buffer.
```
m_pD3DDevice->BeginScene();
    :
// some details shown in Listing 13.4
```
Step 2: initialize selected hardware and set the coordinate system parameters.
```
m_pD3DDevice->SetFVF(D3DFVF_XYZ | D3DFVF_DIFFUSE);
m_pD3DDevice->SetRenderState(D3DRS_CULLMODE, D3DCULL_NONE);
    :
// matrix computation, loading of the WORLD, VIEW and PROJECTION matrix processors
```
details are in Listing 14.4
```
    :
```
Step 3: clear drawing buffer and draw two squares.
```
m_pD3DDevice->Clear( ... ); // detailed in Listing 13.5
    :
// First TRIANGLEFAN: The Large Square
v[0].m_point = D3DXVECTOR3(-4,0,4);    // Vertex V_a
v[1].m_point = D3DXVECTOR3(4,0,4);     // Vertex V_b
    :
```

Source file.
GrfxWindowD3D.cpp file in the *GrfxWindow* folder of the D3D_Rectangles3D project.

Listing 13.2. The GrfxWindowD3D::OnPaint() function of Tutorial 13.1.

```
m_pD3DDevice->DrawPrimitiveUP(D3DPT_TRIANGLEFAN, 2, ... );

// Second TRIANGLEFAN: The Small Square
⋮
v[3].m_point = D3DXVECTOR3(-4,0,9.0);   // Vertex Vg
m_pD3DDevice->DrawPrimitiveUP(D3DPT_TRIANGLEFAN, 2, ... );
⋮

// draw red line along x axis, green along y axis, and
// blue along z axis
```

┌──┐
│ **Step 4:** *present the drawing buffer in the application window.* │
└──┘
```
m_pD3DDevice->EndScene();
m_pD3DDevice->Present(NULL, NULL, NULL, NULL);
}
```

Listing 13.2. (cont.)

with graphics APIs always remains the same. In this case, the only differences between the two OnPaint() functions are the settings of the D3D matrix processors (in Step 2) and the vertex positions of the squares (in Step 3). The difference in vertex positions is simply the result of different coordinate systems: for the sake of convenience, we have chosen different origins and axis directions. The matrix processor settings of Step 2 require the understanding of computer graphics cameras, which is the subject of the next chapter.

This tutorial worked with all the elements we identified earlier in this chapter. In this case, the *model* is defined by the two TRIANGLEFAN primitives, the *camera* is abstractly defined by the operations of Step 2 (to be detailed in the next chapter), and the *scene* arrangements defined the positions of the squares and the camera.

Recall that in 2D, we clearly differentiated the definition of scene hierarchy (model) from the definition of WC window (for displaying). This clear separation allows multiple copies of the same object, for example, rotating CArm as bullets in Tutorial 11.9, with multiple WC windows viewing different parts of the scene. By analogy, in 3D, the definition of the model, the camera, and the arrangement of the scene should be clearly separated. The clear differentiation of these elements will allow multiple cameras to view different parts of the scene consisting of multiple copies of the same model. In the next chapter, we will learn the details and introduce abstraction for computer graphics cameras.

13.3.1 Implementation Details

There are a few more changes involved when extending our program to support the third dimension.

1. **Allocate the Z-buffer.** Listing 13.3 shows part of the OnCreate() function of the GrfxWindowD3D class (defined in GrfxWindowD3D.cpp). The last two lines in Listing 13.3 show that we must enable and allocate the Z-stencil or Z-buffer. As will be discussed later, this buffer is used for resolving visibility in 3D.

2. **Enable the Z-buffer.** At the beginning of rendering, we must make sure Z-buffer testing in the render state is enabled. Listing 13.4 shows some of the details of the CGrfxWindowD3D::OnPaint() function that were omitted in Listing 13.2. Here we see that one of the first operations we perform after BeginScene() is to set the ZENABLE to be true.

3. **Clear the Z-buffer.** Listing 13.5 shows the details of the parameters to the Clear() function during the OnPaint() redraw (once again, this detail is omitted from Listing 13.2). Here we see that when clearing buffers, the Z-buffer must also be cleared.

4. **Define the floor.** Notice that when drawing the rectangles in Step 3 of Listing 13.2, the positions are defined on the xz-plane (e.g., $(4,0,4)$) with the y-coordinate defined to be zero. Recall that in 2D space, we worked with rectangles on the xy-plane. The convention in 3D space reserves y to be the height, and xz to be the horizontal plane.

```
int CGrfxWindowD3D::OnCreate(...) {
    ⋮
    // creation and initialization
    D3DPRESENT_PARAMETERS present_params;
    ⋮
    // Set Windowed to TRUE, since we want to do D3d in a window
    present_params.Windowed = TRUE;
    ⋮
    present_params.EnableAutoDepthStencil = TRUE;
    present_params.AutoDepthStencilFormat = D3DFMT_D24S8;
    ⋮
```

Source file.
GrfxWindowD3D.cpp file in the *GrfxWindow* folder of the D3D_Rectangles3D project.

Listing 13.3. Allocate the Z-buffer.

```
int CGrfxWindowD3D:: OnPaint() {
    ⋮
    if(m_pD3DDevice && width > 0 && height > 0)  {
        //perform all of our drawing
        m_pD3DDevice->BeginScene();
        ⋮
        m_pD3DDevice->SetRenderState(D3DRS_ZENABLE, D3DZB_TRUE);
        m_pD3DDevice->SetRenderState(D3DRS_CULLMODE, D3DCULL_NONE);
        m_pD3DDevice->SetRenderState(D3DRS_LIGHTING, FALSE);
        ⋮
```

Source file.
GrfxWindowD3D.cpp file in
the *GrfxWindow* folder of the
D3D_Rectangles3D project.

Listing 13.4. Enable the Z-buffer.

```
int CGrfxWindowD3D:: OnPaint() {
    ⋮
```

Step 3: *clear drawing buffer and draw two squares.*

```
m_pD3DDevice->Clear(
    0,                  // 0 means clear the entire drawing area
    NULL,               // NULL means the entire drawing area
    D3DCLEAR_TARGET|    // clear target (color)
    D3DCLEAR_ZBUFFER,   // Clear the z-Buffer
    background,         // background color to clear to
    1.0f,               // Z values to clear to
    ⋮
```

Source file.
GrfxWindowD3D.cpp file in
the *GrfxWindow* folder of the
D3D_Rectangles3D project.

Listing 13.5. Clear the Z-buffer.

14

The Camera

This chapter discusses the concepts behind an abstract computer graphics camera. This chapter:

- analyzes the technical requirements of a computer graphics camera;

- explains the perspective and orthonormal visible volumes;

- presents the eye coordinate (EC) and 3D normalized device coordinate (NDC) spaces;

- describes the 3D NDC–to–2D device coordinate space projection.

After this chapter we should:

- understand that computer graphics represents the camera with the VIEW matrix;

- understand the transformation operations defined in the VIEW and the PROJECTION matrix processors.

This chapter does not include any hands-on implementations. Chapter 15 presents the implementation of the abstract concepts learned in this chapter. All objects we have worked with are abstract. For example, the squares in Figure 13.7 are defined by a few lines of code. As we have seen we can define a PrimitiveSquare class to represent the abstract idea of a square. Compared to a few lines of code, the PrimitiveSquare class would be easier to work with because it allows us to program with the characteristics of a square (e.g., size, color).

In a similar fashion, there is not a camera object in computer graphics. For example, in the source code of Tutorial 13.1, there is no camera object, and yet the image of Figure 13.7 clearly presents the results of a camera taking a picture. In this case, the functionality of the camera is realized in Step 2 of Listing 13.2, in the definition of the VIEW and PROJECTION matrix processors. This is true in general that the functionality of a camera is implemented by a few lines of code that compute and load the two matrix processors. However, just as in the case of primitives, we will refer to an abstract camera when discussing the involved functionality. In this way, we can begin analyzing the 3D computer graphics imaging process by referring to our existing experience working with real cameras.

In the real world, after arranging a camera, we count on the physical laws of optics and the chemical processes on the film (or optical properties of the charge-coupled device) to complete the photographic image-capturing process. In computer graphics, we have to algorithmically simulate the laws of physics and the imaging process to convert geometric representation of objects into pixels of an image. This process is referred to as rendering, where geometric objects are rendered into pixels in an image. In this chapter, we learn about the camera and the coordinate transformations of the rendering process. We will continue to refer to the simple 3D scene of Tutorial 13.1 and Figure 13.6 to learn about the details of the mathematics and matrix setups.

14.1   A Computer Graphics Camera

Based on our everyday experience, we know that when taking a photograph, we must consider the following.

- **Camera position**. Where to place the camera.

- **Look-at position**. Where to aim the camera.

- **Up direction**. Whether to rotate the camera for portrait or landscape photographs.

These parameters translate directly to a computer graphics camera.

Camera position.   This is the location of the camera. In typical computer graphics applications, we work with pinhole cameras, where all objects in the resulting image are in focus. In this case, the camera position is actually the location of the pinhole. Figure 14.1 shows that in Tutorial 13.1, the camera is located at (0 cm, 10 cm, −25 cm).

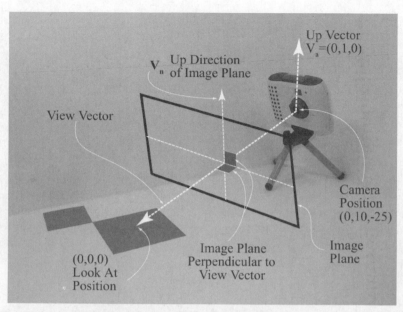

Figure 14.1. Parameters controlling a computer graphics camera.

Look-at position. This is where the pinhole camera is aiming. It is also referred to as the camera focus position. Figure 14.1 shows that the camera is aiming at the center of the large piece of paper, or at the origin of our coordinate system: (0 cm, 0 cm, 0 cm). The *viewing direction* is the direction from the camera (pinhole) position toward the look-at position. The vector describing this direction is referred to as the view vector. As illustrated in Figure 14.1, implicitly defined is the *image plane*, a plane perpendicular to the viewing direction. We can consider the image plane to be the plane upon which the final image is captured. This plane is like the film in the traditional camera, or the charge-coupled device (CCD) sensor array of the contemporary digital camera. In either case, it is a 2D rectangular area that is perpendicular to the viewing direction and upon which the photograph is captured. In the real world, the image plane is a physical part of the camera. For this reason, in computer graphics the term "camera" is sometimes used to refer to "the image taken by the camera." For example, in the following discussion, the "camera up vector" is really referring to the up direction of the image plane. In most cases, the distinction is subtle and unimportant. However, as in the case of the up vector, understanding the distinction helps understand the concept.

Up direction. This is the up direction of the camera and dictates the up direction of the image plane. For example, Figure 14.2 shows that we can change the up

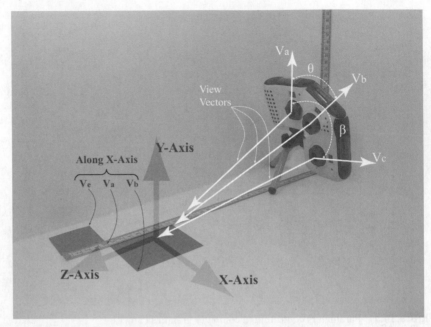

Figure 14.2. Rotating the camera to change the up direction.

Figure 14.3. The top photograph is taken from the camera with $0°$ twist angle (or up vector $= \mathbf{V}_a$); the middle photograph is taken from the camera with $\theta = 45°$ ($\mathbf{V}_b$); the bottom photograph is taken from the camera with $\beta = 90°$ ($\mathbf{V}_c$).

direction of the camera by rotating the camera. Figure 14.3 shows the resulting snapshots taken from the different camera up directions. In computer graphics, we specify the camera up direction as a vector, the up vector. For example, the three different up vectors in Figure 14.2 are

$$\mathbf{V}_a = (0,1,0),$$
$$\mathbf{V}_b = (1,1,0),$$
$$\mathbf{V}_c = (1,0,0).$$

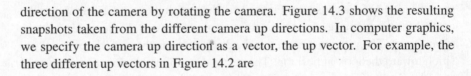

The up vector dictates the y-axis direction of the image plane, and eventually the photograph. For example, in Figure 14.1, the up direction of the image plane $\mathbf{V}_n$ is derived based on the camera up vector $\mathbf{V}_a$. As another example, the $\mathbf{V}_c$ up vector (x-direction) in Figure 14.2 says that the x-direction of WC should be the up direction of the image generated. Notice that in Figure 14.2, the $V_eV_aV_b$ edge is aligned along the x-axis direction. Now if we look at the corresponding image in Figure 14.3 (lowest of the three), we see the edges that correspond to $V_eV_aV_b$ are aligned along the up/down (or y) direction of the image. As programmers, we can specify any direction as the up vector to orientate our camera. In general, the up vector:

- cannot be parallel to the viewing direction;

- does not need to be normalized;

- does not need to be perpendicular to the view vector.

Recall that the image plane is perpendicular to the view vector. The above last point says that although the up direction of the image plane is derived based on the up vector, the two directions do not need to be parallel. For example, in Figure 14.2, we know that the view vector is looking downward from $y = 10$ toward $y = 0$. This means that none of $\mathbf{V}_a$, $\mathbf{V}_b$, or $\mathbf{V}_c$ is perpendicular to the view vector. Figure 14.4 illustrates the details for the case of the $\mathbf{V}_a$ up vector. In this case, $\mathbf{V}_n$ is perpendicular to the view vector and points in the up direction of the image plane. Here we see that although the direction of $\mathbf{V}_n$ is derived from that of $\mathbf{V}_a$, these two vectors are not parallel. We will explore the relationship between these two vectors in much more detail in Section 14.3.

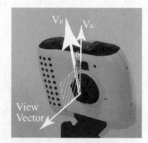

Figure 14.4. The up vector.

In general, it is nontrivial to derive the actual up direction of the image plane. As a result, the up vector we specify is almost never parallel to the actual up direction of the image plane. An alternative approach to specify the up direction is by describing a rotation. A *twist angle* describes a rotation of the y-axis with respect to the view vector. Typically a $0°$ twist angle refers to the y-axis, the default convention for up. For example, Figure 14.2 shows that in this case, the three camera orientations can also be described as angular offsets from the scene's y-axis, with $0°$ corresponding to $\mathbf{V}_a$, $\theta = 45°$ corresponding to $\mathbf{V}_b$, and $\beta = 90°$ corresponding to $\mathbf{V}_c$.

One last note on Figure 14.2: besides changing the camera twist, for the clarity of illustration, the three camera positions are also rotated with respect to the tripod support. In practice, the twist angle is measured with respect to the viewing direction, so changing the twist angle should not alter the camera position.

At the functional level, both the eye and the camera are image-capturing devices. We could have replaced all occurrences of "camera" with "eye" in the above presentation, and all of the discussions would still be valid. For example, "we can define an eye position, a look-at position, and orient our eye based on the up vector to capture an image." In fact, the camera position is often referred to as the eye position. In interactive computer graphics, "eye" and "camera" are often used interchangeably.

Tutorial 14.1. The Viewing Parameters

- **Goal.** Understand the camera parameters and verify the effect of changing these parameters.

Tutorial 14.1.
Project Name:
    AdjustCamera
Library Support:
    UWB_MFC_Lib1

Source file.
GrfxWindowD3D.cpp file in the *GrfxWindow* folder of the D3D_AdjustCamera project.

```
void CGrfxWindowD3D::OnPaint() {
    ⋮
    // Identical to Listing 13.2
    ⋮
```

Step 2: initialize selected hardware and set the coordinate system parameters.
```
    // Set WORLD matrix processor
    ⋮
    D3DXMATRIX matView;
    // camera parameters
    D3DXVECTOR3 camera_pos(...), target_pos(...), up_vector(...);
    // compute matView
A:  D3DXMatrixLookAtRH(&matView,...camera/target/up_vector...);
    // load matView to D3D VIEW processor
    m_pD3DDevice->SetTransform( D3DTS_VIEW, &matView );
    ⋮
    // Set PROJECTION matrix processor
```

Listing 14.1. Details of the VIEW matrix processor settings (Tutorial 14.1).

- **Approach.** Re-implement Tutorial 13.1 to support slider-bar control of the camera parameters. In this way, we can adjust the camera parameters and examine the resulting image.

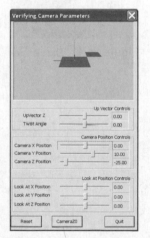

Figure 14.5.   Tutorial 14.1.

Figure 14.5 is a screenshot of running Tutorial 14.1. The implementation of this tutorial is modified from that of Tutorial 13.1 to include GUI slider bars that control the camera parameters. Listing 14.1 shows the programming code for setting the camera view. In this case, the camera parameter variables—camera_pos, target_pos, and up_vector—are controlled by the corresponding GUI slider bars. At label A, these parameters are used for the computation of the matView matrix, and then the matView matrix is loaded into the D3D VIEW matrix processor. The mathematical details of the matView matrix will be discussed in Section 14.3. Here, we are interested in verifying the effects of the camera parameters. Initially, these parameters are set to those as illustrated in Figure 13.6:

$$
\begin{aligned}
\text{camera position} &= (0, \quad 10, \quad -25) \\
\text{look-at position} &= (0, \quad 0, \quad 0) \; . \\
\text{up vector} &= (0, \quad 1, \quad 0)
\end{aligned}
$$

The "Reset" button resets all camera parameters to the above default values. The following discussion assumes the above camera settings.

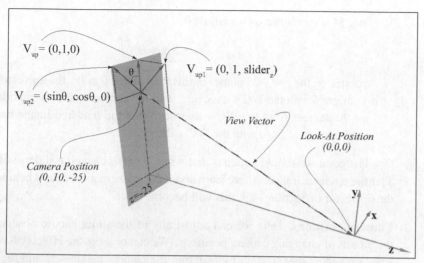

Figure 14.6. Up vector directions of Tutorial 14.1.

1. **Up vector controls.** The "UpVector Z" slider bar returns $slider_z$ value, and the "Twist Angle" slider bar returns θ. The up vector is set according to:

$$\text{up vector} = (\sin(\theta), \cos(\theta), slider_z).$$

- **UpVector Z.** Notice that this slider bar changes the z-component of the up vector without affecting the x- or y-components. For example, as illustrated in Figure 14.6, with $\theta = 0°$, when we change $slider_z$, the up vector will be changed to

$$V_{up1} = (0, 1, slider_z).$$

  Notice that with default initial camera settings, the rendered image does not change for different $slider_z$ values. Here we verify the following.

  (a) The up vector does not need to be normalized. As we change the $slider_z$, the size of the up vector also changes, but the rendered image remains the same.

  (b) The up vector does not need to be parallel to the up direction of the image plane. As we change $slider_z$ values, the direction of the up vector changes, and yet the derived image plane up direction remains the same, and thus the rendered image does not change.

- **Twist angle.** Here we illustrate a simple implementation of the camera twist angle that is defined with respect to the WC y-axis. Figure 14.6 shows that as we adjust θ,

$$V_{up2} = (\sin\theta, \cos\theta, 0)$$

rotates on the $z = -25$ plane. In this way, when $\theta = 0°$, the up vector is aligned with the WC y-axis, and $\theta = 90°$ corresponds to a rotation of 90 degrees from the WC y-axis such that the rendered image has up direction aligned with the WC x-direction.

One last point we should notice is that when $\theta \neq 0°$, changing slider$_z$ will alter the rendered image. As we learn about the mathematical details behind the up vector in Section 14.3, this will become clear.

2. **Camera positions.** Here we can adjust any of the slider bars to observe the effects of changing camera positions. We can observe the effects of *invalid* up vector specification by resetting the camera parameters and then increasing the camera z-position toward 0. Pay attention to the red and blue axes: as the camera position z-value approaches 0, notice that the blue and red axes flip direction as z changes sign and becomes positive. This sudden change of the rendered image is a result of an undefined camera specification. Recall that the default up vector is set to $(0,1,0)$, and as the z-component of the camera position approaches 0, the viewing direction approaches the negative y direction. This means that the up vector will become parallel to the view direction when the camera's z-component becomes zero. As described, the up vector should never be parallel to the view direction, and thus this correspond to an invalid camera definition. Because it can be difficult to adjust the slider bar to get exactly zero, the "CameraZ0" button is provided to set the camera z-component to zero. Click on the button to see that the graphics API is not able to render any object when the camera definition is invalid. Adjusting the camera z-position slider bar slightly in either direction will give us a valid rendered image.

3. **Look-at positions.** Change the look-at position to see the effect in the rendered image.

14.2 The Visible Volume

In the real world, all objects participate in the photographic process because all objects reflect/emit light energy toward the camera. The physical laws of optics govern objects' visibility, size, clarity, and so on in the final photograph. For example, a book behind my camera and a person a mile away from my viewing direction will reflect light energy toward the camera. However, the physics of the real world governs that the reflected energy from the book cannot arrive at the camera lens, and the reflected energy from the person that is too far away would be scattered and/or otherwise attenuated before it arrived at the camera lens. In this way, although both objects participated by reflecting energy toward the camera, neither will show up in the final photograph. In computer graphics, with limited computation resources and representation precision, we define a finite volume, a *visible volume*, to bound the simulation computation. As the name suggests, all objects within this finite volume will participate in the rendering process and thus may be visible in the final image. All objects outside of this volume will be clipped away and thus cannot participate in the rendering process and will not be visible in the final image.

14.2.1   Orthographic Projection: A Rectangular Visible Volume

Figure 14.7 illustrates an intuitive way to define a visible volume with respect to the camera parameters. In this case, a rectangular volume with the dimension of:

$$\text{width} \times \text{height} \times \text{depth} = W \times H \times (f - n)$$

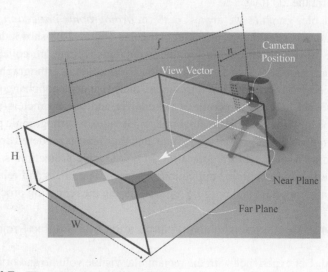

Figure 14.7. The rectangular visible volume.

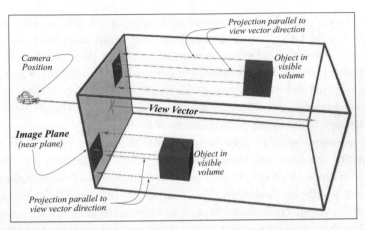

Figure 14.8. Orthographic projection.

is defined *n* units in front of the camera. Along the view vector are two perpendicular planes, the *near plane* and the *far plane*. These two planes are *n* and *f* units away from the camera position, respectively. Both the near and far planes are $W \times H$ units in size. Only objects inside this rectangular volume can participate in the rendering process.

Just like the image plane, the near plane is perpendicular the view vector. It is convenient to consider the near plane as the image plane. In computer graphics, 3D objects inside the visible volume are collapsed, or projected, onto the image plane to form the 2D image.

In computer graphics we always perform *orthographic projection* when the visible volume is specified as a rectangular cube. Figure 14.8 shows that for orthographic projection, objects inside the rectangular volume are collapsed onto the near plane along the view vector direction. Notice that in orthographic projection, as objects move away from the camera, their size does not change. In other words, a soccer ball right in front of the camera and one 20 meters away will appear to be the same size on the final image. Obviously, orthographic projection does not simulate the human vision system, and thus images rendered do not seem natural and do not appeal to regular users. Orthographic projection is important for engineering and scientific applications where measurement and relative sizes of objects are important and must be retained during the rendering process.

Tutorial 14.2. Rectangular Visible Volume and Orthographic Projection

- **Goal.** Get experience with the rectangular visible volume and orthographic projection.

- **Approach.** With the camera settings as in Tutorial 14.1, define a rectangular visible volume with orthographic projection where we can control all aspects of the volume.

Figure 14.9 is a screenshot of running Tutorial 14.2. Although the application window is somewhat larger, the implementation of this tutorial is only slightly different from that of Tutorial 14.1. Listing 14.2 shows the set-up of the PROJECTION matrix processor in the GrfxWindowD3D::OnPaint() function. The only difference between the implementation of this tutorial and that of Tutorial 14.1 is in the computation of the matrix for the PROJECTION processor. The variables that correspond to the parameters of the rectangular visible volume are controlled by the GUI slider bars. At label A, we see the visible volume parameters being referenced for the computation of the matProj matrix, and then the matProj matrix is loaded into the D3D PROJECTION matrix processor. As in Tutorial 14.1, we are not interested in the details of the matProj matrix. Rather, we want to verify the effects of changing the rectangular visible volume parameters.

We see that with the exact same camera setting as in Tutorial 14.1, the two rectangles in the rendered image do not resemble squares in 3D space. The major problem here is the absence of the distance hint. As humans, our visual system expects the farther edge of the squares to be shorter than the closer ones. In the image, those edges are of the same length. We can verify this is indeed an image of the two squares in 3D space by raising the camera position (increasing the value of camera *y*-position slider bar).

Tutorial 14.2.
Project Name:
   D3D_AdjustOrtho
Library Support:
   UWB_MFC_Lib1

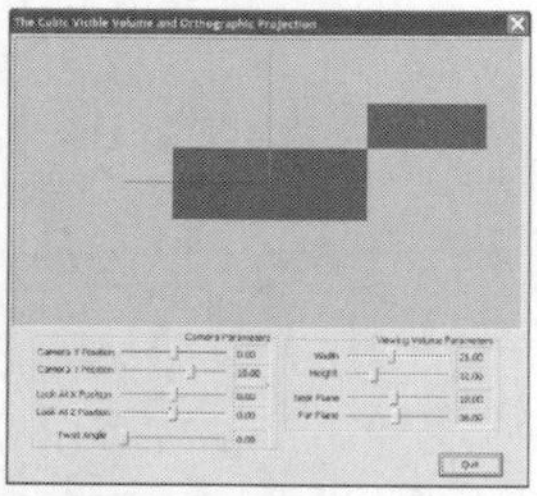

Figure 14.9. Tutorial 14.2.

```
void CGrfxWindowD3D::OnPaint() {
   ⋮
   // Identical to Tutorial 14.1
   ⋮

   Step 2: initialize selected hardware and set the coordinate system parameters.
   // Set WORLD and VIEW matrix processors... Identical to Tutorial 14.1
   ⋮

   D3DXMATRIX matProj;
   // Rect. visible volume parameters: m_ViewWidth, m_ViewHeight, m_ViewNearPlane, m_ViewFarPlane
   // compute matProj
A:  D3DXMatrixOrthoRH(&matProj, width/height/near/far);
   // load matProj to D3D PROJECTION processor
   m_pD3DDevice->SetTransform(D3DTS_PROJECTION, &matProj);
```

Source file.
GrfxWindowD3D.cpp file in the *GrfxWindow* folder of the D3D_AdjustOrtho project.

Listing 14.2. Details of the matrix processors settings (Tutorial 14.2).

As expected, when we increase the camera y-position, we begin to see more of the squares. However, as we continue to increase the camera y-position, we notice that the squares begin to disappear from the top region of the application window. Recall that the visible volume is defined with respect to the camera position. In this tutorial, by default, the visible volume has the near plane located at 18 units and the far plane located at 36 units from the camera position. As we move the camera position, the visible volume, being 18 units in front of the camera, is also moving away from the squares. As the camera and the visible volume move sufficiently far away, the squares are clipped by the far plane. We can verify this by increasing the far plane value to see the squares appearing again. We can also verify the near plane clipping by adjust the near plane slider bar. As we increase the near plane slider bar value, we see the front edge of the squares being cut away and disappear from the image.

The "Width" and "Height" slider bars control the width and height of the near and far plane (and thus the image plane). Notice that if the $\frac{width}{height}$ ratio is different from the aspect ratio of the application window, the squares will appear to be squashed or stretched.

From this tutorial, we verify the rectangular visible volume. We also see that images generated by orthographic projection do not seem natural and do not resemble our expectations of objects in 3D space. However, we also see the strength of size preservation. Notice that we can use a ruler and measure the relative edges of the two squares. For example, the front edge of the large square (8 units) is 1.6 times longer than that of the small square (5 units). In typical non-engineering/non-scientific computer graphics application, we seldom work with orthographic projection. In the rest of this book, we will only work with *perspective projection*.

14.2.2   Perspective Projection: A Viewing Frustum

Field of view (FOV). In practice, depending on the graphics API, field of view may either refer to the *vertical* angle that subtends the height of the image plane or the *horizontal* angle that subtends the width of the image plane. For example, D3D defines the field-of-view angle to be the vertical angle.

Figure 14.10 shows a *viewing frustum*, an alternative way of specifying a visible volume. As we can see, a viewing frustum is a cut-off pyramid where the apex is the camera position, with the view vector piercing from the camera position through the center of the pyramid. As in the case of the rectangular visible volume, the near plane and far plane are n and f units away from the camera, respectively, and are perpendicular to the view vector. The near plane cuts away the top portion of the pyramid. Once again, it is convenient to consider this plane being the image plane. The *field of view (FOV)* is the vertical angle that subtends the height of the near (image) plane from the camera position. As illustrated in Figure 14.10, this angle defines the angular height of the view frustum. The an-

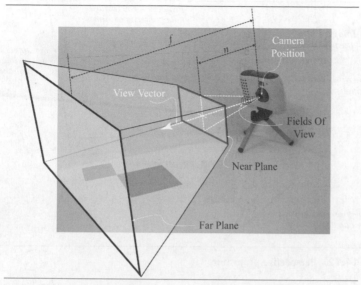

Figure 14.10. The viewing frustum.

gular width of the view frustum is defined by an aspect ratio. Once again, only objects inside this visible volume can participate in the rendering process.

Recall that the aspect ratio describes the width-to-height ratio of the drawing area, or,

$$\text{aspect ratio} = \frac{W_{dc}}{H_{dc}}.$$

As illustrated by Figure 14.11, with half of the vertical field-of-view angle being α, then, at a distance of n, the height of the near plane is

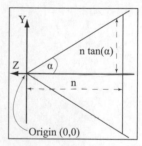

Figure 14.11. Near plane height.

$$n_h = 2n\tan(\alpha).$$

In the same way, the width of the near plane is

$$n_w = 2n\tan(\beta),$$

where β is half of the horizontal field-of-view angle. To maintain proper aspect ratio (so that spheres will appear round), the graphics API ensures that

$$\begin{aligned}
\text{aspect ratio} &= \frac{n_w}{n_h} \\
&= \frac{2n\tan(\beta)}{2n\tan(\alpha)} \\
&= \frac{\tan(\beta)}{\tan(\alpha)},
\end{aligned}$$

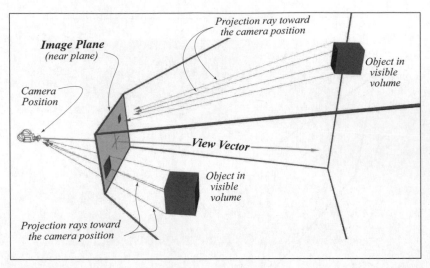

Figure 14.12. Perspective projection.

or

$$\tan(\beta) = \text{aspect ratio} \times \tan(\alpha),$$

or

$$\tan(\beta) = \frac{W_{dc}}{H_{dc}} \times \tan(\alpha). \tag{14.1}$$

It is important to note that although we do not explicitly specify the value for β, the graphics API does ensure the above relationship.

In computer graphics, we always perform *perspective projection* when the visible volume is specified as a viewing frustum. Figure 14.12 shows that perspective projection collapses each object toward the camera position. Notice that the projection direction is from the object toward the camera position. Conceptually, a projection ray is formed from each position on an object. This projection ray is a straight line between the position and the camera position. The position is collapsed onto the image plane along its projection ray. This means that the projection rays are distinct for different parts of an object and for objects located at different locations. This is in contrast to the orthographic projection, where all objects are projected along the same view vector direction. A direct result of per-object projection direction is that the projected object size differs depending on objects' position. As shown in Figure 14.12, in perspective projection, objects that are farther from the camera appear to be smaller. Perspective projection generates images that resemble photographs and thus are appealing to regular users.

Tutorial 14.3. Viewing Frustum and Perspective Projection

- **Goal.** Get experience with the viewing frustum and perspective projection.

- **Approach.** Supply GUI control slider bars for viewing frustum parameters of Tutorial 14.1.

Tutorial 14.3.
Project Name:
  D3D_AdjustPersp
Library Support:
  UWB_MFC_Lib1

Figure 14.13. Tutorial 14.3.

Figure 14.13 is a screenshot of running Tutorial 14.3. This tutorial is exactly the same as Tutorial 14.2 except for the initialization of the D3D PROJECTION matrix processor. Listing 14.3 shows the set-up of the PROJECTION matrix processor in the GrfxWindowD3D::OnPaint() function. The variables that correspond to the parameters of the viewing frustum are controlled by the GUI slider bars. At label A, we see the visible volume parameters being referenced for the computation of the matProj matrix, and then the matProj matrix is loaded into the D3D PROJECTION matrix processor. Once again, details of the mathematics concerning matProj will be discussed in Section 14.6. Here, we are interested in investigating the effects of changing the viewing frustum parameters.

The rendered image of Tutorial 14.3 does resemble the photograph of two squares in 3D space (Figure 13.1). We can observe the familiar property of objects becoming smaller as they are farther from the camera. As previously, we can raise the camera y-position value to look at the squares from a higher position. Once again, we notice that as the camera (and visible volume) moves away, the squares begin to move out of the viewing frustum and get clipped by the far plane. We can increase the far plane setting to continue seeing both of the squares. Just as in the case for Tutorial 14.2, increasing the near plane distance will eventually begin to clip away the front edges of the squares.

Source file.
GrfxWindowD3D.cpp file in the *GrfxWindow* folder of the D3D_AdjustPersp project.

```
void CGrfxWindowD3D::OnPaint() {
    ⋮
    // Identical to Tutorial 14.1 ...
    Step 2: initialize selected hardware and set the coordinate system parameters.
    // Set WORLD and VIEW matrix processors ... Identical to Tutorial 14.1
    ⋮
    D3DXMATRIX matProj;
    // Viewing Frustum parameters: m_ViewFOV, aspec_ratio, m_ViewNearPlane, m_ViewFarPlane
    // compute matProj
A:  3DXMatrixPerspectiveFovRH(&matProj, fov/aspect_ratio/near/far);
    // load matProj to D3D PROJECTION processor
    m_pD3DDevice->SetTransform(D3DTS_PROJECTION, &matProj);
```

Listing 14.3. Details of the matrix processors settings (Tutorial 14.3).

It is interesting that decreasing the FOV value creates a zoom-in effect. This is because as FOV decreases, so do the image plane and the width and height of the viewing frustum. A smaller viewing frustum sees smaller cross-sections of the scene, and the squares in the scene will occupy a more significant proportion of the image plane. When this image plane is mapped onto the application window, the small cross-sections of the screen end up being enlarged into the application window, thus the zoom-in effect. In contrast, increasing the FOV will create a zoom-out effect. Notice that unlike the orthographic projected image, it is difficult to measure relative sizes of objects on a perspective projected image. In this case, we can tell one square is closer to the camera than the other, but it is difficult to determine the relative sizes of these squares.

14.2.3   Discussion

Theoretically, just as in the real world, all objects can participate in the rendering process, whereas the simulation computation will ensure that only those within the view will occupy pixels in the final image. The visible volume optimizes this process by eliminating objects outside of the volume from being rendered. Notice that visible volumes (both the simple rectangular volume and the viewing frustum) are defined by distances measured with respect to the camera position. The far plane distance f must be greater than the near plane distance n, otherwise an invalid visible volume is specified and the output is undefined. The near plane distance must always be greater than 0. A 0 or negative near plane distance will result in an undefined image.

It is important to tightly bound the depth of the visible volume with optimized near and far planes. That is, the near plane should be as far away from the camera as the closest visible object, while the far plane should be as close to the camera as possible. Referring to Figures 14.10 and 14.7, we should maximize n and minimize f to create a visible volume with minimum depth range $(f - n)$. For example, in our scene with the two squares, initially we set the near plane distance to $n = 18$ and far plane to $f = 36$. This depth range of $36 - 18$ is reasonable for viewing the two squares. We have also seen that as we manipulate the camera position, the near/far plane distance settings run the risk of clipping away the squares. The reason to optimize the depth range is that in order to resolve front/back visibility, we must uniquely identify objects' positions in depth. The depth visibility hardware implementation relies on a fixed number of bits to resolve the near/far plane depth range. For example, the hardware may dedicate 16 bits to resolve the near/far depth range. We know that 16 bits can represent

$$2^{16} = 65536$$

unique positions. With a depth range of 18, the hardware will be able to resolve distances of

$$\delta = \frac{18}{65536} \approx 0.000275 \text{ units.}$$

In this case, the hardware will not be able to resolve depth distances of less than δ. That is, if objects are $x \pm \delta$ distances away from the camera, the hardware will *not* be able to determine which is in the front. If we did not optimize the near/far plane settings and set the near plane to 0.1 and far plane to 10^6, we would have the benefit of not having to worry about squares being clipped away by the near/far planes. However, it would also mean that the hardware must represent a 10^6 range based on 16 bits, or,

$$\delta = \frac{10^6}{65536} \approx 15.259 \text{ units.}$$

In this case, the hardware will not be able to determine front/back ordering if objects are less than 15.259 units apart!

Tutorial 14.4. Near/Far Plane Depth Range

- **Goal.** Understand the importance of near/far plane settings.

- **Approach.** Interactively manipulate near/far plane settings to observe the effects of hardware unable to resolve depth range.

Figure 14.14 is a screenshot of running Tutorial 14.4. In this case, we have adjusted the GUI slider bars such that the application window shows two squares where one square seems transparent, with an interesting pattern in the overlapping area. What we are seeing here is actually an error due to hardware precision.

In this tutorial, we change the two squares slightly such that

$$\text{Grey square:} \begin{cases} V_a = & (-4.0, \quad 0.001, \quad 4.0), \\ V_b = & (4.0, \quad 0.001, \quad 4.0), \\ V_c = & (4.0, \quad 0.001, \quad -4.0), \\ V_d = & (-4.0, \quad 0.001, \quad -4.0), \end{cases}$$

and

$$\text{Yellow square:} \begin{cases} V_a = & (-2.0, \quad 0.0, \quad -2.0), \\ V_b = & (6.0, \quad 0.0, \quad -2.0), \\ V_c = & (6.0, \quad 0.0, \quad 6.0), \\ V_d = & (-2.0, \quad 0.0, \quad 6.0). \end{cases}$$

Tutorial 14.4.
Project Name:
  D3D_AdjustDepth
Library Support:
  UWB_MFC_Lib1

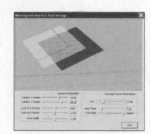

Figure 14.14. Tutorial 14.4.

In this way, the two squares partially overlap, with the gray square slightly above the yellow square. When the tutorial first starts, with the same initial camera and viewing frustum settings as that of Tutorial 14.3, we can see the gray square occluding part of the yellow square.

Near and far plane slider bars. See Figure 14.10. The "Near Plane" slider bar of Tutorial 14.4 controls the n value, whereas the "Far Plane" slider bar controls the f value.

Recall that the depth range is $f - n$. Now, let's increase this depth range by decreasing the value of n to move the near plane close to the camera. Notice that as the value of n reaches around 2.0, portions of the yellow square start to creep above the grey square. With the n value set back to something reasonable (around 18.0), increase the camera y-position to around 30. In this case, with $f = 36$, both of the square are clipped away by the far plane. Now if we increase the f value, we will see the squares again. However, if we continue to increase the f value to beyond 200 or 300, we start to observe the creeping through of the yellow square again. In both cases, we are observing the limitations of hardware precision in resolving large depth ranges. In both cases, we can avoid the problem by optimizing the $f - n$ distance.

The mathematics of the hardware algorithm is especially sensitive to small values associated with the near plane setting. It is always advantageous to maximize the n value. As a rule of thumb, n values of less than 0.1 should be avoided.

14.3　The Coordinate Transformation Pipeline

Just like many abstract concepts we have worked with, for example, transformation, computer graphics supports the camera and visible volume concepts based on coordinate spaces and corresponding transformation matrices. As in the case of geometric transformations, we are interested in the functions and properties of these coordinate spaces and matrices. This knowledge is important because it helps us to work with the matrices with confidence and to understand the behavior of our programs.

Eye versus camera. The terms *eye* and *camera* are often used interchangeably in interactive computer graphics. The EC can also be referred to as the *camera coordinate* space. Since the camera creates a *view*, the EC is also referred to as the *viewing coordinate* space. This book will use EC or eye space.

Before we begin, let's review that the D3D graphics API presents us, the programmers, with three identical matrix processors, the WORLD ($\mathbf{M}_W$), VIEW ($\mathbf{M}_V$), and the PROJECTION ($\mathbf{M}_P$) matrix processors. We have configured D3D to transform all vertices $\mathbf{V}_i$ in a fixed sequence:

$$\mathbf{V}_o = \mathbf{V}_i \, \mathbf{M}_W \, \mathbf{M}_V \, \mathbf{M}_P.$$

In all of the programs we have developed, $\mathbf{V}_i$ represents the vertices on the primitives, or $\mathbf{V}_i$ are vertices in the object coordinate (OC) space. As discussed in Chapter 10, the $\mathbf{M}_W$ matrix processor transforms OC positions to the world coordinate (WC) space. As will be discussed in the next section, in 3D space, $\mathbf{M}_V$

transforms vertices from WC to the *eye coordinate* (EC) space, and $\mathbf{M}_P$ transforms vertices from EC space to the NDC space. In this way, conceptually, $\mathbf{M}_W$ performs the *world transform*, $\mathbf{M}_V$ performs the *eye transform*, and $\mathbf{M}_P$ performs the *projection transform*, or

World transform. Because the result of this transform is the *model* of the world, this is also referred to as the *model transform*.

$$OC(\mathbf{V}_i) \xrightarrow{\overbrace{\mathbf{M}_W}^{\text{world}}} WC \xrightarrow{\overbrace{\mathbf{M}_V}^{\text{eye}}} EC \xrightarrow{\overbrace{\mathbf{M}_P}^{\text{projection}}} NDC(\mathbf{V}_o). \tag{14.2}$$

In computer graphics, we refer to this series of coordinate transformations as the coordinate transformation pipeline, or sometimes simply the transformation pipeline.

As discussed in Section 10.3, most graphics APIs (including OpenGL and D3D) expect the output of this transformation pipeline, $\mathbf{V}_o$, to be in the normalized device coordinate (NDC) space. The graphics API will then automatically transform the $\mathbf{V}_o$ from ± 1 NDC space to the device coordinate (DC) space for displaying on the output device. In other words, for $\mathbf{V}_i$ to be visible on the output display device, the transformed result, $\mathbf{V}_o$, must be in the NDC range, or

$$\mathbf{V}_o = \begin{bmatrix} x_o & y_o & z_o \end{bmatrix}, \text{ where } \begin{cases} -1 \leq x_o \leq +1, \\ -1 \leq y_o \leq +1, \\ -1 \leq z_o \leq +1. \end{cases}$$

We will begin our discussion by learning and reviewing coordinate spaces and how to transform between them. We will then use our first 3D program from Tutorial 13.1 to demonstrate how these coordinate spaces work together.

14.4 The World Transform: OC to WC

In Chapter 11, we defined the SceneNode class to transform primitives and organized the SceneNode objects into tree hierarchies. Recall that the SceneNode class works through the DrawHelper class to manipulate a matrix stack and sets the $\mathbf{M}_W$ matrix processor. In this way, the SceneNode class controls the world transform. Besides the facts that we now work in 3D space and we treat xz as the horizontal plane, all concepts discussed in Chapter 11 generalize to 3D space.

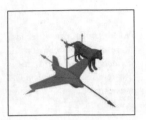

Figure 14.15. The image generated by the camera from Figure 14.16.

14.5   The Eye Transform: WC to EC

This is the second stage of the transformation pipeline where vertices are transformed from WC to EC. To understand this stage, we must first understand what the EC space is.

14.5.1   The Eye Coordinate (EC) Orthonormal Basis

In 3D space, an orthonormal basis is defined to be three perpendicular unit vectors (see the discussion in Section B.4). In this case, we are interested in deriving three perpendicular unit vectors anchored at the eye position.

As illustrated on the left of Figure 14.16, a camera is specified based on three parameters: camera (or eye) position p_e (x_e, y_e, z_e), look-at position p_a (x_a, y_a, z_a), and the up vector ($\mathbf{V}_{up}$). We have defined the view vector ($\mathbf{V}_v$) to point in the direction from the eye position toward the look-at position, or

$$\mathbf{V}_v = p_a - p_e.$$

The sign of the cross product. Remember that

$$\mathbf{V}_1 \times \mathbf{V}_2 = -(\mathbf{V}_2 \times \mathbf{V}_1).$$

Notice the definition for $\mathbf{V}_w$ and $\mathbf{V}_u$. To maintain right-handed coordinate directions, the order of the cross-product operation is important.

If we cross the view vector ($\mathbf{V}_v$) with the up vector ($\mathbf{V}_{up}$),

$$\mathbf{V}_w = \mathbf{V}_{up} \times \mathbf{V}_v,$$

then the vector $\mathbf{V}_w$ is perpendicular to both the view vector and the up vector. Remember that the user-specified up vector, $\mathbf{V}_{up}$, is usually not perpendicular to

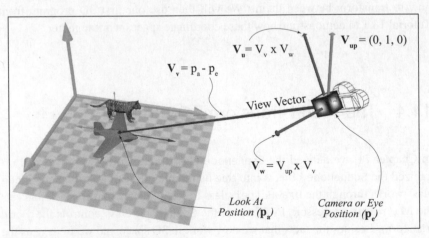

Figure 14.16. The orthonormal basis of eye (camera) space.

the view vector. We can compute the adjusted up vector:

$$\mathbf{V}_u = \mathbf{V}_v \times \mathbf{V}_w.$$

With normalization, we define

EC orthonormal basis: $\begin{cases} \hat{\mathbf{V}}_w = (x_w, y_w, z_w), \\ \hat{\mathbf{V}}_u = (x_u, y_u, z_u), \\ \hat{\mathbf{V}}_v = (x_v, y_v, z_v). \end{cases}$ (14.3)

EC orthonormal basis. The camera space, or camera coordinate, orthonormal basis and the EC orthonormal basis are used interchangeably.

These three unit vectors are perpendicular to each other, and the directions of these three vectors agree with the axes of the right-handed coordinate system. For example, if we consider $\hat{\mathbf{V}}_w$ to be in the x-direction, then $\hat{\mathbf{V}}_u$ is in the y-axis direction, and $\hat{\mathbf{V}}_v$ is in the z-axis direction.

14.5.2   Eye Coordinate (EC) Space

The *eye coordinate* (EC) space is defined with reference to the EC orthonormal basis. As illustrated in Figure 14.17, the EC is a right-handed coordinate system such that

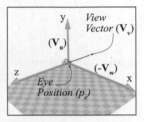

Figure 14.17.   The eye coordinate space.

- **Origin.** The eye position p_e is the origin.

- **Axes directions.** The view vector $\hat{\mathbf{V}}_v$ points in the *negative* z-direction, the adjusted up vector $\hat{\mathbf{V}}_u$ is in the y-direction, and the $\hat{\mathbf{V}}_w$ vector points in the x-direction.

In the EC space with the eye located at the origin looking toward the negative z-axis, the z-components tell us the distance to the eye:

- **Visible volume.** If the near and far planes are n and f units from the camera, then the near plane is located at $z = -n$, and the far plane at $z = -f$. We know that only objects with z-component within the range

$$-f \le \text{object}.z \le -n$$

are inside the visible volume. All other objects are outside of the visible volume and cannot participate in the rendering process.

- **Object depth ordering.** Objects' relative ordering from the camera can be easily determined from their z-component: the larger the value, the closer the object is to the camera. The Z-buffer algorithm takes advantage of this characteristic to resolve object occlusion when projecting 3D objects to the 2D image plane.

14.5.3   Aligning EC and WC Orthonormal Basis

In interactive computer graphics applications, the camera position, look-at position, and up vector are always defined in the WC space. For this reason, the EC orthonormal basis is always defined with respect to the WC space. The WC space is defined based on the basic Cartesian coordinate frame, or

$$\text{WC orthonormal basis:} \quad \begin{cases} \hat{\mathbf{V}}_x & = (1,0,0), \\ \hat{\mathbf{V}}_y & = (0,1,0), \\ \hat{\mathbf{V}}_z & = (0,0,1). \end{cases}$$

wb2eb.   *wb2eb abbreviates world basis to eye basis.*

As discussed in Section B.4, with the EC orthonormal basis as defined in Equation (14.3), the transformation matrix $\mathbf{M}_{wb2eb}$,

$$\mathbf{M}_{wb2eb} = \begin{bmatrix} x_w & x_u & -x_v & 0 \\ y_w & y_u & -y_v & 0 \\ z_w & z_u & -z_v & 0 \\ 0 & 0 & 0 & 1 \end{bmatrix},$$

aligns the EC orthonormal basis with that of WC, where $\hat{\mathbf{V}}_w$ points in the $\hat{\mathbf{V}}_x$ direction, $\hat{\mathbf{V}}_u$ in the $\hat{\mathbf{V}}_y$ direction, and $\hat{\mathbf{V}}_v$ in the $\hat{\mathbf{V}}_z$ direction. Because $\mathbf{M}_{wb2eb}$ is an orthonormal matrix, in this case, the EC-to-WC orthonormal basis transformation is

$$\mathbf{M}_{eb2wb} = \mathbf{M}_{wb2eb}^{-1} = \begin{bmatrix} x_w & y_w & z_w & 0 \\ x_u & y_u & z_u & 0 \\ -x_v & -y_v & -z_v & 0 \\ 0 & 0 & 0 & 1 \end{bmatrix}.$$

Figure 14.18.   The image generated by the camera from Figure 14.19.

14.5.4   The WC-to-EC Transform

With the understanding of EC space, we are now ready to examine the actual WC-to-EC transform. Notice that in the EC orthonormal basis (Equation (14.3)), the view vector $\mathbf{V}_v$ points from the camera toward the look-at position, whereas in the EC space, the viewing direction is defined to be looking toward the negative z-axis. This means that when aligning the EC orthonormal basis with EC space, $\mathbf{V}_v$ should be aligned with the negative z-axis.

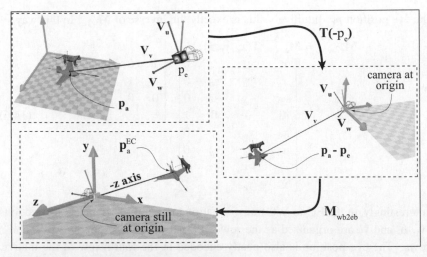

Figure 14.19. WC-to-EC transformation.

Figure 14.19 shows that to transform vertex positions from $\mathbf{V}_{wc}$ (WC) to $\mathbf{V}_{ec}$ (EC), we first translate the eye position p_e to the origin by applying the $\mathbf{T}(-p_e)$ translation and then align the WC and EC orthonormal basis by $\mathbf{M}_{wb2eb}$, or

$$
\begin{aligned}
\mathbf{V}_{ec} &= \mathbf{V}_{wc}\,\mathbf{T}(-p_e)\,\mathbf{M}_{wb2eb} \\
&= \mathbf{V}_{wc}\,\mathbf{M}_{w2e},
\end{aligned}
$$

so

$$
\mathbf{M}_{w2e} = \mathbf{T}(-p_e)\,\mathbf{M}_{wb2eb}. \tag{14.4}
$$

The inverse transform of $\mathbf{M}_{w2e}$ is $\mathbf{M}_{e2w}$, an operator that transforms vertices from EC to WC:

$$
\begin{aligned}
\mathbf{M}_{e2w} &= \mathbf{M}_{w2e}^{-1} \\
&= (\mathbf{T}(-p_e)\,\mathbf{M}_{wb2eb})^{-1} \\
&= \mathbf{M}_{wb2eb}^{-1}\,\mathbf{T}^{-1}(-p_e) \\
&= \mathbf{M}_{eb2wb}\,\mathbf{T}(p_e).
\end{aligned} \tag{14.5}
$$

eb2wb. *eb2wb* is the reverse of *wb2eb* and abbreviates *eye basis to world basis.*

Equation (14.5) says that to transform from EC back to WC, we first apply $\mathbf{M}_{eb2wb}$ to align the EC orthonormal basis with that of the WC, and then we translate by the eye position p_e. Intuitively, this is exactly the inverse of $\mathbf{M}_{w2e}$. In this way,

$$
\begin{aligned}
\mathbf{M}_{e2w} &= \mathbf{M}_{eb2wb}\, \mathbf{T}(x_e, y_e, z_e) \\
&= \begin{bmatrix} x_w & y_w & z_w & 0 \\ x_u & y_u & z_u & 0 \\ -x_v & -y_v & -z_v & 0 \\ 0 & 0 & 0 & 1 \end{bmatrix} \begin{bmatrix} 1 & 0 & 0 & 0 \\ 0 & 1 & 0 & 0 \\ 0 & 0 & 1 & 0 \\ x_e & y_e & z_e & 1 \end{bmatrix} \\
&= \begin{bmatrix} x_w & y_w & z_w & 0 \\ x_u & y_u & z_u & 0 \\ -x_v & -y_v & -z_v & 0 \\ x_e & y_e & z_e & 1 \end{bmatrix}.
\end{aligned}
\tag{14.6}
$$

Interestingly, in the EC-to-WC transformation matrix, the original axis directions ($\hat{\mathbf{w}}$, $\hat{\mathbf{u}}$, and $\hat{\mathbf{v}}$) are organized as the row vectors in the corresponding x, y, and z rows. The eye position is also neatly encoded in the fourth row of the matrix. This information will become important when we need to transform mouse clicks back to WC space (to be discussed in Section 15.4).

14.6 The Projection Transform: EC to NDC

This is the third and final stage of the transformation pipeline where vertices are transformed from EC to NDC space. Let's first review the NDC space. In 3D space, the NDC is defined to be

$$
\text{NDC range} = \begin{cases} -1 \le x \le +1, \\ -1 \le y \le +1, \\ -1 \le z \le +1. \end{cases}
$$

As discussed in Section 10.2, NDC is a well-known coordinate space where the ± 1 range is convenient for performing further transformations. Most modern graphics APIs expect output from the transformation pipeline to be in the NDC space. In this way, the APIs can clip to eliminate all vertices that are outside of the NDC range and convert all primitives inside the NDC range into the application drawing area.

As illustrated in Figure 14.20, the projection transform scales the view frustum into a rectangular cube. Notice that in this transformation, the x/y and z values of vertices are treated differently. The z value of vertices is scaled proportionally from the length far $-$ near to 1.0, or

$$
z_{ndc} = z_{ec}\, \frac{1.0}{\text{far} - \text{near}}.
$$

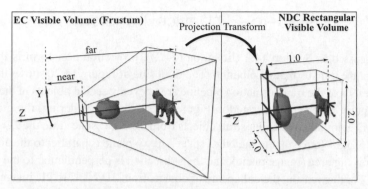

Figure 14.20. View frustum–to-NDC transform.

However, the x/y values of vertices are scaled according to their corresponding z-distance from the origin. Those that are farther away along the z-axis (from the origin) are scaled down more so than those that are closer to the origin. For example, pay attention to the checker floor. In EC space (left of Figure 14.20), the floor is a rectangle where the teapot end is closer to the origin and the tiger end is farther from the origin. After the transformation, in the NDC space (right of Figure 14.20), the rectangular floor has been transformed into a trapezoidal shape with the tiger end being scaled smaller than the teapot end. We see that the projection transform performs disproportional scalings according to the z-distances of objects. Besides the floor, we can further verify this disproportional scaling by comparing the relative sizes of the tiger and the teapot. In the EC space, the tiger is slightly larger. In the NDC space, because the tiger has a large z-distance, it is scaled to be smaller than the teapot. Recall that we are transforming from EC to NDC, and that in EC the eye position is located at the origin. By reducing x/y values of vertices in proportion to the corresponding z-distances, in fact, we are simulating the foreshortening of human vision system where objects that are farther away appear smaller.

As will be discussed in the next section, the image in Figure 14.21 is computed based on collapsing all objects in the NDC cube along the z-axis. In this image, we can observe that the tiger is indeed slightly smaller than the teapot and that the trapezoidal shape does convey a sense that the floor is parallel to our viewing direction. The disproportional scaling of projection transform properly simulates the foreshortening effect of the human vision system.

Just as the view transformation is defined by the WC-to-EC transformation matrix (Equation (14.4)), the projection transform is also defined by a 4×4 matrix. Because this transform is from EC to NDC, we refer to this matrix as the $\mathbf{M}_{e2n}$ matrix.

Figure 14.21. The image generated by the camera from Figure 14.20.

14.7   3D NDC–to–2D Device Transform

As discussed in Section 14.3 (Equation (14.2)), projection transform is the last
stage of the transformation pipeline. The right side of Figure 14.20 shows that the
final results of the transformation pipeline are unevenly scaled objects in the NDC
rectangular cube. As illustrated in Figure 14.22, during rendering, the graphics
API will automatically collapse all objects from 3D NDC space into the 2D image
(near) plane. Notice that in the NDC space, the xy-plane is parallel to the application drawing area (image plane), and the z-direction is perpendicular to the image
plane. For this reason, the collapsing of objects from 3D NDC to 2D image plane
involves the following two steps.

1. Transform NDC (x_{ndc}, y_{ndc}) to the drawing area device (with dimensions of
   $W_{dc} \times H_{dc}$). In Section 10.1, we studied the requirements of this transformation:
   $$\begin{bmatrix} x_{dc} & y_{dc} \end{bmatrix} = \begin{bmatrix} x_{ndc} & y_{ndc} \end{bmatrix} \mathbf{M}_{n2d},$$

   where $\mathbf{M}_{n2d}$ is defined by Equation (10.6) (on p. 264):
   $$\mathbf{M}_{n2d} = \mathbf{S}\left(\frac{W_{dc}}{2}, \frac{H_{dc}}{2}\right) \mathbf{T}\left(\frac{W_{dc}}{2}, \frac{H_{dc}}{2}\right).$$

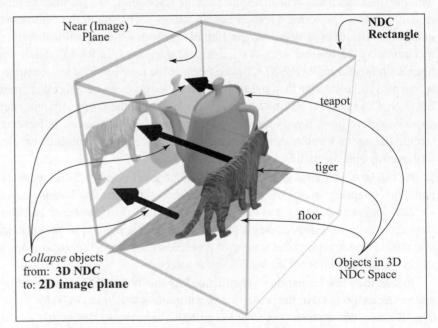

Figure 14.22. Collapsing objects in 3D NDC to 2D DC space.

In this way,

$$
\begin{aligned}
x_{dc} &= x_{ndc} \times \frac{W_{dc}}{2} + \frac{W_{dc}}{2} = (x_{ndc}+1) \times \frac{W_{dc}}{2}, \\
y_{dc} &= y_{ndc} \times \frac{H_{dc}}{2} + \frac{H_{dc}}{2} = (y_{ndc}+1) \times \frac{H_{dc}}{2}.
\end{aligned}
$$

2. Resolve visibility/occlusion along the NDC z-axis. To determine which object is visible on the drawing area, their relative front-to-back ordering must be resolved. For example, from Figure 14.21, we can see that the teapot occludes part of the floor. The graphics API uses the Z-buffer hardware to record the z-value for each pixel. When the Z-buffer depth stenciling is enabled, before a color is assigned to a pixel, the corresponding z-value is compared. A pixel's color will be modified only when the corresponding primitive's z-value is closer to the origin.

The NDC-to-DC transformation described here is the final stage of both the orthographic projection (of Figure 14.8) and the perspective projection (of Figure 14.12). The difference between these two projections is in the EC-to-NDC transform. Orthographic projection proportionally scales all vertices in the EC space into the NDC cube. As discussed in Section 14.6, perspective projection scales vertices in EC space disproportionately according to their z-distance from the origin. In both cases, the NDC-to-DC transformations are identical.

14.8　Re-Examining Tutorial 13.1

Recall that Tutorial 13.1 is our fist encounter with a 3D program (presented in the previous chapter). We are now finally ready to examine Step 2 of Listing 13.2 where we programmed the matrix processors. Listing 14.4 shows the details of Step 2 from Listing 13.2. We see that the matrix processors are set up to transform vertices from object coordinate (OC) space to the NDC:

$$
OC \overset{\mathbf{M}_W}{\longrightarrow} WC \overset{\mathbf{M}_V}{\longrightarrow} EC \overset{\mathbf{M}_P}{\longrightarrow} NDC.
$$

$$
\overbrace{\phantom{OC \overset{\mathbf{M}_W}{\longrightarrow}}}^{\text{Label A}} \overbrace{\phantom{WC \overset{\mathbf{M}_V}{\longrightarrow}}}^{\text{Label B}} \overbrace{\phantom{EC \overset{\mathbf{M}_P}{\longrightarrow}}}^{\text{Label C}}
$$

Because they are set up to transform coordinates, we will refer to the contents of the WORLD, VIEW, and PROJECTION matrix processors as $\mathbf{M}_{o2w}$ (content of the top of matrix stack), $\mathbf{M}_{w2e}$ (Equation (14.4) on p. 401), and $\mathbf{M}_{e2n}$, respectively. In this way, with the input vertex in OC space $\mathbf{V}_{oc}$, the output from the WORLD matrix processor $\mathbf{V}_{wc}$ is a vertex position in WC space:

$$
\mathbf{V}_{wc} = \mathbf{V}_{oc}\,\mathbf{M}_W = \mathbf{V}_{oc}\,\mathbf{M}_{o2w}.
$$

Source file.
GrfxWindowD3D.cpp file in
the *GrfxWindow* folder of the
D3D_Rectangles3D project.

```
// ... From Listing 13.2 ...
```

> ***Step 2:*** *initialize selected hardware and set the coordinate system parameters.*

> **A: $\mathbf{M}_W$:** *Transforms from Object Coordinate (OC) to World Coordinate (WC).*

```
     D3DXMATRIX identity;
     // identity matrix: I4
```

> **A1:** D3DXMatrixIdentity(&identity);

```
     // load I4 to D3D WORLD processor
     m_pD3DDevice->SetTransform( D3DTS_WORLD, &identity);
```

> **B: $\mathbf{M}_V$:** *Transforms from WC to Camera (Eye) Coordinate (EC).*

```
     D3DXMATRIX matView;
     // camera parameters
     D3DXVECTOR3 camera_pos(...), target_pos(...), up_vector(...);
     // compute matView
```

> **B1:** D3DXMatrixLookAtRH(&matView,...camera/target/up_vector...);

```
     // load matView to D3D VIEW processor
     m_pD3DDevice->SetTransform( D3DTS_VIEW, &matView );
```

> **C: $\mathbf{M}_P$:** *Transforms from EC to Normalized Device Coordinate (NDC).*

```
     D3DXMATRIX matProj;
     // view frustum parameters
     float fov=..., aspect=..., near/far_plane=...;
     // compute matProj
```

> **C1:** D3DXMatrixPerspectiveFovRH(&matProj, fov/aspect/near/far);

```
     // load matProj to D3D PROJECTION processor
     m_pD3DDevice->SetTransform(D3DTS_PROJECTION, &matProj);
```

Listing 14.4. Details of matrix processor set-up (Tutorial 13.1).

$\mathbf{V}_{wc}$ is input to the VIEW matrix processor, where the output $\mathbf{V}_{ec}$ is in EC space:

$$\mathbf{V}_{ec} = \mathbf{V}_{wc}\,\mathbf{M}_V = \mathbf{V}_{wc}\,\mathbf{M}_{w2e},$$

and lastly, $\mathbf{V}_{ec}$ is input to the PROJECTION matrix processor with output $\mathbf{V}_{ndc}$ in the NDC space:

$$\mathbf{V}_{ndc} = \mathbf{V}_{ec}\,\mathbf{M}_P = \mathbf{V}_{ec}\,\mathbf{M}_{e2n}.$$

We see that the input vertex in OC space $\mathbf{V}_{oc}$ is indeed transformed by the (coordinate) transformation pipeline:

$$\mathbf{V}_{oc} \xrightarrow{\mathbf{M}_W(\mathbf{M}_{o2w})} \mathbf{V}_{wc} \xrightarrow{\mathbf{M}_V(\mathbf{M}_{w2e})} \mathbf{V}_{ec} \xrightarrow{\mathbf{M}_P(\mathbf{M}_{e2n})} \mathbf{V}_{ndc}.$$

We have worked with OC space extensively via the SceneNode class in Chapter 11. Recall that each SceneNode object has an instance of XformInfo that

takes advantage of the matrix stack in computing appropriate OC-to-WC transformations to load into the D3D WORLD matrix processor. In this case, we did not
define individual OC spaces for the two squares and thus $\mathbf{M}_W$ is set to the identity
matrix at label A.

At label B, the variables that correspond to the camera parameters are initialized to with values that correspond the set up from Figure 13.6. At label B1 the
D3DXMatrixLookAtRH() function uses these values to compute the matView matrix. The computed *matView* would transform vertices from WC to EC in exactly
the same manner as discussed in Equation 14.4. In general graphics APIs support
many alternatives for specifying the camera, for example, the information convey
by look at position can be specified with a view vector; or the up vector can be
replaced with a twist angle, and so on. There are also many ways to compute the
$\mathbf{M}_{w2e}$ matrix. However independent from the approach, the resulting matrix is
always Equation 14.4. The $\mathbf{M}_{w2e}$ matrix encodes all information concerning the
viewing camera, and thus this matrix is also referred to as the *view* or the *viewing*
matrix. The view matrix is essentially our abstract representation for the camera.

At label C the matProj matrix is computed by the D3DXMatrixPerspective
ForRH() function. The computation is based on a viewing frustum that encloses
the two squares. The matProj serves the purpose of the $\mathbf{M}_{e2n}$ matrix (Section 14.6), this matrix transforms the cut-off pyramid into the NDC cube and is
also referred to as the projection matrix. As in the case of the view matrix, there
are many approaches to computing the projection matrix. However and very importantly, unlike the view matrix, some of the contents of the projection matrix are
graphics API-dependent. This is due to the fact that the NDC to DC conversion
process involves graphics hardware and they can be different for implementation
efficiency reasons. For example, OpenGL defines the z range of NDC space to be:

$$-1 \leq z \leq +1$$

whereas the NDC z range for D3D is

$$0 \leq z \leq +1.$$

In this case, because of the different NDC z range, the corresponding projection
matrices are slightly different. Notice that with the same visible volume specifications, the x and y components in the matrices will be the same.

Tutorial 13.1 is a 3D computer graphics program designed to compute the
photograph of Figure 13.1 in 3D. It is interesting that when we compare the implementation to that of Tutorial 3.1, a 2D computer graphics program designed to
draw squares in a 2D window, the only real difference is in the ways the transfor-

mation matrices are computed. In the 2D program, we computed:

$$OC \xrightarrow{\mathbf{M}_W} WC \xrightarrow{\mathbf{M}_V \mathbf{M}_P} NDC$$

with $\mathbf{M}_P$ set to $\mathbf{I}_4$. In the case of 3D, we compute:

$$OC \xrightarrow{\mathbf{M}_W} WC \xrightarrow{\mathbf{M}_V} EC \xrightarrow{\mathbf{M}_P} NDC.$$

Notice that in both 2D and 3D cases, the transformation matrices are setup to transform vertices from OC to NDC space. This is not a coincidence. The graphics API dictates that the output of the transformation must be in NDC space. As programmers, we choose the input to be in OC space to support convenient definition and manipulation of graphical objects.

15

Working with the Camera

This chapter discusses one implementation of the abstract computer graphics camera presented in the previous chapter. This chapter:

- presents the UWBGL implementation of a simple computer graphics camera;

- explains how to build applications that include multiple cameras;

- describes and experiments with approaches to interactively manipulate the camera with the mouse;

- derives the 2D device coordinate to 3D world coordinate transform.

After this chapter we should:

- understand the basics of implementing a computer graphics camera;

- understand the essentials of interactive manipulation of a camera.

In addition, with respect to hands-on programming, we should:

- be able to develop programs with multiple cameras;

- be able to program the manipulation of the camera either interactively by the user or algorithmically by our application;

- be able to support mouse-click selection of 3D objects.

Although the concepts behind the view and projection matrices are new and non-trivial, the graphics API programming mechanisms involved for 3D are actually quite similar to our experience from 2D. In fact, much of what we have learned in 2D applies to 3D:

- **Primitive class.** We will continue to design graphical objects based on the Primitive class.

- **SceneNode class.** We will continue to use the SceneNode class to work with the matrix stack and load the WORLD matrix processor with the proper OC-to-WC transformation matrices.

- **CModel class.** We will continue to define a CModel class to instantiate, arrange, and simulate the interactions of the graphical objects based on the semantics of the application.

In this way, we will continue to use the SceneNode class to define models, and the Model class to arrange the scene of our application. Listing 15.1 shows pseudocode of a typical WindowHandler class we worked with in 2D space. Recall that we designed this class to bind the GUI API drawing area (at label A) with the graphics API device (at label B). A WC window (at label C) is defined to present a different part of the scene to the GUI drawing area. We have defined transformation functions (at label D) to support proper output drawing and input mouse clicks. During each redraw in the DrawGraphics() function, we must set up the matrix processors (at label E) before we can invoke the CModel to draw the scene (at label F). Recall that in our CModel::DrawModel(), we redraw every object in the scene. It is the matrix processor settings, $\mathbf{M}_{w2n}$, that ensures only appropriate objects are transformed into the bounds of the NDC space and thus are visible on the GUI drawing area. Listing 15.2 shows a typical WindowHandler class we would work with in 3D space. We have labeled the programming code to correspond to that of Listing 15.1 for the convenience of clear comparison. Instead of the 2D WC window, at label C a UWB_Camera is defined to present the 3D view in the GUI drawing area. The transformation functions at label D are now defined for 3D cases. During redraw, in the DrawGraphics() function, the only difference between 2D and 3D is how the matrix processors are set up at label E. In the 3D case, we must load both the view and projection matrices to transform from WC to NDC. The tutorials from the rest of this chapter will examine this functionality in more detail.

```
class CDrawHandler : public UWBD3D_WindowHandler {
  public:
    DrawGraphics(); // To draw the application window
  protected:
    // The application window in MFC
```
A: `WBMFC_UIWindow m_Window;`

   To remind ourselves:

```
    // the following are defined in the super classes:
    // UWB_WindowHandler and UWBD3D_WindowHandler


    // This is the link to the D3D Device
```
B: `LPDIRECT3DDEVICE9 m_pD3DDevice;`

   ⋮

```
    // The WC Window bounds
```
C: `UWB_BoundingBox  m_WCWindow;`

```
    // Computes and Loads: Mw2n to MV
```
D: `LoadW2NDCXForm( ... );`

```
    // Transform points from DC to WC
    DeviceToWorld( ... );
}
```

Source file. Pseudocode; no corresponding source file.

```
CDrawHandler::DrawGraphics() {
    ⋮
    // initialized to I4
```
E: `D3DXMATRIX identity; D3DXMatrixIdentity(&identity);`

```
    // MW ⟵ I4 (initialize OC to WC transform)
    m_pD3DDevice->SetTransform(D3DTS_WORLD,&identity);
    // MV ⟵ Mw2n (WC to NDC)
    LoadW2NDCXform();

    // Clears the hardware buffer
    m_pD3DDevice->Clear( ... );
    // draws the scene with models defined by SceneNode and Primitive
```
F: `theApp.GetModel().DrawModel();`

```
    ⋮
}
```

Listing 15.1. The pseudocode of a typical 2D WindowHandler.

Source file.
Pseudocode; no corresponding source file.

```
class CDrawHandler : public UWBD3D_WindowHandler {
    // code similar to Listing 15.1 are not shown here
    To remind ourselves:
    // the following are defined in the super classes:
    // UWB_WindowHandler and UWBD3D_WindowHandler

    // The camera of the drawing area
C:  UWB_Camera   m_Camera;

    // Computes and loads: M_{w2e} to M_V
D:  LoadViewXform();
    // Computes and Loads: M_{e2n} to M_P
    LoadProjectionXform();
    // Transform points from DC to WC (in 3D)
    DeviceToWorld(...);
}
```

```
CDrawHandler::DrawGraphics() {
    ⋮
    // initialize I_4
E:  D3DXMATRIX identity; D3DXMatrixIdentity(&identity);
    // M_W ⟵ I_4 (initialize OC to WC transform)
    m_pD3DDevice->SetTransform(D3DTS_WORLD,&identity);
    // M_V ⟵ M_{w2e} (WC to EC)
    LoadViewXform();
    // M_P ⟵ M_{e2n} (EC to NDC)
    LoadProjectionXform();

    // Clears the hardware buffer
    m_pD3DDevice->Clear( ... );
    // ... exact same drawing prcedure as in 2D
    theApp.GetModel().DrawModel();

    ⋮
}
```

Listing 15.2. The pseudocode of a typical 3D WindowHandler.

15.1 UWBGL Camera Implementation

UWBGL_D3D_Lib14

This is our first library that supports 3D interaction. The major changes in the library include two new classes:

Change summary. See p. 527 for a summary of changes to the library.

- UWB_Camera. To support camera and viewing frustum.

- UWB_PrimitiveAxisFrame. To support drawing of an orthonormal basis.

and modifications to

- UWB_WindowHandler **and** UWBD3D_WindowHandler. To support working with the new UWB_Camera class.

- UWB_XformInfo. To support rotation in 3D.

The details of the UWB_Camera and WindowHandler classes will be explained over the next few tutorials in this chapter. Here is an overview of these two classes. Listing 15.3 shows that the new UWB_Camera class has three major groups

```
class UWB_Camera {
  public:
      A: Setting the camera and matrix processors: to be discussed in Tutorial 15.1
      void SetCameraParameters(const vec3& pos, const vec3 &at, const vec3 &up);
      void SetViewFrustumInDegree(float fov, float n, float f);
      B: Drawing the camera: to be discussed in Tutorial 15.3
      void Draw( eLevelOfDetail lod, UWB_DrawHelper& draw_helper ) const;
      C: Manipulating the camera with mouse: to be discussed in Tutorial 15.3
      void BeginMouseRotate(int x, int y);
      void BeginMouseTrack(int x, int y);
      void BeginMouseZoom(int x);
      :
  protected:
  D:  vec3 m_CameraPos, m_LookAt, m_UpVector;          // parameters for the camera
      float m_ViewFOV, m_ViewNearPlane, m_ViewFarPlane;  // parameters for the view frustum
      :
};
```

Source file. Camera1.h file in the *Common Files/ Camera* subfolder of the UWBGL_D3D_Lib14 project.

Listing 15.3. The UWB_Camera class of Lib14.

```
class UWB_WindowHandler : public UWB_IWindowHandler {
  public:
    ⋮
```

> **A:** *Support for camera and visible volume: to be discussed in **Tutorial 15.1***

```
    virtual void SetCamera(const UWB_Camera &c);
    virtual UWB_Camera& GetCamera();
    virtual void LoadViewXform() const = 0;
    virtual void LoadProjectionXform() const = 0;
```

> **B:** *Support for mouse click input: to be discussed in **Tutorial 15.4***

```
    virtual void DeviceToWorld(int dcX, int dcY, vec3& wcPt, vec3& wcRay) const;
};
```

Listing 15.4. The UWB_WindowHandler class of Lib14.

Source file.
WindowHandler5.h   file
in the *Common Files/Win-dowHandler* subfolder of the
UWBGL_D3D_Lib14 project.

of functionality. At label A are supports for setting and getting the camera and visible volume parameters. At label B is the support for drawing the camera. As we will see, this is an important functionality for visualizing the relative positions between the camera and the scene. At label C are supports for interactive manipulation of the camera. As shown at label D, internally, the UWB_Camera class is represented by the simple parameters of the camera and view frustum. As we will see in subsequent tutorials, the functions under labels A, B, and C interpret and modify the variables at label D. In this way, the UWB_Camera class is an abstract representation of a camera but has no knowledge of any graphics API or any transformation matrices. It is the WindowHandler class that accesses the camera and view frustum parameters, computes the necessary matrices, and loads the graphics API matrix processors to establish the coordinate transformation pipeline necessary for 3D rendering. Listing 15.4 shows the modification to the UWB_WindowHandler class for the proper support of the new UWB_Camera class. At label A are functions that set/get camera association and compute/set the matrix processors. At label B is the support for transforming points from DC to WC space. We will describe the details of these functions with appropriate examples in subsequent tutorials.

Recall that in 2D space, with translation vector **t**, scaling factor **s**, rotation angle θ, and pivot position p, Equation (9.10) says the transformation operator defined by the XformInfo object would be

$$\mathbf{M}_{t1} = \mathbf{T}(-p)\,\mathbf{S}(\mathbf{s})\,\mathbf{R}(\theta)\,\mathbf{T}(p)\,\mathbf{T}(\mathbf{t})\,\mathbf{M}_t,$$

where $\mathbf{M}_{t1}$ is the computed top of matrix stack and $\mathbf{M}_t$ is the initial top of matrix stack. In the 2D case, because we only work in 2D x/y space, the only valid axis of

```
class UWB_XformInfo {
    ⋮
    void SetUpModelStack( UWB_DrawHelper& draw_helper ) const;
    ⋮
    // Access the rotation angle
A:  void GetRotationInRadians(float& x, float& y, float& z) const;
    // Set the variables for rotations
    void SetRotationRadians(float x, float y, float z);
    // Represent rotation angles
B:  float m_xrotation_radians, m_yrotation_radians, m_zrotation_radians;
};
```

Source file.
XformInfo3.h/cpp   file
in   the   *Common   Files/
XFormInfo* subfolder of the
UWBGL_D3D_Lib14 project.

```
void UWB_XformInfo::SetUpModelStack(UWB_DrawHelper& draw_helper) const {
    vec3 rotation(m_xrotation_radians, m_yrotation_radians, m_zrotation_radians);
C:  draw_helper.AccumulateModelTransform(m_translation, m_scale, rotation, m_pivot);
}
```

Listing 15.5. The `UWB_XformInfo` support for 3D rotation.

rotation is the z-axis. For this reason, in 2D space we only need one floating-point number, θ, to represent the rotation angle. The rotation $\mathbf{R}(\theta)$ is a rotation defined with respect to the z-axis. Listing 15.5 shows the expansion to the XformInfo class to support rotation in 3D space. Labels A and B show a straightforward approach to implement rotations in 3D space where we use three floating-point numbers to represent rotation angles with respect to each of the three major axes. At label C, we see that the actual computation of the transformation operator is performed by the AccumulateModelTransform function of DrawHelper. Listing 15.6 shows that we generalize the z rotation of Equation (9.10) with three separate rotations. At label A, we concatenate rotations with respect to the x-, y-, and z-axes consecutively. The computed transformation operator becomes

$$\mathbf{M}_{t7} = \mathbf{T}(-p)\,\mathbf{S}(s)\,\mathbf{R}^z(\theta_z)\,\mathbf{R}^y(\theta_y)\,\mathbf{R}^x(\theta_x)\,\mathbf{T}(p)\,\mathbf{T}(t)\,\mathbf{M}_t, \qquad (15.1)$$

where $\mathbf{M}_{t7}$ and $\mathbf{M}_t$ are the final and initial tops of the matrix stack. Notice that we did not provide any justification for the ordering of the three rotations. Would different rotation orderings, for example, $\mathbf{R}^x\mathbf{R}^y\mathbf{R}^z$ versus $\mathbf{R}^z\mathbf{R}^y\mathbf{R}^x$, produce the same results? As it turns out, it is nontrivial to accomplish intuitive interactive rotation in 3D space, and the above simple rotation support is inadequate. We will examine this topic in much more detail in the next chapter.

Source file.
uwbgl_D3DDrawHelper6.cpp
file in the *D3D Files/
DrawHelper* folder of the
UWBGL_D3D_Lib14 project.

```
bool UWBD3D_DrawHelper::AccumulateModelTransform(vec3 trans,
    vec3 scale, vec3 rotation, vec3 pivot) {
    ⋮
    // the three major axes variables
    D3DXVECTOR3 xaxis(1,0,0), yaxis(0,1,0), zaxis(0,0,1);
    ⋮
    // M_{t1} ← T(t_x,t_y,t_z)M_t
    m_pMatrixStack->TranslateLocal(trans.x, trans.y, trans.z);
    // M_{t2} ← T(p_x,p_y,p_z)M_{t1}
    m_pMatrixStack->TranslateLocal(pivot.x, pivot.y, pivot.z);
    // M_{t3} ← R^x(θ_x)M_{t2}
A:  m_pMatrixStack->RotateAxisLocal(&xaxis, rotation.x);
    // M_{t4} ← R^y(θ_y)M_{t3}
    m_pMatrixStack->RotateAxisLocal(&yaxis, rotation.y);
    // M_{t5} ← R^z(θ_z)M_{t4}
    m_pMatrixStack->RotateAxisLocal(&zaxis, rotation.z);
    // M_{t6} ← S(s_x,s_y,s_z)M_{t5}
    m_pMatrixStack->ScaleLocal(scale.x, scale.y, scale.z);
    // M_{t7} ← T(-p_x,-p_y,-p_z)M_{t6}
    m_pMatrixStack->TranslateLocal(-pivot.x, -pivot.y, -pivot.z);
    // M_W ← M_{t7}
    pDevice->SetTransform( D3DTS_WORLD, m_pMatrixStack->GetTop());
    ⋮
```

Listing 15.6. Lib14 implementation of 3D rotation.

For now, with the above implementation, we can only rotate with respect to one of the axes. That is, we can accomplish intuitive rotation control as long as one and only one of θ_x, θ_y, or θ_z has nonzero value. As we will see in the next tutorial, as soon as more than one θ has nonzero value, the rotation results become almost impossible to interpret.

Tutorial 15.1.
Project Name:
  D3D_CameraLib
Library Support:
  UWB_MFC_Lib1
  UWB_D3D_Lib14

Tutorial 15.1. Integration with UWBGL

- **Goal.** Demonstrate working with the UWB_Camera and UWB_WindowHandler classes and that our simple implementation of rotations in 3D does not support intuitive user interactions.

- **Approach.** Implement the simple 3D scene of Figure 13.1 based on the UWBGL library and support full GUI controls for model manipulations.

Figure 15.1 is a screenshot of running Tutorial 15.1. At the lower portion of the application window, we see all the camera and viewing frustum controls from Tutorial 14.3, and on the right we see the familiar 2D GUI controls for scene nodes, XformInfo, and primitive attributes (e.g., from Tutorial 11.7).

The two squares are defined based on the existing PrimitiveRectangleXZ class. The LargeSq and SmallSq nodes present initial identity transformation operators to allow the user to interactively manipulate the two squares. Now, select the LargeSq node and activate the rotation radio button. Now, if we adjust the x slider bar, as expected we can see the large square rotate with respect to the x-axis of the orthonormal basis. Leave the x slider bar at some nonzero value, e.g., at $x = 50$. Now, adjust the z slider bar. We can see the square rotating with respect to the center of the square, but not with respect to the z-axis of the orthonormal basis. If we leave the z slider bar at some nonzero value (e.g., $z = 65$) and start adjusting the y slider bar, we will see that the square seems to rotate quite arbitrarily with no obvious relationship to the orthonormal basis. At this point, it is virtually impossible to interactively control the rotation of this square. In computer graphics, we refer to this situation as the gimbal lock. As mentioned, we will learn about 3D rotation in detail in the next chapter.

Figure 15.1. Tutorial 15.1.

As described, the UWB_Camera class only stores the parameters for the current camera and view frustum settings. It is up to the WindowHandler class to interpret the parameters, compute the transformation matrices, and load the graphics API matrix processors. Recall that to properly support graphics API–independent programming, we have designed the WindowHandler to be a hierarchy. In this case, the new 3D responsibility is spread among the classes:

Class	Purpose	New functions in 3D
UWB_WindowHandler	API-independent	Set/Get Camera
UWBD3D_WindowHandler (*subclass of* UWB_WindowHandler)	D3D-specific	Compute/Load View/Projection matrix processors
CDrawOnlyHandler CDrawAndMouseHandler (*subclasses of* UWBD3D_WindowHandler)	Output only Input/Output Application-specific	DrawGraphics() Service mouse events

Listing 15.7 shows the implementation of the API-independent UWB_WindowHandler class. At label C, we see an instance of the API-independent UWB_Camera and the corresponding support functions at label A. At label B are important functions that require graphics API knowledge. The implementation of these functions is deferred to API-specific subclasses. The implementation source file, uwbgl_WindowHandler5.cpp at the lower half of Listing 15.7, shows the

Source file.
uwbgl_WindowHandler5.h/cpp
files in the *Common Files/
WindowHandler* subfolder
of the UWBGL_D3D_Lib14
project.

```
class UWB_WindowHandler : public UWB_IWindowHandler {
    // copy camera settings
A:  virtual void SetCamera(const UWB_Camera &c);
    // Get a reference of the camera
    virtual UWB_Camera& GetCamera();
    // Transforms a DC point to WC
B:  virtual void DeviceToWorld(...) const;
    // Compute and load the VIEW matrix processor
    virtual void LoadViewXform() const = 0;
    // Compute and load the PROJECTION matrix processor
    virtual void LoadProjectionXform() const = 0;
  protected:
       ⋮
    // An instance of the camera object
C:  UWB_Camera      m_Camera;
};
```

```
// This is the uwbgl_WindowHandler5.cpp source file.
   ⋮

void UWB_WindowHandler::SetCamera(const UWB_Camera &c) { m_Camera = c; }
UWB_Camera& UWB_WindowHandler::GetCamera() { return m_Camera; }
   ⋮
```

Listing 15.7. The UWB_WindowHandler class of Lib14.

implementation of camera support functions. Listing 15.8 shows the implementation details of the UWBD3D_WindowHandler class, our D3D-specific subclass of the UWB_WindowHandler class. The main responsibilities of this class are to compute/load the view/projection matrices (labels A and B) and support inverse transformation from DC to WC space (label C).

- **View matrix (label A).** The LoadViewXform() function computes the view matrix viewMat (at label A1) and loads this matrix into the VIEW matrix processor (at label A2). The viewMat is computed by the ComputeView Matrix() function, where at label A1a we access the camera parameters (defined in the UWB_WindowHandler superclass) and at label A1b we call the D3DXMatrixLookAtRH() function to compute the actual matrix. Notice that we are calling the exact same function as that of label B1 in Listing 14.4. In this case, we have abstracted the exact same functionality into

```
class UWBD3D_WindowHandler : public UWB_WindowHandler {
  public:
```
```
A:   virtual void LoadViewXform() const;
```
```
B:   virtual void LoadProjectionXform() const;
```
```
C:   virtual void DeviceToWorld(int dcX, int dcY, vec3& wcPt, vec3& wcRay) const;
```
```
    ⋮
};
```

```
void UWBD3D_WindowHandler::LoadViewXform() const {
```
```
A1:   ComputeViewMatrix(viewMat);
```
```
A2:   m_pD3DDevice->SetTransform(D3DTS_VIEW, &viewMat);
```
```
}
```

Source file.
uwbgl_D3DWindowHandler6.h/cpp files in the *D3D Files/ WindowHandler* subfolder of the UWBGL_D3D_Lib14 project.

```
void UWBD3D_WindowHandler::ComputeViewMatrix(D3DXMATRIX &mat) const {
```
```
A1a:   m_Camera.GetCameraPosition(p.x, p.y, p.z); // m_Camera is an instance variable
        m_Camera.GetCameraLookAt(a.x, a.y, a.z);  // defined in the super class: UWB_WindowHandler
        m_Camera.GetCameraUpVector(u.x, u.y, u.z);
```
```
A1b:   D3DXMatrixLookAtRH( &mat, &p, &a, &u );
```
```
A1c:   // now factor in camera rotations ... details to be discussed in Tutorial 15.3
```
```
}
```

```
void UWBD3D_WindowHandler::LoadProjectionXform() const {
```
```
B1:   ComputeProjectionMatrix(projMat);
```
```
B2:   m_pD3DDevice->SetTransform(D3DTS_PROJECTION, &projMat);
```
```
}
```

```
void UWBD3D_WindowHandler::ComputeProjectionMatrix(D3DXMATRIX &mat) const {
```
```
B1a:   m_Camera.GetViewVolumeFOVInRadian(v); // m_Camera is an instance of UWB_Camera class
        m_Camera.GetViewVolumeNearPlane(n);  // defined in the super class: UWB_WindowHandler
        m_Camera.GetViewVolumeFarPlane(f);
```
```
B1b:   D3DXMatrixPerspectiveFovRH(&mat, v, GetAspectRatio(), n, f);
```
```
}
```

```
void UWBD3D_WindowHandler::DeviceToWorld(int dcX, int dcY, vec3& wcPt, vec3& wcRay) const {
```
```
C1:   // details to be discussed in Tutorial 15.4
```
```
}
```

Listing 15.8. The UWBD3D_WindowHandler class of Lib14.

Source file.
DrawOnlyHandler.h/cpp
files in the *WindowHandler*
folder of the D3D_CameraLib
project.

```
class CDrawHandler : public UWBD3D_WindowHandler  {
  public:
    ⋮
A: void DrawGraphics();
    ⋮
  protected:
B: UWBMFC_UIWindow m_window;        // The drawing area
};

  void CDrawHandler::DrawGraphics() {
    ⋮
    BeginDraw();
C: LoadViewXform();
    LoadProjectionXform();
D: D3DXMATRIX identity;  D3DXMatrixIdentity(&identity);
    m_pD3DDevice->SetTransform( D3DTS_WORLD, &identity);
    m_pD3DDevice->Clear( ... );
E: theApp.GetModel().DrawModel();
    EndDrawAndShow();
}
```

Listing 15.9. The CDrawHandler class of Tutorial 15.1.

different classes to support programmability. The resulting matrix is the view matrix $\mathbf{M}_{w2e}$, as defined by Equation (14.4). The final step of computing the view matrix at label A1c involves rotations to support mouse interactions. We will examine this last step in Tutorial 15.3.

- **Projection matrix (label B).** The LoadProjectionXform() function computes the projection matrix projMat (at label B1) and loads this matrix into the PROJECTION matrix processor (at label B2). The projMat is computed by the ComputeProjectionMatrix() function, where at label B1a we access the view frustum parameters from the UWB_Camera class, and at label B1b we call the D3DXMatrixPerspectiveFovRH() function to compute the actual perspective projection matrix. Notice that as above, we are calling the exact same function as that label C1 in Listing 14.4. Once again, the UWBGL library merely reorganizes graphics API function calls to support abstractions.

```
class CTutorialDlg : public CDialog {
    ⋮
A:   virtual BOOL OnInitDialog();      // MFC function to initialize the application
     private:
B:   CDrawHandler m_MainView;          // The WindowHandler from Listing~15.9
C:   CSceneTreeControl m_TreeControl; // GUI controls for SceneNode, XformInfo, and Primitive
    ⋮
```

```
BOOL CTutorialDlg::OnInitDialog() {
D:   if( !m_MainView.Initialize( ... IDC_GRFX_PLACEHOLDER) ) ...
E:   if (!UWBMFC_ReplaceDialogControl(... IDC_PLACEHOLDER, m_TreeControl, ... ) ) ...
F:   m_MainView.GetCamera()...

    ⋮ // initialize camera and GUI controls
```

Source file.
TutorialDlg.h/cpp files
in the *Source Files* and
Header Files folders of the
D3D_CameraLib project.

Listing 15.10. The CTutorialDlg class of Tutorial 15.1.

- **DC-to-WC transform (label C).** We will discuss the details of this function in Tutorial 15.4.

With the above WindowHandler classes support, an application would invoke the proper functions to render a 3D scene. Listing 15.9 shows that the CDrawHandler class of Tutorial 15.1 is a subclass of the UWBD3D_WindowHandler class. The most important function of this class is the DrawGraphics() function (at label A). With the support from superclasses, that is, the camera in UWB_WindowHandler and the view/projection matrix compute/load functions in UWBD3D_WindowHandler, it is straightforward to compute and load the matrices required for the 3D rendering transformation pipeline (at labels C and D) and drawing of the model (at label E).

Recall that in our MFC-based applications, we use the MFC CDialog object as our application window and replace the D3D drawing area and GUI controls into the CDialog object. Listing 15.10 shows that the CTutorialDlg class subclasses from the MFC CDialog class. Recall that in MFC dialog–based applications, the OnInitDialog() function (at label A) will be called to initialize the application. We see that our application window has a CDrawHandler (at label B) for D3D drawing and a CSceneTreeControl (at label C) object supporting user interaction with UWBGL objects (SceneNode, XformInfo, and Primitive). In the implementation of the OnInitDialog() function, we first initialize the CDrawHandler() (at label D). Recall that this function will initialize the D3D rendering context and replace the MFC drawing area (at label B in Listing 15.9) onto the CTutorialDlg window. Similarly, the function call at label E will replace the CSceneTreeControl object into the CTutoralDlg window. At label F, we have the opportunity to initialize the camera.

Notice that the two squares and the associated scene hierarchy are defined in the CModel class and that the instance of CModel is defined in the CTutorialApp class. In this way, we can think of the CModel as the world, and the m_MainView (CDrawHandler) object as a camera with an associated image area looking at the CModel. This agrees with our MVC architecture, where the CModel is the model and the CDrawHandler is an output-only view/controller pair. Now, we should be able to define multiple view/controller pairs to examine the model.

15.2   Working with Multiple Cameras

Tutorial 15.2.
Project Name:
   D3D_TwoCamera
Library Support:
   UWB_MFC_Lib1
   UWB_D3D_Lib14

Tutorial 15.2. Working with Two Cameras

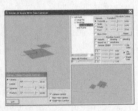

Figure 15.2.   Tutorial
15.2.

- **Goal.** Demonstrate the MVC architecture framework where we can support multiple view/controller pairs looking at the model.

- **Approach.** Instantiate multiple WindowHandler objects to look at the two simple squares CModel scene from multiple viewpoints.

Figure 15.2 is a screenshot of running Tutorial 15.2. This tutorial implements two different cameras looking at the simple square scene, the main view at the left of the application window, and the small view underneath the CSceneTreeControl. To conserve on-screen real estate, the camera and view frustum control parameters have been organized into a pop-up control window. The user can activate the control by clicking on the camera control checkbox and selecting which of the cameras she wishes to control. Listing 15.11 shows that we only need to include an additional CDrawHandler object to support the second camera view (at label B). The new CDrawHandler is also properly initialized and replaced onto the CTutorialDlg window (at label D). Finally, and very importantly, we must render from the new CDrawHandler object during OnTimer services (at label G). At label C is the new camera GUI control object. This object is initialized at label E, where it is default to be invisible and in control of the main view camera.

15.3   Manipulating the Camera

We have learned to describe the camera by specifying the camera position, look-at position, and up vector, and the view frustum by specifying the near/far planes and field of view (FOV). Of these parameters:

```
class CTutorialDlg : public CDialog {
    :
A:  virtual BOOL OnInitDialog(); // MFC function to initialize the application
    private:
B:  CDrawHandler m_MainView;   // camera that renders the large view on the left
    CDrawHandler m_SmallView; // camera that renders the smaller view to the lower right
    :
C:  CCameraControl m_CameraControl; // The Pop-up camera control
    :
```

```
BOOL CTutorialDlg::OnInitDialog() {
D:  if( !m_MainView.Initialize( ... IDC_GRFX_PLACEHOLDER) ) ...
    if (!m_SmallView.Initialize(... IDC_SMALLVIEW_PLACEHOLDER) ) ...
E:  m_CameraControl.Create(IDD_CAMERACONTROL_DIALOG ...); // create the camera GUI control
    m_CameraControl.ShowWindow(SW_HIDE);                  // initialy do not show the control
    m_CameraControl.SetCamera(&(m_MainView.GetCamera())); // default to control main view camera
F:  m_MainView.GetCamera()...

    : // initialize cameras and GUI controls

void CTutorialDlg::OnTimer(UINT nIDEvent) {
G:  m_MainView.DrawGraphics();  // render for the main view
    m_SmallView.DrawGraphics(); // render for the small view
}
```

Source file.
TutorialDlg.h/cpp files in the *Source Files* and *Header Files* folders of the D3D_TwoCamera project.

Listing 15.11. The CTutorialDlg class of Tutorial 15.2.

- The near/far planes bound the rendering computation and have no physical-world analogy.

- The FOV describes the zoom on a telephoto lens, where in our case, the exact same effect can be accomplished by physically moving the camera position toward (or away from) the look-at position.

- The up vector anchors the sense of orientation for the observer and is rarely altered.

In this way, when discussing interactive movement of the camera, we typically pay attention to the camera and the look-at positions. This is not surprising, for we can relate this to our real-world experience using a camera with no zooming capability—we can only move the camera and/or change the position we are looking at. If we think back to our experience using a (video) camera, unless we have special-purpose equipment, we actually seldom move both the camera and the look-at positions simultaneously. Typically, we look through the camera and keep one of the two positions relatively stationary.

1. **Constant camera position.** This is like standing at a fixed position and aiming the camera around. We can pan the environment, search for a subject, or follow a moving subject.

2. **Constant look-at position.** This typically happens when we are examining a subject, where we can move the camera closer/farther from the subject (fixed position), or orbit the camera around the subject.

Of course, we are discussing computer graphics, and we do not need to be constrained by the physical world. For example, we can place a camera and aim it at any position in the scene. In the next chapter, after we re-examine OC space and the involved transformations, we will learn how to place a camera on a moving object and aim at arbitrary positions in our world.

For clarity, we only discuss the changing of camera position with the look-at position kept, in most cases, stationary. The mathematics presented applies to the alternative scenario, where the camera position is kept stationary with changing look-at position. The implementation of the alternative scenario is left as an exercise.

For the following discussion, we will assume the symbols and results from Section 14.3, where

$$
\begin{aligned}
\text{Eye (camera) position:} \quad & p_e = (x_e, y_e, z_e), \\
\text{Look at position:} \quad & p_a = (x_a, y_z, z_a), \\
\text{User specified up vector:} \quad & \mathbf{V}_{up}, \\
\text{View vector:} \quad & \mathbf{V}_v = p_a - p_e, \\
\text{View distance:} \quad & \text{distance from } p_e \text{ to } p_a = v_d = \|\mathbf{V}_v\|,
\end{aligned}
$$

and the EC orthonormal basis is (Equation (14.3)):

$$
\text{EC orthonormal basis:} \quad
\begin{cases}
\hat{\mathbf{V}}_w = (x_w, y_w, z_w), \\
\hat{\mathbf{V}}_u = (x_u, y_u, z_u), \\
\hat{\mathbf{V}}_v = (x_v, y_v, z_v),
\end{cases}
$$

with

$$\begin{aligned}
\mathbf{V}_v &= p_a - p_e, \\
\mathbf{V}_w &= \mathbf{V}_{up} \times \mathbf{V}_v, \\
\mathbf{V}_u &= \mathbf{V}_v \times \mathbf{V}_w.
\end{aligned}$$

Tutorial 15.3. Manipulating Cameras with the Mouse

- **Goal.** Demonstrate and understand the basics of how to manipulate camera parameters, and the simple approaches to visualizing the camera.

- **Approach.** Implement the basic camera manipulation operations: zooming, rotating, and panning; and visualize camera positions in the application windows.

Figure 15.3 is a screenshot of running Tutorial 15.3. The application window appears similar to that of Tutorial 15.2, except that there is a new black line in both views. This line represents the other camera, that is, the black line appearing in the main view represents the camera from the small view, and vice versa. The two ends on this black line represent the eye and look-at positions. This tutorial supports interactive manipulation of the camera parameters with the mouse.

- **Left mouse button.** To rotate the camera. Click and drag with the left mouse button in the main view and notice that left/right movement rotates the camera in the horizontal direction, whereas up/down left mouse button drag rotates the camera in the vertical direction. As you left mouse button drag in the main view, notice the corresponding movements of the black line in the small view. The black line helps us visualize and understand the camera movement. The same functionality is also supported by the small view. This movement is sometimes referred to as tumble.

- **Middle mouse button.** To pan the view. Click and drag with the middle mouse button in the main view and notice how it appears as though we are panning to different regions of the application window with the panning direction corresponding to the mouse movement directions. Once again, by looking at the black line in the small view, we can visualize the actual camera movement. This movement is also referred to as track around the window.

- **Right mouse button.** To zoom the camera. Click and drag with the right mouse button in the main view and notice a leftward drag moves the camera toward the squares and a rightward drag moves the camera away. This movement is also referred to as dolly into or out of a view.

Tutorial 15.3.
Project Name:
   D3D_CameraMouseUI
Library Support:
   UWB_MFC_Lib1
   UWB_D3D_Lib14

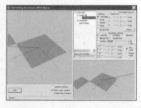

Figure 15.3. Tutorial 15.3.

GUI implementation details. Mouse event service routines are defined in DrawAndMouseHandler.cpp (in the *WindowHandler* folder of the D3D_CameraMouseUI project). The UWB_Camera GUI interaction support functions are defined in uwbgl_Camera_Xform1.cpp (in the *Camera* folder of the UWBGL_D3D_Lib14 project.

Of course, as humans, we usually combine and apply all of the above manipulation operations simultaneously when observing objects. On a computer, we have to be contented with simulating each as distinct operations.

15.3.1   Tumble: Rotating (Orbiting) the Camera

Let's take a moment to do a little experiment. Find a small object on your desk, for example, the eraser on a pencil. Use this object as your fixed look-at position. You want to examine this object without touching it. Notice how you move your head horizontally left to right and vertically up and down when examining this object. Because the object is small and your look at position does not change much, notice that when you move your head, unconsciously, you actually try to maintain the view distance. In effect, you are actually rotating your eye position orbiting the object. As Figure 15.4 shows, we usually orbit the camera position when examining a stationary object.

As depicted in Figure 15.6, when you thought you were moving your head horizontally left to right, you are actually rotating your eye position around the object with respect to the up orientation. Figure 15.5 shows that a vertical up/-down movement corresponds to rotating the eye position with respect to the $\mathbf{V}_w$ vector of the EC orthonormal basis. Recall that $\mathbf{V}_w$ is the vector that is perpendicular to both the view vector $\mathbf{V}_v$ and the up vector $\mathbf{V}_{up}$. In this way, the vertical up/down rotation actually rotates the eye position on the plane defined by the view and up vector.

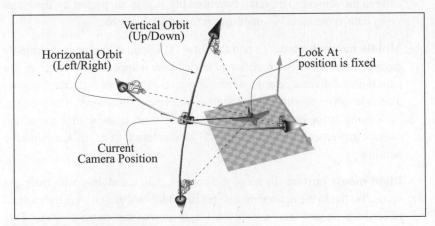

Figure 15.4. Tumble: orbiting of camera position.

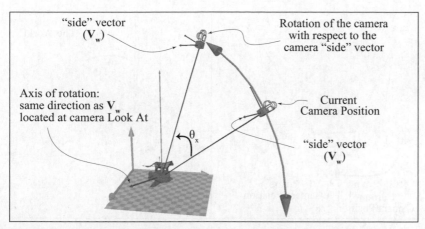

Figure 15.5. Up/down camera rotation.

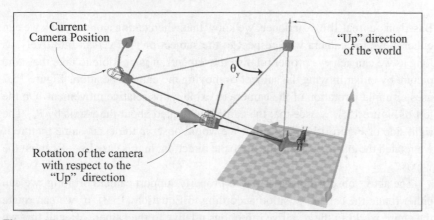

Figure 15.6. Left/right camera rotation.

Let's assume that the camera is rotated horizontally by θ_y and vertically by θ_x. We refer to horizontal rotation as *sub-y* because the rotation is defined with respect to the up orientation, or the y-axis. Similarly, the x of θ_x signifies the axis of rotation. The camera orbiting rotations can be described as

$$\mathbf{M}_{or} = \mathbf{R}^{v_w}(\theta_x)\ \mathbf{R}^y(\theta_y), \qquad (15.2)$$

where $\mathbf{R}$ is the rotation operator, and the superscripts v_w and y represent the $\mathbf{V}_w$ and y axes of rotation. To properly support camera tumbling, for every θ_x and θ_y user input, we need to compute the new camera position p_e^{new}:

$$\begin{aligned} p_e^{new} &= p_e\ \mathbf{M}_{or} \\ &= p_e\ \mathbf{R}^{v_w}(\theta_x)\ \mathbf{R}^y(\theta_y). \end{aligned} \qquad (15.3)$$

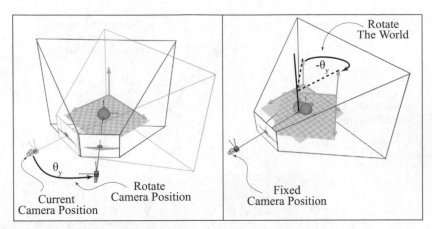

Figure 15.7. Rotating the camera versus rotating the world.

Based on our real-life experience, we know that when taking a photograph we can either move the camera with respect to the subject or vice versa. Intuitively, as long as we can achieve proper relative movements, it is possible to take the same picture by either moving the subject or moving the camera position. Figure 15.7 uses a simple y-rotation of the camera to explain this relative movement. On the left of Figure 15.7, we see that the camera is rotated about the y-axis by θ_y. The right side of Figure 15.7 shows that we would observe the exact same picture if we rotated the entire world in the opposite direction, in this case by $-\theta_y$ about the y-axis.

The above observation says that to properly support camera orbiting, we can either rotate the camera position according to Equation (15.3), or we can rotate the entire world in the negative directions relative to the camera. Recall that we compute the $\mathbf{M}_{w2e}$ matrix based on the camera parameters and that this matrix is loaded in the VIEW matrix processor where all geometries are transformed into the EC. Mathematically, we can implement the rotation of the entire world by augmenting the $\mathbf{M}_{w2e}$ matrix,

$$
\begin{aligned}
\mathbf{M}_{w2e}^r &= [\mathbf{M}_{or}]^{-1}\ \mathbf{M}_{w2e} \\
&= [\mathbf{R}^{v_w}(\theta_x)\ \mathbf{R}^y(\theta_y)]^{-1}\ \mathbf{M}_{w2e} \\
&= [\mathbf{R}^y(\theta_y)]^{-1}\ (\mathbf{R}^{v_w}(\theta_x))^{-1}\mathbf{M}_{w2e},
\end{aligned}
$$

or

$$
\mathbf{M}_{w2e}^r = \mathbf{R}^y(-\theta_y)\ \mathbf{R}^{v_w}(-\theta_x)\ \mathbf{M}_{w2e}. \tag{15.4}
$$

Here we perform the inverse of the camera orbiting rotations, $\mathbf{M}_{or}^{-1}$, before the usual WC-to-EC transform. In this way, all vertices are transformed by the inverse

```
void UWB_Camera::GetMouseRotationsInRadian(float &xRot, vec3 &xRef,
                                            float &yRot, vec3 &yRef) const {
    ⋮ // xRot=-θx, yRot=-θy
A:  view_direction = m_LookAt - m_CameraPos;   // Vv = pa - pe
    xRef = cross(m_UpVector, view_direction); // xRef = Vw = Vup × Vv
    normalize(xRef);
B:  yRef = (0, 1, 0); // yRef is the y-axis
    ⋮

C:  xRot = UWB_ToRadians(m_XRot); // the vertical -θx rotation angle
    yRot = UWB_ToRadians(m_YRot); // the horizontal -θy rotation angle
}
```

Source file.
uwbgl_Camera_Xform1.cpp
file in the *Common Files/
Camera* subfolder of the
UWBGL_D3D_Lib14 project.

Listing 15.12. The **UWB_Camera** support for camera rotation.

camera orbiting rotations, or the entire world is rotated according to the inverse
of the camera orbiting rotations. In our library, we have chosen to implement
Equation (15.4) (over Equation (15.3)) because we have to compute and update
the VIEW matrix anyway. Listing 15.12 shows the UWB_Camera support for camera rotations. We see that in addition to the two angles of rotation (xRot and
yRot), the GetMouseRotationsInRadian() function also returns the two corresponding axes of rotation (xRef and yRef). At label A, the xRef rotation axis
is set to the $\mathbf{V}_w$ vector, and at label B, the yRef rotation axis is set to the y-axis.
m_XRot ($-\theta_x$) and m_YRot ($-\theta_y$) are instance variables of the UWB_Camera class
that record the rotations set by the user. In this case, the left/right left mouse button drag sets m_YRot, and the up/down left mouse button drag changes m_XRot.
Listing 15.13 shows the last stage of view matrix computation that is missing at label A1c from Listing 15.8. Recall that the ComputeViewMatrix() is responsible
for computing the view matrix that will be loaded into the D3D VIEW matrix processor. Once again, here we see that at label A1b, the $\mathbf{M}_{w2e}$ from Equation (14.4)
is computed and stored in the variable mat. Here we see the details of supporting
camera rotation in WC-to-EC transformation matrix. The camera rotation parameters, including the two angles and their corresponding axes are accessed at
label A1d. At label A1e, we invoke the D3DXMatrixRotationAxis() function
to compute the two rotation operators $\mathbf{R}^{v_w}$ and $\mathbf{R}^y$, with results stored in xRotMat
and yRotMat. At label A1f, the operators are concatenated with the view matrix
to compute the $\mathbf{M}'_{w2e}$ of Equation (15.4). The computed WC-to-EC matrix com-
pensates for the horizontal and vertical rotations of the camera, and we can avoid
re-computing the eye position every time the user adjusts the camera rotation.

```
void UWBD3D_WindowHandler::ComputeViewMatrix(D3DXMATRIX &mat) const {
    // Labels A1a and A1b are identical to Listing 15.8
    // Get pe, pa, and Vup
A1a: m_Camera.GetCameraPosition(p.x, p.y, p.z);
        ⋮
    // mat is Mw2e of Equation 14.4
A1b: D3DXMatrixLookAtRH( &mat, &p, &a, &u );
A1c: The following details were not shown in Listing 15.8
    // get camera rotation parameters
A1d: m_Camera.GetMouseRotationsInRadian(xRot, xRef, yRot, yRef);
        ⋮
    // some format conversions not shown
        ⋮
    // xRotMat = Rvw(−θx) (xRot=−θx)
A1e: D3DXMatrixRotationAxis(&xRotMat, &xRef, xRot);
    // yRotMat = Ry(−θy) (yRot=−θy)
    D3DXMatrixRotationAxis(&yRotMat, &yRef, yRot);
    // rotMat = yRotMat * xRotMat
A1f: D3DXMatrixMultiply(&rotMat,  &yRotMat, &xRotMat);
    // Mrw2e = rotMat * Mw2e
    D3DXMatrixMultiply(&mat, &rotMat,  &mat);
}
```

Source file.
uwbgl_D3DWindowHandler6.h/cpp files in the *D3D Files/ WindowHandler* subfolder of the UWBGL_D3D_Lib14 project.

Listing 15.13. $\mathbf{M}_{w2e}$ with camera rotation.

In this section, we simulate the camera orbiting sensation by rotating the world in the inverse directions. The matrix derived and implemented are with respect to the origin of the world. This simulation is correct only when the camera look-at position is located at the origin.

15.3.2   Pan: Tracking the Camera

As illustrated in Figure 15.8, another common operation we often perform on a camera is, with a fixed gaze direction, moving the camera. When compared to orbiting, instead of rotating the camera with a fixed look-at position, we move the camera with a fixed view vector. The effect of this movement is panning on the rendered image, or tracking of the application window.

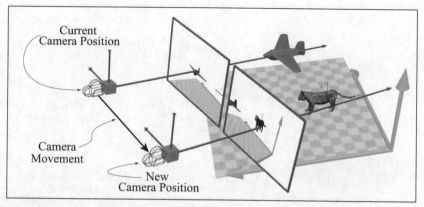

Figure 15.8. Pan: tracking the camera.

To implement tracking, we move the camera and look-at positions by the same displacement vector along directions that are perpendicular to the view vector. With the EC orthonormal basis from Equation (14.3), horizontal movement dx is along the $\mathbf{V}_w$ vector, whereas the vertical movement dy is along the $\mathbf{V}_u$ vector. The displacement $\mathbf{V}_\delta$ for both the camera and look-at positions is:

$$\mathbf{V}_\delta = (-dx \times \mathbf{V}_w) + (dy \times \mathbf{V}_u).$$

Recall that the view vector $\mathbf{V}_v$ in EC points from the camera to the look-at position. With the right-handed coordinate system, this means that the $\mathbf{V}_w$ vector points toward the left. For this reason, we must negate the dx displacement when computing $\mathbf{V}_\delta$. Now, the new camera position p_e^n and look-at position p_a^n are

$$\begin{aligned} p_e^n &= p_e - \mathbf{V}_\delta, \\ p_a^n &= p_a - \mathbf{V}_\delta. \end{aligned}$$

Notice we are taking the negative displacements. Intuitively, when we drag the mouse downward, we expect the content of the scene to lower. As illustrated in Figure 15.9, in order to create the effect of objects lowering, we must move the camera upward. For this reason, we subtract the displacement vectors from the positions. Listing 15.14 shows the UWB_Camera support for the tracking operation. At label A, the dx and dy displacements are computed based on the x/y mouse movements. At label B, the vectors for the EC orthonormal basis are computed. The new camera and look-at positions p_e^n and p_a^n are computed exactly as described above.

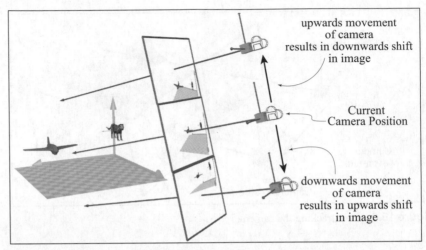

Figure 15.9. Vertical tracking displacement directions.

```
void UWB_Camera::MouseTrack(int x, int y)
     // compute dx/dy using mouse x/y movements
A:   float dx=... dy=...
     // comptue eye axis frame: Vᵥ
B:   view_direction = m_LookAt - m_CameraPos;
     cross_direction = cross(up_direction,view_direction); // V_w
     normalize(cross_direction);                            // V̂_w
     up_direction = cross(view_direction,cross_direction);  // V_u
     normalize(up_direction);                               // V̂_u
     // V_δ = (-dx × V_w) + (dy × V_u)
C:   delta = (-dx*cross_direction) + (dy*up_direction);
     m_CameraPos = m_CameraPos - delta; // p_e^n = p_e - V_δ
     m_LookAt = m_LookAt - delta;        // p_a^n = p_a - V_δ
     ⋮
```

Source file.
uwbgl_Camera_Xform1.cpp
file in the *Common Files/
Camera* subfolder of the
UWBGL_D3D_Lib14 project.

Listing 15.14. The UWB_Camera support for tracking.

15.3.3 Dolly: Zooming the Camera

From real-world experience, we know that the view distance v_d determines the size of the object on the eventual photograph. When we want to take a closer examination of an object, or zoom in on an object, we move the camera closer

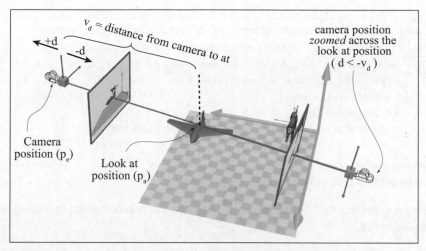

Figure 15.10. Zooming across the look-at position.

to the object. Zooming out corresponds to moving the camera away from the object.

To properly simulate the zooming sensation, we can move the camera position along the view vector. Mathematically,

$$p_e^n = p_a + [(v_d + d)\,\hat{\mathbf{V}}_v], \tag{15.5}$$

where p_e^n is the new camera position and d is the camera movement along the view vector. A d value of 0.0 corresponds to no zooming, a negative d value shortens the view distance and thus create a zoom-in effect, and a positive d value results in a zoom-out effect. In general,

$$
\begin{aligned}
d \le -v_d \quad & \text{move camera beyond look at: no real-world analogy,} \\
-v_d < d < 0 \quad & \text{move camera closer: zooming in,} \\
0 \le d \quad & \text{move camera away: zooming out.}
\end{aligned}
$$

The mathematics of Equation (15.5) is such that a d value of less than $-v_d$ correspond to moving the camera beyond the look-at position. As illustrated in Figure 15.10, because the look-at position is not changed, after the camera moves across the look at position, the view vector flips direction. In this way, the final rendered image appears as though we have moved the camera to the other side of the look-at position while still looking at the same look-at position. Listing 15.15 shows the camera zooming implementation of Equation 15.5. At label A, mouse movement in the x-direction is mapped into displacement along

Source file.
uwbgl_Camera_Xform1.cpp
file in the *Common Files/
Camera* subfolder of the
UWBGL_D3D_Lib14 project.

```
void UWB_Camera::MouseZoom(int x) { // x is a mouse displacement
A:  float dx=...; // convert mouse movement into distance
B:  vec3 view_vec = m_LookAt - m_CameraPos; // Vᵥ = pₐ − pₑ
    float view_distance = length(view_vec); // v_d = ‖Vᵥ‖
    normalize(view_vec);                    // V̂ᵥ ← normalize(Vᵥ)
    // implement Equation 15.5
    m_CameraPos = m_LookAt-((view_distance+dx)*view_vec);
    ⋮
```

Listing 15.15. The UWB_Camera support for zooming.

the view vector. At label B, the new camera position is computed according to Equation (15.5).

15.3.4 Drawing of the Camera

Drawing WindowHandler
camera. It is difficult, if not impossible, to draw and observe the WindowHandler::m_Camera in the same WindowHandler view. For example, a line along the camera viewing direction is a single point in the middle of the drawing area. For this reason, the m_ToDrawCamera is defined to be a reference to a camera from another WindowHandler. In our case, the main view has a reference to the small view camera and vice versa.

The camera and look-at positions are specified in the WC space. In the simplest case, we can simply draw a line from the camera position to the look-at position to represent the camera. The top of Listing 15.16 (label A) shows that in the WindowHandler class, we have defined a m_ToDrawCamera, a reference to the camera to be drawn. For proper visualization, this is a reference to a camera of another WindowHander. In our case, the main view has a reference to the small view camera and vice versa. The lower portion of Listing 15.16 shows that the drawing of the camera can be integrated into the WindowHandler::DrawGraphics() routine. At label B, as previously, the VIEW and PROJECTION matrix processors are loaded with the proper matrices. At label C, we initialize the $\mathbf{M}_{o2w}$ matrix (the WORLD matrix processor) to $\mathbf{I}_4$. Since the $\mathbf{M}_{o2w}$ matrix is identity, we can draw objects in the WC space without further transformations. Thus, at label D, we can simply invoke the camera Draw() function to draw a line between the camera and the look-at position.

As discussed in Section 15.3.1, in the presence of camera tumbling where a user can specify θ_y horizontal camera orbiting and θ_x vertical camera orbiting, the VIEW matrix processor will be loaded with $\mathbf{M}'_{w2e}$ (Equation (15.4)):

$$\mathbf{M}'_{w2e} = [\mathbf{M}_{or}]^{-1} \ \mathbf{M}_{w2e}.$$

In this way, the world-to-eye coordinate transformation matrix is augmented with the inverse of the m_camera orbiting rotations, $[\mathbf{M}_{or}]^{-1}$, to simulate the tumbling of the m_camera. In a similar fashion, to properly visualize the position of

---

```
class CDrawOnlyHandler : public UWBD3D_WindowHandler {
    ⋮
A:  UWB_Camera* m_ToDrawCamera; // camera to be visualized
}
```

```
void CDrawOnlyHandler::DrawGraphics() {
    ⋮
    BeginDraw();
B:  LoadViewXform();        // compute/load M'_{w2e} to VIEW
    LoadProjectionXform(); // compute/load M_{e2n} to PROJECTION
    // initialized M_{o2w} ← I_4
C:  D3DXMATRIX identity;  D3DXMatrixIdentity(&identity);
    // load identity to WORLD
    m_pD3DDevice->SetTransform(D3DTS_WORLD, &identity);
    ⋮
D:  m_ToDrawCamera->Draw(... draw_helper); // Draws the camera
E:  theApp.GetModel().DrawModel();          // Draws the scene
    EndDrawAndShow();
}
```

Listing 15.16. Drawing the camera in the simplest case.

The WORLD matrix processor. Notice that our scene hierarchy is defined by the SceneNode class where the matrix stack is used to store/re-store the WORLD matrix processor before drawing each node. This means that at the end of the DrawModel() (at label E) function call, the WORLD matrix processor is restored to the identity matrix. In this case, we can draw the camera before *or* after drawing the scene.

Source file. Pseudocode; no corresponding source file.

the m_ToDrawCamera, we must also consider its corresponding orbiting rotations. However, in this case, we need to compute and rotate the m_ToDrawCamera (and not the entire world). For this reason, we need to compute the orbit rotation matrix ($\mathbf{M}_{or}^d$) for the m_ToDrawCamera (Equation (15.2)):

$$\mathbf{M}_{or}^d = \mathbf{R}^{v_w^d}(\theta_x^d) \ \mathbf{R}^y(\theta_y^d),$$

where v_w^d is the side vector ($\hat{\mathbf{V}}_w$) and θ_x^d and and θ_y^d are the vertical and horizontal rotation angles, respectively, of the m_ToDrawCamera. In this case, before the drawing of the m_ToDrawCamera, we need to compute

$$\begin{aligned}
&\mathbf{M}_W \ \mathbf{M}_V \ \mathbf{M}_P \\
&= \mathbf{M}_W \ \mathbf{M}_{w2e}^r \ \mathbf{M}_{e2n} \\
&= \mathbf{M}_W \ \mathbf{M}_{or}^d \ [\mathbf{M}_{or}]^{-1} \ \mathbf{M}_{w2e} \ \mathbf{M}_{e2n}.
\end{aligned}$$

Source file.
DrawOnlyHandler.cpp file
in the *Source Files* folder
of the D3D_CameraMouseUI
project.

```
void CDrawOnlyHandler::DrawGraphics() {
    //
    // Everything before Labels D are identical to Listing 15.16
    //
         ⋮
    // m_ToDrawCamera rotation parameters
D:   m_ToDrawCamera->GetMouseRotations(xRot,xRef,yRot,yRef);
    // ... format conversion not shown ...
    // xRotMat = M^{v^d_w}(θ^d_x)  (xRot=-θ^d_x)
    D3DXMatrixRotationAxis(&xRotMat, &xRef, -xRot);
    // yRotMat = M^y(θ^d_y)  (yRot=-θ^d_y)
    D3DXMatrixRotationAxis(&yRotMat, &yRef, -yRot);
    // rotMat = M^d_{or} = xRotMat * yRotMat
    D3DXMatrixMultiply(&rotMat, &xRotMat, &yRotMat);
    // M_W ← M^d_{or} (of m_ToDrawCamera)
    m_pD3DDevice->SetTransform(D3DTS_WORLD, &rotMat);
    m_ToDrawCamera->Draw(... draw_helper);
         ⋮
```

Listing 15.17. Proper support for drawing the camera line.

As illustrated at label C in Listing 15.16, $\mathbf{M}_W$ is initialized to $\mathbf{I}_4$. In our implementation, before drawing the m_ToDrawCamera, we load $\mathbf{M}^d_{or}$ into the WORLD matrix processor:

$$\mathbf{M}_W \, \mathbf{M}_V \, \mathbf{M}_P$$
$$= \mathbf{M}^d_{or} \, [\mathbf{M}_{or}]^{-1} \, \mathbf{M}_{w2e} \, \mathbf{M}_{e2n},$$

to rotate the m_ToDrawCamera orbiting rotations. Listing 15.17 shows that the implementation of camera drawing indeed agrees with the above derivations.

15.4   DC-to-WC Transformation

We have seen that the transformation pipeline introduced many layers of coordinate systems and supported us in designing our scene in 3D space, modeling a camera based on our daily experience, and generating images for our 2D display device. Based on our experience from Chapter 10, we understand that the many layers of coordinate systems mean our geometric objects are not defined in the same space as they appear on the application window. For example, the squares of Tutorial 15.3 are each defined in their own OC space, and yet depending on the

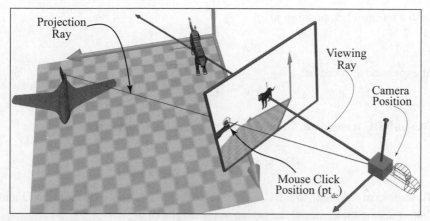

Figure 15.11. 2D mouse position in the 3D scene.

camera positions and scene node transform settings, they occupy different pixel positions in the two views. In Section 10.5, we learned to inversely transform mouse positions from DC back to WC space such that the user can interact with our application through what they can see on the display device.

To transform the 2D mouse position into 3D WC space, we must compute the inverse transform:

$$DC \rightarrow NDC \rightarrow EC \rightarrow WC.$$

Our problem, of course, is that although DC is in 2D, the rest of the coordinate spaces are all in 3D. Recall that the 3D-to-2D perspective projection (from Figure 14.12) collapses objects along individual projection rays toward the camera position onto the image plane. As illustrated in Figure 15.11, given a pixel position, we can reconstruct the projection ray by computing the line that connects this pixel to the camera position. In 3D applications, when the user clicks the mouse in the application window, she actually specifies a ray originating from the camera position into the 3D world. The result of transforming a point in 2D DC space to 3D space is not a position but a ray in 3D space.

Assuming that

$$\text{Device drawing area} = \begin{cases} \text{width} & = W_{dc}, \\ \text{height} & = H_{dc}, \end{cases}$$

then the DC space is

$$\text{DC space:} \begin{cases} 0 \leq x_{dc} \leq W_{dc}, \\ 0 \leq y_{dc} \leq H_{dc}, \end{cases}$$

Perspective projection. Objects are collapsed (or projected) along the projection ray onto the image plane. A projection ray is defined from a position on the object toward the camera position.

with a mouse-click position pt_{dc}:

$$pt_{dc} = (x_{dc}, y_{dc}),$$

or expressed as a vector:

$$\mathbf{V}_{dc} = \begin{bmatrix} x_{dc} & y_{dc} \end{bmatrix}.$$

DC-to-NDC transform.   Recall that in 2D, the NDC space is

$$\text{NDC space:} \begin{cases} -1 \le x_{ndc} \le 1, \\ -1 \le y_{ndc} \le 1. \end{cases}$$

To transform from DC to NDC space, we scale the DC space down to 2×2 and then translate the center of the region to the origin, or:

$$\mathbf{V}_{ndc} = \mathbf{V}_{dc} \, S(\frac{2}{W_{dc}}, \frac{2}{H_{dc}}) \, T(-1, -1).$$

Expanding the scale and translation operators, we get

$$\begin{aligned}
\mathbf{V}_{ndc} &= \begin{bmatrix} x_{ndc} & y_{ndc} \end{bmatrix} \\
&= \begin{bmatrix} x_{dc} & y_{dc} \end{bmatrix} \, S(\frac{2}{W_{dc}}, \frac{2}{H_{dc}}) \, T(-1, -1) \\
&= \begin{bmatrix} \frac{2x_{dc}}{W_{dc}} & \frac{2y_{dc}}{H_{dc}} \end{bmatrix} \, T(-1, -1) \\
&= \begin{bmatrix} \frac{2x_{dc}}{W_{dc}} - 1 & \frac{2y_{dc}}{H_{dc}} - 1 \end{bmatrix},
\end{aligned}$$

or

$$\begin{aligned}
x_{ndc} &= \frac{2 \times x_{dc}}{W_{dc}} - 1, \\
y_{ndc} &= \frac{2 \times y_{dc}}{H_{dc}} - 1.
\end{aligned} \tag{15.6}$$

Because the mouse-click position is in 2D, we cannot compute the z-component for the transformed NDC result. In other words, any z value is valid, or

$$\mathbf{V}_{ndc} = \begin{bmatrix} x_{ndc} & y_{ndc} & z_{ndc} \end{bmatrix},$$

where (from Equation (15.6)):

$$\begin{cases} x_{ndc} = \frac{2 \times x_{dc}}{W_{dc}} - 1, \\ y_{ndc} = \frac{2 \times y_{dc}}{H_{dc}} - 1, \\ -1 \le z_{ndc} \le 0. \end{cases}$$

As illustrated in Figure 15.12, $\mathbf{V}_{ndc}$ actually defines a line in the NDC space. The mouse-click position can be considered to be located on the near plane with $(x_{ndc}, y_{ndc}, 0)$, which defines a line that is parallel to the z-axis and exists from the far plane at $(x_{ndc}, y_{ndc}, -1)$.

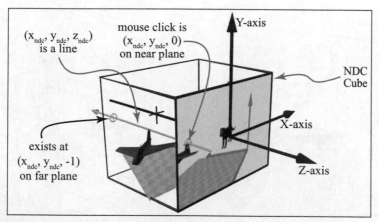

Figure 15.12. DC point is an NDC ray.

NDC-to-EC transform. Remember that the NDC cube is transformed from a view frustum. Figure 15.13 shows the view frustum in EC space and the corresponding NDC cube. From this figure, we see that

$$\overline{p_n^a p_n^b} \overset{\text{transforms}}{\longleftrightarrow} \overline{p_e^a p_e^b}$$

and

$$\overline{p_n^c p_n^d} \overset{\text{transforms}}{\longleftrightarrow} \overline{p_e^c p_e^d}.$$

We see that line segments that are parallel to the z-axis in NDC space transform into projection rays in EC space. Let

$$
\begin{aligned}
p_n^a &= (x_n^a, \quad y_n^a, \quad z_n^a), \\
p_n^c &= (x_n^c, \quad y_n^c, \quad z_n^c), \\
p_e^a &= (x_e^a, \quad y_e^a, \quad z_e^a), \\
p_e^c &= (x_e^c, \quad y_e^c, \quad z_e^c).
\end{aligned}
$$

In general,

$$\frac{y_e^c}{y_n^c} = \frac{y_e^a}{y_n^a},$$

or

$$y_e^c = y_n^c \frac{y_e^a}{y_n^a}. \tag{15.7}$$

In Figure 15.13,

$$
\begin{cases}
y_n^a &= 1.0, \\
y_e^a &= n\tan(\alpha),
\end{cases}
\tag{15.8}
$$

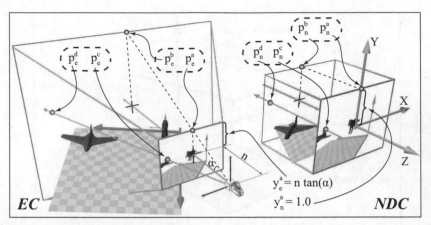

Figure 15.13. The NDC ray transforms to a projection ray in EC.

where n is the near plane distance and α is half of the (vertical) field-of-view angle. Substituting Equation (15.8) into Equation (15.7),

$$y_e^c = n \tan(\alpha) \, y_n^c.$$

This relationship is also true for the x-axis:

$$x_e^c = n \tan(\beta) \, x_n^c.$$

As discussed in Section 14.2.2 and Equation (14.1), β is half of the horizontal field-of-view angle. In this case, we know p_e^c is located at the near plane, or $z_e^c = -n$. So,

$$p_n^c \overset{\text{transforms}}{\longleftrightarrow} p_e^c$$

or

$$\begin{bmatrix} x_n^c & y_n^c & 0 \end{bmatrix} \overset{\text{transforms}}{\longleftrightarrow} \begin{bmatrix} n\tan(\beta)x_n^c & n\tan(\alpha)y_n^c & -n \end{bmatrix}.$$

Remember that our goal is to reconstruct the projection ray. In general, any point

$$p_n = (x_n, y_n, 0)$$

in NDC space will transform to a line in EC space:

$$p_e = \begin{bmatrix} z_e \tan(\beta) \, x_n & z_e \tan(\alpha) \, y_n & -z_e \end{bmatrix}.$$

Substituting from Equation (15.6),

$$p_e = \left[z_e \tan(\beta) \left(\tfrac{2 \times x_{dc}}{W_{dc}} - 1 \right) \; z_e \tan(\alpha) \left(\tfrac{2 \times y_{dc}}{H_{dc}} - 1 \right) \; -z_e \right], \tag{15.9}$$

where
$$\begin{cases} \beta \text{ is half of vertical FOV,} \\ \alpha \text{ is half of horizontal FOV,} \qquad\qquad and \\ n \text{ is distance to near plane } (-n \le z_e \le -1). \end{cases}$$

Equation (15.9) is the projection ray in EC space for the point (x_{dc}, y_{dc}) in DC space. Notice that when $z = 0$, all projection rays will intersect the origin. Remember that in EC space, the camera is located at the origin.

EC-to-WC transform. Finally, we must transform the projection ray of Equation (15.9) to the WC space. A straightforward approach is to transform two points on the projection ray from EC to WC. For example, we can choose $z_e = 0$ and $z_e = 1$ as two convenient points on the projection ray in EC space:

$$\begin{aligned} p_e^0 &= (0, & 0, & & 0), \\ p_e^1 &= (\tan(\beta)(\tfrac{2 \times x_{dc}}{W_{dc}} - 1), & \tan(\alpha)(\tfrac{2 \times y_{dc}}{H_{dc}} - 1), & & -1). \end{aligned} \qquad (15.10)$$

The $\mathbf{M}_{e2w}$ of Equation (14.6) will transform these two points to WC space: p_{wc}^0 and p_{wc}^1. Notice that p_e^0 is the camera position in EC, and thus p_{wc}^0 is the camera position p_e. Recall from Section 14.5.4 that the camera position is neatly encoded in the fourth row of the $\mathbf{M}_{e2w}$ matrix. This means that we can obtain the values of p_w^0 simply by reading the first three elements of the fourth row of the $\mathbf{M}_{e2w}$ matrix. In this way,

Projection ray in EC $(\overline{p_e^0 p_e^1})$ $\overset{transforms}{\longleftrightarrow}$ Projection ray in WC $(\overline{p_w^0 p_w^1})$.

We can then intersect the WC projection ray with the geometries in WC space to compute for intersections. Recall that the projection ray describes a line from the camera position through the mouse position into the scene. We have transformed this line from the DC coordinates, via NDC and EC, to the WC space. Any objects that intersects this ray are objects that are underneath the mouse position. When there is more than one object underneath a pixel, we must compute all the intersections and keep the result that is closest to the camera position p_w^0.

Tutorial 15.4. Mouse Click–to-World Transformation

- **Goal.** Demonstrate the creation of a 3D projection ray in WC space based on the 2D mouse-click position.

- **Approach.** Implement the mathematics presented in Section 15.4 and visualize the WC projection ray with a separate camera.

Tutorial 15.4.
Project Name:
  D3D_CameraInvXform
Library Support:
  UWB_MFC_Lib1
  UWB_D3D_Lib14

```
void CDrawAndMouseHandler::OnMouseMove(unsigned int nFlags, int hwX, int hwY) {
    :
    // hardware (hwXY) -> deviceXY xform
A:  HardwareToDevice(hwX, hwY, deviceX, deviceY);
    // LMB click with Shift Key depressed
    if (nFlags & MK_SHIFT & MK_LBUTTON) {
        :
        // deviceXY -> WC Projection ray xform
B:      DeviceToWorld(deviceX, deviceY, pt, ray);
        // set projection ray in the CModel clss
C:      theApp.GetModel().SetPickRay(pt, ray);
        :
```

Source file.
DrawAndMouseHandler.cpp
file in the *WindowHan-*
dler folder of the
D3D_CameraInvXform
project.

Listing 15.18. Mouse event service routine that defines the WC projection ray.

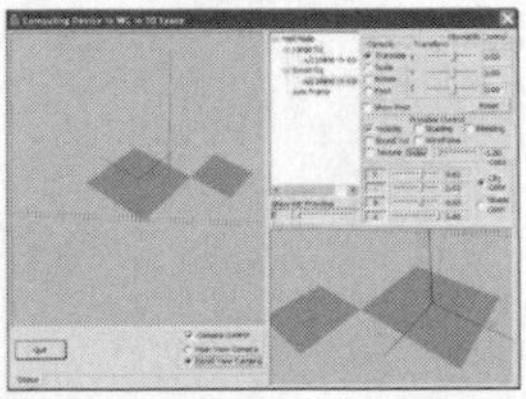

Figure 15.14. Tutorial 15.4.

Figure 15.14 is a screenshot of running Tutorial 15.4. This tutorial appears and works almost exactly the same as that of Tutorial 15.3. The only difference is that the WC projection ray is created and displayed when the left mouse button is depressed with the shift key. For example, similar to Tutorial 15.3, clicking and dragging with the left mouse button orbits the camera. However, with the shift key depressed, clicking and dragging in this tutorial does not manipulate the camera. Instead, we are specifying a DC position for the creation of the projection ray.

With the shift key depressed, when you click and drag the left mouse button in the main view, you will notice a yellow line being drawn in the main view. This yellow line is the computed projection ray based on the mouse position in the main view. We notice that the projection ray is not visible in the window where the mouse is clicked. Recall that the projection ray is a line extending from the camera position through the mouse-click position into the scene. In the window in which the mouse is clicked, the projection ray is projected into a point and thus is not visible. Now, release the shift key and the left mouse button. Notice that the yellow line becomes stationary. We can now left mouse button click and drag in the small view to examine the last WC projection ray that was defined in the main view. Right mouse button click with the shift key depressed clears the yellow line.

The CModel class of Tutorial 15.4 has a m_PickPt and a m_PickRay that represent the WC projection ray origin and direction. These two values are set by the corresponding mouse event service routines in the DrawAndMouseHandler class. Listing 15.18 shows the details of the mouse event service routine. At label A, the mouse click is transformed from hardware coordinate system, (hwX, hwY), to

```
void UWBD3D_WindowHandler::DeviceToWorld(int dcX, int dcY, vec3& wcPt, vec3& wcRay) const {
        ⋮
        // viewMat is M_w2e
A:      ComputeViewMatrix(viewMat);
        // invView is M_e2w
        D3DXMatrixInverse(&invView ... &viewMat);
        // device size: W_dc and H_dc
B:      GetDeviceSize(deviceW, deviceH);
        // get camera vertical fov
C:      m_Camera.GetViewVolumeFOVInRadian(fov);
        // compute tan(α)
        tanAlpha = tanf((fov/2.0f));
        // Refer to Equation 14.1, tan(β) = W_dc/H_dc × tan(α)
        tanBeta = (deviceW/deviceH)*tanAlpha;
        // Compute p_e^1 (of Equation 15.10): (dcX,dcY) is (x_dc,y_dc)
D:      ecPt.x = (((2.0f*dcX)/deviceW)-1)*tanBeta;
        ecPt.y = (((2.0f*dcY)/deviceH)-1)*tanAlpha;
        ecPt.z = -1;
        // wcRayPtD3D is p_w^1
E:      D3DXVec3TransformCoord(&wcRayPtD3D,&ecPt,&invView);
        // wcPt is p_wc^0
F:      wcPt.x = invView._41;     // this is the camera position
        wcPt.y = invView._42;     // which is the 4th row of M_e2w
        wcPt.z = invView._43;
        // wcRay is the projection ray direction
G:      wcRay = wcRayPtD3D - wcPt;
}
```

Source file.
uwbgl_D3DWindowHandler6.cpp file in the *D3D Files/ WindowHandler* subfolder of the UWBGL_D3D_Lib14 project. This is a virtual function defined in the API-independent UWB_WindowHandler class.

Listing 15.19. DC point to WC projection ray transform.

device coordinate system, $(deviceX, deviceY)$. At label B, the DeviceToWorld() function is called to transform the device position to the projection ray where pt is the origin and ray is the projection ray direction. Listing 15.19 shows the DeviceToWorld() function. We can see that at:

1. **Label A.** Compute inverse viewing transformation matrix $\mathbf{M}_{e2w}$.

2. **Label B.** Extract display width (deviceW) and height (deviceH).

3. **Label C.** Compute half of the horizontal and vertical field-of-view angles, α and β.

4. **Label D.** Compute p_e^1 (ecPt) of Equation (15.10) based on the mouse-click position (dcX, dcY) in DC space.

5. **Label E.** Compute P_w^1 (wcRayPtD3D) by applying the $\mathbf{M}_{e2w}$ (invView) matrix on EC position p_e^1.

6. **Label F.** Take advantage of the observation that the WC ray origin is the camera position, and that we know the WC camera position is neatly encoded in the fourth row of the $\mathbf{M}_{e2w}$ matrix.

15.5 2D Versus 3D Coordinate Transformation Pipeline

Recall that in 2D space, Chapter 10 reviewed coordinate systems concepts and introduced world coordinate (WC) space to support a convenient space for composing the scene. In Chapter 11, we introduced the idea of object coordinate (OC) space to support a convenient space for composing complex objects in the scene. To properly support the many coordinate systems, the drawing of each object must undergo a series of transformations that we refer to as the transformation pipeline:

$$\text{Object space} \xrightarrow{\mathbf{M}_{o2w}} \text{WC} \xrightarrow{\mathbf{M}_{w2n}} \text{NDC} \xrightarrow{\mathbf{M}_{n2d}} \text{DC}.$$

Note that the last stage of the pipeline is dictated by the fact that modern graphics APIs (e.g., D3D and OpenGL) automatically transform vertex positions from NDC to DC space.

To implement this transformation pipeline, we took advantage of the matrix processors provided by the graphics API. In the UWBGL library, the SceneNode class is responsible for updating the $\mathbf{M}_W$ matrix processor with an appropriate OC-to-WC transformation, whereas the LoadW2NDCXform() function of the D3D_Window Handler class is responsible for loading the $\mathbf{M}_V$ matrix processor with the appropriate $\mathbf{M}_{w2n}$ matrix. In this way, the UWBGL programs the matrix processors to perform:

$$\text{Object space} \xrightarrow{\mathbf{M}_W} \text{WC} \xrightarrow{\mathbf{M}_V} \text{NDC} \xrightarrow{\text{D3D}} \text{DC}.$$

In this chapter, we have seen that the transformation pipeline for 3D space is slightly more involved:

$$\text{Object space} \xrightarrow{\mathbf{M}_{o2w}} \text{WC} \xrightarrow{\mathbf{M}_{w2e}} \text{EC} \xrightarrow{\mathbf{M}_{e2n}} \text{NDC} \xrightarrow{\mathbf{M}_{n2d}} \text{DC}.$$

The UWBGL introduced the Camera to encapsulate the WC-to-EC and EC-to-NDC transformation information. The Camera class defines parameters that are familiar to the users (e.g., camera position) and methods to support intuitive manipulations of these parameters (e.g., move camera position). The D3D_WindowHandler class references the Camera object, computes the view (WC-to-EC) transformation (M_{w2e}) in ComputeViewMatrix(), and computes the projection (EC-to-NDC) transformation (M_{e2n}) in ComputeProjectionMatrix(). As in the 2D case, the D3D_WindowHandler class is responsible for loading the VIEW (M_V) and PROJECTION (M_P) matrix processors with the computed transformations with the Load ViewXform() and LoadProjectionXform() functions. In the next chapter, we will see how, with minimal modifications, the SceneNode class can continue to be responsible for loading the WORLD (M_W) matrix processor with the OC-to-WC transformation. In this way, in 3D space, we program the matrix processors to support the transformation pipeline:

$$\text{Object space} \xrightarrow{\mathbf{M}_W} \text{WC} \xrightarrow{\mathbf{M}_V} \text{EC} \xrightarrow{\mathbf{M}_P} \text{NDC} \xrightarrow{\text{D3D}} \text{DC.}$$

16

Graphics Programming in 3D

This chapter extends all concepts learned in 2D space into the third dimension. This chapter:

- describes graphics primitive support in 3D;

- analyzes the technical details of rotation in 3D and introduces the quaternion rotation representation;

- presents the mathematics for forward and orientation motion in 3D space;

- demonstrates collision and mouse-click selection support for 3D hierarchical models.

After this chapter we should:

- understand generalizations of all the concepts learned in 2D space;

- understand gimbal lock and the advantages of quaternion rotation representation.

In addition, with respect to hands-on programming, we should:

- be able to build interactive applications in 3D with hierarchical models that are capable of interacting with other objects and with the user;

447

- be able to program simple intelligence in our 3D application where objects can follow or orient toward any given position and/or direction.

It is interesting and encouraging that almost all of the concepts we have learned from the earlier chapters concerning computer graphics in 2D space are valid in 3D space. The only notable exception is rotation, where rotation in 2D space is really a highly restrictive special case of rotation in 3D. In this chapter, we will iterate through all the relevant concepts we have learned in 2D and demonstrate how to extend them into the third dimension. We will pay special attention to rotations in 3D space.

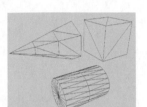

Figure 16.1. Approximating cone, cube, and cylinder with triangles.

16.1   Graphical Primitives for the Third Dimension

So far we have worked with 2D primitives displayed in 3D space. We say 2D primitives because the primitives only have areas but do not occupy volume. For example, a circle and a rectangle are 2D primitives with length and width that define areas. These primitives have zero measurements in the third dimension (height) and thus do not occupy any volume. In the previous chapter, the tutorials viewed these 2D primitives with a camera in 3D environments.

Figure 16.2.   Mesh model of a biplane.

A true 3D primitive must have measurements in all three dimensions: width, length, and height (e.g., spheres, cubes, cylinders). As discussed in Chapter 7, for efficiency concerns all popular modern graphics hardware only support points, lines, and triangles. This means that existing graphics hardware does not support any 3D primitives directly. Instead, just as we have approximated circles with triangles in 2D space, the graphics hardware expects programmers to approximate 3D primitives and objects with triangles. Figure 16.1 shows examples of approximating a cone, a cube, and a cylinder with triangles.

16.1.1   Mesh Objects and Mesh Files

Triangle strip/fan. See Section 7.1.3 for the discussions of these compound primitives.

As discussed in Section 7.1.3 (on p. 161), for efficiency in computation and representation, modern graphics hardware often defines intelligent collection structures for grouping primitives. In the case of triangles, we have seen and have worked with triangle fans and triangle strips. These collection structures are usually referred to as meshes, and geometric objects approximated by meshes are referred to as mesh objects or mesh models. In general, a mesh can consist of polygons with any number of sides. For example, it is possible to define a mesh object based on quadrilaterals. These polygons will be triangulated by the graphics hardware during rendering.

Source file. box.x file in the *MeshFiles* folder.

```
A:  FrameTransformMatrix {              // Define object transform
        1.000000,0.000000, ...          // Default is I₄
B:  Mesh {                              // Define mesh geometric information
        24;                             // There are 24 triangles
        -0.500000;-0.500000;-0.500000;,  //   Geometric position of the 0ᵗʰ vertex
        ⋮                               //   Other vertex positions
C:      12;                             // There are 12 polygons
        3;0,1,2;,                        //   Polygon-0 has 3 vertices: {0ᵗʰ,1ˢᵗ,2ⁿᵈ}
        ⋮                               //   Rest of the polygons (all triangles)
D:  MeshNormals {                       // Define normal vectors
        24;                             // There are 24 unique vectors
        ⋮                               //   Define the vectors for the vertices
E:  MeshMaterialList {                  // Define material properties for the mesh
```

Listing 16.1. Example of a simple D3D mesh file (*.x*).

The top image of Figure 16.2 shows a biplane, and the lower image overlays the triangles that define the geometry. To design such a model, a skillful artist has to spend long hours working with commercial 3D modeling software (e.g., Maya) in perfecting every vertex position. The artist then stores all the triangles and the associated vertices in a mesh file. We notice that the biplane model has interesting wood textures. To accomplish this effect, the artist has to create image files as texture maps for the biplane geometries. Similar to the geometries, these texture image files are usually created by skillful artists spending long hours working with commercial painting software (e.g., Photoshop). The mesh file contains references to the texture image files. Mesh files are typically complex and typically contain geometric information, material properties of the geometry (including file texture information), animations of the geometries, and even transformations and relationships with respect to other objects. Due to the complexity and the fact that much of the information encoded in a mesh file may be closely related to a particular commercial software system, almost all vendors have specialized proprietary file formats. The D3D API defines the .x mesh file format where information is encoded in simple ASCII text. In the following, we use a simple example from this file format to illustrate how information is stored in a mesh file. Listing 16.1 shows fragments from the mesh file that defines the cube shown in Figure 16.1. Although this is a simple example, we can identify some important characteristics common to typical mesh files:

24 versus eight vertices. There are only eight unique vertex positions for a cube. However, each of these vertex positions can have three different directions (*normal*) depending on which triangle they are associated with. For example, the top-front-left vertex has an upward direction when it is part of the top triangle, a leftward direction when it is part of the left triangle, and a frontward direction when it is part of the front triangle. In this way, 24 unique vertex positions and directions (normals) are needed to represent a cube.

- **Transformation.** Mesh files often include transformation information to be applied to part of or the entire mesh object. In this case, label A defines the identify matrix (I_4) to be applied to all the geometries in this file.

- **Geometry.** Mesh files always encode the geometry of an object. In general, the geometry may include components and even animation sequences of the components. In our very simple case, we can see that at label B, the keyword Mesh signifies the beginning of the geometric definition for the cube. After this keyword, we see the number 24 followed by 24 vertex positions. These positions are ordered beginning with index $0^{th}, 1^{st}, \ldots$ to the 23rd. After the 24 vertex positions, the number 12 at label C signifies there will be 12 polygons to follow. We see that each polygon is defined according to:

$$n; i, j, \ldots;,$$

where n is the number of vertices a polygon has and $i, j, \ldots$ are the indices of the vertices. In this case, we see a polygon with three vertices: the 0th, first, and second vertex listed at label B. At label D, 24 normal vectors (or directions) are defined, one for each of the 24 vertex positions.

- **Appearance.** Mesh files often define the appearance (or material properties) for the mesh object. In this case, at label E we see the keyword MeshMaterialList where material properties are defined for the cube. This is where the texture image files will be specified.

Indexed polygons. Listing unique vertices in an ordered list and defining polygons by specifying vertices from this list. When polygons share common vertices, this scheme of encoding geometry optimizes memory.

Material and normal. *Material properties* and *normal directions* at vertices help define the *appearance* of objects. We will examine examples that work with *material* and *normal* direction in Appendix A.

Change summary. See p. 529 for a summary of changes to the library.

UWBGL_D3D_Lib15

This version of the UWBGL library integrates the .x mesh objects as specializations of our Primitive class. There are three main aspects to our implementation: (1) loading of mesh files as resources; (2) managing the mesh resources; and (3) creating mesh specific subclasses to the Primitive class.

Mesh File Resources

Recall that when working with file textures in Lib13 (p. 359), we introduced the Resource class (Listing 12.12) to abstract the interaction with and management of files. For example, we have defined the TextureResource (Listing 12.13) class to interact with and load file textures as a resource. Listing 16.2 shows the MeshResource class where we subclass from the UWBD3D_Resource to inherit the file searching functionality. At label A, the DrawMesh() function

```
class UWBD3D_MeshResource : public UWBD3D_Resource {
  public:
A:   void DrawMesh( ... );                                // Render the mesh with D3D
     ⋮
B:   const UWB_BoundingBox* GetBoundingBox();             // Bounds of the mesh object
     ⋮
  protected:
C:   bool LoadResourceFromFile(fullPathName);             // Loading the .x mesh file
     ⋮
D:   LPD3DXMESH                      m_Mesh;              // D3D-specific mesh storage
     UWB_Array<D3DMATERIAL9>         m_MeshMaterials;     // Materials defined in the .x file
     UWB_Array<LPDIRECT3DTEXTURE9>   m_MeshTextures;      // Textures defined in the .x file
     ⋮
     UWB_BoundingBox                 m_bounds;            // Bounds of the mesh object
```

```
bool UWBD3D_MeshResource::LoadResourceFromFile(const wchar_t* fullPathName) {
     // Loads .x file (fullPathName) into m_Mesh
E:   D3DXLoadMeshFromX(fullPathName, ... m_Mesh)
     ⋮ // if defined, loads file textures into m_MeshTextures
     // Computes m_bound of the mesh object
F:   D3DXComputeBoundingBox(... m_Mesh->GetNumVertices() )
     ⋮
```

Source file.
uwbgl_D3DMeshResource1.h file in the *D3D Files/ D3D_Resources* subfolder of the UWBGL_D3D_Lib15 project.

Listing 16.2. Support for mesh file resource.

will work with D3D to render the geometry defined in a .x mesh file. At label B, proper bound information is maintained for the mesh geometry to support collision computations (to be discussed in Section 16.6). The LoadResoruceFrom File() function at label C will load the mesh file specified by fullPathName into D3D. At label D, LPD3DXMESH is the D3D-specific representation for storing mesh geometries, and the D3DMATERIAL9 and DIRECT3DTEXTURE9 arrays are defined to store the material properties and (potential) file textures defined for the mesh object. Label E shows the implementation of the LoadResourceFromFile() function where the mesh file is loaded into the LPD3DXMESH internal structure by the D3DXLoadMeshFromX() function. Label F shows that we, as programmers, are responsible for computing the bounds of a mesh object.

Mesh Resource Storage Management

Recall from Listing 12.14 that we defined an array of `TextureResource` in the `GraphicsSystem` class to support file texture mapping. Listing 16.3 shows that in a similar fashion, an array of `MeshResource` and the associated mesh loading function are defined (at label B) in the `GraphicsSystem` class. The rest of UWBGL will access the mesh resource via the `.x` mesh filename by calling the `GetMeshResource()` function defined at label A. If a specified mesh filename is not found in the mesh array, loading of the file will occur automatically.

3D Mesh Primitive Objects

With the `MeshResource` class (Listing 16.2) and the associated storage/management support defined in the `GraphicsSystem` class (Listing 16.3), we can perceive a mesh file/object as *just another primitive*. For example, with the support of appropriately defined vertex positions, we have worked with circle as a `Primitive`. In this case, we define the `PrimitiveMesh` class to abstract a mesh file object as a simple mesh primitive. Listing 16.4 shows the definition of the `UWBD3D_PrimitiveMesh` class. We see a simple subclass from the `Primitive`

Source file.
uwbgl_D3DGraphicsSystem5.h
file in the *D3D Files/
D3D_GraphicsSystem*
subfolder   of   the
UWBGL_D3D_Lib15 project.

```
class UWBD3D_GraphicsSystem {
  public:
    // finds mesh MeshResource array
A:  UWBD3D_MeshResource* GetMeshResource(meshname);
    :

  private:
    // MeshResources array
B:  UWB_PointerArray<UWBD3D_MeshResource*> m_mesh_resources;
    // loads if not found in array
    UWBD3D_MeshResource* FindMeshResource(mesh_name);
    :

    // : from Listing 12.14
    UWB_PointerArray<UWBD3D_TextureResource*> m_texture_resources;
    //      file texture support
    UWBD3D_TextureResource* FindTextureResource(texture_name ...);
    :
};
```

Listing 16.3. Array of mesh resources in UWBGL.

```
class UWBD3D_PrimitiveMesh :  public UWB_Primitive {
  public:
A:  UWBD3D_PrimitiveMesh( meshFileName ); // .x file name
    ⋮

  protected:
B:  void DrawPrimitive( ...);              // To draw the Mesh object
    ⋮

C:  std::wstring m_resource_filename;      // Internal representation of mesh object
    ⋮


void UWBD3D_PrimitiveMesh::DrawPrimitive( ... ) {
    ⋮

    // access mesh resource using the file name
D:  UWBD3D_MeshResource* pMesh=...GetMeshResource(m_resource_filename.c_str());
    // Calling D3D Mesh Rendering function
E:  pMesh->DrawMesh( ... );
    ⋮
```

Source file.
uwbgl_D3DPrimitiveMesh1.h
file in the *D3D Files/
D3D_Primitives* subfolder
of the UWBGL_D3D_Lib15
project.

Listing 16.4. UWBGL primitive abstraction over mesh file object.

class. As expected, being a simple `Primitive`, we can work with the new `Primi tiveMesh` just as we have worked with the `PrimitivePoint` or the `Primitive Circle` classes! However, notice the D3D in the `UWBD3D_PrimitiveMesh` class name, and notice that we have placed the source file in the *D3D Files* subfolder. This new primitive class defines a D3D-specific object. The most important implication of this observation is that the drawing of the primitive will not be handled by the `DrawHelper` class. Label B shows that we must override the `DrawPrimitive()` class. The bottom half of Listing 16.4 shows the implementation of `PrimitiveMesh`. At label D, the `GraphicsSystem` class is invoked to `GetMeshResoruce()`, and at label E we call the `MeshResoruce::DrawMesh()` function directly to render the mesh object. There is no new mesh drawing support in the `DrawHandler` class. Listing 16.5 shows the `MeshArrow` class. Once again, this class defines a D3D-specific object. At label A, as in the case of `PrimitiveMesh`, we see that we must override the `DrawPrimitive()` function. In this case, we will approximate an arrow with appropriately scaled cone and cylinder meshes. During `DrawPrimitive()`, at label B, references to the cone and cylinder mesh resources are obtained via the `GraphicsSystem::GetMeshRe source()` function. At labels C and D, the matrix stack is set up to scale and

Source file.
uwbgl_D3DPrimitiveArrow1.h
file in the *D3D Files/
D3D_Primitives* subfolder
of the UWBGL_D3D_Lib15
project.

```
class UWBD3D_PrimitiveMeshArrow : public UWB_Primitive {
  public:
    ⋮

  protected:
    // draws with no internal representation
A:  void DrawPrimitive( ... );
    ⋮
```

```
void UWBD3D_PrimitiveMeshArrow::DrawPrimitive( ... ) {
      ⋮
      // refernce to a cylinder mesh
B:    pCylinderMesh = graphics.GetMeshResource( L"cylinder.x" );
      // reference to a cone mesh
      pConeMesh     = graphics.GetMeshResource( L"cone.x" );
      ⋮
      // init matrix stack for xform
C:    draw_helper.PushModelTransform();
      ⋮
      cylinder_xform.SetScale( ... );         // set up xform for the cylinder
      ⋮                                       // to represent the arrow body
      cylinder_xform.SetUpModelStack( ... ); // load the xform into WORLD matrix
      pCylinderMesh->DrawMesh(... );           // Draw the cylinder
      draw_helper.PopModelTransform();
      ⋮
      // init matrix stack for xform
D:    draw_helper.PushModelTransform();
      ⋮
      cone_xform.SetScale( ... );             // set up xform for the cone
      ⋮                                       // to represent the arrow head
      cone_xform.SetUpModelStack( ... );      // load the xform into WORLD matrix
      pConeMesh->DrawMesh( ... );             // Draw the cone
      draw_helper.PopModelTransform();
      ⋮
```

Listing 16.5. 3D arrow primitive.

```
class UWBD3D_PrimitiveMeshAxis : public UWB_Primitive {
    ⋮
    // physical representations of each arrow
A:  UWBD3D_PrimitiveMeshArrow m_xaxis;
    UWBD3D_PrimitiveMeshArrow m_yaxis;
    UWBD3D_PrimitiveMeshArrow m_zaxis;
};
```

Listing 16.6. Representing the orthonormal basis with three arrows.

Source file.
uwbgl_D3DPrimitiveAxis1.h
file in the *D3D Files/
D3D_Primitives* subfolder
of the UWBGL_D3D_Lib15
project.

orient the drawing of the cylinder and cone mesh objects such that the resulting image resembles an arrow. Here we see that there is actually no internal physical data representing the MeshArrow object. The appearance of the arrow depends entirely on the cylinder.x and mesh.x files. Listing 16.6 shows the definition of three MeshArrow objects representing the three major axes in an orthonormal basis. This example shows an alternative approach to representing mesh objects. Instead of accessing and transforming each individual mesh resources at drawing time, in this case, physical data is defined.

The MeshArrow and MeshAxis classes reaffirm that physical representation of data internal to our program is independent of the graphical rendition of the objects for the user. Representations internal to our program should be based on design guidelines for our system. For example, with no physical memory requirement, the MeshArrow approach of accessing data at drawing time optimizes the program's memory footprint. However, the associated cost is the processing requirements of computing transformation during drawing time.

Tutorial 16.1. Working with Simple Meshes

- **Goal.** Demonstrate working with the new PrimitiveMesh class.

- **Approach.** Implement a simple program with a PrimitiveMesh object.

Figure 16.3 is a screenshot of running Tutorial 16.1. This tutorial is almost exactly the same as the ones from the previous chapter. The only difference here is the tiger.x mesh object. Listing 16.7 shows the constructor for the CModel class for this tutorial. At label A, a tigerMesh primitive object is created based on the corresponding mesh file name (the tiger.x file name). After the instantiation, the resulting primitive reference can be used *just like* any other *UWB_Primitive* references. At label B, the tigerMesh primitive is referenced by a SceneNode object. This means that we should be able to control the transformation of the tiger

Tutorial 16.1.
Project Name:
   D3D_MeshSupport
Library Support:
   UWB_MFC_Lib1
   UWB_D3D_Lib15

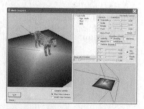

Figure 16.3. Tutorial 16.1.

Source file. Model.cpp file in the *Model* folder of the D3D_MeshSupport project.

```
CModel::CModel() {
    // Create a Mesh Primitive
A:  UWBD3D_PrimitiveMesh* tigerMesh=new UWBD3D_PrimitiveMesh(L"tiger.x");
    UWB_SceneNode* pTigerMeshNode=new UWB_SceneNode(L"tiger_mesh");
    // mesh primitive behaves like a simple UWB_Primitive
B:  pTigerMeshNode->SetPrimitive(tigerMesh);
    m_root_node.InsertChildNode( pTigerMeshNode );
    ⋮
```

Listing 16.7. Constructor of CModel in Tutorial 16.1.

by simply manipulating the corresponding scene node transformation operators. As anticipated, in Tutorial 16.1, with the tiger_mesh scene node selected, we can manipulate the tiger primitive just as any other primitive.

Tutorial 16.2. Working with a Composite Mesh Object

Tutorial 16.2.
Project Name:
  D3D_CompoundMesh
Library Support:
  UWB_MFC_Lib1
  UWB_D3D_Lib15

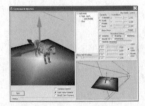

Figure 16.4.   Tutorial 16.2.

- **Goal.** Demonstrate working with the AxisMesh class.

- **Approach.** Implement a simple program that works with an AxisMesh object.

Figure 16.4 is a screenshot of running Tutorial 16.2. This tutorial is identical to Tutorial 16.1 except for the 3D-looking orthonormal basis. Listing 16.8 shows the constructor of the CModel class for Tutorial 16.2. In this case, the scene node that references the orthonormal basis is inserted as a child node of the tiger node. This is to reaffirm that after the initial instantiation, the new D3D-specific mesh primitives can be used in exactly the same manner as all other primitives we have worked with previously, and they behave in exactly the same manner.

Source file. Model.cpp file in the *Model* folder of the D3D_CompoundMesh project.

```
CModel::CModel() {
    ⋮
    // scene node
    UWB_SceneNode* pAxisNode = new UWB_SceneNode( L"axis_frame" );
    // a primitive
    UWBD3D_PrimitiveMeshAxis* pMeshAxis = new UWBD3D_PrimitiveMeshAxis();
    // set scene node primitive
    pAxisNode->SetPrimitive( pMeshAxis );
    ⋮
```

Listing 16.8. Constructor of CModel in Tutorial 16.2.

Gimbal lock. With Tutorial 16.2, select the `tiger mesh` node (under the `root note`) and activate the "Rotate" radio button in the `XformInfoControl`. Adjust the y slider bar to see the tiger mesh rotate about the green (y) axis. We know the rotation is about the green axis because we can observe the entire mesh moving except the position where the green axis intersects the mesh object. Now, leave the y slider bar (θ_{y1}) with a nonzero value and adjust the x slider bar (θ_{x1}). We notice that the tiger mesh does not rotate about the red axis! If we reset the transforms and then adjust the x slider bar, we can see the corresponding rotation about the red (x) axis. In general, after two rotations about different axes, there will be no more clear relationships between the rotation slider bars and the orientation of the tiger mesh, after which it becomes virtually impossible to interactively control the orientation of the mesh. This situation is known as gimbal lock. This is the topic of discussion in the next section.

16.2   Rotation in 3D

Recall that in `Lib14` (on p. 413), when generalizing our library to support 3D graphics, we updated the transformation operator of `XformInfo` (Equation (9.10), p. 249),

$$\mathbf{M} = \mathbf{T}(-p)\,\mathbf{S(s)}\,\mathbf{R}^z(\theta_z)\,\mathbf{T}(p)\,\mathbf{T(t)},$$

to Equation (15.1) (on p. 415),

$$\mathbf{M} = \mathbf{T}(-p)\,\mathbf{S(s)}\,\mathbf{R}^z(\theta_z)\,\mathbf{R}^y(\theta_y)\,\mathbf{R}^x(\theta_x)\,\mathbf{T}(p)\,\mathbf{T(t)},$$

where p is the pivot position, $\mathbf{t}$ is the translation vector, $\mathbf{s}$ is the scaling factor, and $(\theta_x, \theta_y, \theta_z)$ are the angles of rotations about the corresponding axes.

Roll, pitch, yaw.
In some applications, e.g., flight simulators, θ_z is referred to as the *roll*, θ_x is referred to as the *pitch*, and θ_y is referred to as the *yaw*.

16.2.1   Euler Transform and Gimbal Lock

From 2D to 3D, we generalized the rotation from a single angle describing the rotation about the z-axis to three angles describing rotations about the three major axes,

$$\mathbf{R}_e(\theta_x, \theta_y, \theta_z) = \mathbf{R}^z(\theta_z)\,\mathbf{R}^y(\theta_y)\,\mathbf{R}^x(\theta_x). \qquad (16.1)$$

The rotation defined by Equation (16.1) is referred to as the *Euler transform*, and the three angles describing the three rotations about the major axes are referred to as the *Euler angles*. Because of the references to the major axes, the Euler transform is an intuitive way for describing and understanding the orientation of an object. However, as we have already experienced in Tutorial 16.2, describing rotations with Euler transform in interactive manipulations can result in gimbal lock. We can understand the cause of gimbal lock by analyzing the actual rotation operations. In Tutorial 16.2, we performed the following operations:

1. **First rotation.** Rotate about y-axis by θ_{y1}, or $\mathbf{R}^y(\theta_{y1})$.

2. **Second rotation.** Rotate about x-axis by θ_{x1}, or $\mathbf{R}^x(\theta_{x1})$.

Based on the ordering of operators, the rotation we wish to perform should be

$$\mathbf{R}_1 = \mathbf{R}^x(\theta_{x1})\, \mathbf{R}^y(\theta_{y1}).$$

However, our implementation of the Euler transform from Equation (16.1) will compute the rotation

$$\mathbf{R}_{e1}(\theta_{x1}, \theta_{y1}, 0) = \mathbf{R}^y(\theta_{y1})\, \mathbf{R}^x(\theta_{x1}).$$

Clearly,

$$\mathbf{R}_1 \neq \mathbf{R}_{e1}.$$

In more general cases, for example, if we continue the above θ_{y1} and θ_{x1} rotations with a θ_{y2} rotation about the y-axis, the rotation that ought to be performed is

$$\mathbf{R}_2 = \mathbf{R}^y(\theta_{y2})\, \mathbf{R}^x(\theta_{x1})\, \mathbf{R}^y(\theta_{y1}). \tag{16.2}$$

However, the Euler transform will compute the rotation

$$\mathbf{R}_{e2}(\theta_{x1}, \theta_{y1} + \theta_{y2}, 0) = \mathbf{R}^y(\theta_{y1} + \theta_{y2})\, \mathbf{R}^x(\theta_{x1}).$$

Once again,

$$\mathbf{R}_2 \neq \mathbf{R}_{e2}.$$

We see that the Euler transform does not support interactive manipulation of an object's rotational positions. For this reason, our manipulation of the rotation slider bars in Tutorial 16.2 resulted in a gimbal lock. In general, it is virtually impossible to support interactive rotation manipulation based on Euler angles.

To support interactive manipulation of object rotation, as demonstrated in Equation (16.2), we need to represent rotation as a general operator (matrix) and concatenate the operator of each user action in the order that the requests arrive. In UWBLib16 we modify the XformInfo class to support the operations of Equation (16.2). UWBLib17 introduces the quaternion rotation representation to improve storage and computational efficiency.

UWBGL_D3D_Lib16

Change summary. See p. 531 for a summary of changes to the library.

To properly support the concatenation operations as described by Equation (16.2), the `Lib16` library defines an explicit rotation operator (matrix) in the `XformInfo` class. This matrix replaces the three floating-point numbers that represented the Euler angles. Listing 16.9 shows the updated `XformInfo` class where at label C we define a 3×3 matrix to replace the previous three floating-point numbers. At label A and label A1, we see that in this case, the matrix is initialized with the identity matrix ($\mathbf{I}_3$). The function at label B is designed to allow the user to adjust rotation in the x-axis by dx ($\mathbf{R}^x(dx)$). In this case we must compute

$$\texttt{m\_rotation} = \mathbf{R}^x(dx) \times \texttt{m\_rotation}.$$

At label B1, we use the variable m to represent the rotation operator $\mathbf{R}^x$. At label B2, we compute the content of the operator $\mathbf{R}^x(dx)$. At label B3, the new rotation operation is concatenated with the `XformInfo`.

It is important to notice that the rotation matrix in `XformInfo` is an ordered concatenation of all rotation requests. In this case, we do not know the individual steps by which to arrive at this rotation. In addition, we do not have a simple user-

```
class UWB_XformInfo {
  public:
A:   void InitializeRotation();          // initialize rotation
     :
B:   void UpdateRotationXByDegree(dx); // update rotaion by dx about x axis
     :
  protected:
C:   mat3 m_rotation;                     // A 3x3 matrix
     :
```

Source file. uwbgl_XformInfo4.h/cpp file in the *Common Files/* XformInfo subfolder of the UWBGL_D3D_Lib16 project.

```
void UWB_XformInfo::InitializeRotation()
A1:  makeIdentity(m_rotation);            // initialize to identity (I₃)

void UWB_XformInfo::UpdateRotationXByRadian(float dx)
B1:  mat3 m;                              // a 3x3 matrix
B2:  m[1][1]=...; m[1][2]=...             // compute Rˣ(dx)
B3:  m_rotation = m * m_rotation;         // concatenate Rˣ(dx) with the 3x3 matrix
```

Listing 16.9. Supporting 3D rotation with explicit matrix representation.

```
bool UWBD3D_DrawHelper::AccumulateModelTransform(vec3 t, vec3 s, mat3 r,
                                                 vec3 p) {
   ⋮
```

A:
```
   D3DXMATRIX m;                              // D3D matrix representation
   m._11=r[0][0]; m._12=r[0][1]; ... // convert math3d++ to D3D matrix
   ⋮
   m_pMatrixStack->TranslateLocal(t.x,t.y,t.z);      // M_{t1} = T(t)M_t
   m_pMatrixStack->TranslateLocal(p.x,p.y,p.z);      // M_{t2} = T(p)M_{t1}
```

B:
```
   m_pMatrixStack->MultMatrixLocal(&m);              // M_{t3} = RM_{t2}
   m_pMatrixStack->ScaleLocal(s.x,s.y,s.z);          // M_{t4} = S(s)M_{t3}
   m_pMatrixStack->TranslateLocal(-p.x,-p.y,-p.z); // M_{t5} = T(-p)M_{t4}
   ⋮
   // M_W ← M_{t5}
```

C:
```
   pDevice->SetTransform(D3DTS_WORLD,m_pMatrixStack->GetTop());
```

Source file.
uwbgl_D3DDrawHelper8.cpp
file in the *D3D Files/*
D3D_DrawHelper subfolder
of the UWBGL_D3D_Lib16
project.

Listing 16.10. Setting matrix stack with rotation matrix.

friendly representation for the current orientation of our object. In this case, the rotation slider bars are for users to adjust rotation and not set the current rotation. For example, previously a user would manipulate the x-rotation slider bar to set the current x-axis rotation to a certain degree. With the new matrix representation, a user would manipulate the x-rotation slider bar to change the x-axis rotation by a certain amount. We will examine the UI control support requirements in Listing 16.11. Listing 16.10 shows that the D3D_DrawHelper class is modified to support the rotation matrix representation. At label A, the API-independent mat3 is converted to the D3D-specific D3DXMATRIX data type. At label B, the converted matrix is multiplied (pre-concatenated) onto the matrix stack representing the rotation transformation. Label C shows, as previously, that the concatenated transformation operator is loaded to the WORLD matrix processor. When compared to Listing 15.6 (on p. 416), we see that instead of computing (Equation (15.1)),

$$\mathbf{T}(-p)\,\mathbf{S}(\mathbf{s})\,\mathbf{R}^z(\theta_z)\,\mathbf{R}^y(\theta_y)\,\mathbf{R}^x(\theta_x)\,\mathbf{T}(p)\,\mathbf{T}(\mathbf{t}),$$

we now compute

$$\mathbf{T}(-p)\,\mathbf{S}(\mathbf{s})\,\mathbf{R}\,\mathbf{T}(p)\,\mathbf{T}(\mathbf{t}), \tag{16.3}$$

where p is the pivot position, $\mathbf{t}$ is the translation vector, $\mathbf{s}$ is the scaling factor, $(\theta_x, \theta_y, \theta_z)$ are the angles of rotations about the corresponding axes, and $\mathbf{R}$ is a *general* rotation matrix. Notice the similarities between Equation (16.3) and Equation (9.10) (on p. 249). The only difference is the parameter for rotation (θ).

When generalizing from 2D to 3D, we lost the ability to describe rotation with a simple number: instead, we can only describe rotation by a general operator, a matrix in this case.

Tutorial 16.3. Working with Rotation Matrix Representation

Tutorial 16.3.
Project Name:
   D3D_RotateMatrix
Library Support:
   UWB_MFC_Lib1
   UWB_D3D_Lib16

- **Goal.** Demonstrate working with the new matrix rotation operator and understand that the UI controls must report changes in rotation instead of absolute amounts of rotation.

- **Approach.** Work with the scene from from Tutorial 16.2 and identify the difference in implementation.

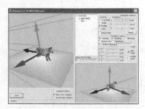

Figure 16.5.   Tutorial 16.3.

Figure 16.5 is a screenshot of running Tutorial 16.3. This tutorial is implemented based on the matrix rotation representation. Now, select the `tiger mesh` scene node and click on the "Rotate" radio button to set the slider bars to control rotations. Adjust the slider bars to notice how the tiger's orientation maintains a constant relationship to the major axes. This constant relationship allows a continuous intuitive manipulation of the tiger's orientation. In this case, we can associate the up direction of the tiger to the y-axis direction, the front of the tiger to the $-z$-axis direction, and the right side of the tiger to the x-axis direction. We can always rotate with respect to y-axis to change the front-facing direction of the tiger. We see that we do not result in gimbal lock by concatenating rotation operators.

Click on the "Reset" button to reset the tiger to the initial orientation. Now, perform the following 4 rotations in order: (1) set the x slider bar to any value (θ_1), (2) set the y slider bar to any value (θ_2), (3) set the x slider bar back to around zero ($-\theta_1$), and finally (4) set the y slider bar back to around zero ($-\theta_2$). The rotations we have performed are

$$\mathbf{R}_a = \mathbf{R}^y(-\theta_2)\mathbf{R}^x(-\theta_1)\mathbf{R}^y(\theta_2)\mathbf{R}^x(\theta_1).$$

Clearly this is not a zero rotation, and the tiger's orientation verifies our observation. However, notice that all three rotation slider bars report 0 rotations. This exercise reaffirms the fact that with the matrix rotation representation, the rotation slider bars are simply a mechanism for specifying changes in rotation and not for reporting the state of the rotation. Listing 16.11 shows our implementation of computing slider bar position changes. At label A are the variables for recording existing values of rotation slider positions. At label B, in the `OnHScroll()` slider bar service routine, the changes in slider bar position are computed (dx) and reported to `XformInfo` for updating the rotation matrix.

Source **file.**
XformInfoControl.h/cpp
files in the *Controls* folder
of the D3D_RotateMatrix
project.

```
class CXformInfoControl : public CDialog {
    ⋮
    // current sldier bar setting
A:  float m_rx, m_ry, m_rz;
    ⋮
```

```
void CXformInfoControl::OnHScroll( ... ) {
    ⋮
    // new values from slider bar
    float x=m_XSlider.GetSliderValue();
    ⋮
    switch(current_control)
        // when radio button is rotation
        case IDC_ROTATE: {
            // compute the change in sldier bar position
B:          float dx = x - m_rx;
            // remember current position
            m_rx = x;
            // send change in position to set rotation
            xform.UpdateRotationXByDegree(dx);
    ⋮
```

Listing 16.11. Capturing rotation differentials.

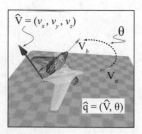

Figure 16.6. The quaternion representation of rotation.

Change summary. See p. 533 for a summary of changes to the library.

Right-handed rotation direction. With the right hand, stick out the thumb and curl the rest of the fingers into a "thumbs up" sign. The thumb direction is along the axis of rotation, and the rest of the fingers point in the positive direction of rotation.

UWBGL_D3D_Lib17

The cost of concatenating operations is the major shortcoming of representing rotation by an explicit matrix. The *quaternion* offers a storage and computationally efficient alternative to representing rotations. As illustrated in Figure 16.6, a quaternion describes a rotation with 4 floating-point numbers:

$$\hat{\mathbf{q}} = (\hat{\mathbf{V}}, \theta) = (v_x, v_y, v_z, \theta), \tag{16.4}$$

where $\mathbf{V}$ is the axis of rotation and θ is the angle to rotate. Notice the right-handed rotation direction and that axes $\mathbf{V}_a$ and $\mathbf{V}_b$ are perpendicular to the axis of rotation $\hat{\mathbf{V}}$. Just as we can describe a series of affine transformations by concatenating corresponding matrices, a series of rotations can be described by

```
class UWB_XformInfo {
  public:
    // New methods for supporting rotation with Quaternion
A:  void InitializeRotation();
    void SetUpModelStack(UWB_DrawHelper&);
    void UpdateRotationXByDegree(float);
    void SetRotation(const mat3&);
    mat3 GetRotation();
  protected:
         ⋮
B:  quat m_rotation; // axis and rotation angle
         ⋮
```

Source file.
uwbgl_XformInfo5.h/cpp
file in the *Common Files/
XformInfo* subfolder of the
UWBGL_D3D_Lib17 project.

```
C:  void UWB_XformInfo::InitializeRotation() {
         ⋮
        m_rotation[0]=...[1]=...[2]=0.0f; // initial axis of rotation
        m_rotation[3] = 1.0f;                   // initial angle of rotation
D:  void UWB_XformInfo::SetUpModelStack(UWB_DrawHelper& dh) const {
         ⋮
        mat3 m = GetRotation(); // Convert quaternion to matrix
        dh.AccumulateModelTransform(... , m, ...); // Set matrix rotation to matrix stack
E:  void UWB_XformInfo::UpdateRotationXByDegree(float dx) {
        quat q = quatFromAA(vec3(1,0,0), dx); // construct Quarternion for R^x(dx)
        m_rotation = m_rotation * q;           // concatenate the rotation (post-multiplication)
F:  void UWB_XformInfo::SetRotation(const mat3 &m) {
        mat3 r(m);                 // ready to compute transpose
        makeTranspose(r);          // transpose of m is post-multiplication
        m_rotation = mat2quat(r); // Convert matrix rotation to Quaternion
G:  mat3 UWB_XformInfo::GetRotation() {
        mat3 r = mat2quat(m_rotation); // convert from quaternion to matrix representation
        makeTranspose(r);              // transpose converts from post to pre-multiplication
        return r;                      // r is pre-multiplication rotation matrix
```

Listing 16.12. Supporting 3D rotation with a quaternion.

concatenating the corresponding quaternion. With the more compact representation, it is computationally more efficient to concatenate quaternions. The major shortcoming of the quaternion representation is that at this point, there is no hardware support for transforming vertices by a quaternion. As programmers, we must maintain the quaternion state in our program and convert the quaternion to a matrix for hardware processing. Listing 16.12 shows representing rotation by a quaternion in the XformInfo class. Label A shows the corresponding supporting methods. At label B, we see the data type quat , the math3d++ support for quaternion. The first three values of a quat data type define the axis of rotation with the fourth value defining the amount to rotate. At label C, we see that zero rotation of a quaternion is defined to be $(0,0,0,1)$. This initial value allows proper subsequent concatenation of quaternion operators. At label D, we see that the quaternion must be converted into a matrix for setting the hardware matrix processor. At label E, we see that to support updating of rotation, similar to matrix operations, we first construct a new quaternion operator to represent the *dx* rotation about the *x*-axis, and then we compute concatenation to represent the composite rotations. At label F, we see that it is possible to convert a rotation represented by a matrix into a quaternion.

Tutorial 16.4. Rotation with a Quaternion

- **Goal.** Demonstrate that working with the quaternion rotation representation can be identical to that of a matrix.

- **Approach.** Port the previous tutorial over and see that no changes in the CModel class or the UI controls are required.

Figure 16.7 is a screenshot of running Tutorial 16.4. The source code for this project is identical to that from Tutorial 16.3. The only difference in this case is the quaternion support in the XformInfo class of Lib17. This tutorial behaves identically to Tutorial 16.3.

16.3   Orientation in 3D

At this point, we are working with UWBGL_LIB17, where rotation is represented with a quaternion in the XformInfo class. Before rendering, the quaternion is converted into a rotation matrix, and the DrawHelper::AccumulateModelTransform() function is invoked to compute Equation (16.3) (on p. 460):

$$\mathbf{M} = \mathbf{T}(-p)\,\mathbf{S}(\mathbf{s})\,\mathbf{R}\,\mathbf{T}(p)\,\mathbf{T}(\mathbf{t}),$$

where *p* is the pivot position, **t** is the translation vector, **s** is the scaling factor, and **R** is the rotation matrix. In this way, the translation vector (**t**) defines the location, the scaling factor (**s**) defines the size, and the rotation matrix defines the orientation of the object drawn.

---

quat.   math3d++ supports post-multiplication   while our   library   implements pre-multiplication. Internally, XformInfo stores rotation in post-multiplication while this representation is converted in pre-multiplication with makeTranspose() to transpose the rotation matrix.

Tutorial 16.4.
Project Name:
   D3D_RotateQuat
Library Support:
   UWB_MFC_Lib1
   UWB_D3D_Lib17

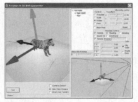

Figure 16.7.   Tutorial 16.4.

It is interesting to note that the computed rotation matrix is guaranteed to be an *orthonormal* matrix. Recall that an orthonormal matrix has normalized row and column vectors that are perpendicular to each other. As discussed in Section B.4, an orthonormal matrix defines the orientation of an object. Our experience from Tutorials 16.3 and 16.4 verify that modifications to the rotation parameters do indeed only change the orientation without changing the position or the size of the tiger. In this section, we examine how to compute and control the rotation matrix to achieve specific orientations for objects.

Tutorial 16.5. Using and Computing the Rotation Matrix

- **Goal.** Demonstrate how to use the rotation matrix in maneuvering objects and understand that we can compute rotation matrices to create custom orientation of objects.

- **Approach.** Implement moving forward, aiming, and homing-in functionality based on using and computing the rotation matrix.

Figure 16.8 is a screenshot of running Tutorial 16.5. The interesting computations here are moving forward, aiming, and homing in.

Moving forward. Before we begin, notice that by default the tiger's head is facing toward the negative z-axis (blue arrow) direction. Now, in preparation for controlling the navigation of the tiger, select the tiger node and click on the "Rotation" radio button in the `XformInfo` control panel. Enable the movement of the tiger by clicking on the "Move Tiger" checkbox. Observe that the tiger moves forward in the direction of its head. We can control the forward direction of the tiger by adjusting the y rotation (y slider bar). The x rotation allows the tiger to move higher or lower from its current level.

To implement this forward-moving functionality, we must first compute the current forward direction $\hat{\mathbf{V}}_f$ of the tiger and then change the tiger position $\mathbf{P}_t$ in the $\hat{\mathbf{V}}_f$ direction. From the orthonormal basis defined in the tiger's object coordinate (OC) space, we can see that the tiger's head is facing the negative z-axis. This observation says that, in the tiger's OC space, the forward direction $\hat{\mathbf{V}}_f^{oc}$ is

$$\hat{\mathbf{V}}_f^{oc} = \begin{bmatrix} 0 & 0 & -1 \end{bmatrix}.$$

The current forward direction (in WC space) is controlled by the user's rotation settings $\mathbf{R}$ such that

$$\hat{\mathbf{V}}_f^{wc} = \hat{\mathbf{V}}_f^{oc} \mathbf{R}.$$

Tutorial 16.5.
Project Name:
  D3D_Orientation
Library Support:
  UWB_MFC_Lib1
  UWB_D3D_Lib17

Figure 16.8.   Tutorial 16.5.

Transforming   directions. Given a transformation matrix $\mathbf{M}$ and a direction vector $\mathbf{V}$, to transform the vector by the matrix, we must compute

$$\mathbf{V}(\mathbf{M}^{-1})^T.$$

In this case, $\mathbf{R}$ is an orthonormal rotation matrix where

$$(\mathbf{R}^{-1})^T = \mathbf{R}.$$

For this reason, we can compute the transformation of $\mathbf{V}_i$ by simply multiplying with the matrix $\mathbf{R}$.

```
void CModel::ComputeTigerPosition(float sec) {
    // Transform operator of the tiger scene node
A:  UWB_XformInfo xf = m_TigerNode->GetXformInfo();
    // user rotation settings (R)
    mat3 tigerM = xf.GetRotation();
    // forward direction in tiger oc space (V̂_f^oc)
B:  vec3 tigerFront(0,0,-1);
    // forward direction in WC (V̂_f^wc)
    vec3 currentFront = tigerFront * tigerM;
    // speed of 0.4 unit per second
C:  float tigerSpeed = 0.4f;
    // tiger's current velocity (V_t)
    vec3 tigerVelocity = currentFront * tigerSpeed;
    // sets the velocity to the scene node
D:  m_TigerNode->SetVelocity(tigerVelocity);
    // computes: P'_t = P_t + (V_t × sec)
    m_TigerNode->MoveNodeByVelocity(sec);
}
```

Source file.
Model_MoveTiger.cpp file in the *Model* folder of the D3D_Orientation project.

Listing 16.13. Moving the tiger forward.

Now, to move the tiger forward, we compute a forward-moving velocity $\mathbf{V}_t$,

$$\mathbf{V}_t = \hat{\mathbf{V}}_f^{wc} \times \text{speed},$$

where speed is some constant, and we change the tiger position $\mathbf{P}_t$:

$$\mathbf{P}'_t = \mathbf{P}_t + \mathbf{V}_t.$$

Listing 16.13 shows the implementation of moving the tiger in its forward direction. The ComputeTigerPosition() function is called from CModel::Update Simulation() during each timer update event. We can see a straightforward implementation of the mathematics we have derived. At label A, we obtain a matrix representation of the user's rotation settings $\mathbf{R}$, the forward direction in WC space $\hat{\mathbf{V}}_f^{wc}$ is computed at label B, the forward velocity $\mathbf{V}_t$ is computed at label C, and finally, the tiger's new position $\mathbf{P}'_t$ is computed at label D.

Aiming with a rotation matrix. Enable plane aiming by checking the "Aim Plane At Tiger" checkbox. Notice that the orientation of the purple plane is changed immediately to face toward the tiger. Now, enable the movement of the tiger by checking the "Move Tiger" checkbox and navigate the tiger. Observe that

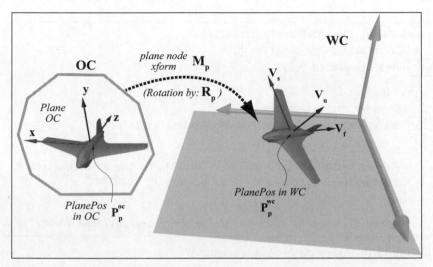

Figure 16.9. The plane OC and WC points.

the plane continuously aims its front toward the tiger. This aiming functionality can be implemented by defining and maintaining an appropriate rotation matrix for the purple plane. In this case, as illustrated in Figure 16.9, by observing the orthonormal basis defined in the plane's OC space:

$$\text{Plane orthonormal basis:} \begin{cases} \hat{\mathbf{V}}_s &= (x_s, \quad y_s, \quad z_s), \\ \hat{\mathbf{V}}_u &= (x_u, \quad y_u, \quad z_u), \\ \hat{\mathbf{V}}_f &= (x_f, \quad y_f, \quad z_f), \end{cases}$$

where the corresponding rotation matrix $\mathbf{R}_p$ for the plane is

$$\mathbf{R}_p = \begin{bmatrix} x_s & y_s & z_s \\ x_u & y_u & z_u \\ x_f & y_f & z_f \end{bmatrix}. \tag{16.5}$$

In this case, the z-axis ($\hat{\mathbf{V}}_f$) is the front direction, the y-axis ($\hat{\mathbf{V}}_u$) is the up direction, and with the right-handed coordinate system, the x-axis,

$$\mathbf{V}_s = \mathbf{V}_u \times \mathbf{V}_f \tag{16.6}$$

and normalizing $\mathbf{V}_s$ to get $\hat{\mathbf{V}}_s$, is the side direction. Now, to aim the plane toward the tiger, we must compute $\hat{\mathbf{V}}_f$ to be the direction toward the tiger. Assuming P_p^{wc} is the plane position in WC and P_t^{wc} is the position of the tiger, then

$$\mathbf{V}_f = -(P_t^{wc} - P_p^{wc}).$$

Source file.
Model_AimPlane.cpp   file
in the *Model* folder of the
D3D_Orientation project.

```
vec3 CModel::ComputePlanePosition() {
    // initial plane position Pₚᵒᶜ
A:  vec3 planePos(0,0,0);
    ⋮

    // plane node transform Mₚ
B:  UWB_XformInfo planeXf=m_PlaneNode->GetXformInfo();
    ⋮

    planeXf.SetUpModelStack(dh); // load Mₚ to top of matrix stack
    dh.TransformPoint(planePos); // compute Pₚʷᶜ = Pₚᵒᶜ Mₚ
    ⋮

    return planePos;                // return plane position in WC: Pₚʷᶜ
```

Listing 16.14. Computing the plane position in WC.

The negation reflects the fact that the initial front direction of the plane points toward the negative z-axis. Notice that the upward direction of the plane is in the y-axis direction of the WC, or

$$\hat{\mathbf{V}}_u' = \begin{bmatrix} 0 & 0 & 1 \end{bmatrix}.$$

Now we can compute $\mathbf{V}_s$ according to Equation (16.6),

$$\mathbf{V}_s = \hat{\mathbf{V}}_u' \times \mathbf{V}_f.$$

In order to ensure $\mathbf{V}_u$ is perpendicular to the other two axes, we must compute

$$\mathbf{V}_u = \mathbf{V}_f \times \mathbf{V}_s.$$

Lastly, we must normalize all three vectors to compute $\hat{\mathbf{V}}_u$, $\hat{\mathbf{V}}_f$, and $\hat{\mathbf{V}}_s$ for components of the rotation matrix in Equation (16.5). Listing 16.14 shows that we can compute the plane WC position (P_p^{wc}) by observing that in OC space, P_p^{oc} is simply the origin. At label A, we initialize the plane OC position P_o^{oc} to be the origin. At label B, we use the plane's scene node transform ($\mathbf{M}_p$) to compute the plane's position in WC space P_p^{wc}.

In the following discussion, we separate the discussion of the ComputePlane Rotation() function into three separate listings: Listing 16.15 presents how we compute the plane-to-tiger direction $\mathbf{V}_f$. Listing 16.16 describes using a rotation matrix to aim the plane toward the tiger. Finally, Listing 16.17 describes using quaternion rotation to aim the plane toward the tiger. Listing 16.15 shows the

```
void CModel::ComputePlaneRotation(float sec) {
    ⋮
A:  UWB_XformInfo tigerXf=m_TigerNode->GetXformInfo(); // tiger scene node transform Mₜ
    vec3 planePos=ComputePlanePosition();              // plane position in WC (Pₚʷᶜ)
    vec3 dirToTiger=tigerXf.GetTranslation()-planePos; // direction to tiger:
                                                       // Vf = Pₜʷᶜ − Pₚʷᶜ
    ⋮
    // distance betwen tiger and plane = ‖Vf‖
B:   float len = length(dirToTiger);
    if (len < 0.1f) return // tiger and plane are too close: done
    dirToTiger /= len;      // normalize Vf
    ⋮
C:  if (this->m_RotateWithMatrix)
        // rotate plane by computing rotation matrix ...
        // details are in: Listing 16.16
        ⋮
    else
        // rotate plane by computing Quaternion ...
        // details are in: Listing 16.17
        ⋮
```

Source file.
Model_AimPlane.cpp   file
in the *Model* folder of the
D3D_Orientation project.

Listing 16.15. Direction from plane to tiger.

implementation of computing the plane-to-tiger direction. At label A, we subtract the WC tiger and plane positions to compute V_f. The computation at label B is a reflection of the fact that it is mathematically impossible to aim an object at itself. In this case, the length of V_f is the distance between the tiger and the plane. When this distance is very small, two objects are very close to each other, and we abort the aim computation. Label C illustrates that there are two ways to implement the aiming functionality. Here, we will pay attention to Listing 16.16, aiming with a rotation matrix. At label A of Listing 16.16, we fist invert V_f to reflect the fact that the plane points in the negative z-direction, after which the side vector V_s is computed using the y-axis as the up direction (Equation (16.6)). At label B, we test for the situation where the tiger is directly beneath or above the plane. In these cases, the plane will be pointing in the y-direction, and we must choose either the x- or the z-axis as the up and side directions. At label C, we ensure that the three vectors are perpendicular to one another and normalize the vectors. Label D fills in the content of rotation matrix R_p according to

Source file.
Model_AimPlane.cpp file
in the *Model* folder of the
D3D_Orientation project.

```
void CModel::ComputePlaneRotation(float sec) {
    ⋮
    // details are in ... Listing 16.15 ...
    // compute direction to tiger (dirToTgr - V̂_f)
    if (this->m_RotateWithMatrix)
        // front is negative z
A:  dirToTgr = -dirToTgr;
        // V̂'_u is the WC y-axis direction
        vec3 upVec(0, 1, 0);
        // V_s = V̂'_u × V̂_f (Equation 16.6)
        vec3 sideVec = cross(upVec, dirToTgr);
        // if V_f and V_u almost parallel
B:  if (length2(sideVec)<0.001f)
            // assign fixed up/side vectors
            ⋮
        // V̂_u perpendicular to V_f and V_s
C:  upVec=cross(dirToTgr,sideVec);
        // normalize all vectors
        normalize(upVec); normalize(sideVec);
        // plane rotation matrix (R_p)
D:  mat3 R;
        // r00 = x_s r01 = y_s r02 = z_s
        R[0][0]=sideVec.x; R[0][1]=sideVec.y; R[0][2]=sideVec.z;
        // r10 = x_u r11 = y_u r12 = z_u
        R[1][0]=upVec.x;   R[1][1]=upVec.y;   R[1][2]=upVec.z;
        // r20 = x_f r21 = y_f r22 = z_f
        R[2][0]=dirToTgr.x;R[2][1]=dirToTgr.y;R[2][2]=dirToTgr.z;
        // M_p.rotation ← R_p
        planeXf.SetRotation(planeRot);
        // plane scene node ← updated M_p
        m_PlaneNode->SetXformInfo(planeXf);
    else
        // details are in: Listing 16.17 ...
        // rotate plane by working with Quaternion
    ⋮
```

Listing 16.16. Aiming the plane with a rotation matrix.

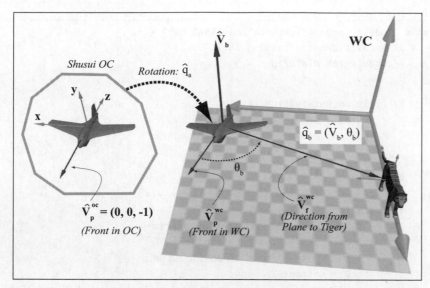

Figure 16.10. Describing plane rotation with a quaternion.

Equation (16.5) to assign the computed axis frame to the plane. When drawing the plane with the $\mathbf{R}_p$ rotation matrix, the plane aims toward the tiger with up in the y-axis direction.

Aiming with quaternion rotations. Restart Tutorial 16.5, click on "Aim Plane At Tiger," and enable rotation with quaternion computation by selecting the "Rotate With Quat" radio button. Now, select the tiger node and set the translation of the tiger to $(10, 10, 10)$. First of all, verify that the plane is still aiming toward the tiger. Now, concentrate on the plane and switch from "Rotate With Quat" to "Rotate With Matrix" to notice the very different upward direction of the plane. As we have seen in Listing 16.16, the matrix rotation computation ensures the upward direction is along the y-axis. As we will see, quaternion computation supports a simple rotation to re-orientate the plane.

Recall from Equation (16.4) that a quaternion $\hat{\mathbf{q}}$ is represented by four floating-point numbers:

$$\hat{\mathbf{q}} = (\hat{\mathbf{V}}, \theta) = (v_x, v_y, v_z, \theta),$$

where $\hat{\mathbf{V}}$ is the axis of rotation and θ is the angle to rotate. As illustrated in Figure 16.10, if we let

$$
\begin{aligned}
\mathbf{V}_p &= \quad \text{plane forward direction,} \\
\mathbf{V}_f &= \quad \text{direction from plane to tiger,}
\end{aligned}
$$

Source file.
Model_AimPlane.cpp   file
in the *Model* folder of the
D3D_Orientation project.

```
void CModel::ComputePlaneRotation(float sec) {
    // details are in: Listing 16.15 ...
    //compute the dirToTiger = V̂_f
        ⋮

    if (this->m_RotateWithMatrix)
        // details are in: Listing 16.16 ...
        // aim the plane with a rotation matrix
        ⋮

    else
            // front dir (V_p) is negative z
A:      vec3 frontDir(0,0,-1);
            // R_a - current plane rotation matrix
        mat3 pm = planeXF.GetRotation();
            // V_p^{wc} = V_p^{oc} R_a - front direction in WC
        frontDir = frontDir * pm;
            // cosTheta is θ_b, where θ_b is the angle between V_p^{wc} and V_f
B:      float cosTheta=dot(frontDir, dirToTiger);
        ⋮

            // convert the angle into degree
        float theta=UWB_ToDegrees(acosf(cosTheta));
            // Two vectors already aligned, done.
        if (theta < 0.001f)  return;
            // rotAxis is: V_b = V_p^{wc} × V_f
C:      vec3 rotAxis=cross(frontDir,dirToTiger);
            // Normaize V_b to V̂_b
        normalize(rotAxis);
            // compute q̂_b = (V̂_b, θ_b)
D:      quat qb = quatFromAA(rotAxis, theta);
            // final plane rotation ← q̂_b concatenate R_a
        planeXf.UpdateRotationByQuat(qb);
            // update plane scene node with new rotation
        m_PlaneNode->SetXformInfo(planeXf);
```

Listing 16.17. Aiming the plane with a quaternion rotation.

then we can consider the aiming operation as a single rotation to align the V_p vector in the V_f direction. We observe that in the original object space, the plane's forward direction is

$$V_p^{oc} = (0,0,-1).$$

As illustrated in Figure 16.10, in the WC space, the plane's current forward direction is rotated by the plane node's `XformInfo` operator $\mathbf{R}_a$:

$$\mathbf{V}_p^{wc} = \mathbf{V}_p^{oc} \, \mathbf{R}_a.$$

By normalizing the vectors into $\hat{\mathbf{V}}_p^{wc}$ and $\hat{\mathbf{V}}_f$, we know the angle θ_b between the two vectors is

$$\theta_b = \mathrm{acos}(\hat{\mathbf{V}}_p^{wc} \cdot \hat{\mathbf{V}}_f).$$

In addition, as shown in Figure 16.10, we know that the axis of rotation $\mathbf{V}_b$ must be perpendicular to both $\mathbf{V}_p^{wc}$ and $\mathbf{V}_f$, or

$$\mathbf{V}_b = \mathbf{V}_p^{wc} \times \mathbf{V}_f.$$

We can normalize the axis of rotation to $\hat{\mathbf{V}}_b$. In this way, we can describe $\mathbf{V}_f$ as the result of rotating $\mathbf{V}_p^{wc}$ about the $\hat{\mathbf{V}}_b$ axis by θ_b. Notice that rotating θ_b about $\hat{\mathbf{V}}_b$ is the quaternion rotation

$$\hat{\mathbf{q}}_b = (\hat{\mathbf{V}}_b, \theta_b).$$

Rotation matrix and quaternion. As discussed in Section 16.2, all rotation (orthonormal) matrices can be converted into corresponding quaternion representations. If $\mathbf{R}_a$ is a rotation matrix that describes a sequence of rotations, then the corresponding quaternion $\hat{\mathbf{q}}_a$ would represent the same rotation.

Listing 16.17 is a continuation of Listing 16.16. This listing shows the same plane-aiming functionality with quaternion rotation implementation. At label A, the initial front direction $\mathbf{V}_p^{oc}$ of the plane is defined to be in the negative z-axis and transformed to $\mathbf{V}_p^{wc}$ in WC space. At label B, we compute the angle θ_b between $\mathbf{V}_p^{wc}$ and $\mathbf{V}_f$ with a dot product. A very small θ_b value says that the two vectors $(\mathbf{V}_p^{wc}, \mathbf{V}_f)$ are almost parallel (in the same direction), and we are done. At label C, the axis of rotation $\mathbf{V}_b$ is computed and normalized. At label D, the quaternion is computed and set to the plane scene node transformation operator.

Slerp: Spherical linear interpolation with quaternion. Restart Tutorial 16.5, enable rotation with quaternion computation by selecting the "Rotate With Quat" radio button, and click on "Aim Teapot At Tiger." Notice that in this case, instead of instantaneous change of orientation, the teapot rotates gradually toward the tiger. As illustrated in Figure 16.11, let the spout of the teapot to be the forward direction and,

$$\mathbf{V}_t \quad = \quad \text{teapot spout direction,}$$
$$\mathbf{V}_f \quad = \quad \text{direction from teapot to tiger.}$$

In the original object coordinate (OC) space, the teapot spout points in the positive x-direction, or

$$\mathbf{V}_t^{oc} = (1,0,0).$$

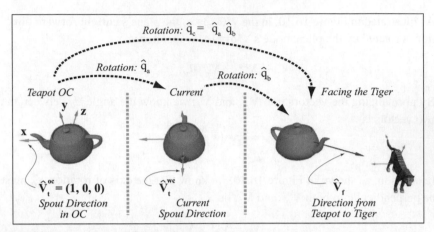

Figure 16.11. Orientation of the teapot.

The current teapot spout direction $\mathbf{V}_t^{wc}$ is the result of applying the XformInfo transformation (rotation $\mathbf{R}_a$ or $\hat{\mathbf{q}}_a$):

$$\mathbf{V}_t^{wc} = \mathbf{V}_t^{oc} \, \mathbf{R}_a.$$

Figure 16.11 shows that the rotation $\hat{\mathbf{q}}_b$, aligns the current $\mathbf{V}_t^{wc}$ with $\mathbf{V}_f$. From previous discussion (Listing 16.17), we know that

$$\hat{\mathbf{q}}_b = (\hat{\mathbf{V}}_b, \theta_b),$$

where

$$\begin{cases} \mathbf{V}_b & = \mathbf{V}_t^{wc} \times \mathbf{V}_f, \\ \theta_b & = \mathrm{acos}(\hat{\mathbf{V}}_t^{wc} \cdot \hat{\mathbf{V}}_f). \end{cases}$$

As illustrated by the topmost arrow in Figure 16.11, the final orientation of the teapot is a rotation,

$$\hat{\mathbf{q}}_c = \hat{\mathbf{q}}_a \, \hat{\mathbf{q}}_b,$$

from the original teapot OC. The effect we need to accomplish is to rotate from the current direction ($\hat{\mathbf{q}}_a$) to facing the tiger ($\hat{\mathbf{q}}_c$) gradually over time.

As illustrated in Figure 16.12, to accomplish a gradual sweeping effect, in subsequent updates we must compute rotations in between $\hat{\mathbf{q}}_a$ and $\hat{\mathbf{q}}_c$, or we need to repeatedly compute $\hat{\mathbf{q}}_{new}$, where

$$\hat{\mathbf{q}}_{new} = \mathrm{LinearInterpolate}(\hat{\mathbf{q}}_a, \hat{\mathbf{q}}_c).$$

The interpolate function must linearly interpolate between two quaternion rotations. Mathematically, this requires the computation of equidistance along a

```
void CModel::ComputeTeapotRotation(float sec) {
    ⋮
    // Compute dirToTiger (Vf): direction from teapot to tiger
    //      (1): compute teapot position in WC: details are similar to Listing 16.14
    //      (2): compute Vf by subtracting teapot from tiger position:
    //           details are similar to Listing 16.15
    // dirToTiger (V̂f) is computed and initialized
    ⋮
    if (m_RotateWithMatrix)
        // Compute teapot aiming with rotation matrix:
        // details are similar to Listing 16.16
        ⋮
    else
        // Vt^oc - teapot spout direction in OC
A:  vec3 teapotFront(1.0f,0.0f,0.0f);
        // the Ra rotation (q̂a)
        mat3 tm = teapotXf.GetRotation();
        // Vt^wc = Vt^oc Ra
        teapotFront = teapotFront * tm;
        // θb = acos(V̂t^wc, V̂f)
        float cosTheta=dot(teapotFront,dirToTiger);
        // convert from radians to degree
        float theta = UWB_ToDegrees(acosf(cosTheta));
        ⋮
        vec3 rotAxis = cross(teapotFront, dirToTiger); // Vb = V̂t^wc × V̂f
        normalize(rotAxis);                            // normalize Vb to get V̂b
        quat qb = quatFromAA(rotAxis, theta);          // q̂b = (V̂b,θb)
B:  quat qa = teapotXf.GetRotationQuat();              // keep a copy of q̂a (or Ra)
        teapotXf.UpdateRotationByQuat(qb);             // concat. to the XformInfo:
                                                       // q̂c = q̂a q̂b
        quat qc = teapotXf.GetRotationQuat();          // q̂c
C:  quat newQ = slerp(qa, qc, 0.05f);                  // newQ=q̂new 5% from q̂a to q̂c
        teapotXf.SetRotationQuat(newQ);                // sets the new rotation q̂new
        m_TeapotNode->SetXformInfo(teapotXf);          // to the XformInfo node
```

Source file.
Model_AimTeapot.cpp file
in the *Model* folder of the
D3D_Orientation project.

Listing 16.18. Slerp: Working with spherical linear interpolation.

spherical arc, or spherical linear interpolation, or simply slerp. Listing 16.18
shows implementation with spherical linear interpolation (slerp). At label A,
we compute the $\hat{q}_b$ rotation that aligns the current V_t^{wc} with V_f (this computa-

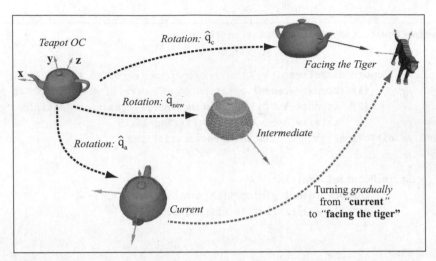

Figure 16.12. Linear interpolation of rotations.

tion is similar to Listing 16.17). At label B, we obtain a copy of the existing $\hat{\mathbf{q}}_a$ rotation and take advantage of the `XformInfo::UpdateRotationByQuat()` function to compute $\hat{\mathbf{q}}_c$ by concatenating $\hat{\mathbf{q}}_b$ with $\hat{\mathbf{q}}_a$. At label C, we invoke the `math3d++::slerp()` function to compute $\hat{\mathbf{q}}_{new}$ as a linear combination of 95% $\hat{\mathbf{q}}_a$ and 5% $\hat{\mathbf{q}}_c$. In this way, the orientation of the teapot will gradually approach the desired $\hat{\mathbf{q}}_c$ rotation.

Homing in with slerp. Click on the "Shoot" button to release an arrow from the plane. Notice that the arrow travels toward the tiger. When this arrow collides with the tiger, it will disappear. Select the tiger node and adjust the slider bars to change the translation of the tiger. Now, release another arrow and see that the arrow now travels toward the new tiger position. In fact, we can change the tiger position at any time to observe the arrow adjusting its flight path to home in on the tiger. This example demonstrates that we can combine moving forward and slerp functionality to implement a home-in flight path.

To implement this functionality, we must release the arrow according to the position and the orientation of the plane. In this way, the arrow begins its flight from the plane location with initial direction aligned to that of the plane. List-ing 16.19 shows the `FireArrow()` function that computes the initial transforma-tion of the arrow. At label A, we define accessors to the `XformIno` of the plane and the arrow. At label B, we set the arrow's position and rotation according to that of the plane's. With the proper transformation settings, home-in behavior can be implemented simply as continuously moving the arrow forward while adjusting the forward direction of the arrow slightly toward the tiger using slerp.

```
void CModel::FireArrow()  {
    // pxf is the plane's transform
A:  UWB_XformInfo pxf = m_PlaneNode->GetXformInfo();
    // axf is the arrow's transform
    UWB_XformInfo axf = m_ArrowNode.GetXformInfo();
    // Arrow translation set to plane WC position
B:  axf.SetTranslation(ComputePlanePosition());
    // Arrow orientation is plane rotation quaternion
    axf.SetRotationQuat(pxf.GetRotationQuat());
    // Update arrow scene node XformInfo
    m_ArrowNode.SetXformInfo(axf);
}
```

Source File.
Model_FireArrow.cpp file
in the *Model* folder of the
D3D_Orientation project.

Listing 16.19. Compute initial transform for the arrow.

Let

$$\mathbf{V}_m = \text{forward direction of arrow,}$$
$$\mathbf{V}_f = \text{direction from arrow toward tiger.}$$

By observation, we know the arrow's original forward direction is along the negative z-axis,

$$\mathbf{V}_m^{oc} = (0, 0, -1).$$

We also know that at any time, the arrow's scene node rotation $\mathbf{R}_a$ will rotate the arrow's forward direction to

$$\mathbf{V}_m^{wc} = \mathbf{V}_m^{oc} \mathbf{R}_a.$$

$\mathbf{R}_a$ **and** $\hat{\mathbf{q}}_a$. $\mathbf{R}_a$ is the rotation matrix of the arrow scene node XformInfo. The corresponding quaternion rotation is $\hat{\mathbf{q}}_a$.

For the arrow to travel forward, we simply change its translation in the $\mathbf{V}_m^{wc}$ direction. Now, we must also adjust the forward direction of the arrow to align $\mathbf{V}_m^{wc}$ with $\mathbf{V}_f$. By now we know the rotation $\hat{\mathbf{q}}_b$,

$$\hat{\mathbf{q}}_b = (\hat{\mathbf{V}}_b, \theta_b) \text{ where } \begin{cases} \mathbf{V}_b = \mathbf{V}_m^{wc} \times \mathbf{V}_f, \\ \theta_b = \text{acos}(\hat{\mathbf{V}}_m^{wc} \cdot \mathbf{V}_f), \end{cases}$$

aligns $\mathbf{V}_m^{wc}$ with $\mathbf{V}_f$. In exactly the same manner as in the teapot's case before,

$$\hat{\mathbf{q}}_a - \text{rotates from OC to WC,}$$
$$\hat{\mathbf{q}}_b - \text{rotates from WC to aim at tiger,}$$
$$\hat{\mathbf{q}}_c - \hat{\mathbf{q}}_a \hat{\mathbf{q}}_b - \text{rotates from OC to aim at tiger,}$$

where we are interested in computing a $\hat{\mathbf{q}}_{new}$ that is a linear combination of the $\hat{\mathbf{q}}_a$ and $\hat{\mathbf{q}}_c$ rotations. Listing 16.20 shows the implementation of the home-in functionality. At label A, we compute $\mathbf{V}_m^{wc}$ according to the arrow's scene node transform. The code under label B is similar to that of Listing 16.13 where we must

```
void CModel::ComputeArrowTransform(float sec) {
```

> *A:*
```
    vec3 arrowFront(0,0,-1);                // V_m^oc initially is -z axis
    mat3 Ra = m_ArrowNode...GetRotation(); // R_a arrow node rotation
    arrowFront = arrowFront * Ra;           // V_m^wc = V_m^oc R_a
    ⋮
```

> *B:*
```
    // Similar to Listing 16.13: Computing forward direction and moving forward
    // arrow velocity is defined by the current V_m^wc
    vec3 arrowV = arrowSpeed * arrowFront;
    // arrow node gets the new velocity
    m_ArrowNode.SetVelocity(arrowV);
    // move the arrow node
    m_ArrowNode.MoveNodeByVelocity( sec );
    ⋮
    // compute V_f
```

> *C:*
```
    vec3 dirToTiger = ...
    // length of V_f. if this is short, then it means
    float dist = length(dirToTiger);
    // the arrow is close to the tiger. Hit! We are done.
    if (dist < 1.0f) return;
    ⋮
```

> *D:*
```
    // Similar to Listing 16.18: Gradual alignment with V_f using slerp
    // to compute θ_b = acos(V̂_m^wc · V̂_f)
    float cosTheta=dot(arrowFront,dirToTiger);
    ⋮
    vec3 rotAxis=cross(arrowFront,dirToTiger); // V_b = V̂_m^wc × V̂_f)
    quat qb = quatFromAA(rotAxis, theta);      // q̂_b = (V̂_b, θ_b)
    // compute and set q̂_a and q̂_c
    ⋮
    // q̂_new is linear combination of q̂_a and q̂_c
    quat newQ = slerp(qa, qc, homeInRate);
    ⋮ // sets the new rotation to the arrow scene node XformInfo
}
```

Listing 16.20. Computing homing-in functionality.

Source file.
Model_FireArrow.cpp file
in the *Model* folder of the
D3D_Orientation project.

re-compute the velocity according to the up-to-date forward direction. At label C, $\mathbf{V}_f$, the vector between the arrow and the tiger is computed and tested. If this vector is short, it means that the tiger and the arrow are close by. We will register that as the arrow having arrived at the tiger and return. The code under label D is similar to that of Listing 16.18, where we compute the interpolated rotation $\hat{\mathbf{q}}_{new}$ to align the arrow front direction toward the tiger.

16.4   Simple Scene Graph in 3D

Everything we learned about scene nodes and scene graphs generalize to 3D space in a straightforward manner. In this section, we use a simple example to refresh and verify our knowledge from Chapter 11.

Tutorial 16.6.
Project Name:
    D3D_SimpleHierarchy
Library Support:
    UWB_MFC_Lib1
    UWB_D3D_Lib17

Tutorial 16.6. Scene Node and Scene Graph in 3D

- **Goal.** Demonstrate that the hierarchical modeling and transformation concepts that we learned from 2D apply in a straightforward manner in 3D.

- **Approach.** Build a simple two-level hierarchy of scene nodes in 3D and demonstrate that all UI transformation applies in an intuitive manner.

Figure 16.14 is a screenshot of running Tutorial 16.6. Figure 16.13 shows that the center object in this tutorial is organized by a simple scene tree hierarchy. On the right of the figure, notice that:

Figure 16.14.   Tutorial 16.6.

1. **The Base node is the root of the hierarchy.** The $\mathbf{M}_1$ transform of the Base node controls the entire scene tree hierarchy. In this case, we want

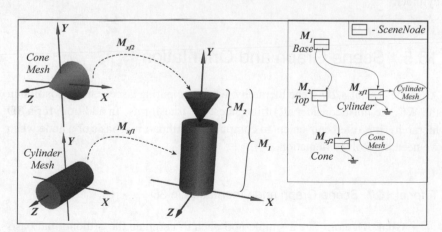

Figure 16.13. Building a simple scene graph in 3D.

the entire object to be transformed with respect to the origin, and thus the pivot of $\mathbf{M}_1$ is located at $(0,0,0)$. Cylinder node is a child of the Base node and thus is only affected by the $\mathbf{M}_1$ transform.

2. **The Top node is a child of the Base node.** The $\mathbf{M}_2$ transform of the Top node only controls the descendent of this node. In this case, the pivot of $\mathbf{M}_2$ is set to be the tip of the cylinder base because we want the top of the object to be transformed with respect to this position. All descendants of the Top node (Cone node) will inherit the concatenated $\mathbf{M}_2\mathbf{M}_1$ transform.

The left of Figure 16.13 shows that the $\mathbf{M}_{xf1}$ transform of the Cylinder node transforms the cylinder mesh from its original position along the z-axis to the standing position along the y-axis. In a similar fashion, the $\mathbf{M}_{xf2}$ transform of the Cone node transforms the cone mesh to the top of the standing cylinder. In this case, despite all the scene node transforms being visible (and manipulatable) via the GUI SceneTreeControl, only the transforms associated with the Base ($\mathbf{M}_1$) and Top nodes ($\mathbf{M}_2$) are designed for the user to manipulate the hierarchy. The transforms associated with the Cylinder ($\mathbf{M}_{xf1}$) and the Cone ($\mathbf{M}_{xf2}$) nodes are required to place the corresponding meshes in their initial positions and are not meant to be manipulated by the user. We can verify the effects of $\mathbf{M}_1$ and $\mathbf{M}_2$ by selecting the Base and Top nodes and manipulating transformation sliders. Listing 16.21 shows the implementation that builds the hierarchy of Figure 16.13. The memory of the four scene nodes is allocated at label A. The parent-child relationships of these nodes are organized at label B. At label C and label D, the $\mathbf{M}_{xf1}$ and $\mathbf{M}_{xf2}$ transforms are computed and loaded into the Cylinder and Cone nodes, respectively. Finally, at label E, the $\mathbf{M}_2$ pivot is set to be the top of the cylinder.

16.5   Scene Graph and Orientation

As in the case of a 2D scene hierarchy, when computing a scene node position in the WC, we must consider all of its ancestors' transforms. In addition, for a 3D hierarchy, it is often convenient to compute the orthonormal basis of a node when we need to resolve orientation.

Tutorial 16.7.
Project Name:
    D3D_SceneGraphIn3D
Library Support:
    UWB_MFC_Lib1
    UWB_D3D_Lib17

Tutorial 16.7. Scene Graph and Orientation in 3D

- **Goal.** Demonstrate a simple approach to compute the orthonormal basis for a scene node in a scene hierarchy.

```
CModel::CModel() : m_root_node( L"root_node" ) {
      ⋮
      // Base node for user interaction
A:    UWB_SceneNode *pBaseNode = new UWB_SceneNode(...);
      // Node for xform Cylinder Mesh
      UWB_SceneNode *pCylinderNode = new UWB_SceneNode(...);
      // Top node for user interaction
      UWB_SceneNode *pTopNode = new UWB_SceneNode(...);
      // Node for xform Cone Mesh
      UWB_SceneNode *pConeNode = new UWB_SceneNode(...);
      ⋮
B:    pBaseNode->InsertChildNode(pCylinderNode); // Cylinder is child of Base
      pBaseNode->InsertChildNode(pTopNode);      // Top is child of Base
      pTopNode->InsertChildNode(pConeNode);      // Cone is child of Top
      m_root_node.InsertChildNode(pBaseNode);    // base is root of hierarchy
      ⋮
C:    pMesh = new UWBD3D_PrimitiveMesh(L"cylinder.x"); // Cylinder mesh primitive
      ⋮
      xf1.UpdateRotationXByDegree(90);              // X rotation of 90 degrees
      xf1.SetScale(vec3(3.0f/2.0f, 3.0f/2.0f, 2.0f)); // Scale to right radius/height
      xf1.SetTranslation(vec3(0.0f, 3.0f, 0.0f));   // ensure one end at origin
      pCylinderNode->SetXformInfo(xf1);             // xform mesh to component location
      ⋮
D:    pMesh = new UWBD3D_PrimitiveMesh(L"OpenCone.x"); // Cone mesh primitive
      ⋮
      xf2.UpdateRotationXByDegree(-90);             // X rotation of -90 degrees
      xf2.SetScale(vec3(2.0f, 2.0f, 2.0f/3.0f));    // scale to right radius/height
      xf2.SetTranslation(vec3(0.0f, 7.0f, 0.0f));   // ensure tip at top of cylinder
      pConeNode->SetXformInfo(xf2);                 // xform mesh to component position
      ⋮
E:    m2.SetPivot(vec3(0.0f, 6.0f, 0.0f)); // pivoted at top of cylinder
      pTopNode->SetXformInfo(m2);          // top node pivoted at top of cylinder
      ⋮
```

Source file. `Model.cpp` file in the *Model* folder of the `D3D_SimpleHierarchy` project.

Listing 16.21. Building a simple hierarchy.

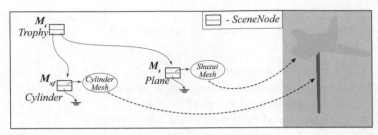

Figure 16.15. Scene graph and orientation in 3D.

Figure 16.16. Tutorial 16.7.

Matrix M_{xf}. Recall from the discussion in Tutorial 16.6 that the transformation M_{xf} in Figure 16.17 is defined to transform the cylinder mesh to the proper component location.

- **Approach.** Implement a simple two-level hierarchy and compute the orthonormal basis for the leaf node to verify the position and orientation.

Figure 16.16 is a screenshot of running Tutorial 16.7. At the center of the application is the "Plane Trophy" object, a green plane on a red cylinder stick. Figure 16.15 shows the two-level scene node hierarchy of the "Plane Trophy" object. We see that the green plane (*shusui*) and the cylindrical base are siblings, both children of the trophy base. In this case, the M_t transform of the Plane Trophy node and the M_s transform of the shusui node are designed to be manipulated by the user, whereas the M_{xf} transformation of the cylinder node is designed to scale and place the cylindrical mesh in the proper initial position.

Click on the "Compute Ref Axis" checkbox to observe that the orthonormal basis drawn at the top of vertical tail wing and a sphere continuously travel from the center toward the front of the plane. Now select and manipulate the transforms of the Plane Trophy (M_t) and shusui (M_s) nodes. Notice that the orthonormal basis drawn at the vertical tail wing always maintains its relative position and the sphere always maintains its relative traveling direction. This functionality can be supported by computing the proper orthonormal basis of the shusui child node.

As illustrated in Figure 16.17, a straightforward approach to compute the general transformation of an orthonormal basis is by identifying and tracking the transformation of the three anchoring positions, where

$$
\begin{cases}
P_o & = (0,0,0), \\
P_y & = (0,1,0), \\
P_z & = (0,0,1).
\end{cases}
$$

In our case, we have a general transformation operator (M) that is the concatenation of the parent trophy (M_t) and the child shusui (M_s) transforms,

$$
M = M_s \, M_t,
$$

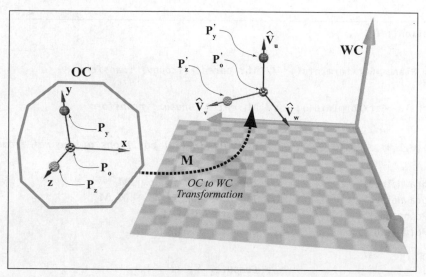

Figure 16.17. Transforming the anchoring positions of an orthonormal basis.

such that

$$\begin{cases} P_o' = P_o\,\mathbf{M}, \\ P_y' = P_y\,\mathbf{M}, \\ P_z' = P_z\,\mathbf{M}. \end{cases}$$

Now, we can compute

$$\begin{cases} \mathbf{V}_y' = P_y' - P_o', \\ \mathbf{V}_z' = P_z' - P_o', \end{cases}$$

and

$$\mathbf{V}_x' = \mathbf{V}_y' \times \mathbf{V}_z'.$$

In this way, the resulting orthonormal basis is

$$\text{Orthonormal basis} = \begin{cases} \hat{\mathbf{V}}_w, \\ \hat{\mathbf{V}}_u, \\ \hat{\mathbf{V}}_v, \end{cases} \quad \text{where} \quad \begin{cases} \mathbf{V}_w = \mathbf{V}_x', \\ \mathbf{V}_u = \mathbf{V}_z' \times \mathbf{V}_x', \\ \mathbf{V}_v = \mathbf{V}_z'. \end{cases}$$

Notice that we must explicitly normalize the vectors $\mathbf{V}_w$, $\mathbf{V}_u$, and $\mathbf{V}_v$. List-ing 16.22 shows the implementation that computes the orthonormal basis of the shusui scene node. At label A, we gain access to the $\mathbf{M}_t$ and $\mathbf{M}_s$ transforms. At label B, the general transformation $\mathbf{M}$ is computed by concatenating $\mathbf{M}_t$ and $\mathbf{M}_s$ transforms on the matrix stack. The orthonormal basis anchor positions P_o, P_y, and P_z are then transformed. The vectors for the orthonormal basis ($\hat{\mathbf{V}}_w$, $\hat{\mathbf{V}}_u$, and

Source file.
Model_Simulation.cpp file in the *Model* folder of the D3D_SceneGraphIn3D project.

```
void CModel::UpdateSimulation() {
    ⋮
A:  UWB_XformInfo pxf = m_Plane->GetXformInfo(); // Mt: parent (Trophy) transform
    ⋮
    UWB_XformInfo cxf = child->GetXformInfo();     // Ms:child (shusui) transform
    ⋮
B:  vec3 pos(0,0,0), yPos(0,1,0), zPos(0,0,1);    // Po,Py,Pz: initial positions of the ref frame
    ⋮
    pxf.SetUpModelStack(drawHelper);               // Top of stack is now: Mt
    cxf.SetUpModelStack(drawHelper);               // Top of stack is now: Ms Mt
    drawHelper.TransformPoint(pos);                // Compute: Po Ms Mt
    drawHelper.TransformPoint(yPos);               // Compute: Py Ms Mt
    ⋮
C:  vec3 Vy = yPos - pos;                          // Compute: V'y = P'y − P'o
    ⋮
    vec3 nVz = pos - zPos;     // Forward direction: this is negative z
    vec3 Vx = cross(Vy, -nVz); // This is the side vector
    Vy = cross(-nVz, Vx);      // Ensure all vectors are perpendicular
    normalize(Vy); ...         // Ensure all vectors are noramlized
    ⋮
D:  R[0][0]=Vx.x;  R[0][1]=Vx.y;  R[0][2]=Vx.z; // The computed orthonomal basis is
    R[1][0]=Vy.x;  R[1][1]=Vy.y;  R[1][2]=Vy.z; // is the rotation matrix
    R[2][0]=-nVz.x;R[2][1]=-nVz.y;R[2][2]=-nVz.z;
    ⋮
E:  UWB_XformInfo rxf=m_RefNode->GetXformInfo(); // Axis Frame objects XformInfo
    ⋮
    rxf.SetTranslation(pos);     // Set the position to draw the axis frame
    rxf.SetRotation(R);          // Orthonormal basis is the rotation matrix
    m_RefNode->SetXformInfo(rxf);
    ⋮
F:  UWB_XformInfo bxf=m_BallNode.GetXformInfo(); // The traveling sphere's XformInfo
    ⋮
    bxf.SetTranslation(pos);                      // Sphere starts at the axis frame position
    ⋮
    m_BallNode.SetVelocity(nVz);                  // Sphere velocity is negative-Z direction
```

Listing 16.22. Computing the orthonormal basis of a scene node.

$\hat{\mathbf{V}}_v$) are computed at label C. At label D, these vectors are used to create a rotation matrix. This rotation matrix is assigned at label E to orient the orthonormal basis according to the transforms. Finally, at label F, the velocity of the traveling sphere is set to the negative-z direction, which is the forward direction of the shusui plane node.

16.6   Collision in 3D

At this point, we understand how to compute the position and orientation (orthonormal basis) of any scene node in a general scene hierarchy. So far, we have worked with examples of using this information to *aim* objects and to *move* objects along predetermined paths. In this section, we examine computing intersection of scene nodes in 3D.

Tutorial 16.8. Collision Computation in 3D

- **Goal.** Demonstrate that we can collide scene nodes in 3D space in similar fashion as in 2D.

- **Approach.** Implement the collision between a simple scene node and the leaf node of a general hierarchy.

Figure 16.18 is a screenshot of running Tutorial 16.8. At the center is the two-level trophy scene node hierarchy from the previous tutorial where the plane shusui is a leaf node. Click on the "Tiger Shoots" checkbox to see the tiger aim toward the hierarchy and continuously release spheres toward the shusui leaf node. Now select the trophy scene node hierarchy and transform the entire hierarchy, e.g., translate the scene node along the *x*-axis. Notice that when missed, the sphere will continue to travel for a few seconds before another sphere is released from the tiger. Now, select and change the transformation of the shusui leaf node. Notice that the tiger is aiming and releasing the sphere toward the shusui leaf node. The implementation of this tutorial combines many of the concepts we have learned from the previous tutorials. For example, Listing 16.22 showed us how to compute the position of the shusui leaf node, Listing 16.16 showed us how to aim the tiger toward the computed shusui position, and Listing 16.13 showed us how to move the sphere along the defined path.

In this tutorial, we are interested in the details of intersecting the sphere with the shusui node. As discussed in Section 7.5, computing accurate collisions between graphical primitives or objects involves tedious mathematics. In computer

Tutorial 16.8.
Project Name:
  D3D_CollisionIn3D
Library Support:
  UWB_MFC_Lib1
  UWB_D3D_Lib17

Figure 16.18.   Tutorial 16.8.

graphics, we typically define collision primitives to perform proximity tests. Now, click on the "Show Collision Sphere" checkbox to see the red wire-frame bound used for collision computation. Instead of performing computation based on the actual geometries, in this case the collision is approximated between the traveling sphere and the red wire-frame sphere. In this way, we have simplified the collision between two scene nodes of arbitrary geometries into a problem of intersecting two spheres in WC space. We know the intersection routine should be:

```
// 1. compute the positions (centers) of the two spheres
// 2. compute the distance between the two centers
// 3. if (computed distance > sum of radius)
//          no collision
//      else
//          collision
```

Listing 16.23. Compute intersection between two spheres.

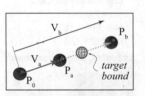

Figure 16.19. Instantaneous positions of the traveling sphere.

To follow the next part of the explanation, you should restart the tutorial such that the positions and distances between scene nodes are at their initial values. Now, adjust the "Ball Speed" slider bar to see that we can control the speed of the sphere that is released from the tiger. Adjust this slider bar such that the speed of the traveling sphere is around 71 units. Notice that with this speed, the released sphere travels right through the plane as though the intersection has failed!

Recall that we simulate the traveling of a sphere by changing its position according to its velocity at each timer update. As illustrated in Figure 16.19, in reality, our implementation positions the traveling sphere at discrete locations along the traveling path. For example, at time t_0, the sphere is located at position P_0. At the subsequent timer update t_1, the sphere's position will depend on its velocity. If the sphere is traveling at velocity V_a, then at t_1, the sphere will be located at position P_a. However, if the sphere is traveling at a higher speed at velocity V_b, then in the same timer update interval the sphere will cover a greater distance. In this example, the sphere is traveling at velocity V_b and thus will be located at P_b at time t_1. Figure 16.19 shows that even though the target bound is located in between positions P_0 and P_b, the collision computation from Listing 16.23 will fail! In this case, we must intersect the target bound with the line segment $\overline{P_0 P_b}$. Refer to the collision results echoed in the Status area:

$$DistHit(F) \quad LineHit(T)$$

where *DistHit* is the result based on distance computation and *LineHit* is the result based on line/sphere intersection.

This tutorial shows us that collision computation in 3D is similar to that in 2D. In particular, we observe:

- **Collision primitive.** Using spherical bound (circular bound in 2D) to approximate collision is efficient.

- **Collision computation.** For objects traveling at high speed, we should intersect the line segment(s) defined by the corresponding velocities.

The source code of the implementation can be found in the `HitTrophy()` function of the `Trophy_Hit.cpp` file in the *Model* folder of the `D3D_CollisionIn3D` project. The details of line-sphere intersection are described in Appendix B.

16.7 Selection in 3D

Mouse-click selection of scene nodes in 3D involves identical issues as discussed in Section 15.4. In both cases, we must construct a 3D ray based on a 2D mouse-click position.

Tutorial 16.9. Mouse-click selection of a scene node.

- **Goal.** Demonstrate that we can support the point-and-click metaphor in selecting objects in 3D space.

- **Approach.** Implement mouse-click selection with a simple scene hierarchy.

Figure 16.20 is a screenshot of running Tutorial 16.9. Click on the "Show Collision Sphere" checkbox to display the spherical wire-frame bound. Now, with the shift key depressed, the left mouse button will generate a selection ray, a line segment from the camera position, through the mouse-click position into the world. In this tutorial, the selection ray is intersected with the wire-frame bound. Notice that we can use the exact same line-sphere intersection routine to detect selection! Notice that in this case, we compute and report the results of intersection between the line and the spherical bound without considering other objects in the scene. For example, rotate (tumble) the camera position such that the floor occludes the trophy scene hierarchy. Now invoke the selection ray (by depressing the shift key and LMB) and drag the mouse around the screen area where the shusui plane is behind the floor. Because we are only intersecting the ray and the spherical bound, our program will report a successful collision even though the floor occludes the object!

Tutorial 16.9.
Project Name:
  `D3D_SelectionIn3D`
Library Support:
  `UWB_MFC_Lib1`
  `UWB_D3D_Lib17`

Figure 16.20. Tutorial 16.9.

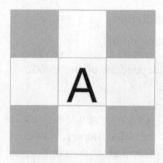

Material and Illumination

In this appendix, we demonstrate how to work with the default illumination model implemented in all of today's graphics hardware. This model is known as the *Phong* illumination model. An illumination model computes a pixel color based on the visible geometry and the lighting conditions of the scene. Typically, input to an illumination mode includes:

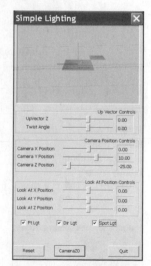

Figure A.1. Tutorial A.1.

- **Object geometry.** Describes the shape of the geometry. This information is typically defined as a normal vector at each vertex.

- **Material property.** Describes the appearance of the visible object (e.g., how incoming light is reflected).

- **Scene lighting conditions.** Describes the light sources that illuminate the scene.

In a traditional computer graphics textbook, the Phong illumination model and the associated lighting computation are typically covered extensively in dedicated chapters. With the recent advancements in graphics hardware technology, the future of a pre-defined default illumination model across all hardware platforms is becoming uncertain. This appendix includes examples that demonstrate how to work with the existing graphics hardware without in-depth discussions.

Tutorial A.1. Simple Example with Lighting Computation

Tutorial A.1.
Project Name:
  D3D_SimpleLighting
Library Support:
  UWB_MFC_Lib1

- **Goal.** Examine how to work with the illumination model.

- **Approach.** Implement a simple program independent of the UWBGL to demonstrate the effect of lighting computation.

Figure A.1 is a screenshot of running Tutorial A.1. This program is similar to Tutorial 14.1 where the source code is independent of the UWBGL library. However, this tutorial includes three extra checkboxes at the lower part of the application window. Each of these checkboxes controls the on/off switch of the corresponding light source. By switching each of the light sources on, we can observe that the point light is green in color, the directional light is purple, and the spot light is blue. All the changes from Tutorial 14.1 are in the GrfxWindowD3D.cpp file, in the OnPaint() function.

UWBGL_D3D_Lib18

Change summary. See p. 533 for a summary of changes to the library.

This library includes support for working with the default Phong illumination model. The new classes introduced by this library are UWB_Material and the UWBD3D_Light hierarchy. UWB_Primitive is modified to contain a UWB_Material as an attribute. This new attribute describes the material property of the primitive. As in any other attribute, before rendering the primitive, the material attribute is copied to the UWB_DrawHelper to be programmed into the graphics API. To observe the results of illumination, a program should create instances of UWBD3D_Light objects, initialize the UWB_Material, and enable the lighting attributes of UWB_Primitive objects.

Tutorial A.2. Lighting with UWBGL

Tutorial A.2.
Project Name:
  D3D_Lighting
Library Support:
  UWB_MFC_Lib1
  UWB_D3D_Lib18

- **Goal.** Demonstrate the support of the illumination model and lighting computation in the UWBGL.

- **Approach.** Implement a simple program based on the UWBGL.

Figure A.2 is a screenshot of running Tutorial A.2. Notice the brighter circular region in the middle of the rendered image; this is the illumination effect from a spot light. You can bring up the "Light Control" window by clicking on the "Light Control" checkbox. On the "Light Control" window, select the "Spot Light" radio button and toggle the "On/Off" checkbox. Notice the circular region appear/disappear with the on/off of the spot light. Now, click on the "Draw Lgt" checkbox and see a blue sphere being drawn. This is the position of the spot light. In similar fashion, we can switch on/off each of the point and directional lights and enable

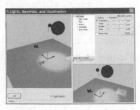

Figure A.2. Tutorial A.2.

the drawing of the lights. Notice that the directional light is drawn as an arrow, whereas the point light is also drawn as a sphere. You can examine the lighting effects by changing their positions and directions. Notice that the directional light's position and point light's direction do not affect the illumination of the scene.

Tutorial A.3. Working with a D3D Mesh

- **Goal.** Demonstrate how to work with the D3D .x mesh file format.

- **Approach.** Create an interface class that allows our program to create and manipulate the vertices of a mesh.

Figure A.3 is a screenshot of running Tutorial A.3. This tutorial is similar to Tutorial A.2 except that in this case, the rectangular floor is implemented by the UWBD3D_PrimitiveMeshCustom mesh.[1] The PrimitiveMeshCustom is a simple 2×2 mesh with uniform $n \times n$ vertex positions centered around the origin on the xz plane. Click on the "Mesh Control" checkbox to bring up the interactive mesh control window. In the interactive mesh control window, click on the "Control Grid" checkbox to see the uniformly distributed control vertices (CV). The top two slider bars let the user select a current CV. Notice that the current CV is drawn as a red box in the application window. The bottom three slider bars let the user manipulate the position of the current CV.

Tutorial A.3.
Project Name:
    D3D_CustomMesh
Library Support:
    UWB_MFC_Lib1
    UWB_D3D_Lib18

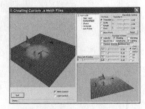

Figure A.3. Tutorial A.3.

Further Reading

We expect graphics hardware and APIs to eliminate the support for a default illumination model in the near future. Readers are encouraged to refer to Peter Shirley's *Fundamentals of Computer Graphics* for a more detailed treatment of this subject.

---

[1] Defined in the D3D_Primitive subfolder of the *D3D Files* folder of the UWBGL_D3D_Lib18 project.

Vectors

This appendix is a review of basic vector math. It is assumed that you have worked with vectors and matrices before. This chapter reviews the application of this knowledge in computer graphics but is not meant as a full coverage of linear algebra.

B.1 Vector Basics

The word "vector" is used for many different entities in different fields, and this can make issues surrounding vectors confusing. For example, in computer graphics, any one-dimensional array might be referred to as a vector. We however restrict our use to mean a geometric entity we might think of as an arrow. The main way we use vectors is as displacements, directions, and locations (points).

A displacement is sometimes called an offset and is a description of a distance and direction. For example, if you point in a direction and say "10 meters that way," you have defined a vector. A direction is simpler in that it lacks a distance. It is often represented as a unit-length displacement. A point, also called a location, is defined in terms of some special location (e.g., the origin). Any point can be defined in terms of an origin and a displacement.

B.1.1 Addition and Subtraction

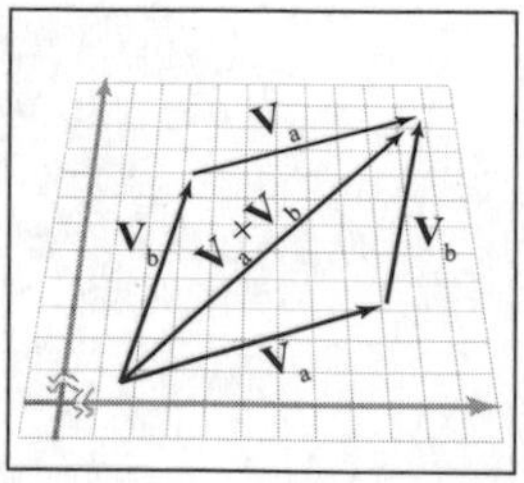

Vectors add the way we expect displacements to. If we "walk 10 steps in direction *A*" and then "walk 5 steps in direction *B*," we can achieve the same instructions by walking toward the two displacements tail to head (see Figure B.1) Subtraction works by "unwalking" and has the expected behavior (see Figure B.2).

B.1.2 Cartesian Coordinates

We often organize directions in the world according to three "special" directions. These are sometimes east/west, north/south, and up/down. Or with respect to one-self, left/right, front/back, and up/down. We usually call these special directions the *x*-, *y*-, and *z*-axes. These can be represented as unit-length vectors $\mathbf{V}_x$, $\mathbf{V}_y$, and $\mathbf{V}_z$ that are mutually perpendicular. Their ordering by convention follows the right-handed coordinate system (see Figure 13.5).

We can uniquely identify a vector by its length measured along the *x*-, *y*-, and *z*-axes. For example, a vector $\mathbf{V}_a$ is just a weighted sum of the Cartesian vectors and the origin (Figure B.3):

$$\mathbf{V}_a = x_a\mathbf{V}_x + y_a\mathbf{V}_x + z_a\mathbf{V}_z.$$

As discussed in Section 8.5.1, we can view the Cartesian vectors as implicit and shared between all vectors and just use a triple of numbers to represent $\mathbf{V}_a$:

$$\mathbf{V}_a = \begin{bmatrix} x_a & y_a & z_a \end{bmatrix}.$$

A point can also be represented by a vector, but it means interpreting the vector as a displacement from an origin point $\mathbf{O}$. Note that if we have a vector $\mathbf{V}_c = \mathbf{V}_a + \mathbf{V}_b$, then we can derive its components by just adding them:

$$x_c = x_a + x_b,$$
$$y_c = y_a + y_b,$$
$$z_c = z_a + z_b.$$

Similarly, subtraction of components corresponds to subtraction of vectors:

$$x_a = x_c - x_b, \quad y_a = y_c - y_b, \quad z_a = z_c - z_b. \tag{B.1}$$

or

$$\begin{bmatrix} x_a & y_a & z_a \end{bmatrix} = \begin{bmatrix} x_c & y_c & z_c \end{bmatrix} - \begin{bmatrix} x_b & y_b & z_b \end{bmatrix},$$

or

$$\mathbf{V}_a = \mathbf{V}_c - \mathbf{V}_b.$$

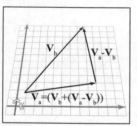

Figure B.1. Vector addition.

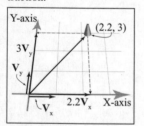

Figure B.2. Vector subtraction.

Figure B.3. Cartesian coordinates.

B.1.3 Magnitude of a Vector

From Pythagoras, we know the distance between V_b and V_c, d_{bc}, is

$$d_{bc} = \sqrt{(x_b - x_c)^2 + (y_b - y_c)^2 + (z_b - z_c)^2}.$$

From Equation (B.1), we can rewrite d_{bc} as

$$d_{bc} = \sqrt{(x_a)^2 + (y_a)^2 + (z_a)^2}.$$

Recall that x_a, y_a, and z_a are the components of vector $\mathbf{V}_a$, the vector that took us from position V_b to V_c. In other words, vector $\mathbf{V}_a$ has moved position V_b by a distance of d_{bc}. Notice that the distance moved by $\mathbf{V}_a$ is the square root of the sum of the squares of all its components. This observation is true in general that given any vector, $\mathbf{V}$,

$$\mathbf{V} = \begin{bmatrix} v_x & v_y & v_z \end{bmatrix},$$

will move any point by a distance of $\|\mathbf{V}\|$, where

$$\|\mathbf{V}\| = \sqrt{v_x{}^2 + v_y{}^2 + v_z{}^2}. \tag{B.2}$$

$\|\mathbf{V}\|$ is defined as the size or magnitude of the vector.

B.1.4 Direction of a Vector

If we scale the components of the vector by the inverse of its magnitude,

$$
\begin{aligned}
\hat{v}_x &= \frac{v_x}{\sqrt{v_x{}^2 + v_y{}^2 + v_z{}^2}} = \frac{v_x}{\|\mathbf{V}\|}, \\
\hat{v}_y &= \frac{v_y}{\sqrt{v_x{}^2 + v_y{}^2 + v_z{}^2}} = \frac{v_y}{\|\mathbf{V}\|}, \\
\hat{v}_z &= \frac{v_z}{\sqrt{v_x{}^2 + v_y{}^2 + v_z{}^2}} = \frac{v_z}{\|\mathbf{V}\|},
\end{aligned}
\tag{B.3}
$$

then the vector $\hat{\mathbf{V}}$,

$$\hat{\mathbf{V}} = \begin{bmatrix} \hat{v}_x & \hat{v}_y & \hat{v}_z \end{bmatrix},$$

has magnitude

$$\|\hat{\mathbf{V}}\| = 1.0.$$

This is because

$$\|\hat{\mathbf{V}}\| = \sqrt{\hat{v}_x^2 + \hat{v}_y^2 + \hat{v}_z^2},$$

where we can substitute from Equation (B.3),

$$\|\hat{\mathbf{V}}\| = \sqrt{(\frac{v_x}{\sqrt{v_x^2+v_y^2+v_z^2}})^2 + (\frac{v_y}{\sqrt{v_x^2+v_y^2+v_z^2}})^2 + (\frac{v_z}{\sqrt{v_x^2+v_y^2+v_z^2}})^2}$$

$$= \sqrt{\frac{v_x^2}{v_x^2+v_y^2+v_z^2} + \frac{v_y^2}{v_x^2+v_y^2+v_z^2} + \frac{v_z^2}{v_x^2+v_y^2+v_z^2}}$$

$$= \sqrt{\frac{v_x^2+v_y^2+v_z^2}{v_x^2+v_y^2+v_z^2}}$$

$$= 1.0.$$

Notations.
V is a position,
$\mathbf{V}$ is the vector, and
$\hat{\mathbf{V}}$ is the normalized vector.

We refer to a vector with magnitude of exactly 1.0 as a normalized vector. A normalized vector tells us the direction of the movement. In general, we can normalize any nonzero magnitude vector $\mathbf{V}$,

$$\mathbf{V} = \begin{bmatrix} v_x & v_y & v_z \end{bmatrix},$$

by computing

$$\hat{\mathbf{V}} = \begin{bmatrix} \hat{v}_x & \hat{v}_y & \hat{v}_z \end{bmatrix}$$

$$= \begin{bmatrix} \frac{v_x}{\|\mathbf{V}\|} & \frac{v_y}{\|\mathbf{V}\|} & \frac{v_z}{\|\mathbf{V}\|} \end{bmatrix} \qquad \text{(B.4)}$$

$$= \frac{1}{\|\mathbf{V}\|}\mathbf{V}.$$

In general, we say the vector $\mathbf{V}$ is capable of moving any point in the $\hat{\mathbf{V}}$ direction by a distance of $\|\mathbf{V}\|$ units. For example, vector $\mathbf{V}_w$,

$$\mathbf{V}_w = \begin{bmatrix} 5 & 0 & 0 \end{bmatrix},$$

has a magnitude of

$$\|\mathbf{V}_w\| = \sqrt{5^2 + 0^2 + 0^2}$$

$$= \sqrt{25}$$

$$= 5.$$

We can normalize $\mathbf{V}_w$ by computing

$$\hat{\mathbf{V}}_w = \frac{1}{\|\mathbf{V}_w\|}\mathbf{V}_w$$

$$= \begin{bmatrix} \frac{5}{\|\mathbf{V}_w\|} & \frac{0}{\|\mathbf{V}_w\|} & \frac{0}{\|\mathbf{V}_w\|} \end{bmatrix}$$

$$= \begin{bmatrix} \frac{5}{5} & \frac{0}{5} & \frac{0}{5} \end{bmatrix}$$

$$= \begin{bmatrix} 1 & 0 & 0 \end{bmatrix}.$$

So, we say the vector $\mathbf{V}_w$ is capable of moving any point in the

$$\hat{\mathbf{V}}_w = \begin{bmatrix} 1 & 0 & 0 \end{bmatrix}$$

direction by a distance of five units.

B.1.5 Velocity: Speed and Direction

In computer graphics applications, we often need to work with objects that are in motion. One convenient way to implement this functionality is by associating a vector, $\mathbf{V}_e$,

$$\mathbf{V}_e = \begin{bmatrix} x_e & y_e & z_e \end{bmatrix},$$

with each moving object representing the corresponding object's velocity. During each timer update, we can update the object's position P_o by

$$P_o \longleftarrow P_o + \mathbf{V}_e.$$

In this way, the object's position will be continuously updated, creating a constant movement, and thus convey a sense of motion for the user. In this case, our object is moving in the $\hat{\mathbf{V}}_e$ direction with a speed of $\|\mathbf{V}_e\|$. It is important to separate the speed from the direction of the movement because:

- **Collision.** When the in-motion object collides with another object, we must define and compute the results of the collision. In our case, we can approximate the collision behavior by working separately with the speed and direction of the colliding objects' velocities. For example, to avoid complex physics, we can approximate a perfectly elastic collision by keeping the speed of the colliding objects constant and only changing the directions of the velocities to repulse the colliding objects away from each other.

- **Acceleration/deceleration.** If we need to speed up or slow down the object, we should change the magnitude of the velocity without altering the direction. For example, to accelerate the object in the same direction by five percent, we can compute the new speed as

$$\text{newSpeed} = \|\mathbf{V}_e\| \times 1.05$$

and compute the new velocity as

$$\mathbf{V}_e \longleftarrow \text{newSpeed} \times \hat{\mathbf{V}}_e.$$

Unit of velocity.

$$\frac{\text{WC unit}}{\text{update interval}}.$$

For all of our tutorials,

$$\text{update interval} = 25 \text{ msec} = 25 \times 10^{-3} \text{ sec} = \frac{25}{1000} \text{ sec} = \frac{1}{40} \text{ sec}.$$

So, the unit is

$$40 \times \frac{\text{WC unit}}{\text{sec}}.$$

That is, a velocity $\mathbf{V}_e$ of

$$\mathbf{V}_e = \begin{bmatrix} 5 & 0 & 0 \end{bmatrix}$$

will move the position of an object in the positive x-axis direction five WC units during each update, or

$$5 \times 40 \, \frac{\text{WC unit}}{\text{sec}} = 200 \, \frac{\text{WC unit}}{\text{sec}}$$

For this reason, if we want to move an object in our world at a speed of $v \frac{\text{units}}{\text{sec}}$, we will make sure the magnitude of the velocity vector is $\frac{v}{40}$.

B.2   Vector Products

The two most common vector operations we work with in computer graphics are the dot product and the cross product.

B.2.1   Dot Product

The vector dot product, sometimes called the scalar product, is written:

$$d = \mathbf{V}_a \cdot \mathbf{V}_b.$$

The dot product has an important geometric property:

$$\mathbf{V}_a \cdot \mathbf{V}_b = \|\mathbf{V}_a\| \|\mathbf{V}_b\| \cos\theta,$$

where θ is the angle between the two vectors. When one of the vectors in the dot product operation is normalized, for example $\hat{\mathbf{V}}_a$, because

$$\|\mathbf{V}_a\| = 1,$$

then

$$\hat{\mathbf{V}}_a \cdot \mathbf{V}_b = \|\mathbf{V}_b\| \cos\theta.$$

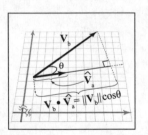

Figure B.4. Dot product.

As illustrated in Figure B.4, geometrically, this is the length of vector $\mathbf{V}_b$ measured along the direction of vector $\hat{\mathbf{V}}_a$. In the case when both of the vectors are normalized, it is especially convenient:

$$\cos\theta = \hat{\mathbf{V}}_a \cdot \hat{\mathbf{V}}_b.$$

We often need to compute cosines in graphics (e.g., for shading), so this formula is extremely useful in practice as we can compute cosines without a call to the expensive math intrinsic functions.

To actually compute a dot product from two vectors represented in Cartesian coordinates, the formula is

$$\mathbf{V}_a \cdot \mathbf{V}_b = x_a x_b + y_a y_b + z_a z_b.$$

B.2.2 Cross Product

Although the dot product produces a real number, the cross product produces a vector. The vector $\mathbf{V}_a \times \mathbf{V}_b$ has three important properties that uniquely define it:

1. Its length is $\|\mathbf{V}_a\|\|\mathbf{V}_b\| \sin\theta$.

2. It is perpendicular to both $\mathbf{V}_a$ and $\mathbf{V}_b$.

3. It follows the right-hand rule.

From these properties, we see that the unit vector along the z-axis is the x-axis vector crossed with the y-axis vector, that is, $(0,0,1) = (1,0,0) \times (0,1,0)$. Note that the angle between x and y is 90 degrees, so the sine of the angle is 1. The lengths are also 1, and the right-hand rule is respected. An implication of the first rule is that the cross product of any two parallel vectors is the zero vector $(0,0,0)$.

On the 2D xy-plane, the right-hand rule property allows us to test relative orientations in the plane. The cross product of any two vectors in the xy-plane is either parallel to the positive or negative z-axis. This allows us to tell "right turns" from "left turns." For example, in Figure B.5, vector $\mathbf{V}_b$ is to the *left* of vector $\mathbf{V}_a$ because the z-component of $\mathbf{V}_a \times \mathbf{V}_b$ is positive. Tutorial 12.1 uses this simple rule to differentiate left from right turns.

Another time when we only care about the direction of the cross product is when computing surface normals. Given two triangle edges, we can get a normal vector by taking the cross product of the two sides.

To actually compute a cross product from two vectors represented in Cartesian coordinates, the formula is simple:

$$\mathbf{V}_a \times \mathbf{V}_b = (y_a z_b - z_a y_b, \ z_a x_b - x_a z_b, \ x_a y_b - y_a x_b).$$

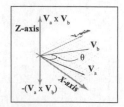

Figure B.5. Left and right turns in 2D space.

B.3 Vector Examples

This section contains a number of examples of using vectors for geometric computations. These map fairly directly into code when you use a library that has functions or operators for things such as vector addition.

B.3.1 Implicit Curves in 2D

An implicit curve in 2D is a real-valued function $f(x,y)$ that divides the plane into positive and negative regions. The boundary where $f(x,y) = 0$ is the curve. The reason it is called "implicit" is that $f()$ can tell you whether a given point is on the curve, but it does not tell you explicitly which points are on the curve. For example, the circle centered at the origin of radius 1 is often written

$$x^2 + y^2 = 1.$$

That is not quite in the form $f(x,y) = 0$. We can subtract 1 from both sides to get

$$x^2 + y^2 - 1 = 0.$$

For points inside the circle, $x^2 + y^2 - 1 < 0$. For points outside the circle, $x^2 + y^2 - 1 > 0$.

Note that for any implicit function $f(x,y) = 0$, the curve is unchanged if we multiply it by a non-zero constant. For example, a unit circle is also described by

$$2x^2 + 2y^2 - 2 = 0$$

and

$$-2x^2 - 2y^2 + 2 = 0.$$

The constant can change how positive or negative points off the circle are, and in the case of a negative constant, it reverses which regions off the curve are positive versus those that are negative. However, points on the curve remain zero.

A more general circle with radius R and center $\mathbf{C}$ is given by:

$$f(x,y) = (x - x_c)^2 + (y - y_c)^2 - R^2 = 0$$

The same principles of implicit equations apply: points where $f(x,y) = 0$ are on the curve, and points where $f(x,y) \neq 0$ are not on the curve. Both in math and in code, vectors give a more compact and less error-prone way to describe a circle:

$$(\mathbf{P} - \mathbf{C}) \cdot (\mathbf{P} - \mathbf{C}) - R^2 = 0.$$

Note that the dot product just expands to $(x - x_c)^2 + (y - y_c)^2$, which is the squared distance between $\mathbf{P}$ and $\mathbf{C}$. Geometrically, that is a nice equation: if the squared distance between and $\mathbf{C}$ is the square of the radius, then $\mathbf{P}$ is on the circle.

The familiar slope-intercept equation of the line in 2D, $y = mx + b$, can also be made into an implicit equation: $y - mx - b = 0$, or equally valid $-y + mx + b = 0$. Unfortunately, neither of these equations is well-suited for computation, as m can be infinite for perfectly valid lines—vertical ones. As we are allowed to multiply an implicit equation by any non-zero value, we can get rid of this degeneracy. Usually, a line in a graphics program is specified by two points $\mathbf{C}$ and $\mathbf{D}$. The slope is

$$\pm \frac{y_d - y_c}{x_d - x_c},$$

with the sign depending on which point is to the right of the other. To eliminate a possible zero denominator we can multiply through by its value:

$$f(x, y) = (x_d - x_c)y - (y_d - y_c)x - (y_d - y_c)b = 0.$$

We can solve for $-(y_d - y_c)b$ by noting that because $\mathbf{C}$ and $\mathbf{D}$ are on the line, $f(x_c, y_c) = f(x_d, y_d) = 0$. Plugging in c:

$$f(x, y) = (x_d - x_c)y_c - (y_d - y_c)x_c - (y_d - y_c)b = 0,$$

so

$$-(y_d - y_c)b = (y_d - y_c)x_c - (x_d - x_c)y_c = x_c y_d - y_c x_d.$$

So our final equation for the line is

$$f(x, y) = (y_c - y_d)x + (x_d - x_c)y + x_c y_d - y_c x_d.$$

This equation can also be derived from a geometric observation. If we have a vector that is perpendicular to a vector parallel to the line, the dot product of that vector and the vector between any two points on the line is zero. This "normal" vector to the line can be derived from the observation that any vector (x, y) is perpendicular to vector $(-y, x)$. This can be verified by noting that their dot product is zero.

The vector $\mathbf{D} - \mathbf{C}$ is parallel to the line. The vector $\mathbf{N} = (y_c - y_d, x_d - x_c)$ is perpendicular to $\mathbf{D} - \mathbf{C}$. If a point $\mathbf{P}$ is on the line, then

$$\mathbf{N} \cdot (\mathbf{P} - \mathbf{C}) = 0.$$

Expanding this gives

$$(y_c - y_d, x_d - x_c) \cot (x - x_c, y - y_c) = 0,$$

which expands to

$$f(x, y) = (y_c - y_d)x + (x_d - x_c)y + x_c y_d - y_c x_d.$$

B.3.2　Parametric Curves

In addition to implicit equations, curves in 2D can also have parametric coordinates. These are curves that are controlled by a single real parameter. For example, the position of a point that changes with time t can be described by two functions $x(t)$ and $y(t)$, or in vector terms $\mathbf{P}(t)$. The parameter can also just be a way to put a coordinate system on the curve, like mileage markers on a highway.

An example of a parametric curve is the circle with parameter θ:

$$\mathbf{P}(\theta) = [x(\theta)\;\; y(\theta)] = [x_c + R\cos\theta\;\; y_c + R\sin\theta].$$

If any θ is allowed, the same point can be generated by many θs. For example, $\mathbf{P}(0) = p(2\pi) = p(-2\pi) = (1,0)$ for a unit radius circle centered at the origin. Often we restrict the parameters to a finite interval (e.g., $-\pi < \theta \le \pi$ for the circle).

We can also write a parametric coordinate for a line through points $\mathbf{C}$ and $\mathbf{D}$. Note that vector addition tells us that $\mathbf{D} = \mathbf{C} + (\mathbf{D} - \mathbf{C})$ where, $(\mathbf{D} - \mathbf{C})$ is the vector from $\mathbf{C}$ to $\mathbf{D}$. We can also add on a scaled copy of $(\mathbf{D} - \mathbf{C})$: the vector $s(\mathbf{D} - \mathbf{C})$ where s is a fraction between 0 and 1 gets us *part way* from $\mathbf{C}$ to $\mathbf{D}$. For example, $\mathbf{C} + 0.5(\mathbf{D} - \mathbf{C})$ gets us halfway between $\mathbf{C}$ and $\mathbf{D}$. In general, we have

$$\mathbf{P}(s) = c + s(\mathbf{D} - \mathbf{C})$$

So given any s between 0 and 1, we get a point $\mathbf{P}$. $p(0) = \mathbf{C}$ and $\mathbf{P}(1) = \mathbf{D}$. For s values less than zero we still get points on the line, but points on the "$\mathbf{C}$ side" of the line. For s greater than 1 we get points on the $\mathbf{D}$ side of the line.

B.3.3　Parametric Curves and Implicit Surfaces in 3D

In 3D we also have implicit equations. Although in 2D these define "zero curves" that divide 2D space into positive and negative areas, in 3D we have "zero surfaces" that divide 3D space into positive and negative volumes. An implicit sphere is an example of a 3D implicit equation:

$$(\mathbf{P} - \mathbf{C}) \cdot (\mathbf{P} - \mathbf{C}) - R^2 = 0.$$

Interestingly, this is exactly the same formula as for the 2D implicit circle! The difference is that the vectors $\mathbf{P}$ and $\mathbf{C}$ are 3D as opposed to 2D. The geometry behind the formula is the same: any point $\mathbf{P}$ a distance R from $\mathbf{C}$ is on the sphere.

The implicit equation for a plane is analogous to the 2D implicit equation for the line. Given a point $\mathbf{C}$ on the plane with surface normal $\mathbf{N}$, the test for whether

P is on the plane is

$$(\mathbf{P} - \mathbf{C}) \cdot \mathbf{N} = 0.$$

Colinear points. Points lying on the same line.

If the plane has three noncolinear points **C**, **D**, and **E**, the normal vector is $\mathbf{N} = (\mathbf{D} - \mathbf{C}) \times (\mathbf{E} - \mathbf{C})$.

There are no implicit curves in 3D because a curve cannot divide 3D space into separate regions like a surface can. However, parametric equations work well for curves in 3D. "Mileage markers" can be places along a road that curve in x, y, and z. The parametric equation for a 3D line is the same as for a 2D line:

$$\mathbf{P}(s) = \mathbf{C} + s(\mathbf{D} - \mathbf{C}).$$

Again, as the real number s varies from 0 to 1, the point **P** varies from **C** to **D**. If s can take on any value, you get the whole line.

B.3.4   Intersection of a Line and a Circle/Sphere

Recall that in vector form, the implicit 2D circle and 3D sphere are the same:

$$(\mathbf{P} - \mathbf{C}) \cdot (\mathbf{P} - \mathbf{C}) - R^2 = 0.$$

Here, **C** and R are fixed, and **P** can be thought of as an argument we are testing. In both 2D and 3D, the parametric equation for a line through points **A** and **B** is

$$\mathbf{P}(s) = \mathbf{A} + s(\mathbf{B} - \mathbf{A}).$$

This can be read, "given s, here is the corresponding point **P** on the line." For any point **P** on the line, there is a unique s and vice versa (an invertible unique mapping like that is called a bijection). This line and circle/sphere intersect if there is some $\mathbf{P}(s)$ where the **P** satisfies the implicit equation for the circle/sphere, that is,

$$(\mathbf{P}(s) - \mathbf{C})(\mathbf{P}(s) - \mathbf{C}) - R^2 = 0.$$

Expanding $\mathbf{P}(s)$ gives

$$(\mathbf{A} + s(\mathbf{B} - \mathbf{A}) - \mathbf{C})(\mathbf{A} + s(\mathbf{B} - \mathbf{A}) - \mathbf{C}) - R^2 = 0.$$

Because the dot product is distributive, we can separate the terms as a polynomial in s:

$$[(\mathbf{B} - \mathbf{A}) \cdot (\mathbf{B} - \mathbf{A})] s^2 + 2[(\mathbf{B} - \mathbf{A}) \cdot (\mathbf{A} - \mathbf{C})] s + [(\mathbf{A} - \mathbf{C}) \cdot (\mathbf{A} - \mathbf{C}) - R^2].$$

This is a quadratic equation, so we can write down the closed-form solution. Recall that for any $as^2 + bs + c = 0$,

$$s = \frac{-b \pm \sqrt{b^2 - 4ac}}{2a}.$$

Because there is a square root, there may be no real solution (if the number under the $\sqrt{}$ is negative), which occurs when the line misses the circle/sphere. If the square root term is zero, there is one solution, which means the line grazes the circle/sphere and thus hits it at exactly one point. If the square root is real, the $\pm$ means there are two real solutions, which correspond to the two points where the line hits the circle/sphere. If the value of s is between zero and one for either or both of the solutions, then the line segment between $\mathbf{A}$ and $\mathbf{B}$ hits the circle/sphere.

B.3.5   More Small Examples

Here are more simple examples of the power of vector math. Remember that all of these operations should look very similar in code once you have dot, vector add, and so on as functions and operators.

2D distance of a point and a line.   Given a line through points $\mathbf{C}$ and $\mathbf{D}$ and a point $\mathbf{P}$, we can compute the signed distance between the point and the line via the implicit equation

$$(\mathbf{P} - \mathbf{C}) \cdot \mathbf{N} = 0.$$

For a point $\mathbf{Q}$, the distance is

$$\text{distance} = \frac{\|\mathbf{Q} - \mathbf{C}\| \cdot \mathbf{N}}{\|\mathbf{N}\|}.$$

If it is on one side of the line, the distance will be positive, and on the other negative.

Projection of a point onto a plane.   After finding the signed distance d to the plane, translate the point along $\mathbf{N}$:

$$\mathbf{Q}_{\text{plane}} = \mathbf{Q} - d \frac{\mathbf{N}}{\|\mathbf{N}\|}.$$

Reflection direction.   Given a vector $\mathbf{E}$ in the direction of the viewer, and a unit normal vector $\hat{\mathbf{N}}$, the reflection vector $\mathbf{R}$ is

$$\mathbf{R} = -\mathbf{E} + 2(\mathbf{E} \cdot \hat{\mathbf{N}})\hat{\mathbf{N}}.$$

Intersection of line and plane. Given parametric line $P(s) = \mathbf{A} + s(\mathbf{B} - \mathbf{A})$ and implicit plane (or 2D line) $(\mathbf{P} - \mathbf{C}) \cdot \mathbf{N} = 0$, we find s_{plane} such that $(\mathbf{A} + s_{\text{plane}}(\mathbf{B} - \mathbf{A}) \cdot \mathbf{N} = 0$. This yields

$$s_{\text{plane}} = \frac{-\mathbf{A} \cdot \mathbf{N}}{(\mathbf{A} - \mathbf{B}) \cdot \mathbf{N}}.$$

Smallest distance between two lines. Given two lines, one through $\mathbf{A}$ and $\mathbf{B}$ and one through $\mathbf{C}$ and $\mathbf{D}$, we first find a vector perpendicular to each of the lines:

$$\mathbf{N} = (\mathbf{B} - \mathbf{A}) \times (\mathbf{D} - \mathbf{C})$$

If this vector has zero length then the lines are parallel, and we can compute the minimum distance from the point $\mathbf{C}$ to the line through $\mathbf{A}$ and $\mathbf{B}$. If the length is not zero, we can write an equation of a plane that contains the line $\mathbf{A} \mathbf{B}$ and is parallel to the other line: $(p - a) \cdot n = 0$. Now simply compute the minimum distance from $\mathbf{C}$ to that plane.

B.4 Orthonormal Matrices

We have seen the Cartesian coordinates with our familiar xyz axes. We could also pick a different set of three mutually perpendicular axes uvw. Although a vector does not change when going back and forth between xyz and uvw, its three components in Cartesian representation do. Recall that the components just give you a way to say how the axis vectors combine. If you want the same vector in each coordinate system, that means

$$x\hat{\mathbf{V}}_x + y\hat{\mathbf{V}}_y + z\hat{\mathbf{V}}_z = u\hat{\mathbf{V}}_u + v\hat{\mathbf{V}}_v + w\hat{\mathbf{V}}_w.$$

So the vectors (x, y, z) and (u, v, w) are the same in the two coordinate systems, but you need to be sure to turn them into vectors by multiplying by the appropriate axis vectors for that coordinate system.

Suppose you have the uvw basis vectors stored in xyz coordinates (as will almost always be the case):

$$\hat{\mathbf{V}}_w = (x_w, y_w, z_w),$$
$$\hat{\mathbf{V}}_u = (x_u, y_u, z_u),$$
$$\hat{\mathbf{V}}_v = (x_v, y_v, z_v).$$

And now suppose you wanted a matrix that would take an (x, y, z) and produce the equivalent (u, v, w) or vice-versa. That matrix would be a rotation because you would never want the length of a vector to change just by changing coordinate systems. Rotation matrices have the interesting property of being orthonormal, which means that their rows are a set of three mutually perpendicular unit vectors (the same is true for their columns). There is an easy way to get two such matrices, and in fact they are all we need:

$$\mathbf{M}_1 = \begin{bmatrix} x_u & y_u & z_u \\ x_v & y_v & z_v \\ x_w & y_w & z_w \end{bmatrix}$$

and

$$\mathbf{M}_2 = \begin{bmatrix} x_u & x_v & x_w \\ y_u & y_v & y_w \\ z_u & z_v & z_w \end{bmatrix}.$$

Note that these two matrices are the transposes of each other (rows and columns exchanged). For rotation matrices such as these, the transpose is the inverse. Thus each matrix is the geometric opposite of the other and "unrotates" the action of its partner. Now suppose that $(u, v, w) = (2, 0, 0)$ so the vector is just in the direction of $\mathbf{V}_u$ but has length 2. If we apply M_2 to that vector, we get $(2x_u, 2y_u, 2z_u)$, so for that vector, M_2 seems to rewrite the uvw into the right xyz. Try this with other simple uvw cases. In fact, in general, M_2 takes uvw coordinates and converts them into the equivalent xyz coordinates. The matrix M_1 does the opposite: it takes xyz coordinates to uvw coordinates.

If you ever have three coordinate systems, you can either pass through two matrices $\mathbf{A}$ and $\mathbf{B}$ or note that passing through the matrix product $\mathbf{C} = \mathbf{BA}$ is equivalent.

One question that arises is whether all vectors transform the same. The answer is no. Surface normal vectors transform using $(\mathbf{M}^{-1})^T$ instead of $\mathbf{M}$. Fortunately, for rotation matrices, those are the same. However, if your matrix ever has any nonuniform scaling in it (e.g., a scaling that would take a sphere to an ellipsoid), then you will need to use the inverse transpose.

Summary of Library Version Changes

Starting from Chapter 5, we begin developing and evolving three software libraries. Tutorials will be developed based on these libraries: an MFC library for GUI support, and two graphics libraries (OpenGL and D3D) to support graphics. Here we provide a summary of all the libraries, with very brief descriptions. This information is provided for references only. Readers must read the corresponding chapters/tutorials to understand the details of each version of the library.

Because all filenames begin with uwbgl_, we will omit this string when listing filenames. For example, uwbgl_Common.h will be listed as Common.h. In addition, we will omit the header (.h) and source (.cpp) extensions when both are present. For example, we will list filename: CircleGeom to represent uwbgl_CircleGeom.h/.cpp. However, we will list D3D_Lib1.h since there is no corresponding .cpp file.

From library to library, only changes to source files are listed. Unlisted or otherwise unmentioned files are assumed to be unchanged from previous versions.

UWBGL_MFC_Lib1

Supports. All tutorials from
Chapter 5 onward.

First introduced in Chapter 5 (on p. 124) to support Tutorial 5.1, this will be the
only GUI API library we work with. Figure C.1 is the static class diagram of this
library. Files in this library include:

Filename	Purpose
MFC_Lib1.h	header file for using this library
MFCDefines.h	compile parameters for this library
MFCUIWindow	UI drawing area for the graphics API
MFCUtility	defines ReplaceDialogControl() function
MFCSliderCtrlWithEcho	slider bar with numeric echo

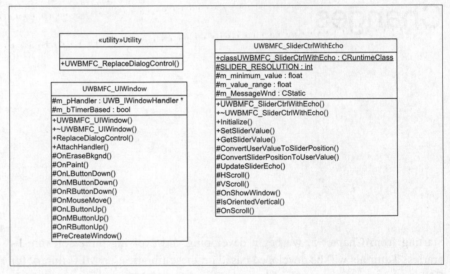

Figure C.1. UWBGL_MFC_Lib1: Classes.

UWBGL_D3D_Lib1

Introduced in Chapter 5 (on p. 124), this is the first version of our own graphics library. This library is designed to present the WindowHandler class as an abstraction of the view/controller pair. Figure C.2 is the static class diagram for this library. File in this library include:

Supports. The tutorial that is based on this library: Tutorial 5.1.

Filename	Purpose
Header Files folder: library header files	
D3D_Lib1.h	header file for using this library
D3DDefines.h	compile parameters for this library
math3d++ folder: API-independent math library	
All math operations in the UWBGL library and in all tutorials use classes (e.g., vec3, mat4) from this library.	
Common Files folder: API-independent files	
Common.h	header file for files in this folder
Common Files/WindowHandler folder: view/controller pairs	
IWindowHandler.h	virtual base class for view/controller pair
WindowHandler	API-independent view/controller pair
D3D Files folder: D3D-specific source files	
D3D Files/D3D_Geoms folder:	
D3DCircleGeom1	abstraction of circle geometry
D3DRectangleGeom1	abstraction of rectangle geometry
D3D Files/D3D_GraphicsSystem folder:	
D3DGraphicsSystem1	interface to D3D graphics API
D3D Files/D3D_WindowHandler folder:	
D3DWindowHandler1	abstraction of view/controller pair

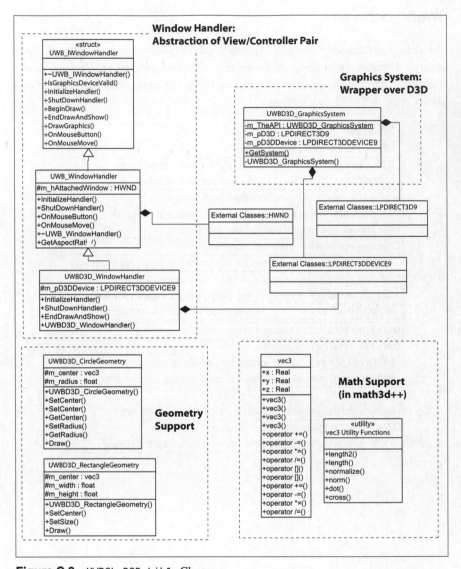

Figure C.2. `UWBGL_D3D_Lib1`: Classes.

UWBGL_D3D_Lib2

Introduced in Chapter 5 (on p. 134), this library provides a better UI support. It modifies from the previous version:

Supports. The tutorials that are based on this library: Tutorials 5.2 and 5.3.

- Defines `WindowHandler::HardwareToDevice()` for hardware-to-device transformation to support mouse input.

- Adds `EchoToStatusArea()` function (in `Utility1.h/.cpp`) to support output of status strings to application window status area.

Because of the relatively minor and localized changes, the static class diagram for this library is not shown. Files changed include:

Filename	Purpose
Header Files folder: library header files	
`D3D_Lib2.h`	header file for using this library
Common Files folder: API-independent files	
Common Files/Utilities folder: General utilities	
`Utility1`	`EchoToStatusArea()` function
Common Files/WindowHandler folder: view/controller pairs	
`WindowHandler2`	API-independent view/controller pair
D3D Files folder: D3D-specific source files	
D3D Files/D3D_WindowHandler folder:	
`D3DWindowHandler2`	abstraction of view/controller pair

UWBGL_D3D_Lib3

Supports. The tutorials that are based on this library: Tutorials 5.4, 5.5, and 5.6.

Introduced in Chapter 5 (on p. 141), this library modifies the previous version to support multiple view/controller pairs and to provide a more comprehensive utility functionality.

The important changes are in the `GraphicsSystem` class, where we added functions for creating and activating swap chains, D3D's mechanism for supporting multiple drawing areas on the application window.

Figure C.3 highlights the updated `GraphicsSystem` and `WindowHandler` classes, and Figure C.4 depicts the new utility classes in this library. The following files are modified from the previous version of the library:

Filename	**Purpose**
Header Files folder: library header files	
`D3D_Lib3.h`	header file for using this library
Common Files folder: API-independent files	
Common Files/Utilities folder: General utilities	
`Containers.h`	customized `STL vector`
`Utility2`	random functions
`Color1`	packing RGBA as 32-bit int
`Clock`	stopwatch for wall clock in seconds
D3D Files folder: D3D-specific source files	
D3D Files/D3D_Geoms folder:	
`D3DCircleGeom2`	circle geometry for working with swap chains
`D3DRectangleGeom2`	rectangle geometry for working with swap chains
D3D Files/D3D_GraphicsSystem folder:	
`D3DGraphicsSystem2`	create/activate swap chains
D3D Files/D3D_WindowHandler folder:	
`D3DWindowHandler3`	view/controller working with swap chains

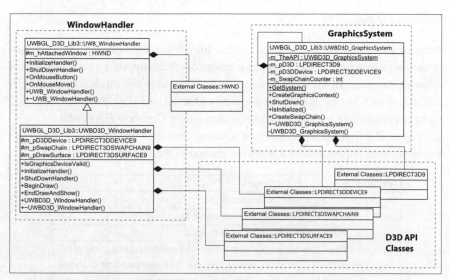

Figure C.3. `UWBGL_D3D_Lib3:` `GraphicsSystem` and `WindowHandler` changes.

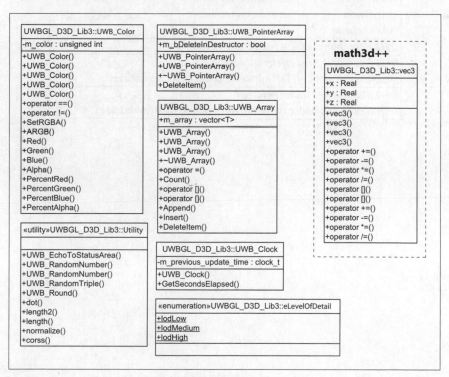

Figure C.4. `UWBGL_D3D_Lib3:` Utility classes and methods.

UWBGL_D3D_Lib4

Supports. The tutorial that is based on this library: Tutorial 7.1.

Introduced in Chapter 7 (on p. 163), this library presents the DrawHelper abstraction to separate general primitive behaviors from the API-specific graphics drawing routines. Besides the DrawHelper abstraction, the other significant difference of this library is that the geometry abstractions (i.e., Point, Line, and Circle classes) are moved to the API-independent *Common Files* folder.

Figure C.5 highlights the new and updated classes in this library. The following files are modified from the previous version of the library:

Filename	Purpose
Header Files folder: library header files	
D3D_Lib4.h	header file for using this library
Common Files folder: API-independent files	
Common Files/DrawHelper folder: API-independent drawing support	
DrawHelper1	virtual abstraction for API-independent drawing
Common Files/Geoms folder: abstraction of geometries	
PointGeom	abstraction for points
LineGeom	abstraction for lines
CircleGeom	abstraction for circles
D3D Files folder: D3D-specific source files	
D3D Files/D3D_DrawHelper folder:	
D3DDrawHelper1	D3D drawing routines for geometries
D3D Files/Geoms folder **removed**	
All files in this folder are **removed** (replaced by DrawHelper)	

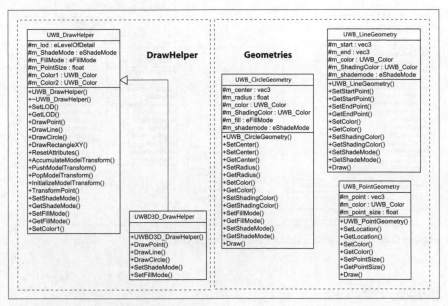

Figure C.5. `UWBGL_D3D_Lib4`: New classes.

UWBGL_D3D_Lib5

Introduced in Chapter 7 (on p. 173), this library presents the `Primitive` class hierarchy. All source files for the `Primitive` hierarchy are located in the *Common Files/Primitives* folder. This new folder replaces the previous *Common Files/ Geoms* folder.

Figure C.6 highlights the new and updated classes in this library. The following files are modified from the previous version of the library:

Supports. The tutorial that is based on this library: Tutorial 7.2.

Filename	Purpose
Header Files folders: library header files	
`D3D_Lib5.h`	header file for using this library
Common Files folder: API-independent files	
Common Files/Geoms folder **removed**	
All files in this folder are **removed**	
(replaced by the following `Primitive` hierarchy)	
Common Files/Primitives folder: abstraction of primitives	
`Primitive1`	virtual base class for all primitives
`PrimitivePoint1`	abstraction for points
`PrimitiveLine1`	abstraction for lines
`PrimitiveCircle1`	abstraction for circles

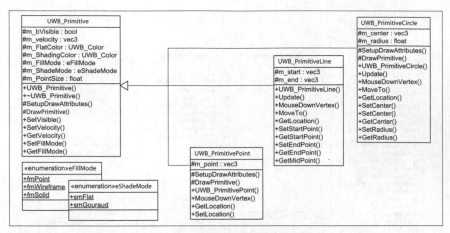

Figure C.6. `UWBGL_D3D_Lib5`: Primitive hierarchy.

UWBGL_D3D_Lib6

Supports. The tutorial that is based on this library: Tutorial 7.3.

Introduced in Chapter 7 (on p. 185), this library presents the `BoundingVolume` abstraction to support collision behavior for the `Primitive` hierarchy. A new `BoundingVolumes` subfolder is defined in the *Common Files* folder for the new source files. All source files in the entire `Primitive` hierarchy are updated to support `BoundingVolume` collision behavior.

Figure C.7 highlights the new and updated classes in this library. The following files are modified from the previous version of the library:

Filename	Purpose
Header Files folders: library header files	
`D3D_Lib6.h`	header files for using this library
Common Files folder: API-independent files	
Common Files/BoundingVolumes folder:	
`Intersect1`	defines bounding volume hierarchy to support collisions
Common Files/Primitives folder: abstraction of primitives	
all primitives are updated to support bounding volumes:	
`Primitive2, PrimitivePoint2, PrimitiveLine2, PrimitiveCircle1`	

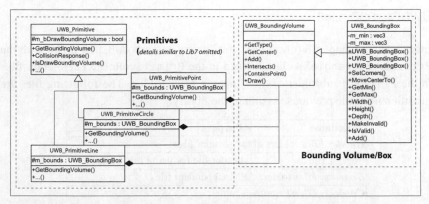

Figure C.7. `UWBGL_D3D_Lib6`: BoundingBox and the `Primitive` hierarchy.

UWBGL_D3D_Lib7

Introduced in Chapter 7 (on p. 189), this library presents the `PrimitiveList` abstraction for coherently grouping primitives. The important change from the previous library is the addition of `PrimitiveList1.h/.cpp` into the *Primitives* subfolder of the *Common Files* folder.

Figure C.8 highlights the new and updated classes in this library. The following files are modified from the previous version of the library:

Supports. The tutorials that are based on this library: Tutorials 7.4 and 7.5.

Filename	Purpose
Header Files folder: library header files	
`D3D_Lib7.h`	header file for using this library
Common Files folder: API-independent files	
Common Files/Primitives folder:	
`PrimitiveList1`	support list of primitives

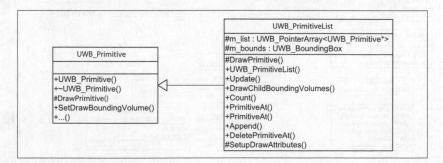

Figure C.8. `UWBGL_D3D_Lib7`: PrimitiveList class.

UWBGL_D3D_Lib8

Supports. The tutorials that are based on this library: Tutorials 8.1, 8.2, 8.3, 8.4, 9.1, 9.2, 9.3, 9.4, and 9.5.

Introduced in Chapter 8 (on p. 216), this library extends `UWB_D3D_Lib7` with the `PrimitiveRectangleXY` class defined in the `PrimitiveRectXY1.h/.cpp` files in the *Primitives* subfolder of the *Common Files* folder. The following files are modified from the previous version of the library:

Filename	Purpose
Header Files folder: library header files	
`D3D_Lib8.h`	header file for using this library
Common Files folder: API-independent files	
Common Files/Primitives folder:	
`PrimitiveRectXY1`	rectangle primitive on the *xy*-plane
D3D Files folder: D3D-specific source files	
D3D Files/D3D_DrawHelper folder:	
`D3DDrawHelper2`	support drawing of rectangle

So far we have only highlighted incremental changes in between libraries. For reference, and for completeness, Figure C.9, Figure C.10, and Figure C.11 illustrate all of the classes that are in the `UWB_D3D_Lib8` Library.

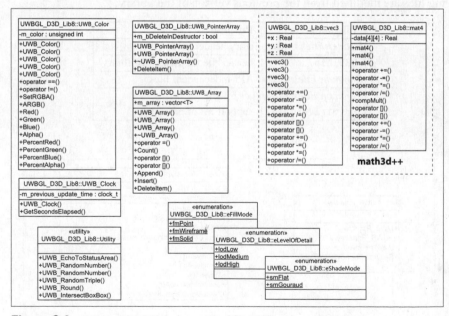

Figure C.9. `UWBGL_D3D_Lib8` classes (1 of 3): Utility classes/functions.

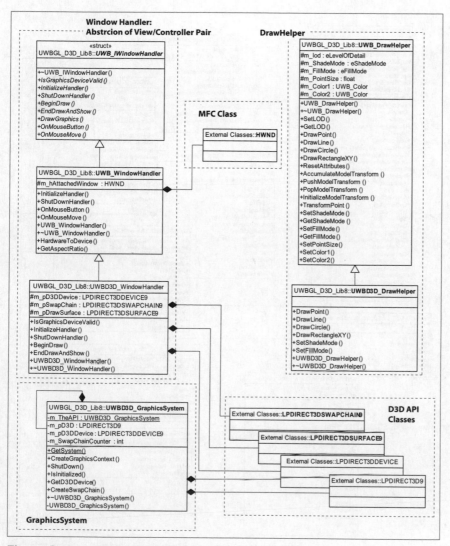

Figure C.10. UWBGL_D3D_Lib8 classes (2 of 3): WindowHandler, GraphicsSystem, and DrawHelper.

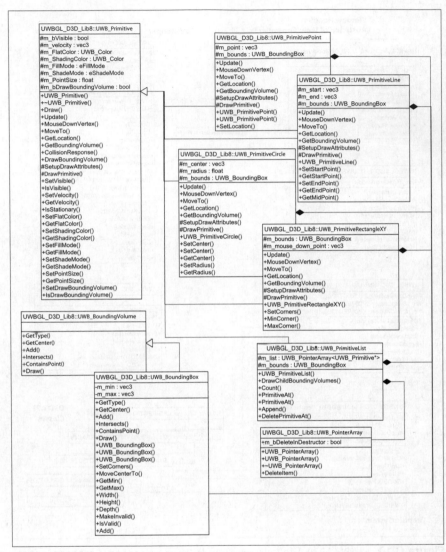

Figure C.11.   UWBGL_D3D_Lib8 classes (3 of 3):   Primitive hierarchy and BoundingVolume.

UWBGL_D3D_Lib9

Introduced in Chapter 9 (on p. 247), this library presents pivoted transformation operations via the XformInfo class. The D3DDrawHelper class is updated to support the new XformInfo with the D3D matrix stack.

Figure C.12 highlights the new and updated classes in this library. The following files are modified from the previous version of the library:

Supports. The tutorials that are based on this library: Tutorials 9.6, 9.7, 9.8, 9.9, 10.6, 10.7, and 10.8.

Filename	Purpose
Header Files folder: library header files	
D3D_Lib9.h	header file for using this library
Common Files folder: API-independent files	
Common Files/XformInfo folder:	
XformInfo1	support for pivoted transformation
D3D Files folder: D3D-specific source files	
D3D Files/D3D_DrawHelper folder:	
D3DDrawHelper3	work with D3D WORLD matrix with matrix stack

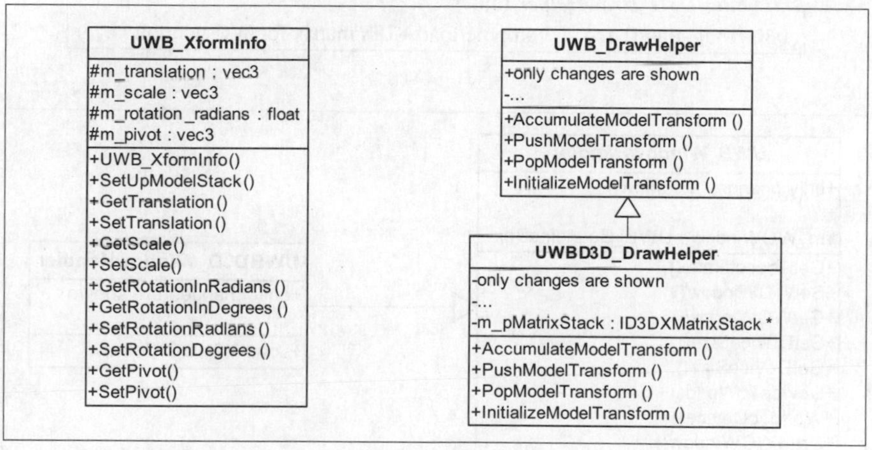

Figure C.12. UWBGL_D3D_Lib9: XformInfo and modifications to DrawHelper.

UWBGL_D3D_Lib10

Supports. The tutorials that are based on this library: Tutorials 10.9, 10.10, 10.11, 10.12, 10.13, 10.14, 11.1, and 11.2.

Introduced in Chapter 10 (on p.e 276), this library presents the support for coordinate systems, in particular the definition and manipulation of the world coordinate (WC) window. The WindowHandler class is extended to support the definition of the WC window and programming of the M_{w2n} operator. The D3D subclass D3D_WindowHandler is also updated to reflect the changes.

Figure C.13 shows that the LoadW2NDCXform() function is defined in Window Handler and implemented in D3D_WindowHandler. The following files are modified from the previous version of the library:

Filename	Purpose
Header Files folder: library header files	
D3D_Lib10.h	header file for using this library
Common Files folder: API-independent files	
Common Files/WindowHandler folder:	
WindowHandler3	support definition/programming of WC window
D3D Files folder: D3D-specific source files	
D3D Files/D3D_DrawHelper folder:	
D3DWindowHandler4	compute/load VIEW matrix for WC window

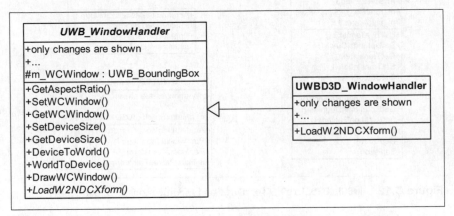

Figure C.13. UWBGL_D3D_Lib10: The LoadW2NDCXform() of WindowHandler.

UWBGL_D3D_Lib11

Introduced in Chapter 11 (on p. 300), this library presents the scene node and scene hierarchy functionality via the SceneNode class.

Figure C.14 highlights the new and updated classes in this library. The following files are modified from the previous version of the library:

Supports. The tutorials that are based on this library: Tutorials 11.3, 11.4, 11.5, and 11.6.

Filename	Purpose
Header Files folder: library header files	
D3D_Lib11.h	header file for using this library
Common Files folder: API-independent files	
Common Files/SceneNode folder:	
SceneNode1	scene graph for hierarchical modeling

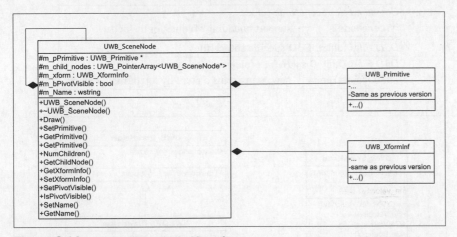

Figure C.14. UWBGL_D3D_Lib11: New classes.

UWBGL_D3D_Lib12

Supports. The tutorials that are based on this library: Tutorials 11.7, 11.8, 11.9, 12.1, and 12.2

Introduced in Chapter 11 (on p. 323), this library extends `UWB_D3D_Lib11` to support scene node selection and collision. The `SceneNode` class is extended to support the building of bounding volumes. The `D3DDrawHelper` class is extended to support transforming a point by the top of the matrix stack.

In this case, changes are localized to the `SceneNode` and `WindowHandler` classes (Figure C.15). The following files are modified from the previous version of the library:

Filename	Purpose
Header Files folder: library header files	
`D3D_Lib12.h`	header file for using this library
Common Files folder: API-independent files	
Common Files/SceneNode folder:	
`SceneNode2`	support bounding volume for the node
D3D Files folder: D3D-specific source files	
D3D Files/D3D_DrawHelper folder:	
`D3DDrawHelper4`	new: transforms a point by top of matrix stack

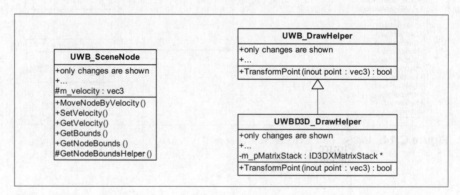

Figure C.15. `UWBGL_D3D_Lib12`: Changes to `XformInfo` and `DrawHelper` classes.

UWBGL_D3D_Lib13

Supports. The tutorials that are based on this library: Tutorials 12.3 and 12.5.

Introduced in Chapter 12, this library presents the alpha blending (on p. 348) and texture mapping (on p. 359) functionality to the programmers. Figure C.16 highlights the new and updated classes in this library. The following list summarizes the changes from the previous version of the library:

- UWBD3D_Resource. This is a new class introduced to support searching and loading of files. A *loadable* file is considered as a resource. For now, we support loading of file textures as resources.

- UWBD3D_GraphicsSystem. This class is modified to include an array of file texture resources. New functionality is added to search, and to trigger lazy loading of file texture resources.

- UWB_Primitive. This class is modified to support attributes associated with alpha blending and file textures.

- DrawHelper. The classes in the *Common Files* and *D3D Files* folders are both modified to support the new alpha blending and file texture attributes and rendering.

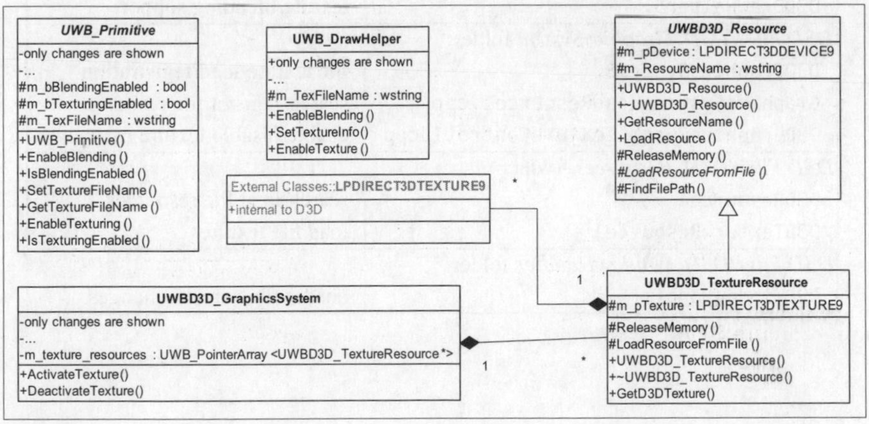

Figure C.16. UWBGL_D3D_Lib13: Resource classes and modifications for resource support.

The above changes are reflected in new header file versions (e.g., `DrawHelper 1.h` to `DrawHelper2.h`). As a result, many of the files that depend on these new header files must also be updated. The phrase "header file version changes" signifies that the only change in a file is in a new header file version. The following is the list of all files that are changed:

Filename	Purpose
Header Files folder: library header files	
`D3D_Lib13.h`	header file for using this library
Common Files folder: API-independent files	
Common Files/BoundingVolumes folder:	
`Intersect2`	header file version changes
Common Files/DrawHelper folder:	
`DrawHelper2`	texture/blending support
Common Files/Primitives folder:	
`Primitive3`	texture/blending support
All primitive files are updated to reflect header file version changes:	
`PrimitivePoint3, PrimitiveLine3, PrimitiveCircle3` `PrimitiveList2, PrimitiveRectXY2`	
Common Files/SceneNode folder:	
`SceneNode3`	header file version changes
Common Files/WindowHandler folder:	
`WindowHandler4`	header file version changes
Common Files/XformInfo folder:	
`XformInfo2`	header file version changes
D3D Files folder: D3D-specific source files	
D3D Files/D3D_DrawHelper folder:	
`D3DDrawHelper5`	texture/blending support
D3D Files/D3D_GraphicsSystem folder:	
`D3DGraphicsSystem3`	file texture load/registration
`GraphicsSystem_LoadResource1.cpp`	search/register file resources
`D3DGraphicsSystm_TextureControl1.cpp`	enable/disable texture map
D3D Files/D3D_Resources folder:	
`D3DResource1`	search/load file resources
`D3DTextureResource1`	load file textures
D3D Files/D3D_WindowHandler folder:	
`D3DWindowHandler5`	header file version changes

UWBGL_D3D_Lib14

Introduced in Chapter 15 (on p. 413), this is the first library that supports 3D.

Figure C.17 highlights the new and updated classes in this library. The following list summarizes the changes from the previous version of the library:

Supports. The tutorials that are based on this library: Tutorials 15.1, 15.2, 15.3, and 15.4.

- UWB_Camera. This is a new class defined to support basic camera and view frustum specification; draws camera/view parameters; and implements interactive manipulation of the camera (rotate/track/zoom).

- UWB_WindowHandler **and** UWBD3D_WindowHandler. These classes are modified to support the UWB_Camera; compute/load view and projection matrices; implement 3D transformations.

- UWBD3D_GraphicsSystem. This class is modified to support D3D creation/initialization of Z-buffer for 3D applications.

- UWB_XformInfo. This class is modified to support rotation in 3D.

- UWBD3D_DrawHelper. This class is modified to support the new 3D rotation functionality of UWB_XformInfo.

- UWB_PrimitiveAxisFrame. This is a new class defined to draw the 3D orthonormal basis.

- UWB_PrimitiveRectangleXZ. Recall that the floor of our 3D world is the *xz*-plane, yet PrimitiveRectrangleXY only draws rectangles on the *xy* plane. This new class makes it easier for us to draw the *xz* floor.

Once again, many files are changed to reflect updated versions of the latest header files. In such cases, the phrase "header file version changes" is used to describe the purpose of changes. The following is the list of all files that are changed:

Filename	Purpose
Header Files folders: library header files	
D3D_Lib14.h	header file for using this library
Common Files folder: API-independent files	
Common Files/BoundingVolumes folder:	
Intersect3	draw box in 3D
Common Files/Camera folder:	
Camera1	camera and view frustum parameters set/get
Camera_Draw1.cpp	draw the camera and view parameters
Camera_Xform1.cpp	rotate/track/zoom camera parameters
Common Files/DrawHelper folder:	
DrawHelper3	draw xz rectangle
Common Files/Primitives folder:	
Primitive4	header file version changes
PrimitiveAxisFrame1	draw an orthonormal basis
PrimitiveRectangleXZ1	draw rectangle on xz-plane
All primitive files are updated to reflect header file version changes:	
PrimitivePoint4, PrimitiveLine4, PrimitiveCircle4	
PrimitiveList3, PrimitiveRectXY3	
Common Files/SceneNode folder:	
SceneNode4	draw bounding box in wire-frame
Common Files/WindowHandler folder:	
WindowHandler5	support camera and 3D xform
Common Files/**XformInfo** folder:	
XformInfo3	support rotation in 3D
D3D Files folder: D3D-specific files	
D3D Files/D3D_DrawHelper folder:	
D3DDrawHelper6	support rotation in 3D + xz rectangle
D3D Files/D3D_GraphicsSystem folder:	
D3DGraphicsSystem4	D3D initialization for 3D drawing
D3DGraphicsSystem_LoadResource2	header file version changes
D3DGraphicsSystem_TextureControls2	header file version changes
D3D Files/D3D_WindowHandler folder:	
D3DWindowHandler6	support camera and 3D xform

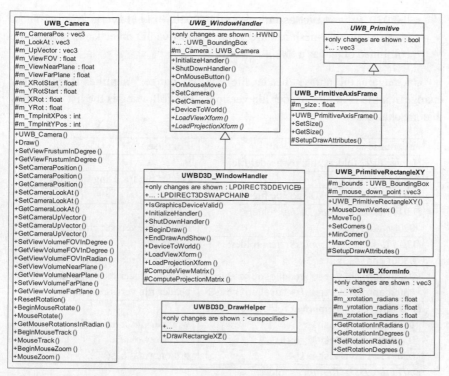

Figure C.17. `UWBGL_D3D_Lib14`: The `Camera` class and modification for 3D support.

UWBGL_D3D_Lib15

Introduced in Chapter 16 (on p. 450), this library presents the programmer with the functionality of working with D3D `.x` mesh objects. This library implements the loading of D3D mesh files (the `.x` mesh files) based on the `UWBD3D_Resource` utilities (introduced in `Lib13`).

Supports. The tutorials that are based on this library: Tutorials 16.1 and 16.2.

Figure C.18 highlights the new and updated classes in this library. The following list summarizes the changes from the previous version of the library:

- `UWBD3D_MeshResource`. This is a new class that subclasses from the `UWBD3D_Resource` to load D3D `.x` mesh objects as resources.

- `UWBD3D_GraphicsSystems`. This class is modified to include an array of mesh resources. New functionality is added to search and to trigger lazy loading of mesh resources.

- `UWBD3D_PrimitiveMesh`. This is a new class that *wraps* `UWB_Primitive` functionality over mesh resources.

- `UWBD3D_PrimitiveMeshArrow` **and** `UWBD3D_PrimitiveMeshAxis.` These classes combine mesh resources into respective 3D objects and present the combined object as a `UWB_Primitive`.

Once again, the phrase "header file version changes" signifies that the only change in a file is in new header file versions. The following is the list of all files that are changed:

Filename	Purpose
Header Files folders: library header files	
`D3D_Lib15.h`	header file for using this library
D3D Files folder: D3D-specific files	
D3D Files/D3D_DrawHelper folder:	
`D3DDrawHelper7`	header file version changes
D3D Files/D3D_GraphicsSystem folder:	
`D3DGraphicsSystem5`	mesh resource support
`D3DGraphicsSystem_LoadResource3`	search/register mesh resource
`D3DGraphicsSystem_TextureControls3`	header file version changes
D3D Files/D3D_Primitives folder: ***new folder***	
`D3DPrimitiveMesh1`	wrapper of `.x` mesh file
`D3DPrimitiveMeshArrow1`	3D arrow object
`D3DPrimitiveMeshAxis1`	orthonormal basis
D3D Files/D3D_Resources folder:	
`D3DMeshResource1`	load mesh resource
D3D Files/D3D_WindowHandler folder:	
`D3DWindowHandler7`	header file version changes

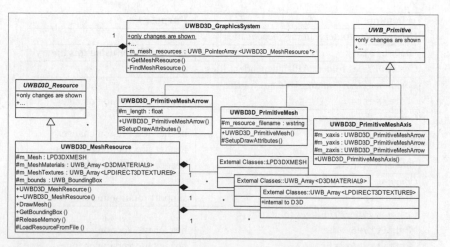

Figure C.18. `UWBGL_D3D_Lib15`: `MeshResource` class and modifications for mesh support.

UWBGL_D3D_Lib16

Supports. The tutorial that is based on this library: Tutorial 16.3.

Introduced in Chapter 16 (on p. 459) to support interactive manipulation of rotation based on an explicit rotation matrix. Because of the relatively minor and localized changes, the static class diagram for this library is not shown. Files changed include:

- `UWB_XformInfo`. This represents rotation with an explicit 3×3 matrix instead of the three floating-point Euler angles.

- `UWB_DrawHelper` **and** `UWBD3D_DrawHelper`. Both of these are updated to support setting the matrix stack based on the rotation matrix from the new `XformInfo` class.

Again, in the following table, the phrase "header file version changes" signifies that the only change in a file is in new header file versions. The following is the list of all files that are changed:

Filename	Purpose
Header Files folders: library header files	
`D3D_Lib16.h`	header file for using this library
Common Files folder: API-independent files	
Common Files/BoundingVolumes folder:	
`Intersect4`	header file version changes
Common Files/Camera folder:	
`Camera2`	header file version changes
`Camera_Draw2`	header file version changes
`Camera_Xform2`	header file version changes
Common Files/DrawHelper folder:	
`DrawHelper4`	support rotation matrix
Common Files/Primitives folder:	
`Primitive5`	header file version changes
`PrimitiveAxisFrame2`	header file version changes
`PrimitiveCircle5`	header file version changes
`PrimitiveLine5`	header file version changes
`PrimitiveList4`	header file version changes
`PrimitivePoint5`	header file version changes
`PrimitiveRectangleXY2`	header file version changes
`PrimitiveRectangleXZ2`	header file version changes
Common Files/SceneNode folder:	
`SceneNode5`	header file version changes
Common Files/WindowHandler folder:	
`WindowHandler6`	header file version changes
Common Files/XformInfo folder:	
`XformInfo4`	represent rotation with matrix
D3D Files folder: D3D-specific files	
D3D Files/D3D_DrawHelper folder:	
`D3DDrawHelper8`	support of rotation matrix
D3D Files/D3D_GraphicsSystem folder:	
`D3DGraphicsSystem6`	header file version changes
`D3DGraphicsSystem_LoadResource4`	header file version changes
`D3DGraphicsSystem_TextureControls4`	header file version changes
D3D Files/D3D_Primitives folder:	
`D3DPrimitiveMesh2`	header file version changes
`D3DPrimitiveMeshArrow2`	header file version changes
`D3DPrimitiveMeshAxis2`	header file version changes
D3D Files/D3D_Resources folder:	
`D3DMeshResource2`	header file version changes
D3D Files/D3D_WindowHandler folder:	
`D3DWindowHandler8`	header file version changes

UWBGL_D3D_Lib17

Supports. The tutorials that are based on this library: Tutorials 16.4, 16.5, 16.6, 16.7, 16.8, and 16.9.

Introduced in Chapter 16 (on p. 462) to support interactive manipulation of rotation based on the more efficient quaternion representation. In this case, all changes are localized to the XformInfo class. Because of the limited and localized modifications, the static class diagram for this library is not shown. Besides the wubgl_XformInfo file, all changes in other files are results of header file version changes.

Filename	Purpose
Header Files folders: library header files	
D3D_Lib17.h	header file for using this library
Common Files/SceneNode folder:	
SceneNode6	header file version changes
Common Files/XformInfo folder:	
XformInfo5	represent rotation with quaternion
D3D Files folder: D3D-specific files	
D3D Files/D3D_Primitives folder:	
D3DPrimitiveMeshArrow3	header file version changes
D3DPrimitiveMeshAxis3	header file version changes

UWBGL_D3D_Lib18

Supports. The tutorials that are based on this library: Tutorials A.2 and A.3.

Introduced in Appendix A (on p. 490) to support per-vertex lighting computation and definition of custom .x mesh. The following are the new classes introduced in this version of the library:

- UWB_Material. As illustrated on the right of Figure C.19, this new class abstracts the material property required in a typical Phong lighting computation.

- UWBD3D_Light. As illustrated on the left of Figure C.19, this new class defines simple accessor functions to the D3DLIGHT9 class. UWBD3D_PointLight, UWBD3D_DirectionalLight, and UWBD3D_SpotLight all subclass from this class. The subclasses define simple functions to draw the corresponding light types.

- UWBD3D_MeshPrimitiveCustom. A wrapper class over simple .x mesh definition. This class defines a mesh with $n \times n$ vertices on the xz-plane in the ± 1 range. Drawing and editing functions are defined to allow interactive manipulation of each of the vertices.

The following classes are modified to support lighting computation and a custom .x mesh:

- **UWB_Primitive.** As shown on the left of Figure C.19, all primitives now have an instance of UWB_Material, which serves as the parameter to the lighting computation.

- **UWBD3D_PrimitiveMesh.** Modified to include accessors to change the first submesh's material. When lighting is enabled, the first submesh of a .x mesh file will be drawn based on the material attribute defined in the Primitive class.

- **UWB_DrawHelper.** As shown on the left of Figure C.19, this class now has an instance of UWB_Material to properly support the lighting attribute of the UWB_Primitive class.

- **UWBD3D_DrawHelper.** Modified to allow per-vertex normal specification and to support lighting computation. Together with the material, this information is forwarded to D3D to support Phong illumination computation.

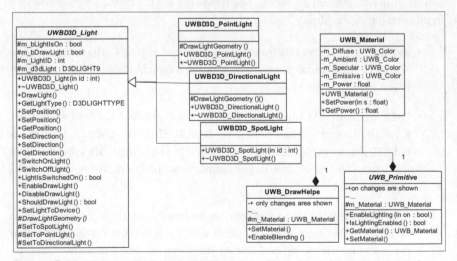

Figure C.19. UWBGL_D3D_Lib18: UWBD3D_Light hierarchy and UWB_Material class.

- **UWBD3D_GraphicsSystem.** Modified to enable specular computation and to define source of materials.

- **UWBD3D_MeshResource.** Modified to allow access to the `MeshPrimitive Custom` class.

Once again, "header file version changes" signifies that the only change in a file is in new header file versions. The following is the list of all files that are changed:

Filename	Purpose
Header Files folders: library header files	
`D3D_Lib18.h`	header file for using this library
Common Files folder: API-independent files	
Common Files/DrawHelper folder:	
`DrawHelper5`	support lighting/material attributes
Common Files/Material folder:	
`Material1`	support lighting computation
Common Files/Camera folder:	
`Camera3`	header file version changes
`Camera_Draw3`	header file version changes
`Camera_Xform3`	header file version changes
Common Files/Primitives folder:	
`Primitive6`	support lighting/material attributes
All other primitives files are updated to reflect header file version changes:	
`PrimitivePoint6`, `PrimitiveList5`, `PrimitiveLine6`, `PrimitiveCircle6` `PrimitiveRectXY5`, `PrimitiveRectXZ3`, `PrimitiveAxisFrame3`	
Common Files/SceneNode folder:	
`SceneNode7`	header file version changes
Common Files/BoundingVolumes folder:	
`Intersect5`	header file version changes
Common Files/WindowHandler folder:	
`WindowHandler7`	header file version changes
Common Files/XformInfo folder:	
`XformInfo6`	header file version changes

D3D Files folder: D3D-specific files	
D3D Files/D3D_Lights folder:	
`D3DLight1`	support interaction with D3DLIGHT9
`D3DPointLight1`	draws a sphere at the light
`D3DSpotLight1`	draws a sphere at the light
`D3DDirectionalLight1`	draws an arrow at the light
D3D Files/D3D_DrawHelper folder:	
`D3DDrawHelper9`	support vertex normal and lighting
D3D Files/D3D_GraphicsSystem folder:	
`D3DGraphicsSystem7`	enable specular computation
`D3DGraphicsSystem_LoadResource5`	header file version changes
`D3DGraphicsSystem_TextureControls5`	header file version changes
D3D Files/D3D_Resources folder:	
`D3DMeshResource3`	support custom .x mesh
D3D Files/D3D_WindowHandler folder:	
`D3DWindowHandler9`	header file version change
D3D Files/D3D_Primitives folder:	
`D3DPrimitiveMesh3`	drawing submesh with lighting
`D3DPrimitiveMeshArrow4`	head file version change
`D3DPrimitiveMeshAxis4`	head file version change
D3D Files/D3D_Primitives/Custom Mesh folder:	
`D3DMeshPrimitiveCustom1`	custom .x mesh
`D3DMeshPrimitiveCustom_Draw1`	draw custom mesh
`D3DMeshPrimitiveCustom_Select1`	interaction with vertices

Index

Affine transformation, 209, 264
Alpha blending, 345
    Alpha channel, 346
    Blending factors, 348
    Blending functions, 348
    Programming, 348
    Tutorial, 350
Aspect ratio, 284
    Frustum, 391
    Rectangular visible volume, 390
    Tutorial, 285

Bounding volumes, 183
    Implementation, *see* UWBGL_D3D_Lib6

Camera, 379
    Focus, 381, *see also* Viewing parameters
    Frustum, 390, *see also* View frustum
    Implementation, *see* UWBGL camera
    Parameters, *see* Viewing parameters
    Visible volume, 386, *see also* Visible volume

Camera coordinate system, *see* Eye coordinate system (EC)
Cartesian coordinate system, 77, 265, 371, *see also* Coordinate systems
Charge-coupled device (CCD), 380, 381
Circle class, 90
Collision, *see also* Object coordinate system (OC), *see also* Primitives
    3D, 485
        Tutorial, 485
    Missing collisions, 486
Colors, 162
    Channels, 162
    Components, 162
        Alpha, *see* Alpha blending
    Unsigned integers, 162
Control-driven programming, 14
    main(), 14
Controlling primitives, 295
    Parent/child, 297
Coordinate positions, 78, *see also* Vertex
Coordinate spaces, *see* Coordinate systems

Coordinate systems, 78, 257, 505
　　2D convention, 77
　　3D, 371
　　　　z-axis direction, 371
　　Axes, 77, 373
　　Camera space, *see* Eye coordinate
　　　　system (EC)
　　Device, *see* Device coordinate system
　　　　(DC)
　　Eye space, *see* Eye coordinate system
　　　　(EC)
　　Hardware, *see* Hardware coordinate
　　　　system
　　Left-handed, 372
　　Normalized, *see* Normalized device
　　　　coordinate system (NDC)
　　Object, *see* Object coordinate system
　　　　(OC)
　　Origin, 77, 373
　　Right-handed, 372, 494
　　Transform, *see* Coordinate
　　　　transformation
　　Units, 78, 373
　　Vertex, 273
　　World, *see* World coordinate system
　　　　(WC)
Coordinate transformation, 97
　　3D NDC to DC, 404
　　DC to OC, 321
　　DC to WC, 288
　　EC to NDC, 402
　　EC to WC, 401
　　Hardware to DC, 132, 134, 287, 511
　　Inverse transform, 287
　　　　Tutorial, 289
　　$\mathbf{M}_{d2w}$, 288
　　$\mathbf{M}_{e2n}$, 403
　　$\mathbf{M}_{e2w}$, 401
　　$\mathbf{M}_{n2d}$, 264
　　$\mathbf{M}_{w2d}$, 274
　　$\mathbf{M}_{w2e}$, 401
　　$\mathbf{M}_{w2n}$, 218, 258, 260, 261, 264, 266,
　　　　273, 278, 294

　　NDC to DC, 264
　　OC to WC, 319, 397
　　Pipeline, 396, 397
　　　　2D versus 3D, 444
　　WC to DC, 274, 279
　　WC to EC, 398, 400
　　WC to NDC, 218
Cross product, 499
Curves, 500, 502

D3D, 38
　　CreateDevice(), 101
　　Example, 79
　　GetAdapterDisplayMode(), 101
　　ID3DXMatrixStack, 239
　　Matrix processors, 216, 396, *see also*
　　　　Graphics API
　　　　Initialization, 217
　　　　PROJECTION ($\mathbf{M}_P$), 216, 389, 393,
　　　　　　420
　　　　VIEW ($\mathbf{M}_V$), 216, 218, 278, 418
　　　　WORLD ($\mathbf{M}_W$), 216, 218, 247, 397
　　Matrix stacks, *see also* Graphics API
　　　　Top of, 249
　　　　Tutorial, 240
　　Programming model, 99
　　SetFVF(), 83
　　Swap chains, 139
　　Transformation pipeline, 226, 294
　　Z-buffer, 377
　　　　Example, *see* Z-buffer
Device coordinate system (DC), 264, 265,
　　　　397
　　Transform, *see* Coordinate
　　　　transformation
Direction
　　Front facing, 342
　　Left/right turns, 342
Dot product, 498
Double buffering, 84, 87

Euler transform, 457, *see also* Rotation
　　Euler angles, 458

Event-driven programming, 13, 19
  Application state, 22
  Callback functions, 30
  Complexity, 18
  Efficiency, 18
  Event service registration, 19, 21, 30
  Event service routines, 19, 30, 35
  Events, *see* GUI events
  MainEventLoop(), 19
  RedrawRoutine(), 35
Events, *see* GUI events
Eye coordinate system (EC), 397, 399
  Align with WC, 400
  Axes, 399
  Origin, 399
  Orthonormal basis, 398
  Transform, *see* Coordinate
      transformation
  Visible volume, 399
Eye transform, 397, *see also* Coordinate
      transformation

File texture mapping, *see* Texture mapping
FLTK Fluid, *see* GUI builder

Geometries, 489, *see also* Primitives
Gimbal lock, 457
Gouraud shading, 160
Gradual movements, 343
  Automatic aiming, 343, 473
  Home in, *see* Home in
Graphical user interface (GUI), 14
Graphics API, 75, 93
  DirectX Direct3D (D3D), 38, *see also*
      D3D
  Graphics hardware context (GHC), 96,
      123, 138
  Java 3D, 38
  Matrix processors, 97, 216, *see also*
      D3D
  Matrix stacks, 239
  OpenGL, 38, *see also* OpenGL
  Programming model, 96

  Example in 2D (D3D), 99
  Example in 2D (OpenGL), 100
  Example in 3D, 374
  Relation to GUI API, 95
  Rendering context (RC), 97, 123, 138,
      215
  Rendering pipeline, 97
Graphics hardware context (GHC), *see*
      Graphics API
Graphics scenes, 369, 372
  3D, 479
  Camera, 370
  Light source, 370
  Model, 370, 372
  Scene, 370
  Scene graph, *see* Scene trees
  Scene tree, *see* Scene trees
  Tutorial, 374
GUI, *see* Graphical user interface
GUI API, 14, 25, 37, 38
  FLTK, 38
  GLUT, 14, 38
  Java Swing, 14, 38
  MFC, 14, 38
  Relation to graphics API, 95
GUI builder, 41
  FLTK example, 43
  MFC example, 44
GUI elements, 11, 25, 39, 46
  Back-end programming, 41
  Control variables, 40, 43
  Front-end layout, 41
  Input/output functionality, 46
GUI events
  Categories of events, 27
  Event propagation, 24
  Event translation, 24
  Implicit events, 45
  OnIdle events, 47
  Paint events, 29, 47
  Redraw events, 29, 47
  Timer events, 28

Hardware coordinate system, 112, 287
    Transform, *see* Coordinate
        transformation
Hexadecimal number, 162
Hierarchical modeling, 293
Home in, 476, *see also* Gradual movements
    Example implementation, 477
Homogeneous coordinate systems, 214

Illumination, 97, 160, 489
    Tutorial, 490
Image files, 351, *see also* File texture
        mapping
    Formats, 352
Implicit functions, 500

Lighting, 489, *see also* Illumination
Linear algebra, 194

Material properties, 489, *see also*
        UWBGL_D3D_Lib18
Matrix, 97, 211
    Identity, 212
    Multiplication order, 212
    Orthonormal, 505
    Rotation, *see* Rotation, 506
    Scaling, *see* Scaling
    Transforming vectors, 213
    Translation, *see* Translation
Matrix processors, *see* Graphics API
Matrix stacks, *see* Graphics API
Mesh, 448
    Compound mesh
        Tutorial, 456
    Files, 449
        Example, 449
        Format, 449
    Implementation, 450, *see also*
        UWBGL_D3D_Lib15
    Tutorial, 455
MFC
    `CDialog` class, 63
    Control variables, 55
    `CWnd` class, 123, 124

GUI elements, 55
    Container window, 70
GUI IDs, 51, 55
Input/output GUI elements, 65
Mouse events, 63
`OnInitDialog()`, 54, 129
`OnPaint()`, 54
`OnTimer()`, 63, 129
Output GUI elements, 58
Resource Editor, *see* GUI builder
`Resource.h`, 51
Slider bars, 58
    `OnHScroll()`/`OnVScroll()`, 60
    `OnScroll()`, 60
Source code structure, 50
`theApp`, 55
Timer events, 63
Microsoft Visual Studio, 3
    `.aps/.ncb` temporary files, 50
    Debug/Release folders, 51
    `Stdafx.h/.cpp` precompile header
        files, 52, 68, 126
    `.vcproj/.sln` project files, 50
Model transform, 397, *see also* Coordinate
        transformation
Model-view-controller (MVC), 109
    Component interactions, 120
    Components, 110
    Controller, 111, 112, 116
        Implementations, 130
    Framework, 110, 120
    Model, 111, 113
        Implementations, 130
    View, 111, 112, 115
    View/controller pairs, 118, 120
        Implementations, 122, 130
Modeling coordinate system, 318, *see also*
        Object coordinate system (OC)

Normal vector
    Transforming, 506
Normalized device coordinate system
        (NDC), 261, 263, 265, 397

3D, 402

Transform, *see* Coordinate
    transformation

Tutorial, 263

Normalized numbers, 162

Object coordinate system (OC), 317, 397

  Collision, 319, 329

    Tutorial, 329

  Drawing, 318

  Selection, 318, 320

    Tutorial, 327

  Transform, *see* Coordinate
    transformation

Opacity, *see* Alpha blending

OpenGL, 38

  `ChoosePixelFormat()`, 102

  Example, 85

  `GetDC()`, 102

  Programming model, 100

  `SetPixelFormat()`, 102

  `wglCreateContext()`, 102, 139

Operating system

  `.a`, `.dso`, `.lib`, and `.dll` library files,
    68

  Static/dynamic linking, 68

Operating system (OS), 25

Orientation

  3D, 464

  Aiming, 338, 466

    Matrix rotation, 469

    Quaternion rotation, 471

    Tutorial, 338

  Move forward (2D), 340

  Move forward (3D), 465

    Source code, 466

  Scene nodes, 343, 480

    Tutorial, 480

  Slerp, *see* Quaternion

  Tutorial (3D), 465

Orthographic projection, 387, 388, 405, *see
    also* Rectangular visible volume

  Tutorial, 388

Orthonormal matrix, 505

OS, *see* Operating system

Panning, *see* World coordinate system
    (WC)

Parametric curves, 502

Particle systems, 159

Persistent application state, 111

Perspective projection, 390, 392, 405, 437,
    see also View frustum

  Projection ray, 392, 437, 440

  Tutorial, 393

Photographs, 369, *see also* Graphics scenes

Pinhole camera, 380, *see also* Camera

Primitives, 157

  3D, 448

  Attributes, 158, *see also* Colors

    Colors, 158–161

    Fill styles, 162

    Material properties, 160, 161, *see
      also* Material properties

    Normal vector, 160

    Size, 159

    Style/width, 160

    Texture coordinates, 159, 160, *see
      also* Texture mapping

  Behaviors

    Collection, 158, 188

    Collision, 158, 182

    Motion, 158

  Drawing commands, 158

  Implementation, 172, *see also*
    `UWBGL_D3D_Lib5`

  Per–drawing command attributes, 160

  Per-vertex attributes, 160

  Types, 158

    Line strips, 159

    Lines, 159

    Meshes, *see* Mesh

    Points, 159

    Polylines, 159

    Triangle fans, 161, 376

    Triangle lists, 161

Triangle strips, 161
Triangles, 161, 210
Programming models
    External control, *see* Event-driven
        programming
    Internal control, *see* Control-driven
        programming
Projection ray, *see* Perspective projection
Projection transform, 397, 404, *see also*
    Coordinate transformation

Quaternion, 462
    Slerp, 473
        Home in, *see* Home in
        Working with, 475
    Tutorial, 464

Rectangle class, 88
Rectangular visible volume, 387, *see also*
    Orthographic projection
    Aspect ratio, *see* Aspect ratio
    Clipping, 390
    Far plane, 388
    Image plane, 388
    Near plane, 388
    Tutorial, 388
Render buffer, 81, 97, *see also* Graphics
    API
Rendering, 81, 380
Rendering context (RC), *see* Graphics API
Rendering pipeline, 97, *see also* Graphics
    API
Rotation, 204, 506
    3D, 457, *see also* Gimbal lock
        Quaternion, *see* Quaternion
        Tutorial, 461
    Direciton of rotation, 205
    Properties, 208
    Rotation matrix, 212
    Tutorial, 222
Rotation matrix, 506

Scaling, 198
    Negative factors, 202

Properties, 203
Reflection, 202
Scaling matrix, 212
Tutorial, 222
Scene hierarchy, *see also* Scene trees
    Instancing, 314
        Sharing geometries, 316
        Sharing node references, 314
    Orientation, *see* Orientation
Scene nodes, 303, *see also*
        UWBGL_D3D_Lib11, SceneNode
        class
    Animation, 333
        Tutorial, 334
    Orientation, *see* Orientation
Scene trees, 311
    nodes, *see* Scene nodes
    Orientation, *see* Orientation
    Tutorial, 312
Selection, *see also* Object coordinate
        system (OC)
    3D, 487
        Selection rays, 487
        Tutorial, 487
Shading, 489
    Gouraud shading, 160
Slider bars, *see* MFC

Texel, *see* Texture mapping
Texture mapping
    File texture mapping, 351
        Texture files, 351
    Implementation, 360, *see also*
        UWBGL_D3D_Lib13
    Procedural texture mapping, 351
    Texel, 351
    Texel look-up, 353
    Texture coordinate, 352
        Explicit *uv*, 353
        Implicit *st*, 352
    Texture maps, 351
    Textures, 351
    Tutorials

DeviceVertexFormat, 355, *see also*
   UWBGL
No library, 355
uv coordinate, 357
UWBGL_D3D_Lib13, 364
Transform
Normal vector, 506
Transformation, 193
Concatenations, 225, 226
   Costs, 228
   Implementation, *see*
      UWBGL_D3D_Lib11
   Order of, 228
   Order of (tutorials), 238
   Tutorial, 236
Coordinate, *see* Coordinate
   transformation
Inverse transforms, 229
Linearity, 209, 264
Operators, 194
   Reflection, *see* Scaling
   Rotation, *see* Rotation
   Scaling, *see* Scaling
   Translation, *see* Translation
   Tutorial, 215
Pipeline, 397
Pivoted transforms, 231
   Pivot position, 234, 235
   Rotation, 235
   Scaling, 233
   Tutorial, 242
Properties, 210
Uniqueness, 230
Vertex, 273
Translation, 194
Properties, 196, 197
Translation matrix, 212
Tutorial, 216, 220
Transparency, *see* Alpha blending

UWBGL, 3
2D
   Matrix processors set-up, 444

WindowHandler class, 410
3D
DC to NDC, 438
DC to WC, 436, 441
EC to WC, 441
GrfxWindow class, 374, 389, 393
Matrix processors set-up, 405, 445
NDC to EC, 439
Projection ray, 441, 443
WindowHandler class, 410
All libraries
DeviceVertexFormat, 83
EchoToStatusArea(), 134
EchoToStatusArea(), 511
math3d++, 124
WindowHandler class hierarchy, 126
All projects
DrawAndMouseHandler class, 132
DrawOnlyHandler class, 127, 128
OnInitDialog(), 129
OnTimer(), 130
Before libraries
GraphicsSystem class, 103
GraphicsSystem class (D3D), 105
GraphicsSystem class (OpenGL),
   108
GrfxWindow class (D3D), 99, 374
GrfxWindow class (OpenGL), 102
SetFVF(), *see* D3D
Naming conventions, 3
Projects (Lib8 and after)
DrawOnlyHandler class, 218
Projects (Lib9 and after)
CXformInfoControl class, 252
Projects (Lib11 and after)
CPrimitiveControl class, 311
CSceneTreeControl class, 308, 309
UWBGL camera, 409, 417
Dolly/zoom, 432
   Equation, 433
   Source code, 433
Drawing, 434
   Matrix, 435

Manipulation, 422
  Tutorial, 425
Orbit/rotate, 426
  Matrix, 428
  Source code, 429
Pan/track, 430
  Equations, 431
  Source code, 431
Tutorial, 416
Two cameras, 422
UWBGL_D3D_Lib1, 124, 509
  D3DWindowHandler class, 126
  First library support, 509
  GraphicsSystem class, 123
  IWindowHandler interface, 125
  Source files, 124
  WindowHandler class, 122, 123, 126
    BeginDraw(), 128
    EndDrawAndShow(), 128
  WindowHandler class hierarchy, 126
UWBGL_D3D_Lib2, 134, 511
  D3DWindowHandler class, 132
  Utilities support, 511
  WindowHandler class, 132
    HardwareToDevice(), 511
    HardwareToDevice(), 132, 134
UWBGL_D3D_Lib3, 141, 512
  GraphicsSystem class, 138
    CreateGraphicsContext(), 139
  View/controller support, 512
  WindowHandler class
    BeginDraw(), 140
    EndDrawAndShow(), 140
    InitializeHandler(), 140
UWBGL_D3D_Lib4, 163, 514
  D3DDrawHelper class, 164
  D3DGraphicsSystem class, 164
  D3DWindowHandler class, 164
  DrawHelper class, 163, 164
  Geometry support, 514
  OGLDrawHelper class, 164
UWBGL_D3D_Lib5, 173, 515
  Files, 173

Primitive class
  Draw(), 173
  DrawPrimitive(), 173
  SetDrawAttributes(), 173
  Update(), 174
Primitive class hierarchy, 173
  Tutorial, 172
Primitive support, 515
UWBGL_D3D_Lib6, 185, 516
  BoundingBox class, 186
  BoundingVolumes class
    Add(), 185
    CollisionResponse(), 186
    Draw(), 185
    Intersects(), 185
  BoundingVolumes class hierarchy, 185
  Collision support, 516
UWBGL_D3D_Lib7, 189, 517
  Collection of primitives support, 517
  PrimitiveList class, 189
UWBGL_D3D_Lib8, 216, 518
  GraphicsSystem class
    Initialization, 218
  Primitives class
    Transform tutorial, 245
  Rectangle primitives support, 518
UWBGL_D3D_Lib9, 247, 521
  D3DDrawHelper class, 247, 521
    AccumulateModelTransform(),
    248
    InitializeModelTransform(),
    248
    User interaction, 251
  M_W settings, 247
  Pivoted transform support, 521
  XformInfo class, 249, 521
    Tutorial, 250
UWBGL_D3D_Lib10, 276, 522
  M_V settings, 277
  Tutorial, 278
  WC window support, 522
  WindowHandler class, 278, 522
    DeviceToWorld(), 289

LoadW2NDCXform(), 278, 282, 294, 522

UWBGL_D3D_Lib11, 300, 523
  Scene tree support, 523
  SceneNode class, 299, 523
    Concatenate transform operators, 301
    Subclass from, 305
    Tutorial, 303
    User interaction, 308

UWBGL_D3D_Lib12, 323, 524
  Scene node selection/collision support, 524
  SceneNode class
    GetBounds(), 324
    GetNodeBounds(), 323

UWBGL_D3D_Lib13, 348, 525
  D3DResources class
    LoadResource(), 360
  D3DTextureResource class, 360
  DeviceVertexFormat, 359
  DrawHelper class, 360, 362
    Blending support, 348
  GraphicsSystem class, 360, 361
  Primitive class
    Blending support, 348
  Texture support, 359
  uv coordinates, 359

UWBGL_D3D_Lib14, 413, 527
  3D and camera support, 527
  3D rotation, 415
  Camera class, 413, see also UWBGL camera, 527
  D3DWindowHandler class, 418
    LoadProjectionXform(), 420
    LoadViewXform(), 418
  DrawHelper class, 415, 527
  Tutorial, 416, 417
  WindowHandler class, 413, 417, 527
  XformInfo class, 415, 527

UWBGL_D3D_Lib15, 450, 529
  D3DMeshResource class, 450, 529
  GraphicsSystem class, 452
  Mesh support, 529

Tutorial, 455
UWBGL_D3D_Lib16, 459
  3D rotation with matrices, 459
  D3DDrawHelper class, 460
  Rotation matrix support, 531
  XformInfo class, 459

UWBGL_D3D_Lib17, 462, 533
  Quaternion support, 464
  Tutorial, 464
  XformInfo class, 464, 533

UWBGL_D3D_Lib18, 490, 533
  Illumination support, 533
  Light class hierarchy, 490, 533
  Material class, 490, 533
  Mesh, 491
  Tutorial, 490

UWBGL_MFC_Lib, 67, 124
  ReplaceDialogControl(), 69, 72, 124
  SliderCtrlWithEcho class, 66, 68, 124
  UIWindow class, 123, 124

UWBGL_MFC_Lib1, 508
  Source files, 508

Vectors, 210, 493, 494
  Column/row representations, 194, 211
  Cross product, 499
    Sign, 398
  Dot product, 498
  Transforming vectors, 213
Vertex, 78
  Coordinate spaces, 273
  Edge angles, 196
  Edge directions, 196
  Edges, 196
  Specification order
    Counterclockwise, 78, 374
  Transform vertex, see also Transformations
    DC to NDC, 274
    World to NDC, 273
  Vector representations, 194, see also Vectors

View frustum, 390, *see also* Perspective
        projection
    Aspect ratio, *see* Aspect ratio
    Clipping, 393
    Far plane, 390
    Field of view (FOV), 390
    Image plane, 392
    Near plane, 390
    Near/far optimization, 394
        Tutorial, 395
    Tutorial, 393
Viewing parameters, *see also* Camera
    Look-at, 381
        Example, 386
    Position, 374, 380
        Example, 386
    Tutorial, 383
    Twist angle, 383
        Example, 385
    Up direction, 381
    Up vector, 383
        Example, 385
    View vector, 381
    Viewing direction, 381
    Visible volume, *see* Visible volume

Visible volume, 386
    Clipping, 390, 393
    Frustum, 390, *see also* View frustum
    Image plane, 381
    Rectangular, 387, *see also* Rectangular
        visible volume

Window manager, 25, 286
WindowHandler class, *see* UWBGL, All
        libraries
Wire frame, 162
World coordinate system (WC), 266, 268,
        397
    Aspect, *see* Aspect ratio
    Transform, *see* Coordinate
        transformation
    WC window, 273
        Panning (translate), 271, 275, 279
        Zooming (scaling), 275, 283
World transform, 397, *see also* Coordinate
        transformation

Z-buffer, 377, 399, 405
    Impelementation example, 377
Zooming, *see* World coordinate system
        (WC)